Iran

Andrew Burke
Mark Elliott

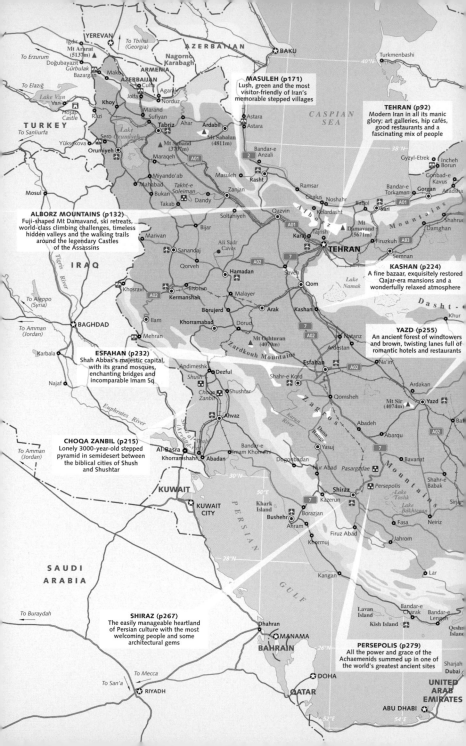

MASULEH (p171)
Lush, green and the most visitor-friendly of Iran's memorable stepped villages

TEHRAN (p92)
Modern Iran in all its manic glory; art galleries, hip cafés, good restaurants and a fascinating mix of people

ALBORZ MOUNTAINS (p132)
Fuji-shaped Mt Damavand, ski retreats, world-class climbing challenges, timeless hidden valleys and the walking trails around the legendary Castles of the Assassins

KASHAN (p224)
A fine bazaar, exquisitely restored Qajar-era mansions and a wonderfully relaxed atmosphere

YAZD (p255)
An ancient forest of windtowers and brown, twisting lanes full of romantic hotels and restaurants

ESFAHAN (p232)
Shah Abbas's majestic capital, with its grand mosques, enchanting bridges and incomparable Imam Sq

CHOQA ZANBIL (p215)
Lonely 3000-year-old stepped pyramid in semidesert between the biblical cities of Shush and Shushtar

SHIRAZ (p267)
The easily manageable heartland of Persian culture with the most welcoming people and some architectural gems

PERSEPOLIS (p279)
All the power and grace of the Achaemenids summed up in one of the world's greatest ancient sites

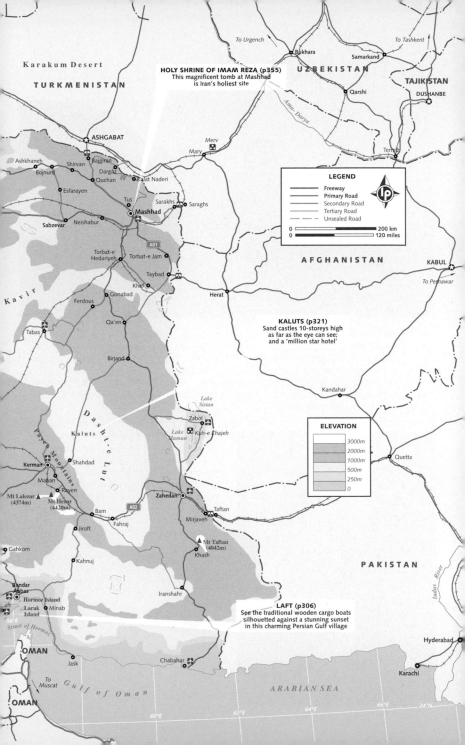

Karakum Desert

TURKMENISTAN

ASHGABAT

Ashkhaneh
Shirvan
Bajgiran
Bojnurd
Quchan
Kalat Naderi
Dargaz
Esfarayen
Tus
Sarakhs
Saraghs
Mashhad
Sabzevar
Neishabur

Torbat-e
Hedariyeh
A01
Torbat-e Jam
Taybad
Khaf

Ferdous
Gonabad
Kavir
Qa'en
Tabas
Birjand

Kaluts
Dasht-e Lur
Zabol
Lake Sistan
Kuh-e Khajeh
Lake Hamun

Zagros Mountains
Kerman
Shahdad
Mahan
Rayen
Mt Lalezar
(4374m)
Mt Hezar
(4420m)
Bam
Fahraj
Zahedan
Taftan
Jiroft
Mirjaveh
Gahkom
Mt Taftan
(4042m)
Kahnuj
Khash

Bandar Abbas
Hormoz Island
aft
Larak Island
Minab
Iranshahr

Strait of Hormoz
56°E

OMAN
Jask
Chabahar

To Muscat
Gulf of Oman
ARABIAN SEA
60°E
62°E
64°E

To Urgench
Bukhara
Samarkand
To Tashkent

UZBEKISTAN
Qarshi
TAJIKISTAN
DUSHANBE

HOLY SHRINE OF IMAM REZA (p355)
This magnificent tomb at Mashhad
is Iran's holiest site

Merv
Mary
Termez

AFGHANISTAN
KABUL
To Peshawar
Herat

KALUTS (p321)
Sand castles 10-storeys high
as far as the eye can see;
and a 'million star hotel'

Kandahar
Quetta

PAKISTAN

Indus River

Hyderabad

LAFT (p306)
See the traditional wooden cargo boats
silhouetted against a stunning sunset
in this charming Persian Gulf village

Karachi

24°N
66°E

On the Road

ANDREW BURKE Coordinating Author
It was at the end of a long day exploring ancient Sassanian cities that Kazem suggested we stop for a picnic by a lake south of Shiraz. 'A picnic? What with?' I asked. 'Don't worry, I have everything in the car,' he replied. And he did. Kazem proved to be a veritable professor of the picnic, producing a plastic blanket, hot water, tea, coals, qalyan, biscuits, sugar and a wire cage in which he swung the coals until they lit in a sea of sparks. We sat, smoked, sipped tea and just enjoyed life as the sun settled behind the hills…it was pure Iranian hospitality.

MARK ELLIOTT Arriving in Paveh, I'd been invited home by a delightful fellow savari-passenger. 'Lunch' had turned into a whole day of feasting, meeting families, smoking qalyan and – as the evening wore on – dancing in a whirl of Kurdish cummerbunds. We got to sleep at 4am, making next morning's 7am departure something of a tall order. But the dawn was spectacular and not a cloud blemished the sky as my chartered taxi lurched and bounced through the spectacular valleys towards Howraman-at-Takht (p194). En route a passing pedestrian wanted to be photographed with the odd-looking stranger. Guess which one is me.

for all author biographies, see page 431

Iran Highlights

A journey to Iran is a chance to peel away the layers of a country with a serious image problem. Beyond the stereotypes you'll experience a country desperate to been seen for what it is, rather than what it is perceived to be. Whether you're travelling in the cities, mountains or deserts, admiring monuments to glories past or witnessing the confounding present, the real Iran will be revealed. At its core you'll discover a country of warm and fascinating people living within an ancient and sophisticated culture. Embrace Iran, and allow the Iranians to embrace you – it's the most priceless of experiences.

ANDREW BURKE

❶ REDEFINE HOSPITALITY

It's the people you meet who will leave the most lasting impressions. You will regularly be asked 'What do you think of Iran?', and be bought tea and food with intonations that 'You are our guest'. Even the act of buying *fereni* (a delicious dessert made of rice flour, milk, sugar and rose water) can end in your being the subject of a poetic serenade.

PATRICK SYE

2 THE STEREOTYPICAL...

From watching the TV news you could be forgiven for thinking all Iranians were America-hating fundamentalists and all Iranian women wear the black, all-encompassing chador. There are certainly elements of truth to these stereotypes, but they are the exception rather than the rule.

ANDREW BUR

3 ...GIVES WAY TO SURPRISES

Instead of two-dimensional media stereotypes, you'll find at every turn a complex, millennia-old Iranian culture that is markedly different to the Arabian culture for which it is often mistaken. The Iranians have found room for both tradition and an (at first) surprising level of modernity. Experience it discussing philosophy and contemporary art with Tehran's café society, or head up the hill to go skiing with the young.

ANCIENT TRADITIONS

Many of the festivals celebrated in pre-Islamic times are still enjoyed today. The biggest is No Ruz (p384), the Iranian New Year, which begins with jumping over fires to burn away bad luck on Chaharshanbe Soori, and continues to the new year itself, when you might be adopted by a family for a feast of fish and vegetable rice.

4

ANDREW BURKE

PHIL WEYMOUTH

5

ANCIENT PERSEPOLIS

The ancient glories of the Persian empire reached their peak at Persepolis (p279) and nearby Naqsh-e Rostam (p283), the showpiece city and monolithic rock tombs of kings Darius and Xerxes (respectively). Climbing the monumental staircases and admiring the artistic harmony of the imposing gateways and exquisite reliefs leaves you in little doubt that in its prime Persepolis was indeed the very centre of the known world.

PATRICK SYDER

6

ISLAMIC REPUBLIC

Iran is an Islamic Republic and while Islam is not as all-pervasive as you might believe, the Shiite faith remains an important aspect of Iranian life (see p54). It is at its most obvious in the passionate devotion seen at monuments, such as the Holy Shrine of Imam Reza (p355) or Ayatollah Khomeini's tomb (p130). But there is another, more contemplative, face that can often be found in the quiet courtyards of Iran's madrasehs.

MARK DAFF

7 HALF OF THE WORLD

Esfahan has been called 'half of the world', and when you're standing in its vast Imam Sq (p238) it can be hard to argue that it's not. For this square is home to arguably the most majestic collection of buildings in the Islamic world: the perfectly proportioned blue-tiled dome of the Imam Mosque (p239), the supremely elegant Sheikh Lotfollah Mosque (p240) and the indulgent and lavishly decorated Ali Qapu Palace (p241). And a little rooftop teahouse (p249) from which to take it all in.

ANDREW BURKE

COEXISTENCE

Few places have adapted to their environment as well as the desert city of Yazd (p255). It's a gem of winding lanes, blue-tiled domes, soaring minarets, covered bazaars and fine old homes topped by *badgirs* (windtowers) and watered by the ingenious *qanats* (underground canals). Today some of these homes have been restored and converted into marvellously evocative hotels.

9

ANDREW BURKE

8

COUNTRY OF POETS

Iranians like to say that even in the poorest home you'll find two books: a Quran and the poetry of Hafez. It's appropriate for a country whose most celebrated sons are poets, and where almost every person can quote their favourite poet – and often does. Men such as Hafez, Ferdosi, Sa'di and Khayyam (see p74) are commemorated in street names across Iran, and their grand mausoleums draw pilgrims from around the country.

PHIL WEYMOUTH

10

BAZAAR KIND OF LIFE

In the age of the superstore, most Iranians continue to rely on these mazes of covered lanes, madrasehs and caravanserais for much of their shopping. Join them in dodging carts and motorbikes in Tehran's buzzing bazaar (p100), walking under the domed ceilings of Esfahan's Bazar-e Bozorg (p238) or stopping for tea and a chat in Shiraz, Kashan or Tabriz.

PHIL WEYMO

11 THE ART MARKET

The bazaars are home to a dizzying array of arts and crafts. You'll find fine miniatures, marquetry, ceramic and glasswork and, of course, the most famous of all Iranian arts, a huge array of Persian carpets and kilims (see p61).

ANDREW BL

12 IT HAS NOTHING, IT HAS EVERYTHING

The welcome is rarely warmer than in the vast, empty silence of Iran's two great deserts. In tiny Toudeshk (p253) the locals welcome travellers with tea and communal bathing as they have done for centuries. The giant sand castles of the Kaluts (p321) make fine bedroom walls in the 'million star hotel'. And then there is the oasis village of Garmeh (p254), where almost nothing feels like everything you'll ever need.

OFF THE BEATEN TRACK

Travel is as much about the journey as the destination. Places that see few travellers but are stunningly beautiful include the mountains of Kordestan (p134) in western Iran and the Alamut Valley (p180) – perfect for trekking and home to the ruined Castles of the Assassins (p182). Nearer to the sea you could venture to tiny Laft (p306) on Qeshm Island for a taste of Bandari Arab life.

13

ANDREW BURKE

TWO MILLION NOMADS

About two million Iranians from several different ethnic groups still live a nomadic existence, travelling with their goats in spring and autumn in search of pasture. A good proportion of nomads spend half the year in the Zagros Mountains near Shiraz, and it's possible to visit these people and get a taste of life in a tent in remote settings, such as the Bavanat area (see p285).

14

PATRICK SYDER

ANDREW B...

15 DELICIOUS SURPRISE

Like peeling the layers of the ubiquitous lunchtime raw onion (which tastes pretty good and keeps nasties at bay), Iranian food is one delicious surprise after another (see p78). Once you've tried several varieties of kabab, *khoresht* (stew) and flat bread, ask for *fesenjun* (chicken in walnut and pomegranate sauce) or anything with *bademjan* (eggplant). Then you can try the *shirin* (sweets)…

ANDREW B...

16 JUST SAY 'YES'

The key to experiencing the best of what Iran has to offer is to open yourself to it. Engage. When you are invited into the home of a near-total stranger, just say 'yes'. Like us, you'll find your photographs will be the ultimate answer to those friends who exclaimed: 'Iran! But isn't it dangerous?'

Contents

Regional Map Contents

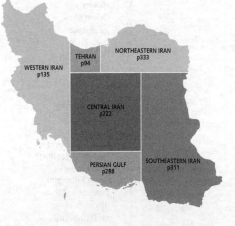

WESTERN IRAN
p135

TEHRAN
p94

NORTHEASTERN IRAN
p333

CENTRAL IRAN
p222

PERSIAN GULF
p288

SOUTHEASTERN IRAN
p311

Getting Started

WHEN TO GO

When deciding when to go to Iran you must first work out where you'd like to go. Temperatures can vary wildly: when it's -5°C in Tabriz it might be 35°C in Bandar Abbas, but for most people spring and autumn are the most pleasant times to visit. At other times, the seasons have advantages and disadvantages depending on where you are. For example, the most agreeable time to visit the Persian Gulf coast is during winter, when the humidity is low and temperatures mainly in the 20s. At this time, however, the more elevated northwest and northeast can be freezing, with mountain roads impassable due to snow. Except on the Persian Gulf coast, winter nights can be bitterly cold, but we think the days (often clear and about 15°C in much of the country) are more pleasant than the summer heat.

See Climate Charts (p376) for more information.

And when we say 'heat', we mean it. Between May and October temperatures often rise into the 40s, and in the deserts, southern provinces

---

DON'T LEAVE HOME WITHOUT...READING THIS FIRST

The best preparation for visiting Iran is to read as much of the front and back chapters in this guide as you can. If you can't read everything, at least read the following:

- How do I get a visa and how long can I stay? (p393)
- Credit cards and travellers cheques don't work. Bring cash. (p387)
- This money is confusing. Rials or toman? (p387)
- Prices will be higher than what we have in this book; see p25 and p388.
- How do Iranians think? Read about the National Psyche, p45.
- Is he really giving me that for free? See the boxed text Ta'arof (p45).
- As a woman, what should I wear? (p398)
- Books to take with you (see Reading Up, p17).

There is not much you can't buy in Tehran or the other big cities, though the selection can be limited. Things you should consider bringing:

- Sunscreen and a hat
- A head-lamp
- A short-wave radio
- A universal plug
- A small stash of toilet paper (to be replenished throughout the trip)
- A phrasebook and pictures of your family to better communicate with your new Iranian friends
- A couple of decent books to soak up the free hours at night and on transport (but nothing with pictures of scantily clad women on the cover)
- Earplugs for when you've finished reading and want to sleep, or if you'd prefer to sleep than watch that Bollywood flick on the overnight bus
- Tampons: they're hard to find, so if you use them it's worth bringing enough to last the trip

There's just one more important thing: try, as much as possible, to leave your preconceptions at home.

and along the Gulf coast, very little is done between noon and 4pm or 5pm. For women, who need to wear head coverings whenever they're outside (see p398), summer can be particularly trying.

Seasons & Holidays

Iran has two main seasons. High season begins with the mass national movement accompanying No Ruz (p385), the Iranian New Year holiday that begins on March 21 and runs for two weeks. During this period cities such as Esfahan, Shiraz and Yazd are packed. Hotels in these cities and resort destinations, such as Kish Island, charge their rack rates, and finding a room can be harder than finding a stiff drink in Qom. But it's a great time to be in Tehran, which is virtually empty.

No Ruz also marks the annual government-mandated price rise in hotels, usually about 20%, and in most of the country a change in opening hours. For the sake of clarity, in this book when you see 'summer' opening hours it refers to the period from March 21 to mid-October. Mid-October until mid-March is 'low season' (referred to as 'winter' in this book) in most of Iran, and brings shorter opening hours at sights and hotel prices about 10% to 20% lower, or much more in holiday destinations.

Some travellers prefer not to visit Iran during Ramazan (p384), the Muslim month of fasting, when many restaurants close between dawn and dusk, and tempers can be strained. However, most people (including us) think travelling during Ramazan isn't as tough as reputation would have it: restaurants in hotels and bus terminals still operate and while buses might be less frequent, Ramazan is the least-crowded time on trains and planes.

COSTS & MONEY

It's not quite Zimbabwe, but inflation is running at about 25% in Iran, so expect just about every price in this book to rise – repeatedly – in the coming years (for details, see p25). Inflation or no inflation, Iran remains an eminently affordable place to travel and great value by Western standards.

Backpackers can get by on as little as IR150,000 to IR200,000 (US$16 to US$22) a day, even less if all luxuries are foregone. To do this, however, 'surviving' is the operative word; you need to stay in basic lodgings, such as a dorm or basic hotel, known as a *mosaferkhaneh* (p371, from about IR50,000/US$5.50), eat the simplest food in local restaurants (preferably only twice a day) and take the cheapest, slowest transport.

If you're not a complete ascetic you'll be looking at about IR250,000 to IR400,000 (US$27 to US$43) a day. This will usually be enough for budget or simple midrange accommodation (with a bathroom), one good cooked meal a day, transport by Volvo buses (see the boxed text, p408) or savari (p415), chartered taxis around town (and sometimes in the countryside) and visits to all the important tourist attractions.

For about IR400,000 to IR500,000 (US$43 to US$54) a day you could take a couple of internal flights, eat at restaurants serving 'exotic' Western fare, and lodge in midrange hotels with Western toilets and satellite TV.

THE END OF DUAL-PRICING IN HOTELS?

As this book went to press, Iran was in the midst of a fight about the future of dual pricing in hotels – where foreigners pay significantly more for hotel rooms than Iranians do. Dual pricing has been in force for years, but in early 2008 the government tourism organisation ordered all hotels to use one rate for everyone. For full details, see p388.

If you prefer upper midrange or top-end hotels you'll be looking at somewhere more than IR700,000 (US$76) a day. Single and twin/double rooms cost virtually the same, so couples should expect to pay considerably less than double the figures quoted here.

Getting around Iran is cheap; comfortable buses work out at less than IR9200 (US$1) per 100km, while a bed on an overnight train starts at IR92,000 (US$10). Domestic flights are no longer as ridiculously cheap as they were, but you can still fly from Tehran to Esfahan, for example, for only IR245,000 (US$27).

In 2004 the government ended dual-pricing at museums and historical sites, so admission fees won't hurt too much either – between about IR1500 and IR6000 for most places.

Remember that travellers cheques and credit cards don't work in Iran, so bring all the money you'll need in cash (see p387).

READING UP

Travellers have been writing about Iran for millennia so there are plenty of evocative travelogues worth hunting down. And while English-language fiction is scarce, Iran has been the subject of dozens of political and historical books in recent years. For books by Iranian writers, see p73.

Most of these books are not available or are banned in Iran, but bringing them or any other book into the country shouldn't be a problem. Notable exceptions are *Not Without My Daughter,* which is despised by most Iranians, or anything by Salman Rushdie. For more on customs restrictions, see p377.

Travel Literature

In the Land of the Ayatollahs Tupac Shapur is King: Reflections from Iran and the Arab World, by Shahzad Aziz, combines travelogue and humour in its often insightful observations of the modern Middle East.

Journey of the Magi, by Paul William Roberts, is the author's thought-provoking, spiritual and often humorous account of his own journey 'in search of the birth of Jesus'.

Neither East Nor West, by Christiane Bird, is an American woman's sometimes painfully honest account of her travels in Iran, and does a decent job of getting behind the veil.

Persia Through Writers Eyes, edited by David Blow, gathers together some of the best descriptive writing about Iran from throughout history. Extracts from works by Herodotus, Xenophon, Freya Stark, Robert Byron, John Chardin, Isabella Bird and EG Browne, among others, make this like a sample bag of largely hard-to-find works.

Searching for Hassan, by Terence Ward, recounts the author's return to Iran with his family in search of Hassan, the family's 1960s housekeeper. However, looking for Hassan is really a subplot to a revealing look at the history and culture of Iran. Some have criticised Ward's soft approach to the Islamic government.

The Road to Oxiana, by Robert Byron, is a classic. A vividly observed travel diary of the author's 1930s passage from England to Afghanistan via Iran. Famous for its descriptive prose and often biting sketches of local people, its tone can verge uncomfortably close to racism by today's standards.

The Valleys of the Assassins: and Other Persian Travels, by Freya Stark, was first published in 1934 but remains the archetypal travelogue – adventurous, challenging perceptions and illuminating reality.

HOW MUCH?

Meal in a cheap restaurant IR20,000

One hour online IR10,000

Short taxi ride IR6000-10,000

Average museum ticket IR4000

Two-pack of toilet paper IR700

GREAT READS

Iran's complex culture and long history have seen plenty of words written about them, with most authors finding the truth far more interesting than fiction – there aren't many novels. Check out the following titles.

1 *All the Shah's Men* by Stephen Kinzer (p37)

2 *In Search of Zarathustra* by Paul Kriwaczek

3 *Journeys in Persia & Kurdistan* by Isabella Bird

4 *My Uncle Napoleon* by Iraj Pezeshkzad (p38)

5 *Persepolis: The Story of a Childhood* by Marjane Satrapi (p73)

6 *Persian Fire* by Tom Holland (p30)

7 *Reading Lolita in Tehran* by Azar Nafisi (p39)

8 *Shah of Shahs* by Ryszard Kapuscinski (p39)

9 *The Soul of Iran: A Nation's Journey to Freedom*, by Afshin Molavi

10 *We Are Iran: The Persian Blogs* by Nasrin Alavi (p54)

MUST-SEE MOVIES

These are a few standout Iranian films. For more general information on Iranian cinema, see p75.

1 *A Moment of Innocence* (1996) by Mohsen Makhmalbaf

2 *The Apple* (1998) by Samira Makhmalbaf (p76)

3 *Bashu, The Little Stranger* (1986) by Bahram Beizai (p40)

4 *Children of Heaven* (1997) by Majid Majidi (p77)

5 *Gabbeh* (1996) by Mohsen Makhmalbaf (p50))

6 *Offside* (2006) by Jafar Panahi (p51)

7 *A Time for Drunken Horses* (2000) by Bahman Ghobadi (p50)

8 *Taste of Cherry* (1997) by Abbas Kiarostami (p77)

9 *Turtles Can Fly* (2004) by Bahman Ghobadi (p50)

10 *The White Balloon* (1995) by Jafar Panahi (p77)

WHERE NOTHING IS EVERYTHING

The warmest welcomes and most memorable experiences are often found in the little villages in the middle of nowhere. These few have at least one place to stay but are just a guide – countless more are waiting to be found...

1 Abyaneh (p231)

2 Baghestan-e Olia (p255)

3 Bavanat Area (p285)

4 Garmeh (p254)

5 Gazor Khan (p182)

6 Kalat (p366)

7 Paveh (p194)

8 Masuleh (p171)

9 Meymand (p311)

10 Toudeshk (p253)

Other Books

As well as the books recommended in Great Reads (opposite), the following works are worth considering.

- *Strange Times, My Dear: The PEN Anthology of Contemporary Iranian Literature,* edited by Nahid Mozaffari and Ahmad Karimi Hakkak
- *Guests of the Ayatollah: The First Battle in the West's War on Militant Islam* by Mark Bowdeno
- *My Father's Notebook* by Kader Abdolah
- *The Prince* by Hushang Golshiri
- *Tehran Blues: Youth Culture in Iran* by Kaveh Basmenji
- *The Shia Revival,* by Vali Nasr, includes an insightful and highly readable introduction to the complexities of Shia Islam.

INTERNET RESOURCES

Easypersian (www.easypersian.com) Learn a few words of Farsi and have a better trip.

Iran Chamber Society (www.iranchamber.com) Historical and cultural summaries about Iran.

Iranian Visa (www.iranianvisa.com) Detailed feedback on visas from applicants across the globe.

Lonely Planet (www.lonelyplanet.com) Destination information plus the latest feedback from travellers on the Thorn Tree bulletin board.

Pars Times (www.parstimes.com) Encyclopaedia of links to sites on just about everything you need to know before you go to Iran.

Tehran Times (www.tehrantimes.com) English-language newspaper and archive.

Itineraries
CLASSIC ROUTES

IN THE FOOTSTEPS OF EMPIRE
Two Weeks / Tehran to Tehran

Two busy weeks is just long enough to get a taste of the jewels of Iran's rich history. Fly into **Tehran** (p92) and spend two days seeing the major sights, including the **Golestan Palace** (p101), **National Museum of Iran** (p104) and **Tehran Bazar** (p100). Fly to **Shiraz** (p267), where in three days you can see the Zand-era mosques, gardens and bazaar, and magnificent **Persepolis** (p279).

Take a bus or taxi and stop in **Abarqu** (p267) on the way to **Yazd** (p255). Spend a day wandering the maze of lanes in this ancient desert city, gaping at the **Jameh Mosque** (p259) and taking in the Zoroastrian **Towers of Silence** (p262). On your second day, tour **Meybod** (p266), the Zoroastrian pilgrimage site at **Chak Chak** (p266) and the mud-brick village of **Kharanaq** (p266).

Catch a bus to **Esfahan** (p232), Iran's most architecturally stunning city, and explore Shah Abbas' **Imam Sq** (p238), the **Bazar-e Bozorg** (p238), the sublime **bridges** (p242) across the Zayandeh River and the Armenian community at **Jolfa** (p243). An easy bus trip brings you to **Kashan** (p224), where you can scramble over the roofs of both the bazaar and the opulent Qajar-era **traditional houses** (p226), and take a day trip to **Abyaneh** (p231), before heading back to Tehran.

This 1500km-long loop takes in most of Iran's highlights. Without getting too far off the beaten track, you'll get a taste of manic Tehran, Persia's glorious pre-Islamic legacy, and the stately former capitals. Most journeys are along busy transport routes; still, it pays to plan your next leg as soon as you arrive.

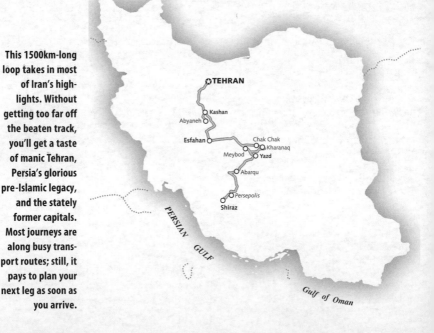

EAST BY SOUTHEAST   One Month / Turkey to Pakistan

Travellers with an adventurous bent have been following this classic overland route from Europe to subcontinental Asia for centuries. A month is the minimum time needed to do it justice. **Maku** (p136) makes a pleasant introduction on the way to **Tabriz** (p146), from where you can spend three days and check out **Jolfa** (p156) and **Kandovan** (p155), before heading for **Zanjan** (p184) for a look at **Soltaniyeh** (p184).

Historic **Qazvin** (p176) is the staging point for excursions into the spectacular Alamut Valleys to walk among the ruined **Castles of the Assassins** (p182). Head north of Qazvin via Rasht to lush **Masuleh** (p171), a charming village ideal for chilling out before dashing along the dreary Caspian Coast. From **Chalus** (p173) or **Kelardasht** (p175) zigzag up through the dramatic Alborz Mountains to Tehran. Spend three days in **Tehran** (p92) seeing the museums and taking in the hustle and bustle, and then head south for two days in **Kashan** (p224) and **Abyaneh** (p231). Bus it to **Esfahan** (p232) where you'll need at least three days to see the sights, and then head off to **Shiraz** (p267), where one of your three days will be spent gaping at the ruins of magnificent **Persepolis** (p279). You could spend a night in **Abarqu** (p267) en route to **Yazd** (p255), where three days should include a trip to the historic towns of **Meybod** (p266) and **Kharanaq** (p266), plus the spectacular Zoroastrian pilgrimage site at **Chak Chak** (p266).

Splurge on a night in the restored **Caravanserai Zein-o-din** (p267) on the way to **Kerman** (p312), where three days will be enough to see **Mahan** (p319) the 'New Arg' at **Rayen** (p321) and maybe the **Kaluts** (p321). Stop in **Bam** (p322) to see what remains of the Arg and just chill out a bit before the long trip to Quetta in Pakistan, and blast through **Zahedan** (p326), en route to the border at **Mirjaveh** (p330).

En route you'll absorb and appreciate Iran's diversity: this 4420km-long traverse passes through rocky mountain gorges, green hillsides, the grand cities of central Iran and the great expanse of the arid southeast. Check the security situation before travelling beyond Kerman.

ROADS LESS TRAVELLED

CANYONS, FORESTS & PADDYFIELDS...IN IRAN?!

10 Days /
Tabriz to Masuleh

Challenge Iran's desert image in the lush and rarely visited mountains of northwestern Iran. In the remotest sections you'll need to charter taxis, but with rides at about US$6 per hour they're an affordable luxury.

Start in **Tabriz** (p146), where you can explore the brilliant covered **bazaar** (p150) and the contrasting **Valiasr District** (p151). Allow a day or two for an excursion to the quaint troglodyte village of **Kandovan** (p155). Head to **Jolfa** (p156) and spend the afternoon at the ancient **Church of St Stephanos** (p157) and in nearby canyons. In Jolfa arrange a taxi for the next morning's early start: reaching Kaleybar along the fascinating **Aras River Valley** (p157) will take a long day. Unwind in **Kaleybar** (p159) after hiking up the soaring crag of nearby **Babak Castle** (p159).

Take a savari from nearby **Ahar** (p158) via **Meshgin Shahr** (p160) to Ardabil for impressive views of Mt Sabalan. While in **Ardabil** (p160) visit the **Sheikh Safi-od-Din Mausoleum** (p162), one of western Iran's finest monuments. Descend to the Caspian Sea coast either via **Astara** (p165), or through nomad country via **Kivi** and **Khal Khal** (both p164). Stop in **Bandar-e Anzali** (p170) or **Rasht** (p165) to enjoy the garlic-stoked food, then escape through paddyfields and thick forests to the mountain village of **Masuleh** (p171).

This intriguing 1000km-long meander through alternative Iran is ideal for those who've already seen the main desert city sites and who are confident in navigating through areas unaccustomed to foreign visitors. A sizable chunk (265km) is covered during one long day on the splendid taxi ride between Jolfa and Kaleybar.

DESERT DETOUR   10 Days / Esfahan to Kerman

After a few days in bustling cities, the wide open spaces, ancient mud-and-straw towns and tiny oasis villages in and around the Dasht-e Kavir desert are a tonic for the soul. Start this detour when you've finished in **Esfahan** (p232) and take a short bus trip to **Na'in** (p253), on the edge of the desert.

From Na'in hitch or take the bus east to Khur, and a taxi or any transport you can find to take you the last 38km to **Garmeh** (p254). The silence in this oasis village is profound, and the hospitality at **Ateshoni** (p254) heartfelt; you'll likely be here longer than planned.

Take a bus to **Yazd** (p255) and check into one of the atmospheric traditional hotels in the old town. Explore the old city, visit the Zoroastrian **Towers of Silence** (p262) and a **qanat** (p260), the underground water veins that keep these desert cities alive.

Take a day trip to **Meybod** (p266), **Chak Chak** (p266) and the mud-brick ghost town of **Kharanaq** (p266), and if you're fit perhaps a one- or two-day trek into the deserts around Yazd. Continue south and – having called ahead – stop in for one night of Safavid-era luxury in the restored **Caravanserai Zein-o-din** (p267), a wholly unforgettable experience that's worth the money.

Move to **Kerman** (p312), where you can arrange camel or 4WD tours to the beautiful sand castles at **Kaluts** (p321).

Do not even think of doing this trip during summer. October to April is the best time to travel, carrying something warm for the cold nights.

If you've ever dreamt of the oasis towns of the 1001 Nights, or are drawn to the vast expanses of emptiness, this 1330km-long trip is for you. Transport isn't always frequent, so try to plan ahead and brace yourself for some long waits – or consider renting a taxi.

TAILORED TRIPS

THE CRADLE OF PRE-ISLAMIC RELIGIONS

Two Weeks / Off the Beaten Track in Western Iran

Fire your imagination with millennia of religious history and myth. Start in ancient **Shush** (p214), visiting the tomb of the Jewish hero Daniel as well as the nearby **Choqa Zanbil** (p215), a magnificent 3000-year-old Elamite ziggurat (stepped pyramid). Climb into the mountains along the Babylonian 'Royal Road' via **Kermanshah** (p195) to **Hamadan** (ancient Ecbatana; p200) to see the tomb of biblical Jewish Queen Esther. Alternatively, from Kermanshah (via Paveh) roller-coaster the bumpy hairpins of the valleys of **Howraman** (p194), where the spectacularly set **Howraman-at-Takht** (p194) holds the last extant Mithraic midwinter festival. Further north, amid idyllic rural villages, explore the lonely ruins of **Takht-e Soleiman** (p187), once the world's greatest Zoroastrian fire-temple complex.

David Rohl's book *Legend* claims that the area around bustling **Tabriz** (p146) is the historical Garden of Eden, and that Mt Sahand, above the lovely village of **Kandovan** (p155), is the Old Testament's Mountain of God. Northwest of Tabriz is **Bazargan** (p136), from where Mt Ararat (Noah's Ark crash-landing spot) is clearly visible. Nearby **Jolfa** (p156), in the beautiful valley of the **Aras River** (the Bible's Gihon; p157), charming **Church of St Stephanos** (p157) was originally founded just a generation after Christ. To the east of Tabriz, around **Ardabil** (p160), is Genesis' Land of Nod guarded by the magnificent volcanic peak of **Mt Sabalan** (p163), the metaphorical fire-sword of the Cherubim.

THE TRANSIT-VISA DASH   Five Days / Turkey to Pakistan

The days of extendable transit visas are over. But if a transit visa is all you can get, overnight buses mean that you can still get a taste of Iran's two gem-cities while crossing the country for barely US$30 all in. On day one, leave Van (Turkey) in the early morning, cross the border at **Sero** (p139) to arrive in **Orumiyeh** (p140) by early afternoon. At 3.30pm take the overnight bus to glorious **Esfahan** (p232), avoiding Tehran. Spend two days in Esfahan then on the third evening take a night bus (six hours) to wonderful **Yazd** (p255). Book the next night's ticket to Zahedan before spending the day exploring Yazd. With luck you're not too tired to enjoy its splendid alleys and *badgirs* (windtowers). You'll arrive in unpleasant **Zahedan** (p326) early and head straight through to the Pakistani border.

Snapshot
Andrew Burke

'Come, come, drink *chay,*' says Reza, seating me and settling cross-legged on the carpet nearby. 'So, what do you think about Iran?'

I love Iran, Reza. But what do you think about Iran?

'I love Iran too, of course, this is my land and it is a great country. But I tell you, we have many problems. Especially with this president. Many people from other countries think we're crazy, and sometimes when I look at the TV, I think Ahmadinejad is crazy, too. All this rhetoric he spouts when he is overseas, talking about Israel all the time and saying Iran has no…you know…homosexuals. Hah! Who does he think he is kidding? Sure, the Arabs might like what he says and in some ways it is good to see him standing up to arrogant George Bush. But I ask you, how different is Mahmoud Ahmadinejad? A couple of my friends like him; they say he's honest and he is not part of the revolutionary establishment. But most of us Iranians have heard enough promises from him and his government to know better. He promised to be different from all the mullahs of the last 25 years, who have just become rich on oil. He said he'd put oil money on the dinner tables of ordinary Iranians. I tell you, there's no oil on my table. My wife is still making *ghorme sabzi* and the cooking oil costs more than ever. Do you know what is the inflation in Iran? It's 25%! *Bist o panj!* The government says 13% but you can't trust them, they're worse than the *bazaris.*'

Yes, I can relate to you on that one, sounds like politicians everywhere. But what about this nuclear program? I see the Bushehr reactor is opening soon and everyone in America and Europe is worried about it…even the Chinese are unhappy. What do you think? Does Iran really need nuclear energy? I mean, you have the second-largest reserves of oil and gas of any country on earth, isn't that enough to keep all those Paykans running? And as for nuclear weapons, do you think they are really trying to build a bomb?

'*They* have the oil, not us…remember. But anyway, Iran absolutely has the right to nuclear power. Absolutely! Lots of other countries have nuclear power so why shouldn't Iran have it? We might have a lot of oil but the refineries are so old that a lot of it actually gets drilled here, then exported, and then we have to buy it back as petrol. Ridiculous, isn't it? And you know how dirty those Paykans are, look at the pollution. If nuclear energy

FAST FACTS

Population: about 70 million

Part of population aged under 30: 70%

Surface area: 1,648,000 sq km

Highest point: Mt Damavand (5671m)

Lowest point: Caspian Sea (-28m)

Rate of inflation: 13/25% (official/unofficial)

Per capita GDP: US$2440/8700 (nominal/PPP)

Population living in towns and cities: 70%

University places taken by women: 65%

Women as a percentage of paid workforce: about 13%

INFLATION, RISING PRICES & YOU

Whether you choose to believe the official inflation rate of 13% or the more widely agreed 25%, the reality for Iranians – and for travellers – is that prices are rising steadily and look likely to continue to do so through the life of this book. As much as we'd love for our prices to be exact, they won't be. All prices are a guide, not gospel. The reality is that many transport, hotel and food prices will have risen before this book has even been published.

The good news for travellers is that costs in Iran are very reasonable by Western standards, so rises shouldn't break the bank. And with the Iranian rial losing value against most other currencies (yes, even the US dollar), 25% inflation shouldn't mean a full 25% rise in dollar/euro/pound terms. Within a short time you'll know approximately by how much prices have risen and can factor that into negotiations for whatever goods or services you're seeking.

Prices *will* rise. Accepting and expecting it will make your journey less argumentative, suspicious and much more enjoyable.

Reza isn't real, but this conversational snapshot of issues in Iran comes from dozens of encounters with real people in Iran and is broadly representative of opinion – and of course like any country there is a range of ideas.

In the 1980s Iranian women had an average of six children each and the population doubled. Today that average is just 1.7 and population growth is the lowest in the region, and similar to many European countries.

For two sides of political debate in Iran, see and contribute to President Mahmoud Ahmadinejad's blog at www.ahmadinejad.ir, and search for dissident Akbar Ganji's manifesto for the alternative view.

is cleaner isn't that good? You know, what annoys me most is that despite all the president's rhetoric, Iran has not actually broken the rules of this Nuclear Non-Proliferation Treaty we keep hearing about; but still the Americans and Europeans impose sanctions that make the economy even worse. I don't want a nuclear bomb and I don't think we should have one – it's too dangerous. Now that the CIA says we're officially not making one, do you think they'll lift the sanctions?'

I don't know, Reza, not everyone in the US and Europe is convinced, though at least now a military attack seems less likely. If America and Iran started talking a bit more that could help, and maybe then the sanctions could be lifted, which would help the economy. Being so isolated must be a big problem, especially for a country where millions of kids are finishing school and looking for jobs every year.

'Yes, there are not enough jobs for the young people – and two thirds of the population are young people. Look at my children. My son is doing military service in Kermanshah, thankfully, because for now I don't have to pay for him and he's not going to get shot like those poor boys fighting drug smugglers on the Afghanistan border. My daughter is studying engineering at university. I wanted her to get married and give us some grandchildren, but the women today are different. She was smart enough to get into university and that is not easy, so if she really wants to study then I suppose I should support her – that's what my wife says, anyway. But I do worry about her because it's harder for women to find good jobs than it is for men. I don't want her to have to emigrate to find a job. Already too many young people are going off to Canada, America and Europe, and it's always the smartest who leave. Still, she is a good girl, she hasn't been arrested for showing too much hair yet and hasn't asked me to buy her a new nose…I'm serious, that's what my friend's daughter did.'

But, they're not just leaving to find work, are they? My friends here tell me a lot of the strict old laws about how people dress and what they say have come back. Newspapers and bookshops are being closed, editors and dissidents sent to jail, the Majlis even passed a bill promoting Islamic fashion. Is that what young people want from the Islamic Republic?

'You must remember that this country is not all black and white. Yes, it is 30 years since the revolution and most of us want to move on. But a lot of less influential people, like my cousin who lives in a village, have better lives thanks to the revolution. Though I am worried. These crackdowns are taking us back 10 years. Even some ayatollahs in Qom are saying that arresting women for showing a bit of hair, all in the name of the Islamic Revolution, is ridiculous and will only turn more people away from Islam. But, what can we do? We must solve our own problems – we certainly don't need George Bush to solve them for us – and we must hope that the Guardian Council will allow good candidates to run in the next elections. That is all we can do.'

History

Historians are still debating when the first inhabitants settled in what is now Iran, but archaeologists suggest that during Neolithic times small numbers of hunters lived in caves in the Zagros and Alborz Mountains and in the southeast of the country.

THE ELAMITES & MEDES

Iran's first organised settlements were established in Elam, the lowland region in what is now Khuzestan province, as far back as the middle of the 3rd millennium BC. Elam was close enough to Mesopotamia and the great Sumerian civilisation to feel its influence, and records suggest the two were regular opponents on the battlefield. The Elamites established their capital at Shush (p214) and derived their strength through a remarkably enlightened federal system of government that allowed the various states to exchange the natural resources unique to each region. The Elamites' system of inheritance and power distribution was also quite sophisticated for the time, ensuring power was shared by and passed through various family lines.

The Elamites believed in a pantheon of gods, and their most notable remaining building, the enormous ziggurat at Choqa Zanbil (p215), was built around the 13th century BC and dedicated to the foremost of these gods. By the 12th century BC the Elamites are thought to have controlled most of what is now western Iran, the Tigris Valley and the coast of the Persian Gulf. They even managed to defeat the Assyrians, carrying off in triumph the famous stone inscribed with the Code of Hammurabi, a battered copy of which is in the National Museum of Iran (p104), the original having been carried off to the Louvre in Paris.

About this time Indo-European Aryan tribes began to arrive from the north. These Persians eventually settled in what is now Fars province, around Shiraz, while the Medes took up residence further north, in what is today northwestern Iran. The Medes established a capital at Ecbatana, now buried under modern Hamadan (p200), and first crop up in Assyrian records in 836 BC. But little more is heard of them until Greek historian Herodotus writes of how Cyaxares of Media expelled the Scythians, who had invaded from the Caucasus, in about 625 BC. According to Herodotus, whose histories are notoriously colourful, the Scythians were defeated when their kings attended a party and became so drunk they were easily disposed of.

Under Cyaxares, the Medes became a most formidable military force, repeatedly attacking the neighbouring Assyrians. In 612, having formed an alliance with the Babylonians, the Medes sacked the Assyrian capital of Nineveh and chased the remnants of this once-mighty empire into history. Exactly how the conquering powers divided the spoils of this heady success is uncertain, but it is believed the Medes assumed control of the highland territories. This meant that at his death in 575 BC Cyaxares is thought to have controlled an area that stretched from Asia Minor in the west as far as present-day Kerman in the east. Within a few years, though, this would seem very modest indeed.

THE ACHAEMENIDS & THE FIRST PERSIAN EMPIRE

In the 7th century BC the king of one of the Persian tribes, Achaemenes, created a unified state in southern Iran, giving his name to what would

Ancient Persia, by Josef Wiesehöfer, is a study of the country's origins and why it collapsed so dramatically after the Arab invasions of the 7th century.

IRAN'S DYNASTIES & NOTABLE RULERS

Achaemenids 550–330 BC
Cyrus II (the Great) r 559–530 BC
Cambyses r 529–522 BC
Darius I (the Great) r 522–486 BC
Xerxes r 486–465 BC
Artaxerxes I r 465–425 BC
Darius II r 424–405 BC
Artaxerxes II r 405–359 BC
Capitals in Shush, Babylon & Persepolis

Seleucids 323–162 BC

Parthians 247 BC–AD 224
Mithridates r 171–138 BC
Mithridates II r 123–88 BC
Capitals in Rey and Ctesiphon

Sassanians AD 224–642
Ardashir I r 224–41
Shapur I r 241–72
Shapur II r 310–79
Khusro II r 590–628
Capitals at Firuz Abad, then Ctesiphon

Arabs & Turks arrive 642–1051
Umayyad Caliphate r 642–750, capital in Damascus
Abbasid Caliphate r 750–830s, capital in Baghdad 9th century, rule fragments
Tahirids, r 820–72
Saffarids, r 868–903
Samanids, r 874–999
Ziarids, r 928–1077
Buyids, r 945–1055
Qaznavids, r 962–1140

Seljuks 1051–1220
Toghrol Beik r 1037–63

Malek Shah r 1072–92
Capital in Esfahan

Mongol Ilkhanids 1256–1335
Hulagu Khan r 1256–65
Ghazan Khan r 1295–1304
Oljeitu Khan r 1304–16
Capitals in Maraghe, Soltaniyeh

Timurids 1380–1502
Tamerlane r 1380–1405
Shahrokh r 1405–47
Govern from Samarkand, Herat and Qazvin

Safavids 1502–1736
Ismail Savafi r 1502–24
Tahmasp r 1524–76
Abbas I (Abbas the Great) r 1587–1629
Capitals in Tabriz, Qazvin then Esfahan

Nader Shah 1736–1747
Capital in Mashhad

Zand Period 1750–1795
Karim Khan Zand r 1750–79
Lotf ali Khan r 1779–95
Capital in Shiraz

Qajars 1795–1925
Aga Mohammad Khan r 1795–6
Fath Ali Shah r 1797–1834
Nasser al-Din Shah r 1848–96
Capital in Tehran

Pahlavis 1925–1979
Reza Shah r 1925–41
Shah Mohammad Reza r 1941–79

become the First Persian Empire, that of the Achaemenids. By the time his 21-year-old great-grandson Cyrus II ascended the throne in 559 BC, Persia was clearly a state on the up. Within 20 years it would be the greatest empire the world had known.

Having rapidly built a mighty military force, Cyrus the Great (as he came to be known) ended the Median Empire in 550 BC when he defeated his own grandfather – the hated king Astyages – in battle at Pasargadae. Within 11 years, Cyrus had campaigned his way across much of what is now Turkey, east into modern Pakistan, and finally defeated the Babylonians. It was in the aftermath of this victory in 539 BC that Cyrus marked himself out as something of a sensitive, new age despot. Rather than putting the Babylonians to the sword, he released the Jews who had been held there and, according to Herodotus in *The Persian Wars*, declared, among other things, that he would 'respect the traditions, customs and religions of the nations of my empire and never let any of my governors and subordinates look down on or insult them... I will impose my monarchy on no nation. Each is free to accept it, and if any one of them rejects it, I never resolve on war to reign.'

Cyrus colonised the old Median capital at Ecbatana, redeveloped Shush and built for himself a new home at Pasargadae (p284), establishing the pattern whereby Persian rulers circulated between three different capitals. Unfortunately for him, the Massagetae from the northeast of the empire decided he was indeed imposing his monarchy on them and they didn't like it. Herodotus writes that Cyrus incurred the wrath of the Massagetae queen, Tomyris, after he captured her son and slaughtered many of her soldiers in a battle made especially one-sided because the Massagetae army were all drunk – on wine strategically planted by the Achaemenids. Herodotus writes:

> When Tomyris heard what had befallen her son and her army, she sent a herald to Cyrus, who thus addressed the conqueror: 'Thou bloodthirsty Cyrus, pride not thyself on this poor success: it was the grape-juice...it was this poison wherewith thou didst ensnare my child, and so overcamest him, not in fair open fight. Now hearken what I advise, and be sure I advise thee for thy good. Restore my son to me and get thee from the land unharmed... Refuse, and I swear by the sun, the sovereign lord of the Massagetae, bloodthirsty as thou art, I will give thee thy fill of blood'.

Cyrus paid no heed to Tomyris, who gathered all the forces of her kingdom for what Herodotus described as the fiercest battle the Achaemenids had fought. Cyrus and most of his army were slain. When his body was recovered she ordered a skin filled with human blood and, making good on her threat, dunked Cyrus's head in it. Cyrus's body was eventually buried in the mausoleum that still stands at Pasargadae (p284).

In 525 BC Cyrus's son, Cambyses, headed west to capture most of Egypt and coastal regions well into modern Libya. It was later recorded

Cyrus the Great, by Jacob Abbott, tells the story of the fair-minded empire builder through the writings of Greek historian Herodotus and general Xenophenon, with extensive commentary from Abbott.

THE FIRST CHARTER OF HUMAN RIGHTS...OR NOT

In 1879, Assyro-British archaeologist Hormuzd Rassam unearthed a clay cylinder during a dig in the ancient Marduk temple of Babylon. What became known as the 'Cyrus Cylinder' bears a cuneiform inscription recording, among other things, that Cyrus 'strove for peace in Babylon and in all his [the god Marduk's] sacred sites' and 'abolished forced labour for those (Jews) who had been enslaved in Babylon.

These passages have been widely interpreted as a reflection of Cyrus's respect for human rights, and many consider it the world's first charter of human rights. Indeed, a replica remains on permanent display at UN headquarters in New York (the original is in the British Museum), and in 1971 the cylinder became the symbol of the 2500th anniversary of Iranian royalty. However, not everyone agrees. Many scholars argue the cylinder is not a charter of human rights, but rather that such statements were common populism among kings at the time. They say that Mesopotamian kings had a tradition dating back to the 3rd millennium BC of making grand and popular statements espousing social reform when they came to the throne, meaning Cyrus's declaration was neither new nor unique.

Whether the cylinder was the world's first declaration of human rights or not, it seems fair to say that Cyrus was an unusually benevolent ruler for his time, and he's well-remembered across the faiths. In the Bible both Ezra and Isaiah speak of Cyrus as a benign ruler responsible for the restoration of the temple in Jerusalem. And he is the only Gentile (non-Jew) designated as a divinely appointed king, or messiah, in the Tanakh.

that Cambyses had quietly arranged the assassination of his brother, Smerdis, before he left. The story goes that while Cambyses was distracted in Egypt, a minor official called Magus Gaumata, who had an uncanny resemblance to Smerdis, seized the throne. Cambyses died mysteriously in 522 BC while still in Egypt. With the king dead, Darius I, a distant relative, moved quickly and soon had 'Gaumata' murdered. This 'justice' was glorified in a giant relief at Bisotun (p199), near Hamadan, where you can see Darius's foot on Gaumata's head. What we will probably never know is whether Darius rid Persia of the so-called 'False Smerdis', or whether he murdered the real Smerdis and cooked up this unlikely story to justify his regicide.

Persian Fire, by Tom Holland, is a page-turning history of the Persian Wars, the first battles between East and West, and the Achaemenid empire at its most powerful. Recommended reading before visiting Shush or Persepolis.

Darius had won an empire in disarray and had to fight hard to re-establish it, dividing his sprawling inheritance into 23 satrapies to make it easier to govern. The magnificent complex at Persepolis (p279) was created to serve as the ceremonial and religious hub of an empire whose primary god was Ahura Mazda, also the subject of Zoroastrian worship. The Median capital at Shush became the administrative centre, but Persepolis was the imperial showcase, extravagantly decorated to intimidate visitors and impress with its beauty. The Apadana Staircase (p281), which depicts 23 subject nations paying tribute to the Achaemenid king, is arguably the artistic apex of the site. Darius eventually expanded the empire to India and pushed as far north as the Danube River in Europe.

It was the greatest of the early civilisations. Paved roads stretched from one end of the empire to the other, with caravanserais at regular intervals to provide food and shelter to travellers. The Achaemenids introduced the world's first postal service, and it was said the network of relay horses could deliver mail to the furthest corner of the empire within 15 days.

But it wasn't all smooth sailing. When the Greek colonies of Asia Minor rebelled against their Persian overlord, Darius decided to invade mainland Greece to make an example of those states that refused to subject themselves. It didn't work. In 490 BC Darius's armies were defeated at Marathon near Athens. He died in 486 BC.

The subsequent defeat of Darius's son Xerxes at Salamis in Greece in 480 BC marked the beginning of a long, slow decline that would continue, with glorious interludes, for another 150 years.

ALEXANDER THE GREAT & THE END OF PERSEPOLIS

The end of the First Persian Empire finally came at the hands of Alexander the Great, king of Macedonia. Having defeated the Greeks and Egyptians, Alexander saw off Persian armies at Issus in Turkey (333 BC) and Guagamela in present-day Iraq (331 BC). By the time he arrived in Persia proper the end of the Achaemenid empire was almost inevitable, and it wasn't long before the last remaining armies of Darius III were swept aside. Darius himself fled east to Bactria, only to be murdered by his cousin. In the wake of his victory, Alexander spent several months at Persepolis, before the finest symbol of Achaemenid power was burned to the ground. Even today experts argue whether this was the accidental result of a drunken party or deliberate retaliation for the destruction of Athens by Xerxes.

In 311 BC the Macedonian ruler Cassander had Alexander the Great's Persian widow, Roxana, and their son, Alexander IV, put to death to stave off any threat to his rule.

Alexander's empire soon stretched across Afghanistan, Pakistan and into India, but after his death in 323 BC it was divided between three squabbling dynasties, with Persia controlled by the Macedonian Seleucids. Gradually the Greek language replaced Aramaic as the lingua franca, new towns were set up all over the region and Greek culture stamped itself on the older Persian one. However, ambitious satraps and feisty ethnic minorities were bucking the system, particularly the nomadic Parthians.

THE PARTHIAN TAKEOVER

The Parthians had settled the area between the Caspian and Aral Seas many centuries before. Under their great king Mithridates (171–138 BC), they swallowed most of Persia and then everywhere between the Euphrates in the west and Afghanistan in the east, more or less re-creating the old Achaemenid Empire. They had two capitals, one at what is now Rey (p131), the other at Ctesiphon, in present-day Iraq.

Expert horsemen and archers, the Parthians spent much energy fighting with Rome for control of Syria, Mesopotamia and Armenia – territories the Romans felt were rightly theirs. This largely ended, however, after the Roman general Crassus, who had defeated Spartacus 20 years earlier and was now one of three men controlling Rome, wrongly concluded his armies had the measure of their Parthian counterparts. In 53 BC Crassus saw his armies routed at Carrhae, in modern-day Turkey (he was then captured, had molten gold poured down his throat to mock his greed, and eventually lost his head). Extended periods of peace followed, though the Romans and Parthians were only ever an ambitious leader away from a fight.

More enlightened than later dynasties, the Parthians oversaw significant progress in architecture and the arts, though little remains today.

The modern term 'parting shot' derives from the ancient 'Parthian shot'. As Parthian horsemen rode away from their enemy they would turn in their saddles and fire arrows at their pursuers. This was the 'Parthian shot'.

THE SASSANIANS & THE SECOND PERSIAN EMPIRE

Like the Achaemenids before them, the Sassanian rise from small-time dynasty to empire was nothing short of staggering. Beginning in their home province of Fars in AD 224, Ardashir I (r 224–41) led a push that saw the Sassanians replace the ailing Parthians in Persia and within 40 years become a renewed threat to the Roman Empire.

Between 241 and 272 Ardashir's son, Shapur I, added Bactria to the empire and fought repeatedly with the Romans. In one of the most celebrated of all Persian victories, Shapur's armies defeated the Romans at Edessa in 260 and took the Roman emperor Valerian prisoner. You can still see the city of Bishapur (p286), where Valerian was kept until he died, and bas-reliefs depicting the victory at Naqsh-e Rostam (p283).

The Sassanians re-formulated Zoroastrianism into a state religion incorporating elements of Greek, Mithraic and ancient animist faiths. They then indulged in sporadic bursts of repression against other religions, including newly emerging Christianity. The Sassanians spoke their own language, Pahlavi, the root of modern Farsi. Several fire temples and other important and imposing structures remain from the Sassanid period. Among the most impressive are the largely intact Ardashir's Palace at Firuz Abad (p285); the crumbling adobe city at Kuh-e Khajeh (p331); the city of Bishapur and the giant Statue of Shapur I (p286) in a nearby cave; and the Arg-e Bam (p322), where investigations following the 2003 earthquake have revealed the outer walls and several other structures were built by the Sassanians. The Sassanian capital was at Ctesiphon in modern Iraq.

The Sassanians developed small industries, promoted urban development and encouraged trade across the Persian Gulf but eventually they, too, were weakened by seemingly never-ending conflict with Byzantium. Ironically it was in its last years that the empire was at its largest, when Khusro II (590-628) recaptured parts of Egypt, Syria, Palestine and Turkey. However, after Khusro was murdered by his son in 628, at least six rulers, including Persia's only two women monarchs, came and went in the following five years. Persia was in no state to resist when the Arabs attacked in 633.

Those Roman soldiers fortunate enough to survive the carnage at Carrhae reported that the Parthians fought under dazzlingly bright flags. It was Europe's first glimpse of silk.

In 387 the Persian and Byzantine empires agree to solve their long-running dispute over control of Armenia by carving it up; it was one of the first (and ultimately unsuccessful) examples of partition.

THE ARABS & ISLAM

A crucial chapter in Persian history started when the Arabs defeated the Sassanians at Qadisirya in AD 637, following up with a victory at Nehavand near Hamadan that effectively ended Sassanian rule.

In the late 5th century a socialist called Mazdak won a huge following by preaching that nobles should share their wealth and their women with the oppressed masses.

By the time of Mohammed's death in 632 the Arabs were firm adherents of Islam. The Persians found plenty to like in Islamic culture and religion, and happily forsook Zoroaster for the teachings of Mohammed without much need of persuasion. Only Yazd and Kerman (both of which clung to Zoroastrianism for a few centuries more) and a few isolated tribes in the mountains near the Caspian Sea held fast to their old religions. As they rapidly spread across the Middle East, the Arabs adopted Sassanians' architecture, arts and administration practices.

The Umayyad caliphs initially governed Persia from their capital in Damascus, but in 750 a Shiite rebellion led to the elevation of the Abbasid dynasty, which set up its capital near Baghdad. The Abbasid caliphs presided over a period of intellectual exuberance in which Persian culture played a major role. Persians also held many high offices at court, but the Arabic language and script became the norm for day-to-day business.

During the 9th century Abbasid power crumbled and, one by one, regional governors established their own power bases. In eastern Iran these new Iranian dynasties included the Safarrids (868–903), the Tahirids (820–72) and the Samanids (874–999), who set up their capital at Bukhara and revived the Persian language.

Ferdosi wrote his epic poem, the *Shahnameh* (Book of Kings), between about 990 and his death in around 1020. Its 60,000 couplets are considered the foundation stone of modern Farsi, in the same way Shakespeare is considered the father of English.

THE COMING OF THE SELJUKS

Inevitably, these local dynasties could not hold onto their power. The Samanids became fatally dependent on Turkish soldiers, one of whom soon elbowed them aside to found his own Qaznavid dynasty (962–1140); his son Mahmud spread the realm deep into India, introducing Islam as he went.

In turn they were ousted by the Seljuk Turks who pushed on through Persia, capturing Esfahan in 1051 and turning it into their capital. Within a few years they had added eastern Turkey to their empire and, despite numerous rebellions, managed to maintain control with a large and well-paid army.

The Seljuk dynasty heralded a new era in Persian art, literature and science, distinguished by geniuses such as the mathematician and poet Omar Khayyam (p74). Theological schools were also set up throughout Seljuk territories to propagate Sunni Islam. The geometric brickwork and elaborate Kufic inscriptions of Seljuk mosques and minarets can still be seen across Iran, though they're arguably at their finest in Esfahan's Jameh Mosque (p236).

In 1079 mathematician and poet Omar Khayyam calculated the length of the year as 365.242198 days. This preceded the Gregorian calendar by almost 500 years.

The death of Malek Shah in 1092 marked the end of real Seljuk supremacy, and once again a powerful empire splintered into weaker fragments.

GENGHIS KHAN & TAMERLANE

In the early 13th century, the Seljuk Empire came to a final and bloody end when the rampaging Mongols swept across the Iranian plateau on their horses, leaving a trail of cold-blooded devastation and thousands of dismembered heads in their wake.

Under the leadership first of Genghis Khan, and then his grandsons, including Hulagu, the Mongol rulers managed to seize all of Persia, as well as an empire stretching from Beijing (China) to İstanbul (Turkey). Eventually they established a capital at Tabriz (too close, as they later found out, to the Turks). It was Hulagu Khan who put an end to the stealthy power of the Assassins, destroying their castles around Alamut (p182). After a flirtation with Christianity and Buddhism, Hulagu was forced by social pressures in Persia to adopt Islam. He called himself *il khan* (provincial khan or ruler), a name later given to the entire Ilkhanid dynasty (1256–1335).

Tragically, the Mongols destroyed many of the Persian cities they conquered, obliterating much of Persia's documented history. Perhaps feeling guilty about all the violence, they became great arts patrons, leaving many fine monuments, including the wonderful Oljeitu Mausoleum (Gonbad-e Soltaniyeh, p184), near Zanjan. During Mongol rule Farsi definitively replaced Arabic as the lingua franca and Marco Polo followed the Silk Road across Persia (see the boxed text, p34). In 1335 the Ilkhanid empire came to an end when the death of Sultan Abu Said left it with no successor.

The fragmented empire succumbed to invading forces from the east led by Tamerlane (Lame Timur), who swept on to defeat the Ottoman Turks in 1402. Tamerlane came from a Turkified Mongol clan in what is now Uzbekistan. Tamerlane managed to stop the constant warring in Iran and moved the capital from Tabriz to Qazvin (p176). He was yet another of the great contradictions who ruled Persia over the years: an enthusiastic patron of the arts and one of history's greatest killers (after one rebellion 70,000 people are said to have been executed in Esfahan alone).

When he died in 1405, Tamerlane's empire immediately started to struggle. The Timurids in eastern Iran clung to varying degrees of power for several decades, maintaining their support of Persian art, particularly the miniaturists of Shiraz. Gohar Shad, the wife of one of the Timurid rulers, was responsible for the beautiful mosque at the heart of Mashhad's Holy Shrine to Imam Reza (p354).

The pattern of strong ruler, decline and the fragmentation of empire is a recurring theme in Persian history. The years following the Mongol and Timurid periods were no different, with the power divided and fought over by several blocs. Among the more notable groups were the Kara Koyunlu (Black Sheep) tribe, which managed to set itself up in Tabriz and grab power from the Mongols in eastern Turkey. Having held strong for almost two centuries (1275–1468), they, in turn, gave way to the Ak Koyunlu (White Sheep) tribe, which ruled the northeast until 1514.

THE SAFAVIDS & THE THIRD PERSIAN EMPIRE

A Sufi called Sheikh Safi od-Din (d 1334) was the inspiration for and progenitor of the Safavi, a powerful sect of Shiite followers from Ardabil (p160). Ismail Savafi, a distant descendent of Safi od-Din, was eventually to conquer all the old Persian imperial heartlands, from Baghdad to Herat. He ruled as Persian Shah (r 1502–24) and although forced out of western Iran by the Ottoman sultan, Selim the Grim, at the disastrous battle of Chaldoran, his Safavid dynasty ushered in a great Iranian revival.

Under Ismail's son Tahmasp (r 1524–76), the capital was moved from Tabriz to Qazvin, and European monarchs started to take an interest in Persia. The Safavids reached their peak under the brilliant Shah Abbas I (Abbas the Great; r 1587–1629), who, with military advice from English adventurer Robert Shirley, finally crushed the assorted Turkmen and Turkish factions to create what is considered the Third Persian Empire.

The Safavids oversaw a renewed flowering of Persian art and architecture. Abbas moved the capital to Esfahan and promptly set about rebuilding the city around what is today Imam Sq (p238). The splendour of the

Marco Polo crossed Iran while travelling to and from China in the 13th century, stopping in Tabriz, Kashan, Yazd, Kerman, Hormoz, Bam, Tabas and Neishabur, among others.

Genghis Khan took the most beautiful women from the lands he defeated and made them wives or concubines, fathering hundreds of children. A recent study across Asia found that some 16 million men living today can likely trace their heritage back to the loins of the great ruler.

Safavid court can still be seen in the fantastic frescoes of the Chehel Sotun Palace (p241). Shiism was enshrined as Persia's state religion, bringing it into direct conflict with the Sunni Ottoman Empire.

European powers began looking on Persia as a market. English companies were given business concessions, although the Portuguese, who

THE SILK ROAD

Silk first began moving westward from China more than 2000 years ago, when the Parthians became quite enamoured with the soft, fine fabric. By about 100 BC, the Parthians and the Chinese had exchanged embassies and inaugurated official bilateral trade. The Romans developed an expensive fixation with the fabric after their defeat at Carrhae in 53 BC, and within a few centuries it would become more valuable than gold. The Romans even engaged in some early industrial espionage when the Emperor Justinian sent teams of spies to steal silk worm eggs in the 6th century.

It took many months to traverse the 8000km Silk Road route, though geographically it was a complex and shifting proposition. It was no single road, but rather a web of caravan tracks threading through some of the highest mountains and harshest deserts on earth. The network had its main eastern terminus at the Chinese capital Ch'ang-an (now Xian). Caravans entered present-day Iran anywhere between Merv (modern Turkmenistan) and Herat (Afghanistan), and passed through Mashhad, Neishabur, Damghan, Semnan, Rey, Qazvin, Tabriz and Maku, before finishing at Constantinople (now İstanbul). During winter, the trail often diverted west from Rey, passing through Hamadan to Baghdad. Caravanserais every 30km or so acted as hotels for traders; Robat Sharaf (p365) northeast of Mashhad is a surviving example.

Unlike the Silk Road's most famous journeyman, Marco Polo, caravanners were mostly short- and medium-distance hauliers who marketed and took on freight along a given beat. Goods heading east included gold, silver, ivory, jade and other precious stones, wool, Mediterranean coloured glass, grapes, wine, spices and – early Parthian crazes – acrobats and ostriches. Going west were silk, porcelain, spices, gems and perfumes. In the middle lay Central Asia and Iran, great clearing houses that provided the horses and Bactrian camels that kept the goods flowing.

The Silk Road gave rise to unprecedented trade, but its glory lay in the interchange of ideas. The religions alone present an astounding picture of diversity and tolerance: Manichaeism, Zoroastrianism, Buddhism, Nestorian Christianity, Judaism, Confucianism, Taoism and shamanism coexisted along the 'road' until the coming of Islam.

The Silk Road was eventually abandoned when the new European powers discovered alternative sea routes in the 15th century.

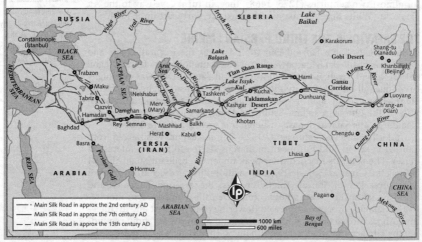

had controlled Hormoz Island (p306) in the Persian Gulf, were eventually expelled.

The death of Abbas was the signal for the predictable period of bickering and infighting, which eventually left the door wide open for the Afghans, who invaded in 1722. The Afghans besieged Esfahan and eventually took control of the city, slaughtering thousands but sparing the architectural wonders. The first Afghan ruler, Mahmud, went mad and was murdered by a member of his own army.

NADER SHAH & KARIM KHAN ZAND

The Safavids were briefly rescued from oblivion by a soldier of fortune, Nader Shah, who in 1729 scattered the Afghans, along with the Russian and Turkish forces that were encroaching in the north. Nader Shah ruled Persia in all but name until 1736, when he grew tired of the pretence and installed himself as shah, thus ending once and for all the Safavid dynasty. To describe Nader Shah as a brilliant but war-loving mercenary is something of an understatement. He was a megalomaniac who, in a show of supreme self-confidence, invaded India in 1738 and returned with loot that included the Kuh-e Nur and Darya-e Nur diamonds; see the latter in the National Jewels Museum (p105). His constant warring rapidly wore out the country and it was a relief to everyone when he was assassinated in 1747.

A Lor from western Iran (for more on the Lors, see the boxed text, p207), Karim Khan Zand (r 1750–79) grabbed power. Almost uniquely, he had little interest in warfare. Instead he is remembered for moving the capital to Shiraz, where he built the impressive Arg-e Karim Khan (p271) and the Regent's Mosque (Masjed-e Vakil; p271).

THE QAJARS & THE CONSTITUTIONAL REVOLUTION

The Qajar dynasty was a disaster for Iran, transforming more than 2000 years of empire and influence into an international laughing stock in just a few decades. Following Karim Khan's death in 1779, bitter and twisted eunuch Aga Mohammad Khan united the Azari Qajars and created a new capital in the village of Tehran. By 1795 he had wrested control of Persia from Lotf Ali Khan, but just a year later Aga Mohammad Khan was murdered by his own servants.

Both the Russians and British had their eyes on Iran. Russia was determined to gain access to the Persian Gulf and India, while Britain was equally determined to deny them. During the undistinguished reign of big-bearded Fath Ali Shah (r 1797–1834) Russia captured Georgia, Shirvan (today's Azerbaijan), eastern Armenia and Daghestan, all semi-independent entities previously within Persia's sphere of influence.

While responsible for a broad campaign of modernisation, Nasser al-Din Shah (r 1848–96) was generally more interested in collecting art, building museums and servicing his numerous wives. He sired hundreds of princes, all of whom took from the national treasury at will. Inevitably, the Russians asserted control over northern Iran while the British ran things in the south.

The Qajar shahs spent so much on luxuries – such as the Golestan Palace (p101) – that the treasury needed constant topping up through hasty sales of state assets. Foreign buyers were more than happy to pick up the bargains. In one notorious incident, Nasser al-Din tried to sell exclusive rights to exploit all Iran's economic resources (including all the banks, mines and railways) for a one-off sum of UK£40,000 to be followed by payments of UK£10,000 for the next 25 years. He was made to cancel the deal once news of its absurdity leaked out.

A steady trickle of European travellers and adventurers came, saw and wrote about Safavid Persia, most notably the French jewellers Jean-Baptiste Tavernier (1605–1689) and John Chardin (1643–1713), and English buccaneers Sir Anthony Shirley (1565–1635) and Sir Robert Shirley (1581–1628), in the early 17th century.

Karim Khan Zand rose to rule much of Persia from a power base of just a few rural families. He is renowned as a more compassionate, humble ruler than any in Persian history, and he insisted upon being called *vakil* (regent) rather than shah.

When news broke of an attempt to sell the tobacco monopoly, discontent boiled over into revolt. In 1906 the third-last Qajar shah, Muzaffar al-Din (r 1896–1907), was forced to introduce an embryo parliament, the first Majlis, and a constitution. It became known as the Constitutional Revolution.

When Cossack-soldier-turned-king Reza Shah moved into the Green Palace (p111) he found the dazzling mirrored tiles and four-post bed to be a bit too much, so slept on the floor.

Worried that such a helpful shah was being weakened, Russia persuaded him to backtrack on his promises. The Majlis was attacked with artillery and in 1908 martial law and dictatorship were introduced by his ruthless son Shah Mohammad Ali, leading to an uprising in Tabriz in 1909 (p146). Shah Mohammad Ali was forced to abdicate in favour of his son, who was still a child. The furore soon died down and in 1911 Shah Ahmad quietly abolished the second Majlis.

During WWI both Britain and Russia occupied parts of Iran while the Turks ravaged the partly Christian northwest. Inspired by the new regime in Russia, Gilan (the west Caspian area) broke away in 1920 to form a Soviet republic under Kuchuk Khan. The weak Qajar shah seemed unable to respond, so Britain backed charismatic army officer Reza Khan, who swiftly retook Gilan before ousting Shah Ahmad.

THE PAHLAVIS

From the moment in 1921 that Reza Khan staged a coup d'etat to, in effect, end Qajar rule, the poorly educated but wily soldier was king of Persia in all but name. Initially he installed a puppet prime minister, but in 1923 he took that role himself and in 1925 crowned himself, Napoleon-like, as the first shah of the Pahlavi line.

Reza Shah, as he became known, set himself an enormous task: to drag Iran into the 20th century in the same way his neighbour Mustafa Kemal Atatürk was modernising Turkey. Literacy, transport infrastructure, the health system, industry and agriculture had all been neglected and were pathetically underdeveloped. Like Atatürk, Reza Shah aimed to improve the status of women and to that end he made wearing the chador (black cloak) illegal. Like Atatürk, too, he insisted on the wearing of Western dress and moved to crush the power of the religious establishment.

Unlike his royal predecessors and the clerics who followed, who concentrated on religious architecture, Shah Mohammad Reza Pahlavi commissioned secular buildings in strikingly modern styles. Tehran's Carpet Museum of Iran (p108), Museum of Contemporary Art (p108), Tezatre Shahr (City Theatre; p122) and monolithic Azadi Tower (p114) are among the best.

However, Reza had little of the subtlety of Atatürk and his edicts made him many enemies. Some women embraced his new dress regulations, but others found them impossible to accept. Even today, some older Iranians talk of how their mothers didn't leave home for six years; too scared of prosecution to go outside wearing a head-covering, too ashamed to leave home without one.

Despite being nominally neutral during WWII, Reza's outspoken support of the Nazis proved too much for Britain and Russia. In 1941 Reza was forced into exile in South Africa, where he died in 1944. The British arranged for his 22-year-old son, Mohammad Reza, to succeed him. In 1943 at the Tehran Conference, Britain, Russia and the USA signed the Tehran Declaration, accepting the independence of Iran. The young Mohammad Reza regained absolute power – under heavy influence from the British.

By now the Anglo-Iranian Oil Company (later British Petroleum) was churning out petro-dollars by the million and there were calls for it to be nationalised. When prime minister Ali Razmara was assassinated in 1951, 70-year-old nationalist Dr Mohammad Mossadegh, leader of the National Front Movement, swept into office on the back of promises to repatriate that money. Mossadegh succeeded in nationalising Anglo-Iranian as the National Iranian Oil Company, but in 1953 he was removed in a coup organised by the USA and Britain (see the boxed text, opposite).

With Mossadegh gone, the US government encouraged the shah to press ahead with a program of social and economic modernisation dubbed the White Revolution because it was intended to take place without bloodshed. Many Iranians remember this period fondly for reforms including the further emancipation of women and improved literacy. But for a conservative, mainly rural Muslim population it was all too fast. The religious establishment, the ulema, also took exception to land reforms depriving them of rights and electoral reforms giving votes to non-Muslims.

By 1962 Ayatollah Ruhollah Khomeini, then living in Qom, had emerged as a figurehead for opposition to the shah. In 1964 the shah approved a bill giving US soldiers in Iran complete immunity from arrest. Khomeini responded by claiming the shah had 'reduced the Iranian people to a level lower than that of an American dog', because if anyone ran over a dog in America they would be prosecuted for doing so, but if an American ran over an Iranian he could do so with impunity. The shah reacted by banishing Khomeini, who fled first to Turkey and then to Iraq.

In 1971 the shah organised lavish celebrations for the 2500th anniversary of the founding of the Persian Empire, hoping to make himself more popular by fanning the flames of nationalism. More than 60 international monarchs and heads of state came to the party, held in a purpose-built tent city (p283) at Persepolis. The news coverage brought Iranian culture to the world, but at home it encouraged those who saw the shah as wasteful and became a rallying call for opposition groups.

Ironically, the 1974 oil price revolution also contributed to the shah's undoing. In just one year the income from oil shot from US$4 billion to US$20 billion, but the shah allowed US arms merchants to persuade him to squander much of this vast new wealth on weapons that then stood idle

All The Shah's Men, by Stephen Kinzer, is the incredible true story of the CIA's coup to overthrow Mohammad Mossadegh. It reads like a thriller and draws a line between the coup and the rise of Islamic terrorism. Highly recommended.

MOHAMMAD MOSSADEGH & THE CIA'S FIRST COUP

Before Lumumba in Congo, Sukarno in Indonesia and Allende in Chile, Mohammad Mossadegh was the first democratically elected leader toppled by a CIA coup d'etat. Mossadegh, a highly educated lawyer, paid the price for seeking a better deal for Iran from the hugely profitable oilfields run by the Anglo-Iranian Oil Company. When the British refused Iran a fairer share, he nationalised the company and expelled British diplomats, whom he rightly suspected of plotting to overthrow him. The significance of this act went far beyond the borders of Iran, and Mossadegh was named *Time* magazine's Man of the Year in 1951 for his influence in encouraging developing nations to shake off the colonial yoke.

The British were desperate to get 'their' oil back. They encouraged a worldwide boycott of Iranian oil and worked hard to muddy Mossadegh's name in Iran and internationally. After arch-colonialist Winston Churchill was re-elected in 1952, he managed to persuade the new Eisenhower administration in the USA that Mossadegh had to go. The CIA's Operation Ajax was the result. Kermit Roosevelt, grandson of former president Theodore Roosevelt and one of the agency's top operatives, established a team in the basement of the US Embassy in Tehran and soon won the shah's support. But that alone wasn't enough and another US$2 million was spent buying support from senior clerics, military officers, newspaper editors and thugs.

The CIA was new at the coup game – it started badly when Mossadegh loyalists arrested the coup leaders on 16 August. The shah promptly fled to Rome, but three days later there was a second attempt and Mossadegh was toppled. The shah returned and the oil industry was denationalised, but the British monopoly was broken and for its trouble the USA claimed a 40% stake.

Check out www.nytimes.com/library/world/mideast/041600iran-cia-index.html for the 96-page CIA history of the coup.

in the desert. As the world slipped into recession, oil sales slumped and several planned social reforms were cut. The public was not happy.

THE REVOLUTION

Since the beginning of the Pahlavi dynasty, resistance had smouldered away and occasionally flared into violence. Students wanted faster reform, devout Muslims wanted reforms rolled back, and everyone attacked the Pahlavis' conspicuous consumption.

The opposition came from secular, worker-communist and Islamic groups whose common denominator was a desire to remove the shah. Exiled Ayatollah Khomeini was an inspirational figure, but contrary to the official Iranian portrayal other people did most of the organising. Among the most prominent was Ayatollah Mahmoud Taleqani, a popular Islamic reformist whose ideas were considerably less fundamental than Khomeini's.

As the economy faltered under the shah's post oil-boom mismanagement, the opposition grew in confidence and organised massive street demonstrations and small-scale sabotage. The shah responded with brutal force and his security agency, Savak, earned a horrific reputation for torture and killing. In November 1978, he imposed martial law and hundreds of demonstrators were killed in Tehran, Qom and Tabriz. America's long-standing support began to falter and in December the now-desperate shah appointed veteran opposition politician Shapur Bakhtiar as prime minister. It didn't work. On 16 January 1979 (now a national holiday), Shah Mohammad Reza Pahlavi and his third wife, Farah Diba, finally fled. He died in Egypt in 1980.

Khomeini's frequent broadcasts on the BBC's Persian Service had made him the spiritual leader of opposition. But at 77 years old, everyone expected that once the shah was ousted he would assume a more hands-off, statesman-like role. They were wrong. On his return to Iran on 1 February 1979, Khomeini told the exultant masses his vision for a new Iran, free of foreign influence and true to Islam: 'From now on it is I who will name the government'.

> In 1971 the Arabic Islamic calendar was replaced by a 'Persian' calendar (p375).

> *My Uncle Napoleon*, by Iraj Pezeshkzad and published in the early 1970s, was an instant bestseller. In 1976 it became a TV series, and its story – of three families living under the tyranny of a paranoid patriarch – became a cultural reference point in the lead-up to revolution.

AYATOLLAH RUHOLLAH KHOMEINI

An earnest, belligerent and intensely committed man, Ayatollah Ruhollah Khomeini is reviled and little understood in the West but revered as a saint by many Iranians. Khomeini was a family man of modest means whose wife hennaed her hair orange until his death; a religious leader who reduced the age at which 'women' could marry to nine; a war leader who sent young men to their deaths on the Iraqi front by persuading them they would go straight to paradise as martyrs; the man who proclaimed the infamous fatwa against Salman Rushdie.

Born in the village of Khomein in central Iran about 1900, Sayyed Ruhollah Musavi Khomeini followed in the family tradition by studying theology, philosophy and law in the holy city of Qom. By the 1920s he had earned the title of ayatollah (the highest rank of a Shiite cleric) and settled down to teach and write.

He first came to public attention in 1962 when he opposed the shah's plans to reduce the clergy's property rights and emancipate women. In 1964 he was exiled to Turkey, before moving on to Iraq. In 1978 Saddam Hussein expelled Khomeini and he moved to Paris. When the shah fled in 1979, Khomeini returned to take control of Iran through force of character and ruthless efficiency, and remained leader of the world's first Islamic theocracy until his death in 1989 (p131).

Today, Khomeini is officially known as Imam Khomeini, raising him to the level of saint, and almost every town in the country has a street or square named after him. His portrait, with prominent eyebrows and stern expression, is everywhere, often beside and thus legitimising that of the current leader, Ayatollah Ali Khamenei.

THE AFTERMATH OF THE REVOLUTION

Ayatollah Khomeini soon set about proving the adage that 'after the revolution comes the revolution'. His intention was to set up a clergy-dominated Islamic Republic, and he achieved this with brutal efficiency.

Groups such as the People's Feda'iyin, the Islamic People's Mojahedin, and the communist Tudah had been instrumental in undermining the shah and his government. But once the shah was safely out of the way they were swept aside. People disappeared, executions took place after brief and meaningless trials, and minor officials took the law into their own hands. The facts – that the revolution had been a broad-based effort – were revised and the idea of the Islamic Revolution was born. Leaders such as Ayatollah Taleqani were sidelined or worse. Taleqani is still revered as a hero of the revolution, but many Iranians believe he died because Khomeini refused him the asthma inhalers he needed to survive.

Following a referendum in March 1979, in which 98.2% of the population voted in favour, the formation of the world's first Islamic Republic was announced on 1 April 1979. Ayatollah Khomeini became the Supreme Leader.

Almost immediately, the Islamic Republic was viewed suspiciously and accused of adopting confrontational policies designed to promote other Islamic revolutions. In November 1979, conservative university students burst into the US embassy and took 52 staff hostage, an action blessed by Khomeini. For the next 444 days the siege of the US embassy dogged US president, Jimmy Carter. Worse still, a *Boy's Own*–style attempt to rescue the hostages ran aground quite literally when the helicopters supposed to carry them to safety collided in the desert near Tabas. Amid the crisis, presidential elections were held and Abol Hasan Bani-Sadr, Khomeini's friend since the days of his Paris exile, was elected, with Mohammad Ali Rajai as his prime minister.

THE IRAN–IRAQ WAR

In 1980, hoping to take advantage of Iran's domestic chaos, Iraq's President Saddam Hussein made an opportunistic land grab on oil-rich Khuzestan province, claiming it was a historic part of Iraq. It was a catastrophic miscalculation that resulted in eight years of war and up to 500,000 deaths on each side.

Ironically, the invasion proved to be pivotal in solidifying support for the shaky Islamic Revolution by providing an obvious enemy to rally against and an opportunity to spread the revolution by force of arms. Iraq was better equipped and better supplied, but Iran could draw on a larger population and a fanaticism fanned by its mullahs.

Fighting was fierce, with poison gas and trench warfare being seen for the first time since WWI. A group of Islamic volunteers called Basijis, many as young as 13, chose to clear minefields by walking through them, confident they would go to heaven as martyrs. By July 1982 Iran had forced the Iraqis back to the border, but rather than accept peace Iran adopted a new agenda that included occupying Najaf and Karbala, important Shia pilgrimage sites. The war dragged on for another six years, ending shortly after an Iranian airliner was shot down by the US Navy over the Persian Gulf.

During the war Iraq bombed nearly 3000 villages and 87 Iranian cities, virtually obliterating Abadan and Khorramshahr. Millions of Iranians lost their homes and jobs, and some 1.2 million fled the battle zone, many moving permanently to far-away Mashhad. A cease-fire was finally negotiated in mid-1988, though prisoners were still being exchanged in 2003. Iranians

Modern Iran: Roots and Results of Revolution, by Nikki R Keddie, is a thorough analysis of the causes and effects of the revolution, focusing more on economic than religious factors.

Shah of Shahs, by journalist Ryszard Kapuscinski, is a fast-paced yet perceptive account of Iran in the decade leading to the revolution, written in a style that draws attention to the absurdities of a deadly serious situation.

Although nominally *Reading Lolita in Tehran*, by Azar Nafisi, is a work of literary criticism, in reality Nafisi writes a beautiful and powerfully moving memoir of her life in Iran after the revolution.

refer to the war as the 'Iraq-imposed war' and it remains a huge influence on the country. Pictures of martyrs can be seen in every city, and barely a day passes without TV broadcasting interviews with veterans.

Bashu, the Little Stranger, Behram Beiza'i's 1986 film, tells the story of a little boy finding a new mother in southern Iran. It was the first antiwar film, made at the height of the Iran–Iraq War.

While war was raging, different factions within Iran continued to jostle for supremacy. In June 1981 a bomb blast at the headquarters of the Islamic Republican Party killed its founder Ayatollah Beheshti and 71 others, including four cabinet ministers. A second bomb in August killed President Rajai and the new prime minister. The Islamic People's Mojahedin, once co-revolutionaries but now bitter enemies of the clerics, were blamed. By the end of 1982 all effective resistance to Khomeini's ideas had been squashed.

AFTER KHOMEINI

When Ayatollah Khomeini died on 4 June 1989 he left an uncertain legacy. Khomeini's position as Supreme Leader passed to the former president, Ayatollah Ali Khamenei. The presidency, which had previously been a largely ceremonial post, was transformed with the election of the cleric Ali Akbar Hashemi Rafsanjani, who began a series of much-needed economic reforms. Despite being widely seen as the richest – and most corrupt – man in the country, Rafsanjani was re-elected in 1993. Social and religious conservatism remained firmly ingrained in Iranian society and he could never be described as a liberal, but domestic policy took on a far more pragmatic tone. This included an aggressive campaign to curb sky-rocketing population growth through contraception. A greater focus on the poor brought electricity, running water, telephone and sealed roads to rural areas long ignored under royal rule.

At the urging of the new Islamic government, Iranian women had, on average, six children each during the 1980s; the population almost doubled in a decade.

On the international front, however, Iran continued to be unpopular. In 1995 the USA slapped a trade embargo on Iran on the grounds that it was a state sponsor of terrorism.

KHATAMI & THE REFORMISTS

In 1997 the moderate, reform-minded Ayatollah Hojjat-ol-Eslam Sayyed Mohammad Khatami won the presidency in a landslide. Almost everyone, and especially the ruling clerics, was shocked. Khatami was a liberal by Iranian standards, but he was also an insider. He had studied theology in Qom, had held important posts during the Iran–Iraq War and served as Minister of Culture and Islamic Guidance for 10 years until he was forced to resign in 1992 – for being too liberal.

During the 1980s and early '90s several high-profile opposition leaders were assassinated while in exile in Europe. These included Kurdish human rights activist Dr Kazem Rajavi, shot in Switzerland in 1990, and former prime minister Shapur Bakhtiar, stabbed to death in Paris in 1991.

His election sent an overwhelming message of discontent to the ruling Islamic conservatives and resulted in a spontaneous, unlegislated liberalisation. Suddenly, harsh laws on dress and social interaction were no longer being strictly enforced and women, especially those in Tehran and other major cities, embraced make-up, figure-hugging manteaus and hair-colouring products with unbridled enthusiasm.

Khatami promised 'change from within', a policy of avoiding confrontation with the clerics and engineering change from within the theocratic system. When reformers won a large majority in the Majlis in 2000 and Khatami was re-elected with 78% of the vote in 2001, hopes were high. But what the public wanted and what Khatami and the Majlis were able to deliver proved to be very different. Of the hundreds of pieces of legislation the Majlis passed during its four-year term, more than 35% were vetoed by the conservatives on the Guardian Council (see Government, p42).

The conservative backlash didn't stop there. Reformist intellectuals were assassinated, students beaten for protesting, dozens of reform-minded newspapers were closed and editors imprisoned. It was an effective campaign. With the reformers either unable or too scared to institute their promised reforms, the public lost faith in them and the idea of 'change from within'.

By 2004 living in Iran had become significantly easier than it had been before Khatami's election. Women had won greater freedoms, limited economic liberalisation had spurred economic growth, and art and cultural activities were (relatively) thriving. Huge amounts of money were being spent on infrastructure, with new roads, railways and, in four cities, underground railways. But many Iranians were disheartened. So many promised reforms – both economic and social – had not been delivered that they lost sight of what had been achieved. The Majlis elections in February 2004 saw more than 2000 mostly Reformist candidates, including 82 sitting members, barred from running by the Guardian Council and many chose not to vote as a means of protesting. The conservatives were swept back into power and for the last year of his presidency, Khatami was almost powerless.

IRAN TODAY

In May 2005 Mahmoud Ahmadinejad was elected president. The former Republican Guard member and Tehran mayor was seen as a lightweight compared with the seven alternative candidates and his populist campaign had been ignored by most 'experts'. Which is exactly why he won.

Despite his religious conservatism, Ahmadinejad's man-of-the-people image appealed to a population frustrated and angry with the clique of clerics, military and their cronies that had become Iran's new elite. His message was summed up in an advertisement showing Ahmadinejad sitting in his sparsely furnished 750-square-foot south Tehran apartment while a narrator asked: 'Where's the swimming pool?' The contrast with his opponent in the run-off, ex-president Rafsanjani, was stark: everyman versus the wealthiest man in Iran. Sure, Ahmadinejad would be a gamble, but what did the poor have to lose?

From the outset Ahmadinejad's presidency has been unconventional, even by Iranian standards. Regular promises to 'put petroleum income on people's tables', stimulate the economy and create jobs went down well initially (for more details on Iran's economy, see p43). But within months, Ahmadinejad replaced many experienced bureaucrats with his own ex-Revolutionary Guard cronies, and the impossible promises were being seen for what they were. Employment wasn't rising but inflation was. Social crackdowns were more frequent and strict. Ahmadinejad might be honest and have good intentions, Iranians were saying, but he's incompetent.

The only issue on which he had wide-ranging support was the nuclear energy program (not bombs). Also see the Nuclear Issue (p42) and Snapshot (p25). In a region where the USA is widely perceived as arrogant and overbearing, Ahmadinejad's high-profile refusals to be pushed around (or negotiate) brought him and his stone-white 'Ahmadinejad jacket' celebrity status. His statements about Israel were more controversial, but the international spotlight rarely wavered.

The majority of Iranians were less than impressed, if not outright cynical. What was their president doing gallivanting across the world stage, provoking sanctions and perpetuating the perception that Iranians were all crazy, when things at home were not good at all? And, thanks to the growing isolation, getting worse. Petrol prices rose and quotas were introduced. Getting a visa to travel had become even harder and dissent was punished. Where was the promised oil money on the table?

Shortly after the 1989 publication in Iran of *Women Without Men*, the author, Shahrnush Parsipur, was arrested and jailed. Banned in Iran, the novel is an allegory of women's lives, following five women who come to live around a garden.

On 26 December 2003, the oasis city of Bam was devastated by an earthquake that killed more than 31,000 people and destroyed the ancient Arg-e Bam. See p322 for details.

WHY IS IRAN SO UNPOPULAR?

From the moment the Islamic Republic was formed Iran has been a pariah state. The reasons seem simple enough. Three decades of outrageously provocative statements and, less often, actions dominate Iran's media image and the response of foreign governments to it. Think of Iran and most people think burning flags, chador-clad women and bearded men demanding 'Death to America, Down With Israel', support for 'terrorist' organisations in Lebanon and Palestine, and American hostage diplomats. More recently, President Ahmadinejad and his pronouncements on nuclear power and Israel, in particular, have dominated coverage.

Unfortunately for the rest of Iran, it is rarely reported that many of the president's views are out of step with average Iranians. Following is a brief summation of Iran's stated policies on key issues of discord.

The Nuclear Issue

Iran says it is developing a nuclear energy program as an alternative to fossil fuels. It says nuclear weapons are not part of the plan. But Iran's refusal to declare the program for years, or to allow full or timely inspections by the International Atomic Energy Agency, has raised persistent doubts. For most Iranians, completing the nuclear fuel cycle is a matter of national pride, but few want the bomb. Iran sticks vehemently to its 'peaceful purposes' line. Why build a nuclear reactor and need another country to supply the fuel, it asks, when we can produce it ourselves? It's hard to argue with that but if, after all the denials, Iran does produce a nuclear bomb, whatever little credibility the Iranian government retains in the international community will be gone.

Israel

Israel, and the Israeli role in the problems in Palestine, has been the subject of verbal attacks by Iranian leaders for 30 years. Throw in the nuclear fears and it becomes even more combustible. Ahmadinejad was reported as saying Israel should be 'wiped off the map'. The translation of what he actually said in Farsi has been widely debated, but the message that went out was fairly clear: Iran wants to nuke Israel. Fortunately, about 99% of Iranians – and perhaps even Ahmadinejad himself – don't want this at all; see Snapshot (p25).

'State sponsor of terrorism'

Another old chestnut – Iran has long been accused of establishing and funding Palestinian 'terror' groups Hezbollah and Hamas. Iran has never admitted this, though the evidence is strong. Exactly how much influence Iran has over these groups is unknown, though that didn't stop George Bush describing Iran as a 'state sponsor of terror' as he lumped it into the Axis of Evil.

In early 2008 Majlis elections saw conservative candidates retain a clear majority after many Reformist candidates were barred from running. The most notable change was that supporters of President Ahmadinejad did badly, often being defeated by more pragmatic conservatives. Presidential elections are scheduled for May 2009. For more on Iran today, see Snapshot (p25).

Government

All Iranian men and women can vote after the age of 15.

Iran's system of government, the Islamic theocracy, is unique in the world. In effect, it is two parallel governments: one elected and comprised of the usual ministries and bureaucracies found in any country; and another that exists in the shadows, controlled largely by Islamic clerics, rarely reported about in the media and answerable only to the Supreme Leader – Ayatollah Ali Khamenei since 1989.

The 'normal' branch of government comprises a president and the Majlis, Iran's parliament. The president is elected in a direct vote, as in the US. The 290-member Majlis is elected at a different time. Both serve four-year terms, with the president serving a maximum of two terms.

Lower levels of government are a mix of elected – such as city mayor – and appointed officials.

The relationship between the president, his government and the Majlis is similar to that of the US President, his administration and the Senate. The president is head of government and can fill government posts from the level of minister right down to provincial positions. He can set and pursue policy, but does not always have the final say because he is not the head of state.

That role belongs to the aptly-named Supreme Leader. Unlike constitutional monarchs or ceremonial heads-of-state, Iran's Supreme Leader is supremely powerful, though the influence he chooses to exercise is seldom reported in the press.

He sits above the Guardian Council, a 12-man group that interprets the constitution and can veto any law passed by the Majlis. This was a power regularly exercised when the Reformists dominated the Majlis between 2000 and 2004. The Guardian Council also decides who can run for president or seats in the Majlis; in 2008 more than 2000 out of a total of 7597 would-be candidates, meaning only about one third of seats had a Reformist on the ballot. The make-up of the Guardian Council illustrates just how concentrated power is at the top of Iranian politics. Six of the men are Islamic jurists appointed by the Supreme Leader, while the other six are Islamic jurists elected by the Majlis from men appointed by the head of the judiciary – who is himself appointed by the Supreme Leader.

The influence of this unelected branch of government extends far beyond the power of veto. The Basij (Volunteers), Sepah and Pasdaran are hardline armed militias with hundreds of thousands of members, and they report not to the president but to the Supreme Leader. They are, in effect, a second police force, though one that is more influential than the formal uniformed police. For example, during the 2000–2004 Reformist-dominated Majlis, they worked tirelessly to undermine both Khatami and the parliament. For months Basijis followed sitting Majlis members around, building dossiers that 'proved' they were unworthy of office. Presented with such evidence, the Guardian Council then banned them from standing in the next election.

> For millennia Iran was called Persia. However, Reza Shah hated the name and in 1934 changed it to Iran – derived directly from Aryan (meaning 'of noble origin').

Economy

Although Iran is traditionally an agrarian society, the world's second-largest known reserves of both oil and natural gas have made fossil fuels the energy behind the whole economy. Oil accounts for 80% of export earnings and about 45% of gross domestic product. Record high oil prices have been a boon for Iran, with much revenue spent on large infrastructure projects. But Iran is dangerously reliant on this single source of income and, unlike its Persian Gulf neighbours, has done little to address the issue.

At a glance, the numbers don't sound so bad. The Iranian economy has been growing at a respectable 5% a year, foreign debt is less than US$10 billion, and a relatively small 16% of people live below the poverty line. Look deeper at this state-dominated economy, however, and it's much less encouraging. More than 25% of GDP is spent on subsidies, the vast majority on making petrol and electricity cheap. Such cheap fuel has led to a 10% annual increase in consumption. And with Iran's creaking old refineries only able to pump two thirds of what they could 30 years ago, Iran had been forced to import about 45% of its refined oil – mostly as petrol. Local critics ask why some of these subsidies haven't been used to upgrade existing infrastructure.

> President Ahmadinejad has said he prays to God he will 'never know about economics'. His populist ideas include privatising state-run industries and giving 'justice shares' to ordinary citizens. These people, however, are sceptical.

That the government controls more than 60% of the economy is another factor stifling growth. Much of this control is in the hands of *bonyads*, shadowy state-religious foundations that are well-connected and exempt from tax, thus out-competing most private business. The main nongovernment industries are agriculture (especially pistachios), carpet weaving and manufacturing.

Economic sanctions have made doing business significantly more difficult for Iranians and reduced foreign investment to a trickle. But after years of isolation and the experience of surviving eight years of war, Iran's economy is betterequipped to withstand sanctions than most.

The Culture Kamin Mohammadi & Andrew Burke

THE NATIONAL PSYCHE

Iranians are the most surprising people. Where you might expect them to be austere, they are charming; rather than dour, they are warm; and instead of being hostile to foreigners, they are welcoming and endlessly curious.

The truth of the Iranian national psyche lies in the gap between reality and Western perception. Before the revolution, the West's experience of Iranians was drawn from the country's elite that travelled and came abroad for their education. The revolution turned that image on its head. Suddenly Iranians were scary, hysterical people chanting 'Death to America', covering their women in black chadors, and supporting a fundamentalist regime that apparently took their society back to the Middle Ages.

Let's dispel these images. Despite the Islamic government and the Sharia laws that rule the country, Iranians are not frightening people. They are generally warm and welcoming to a degree that can be, and often is, embarrassing to Westerners. Any rhetoric that comes from the regime regarding countries such as the USA rarely extends to individuals from those countries.

Iranians take their role as hosts very seriously; there are well-developed rules governing social conduct and interaction. This comes from a genuine desire to put others' needs first and please where possible. *Ta'arof*, the Iranian system of courtesy, can be a minefield if unknown (see below),

The area of land that is Iran has been continuously inhabited by a single nation for longer than any other land.

TA'AROF

At the end of your first taxi trip in Iran, there's a good chance you'll ask the driver *'chand toman'* (how many tomans?) and he'll reply *'ghabeli nadari'*. His words mean 'it's nothing', but the taxi driver still expects to get paid. This is *ta'arof*, a system of formalised politeness that can seem very confusing to outsiders, but is a mode of social interaction in which everyone knows their place and their role.

Despite the apparent contradictions in the taxi, you'll soon learn that *ta'arof* is more about people being sensitive to the position of others than mere routine politeness. *Ta'arof* gives everyone the chance to be on equal terms: this ritual display of vulnerability is never abused. So for example, an offer of food will be turned down several times first, giving the person making the offer the chance to save face if in reality they cannot provide a meal. A good rule is to always refuse any offer three times but, if they continue to insist, do accept. When a shopkeeper, restaurateur or (less often) a hotel manager refuses payment when asked for a bill, do remember that this is just *ta'arof* – don't leave without paying! If you accept an offer that is in fact *ta'arof*, the shocked look on the vendor's face should soon reveal your error.

Ta'arof also involves showing consideration of others in your physical actions, so try not to sit with your back to people, especially your elders, and be prepared for a delay at every doorway as Iranians insist that whoever they're with goes through the door first with repeated *'befarmayid'* (please). Be prepared for lots of small talk at the beginning of any exchange, as the health of every member of your family is enquired after. Try to return this courtesy as it will be well appreciated. Also be prepared for questions considered quite personal in the West, such as your salary, marital status, why you don't have children and so on. This is quite normal. Steer away from politics or religion unless your Iranian host broaches the subject first.

And don't forget to pay the taxi driver…think of it this way: it would be bad form for the taxi driver to not offer you the trip for free, and worse form for you to accept his offer.

but it makes Iran a haven for travellers – you will be treated with unfailing politeness wherever you go.

A glance at Iran's history will give another insight into the Iranian character. Despite several devastating invasions, Iranians have always managed to keep their own unique culture alive and somehow subvert the invading culture and assimilate it with their own. Thus the Iranian way is to bend to the prevailing wind only to spring back in time with regained poise. Ever-changing fortunes have taught Iranians to be indirect people, unwilling to ever answer with a bald negative and unable to countenance rudeness or public displays of anger.

Iran's attitudes to the West are contradictory. Whereas most Iranians can talk at length about the faults of Western governments, holding first the British and then the Americans responsible for much of Iran's 20th-century history (with some justification), they can nonetheless admire Western attitudes. They will alternately boast of Iran's superiority in terms of culture, home life and morality and then apologise for Iran's inferiority.

Remember that Iranians are proud of their Aryan roots, which distinguish them from the people of south Asia or the Middle East. Iranians intensely dislike being classed as Arabs, who remain unforgiven for their invasion of Iran in the 7th century. Iranian racism is reserved for Afghan refugees and the Arabs of neighbouring countries, who are regarded as having no culture aside from what their invasion of Iran gave them. But such is the power of Iranian courtesy and hospitality that you will rarely see such attitudes displayed openly and especially not extended to travellers.

The Iranian spirit is tolerant and eternally buoyant. The Iranian plateau can be a harsh land, hence the necessary creativity of the Iranian soul. The traditional Persian garden, walled in from the desert and divided by water channels, occupies a profoundly primal place in the Iranian heart, inspiring the designs of rugs, informing the brilliance of miniatures and lending its colours to the tiled domes of mosques. The play of light and colour preoccupies all aspects of Iranian art and even Shiism can be seen as an expression of this, based as it is on the 'Light of Mohammad', a spiritual thread passed on through the imams.

In essence the Iranian soul is a deeply sensual one – perhaps the biggest surprise for Westerners expecting religious fanaticism and austerity. What is universal in the Iranian character is the enjoyment of the cadences of poetry read aloud, their wonderful food and their admiration of natural beauty. They are tied absolutely to the land, although most now live urban lives.

Somewhere in every modern Iranian the desires expressed by Omar Khayyam (p74) in his 12th-century poem *Rubaiyat* still resound:

> A book of verses underneath the bough
> A jug of wine, a loaf of bread and thou
> Beside me singing in the wilderness
> And wilderness is paradise enow.

LIFESTYLE

The majority of Iran's urban dwellers live in flats, and more and more houses in Tehran and the major cities are being razed, with apartment blocks taking their place. Land in Tehran is as expensive as many North American and European cities, and the cost of living increasingly prohibitive, particularly for young couples who can rarely afford their own

---

The name Iran – from the Middle Persian 'Eran' – comes from the term for Aryan, 'the land of the nobles'. It was first used in the 1st millennium BC.

Shiites were historically persecuted by the Sunni majority and so developed a doctrine whereby it is fine to conceal one's faith in order to escape persecution.

'WHAT IS YOUR IDEA ABOUT IRAN?' *Andrew Burke*

It's a question I've been asked hundreds of times while travelling in Iran, and one that simultaneously reflects a strong sense of national pride and an equally strong insecurity about Iran's place in the world. Iranians are well aware the rest of the world has a one-dimensional understanding of their country and culture. It's something they don't like, and something that many feel makes them – undeservedly – second class citizens of the world. Iranians like to think of themselves as equals to Europeans, and don't like being treated as second-rate or somehow fanatic when they visit these places.

So when you're inevitably asked what you think about Iran, remember it's a genuine question and you're expected to give a genuine answer. Quite often it leads to further conversation, particularly among young people who speak (and want to practise) English. These conversations are a great way to get a little further inside the Iranian way of thinking, and way of life, and for Iranians to better understand your way of life.

---

place. Many newly married couples will live with parents for years before they can afford their own place. With the monthly rent for an average two-bedroom property in Tehran coming in at around US$600, and the salary of a mid-ranking civil servant US$250 a month, the struggle to make ends meet dominates many lives. Hence, many ordinary Iranians work more than one job and, in the case of the middle classes, often both men and women work.

The gap between rich and poor is huge, with the middle class shrinking. Teachers, earning not much more than US$200 a month, are the sort of state employee hardest hit by inflation rates running at between 13% and 25% per annum, depending on which arm of government you believe (see p25); unofficial figures are higher. On the other hand, a fortunate minority, some of whom have made a fortune from land and property speculation, continue to build lavish villas with swimming pools behind high walls in Tehran's breezy northern suburbs. Or they live in one of the many glistening new apartment towers punctuating the hilly north of Tehran, in marble-and-glass apartments filled with cappuccino machines, Le Corbusier chairs and home gyms. The women of such families tend not to work but instead lead lives revolving around their children, visiting parents and friends and working out with personal trainers.

In contrast a middle-class couple may leave their modest apartment together in the morning after the typical Persian breakfast of bread, cheese, jam and tea. Their children, if small, will mostly be looked after by grandparents while the couple go to work. One or the other may make it back for lunch, unless living in Tehran where distances are greater and traffic hideous. In the evening the family meal will be taken together, often with the wider family and friends. Iranians are social creatures and many visits take place after dinner.

In poorer or more traditional families it is likely that the woman will stay at home, in which case her whole day revolves around housework, providing meals for her family and shopping (in ultraconservative families the men may do the shopping).

Iranian meals can take time to prepare and though supermarkets exist and some pre-packaged ingredients are available, mostly there is no convenience food. Just buying, cleaning and chopping the herbs served with every meal can take a good chunk of the afternoon. Working women generally see to these tasks in the evenings, when they may prepare the next day's lunch. Perhaps in more enlightened families men help with the cooking and housework, but as both the mother and grown sons of

Dara and Sara are dolls developed by a government agency to promote traditional values and rival Barbie (though so far Barbie is winning hands down!).

Jafar Panahi directs a Kiarostami script in *Crimson Gold*. This Cannes award-winning film is a dark tale of the ruin of a young pizza delivery boy and the madness of modern life in Tehran.

one Iranian family we know told us: 'men who cook are not real men'. Mostly it is safe to say that men's role in the home is largely confined to appreciating the quality of the cooking. Which they do well, Iranians being true gourmands.

Family life is still of supreme importance although there is ongoing talk of the erosion of family values. Often families include children, parents, grandparents and other elderly relatives. As a result Iranian society is more multigenerational than Western society, something that's most obvious on holidays and weekends when you'll see multigenerational families walking, laughing and picnicking together.

It's extremely unusual to live alone and unmarried children only leave home to attend university in another town or for work. Although the young people of Iran long for independence and their own space, just like their Western counterparts, there is not much cultural precedence for this. Those who do live alone – mostly men – are pitied. Women living alone are regarded with extreme suspicion, the presumption being that they are of dubious moral character. Being married and having a family is regarded as the happiest – not to mention the most natural – state of being.

Education is highly regarded; literacy is well above average for the region at 77%, according to Unesco. Many middle-class teenagers spend up to two years studying for university entrance exams, though the sheer number of entrants, ideological screening and places reserved for war veterans and their offspring make it very hard to get in. And once out of university, there is no guarantee of work. With the sexes segregated at school and boys and girls discouraged from socialising together, trying to get to know members of the opposite sex is a huge preoccupation for Iranian teenagers. They hang around shopping malls, in cafés and parks, parade up and down boulevards and spend lots of time cruising around in cars. This is especially noticeable in Tehran.

Drugs are available and increasingly a problem, from the army of war-veteran addicts to middle-class kids with nothing better to do, via a wide range of social problems, including a lack of jobs and opportunity. Social taboos make it hard for parents to seek help for addicted children, though when they do, they find Iran has some of the most progressive addiction treatment practices on earth. The phenomena of teenage runaways, especially girls, is another social problem that gives weight to those decrying the breakdown of traditional family structures.

For the most part, though, the average Iranian family is a robust unit and, despite economic and social differences, most operate in broadly the same way. They provide an essential support unit in a country with no state benefit system.

POPULATION

When Iranians meet they inevitably ask: 'Where are you from?' This is because Iran has a multiplicity of distinct ethnic identities who are all, nevertheless, Iranian. It is important to understand that though the indigenous ethnicities are very much part of life, there is a unifying Iranian identity that keeps all these separate peoples part of a bigger whole.

Iran's population has more than doubled since the revolution, as contraception was outlawed and large families encouraged. This policy was hastily reversed when the economic implications became clear and in recent years population growth has fallen sharply. Having said that, the number of Iranians is still growing and with all those born in the 1980s now beginning to have children of their own, expect that growth to

Estimates suggest Iran has more than one million drug addicts, even though drug dealing and even drug use can be punishable by death. However, Iran has enlightened policies for treating addiction, including methadone programmes and clean needles for addicted prisoners.

More than 97% of all children are enrolled in schools, with the rations being almost equal among girls and boys.

The population of greater Tehran is about 14 million – almost one-fifth of Iran's population. That's comparable to 50 million people living in New York City.

continue. In 2007 the population was more than 70 million, with almost 70% of those under 30 years old and about one-third under 15, creating serious issues with unemployment and underemployment; (see Iran's Big Brain Drain, p53).

The rapid urbanisation of Iranian society started well before 1979, but was intensified by the Iran–Iraq War. Now an estimated 70% of the population live in cities and large towns. Traditional rural life is becoming a thing of the past.

The following are brief summaries of the main ethnic groups you'll find in Iran. For more detailed descriptions, follow the cross-references to the relevant chapters.

> Rakhshan Bani Etemad's latest film, *Mainline* (2006), looks at drug addiction among a middle-class Iranian family, with the protagonist, Sara, played by her daughter, actress Baran Kosari.

Persians

Persians are the descendents of the original Elamite and Aryan races who arrived in what is now Iran during the 3rd millennium BC. The Persians, or Farsis, were originally the tribes that came to establish the Achaemenid Empire and now make up about 50% of the population. Persians are found across Iran, but Tehran, Mashhad, Esfahan, Yazd and particularly Shiraz have the highest concentrations. Farsi is the main Iranian language and Persian culture is often considered Iranian culture. For more on Persian culture, see Lifestyle (p46) and the National Psyche (p45).

Azaris

Commonly called 'Turks' in Iran, the Azaris make up about 25% of the population. They speak Azari Turkish, a dialect mixing Turkish with Farsi. They are concentrated in northwest Iran, in the Azarbayjan provinces around Tabriz. See p146 for more.

Kurds

Iran has more than six million Kurds. The Kurds lay claim to being the oldest Iranian people in the region, descended from the Medes. In Iran, Kurds live in the mountainous west, particularly Kordestan province near the Iraqi border. Kurds also live in Iraq, Syria and Turkey. Kurds are widely feared and misunderstood by other Iranians. For more on the Kurds, see p190.

> As the largest and most influential ethnic group, Persians fill most of Iran's senior government posts. However, people from most other ethnic groups (as opposed to religions) can still reach the top – Iran's Supreme Leader, Ali Khamenei, is an ethnic Azari.

BUTT OF THE JOKE *Mark Elliott*

'If you drop your wallet in Qazvin, don't bend down to pick it up!' Political correctness has yet to touch the Iranian sense of humour and poor Qazvin, 'where birds fly on one wing', suffers constantly from jibes about predatory homosexuality. Other regions are equally unfairly stereotyped for jocular effect. Men from Rasht are portrayed as sexually liberal and constantly cuckold, Shirazis as lazy and fun-loving (in reality, everyone loves Shirazis), Turkmen as vengeful, Kurds as hot blooded and the Loris of Lorestan as congenitally untrustworthy. In common jokes Azaris are supposedly slow-witted yet cash-canny with Tabrizis surly and religious, but those from Orumiyeh, by contrast are relaxed and open-minded. Within their loose-fitting *dishdasha* robes, Iranian Arab men are whispered to be endowed with an especially impressive set of wedding tackle.

But it's Esfahanis, who are reputed to be cunning and tight with money, that you're most likely to hear about. One Yazdi man gleefully told us that Esfahanis are 'like the Scots; they'll do anything to save a few tomans'. While in Shahr-e Kord we were told a supposedly true story of how a tired truck driver from Shahr-e Kord had run into a brand new Mercedes driven by a Yazdi. The furious Yazdi's first accusatory question was: 'Are you Esfahani?' When the driver replied 'No, I'm from Shahr-e Kord', the Yazdi's mood immediately softened. 'Okay, then,' he's reported to have said, 'You're not Esfahani, you can go.'

Arabs

Bahman Ghobadi's film *A Time for Drunken Horses* shared Cannes' 2000 Caméra d'Or prize with Hassan Yektapanah's *Djom'eh,* another masterful film using children and nonprofessional actors to follow the story of Kurdish orphans living in a border village. Ghobadi has since had hits with *Turtles Can Fly* and *Half Moon.*

Arabs make up about 3% of the Iranian population and are settled mostly in Khuzestan, near the Iraq border, and on the coast and islands of the Persian Gulf. They are often called *bandari* (*bandar* means port), because of their historical links to the sea. Their differing language (a dialect of Arabic), dress and faith (many are Sunni Muslims) mean other Iranians consider them exotic. See also p291.

Lors

These proud people constitute about 2% of Iran's population and are thought to be descendants of the first peoples in the region, the Kassites and Medes. Many speak Lori, a mixture of Arabic and Farsi, and about half remain nomadic. Most of the rest live in or near the western province of Lorestan; see the boxed text, p207.

Turkmen

Making up about 2% of the population, Iranian Turkmen are descended from the nomadic Turkic tribes that once ruled Iran. They live in the northeast of the country, especially around Gorgan and Gonbad-e Kavus. They speak their own Turkic language; see the boxed text, p343.

Baluchis

Gabbeh, directed by Mohsen Makhmalbaf, is a beautiful film centred on a *gabbeh,* a type of Persian carpet made by Qashqa'i nomads, and the love story of a nomad girl with the same name.

The population of dry, barren Sistan va Baluchestan province is largely Baluchi. Baluchis comprise around 2% of Iran's population and are part of a greater whole that spreads into western Pakistan and Afghanistan. Their culture, language and dress are more associated with Pakistan than Iran; see p315.

Nomads

About a million people still live as nomads in Iran despite repeated attempts to settle them. Most migrate between cooler mountain areas in summer and low-lying warmer regions during winter, following pasture for their goats and sheep. Their migrations are during April and May, when they head uphill, returning during October and November. The majority of nomads are Turkic Qashqa'i and Bakhtiyari, but there are also nomadic Kurds, Lors and Baluchis; see Nomads, p285.

ESTEGHLAL OR PERSEPOLIS?   Andrew Burke

The departure lounge at Mehrabad airport in Tehran is packed as I wait for one or another delayed domestic flight. But rather than reading books or arguing with ground staff, the vast majority of people (both men and women) are glued to the football on the big screens.

It's red versus blue, and as a shot whizzes past the post the entire departure lounge seems to simultaneously inhale or exhale, depending on who they're supporting. But this is not Man U and Chelsea, it's Iran's two biggest football clubs, Esteghlal and Persepolis.

Both teams are based in Tehran. Persepolis (pronounced 'perspolis' and playing in a red home strip) is known as the working-class team and has the dubious honour of being both the most-loved and most-hated team in Iran – by a considerable margin; Persepolis has won five national titles. Esteghlal (blue home strip) is the wealthy club and has won seven titles. Just to confuse you, Esteghlal Ahwaz also plays in the Persian Gulf Cup – the fourth name for the national league since its inception in the early 1970s.

If you're a football fan, it might be worth adopting one of these teams and boning up on the names of their top players if you fancy some lively debate. If that sounds too hard, don't worry – most Iranian football fans are fully conversant on the major European leagues.

SPORT

Iran is not a country you'll automatically associate with sport. And while football is a national obsession and you'll see kids playing in streets and squares across Iran, you won't see too many pitches. This is partly because religious strictures mean women should not see unrelated men in shorts, so most grounds are behind large walls. Women are barred from attending men's sporting events even though they are, conversely, free to watch them on TV; this oft-debated issue is dealt with in Jafar Panahi's film *Offside*.

Modern-day restrictions aside, Iran does have an interesting sporting history. Polo is believed to have originated in Iran and was certainly played during the reign of Darius the Great. A couple of millennia later, the huge main square of Esfahan was used for polo matches that would be watched by the Safavid Shah Abbas I from the balcony of the Ali Qapu Palace. Today you can still see the burly stone goal posts at either end of the square – see p238 – while stylised polo matches can be seen in thousands of miniature paintings. Real-life polo has made a tentative comeback in recent years, though you'll do very well to see it.

Another ancient sport peculiar to Iran is the *zurkhaneh* (literally, 'house of strength'); for details, see p52.

On the international stage, Iran has enjoyed considerable success in wrestling, weightlifting and tae kwon do – all of Iran's 46 Olympic medals (including 10 gold) have been won by men competing in these sports. As well as football, Iran competes internationally in volleyball, fencing, track, shooting and martial arts. Shooting and tae kwon do have become popular with women because it's possible to compete while wearing hejab.

Skiing (p373) is the sport travellers are most likely to participate in. Iran has sent both cross-country and downhill skiers to the Winter Olympics, though with limited success so far. Mountaineering is also becoming more popular, which is not surprising given how many Iranians hike in the mountains or take a leisurely walk (accompanied by elaborate picnics) in the city parks on holidays.

Football

Iran has been competing in international football since 1941 and won three Asian Cups during the '60s and '70s. But it wasn't until the 1998 World Cup that it really made its mark on the world stage. Having been the last country to qualify after a dramatic away goals victory over Australia (a victory we're still being gleefully reminded of 10 years later!), Iran faced up to the USA and won a match charged up with two decades of political enmity. In Iran the success was greeted by the largest crowds since the revolution; so big, in fact, that the government became seriously worried that all this unity might morph into something more dangerous to the regime.

As it happened the team didn't progress beyond the group stage but when it returned home hundreds of women forced their way into the Azadi Sports Complex in Tehran to welcome them, to which the authorities turned a blind eye. That same year a women's football league was formed. All-women football matches are held indoors and no males – including male managers – are allowed to watch. In 2008 the Iranian women's team will compete in its first Asian Women's Cup.

Iran's men's professional league has 18 teams in the top division and runs from August to May, with games played most Thursdays and Fridays. For a word on the teams you need to know about, see the boxed text Esteghlal or Persepolis?, opposite.

Chess (shatranj) originally came from India, but it was refined into the version that is played today in ancient Persia.

As of February 2008, Iran ranked 39 in the FIFA World Rankings, making it the second highest-ranking team in Asia, after Japan. Iran's highest ever ranking was 15.

Offside, Jafar Panahi's 2006 film, follows a handful of women who disguise themselves as men to get into Azadi Stadium to watch Iran's 2006 World Cup qualifying match. It is funny, eloquent and offers a fascinating glimpse into the realities of life in Iran.

ZURKHANEH

Unique to Iran, the *zurkhaneh* (literally, 'house of strength') dates back thousands of years. As it was refined through the ages, the *zurkhaneh* picked up different components of moral, ethical, philosophical and mystical values of Iranian civilisation, making it unique. Incorporating the spiritual richness of Sufism, traditional rituals of Mithraism and the heroism of Iranian nationalism, its appeal lies somewhere between sport, theatre and religion. A group of men, standing around the perimeter of a lowered pit, perform a series of ritualised feats of strength, all to the accompaniment of a leader pounding out a frenetic drumbeat. The leader sings verses from epics such as the *Shahnameh* and recites poetry by Hafez, while the performers whirl dervishlike in the centre of the floor. The performance, which takes place in a small, traditional gymnasium often decorated like a shrine, is open to the public and usually free (a small donation is sometimes expected); Esfahan, Yazd and Kerman are good places to look. You won't see too many local women in attendance – Western women are welcomed as honorary men.

For more information about *zurkhaneh*, see www.pahlavani.com.

IMMIGRATION & EMIGRATION

For almost three decades Iran has hosted huge populations of refugees with little international assistance. In 2007 more than 950,000 refugees were officially registered with the UNHCR, but it's believed the real number is closer to two million. The vast majority of these are Afghans, though there are also Iraqi Shiites and Kurds.

Afghan refugees started arriving in Iran in 1980 and soon spread out from camps on the eastern border into larger towns. Most have settled onto Iranian society's lowest rungs, living in the oldest and cheapest parts of Iranian cities and working menial jobs that Iranians don't want to do; almost every construction worker in the country is Afghan. Unlike Iraqis, Afghans don't have full access to health and education in Iran. In short, while the Iranian economy relies on the cheap labour provided by Afghans, they are widely distrusted and treated as second-class citizens.

Since the fall of the Taleban Iran has encouraged Afghans to go home. At the same time it has started fining and imprisoning employers who provide jobs to foreigners – usually Afghans – without work permits. By choice or otherwise, many Afghans have gone back to their homeland, but a good percentage of them cannot find jobs or secure lodgings and are soon back in Iran.

Most of the 1.5 million Iraqi Kurds who took refuge in Iran during the 1990s have since been repatriated. However, many of the more than 200,000 ethnic Iranians expelled from Iraq during the Iran–Iraq War have now settled permanently in Iran. Many were descended from Iranians who had settled in Iraq centuries before. Along with Iraqi Shiites who fled Saddam's Iraq, Iran resettled them all, despite the war-torn economy.

Since the revolution of 1979, there has been a steady emigration of educated Iranians abroad. Estimates of the number vary from 750,000 to 1.5 million. Most have settled in Western Europe, North America and, to a lesser extent, Australia and Turkey. Some of these early Iranian emigrants were members of the prerevolutionary political elite who succeeded in transferring much of their wealth out of Iran.

Other émigrés included members of religious minorities, especially Baha'is and Jews; intellectuals who had opposed the old regime, which they accused of suppressing free thought and who found the Islamic Republic no better; political opponents of the government in Tehran; and young men who deserted from the military or sought to avoid conscription.

MEDIA

The struggle for influence and power is increasingly played out in Iran's media. The relative freedom of the press, an achievement of President Khatami's government, saw a blossoming of ideas and opinions that challenged the official line. During the late 1990s dozens of proreform newspapers were opened. Many, however, were soon shut down and reformist writers and editors were jailed.

Officially, the constitution provides for freedom of the press as long as published material accords with Islamic principles. The publisher is required by law to have a valid publishing licence and those perceived as being anti-Islamic are not granted a licence. In practice, the criteria for being anti-Islamic have been broadly interpreted to encompass all materials that include anti-regime sentiment.

During his high-profile visit to New York in September 2007, President Ahmadinejad described Iranian people as 'the freest in the world'. As Paris-based NGO Reporters Sans Frontiers responded in an open letter to Mr Ahmadinejad, in the year prior to this statement 73 journalists had been arrested and 10 remained in prison when he made the claim. Two of these, magazine journalists working in Kordestan, had been sentenced to death by a revolutionary tribunal for conducting 'subversive activities against national security' and peddling 'separatist propaganda'.

Broadcast Media

In the broadcast media, satellite TV has provided many Iranians with a welcome window on the world. Although still officially banned, stand on the roof of any building in Tehran and you'll see a forest of dishes pointing skyward. For many, access to foreign broadcasters is almost unlimited. One Tehrani told us 'I just got rid of 200 stations, so now I only have about 800'. More than a dozen opposition TV stations beam Persian-language broadcasts into Iran, mostly from the USA. Arab and

IRAN'S BIG BRAIN DRAIN

Iran suffers from what has been described as the worst 'brain drain' in the world. The country's lack of internationally recognised educational facilities, high unemployment and restrictions on personal freedom mean many of its educated young people feel forced to leave. Economists reckon Iran needs to create more than a million jobs a year just to keep pace with its growing population. In reality, though, less than half this number is added. Unemployment is generally believed to be about 25% and much higher for young people – the government's own figures put unemployment among 25- to 29-year-olds, many of them recent graduates, at almost 50%. Hidden in the statistics is massive underemployment, with graduates forced to take jobs below their qualifications.

Faced with such prospects, and a long-held government attitude that anyone who doesn't like life in Iran 'should just leave', every year more than 150,000 educated young people leave Iran for countries such as the UK, Australia, the USA and Canada, where Iranians are the most educated group of immigrants. Among these are many of the country's brightest minds. Foreign embassies in Tehran keep a keen eye out for graduates of the best universities, and we have even heard of bidding wars between countries for top students. Estimates put the economic loss to Iran at tens of billions of dollars a year.

At least four million Iranians now live abroad. Few of these will ever return, though on this research trip we did meet some who had come home after living more than 10 years in the US or Europe. But the more common message was summed up by one man we met in Tehran: 'I came back to see whether I'd be able to live here again, but I can't do it. Going from the freedom I have had in London for the last two years to the restrictions here would just be too hard.'

Turkish stations are also picked up as are some news channels, such as BBC and Euronews. Indeed, the BBC thinks the Iranian market is important enough that it will launch a Persian-speaking satellite channel in 2008. As with the liberal newspapers, there are periodic clampdowns when uniformed men armed with hacksaws confiscate satellite dishes.

Of course, not everyone can afford satellite TV. Those going without are limited to five or six pretty dire state-run channels; four national networks and one or two provincial channels run by the Islamic Republic of Iran Broadcasting (IRIB) service. On these you'll see constant reminders of the Iran–Iraq War, martyrs, political propaganda, prayer, preaching mullahs, football (local and European), news, and lots of jarring reminders of the social conventions, such as women-only game shows and soap operas in which women wear hejab in bed. All up, more than 80% of the population watches TV from one source or another.

IRIB's main radio channel broadcasts around the clock. IRIB also operates a parliamentary network and Radio Koran. Many foreign broadcasters target listeners in Iran. The BBC World's Persian service is universally popular and easily picked up throughout the country.

Internet

Internet access is easy to arrange and affordable for middle-class Iranians, about 15% of whom have regular access. As such, the web has become the main medium for circumventing the barriers of censorship. Farsi is one of the most used languages in the blogosphere, with bloggers both inside and outside Iran being widely read. Some of these voices were captured in Nasrin Alavi's 2005 book *We Are Iran: The Persian Blogs*.

However, life for bloggers contains many of the risks faced by regular Iranian journalists, without any of the financial rewards. In 2004 at least 20 bloggers were jailed and had their sites banned. These are among the '10 million' websites the government claims to have blocked, ranging from porn to anti-Islamic sites, via some foreign media. However, Iran is also home to some talented hackers, and codes to break the blocks are quickly developed, some even appearing as graffiti on public transport.

RELIGION

The Islamic Republic of Iran is the only Shiite Muslim regime in the world, distinguishing it from its Sunni neighbours. Ninety-nine percent of the population are Muslim, made up of around 89% Shiites and 10% Sunnis. There are other religions followed in Iran, with Zoroastrians, Jews, Christians and Baha'is making up the numbers. Although freedom of worship is guaranteed in the constitution (apart from the open practice of the Baha'i religion, which is outlawed), it is safe to assume that the minorities number more than the official statistics allow because calling yourself a Shiite Muslim, even if you're not, means you'll probably face fewer hurdles when dealing with Iran's huge and potentially tricky bureaucracy.

Iranians will happily accept that visitors are Christians, but in certain circumstances it may be best not to admit to being Jewish. Even among better educated Iranians, admitting to being atheist or agnostic can result in blank-faced incomprehension.

Islam

Muslims accept that there is no God but Allah and that Mohammed was his final prophet. These two precepts form the first pillar of Islam, the *shahada*. The other four pillars, which a Muslim must try to follow, are *salat* (*namaz*; praying five times a day, though Shiites only pray three times), *zakat* (alms-

---

Photojournalist Kaveh Golestan's documentary on the plight of Iranian intellectuals, Recording the Truth, made for British television, led to his two-year house arrest. He joined the BBC in 1999 and was killed in 2003 in Iraq. See some of his images at www.kavehgolestan.com.

Aryana Farshad's lovely documentary, Mystic Iran: The Unseen World, claims to journey to the heart of spiritual Iran, but is most remarkable for its unique footage of the sacred trance dances of dervishes in Kordestan.

giving), *sawm* (*ruzeh*; fasting during Ramazan) and *haj* (the pilgrimage to Mecca that those able should perform at a given time).

All Muslims, regardless of whether Sunni or Shiite, are forbidden to drink alcohol or eat anything containing pork, blood or any meat that died in any way other than being slaughtered in the prescribed manner (halal).

Every town of any size has a Jameh Mosque (Masjed-e Jameh), which literally means Congregational Mosque. It serves as the local centre of worship and Islamic discussion and was traditionally a centre of much social interaction as well; for more on Jameh Mosques, see p316.

> Muslims believe that Jesus was a prophet second only to Mohammed. The concept that he is the son of God is considered heretical.

SHIISM

When the Prophet Mohammed died in AD 632, there was disagreement over his successor. The majority backed Abu Bakr, the prophet's father-in-law and friend. He became Caliph. However, there were those who backed the claim of the prophet's son-in-law and cousin, Ali bin Abi Taleb, one of the first converts. Ali was passed over a total of three times before eventually becoming the fourth Caliph in 656, only to be assassinated five years later. The Muslim community was by now divided into two factions, the Sunnis, who followed the Umayyad Caliphate, and the Shiite (from 'Shiat Ali', meaning 'Partisans of Ali' or 'followers of Ali'). When Ali's second son Hossein and his supporters were slaughtered by the Caliph's troops at the Battle of Karbala in 680, the division became permanent.

Shiism reached its greatest influence in Iran. Iranian converts to Islam were attracted by the idea of the imam as a divinely appointed leader possibly because the Iranians possessed a long heritage of government by a divinely appointed monarch. For more on the history and structure of Shiism, see The 12 Imams, p56.

> A popular part of Shiism is the representation of its imams. You will see pictures of Imam Hossein everywhere.

SUNNISM

Sunni comes from the word *sonnat*, which means tradition and refers to the fact that the Sunnis follow the traditional line of succession after the Prophet Mohammad. Sunnism has developed into the orthodox branch of Islam and most of the world's Muslims are Sunni, except in Iran.

SUFISM

A mystical aspect of Islam that is particularly close to Iranian hearts, *tassawof* (mysticism) is a discovery made by Iranians within Islam, and derived from the Quranic verses. According to Sufis, God must be felt as a light that shines in the believer's heart and the heart must be pure enough to receive the light. The two are the same, but separated: man's soul is in exile from the Creator and longs to return 'home' to lose himself again in Him. Sufism has various orders and throughout Iran you can find *khaneqas* (prayer and meditation houses) where people go to worship. Sufism in no way conflicts with Shiism or Sunnism.

> Ayatollah Khomeini was a published Sufi poet.

Some of Iran's greatest thinkers, poets and scholars have had Sufi mystic tendencies, including Sohrevardi, Ghazali, Attar, Rumi, Hafez and Sa'di (p74).

Other Religions

Throughout history Iranians have shown tolerance towards other people's religious beliefs (with the exception of Baha'is), and since the adoption of Islam they have been particularly tolerant of Christians and Jews, who are 'People of the Book'. Christians, Jews and Zoroastrians are all officially recognised and exempt from military service, and have guaranteed seats in the Majlis (parliament). The Islamic theocracy is happy to tolerate, if not indulge, most of these minorities, though that tolerance falls far short of encouragement – minorities are free to convert to Islam, but conversion from Islam to another faith is punishable by death.

ZOROASTRIANISM

Zoroastrians, the followers of Iran's pre-Islamic religion, are based mainly around Yazd with its fire temple (where the fire is said to have

---

THE 12 IMAMS

Shiism has several sub-branches but the Twelvers are by far the largest group, and make up the vast majority in Iran. Twelvers believe that following the death of Mohammed the rightful spiritual leadership of the Islamic faith passed to 12 successive descendants of the prophet. These were known as imams ('leaders' or more loosely, 'saints') and apart from Ali, the first imam, they weren't recognised by the caliphate.

The most devout Shia Muslims might celebrate the death days of all 12 imams, but in Iran the majority concentrate on the first, Ali, the third, Hossein, and the eighth, Reza (p353) – the only one of the 12 who is buried in Iran, in the lavish Haram-e Razavi (p354) in Mashhad.

The defining episode is the schism between Sunni and Shia is the death of the third imam, Hossein. On the first day of the month of Moharram in 661 Imam Hossein and 72 followers set up camp at Karbala, in present-day Iraq. They were besieged for nine days, and on the 10th Hossein and most of his followers were killed. Hossein's martyrdom is commemorated in a 10-day anniversary that culminates on Ashura – the final day. It's during Ashura that the Iranian culture of martyrdom is most evident. It's not unusual to see men walking through the streets flailing themselves with chains, and others crying genuine tears for their lost hero.

Almost as important is the 12th Imam, known as the Mahdi or Valiasr (Leader of Our Time). Mahdi is the Hidden Imam, believed to have disappeared into a cave under a mosque at Samarra in 874 AD. He is believed to live on in occultation, continuing as Valiasr, the leader of the Shia in the present time. It is believed Mahdi will eventually return when, with the prophet Jesus by his side, he will guide the world to peace and righteousness. The Shia militia of Muqtadr al Sadr in Iraq, known as the Mehdi Army, is named after the 12th Imam.

Shias believe only the imams can interpret the Quran and the clergy act as their representatives until the Hidden Imam returns. Ayatollah Khomeini was given the honorary title imam after his death, and when you hear people talking about 'the Imam' today it's usually a reference to him.

Exactly how much the martyrdom of the 12 Imams, allegedly at the hands of Sunni supporters of the caliphate, is responsible for modern Iranian cultural traits is impossible to say. What is more certain is that the culture of martyrdom remains a powerful motivator in Iran. During the Iran–Iraq War (p39) thousands of men and boys quite literally sacrificed their lives (some chose to clear mine fields by walking through them) in the name of country and/or religion.

The 12 Imams, their commonly understood names in Iran, birth and death years, and where they are buried:

1 Imam Ali (600–661) Buried in Najaf, Iraq

2 Imam Hasan (625–669) Medina, Saudi Arabia

3 Imam Hossein (626–680) Karbala, Iraq

4 Imam Sajjad (658–713) Medina, Saudi Arabia

5 Imam Mohammad Bagher (676–743) Medina, Saudi Arabia

6 Imam Jafar Sadegh (703–765) Medina, Saudi Arabia

7 Imam Musaye Kazem (745–799) Baghdad, Iraq

8 Imam Reza (765–818) Mashhad, Iran

9 Imam Javad (810–835) Baghdad, Iraq

10 Imam Hadi (827–868) Samarra, Iraq

11 Imam Hasan Askari (846–874) Samarra, Iraq

12 Imam Mahdi (868–?) In occultation

been burning for 4000 years) and the Chak Chak (p266) pilgrimage site in its desert mountain setting. Sizable communities also live in Tehran. Estimates as to the number of Zoroastrians in Iran vary, anywhere from 30,000 to 100,000. Zoroastrianism is the world's first monotheistic religion and has influenced those who have followed religions such as Judaism, Christianity and Islam.

Several traditions and ceremonies dating from Zoroastrian times are important in modern Iranian culture. The Iranian New Year, No Ruz, is Iran's main festival celebrated on the spring equinox, and is descended directly from a Zoroastrian festival, as is Chaharshanbe Soori, which takes place on the Wednesday before New Year and involves people jumping over a series of small bonfires. Shab-e yalda, celebrated on the winter solstice, is another Zoroastrian festival still observed by Iranians.

Religious Minorities in Iran, by Eliz Sanasarian, is drawn from a large number of interviews. This useful book explores the relationship between Iran's religious minorities and the state from the beginning of the Islamic Republic to the present day.

CHRISTIANITY

The Christian community in Iran consists mainly of Armenians who settled, historically, at Jolfa, in the north of Iran, and were then moved to New Jolfa in Esfahan in Safavid times. Many also live around the northwestern city of Orumiyeh (p140). Christians were present in Iran before the arrival of Islam and some Christian saints were martyred here.

Today, Iran's 250,000 Christians also include Roman Catholics, Adventists, Protestants and Chaldeans as well as about 20,000 Assyrians. There are churches in most large towns. Christians are allowed to consume alcohol and hold mixed-sex parties with dancing, just as long as no Muslims can see the revelry, let alone partake. They also have a nonsegregated sports centre in Tehran, where women can play sports unencumbered by hejab.

JUDAISM

Iran has been home to a healthy population of Jews since about the 8th century BC – even before Cyrus the Great famously liberated the Jews who had been enslaved at Babylon (p28). Today Iran is home to about 25,000 Jews, the second-largest Jewish population in the Middle East, after Israel.

More than 50,000 Jews left Iran when life became more difficult following the revolution – the majority migrating to the USA. In 2007 Israel tried to prompt a mass migration of those remaining in Iran by offering cash incentives of up to US$60,000 per family. However, the Society of Iranian Jews snubbed the offer, saying the 'identity of Iranian Jews is not tradable for any amount of money'.

Traditionally active in the bazaars and jewellery trade, Iranian Jews tend to live in the large cities such as Tehran, Esfahan and Shiraz. About 30 synagogues remain in Iran, but they are not easy to find.

Esther's Children: A Portrait of Iranian Jews, by Houman Sarshar, is a comprehensive history of Iran's Jews from the Achaemenid Empire to the community that remains following the revolution of 1979.

BAHA'ISM

The most persecuted religious minority in Iran, Baha'is suffered greatly after the revolution. Today, it remains illegal to practise the religion in public and Baha'is are routinely discriminated against when it comes to jobs and education. Of the world's five million Baha'is, around 300,000 remain in Iran – they form the country's largest religious minority. Most Baha'is are urban, but there are some Baha'i villages, especially in Fars and Mazandaran provinces.

Baha'ism originated in Iran during the 1840s as a Shia Islamic reform movement. Iran's political and religious authorities were not impressed and tried to suppress the movement, massacring followers and executing

The website www.bahai .org is a comprehensive site for and about the Baha'i religion and community.

the founding prophet The Bab in Tabriz in 1850. Hostility to Baha'ism has remained intense ever since. Baha'i doctrines are strictly egalitarian, teaching the complete equality of men and women and the unity of all humanity. The headquarters of the Baha'i are in Haifa, Israel.

MANDAEISM

The sites www.mandaean world.com and www .iranmanda.com are good sites for those interested in finding out more about Mandaeism.

An ancient gnostic religion, the exact origin of Mandaeism is unknown. Because they speak a form of Aramaic, some credence is given to the Mandaeans' claim that they are descended from followers of John the Baptist; others believe they may be descended from the Essene sect. They practise weekly baptisms as a sacrament, and claim to follow the teachings of John the Baptist. They are considered by Muslims to be 'People of the Book' and identified as the Sabeans of Quranic legend. The small community of around 10,000 is centred on the Shatt al Arab in Khuzestan.

WOMEN IN IRAN

When Samira Makhmalbaf's first film *The Apple* (1998) made waves in the West, people were confused. How could Iran – the land of female oppression and Sharia law – produce an 18-year-old female film-maker of such vision? Samira Makhmalbaf's answer was simple: 'Iran is a country where these two contrasts coexist'.

Nowhere are the contradictions in Iranian society more apparent than in the position of women. Historically, women in Iran have lived in a progressive society and enjoyed more equality and freedom than their neighbours. In Iran women are able to sit in parliament, to drive, to vote, to buy property and to work.

The One Million Signatures Campaign, headed by well-known women activists such as Shirin Ebadi, aims to educate Iranian women in their rights under the law as well as collecting signatures demanding equal rights.

There is a long precedence for this. In pre-Islamic Iran, archaeological evidence suggests that ordinary women were able to work, own, sell and lease property and that they paid taxes. Women managers were mentioned at work sites and women were also known to have held high level military positions. By the Sassanian period, though, women's rights were not formally enshrined.

The Prophet Mohammed was the first to specifically address women's rights, recognising men and women as having different (rather than unequal) rights and responsibilities. Men are expected to provide financially, therefore women are not seen as needing legal rights as men are there to protect and maintain them.

In reality, for Iranian women, the arrival of Islam after the Arab conquest saw a decline in their position at every level. Most of their rights evaporated, the Islamic dress code was imposed, polygamy was practised and family laws were exclusively to the advantage of the male.

Reza Shah started legislating for women when in 1931 the Majlis approved a bill that gave women the right to seek divorce. The marriage age was raised to 15 for girls. In 1936, a system of education was formed for boys and girls equally and in the same year, controversial legislation was passed to abolish the veil, a move that polarised opinion among women. Reza Shah also encouraged women to work outside the home.

Nine Parts of Desire, by Geraldine Brooks, is an insightful look into Muslim women's lives. The author interviews women throughout the Middle East, including, in Iran, Faeze Rafsanjani and Khomeini's widow.

The last shah gave women the vote in 1962 and six years later the Family Protection Law, the most progressive family law in the Middle East, was ratified. Divorce laws became stringent and polygamy was discouraged. The marriage age was raised to 18.

Many Iranian women were active in the revolution that overthrew the shah, but it's safe to say that few foresaw how the adoption of a version of Sharia law and the Islamic Republic would affect their rights.

Within a couple of years of the revolution women were back in the hejab (veil) – and this time in public with a man who was not compulsory. The legal age of marriage for girls had plummeted to nine (15 for boys), and society was strictly segregated. Women were not allowed to appear in public with a man who was not a husband or a direct relation, and they could be flogged for displaying 'incorrect' hejab or showing strands of hair or scraps of make-up. Travel was not possible without a husband or father's permission and a woman could be stoned to death for adultery, which, incidentally, included being raped. Family law again fell under the jurisdiction of the religious courts and it became almost impossible for a woman to divorce her husband without his agreement, and in any case of divorce she was almost certain to lose custody of her children. Women holding high positions – such as Shirin Ebadi, who became a judge in 1979 and won the Nobel Peace Prize in 2003 – lost their jobs and many gave up promising careers.

Daughter of Persia, by Sattareh Farman Farmaian, is an engaging memoir by the daughter of a Qajar prince who introduced social work to Iran. It covers much of Iran's modern history and illustrates the changing roles of women.

However, women did not disappear behind a curtain this time. Iranian women had tasted emancipation, and they resisted a total return to the home. There were many rights that women did not lose – such as the right to vote and the right to hold property and financial independence in marriage. In fact, the rates of education and literacy for women have shot up since the revolution for the simple reason that many traditional families finally felt safe sending their daughters to school once Iran had adopted the veil. Women make up about two-thirds of all university entrants, though their subsequent employment rate is well below 20%. Although women's importance in the workforce is acknowledged – maternity leave, for example, is given for three months at 67% of salary – there is still widespread discrimination.

The website www .badjens.com is an Iranian feminist online magazine mainly addressing readers outside Iran.

In 1997 Reformist president Khatami was voted in by mostly women and young people, promising change. By 2001, there were 14 women in the Majlis and calls to improve women's rights became louder. Among the most prolific Islamic feminists is Faezeh Rafsanjani, the daughter of the ex-president, who herself was a member of parliament, a magazine proprietor, an academic, a mother and an Olympic horse rider.

The Khatami period brought a series of hard-fought minor victories. The Reformists managed to win the right for single women to study abroad, to raise the legal age for marriage from nine to 13 for girls (though they had proposed 15), to defeat an attempt to limit the percentage of female students entering university and to improve custody provisions for divorced mothers. However, a woman's testimony is still only worth half that of a man in court and in the case of the blood money that a murderer's family is obliged to pay to the family of the victim, females are estimated at half the value of a male. *Sigheh* (the Islamic practice of temporary marriage) is seen by many as a sort of legalised prostitution.

In the Eye of the Storm: Women in Post-Revolutionary Iran, edited by Mahnaz Afkhami and Erica Friedl, explores issues such as temporary marriage, education and the strategies used by women to gain control.

On the street, especially in Tehran, you will see that superficially the dress code has eased and the sea of black chadors is offset by shorter, tighter, brightly coloured coats and headscarves worn far back on elaborate hairstyles. Young girls have lost the fear of being seen outside the home with unrelated men, and many defy the regular clampdowns. Activists such as Shirin Ebadi, who works as a lawyer and champions human rights, are insistent that within Islam are enshrined all human rights and that all that is needed is more intelligent interpretation.

Any visit to an Iranian home will leave you in no doubt as to who is really in charge of family life – which is the most important institution in Iran. Iranian women are feisty and powerful and they continue to educate themselves. Most women in Iran will tell you that the hejab is the least of their worries; what is more important is to change the institutional discrimination inherent in Iranian society and the law. As ex-Reformist MP Elaheh Koulaie says: 'We have to change the perceptions that Iranians have of themselves, the perception of the role of men and women'.

After conservatives regained control of the Majlis in 2004 (p40), and hardline Mahmoud Ahmadinejad was elected president in 2005, many feared the recently won reforms would be rescinded. For two years nothing much changed. But in mid-2007 the government began acting on restrictive laws that hadn't been enforced for years. In Tehran women wearing too much make-up and not enough scarf were arrested; across the country female university students were told to start wearing a *maqneh* or stop coming to class. It was part of a broader crackdown that also targeted satellite TV dishes and opposition media.

These sort of crackdowns happen periodically in Iran, often as a means to divert the public focus from other domestic political issues (this one coincided with a deeply unpopular petrol price rise). But by late 2007 it seemed there had been a lasting tightening of official attitudes.

For women, the immediate future looks much less optimistic than it was a few years ago. However, no matter how Iran's political landscape changes, it seems certain Iranian women will continue to assert their rights and slowly chip away at the repressive system, be it with a defiant splash of red lipstick, making visionary movies or becoming expert at interpreting the law and winning the Nobel Peace Prize.

Through its portrayal of Behnaz Jafari, an ambitious young Tehran actress, Pirooz Kalantari's 1999 film *Alone in Tehran* shows the difficulty of being an independent woman in Iran.

Arts Kamin Mohammadi

Most Iranian art forms predate the Arab conquest, but since nearly all of them reached their peak within the Islamic era, religious influences are rarely completely absent. What distinguishes Iran from other Islamic countries, however, is that the Persian culture that predates the Islamic conquest was already over a thousand years old when the Arabs arrived.

In Iran Islamic art favours the non-representational, the derivative and the stylised over the figurative and the true-to-life. Geometrical shapes and complex floral patterns are especially popular in Iranian art. Traditionally, Islam has forbidden the representation of living beings, but if you're more used to travelling in Sunni Islamic countries, where such images rarely appear, the portraiture and images of animals in Iran might come as a surprise.

CARPETS

The best-known Iranian cultural export, the Persian carpet, is far more than just a floor covering to an Iranian. A Persian carpet is a display of wealth, an investment, an integral part of religious and cultural festivals, and is used in everyday life.

History

The oldest surviving carpet is the 'Pazyryk' rug, believed to date from the 5th century BC and discovered in the frozen tomb of a Scythian prince in Siberia in 1948. While the rug's exact origins are unknown, some scholars believe it is in the style of carpets found in the Achaemenid court. Today it's kept in the Hermitage (www.hermitagemuseum.org) in St Petersburg.

Early patterns were usually symmetrical, with geometric and floral motifs designed to evoke the beauty of the classical Persian garden. Stylised animal figures were also woven into carpets, and along with human figures (often royalty), became more popular in the later pre-Islamic period. After the Arab conquest, Quranic verses were incorporated into some carpet designs, and prayer mats began to be produced on a grand scale; secular carpets also became a major industry and were highly prized in European courts. However, very few examples dating from before the 16th century remain.

During the 16th and 17th centuries, carpetmaking was patronised by the shahs and a favoured designer or weaver could expect great privileges. Sheep were bred specifically to produce the finest possible wool, and vegetable plantations were tended with scientific precision to provide permanent dyes of just the right shade. Carpet designs were inspired by book illumination, which had, by this period, reached a degree of unsurpassed sophistication and elegance. The reign of Shah Abbas I (Abbas the Great; r 1587–1629) marks the peak of Persian carpet production, when the quality of the raw materials and all aspects of the design and weaving were raised to a level never seen before or since. As demand for Persian carpets grew, standards of production began to fall and designs became less inspired, though they still led the world in quality and design.

Today, Persian carpets remain a hugely important industry in Iran. According to the National Iranian Carpet Center, more than five million Iranians work in the industry and carpets are the country's largest non-oil export by value. The trade relies on the prestige evoked by the term

Arguably the most famous Persian carpets are the twin 'Ardabil carpets', vast rugs (10.7m x 5.34m) woven with 30 million knots in the 16th century for the Sheikh Safi-od-Din Mausoleum (p162). They are now kept in London's Victoria & Albert Museum (www.vam.ac.uk) and the Los Angeles County Museum of Art (www.lacma.org).

'Persian carpet', but maintaining the 'brand' is increasingly difficult with cheaper 'Persian carpets' being produced in India and Pakistan. Fewer young Iranians are interested in learning to weave, so expect the cost of making genuine handmade rugs – and their price in the bazaar – to rise steadily.

The *Iran Carpet* map, produced by Ramezani Oriental Carpets and sometimes available at the Gita Shenasi (p95) map shop in Tehran, is 10 years old but the location of carpet-weaving centres hasn't changed much.

Types of Carpets & Rugs

To most people (including us in this chapter), the words 'carpet' and 'rug' are used interchangeably. But there is a difference – a carpet is bigger than a rug. Anything longer than about 2m is considered a carpet, while anything shorter is a rug. As well as carpets, which are made using thousands or even millions of knots, you will also find kilims, which are thinner, flat-woven mats without knots and thus, no pile.

Carpets come in a huge variety of designs. Some are inspired by religion, such as those on prayer rugs, usually displaying an arch representing the main arch of the Al Haram Mosque in Mecca and perhaps a lamp symbolic of the statement in the Quran that 'Allah is the light of Heaven'. Other common motifs include amulets to avert the evil eye and other, pre-Islamic motifs, such as stylised Trees of Life, hunting scenes and pictorial depictions of epic poems. They may also be inspired by whatever surrounds the weaver, eg trees, animals and flowers, particularly the lotus, rose and chrysanthemum. Gardens are commonly depicted and, in the case of a tribal nomad, such a carpet will be the only garden the weaver will ever own.

In 2007 the world's largest hand-woven carpet was unveiled in Tehran. The green-coloured carpet has an area of 1020 sq m and was woven for a mosque in Abu Dhabi, UAE.

In general, these designs are classified as either 'tribal' or 'city' carpets. Tribal designs vary greatly depending on their origin (see Know Your Persian Rugs, p64), but are typically less ornate. 'City carpets' are the classic Persian rugs you'll have seen across the world, usually highly ornate floral designs around one or more medallions.

Most Iranians aspire to own fine, formal city rugs of Tabriz, Esfahan, Kashan, Qom or Kerman. They consider tribal carpets the work of peasants, and those who cannot afford hand-woven city carpets would buy a carpet made on a machine using chemical dyes and inferior wool (or even synthetic fibres) before they'd buy a tribal carpet.

WEAVING

Most handmade carpets are woven from wool. The wool is spun, usually by hand, and then rinsed, washed, dried and dyed. Each rug is woven around a vertical (warp) and horizontal (weft) foundation, usually made of cotton – the skeleton of the rug.

The best are made from sheep wool, with quality varying from region to region. Occasionally goat or camel hair is used, usually by tribal weavers in the warps or selvedges (edge bindings) of rugs, kilims or saddle bags to give them strength. Silk carpets are magnificent but they're largely decorative, while wool and silk mixtures are more practical and look beautiful. Weavers are often, but not always, women.

Oriental Rugs in Colour, by Preben Liebetrau, is probably the most useful carpet guide to carry around. This pocket-sized book includes an explanation of the carpets and rugs of Iran and Turkey.

Dyes

Dyeing is often done in large vats in small, old-style buildings in the older parts of towns; walk the old town streets of Kashan (p224), in particular, to see it in action. The dyes themselves are the product of centuries of innovation and experimentation. Colours are extracted from natural sources available locally, including plants (such as herbs, vegetables and fruit skins), insects and even shellfish.

In 1859 chemical dyes such as aniline and chrome were introduced. They caught on quickly because they were cheap and easy to use, though

---

MEASURING UP

Persian carpets can be woven to almost any size, from modest little prayer rugs (usually about 1.5m x 1m) to the vast works decorating the last shah's Niyavaran Palace (p112) in Tehran. However, as you explore the bazaars and carpet shops, sipping tea and watching rug after rug being dramatically unfurled for your perusal, you'll find most are one or another standard size. Other common sizes are 3m x 2m and 4m x 3m. Anything larger than this is usually made to order. The following dimensions (length by width) are approximate:

- *Balisht* or *phosti* – cushion sized
- *Ja Namaz* or *namazlik* – prayer rug, 1.5m x 1m
- *Kenareh* – 3m x 1m

- *Mian farsh* – 3m long and up to 2.5m wide
- *Kellegi* – 3.5m x 2m

The following rugs are measured using an old Persian linear measure called a *zar*.

- *Zarcharak* – 1.25 *zars* or 1.5m x 1m
- *Zaronim* – 1.5 *zars* or 2m x 1m

- *Dozar* – two *zars* or 2m x 1.5m

---

rarely actually better. Not everyone abandoned the old ways, however, and indeed some weavers, notably those in the Chahar Mahal-va Bakhtiari region west of Esfahan, have continued using natural dyes almost uninterrupted to the present day.

Today Iranian rug producers big and small are turning back to natural dyes because buyers in the West are more attracted to their subtle, pleasing shades. The Iranian government is encouraging the producers with subsidies and concessions.

Looms

Traditionally, nomadic carpet-weavers used horizontal looms, which are lightweight and transportable. Their carpets and rugs were less detailed and refined but the quality of wool was often high. Designs were either conjured up from memory, or made up as the weaver worked. These carpets and rugs were woven for domestic use or occasional trade and were small because they had to be portable.

In the villages, small workshops have simple upright looms where weavers can create better designs, with more variety. Designs are usually standard or copied from existing carpets or designs.

Over the last 150 years or so larger village workshops and city factories have begun using bigger and more modern looms. Some still require people to do the weaving, while others are fully mechanised – producing 'machine carpets' that cost about half as much as their hand-woven equivalents.

Persian Kilims, by A Hull & N Barnard, is a lavishly illustrated volume covering most of what you'll need to know about Persian kilims (not carpets).

Knots

You may come across the terms 'Persian (or *senneh*) knot' (known in Farsi as a *farsi-baf*) and 'Turkish (or *ghiordes*) knot' *(turki-baf)*. Despite the names, both are used in Iran: the Turkish knot is common in the Azarbayjan provinces and western Iran.

As a rough guide, an everyday carpet or rug will have up to 30 knots per sq cm, a medium-grade piece 30 to 50 knots per sq cm, and a fine one 50 knots or more per sq cm. A prize piece might have 500 or more knots per sq cm. The higher the number of knots, the better the quality. Nomad weavers tie around 8000 knots a day; factory weavers about 12,000 knots a day.

Buying Carpets & Rugs

Iranians have had more than 2500 years to perfect the art of carpet-making – and just as long to master the art of carpet-selling. If you don't know your warp from your weft, it might be worth reading up before visiting Iran, or taking an Iranian friend when you go shopping (bearing in mind that professional 'friends' who make a living from commission are a fact of life in Iran).

If you know what you're doing, you might pick up a bargain, but it's worth remembering that dealers in Western countries often sell Persian carpets for little more than you'd pay in Iran. Unless you're an expert, don't buy a carpet or rug as an investment – buy it because you like it.

Before buying, lie the carpet flat on the floor and check for bumps or other imperfections. Small bumps will usually flatten out with wear but

---

KNOW YOUR PERSIAN RUGS *Andrew Burke*

Persian carpets come in almost as many different designs as there are ethnic groups and major urban centres. Usually the name of a carpet indicates where it was made or where the design originated. What you will like is purely subjective, though tribal and nomadic carpets generally appeal more to Western tastes than city carpets. The widest range can be found in the bazaars of Tehran (p100), Esfahan (p238), Shiraz (p272), Mashhad (p361) and Tabriz (p150).

Azari Weavers in Tabriz are renowned for being able to reproduce any type and quality of carpet, ranging from fine works in silk or with silk highlights, to simpler weaves from the village and tribal groups of the region.

Bakhtiari These carpets are popular with Westerners. Named after the Bakhtiari people, some of whom remain nomadic, they are woven in more than 200 villages in the Zagros Mountains west of Esfahan, notably in the Chahar Mahal region. Wool quality is high, natural dyes are used and the *kheshti* design, a garden carpet with flower- and tendril-filled compartments, is famous. Most available in Esfahan.

Esfahani The Esfahani carpets are internationally famous for their quality. In the best examples, soft wool and tight knotting is woven around a silk warp and cotton, wool or silk weft. Esfahani designs are noted for their symmetry, usually comprising a single medallion surrounded with vines and palmettos in typical 'city' style. They often have ivory backgrounds with blue, rose, and indigo motifs.

Kashani The Kashani carpets are the classic city rugs. The Kashani design is probably the most common in Iran: a central medallion surrounded by dense floral motifs, including palmettos, flower stems and arabesques on fields of red, light green, clear blue and ivory. They are woven of fine wool using tight Persian knots.

Kermani These carpets have long been renowned for their remarkable quality and large sizes. They remain highly sought-after and relatively expensive. They come in myriad designs, the most famous of which are the eski-Kerman (a single medallion with an arabesque form) and the Tree of Life. Colours are primarily red, blue, green and ivory.

Kordish This style of weaving is centred in Bijar and, more famously, Sanandaj. The carpet terminology here is a bit confusing: Sanandaj carpets are woven using Turkish knots, but they're still known as *senneh* carpets (elsewhere, *senneh* refers to Persian knots). These *senneh* carpets feature predominantly tribal patterns that are primarily geometric – hexagonal medallions are common. *Senneh* are reputed as relatively large, hard-wearing rugs and are made of natural dyes, often deep red with ivory highlights.

Hamadan This is the collection point for the tribal weavings of about 500 villages. Patterns are usually simple geometric designs woven of particularly durable wool from local mountain sheep. They are primarily mid-sized (between 1.5m x 2m and 2.5m x 3.5m), with vibrant reds and blues, usually flat-woven by hand using Turkish knots.

Qashqa'i These carpets are named after the confederation of six major subtribes concentrated in the mountains around Shiraz, who have been famous for their weaving for centuries. Their rugs, runners, kilims and saddle bags, in particular, are popular in bazaars in Shiraz and elsewhere. Patterns are usually geometric, including stylised animals and birds and floral designs in the borders. Pile is tight and thin but natural dyes are not always used – ask. The Qashqa'i also weave fine *gabbeh*, small, thick flat-woven rugs with loose pile. Designs are geometric but simple; khaki, green and red are common colours.

big ones are probably there to stay; if you're still sold on the carpet, look disappointed and expect a price cut. To check if a carpet is handmade, turn it over; on most handmade pieces the pattern will be distinct on the underside (the more distinct, the better the quality).

TAKING THEM HOME
Export regulations for carpets are notoriously changeable; ask a reputable dealer for the latest. At the time of writing there was no limit to the number of carpets you could take home. However, some larger, older and more valuable carpets cannot be exported without special permission. See also Export Restrictions (p377) for other details.

For a more complete description of which carpets come from where, see www.oldcarpet.com and click through to Carpet By Zone.

So you've got your carpet(s), and now it's time to get them home. It's usually cheaper carrying your carpets than posting them because you're less likely to have to pay duty if you can get them through airport customs at home. Alternatively, most carpet dealers can arrange postage and costs are not outrageous. In most countries you can import up to 25 sq metres of Persian carpets before they start looking at you (and charging you) as a merchant; though you will probably still have to pay some duty. Allow between one and two months for it to land on your floor.

One reader reported that sanctions mean US customs are 'quite strict' about anything bought in Iran for more than US$100 – meaning most carpets.

ARCHITECTURE

Persian architecture has a long and complex history, and is often regarded as the field in which Persia made its greatest contribution to world culture. As you travel through Iran its rich history – from home-grown empire to foreign domination – is dramatically chronicled in thousands of years' worth of distinctive architecture.

Although Persian styles differ sharply from those of other Islamic architectural traditions, they have strongly influenced building throughout much of the Islamic world, especially in Central Asia, Afghanistan, Pakistan and India. The two important religious influences on Persian architecture have been Zoroastrianism and Islam (after AD 637). Most of the greatest buildings were built for religious purposes, and religious influences are rarely entirely absent in secular and non-Islamic buildings – even Persian churches use Islamic features.

What Makes Persian Architecture Unique?

The defining aspects of Persian architecture are its monumental simplicity and its lavish use of surface ornamentation and colour. The ground plans of ordinary Persian buildings are usually very simple, mixing only a few standard elements: a courtyard and arcades, lofty entrance porticoes and four *iwan* (barrel-vaulted halls opening onto the courtyard).

The typical Persian mosque design consists of a dome above an entrance *iwan* that leads into a large courtyard surrounded by arched cloisters. Behind these are four inner *iwan,* one of them featuring a decorated niche indicating the direction of Mecca. In the Islamic world in general this is usually called a mihrab although in Iran this term is also used to refer to the cut-out space in the ground in front of it. According to many commentators, the four-*iwan* design can be traced back to old Zoroastrian ideas about the four elements and the circulation of life.

These basic features are often so densely covered with decoration that observers are led to imagine the architecture is far more complex than it actually is. The decorations are normally geometric, floral or calligraphic.

A wall's decoration sometimes consists of nothing but mosaics forming the names of Allah, Mohammed and Ali, repeated countless times in highly stylised script.

TILES

The tiled domes of Iranian mosques, reminiscent of Fabergé eggs in the vividness of their colouring, are likely to remain one of your abiding memories of Iran.

The art of Persian tile production dates back to the Elamite period. However, the glorious period of tile-making came during the Safavid era (1502–1736). Tiles from that period come in two main forms. The very best are *moarraq kashi* (mosaics) – patterns are picked out in tiny pieces of tile rather than created in one piece. Less fine are the *haft rangi* (seven-coloured) tiles, which are square with a painted surface and first appeared in the early 17th century; see Shah in a Hurry, p240. *Haft rangi* tiles normally appear only on the inside of buildings.

By the time of the Qajars, Persian tile-making had passed its prime. But Qajar buildings often make up in quantity of colourful tiles for what they lack in quality. Examples are the courtyard walls of the Golestan Palace (p101) in Tehran and the walls of the wonderful Takieh Mo'aven ol-Molk (p197) in Kermanshah.

Pre-Islamic Architecture

The only substantial remains left from before the 7th century BC are those of the remarkable Elamite ziggurat at Choqa Zanbil (p215). The ancient inhabitants of Persia imbued their mountains with great religious symbolism and built the characteristic pyramidal ziggurats to imitate them. The earliest builders used sun-dried mud bricks; baked brick was already being used for outer surfaces by the 12th century BC, as evidenced by the bricks at Choqa Zanbil, which look like they came out of the kiln last week.

The surviving sites from the Achaemenid era (550–330 BC) include the magnificent ceremonial palace complexes and royal tombs at Pasargadae (p284), Naqsh-e Rostam (p283), Persepolis (p279) and Shush (p214). These are decorated with bas-reliefs of kings, soldiers, supplicants, animals and the winged figure of the Zoroastrian deity Ahura Mazda.

Remains from the Achaemenid era show links with the old ziggurats in their shape and decoration. The Achaemenid style also incorporated

---

QUIRKS OF PERSIAN ARCHITECTURE

All along the great trade routes from east to west caravanserais (an inn or way-station for camel trains, usually consisting of rooms arranged around a courtyard) were set up to facilitate trade. Although the earliest caravanserais date to Seljuk times, many of those surviving date from the reign of Shah Abbas I who was credited with establishing a network of 999 such structures; Caravanserai Zein-o-din (see p267) is a fine restored example. In cities they were typically built right beside the bazaar to facilitate the transfer of goods from beast to shelf and back again. It's easy to see this arrangement in Esfahan (p238) and Kerman (p315), in particular.

In the hot southern deserts you will see the remains of *yakh dans* (mud-brick ice houses) built to store ice through the summer. Water, often from a *qanat* (p260), was left outside to freeze during winter – the ice that formed was scraped off and then moved to an adjoining building, often a stepped dome. The *yakh dan* at Meybod (p266) near Yazd resembles a circular ziggurat outside and a vast hollow egg inside. Yazd is also famous for its *badgirs* (windtowers; p257), while Esfahan still has many curious-looking circular towers used to rear pigeons for meat and manure.

DOMES & MINARETS

The development of the dome was one of the greatest achievements of Persian architecture. The Sassanians (AD 224–642) were the first to discover a satisfactory way of building a dome on top of a square chamber by using two intermediate levels, or squinches – the lower octagonal and the higher 16-sided – on which the dome could rest. Later domes became progressively more sophisticated, incorporating an inner semicircular dome sheathed by an outer conical or even onion-shaped dome. Externally the domes were often encased in tiles, with patterns so elaborate they had to be worked out on models at ground level first.

The minaret started life as an entirely functional tower, from the top of which the muezzin called the faithful to prayer. However, during the Seljuk period (AD 1051–1220) minarets became tall, tapering spires, which were far more decorative than practical. Since it is feared that someone standing atop a minaret can look into the private family areas of nearby houses, Shiite mosques often have a separate hut-like structure on the roof from where the muezzin makes the call to prayer (azan; though these days it's more likely to be a tape recording). Most minarets still have a light, often green (the colour of Islam), in the uppermost gallery. Traditionally these lights and indeed the minarets themselves acted as a beacon to direct people coming to town to pray.

features taken from Egyptian and Greek architecture. They built colossal halls supported by stone and wooden columns with typically Persian bull's-head capitals. The most usual building materials were sun-dried brick and stone.

Alexander the Great's arrival in 331 BC effectively ended the Achaemenid style of architecture in Persia. Instead the influence of Greece and Macedonia grew even stronger. No great examples remain today, although the now-ruined Anahita Temple (p208) at Kangavar was built with Greek capitals to honour a Greek goddess. Under the Parthians (from 247 BC to AD 224) a few characteristically Persian features, including the *iwan*, began to appear.

In the Sassanian period (AD 224–642), buildings became larger, heavier and more complex; Ardashir's Palace (p286) at Firuz Abad is one monumental example. The four-*iwan* plan with domed, square chambers became increasingly common, with the distinctive Persian dome seen for the first time. The Sassanians built fire temples throughout their empire and the simple plan of the earliest examples was retained throughout the pre-Islamic era, even in the design of churches.

The Arab Conquest & Early Persian Islamic Style

The Arab conquest didn't supplant the well-developed Sassanian style but it did introduce the Islamic element that was to have such a pervasive impact on Persian arts. Not only did the Arab period (AD 642–1051) shape the nature and basic architectural plan of religious buildings, but it also defined the type of decoration – no human representation was to be permitted, and ceremonial tombs or monuments also fell from favour. In place of palace complexes built as symbols of royal majesty came mosques designed as centres of daily life for ordinary people.

As Sassanian and Arab ingredients merged, a distinctly Persian style of Islamic architecture evolved. From the mid-9th century, under the patronage of a succession of enlightened rulers, there was a resurgence of Persian nationalism and values. Architectural innovations included the high, pointed arch, stalactites (elaborate stepped mouldings used to decorate recesses) and an emphasis on balance and scale. Calligraphy became the principal form of architectural decoration. A good example is the Jameh Mosque (p253) in Na'in.

In desert cities, such as Yazd and Esfahan, minarets are quite tall because they traditionally acted as a landmark for caravans crossing the desert. In mountainous areas or places surrounded by hills, such as Shiraz, where this function was impossible, most minarets are short.

The period also marks the emergence of a series of remarkable towers, more secular than religious in purpose. Built of brick and usually round, the towers show a development of ornamentation starting with little more than a single garter of calligraphy and graduating to elaborate basket-weave brickwork designed to deflect the harsh sunlight. Today these are commonly referred to as tombs, but some, such as Radkan Tower (p364), were important early astronomical observatories.

The Steppe Peoples: the Seljuks, Mongols & Timurids

Many of the Seljuk rulers (1051–1220) took a great personal interest in patronage of the arts. Architectural developments included the double dome, a widening of vaults, improvement of the squinch and refinement of glazed tilework. A unity of structure and decoration was attempted for the first time, based on rigorous mathematical principles. Stucco, incorporating arabesques and Persian styles of calligraphy, was increasingly used to enhance brick surfaces.

During the Safavid period Shah Abbas the Great ordered 999 caravanserais to be built. Of them, only two were circular, one near Esfahan and the other at Zein-o-din, south of Yazd. The latter has been restored and turned into a hotel (see Caravanserai Zein-o-din, p267).

Although often seen as a dark age in Iranian history, the Mongol period (1220–1335) saw new developments in Persian architecture. The conquest by Genghis Khan's rampaging hordes was initially purely destructive, and many architects fled the country, but later the Mongols, too, became patrons of the arts. The Mongol style, designed to overawe the viewer, was marked by towering entrance portals, colossal domes, and vaults reaching up into the skies. It also saw a refinement of tiling, and calligraphy, often in the formal angular Kufic script imported from Arabia. Increasing attention was paid to the interior decoration of domes.

The Timurids (1380–1502) went on to refine the Seljuk and Mongol styles. Their architecture featured exuberant colour and great harmony of structure and decoration. Even in buildings of colossal scale, they avoided the monotony of large empty surfaces by using translucent tiling. Arcaded cloisters around inner courtyards, open galleries, and arches within arches were notable developments.

The Safavids

Under a succession of enlightened and cultivated rulers, most notably Shah Abbas I, came the final refinement of styles that marked the culmination of the Persian Islamic school of architecture. Its greatest expression was Abbas' royal capital of Esfahan, a supreme example of town planning with one of the most magnificent collections of buildings from one period anywhere in the world – the vast and unforgettable Imam Sq (p232).

Other fine examples of Safavid architecture are at Qazvin (p176), while the Holy Shrine (p355) of Imam Reza at Mashhad gained much of its present magnificence in Safavid times.

The Qajars

During the Qajar period a European style of painting became popular as the shahs created a royal iconography with life-sized portraits, rarely seen in the Middle East. For more information, read *Royal Persian Paintings: The Qajar Epoch*, edited by Layla Diba.

The Qajar period (1795–1925) marks the rather unhappy transition between the golden age of Persian Safavid architecture and the creeping introduction of Western-inspired uniformity from the mid-19th century. Now widely regarded as tasteless, flimsy and uninspired, the often-colourful Qajar style did produce some fine buildings, including the Golestan Palace (p101) in Tehran and the stately mansions in Kashan (p226).

PAINTING

The earliest known distinctively Persian style of painting dates back to the Seljuk period (1051–1220) and is often referred to as the Baghdad School. Early painting was mainly used to decorate manuscripts and

---

A CONNOISSEUR'S GUIDE TO PERSIAN ARCHITECTURE

Listed chronologically.

Choqa Zanbil (p215) A huge brick ziggurat from before the 7th century BC.

Persepolis (p279) The full glory of the Achaemenid period in one place.

Ardashir's Palace (p286) South of Shiraz, Ardashir's monumental palace was one of the earliest Sassanian architectural triumphs, and the most impressive of what's left.

Mil-e Gonbad (p342) A soaring, almost unfeasibly bold 11th-century brick tower.

Jameh Mosque (p236) Esfahan's congregational mosque is the finest remaining Seljuk building.

Oljeitu Mausoleum (p184) The most magnificent surviving Mongol structure in Iran, and probably the world.

Azim-e Gohar Shad mosque (Mashhad; p357) and **Blue (Kabud) Mosque** (Tabriz; p150) Timurid architecture at its finest.

Imam Sq (p238) The lasting glory of the Safavids is enshrined in this grand square, containing arguably the greatest concentration of Islamic buildings anywhere on earth.

Golestan Palace (Tehran; p101) and **Takieh Mo'aven ol-Molk** (Kermanshah; p197) The finest examples of overblown Qajar style.

Qurans, though some fine 13th-century pottery found near Tehran also reveals a unique early Persian style of art. During the Mongol period (1220–1335), paintings were used to decorate all sorts of books, especially poetry books.

In the 16th century an important school of Persian art developed in Tabriz, under the guidance of Sultan Mohammed. Designs and patterns produced by this school also influenced carpet design. Persian art later flourished under Shah Abbas I, who turned Esfahan into a centre for the arts. By the 18th century artists fell under the influence of India and Europe. Persian artists rarely signed their works so little is known about most of the artists.

CALLIGRAPHY

With the arrival of Islam several distinctly Persian calligraphic styles emerged, some of them so elaborate that they are almost illegible, eg *nashki*, which later developed into another renowned style known as *thulth*. Not only was the Quran faithfully reproduced as a whole in calligraphic form, but verses from it, and the holy names of Allah and Mohammed, were used as decorations on religious buildings and elsewhere, as they are to this day.

By about the 16th century, Shiraz and Esfahan were producing some of the finest calligraphy in the Islamic world. Some of the very best examples of ancient and modern calligraphy can be seen at Tehran's Reza Abbasi Museum (p114), named for the renowned 16th-century calligrapher.

The word Persian doesn't exist in Farsi. It is the ancient Greek word for Iranians.

MINIATURES

The Persian miniature-painting *(minyaturha)* tradition began after the Mongol invasion, influenced by artisans brought to the royal court from China. It reached its peak during the 15th and 16th centuries. Later, artists from eastern Iran, who had studied under the great Mohammadi in Herat (now in Afghanistan), also started to influence this art form.

Persian miniature paintings are now deservedly famous throughout the world. The best examples show great intricacy and attention to detail. Favourite subjects include courting couples in traditional dress (usually figures from popular poetry), polo matches and hunting scenes. Some of the best modern miniatures come from Esfahan, where the tourist market keeps hundreds of miniaturists busy.

ILLUSTRATED MANUSCRIPTS

Bihzad, Master of Persian Painting, by Ebadollah Bahari, is the lavishly illustrated life of Kamal al-Din Bihzad, the great 15th-century Persian artist and manuscript illustrator.

Neatly combining Persia's two traditions of fine penmanship and miniature painting are the illustrated manuscripts you can see on display at the Reza Abbasi Museum (p114) in Tehran. Most of the manuscripts are books of poetry with the themes beautifully illustrated alongside the text. However, some manuscripts are decorated Qurans that, while still nonfigurative, go beyond just beautiful handwriting.

GLASSWARE

Small, translucent glass vessels dating back to the 2nd millennium BC have been found at Choqa Zanbil (p215). During the Sassanian era Persian glassware *(shisheh alat)* became a sought-after luxury that was traded as far away as Japan. By early Islamic times, two principle techniques were used: mould-blown to produce thicker items, and free-blown for more delicate articles. Glassware was usually green, lapis lazuli, light blue or clear with a tinge of yellow, and decorations were cut into the glass. The art reached its peak during the Seljuk era when the manufacture of enamelled and gilded glassware flourished.

The world's first ever 'pane' glass was produced at Choqa Zanbil. It was used to cover the panels of doors and windows of the ziggurat.

Under the Safavids Shiraz became an important centre of glass production, with rose-water sprinklers, long-necked wine bottles, flower vases and bowls particularly popular. By the reign of Karim Khan Zand, the famous wine from Shiraz was exported in locally crafted jugs and bottles. Typical decorations now include gilded or enamelled floral patterns, sun and lion emblems, or glass strings wound around a tall necked vessel. See Iran's history of glassware in Tehran's excellent Glass & Ceramics Museum (p106).

LACQUER WORK

Some consider this the most interesting of Iran's decorative arts; it can be traced back to early Islamic times as an independent art form, decorating smaller private objects. Wooden or papier-mâché objects are painted, then a transparent sandarac-based varnish is applied in successive layers from three to more than 20 coats. The result gives an impression of depth and provides great durability. Common designs are the popular Persian motif of the nightingale and the rose, flowers, hunting scenes, battles or classic love stories. Pen boxes are the most common form of lacquer work.

MARQUETRY

One of the most intricate styles of woodwork is a form of marquetry *(moarraq)* called *khatam*. A Persian style of marquetry slowly developed through the centuries and by the 17th century *khatam* was so prestigious that several Safavid princes learned the technique.

A pair of doors from 1590, now in the Islamic Museum of Berlin, is one of the earliest existing examples of Persian *khatam* (a form of marquetry).

Several different woods, including betel, walnut, cypress and pine are used, with the inlaid pieces made from animal bones, shells, ivory, bronze, silver and gold. The final product is coated with varnish. Genuine Persian *khatam* contains no paint; the colours come from the inlaid pieces. *Khatam* can be used for furniture but visitors usually buy it in the form of ornamental boxes or picture frames. Most of what you'll see for sale in souvenir shops is not genuine.

METALWORK

Persian metalworking can be traced back at least to Achaemenid times when silverware was commonly used in the royal court. As well as working with copper, bronze, silver and gold, Iranian metalworkers were unique in producing a wide variety of steel objects, as well as arms and armour. The shapes and decorative motifs used then still survive in the bazaars, where there are alleyways of copperworkers, tinsmiths and engravers producing trays and table tops with scenes depicting hunts or calligraphy.

Enamelling (minakari) is another way of working with metal, the earliest-known example being an enamelled copper mihrab dating from 1556. The metal surface is painted with fine patterns usually in turquoise, white and black and then varnished. It is delicate work, easily chipped and needs to be handled with care. The best examples come from Esfahan and are usually bought as small vases or decorative plates.

POTTERY

Pottery is one of the oldest Persian art forms and examples have been unearthed from burial mounds dating from the 5th millennium BC. Early pieces were probably ornamental rather than for domestic use, with elaborately detailed animals dominating the design. Persian pottery was initially unglazed, but glazed pottery dating back to the Elamite period has been unearthed from Choqa Zanbil. In the 1st millennium AD, pottery was painted with the simple geometric, floral and animal motifs that developed into the characteristic Persian style. The lotus flower (niloofar in Farsi) featured heavily as a symbol of life and of women.

From the 9th century onwards, Persia's detailed and colourful (mainly blue and green) glazed pottery became world famous. The nomads of northeastern Khorasan province had by then created their own style of glazing, adding early Islamic lettering styles such as Kufic to the design. Persian pottery reached its zenith in the 13th century, when a new type of clay improved durability and several dazzling new colours were introduced. Chinese influences became strong during the Mongol period, when figurative designs became commonplace.

The earliest evidence of textiles comes from Seh Gabi in Kordestan province where 5th-millennium-BC pottery vessels have imprints of fabric wrapped around them as textile fragments.

TEXTILES

You will see hand-printed cloth everywhere you go, mostly made in Esfahan, and used as bedspreads or tablecloths. Wooden blocks are used to apply patterns in black, red, blue, yellow and green to what are basically beige cloths. These are then washed in the river to fasten the colours. It is thought that textile printing has been practised since Sassanian times. Other parts of Iran have their own textile traditions, for example in Yazd you can buy intricately woven textiles known as termeh, with paisley patterns worked in cotton and silk.

MODERN ART

Contemporary art in Iran is concentrated in Tehran, where a small but sophisticated community of artists produce and exhibit work in a variety of media. Their work is not always appreciated by the people in power, and several, including Tehrani artist Khosrow Hassanzadeh, have found greater acclaim internationally than at home.

Despite the limited resources available to Iranian artists – there are few professional galleries and institutions capable of launching an artist's career – the restrictions themselves seem to inform their aesthetic. Established modern artists include Aidin Aghdashlou, Habibollah Sadeqi and Gholamhossein Nami.

The Tehran Museum of Contemporary Art (p108) has a formidable collection of international work believed to be worth more than US$2 billion, including world-famous works by Renoir, Monet, Gauguin, Van Gogh, Pissarro, Toulouse-Lautrec, Magritte, Miró, Dali, Picasso, Jackson

One of the best-known and loved modern Iranian artists and sculptors is Sayyed Ali Akhbar Sanati, whose work is on display in the Sanati Museum of Contemporary Art (p316) in Kerman.

and Warhol. At the time of writing, however, the museum was only exhibiting works by Iranian artists – all foreign works had been sent to the basement. This may change if there is a change in government. For a short list of Tehran galleries, see p122.

MUSIC

Most Iranians are familiar with the big names of Western pop, thanks to satellite TV and the internet. Almost every taxi driver, especially in Tehran, seems to keep a cache of Turkish pop classics stashed under the dashboard. Increasingly, shops selling CDs are taking their place on main streets, complemented by the usual developing world array of hawkers flogging pirated copies from footpath stalls. Most of the musicians are Iranian, either home-grown or from outside Iran, usually 'Tehrangeles' (aka Los Angeles).

There are occasional music festivals, particularly during the annual 10 Days of Dawn (1 to 11 February). Festivals can be hard to track down; the website www.tehranavenue.com might have details. Women performers were banned for many years but now women-only concerts are commonplace.

Classical

For Iranians there is no distinction between poetry and lyrics, and traditional Persian music is poetry set to a musical accompaniment. Like epic poems, some 'epic songs' are very long and masters can spend most of their lives memorising the words.

Classical Persian music is almost always downbeat and can sound decidedly mournful or, as one young Shirazi told us, 'depressing'. Despite this, it remains hugely popular and you'll hear it in taxis and teahouses across the country. Two singers particularly worth listening out for are Shajarian and Shahram Nazeri, both of whom have helped promote interest in classical Persian music internationally.

While the voice is usually central to this form of music, it is backed by several instruments that have deep roots in Persian culture. Among the most common:

- *tar* – a six-string instrument, usually plucked
- *setar* – similar to the *tar* but with four strings
- *nay* – generic name for various types of flute
- *sorna* – similar to an oboe
- *kamancheh* – a kind of four-stringed viola played like a cello
- *daf* and *daryereh* – different sizes of outsized tambourine
- *santur* – dulcimer played with delicate wooden mallets
- *tombak* – vase-shaped drum with a skin at the wide end
- *dahol* and *zarb*– large and small drums respectively

Folk

The most appealing and melodious traditional music is heard among ethnic minorities, such as the Turkmen in northern Iran. Azaris favour a unique style of music, often based around a love song, whereas Kurds have a distinctively rhythmic music based mainly around the lute and their own versions of epic songs, called *bards*.

Folk music employs most of the instruments mentioned above, with regional variations; along the Persian Gulf a type of bagpipe called the *demam* is popular. The music of Sistan va Baluchestan is understandably similar to that of Pakistan and typically uses instruments such as the *tamboorak* (similar to the Pakistani *tambura*, a type of harmonium).

To hear the varying types of Iranian music, both new and old, listen to free tracks available on www.iranian.com/music.html, www.persia.org/audio.html or www.theiranianradio.com. To buy Persian music, and make sure your money goes to the artists, check out www.cdbaby.com.

Sima Bina was born in Khorasan province and first performed publicly at the age of nine. She continues to record the folk music of Khorasan, holds women-only concerts in Iran and tours worldwide.

The Kamkars, a Kurdish family ensemble, started as a semi-professional group in 1967. Since then, they have been celebrated for their concerts featuring traditional Iranian music, and rousing Kurdish folk songs. They tour in Iran and worldwide.

Perhaps not surprisingly, the lyrics of most traditional music revolve around Islam, though some are based on love or celebrate ancient military victories.

Pop

Iranian pop music has re-emerged under the watchful eye of the Iranian authorities. Many of the best Iranian musicians fled Iran after the Islamic Revolution. They now perform abroad, with '70s superstar Googosh, in particular, playing regularly in North America, Europe, Australia and Dubai. Their music still circulates illicitly within Iran.

Nine-piece Arian was the first mixed-gender band to get official approval after the revolution. Their debut album, *Gole Aftabgardoon* (The Sunflower) was released in 2000 and soon they were playing to crowds of more than 50,000. Other favourite artists include Benyamin Bahadori, Moin and Omid.

Rock & Rap

Iran's rock and rap scene is mainly underground but an ever-growing number of bands and musicians are finding a Persian way to rock. Groups such as O-Hum set the scene with 'Persian rock', a mix of familiar and Iranian instruments and the poetic lyrics of Hafez. The result is like '90s grunge rock with an Iranian flavour; download free tracks at www .iranian.com. Other popular rock acts include Barad, Meera, The Technicolor Dream and Hypernova. Home-grown rap is popular, with lyrics in Farsi extolling the joys of sex and drugs as in the West. Not surprisingly, the authorities don't approve but millions of young Iranians do. Zed Bazi has the biggest following.

LITERATURE

Iran is a nation of poets and overwhelmingly the most important form of writing is poetry. Familiarity with famous poets and their works is universal: ask almost any man on the street and he will quote you lines from Hafez or Rumi. The big-name writers are all primarily poets, eg Omar Khayyam, Sa'di and, above all, Ferdosi (see The Great Iranian Poets, p74). Many Iranians write poetry themselves and the Sufi form, poems addressed to the divine beloved, are still popular.

While writers have long been persecuted in Iran, their numbers increased dramatically during the Khatami years, particularly women novelists who regularly topped best-seller lists. But writers haven't fared so well under the conservative Ahmadinejad government. All books must be approved by government censors before publication and thousands of new and old works have been banned; from Dan Brown's *The Da Vinci Code* to all works by Sadeq Hedayat, one of Iran's most famous pre-revolutionary novelists.

Poetry

While no-one knows the exact date of origin of the *Avesta*, the first-known example of Persian literature, it is known that various forms of Persian poetry developed around the 9th century AD. Typical were the *masnavi*, with its unique rhyming couplets, and the *ruba'i*, similar to the quatrain (a poem of four lines). Poems of more than 100 nonrhyming couplets, known as *qasideh*, were first popularised by Rudaki who flourished under the Samanid ruler Nasr II (913–43).

These styles later developed into long and detailed 'epic poems', the first of which was Ferdosi's *Shahnamah*, (see Ferdosi, p74). Many epic

Underground rockers Kiosk regularly tour the US. Reminiscent of Dire Straits, their lyrics are witty and wry. Their videos are excellent with young Iranian artists working on 'To Kojaiee'. The video for 'Esgh-e Sorat' lays bare issues facing contemporary Iran; for a subtitled version visit www.kiosk-music.com.

Farsi (Persian) has changed less since the 10th century than English since Shakespeare's day.

Persepolis: The Story of a Childhood is Marjane Satrapi's autobiographical graphic novel about growing up through the revolution and the formation of the Islamic Republic. It's compelling, funny and, ultimately, heart-rendingly sad. The movie version, *Persepolis*, was released late 2007.

THE GREAT IRANIAN POETS

Iranians venerate their great poets, who are often credited with preserving the Persian language and culture during times of occupation. Streets, squares, hotels and *chaykhanehs* (teahouses) are named after famous poets, several of whom have large mausoleums. Ferdosi (p363) and Omar Khayyam (p364) are buried in huge (separate) gardens near Mashhad, and Sa'di (p274) and Hafez (p274) have mausoleum complexes in Shiraz; all are popular pilgrimage sites.

Ferdosi

Hakim Abulqasim Ferdosi, first and foremost of all Iranian poets, was born in about AD 940 near Tus. He was famous for developing the *ruba'i* (quatrain) style of 'epic' historic poems. He is most famous for the *Shahnamah* (Book of Kings), which he started when he was 40 and finished some 30 years later. When completed, this truly epic poem included almost 60,000 couplets. However, the Turkish king to whom he presented it was incensed that it contained no references to Turks and so rejected it. Ferdosi died old, poor and grief-stricken.

These days Ferdosi is seen as the saviour of Farsi, which he chose to use at a time when the language was under threat from Arabic. Without his writings many details of Persian history and culture might also have been lost. All in all, Ferdosi is credited with having done much to help shape the Iranian self-image.

Hafez

Khajeh Shams-ed-Din Mohammed, or Hafez (meaning 'One Who Can Recite the Quran from Memory') as he became known, was born in Shiraz in about 1324. His father died while he was still young so the boy was educated by some of the city's leading scholars. Apart from memorising the Quran at an early age, he also became interested in literature and wrote many verses still used in everyday speech. His collection of poems, known as *Divan-e Hafez,* has a strong mystical quality and is often virtually untranslatable; much of it was also about nightingales, courtship and wine. Although he lived in turbulent times, Hafez refused many generous invitations to some of the great courts of the day, both inside and outside Iran, because of his love for his birthplace. He died in 1389.

Omar Khayyam

Omar Khayyam (Omar the Tentmaker) was born in Neishabur in about 1047. He is probably the best-known Iranian poet in the West because many of his poems, including the famous *Rubaiyat,* were translated into English by Edward Fitzgerald; in Iran he is more famous as a mathematician, historian and astronomer, in particular for his studies of the calendar and algebra. Although there is some speculation about what he actually wrote, Omar Khayyam is famous for his *ruba'i* poems. He died in 1123.

Rumi

Born Jalal ad-Din Mohammad Balkhi – known as Rumi – in 1207 in Balkh (in present-day Afghanistan). His family fled west before the Mongol invasions and eventually settled in Konya in present-day Turkey, where first his father and then he retreated into meditation and study of the divine. His first great work was the *Masnevi*. He was inspired by a great dervish, Shams-e Tabrizi, and many of his poems of divine love are addressed to him. He is credited with founding the Maulavi Sufi order – the whirling dervishes. He is also known as Maulana ('the Master' in Arabic).

Sa'di

The other great Shirazi poet, Sheikh Mohammed Shams-ed-Din (known as Sa'di), lived from about 1207 to 1291. Like Hafez, he lost his father at an early age and was educated by some of the leading teachers of Shiraz. Many of his elegantly phrased verses are still commonly used in conversation. His most famous works, the *Golestan* (Rose Garden) and *Bustan* (Garden of Trees), have been translated into many languages.

poems celebrated the glories of the old Persia before whichever foreigners had most recently invaded and occupied the country. The last truly great 'epic poem', *Zafarnamah*, by Hamdollah Mostowfi, covered the history of Islam from the birth of Mohammed to the early 14th century.

Moral and religious poetry became enormously popular following the success of Sa'di's most famous poems, the *Bustan* and *Golestan*. By the 14th century, smaller *qazal* poems, which ran to about 10 nonrhyming couplets, were still being used for love stories. *Qazal* poetry, which developed around the same time as *qasideh,* was made famous by Hafez and is still practised today.

Early in the last century modernist Persian poetry changed the poetic landscape. This style is exemplified by the work of Nima Yushij. Poets such as Forough Farrokhzad and Sohrab Sepehri were influential from the 1950s onwards. Ahmad Shamloo's *Fresh Air*, a book of poems published in 1957, marked the introduction of a lyrical style that was also political and metaphoric. Parvin E'tesami is a noted female poet, renowned for her religious poems, *Mecca of the Heart* and *Eye and Heart*. She died in 1941 at 35.

Modern Persian Poetry (An Anthology in English), edited by Mahmud Kianush, is a thorough anthology that includes 129 poems by 43 poets of the 20th century. Featured poets include all the modern innovators, such as Nima Yushij, Fereydun Tavalloli and Forough Farrokhzad.

Novels

More and more Iranian novels are now available in English. The 20th-century writer Sadeq Hedayat is the best-known Iranian novelist outside Iran, and one whose influence has been most pervasive in shaping modern Persian fiction.

A 2005 study found 370 Iranian women had published novels – 13 times the number in 1995 and about equal with the number of published male novelists. Among the most popular is Fataneh Haj Seyed Javadi, whose 1998 novel *Drunkard Morning* is about a woman who defies her aristocratic family to marry a carpenter in the 1940s, then leaves him when he becomes abusive. Another is Simin Daneshvar, whose novel *A Persian Requiem* (*Shavushun* in Farsi) deals with life in Iran between the two world wars. Her husband was the prominent social commentator Jalal Al-e Ahmad whose novels – *The School Principal* and *The Pen* – have also been translated into English.

Iranians themselves tend to prefer short stories to novels. A selection of these are included in Minou Southgate's compendium *Modern Persian Short Stories*.

The Blind Owl, by Sadeq Hedayat, published in 1941, a seminal and influential book, is a dark and powerful portrayal of the decadence of a society failing to achieve its own modernity.

CINEMA

Iran's love affair with cinema started at the dawn of the last century. Mirza Ebrahim Khan Akkas-Bashi recorded a royal visit to Belgium in 1900, and in the same year the country's first public cinema opened in Tabriz. By 1904 a cinema had opened in Tehran, and it has been the most popular form of artistic entertainment ever since. Avanes Oganian's *Abi & Rabi* (1930) was the first silent Iranian movie, and *The Lor Girl* (1933), directed by Ardashir Irani in India, the first talkie. Producer Abdolhossein Sepanta's love for Iranian history and literature helped him to craft films that appealed to Iranian tastes. Esmail Kushan's 1948 *The Tempest of Life* was the first film to be made in Iran and since then, the home-grown industry has not looked back.

It was not until the 1960s, however, that the first signs of a very distinctive Iranian cinematic language emerged. Poet Forough Farrokhzad's 1962 film of life in a leper colony, *The House is Black*, anticipated much of what was to come. Darius Mehrjui's 1969 film *Gaav*, based on a story by modern playwright Gholamhossien Sa'edi, was the period's most

For news and history of Iranian cinema, see the Farabi Cinema Foundation's site at www.fcf .ir/english.

THE MAKHMALBAF FAMILY – A CINEMA DYNASTY

Born in 1957 in Tehran, Mohsen Makhmalbaf first gained infamy when he was imprisoned for five years after fighting with a policeman. He was released during the Islamic Revolution in 1979 and started to write books before turning to film-making in 1982. Since then he has produced more than a dozen films, including *Boycott, Time for Love, Gabbeh* (p50) and, more provocatively, *Salaam Cinema*. Many of his films are based on taboo subjects: *Time for Love* was filmed in Turkey because it broached the topic of adultery; and *Marriage of the Blessed* was a brutal film about the casualties of the Iran–Iraq War.

Makhmalbaf refuses to follow the strict Islamic guidelines for local film-making and has become a virtual exile from Iran because of overzealous censorship. In 1997 Makhmalbaf's daughter Samira produced her first film, *The Apple*, to critical acclaim. In 2000 her second film, *Blackboards*, was a smash hit at the Cannes Film Festival; she was the youngest director ever to have shown a film there.

The Makhmalbaf movie factory continues to churn out winners. Samira's younger brother made a 'making-of' documentary about *Blackboards;* then younger sister Hana directed a feature about the shooting of *At Five in the Afternoon.* On the strength of that film, *Joy of Madness,* Hana beat Samira to a 'youngest-ever' record by being invited to the Venice Film Festival at the age of 14. Even Mohsen Makhmalbaf's second wife (the sister of his first wife, who died tragically), Marzieh Meshkini, has directed an acclaimed film, *The Day I Became A Woman,* a film featuring three linked short stories that examine what it is to be a woman in Iran.

However, life for the Makhmalbaf's has a darker side. Mohsen Makhmalbaf survived two assassination attempts while filming *Kandahar* in Iran, and in 2007 the whole family was attacked while on location in Afghanistan for Samira's latest film, *The Two-legged Horse.* A man posing as an extra threw a bomb onto the set, wounding six actors and several extras and killing the horse in the film's title. Filming was eventually finished in June 2007. For more on the Makhmalbafs, see www.makhmalbaf.com.

important landmark film. Sohrab Shahid Sales' early 1970s films, such as *Still Life,* introduced a new way of looking at reality; the influence of his still camera and simple stories is seen in Abbas Kiarostami and Mohsen Makhmalbaf's work.

The first 'new wave' of Iranian cinema is marked by the work of those who first captured the attention of arthouse movie fans around the world: Kiarostami, Dariush Mehrjui and Bahram Beiza'i, Khosrow Haritash and Bahram Farmanara. The post-revolutionary directors, such as Makhmalbaf, Rakhshan Bani Etemad and Jafar Panahi, have helped develop a reputation for Iranian cinema as arthouse, neorealist and poetic – the second 'new wave'. Arguably, film-makers such as Kiarostami are continuing the great tradition of Persian poetry, albeit in a visual medium. The strict censorship of the post-revolutionary state has encouraged use of children, nonprofessional actors and stories that are fixated on the nitty-gritty of life, and which have proved popular overseas.

Friendly Persuasion: Iranian Cinema After the Revolution, by Jamsheed Akrami, is a feature-length documentary that examines the phenomenon of Iranian post-revolutionary cinema. Those interviewed represent three generations of Iranian filmmakers.

Iranians have finally learned to love their own cinema and flock to it in droves. But many internationally acclaimed 'arthouse' films never get released at home, and instead get distributed on the bootleg market. Some Iranians feel the masters are making movies specifically for foreign markets and film festivals.

Dozens of films are churned out every year for the domestic market, many of them action flicks. There are, however, signs of improvement here, too, with social issues increasingly taking centre stage, as in Rakhshan Bani Etemad's films. Female director Tahmineh Milani's most recent film, *Atash Bas* (Cease Fire; 2006), is a screwball comedy that deals with the difficulties of a newly-wed couple and features two of Iran's biggest film stars. It was that year's biggest hit, breaking box office records.

Other worthy Iranian films include *Crimson Gold* (p47), *Mainline* (p49) and *Alone in Tehran* (p60). *Children of Heaven*, Majid Majidi's film, was nominated for the Best Foreign Language Film Oscar in 1998. It is a delicate tale focussing on two poor children losing a pair of shoes. Humorous and tender. *The White Balloon*, written by Abbas Kiarostami and directed by Jafar Panahi, tells the story of a young girl who loses her money while on the way to buy a goldfish. The film won several international awards. Also see Must-see Movies (p18), which lists our top 10.

Several books take a detailed look at Iranian cinema, including *Iranian Cinema: A Political History* by Hamid Reza Sadr (2006); *The New Iranian Cinema: Politics, Representation and Identity* by Richard Tapper (2002); and *Close Up: Iranian Cinema, Past, Present and Future* by Hamid Dabashi.

Taste of Cherry, directed by Abbas Kiarostami, was co-winner of the prestigious Palme d'Or at the 1997 Cannes Film Festival, despite being very controversial inside Iran because it deals with suicide, a taboo subject in Islam.

THEATRE

The most important and prevalent form of Iranian theatre is the *ta'ziyeh* (passion play), which means 'mourning for the dead', and actually predates the introduction of Islam into Iran. These plays are staged in every Iranian city, town and village during Ashura (see p383), the anniversary of the battle in AD 680 in which Imam Hossein, the grandson of the Prophet, was murdered at Karbala.

During the two days of mourning, boys and men dressed in black walk through city streets, hitting their chests and backs with chains called *shallagh*. Others play drums and brass instruments, lead the chanting, and carry flags and weapons symbolising the struggle against the infidels. The highlight for both participants and spectators comes when mounted warriors dressed in traditional fighting outfits re-enact the martyrdom of Hossein.

The groups then move to a public place where a temporary platform or stage has been erected. Here actors carrying dangerous-looking weapons continue to re-enact the martyrdom. The followers of Hossein are usually dressed in green (the colour of Islam), while the followers of his enemy Yezid are dressed in red. One actor has to play Shemr, the man believed to have killed Hossein. It's a dangerous role because passions run high and audiences have become so caught up in the play that they have actually killed 'Shemr'. Traditional poems are recited and dramatic songs sung to an accompaniment of Iranian flutes and drums. Many spectators openly weep while others pray.

Tehran's Film Museum of Iran (p109) shows Iranian films and you can request subtitles (if available), and buy a huge array of DVDs. The annual Fajr Film Festival (p382) showcases the latest Iranian films.

Food & Drink

Far more than simply the fuel of empires, food in Iran has as long a story as the country itself. The dishes you eat today have evolved over three millennia, influenced by culture and environment.

Food plays a central role in honouring guests and celebrating special events, such as No Ruz (see p385). The way food is served draws on the ideas of ancient physicians, who carefully combined food and drink to maintain strength in both body and mind. Long before Weight Watchers, these wise Persians concluded that a good diet did not involve an excess of fats, red meats, starch or alcohol – these transformed men into wicked, selfish brutes. Instead, fruit, vegetables, chicken and fish were encouraged as the food of gentler, more respectable people. In practice, this philosophy is governed by a classification of foods dating back to Achaemenid times; see Persian Food Philosophy: It's 'Hot' & 'Cold' (below).

Despite this, outside Tehran most restaurant menus are dominated by kababs (see opposite) and fast food. To enjoy the best cooking you really need to be invited into an Iranian home. Fortunately there's a good chance that will happen. When it does, just say 'yes'. As a guest you will be a 'gift of God' and the fabulous food and humbling hospitality should make for a meal you'll remember for a lifetime. (Make sure you have a read up on etiquette; see p83.)

PERSIAN FOOD PHILOSOPHY: IT'S 'HOT' & 'COLD'

The Persian philosophy of food is to eat a balance of 'hot' and 'cold' foods to maintain good health. It's not about the temperature a food is served at, but rather the 'heating' and/or 'cooling' effect food has on the body. As an ancient philosophy largely passed down by word of mouth, it's not known exactly where or why these ideas originated. But the general belief is that 'hot' foods 'thicken the blood' and speed metabolism, while 'cold' foods 'dilute the blood' and slow the metabolism.

The philosophy extends to personalities and weather, too. Like foods, people are believed to have 'hot' and 'cold' natures. People with 'hot' natures should eat more 'cold' foods, and vice versa. And on cold days it's best to eat 'hot' foods, and vice versa.

So what's 'hot' and what's not? Classifications vary across the country but it's generally agreed that animal fat, wheat, sugar, sweets, wine, all dried fruits and vegetables, fresh herbs including mint and saffron, and most meats are 'hot' (though beef and mutton are debated). 'Cold' foods include fish, yogurt and watermelon (all 'very cold'), rice, some fresh vegetables (particularly radishes) and fruits, beer and other nonwine alcohol. Some foods are hotter or colder than others, and some, such as onion and tomato, are fairly neutral.

As you travel, you'll see the balance in dishes such as *fesenjun* (sauce of grated pomegranate, walnuts, eggplant and cardamom served over roast chicken and rice), where the pomegranate (cold) is balanced by the walnuts (hot). You'll also see this balance on the table, where *mast* (yogurt), cheese, radishes and greens – all cold – are served with 'hot' kababs (opposite), chicken and sweets. Getting the balance right is what is most important. Too much 'cold' food is thought to be particularly unhealthy. We were told of one man in his 30s who, in an effort to lose weight, ate only yogurt for dinner for six months. When he ate watermelon after his yogurt one night he promptly died of a heart attack (yes, he might just have had a dicky ticker). 'Hot' foods are apparently not so dangerous: too much of 'hot' and you might end up with a cold sore, if you're prone to them.

So think twice before ordering *dugh* (churned sour milk or yogurt mixed with water) with your fish meal, unless the *dugh* comes with chopped herbs to balance it out. And be careful with that watermelon!

STAPLES & SPECIALITIES

Almost every meal in Iran is accompanied by *nun* (bread) and/or *berenj* (rice). *Nun* is dirt cheap and usually fresh. There are four main varieties: *lavash* is common for breakfast and is flat and thin (it's mouthwatering when fresh but soon turns cardboard-like); *barbari* is crisp and salty and more like Turkish bread (and is often covered with sesame seeds); *sangak* is the elite of Iranian breads, long and thick and baked on a bed of stones to give it its characteristic dimpled appearance (check carefully for rogue chunks of gravel); and *taftun* is crisp with a ribbed surface.

Chelo (boiled or steamed rice) forms the base of many an Iranian meal, and especially at lunch is served in vast helpings. Rice cooked with other ingredients, such as nuts, spices or barberry (small, red berries), is called *polo* and is worth asking for specifically. Saffron (*za'feran*) is frequently used to add flavour and colour. If rice is served with a knob of butter on top, blend this in as the Iranians do. *Tahdig*, the crunchy, savoury crust at the bottom of the pan, sometimes served with slices of potato, is the favourite of almost every Iranian.

> *New Food of Life: Ancient Persian and Modern Iranian Cooking and Ceremonies*, by Najmieh Khalili Batmanglij, is so good – clear, concise and accurate – it's on the gift table at almost every Iranian wedding in the US.

IRANIAN MEALS

STARTERS

A standard Iranian meal starts with a basic, prefabricated green salad, radioactive-pink dressing and *ash-e jo* (soup of pearl barley). Some places include these in a total set-meal price but usually they are charged separately.

MAINS

Even in a restaurant with a long menu, 90% of the main-dish options are likely to be kababs. These are served either on bread (preferably hot from the *tandir* clay oven) or as *chelo kabab* (on a mound of rice) with a pair of grilled tomatoes. Contrasting with the greasy doner kebabs inhaled after rough nights in the West, Iranian kababs are tasty, healthy and cooked shish-style over hot charcoals. The cheapest, standard version is *kubide* (literally, 'ground') kabab, made out of pressed, minced meat mixed with a variable proportion of breadcrumbs. *Kabab-e barg* (literally, 'leaf kabab') is thinner and more variable in quality, and *fille kabab* uses lamb fillet, while *juje kabab* are chunks of marinated chicken. Kababs are usually sprinkled with spicy *somaq* (sumac; dried extract from fruits of the rhus genus) and accompanied by raw onion and, for small extra fees, a bowl of *mast* (yogurt) and grilled tomato.

After a couple of weeks, many travellers start suffering from what could be called 'kabab shock'. However, it's not too hard to find treatment. Even when not on the menu it's worth asking for the common

---

GETTING DIZI

Known alternatively as *abgusht* (or as *piti* in Azerbaijan), *dizi* is a cheap soup-stew meal named for the earthenware pot in which it's served. It's considered by many Iranians as the food of the poor. But assuming you're neither a vegetarian nor obsessive about cholesterol, it's actually a delicious and filling dish. There is, however, an art to eating it. First, drain off the soupy broth into a bowl full of bread that you've previously ripped into bite-sized morsels. Eat this stew then turn to the main ingredients: chickpeas, potatoes, tomatoes and soft-boiled mutton. Grind these together using a provided metal pestle that looks disturbingly like a stylised toilet plunger. Do include the inevitable chunk of fat; it might look unappetising but adds taste and texture. Eat the resulting mush with a spoon or bread.

IRAN'S TOP TRADITIONAL RESTAURANTS

■ **Malek-o Tojjar** (Yazd; p264) In a restored mansion in the middle of the bazaar, this place is romance on a stick, and the food's pretty good, too.

■ **Haji Dadash** (Zanjan; p185) Cosy, characterful tea-cavern in Zanjan's brilliant bazaar.

■ **Yord Cultural Complex** (Shiraz; p277) A Bakhtiari nomad restaurant in a giant tent, with delicious food served on dozens of carpets accompanied by traditional music.

■ **Sofrekhane ye Sonnati Ebrahimabad** (Ardabil; p163) With truly excellent food served in a superb medieval former-*hammam* (bathhouse), this place is by itself reason enough to visit Ardabil.

■ **Sofrekhane ye Sonnati Darvish** (Gorgan; p340) Great for traditional music.

■ **Sofrekhane Sonnati** (Esfahan; p248) Not as traditional as some, but a vast menu of delicious dishes (plenty of *bademjan* – eggplant – options), Imam Sq location and value make it a must.

■ **Hezardestan Traditional Teahouse** (Mashhad; p360) Fabulous if somewhat pricey.

---

stand-by *zereshk polo ba morgh* (chicken on rice made tangy with barberries), *ghorme sabzi* (a green mix of diced meat, beans and vegetables, served with rice) or various mouthwatering dishes made from *bademjan* (eggplant; see Vegetarians & Vegans p82).

But it doesn't end there. Certain (usually down-market) eateries and many *chaykhanehs* (teahouses) specialise in underrated *dizi* (see Getting Dizi, p79). Most restaurants will also serve one or another variety of *khoresht* (thick, usually meaty stew made with vegetables and chopped nuts, then served with rice and/or French fries). However, in some less popular restaurants *khoresht* has been known to live in big pots for days before reaching the plate, so if you have a suspect stomach think twice.

Dolme (vegetables, fruit or vine leaves stuffed with a meat-and-rice mixture) makes a tasty change. *Dolme bademjan* (stuffed eggplant) is especially delectable. The Persian classic *fesenjun* (sauce of grated pomegranate, walnuts, eggplant and cardamom served over roast chicken and rice) is rarely found in restaurants, but you might get lucky and be served *fesenjun* in an Iranian home, which is quite an honour.

In Western Iran and on the Persian Gulf coast *chelo mahi* (fried fish on rice) is quite common in season while on the Caspian coast it's relatively easy to find the heavenly *mirza ghasemi* (mashed eggplant, squash, garlic, tomato and egg, served with bread or rice).

> '*Khosh ma-ze*' means 'delicious'. Even if your Farsi is terrible, being able to tell the cook/chef their food is *khosh ma-ze* will be fun for you and greatly appreciated by them.

Dessert & Sweets

After-meal dessert is usually a bowl of delicious fruit. However, Iran produces a head-spinning array of freshly made *shirini* (sweets) with many places famous for a particular sweet: Esfahan (p248) is famed for its nougat-like *gaz*; Qom (p223) for *sohan* (a brittle concoction of pistachio and ginger); Orumiyeh (p143) for *noghl* (sugar-coated nuts); and Kerman (p318) for (our favourite) *colompe* (a soft, date-filled biscuit). Other sweets worth trying include refreshing *palude* or *falude* (a sorbet made of rice flour, grated fresh fruit and rose water) and *bastani,* Iranian ice cream.

DRINKS
Nonalcoholic Drinks
TEA

Socialising in Iran almost inevitably involves *chay* (tea). Whether you're in a *chaykhaneh*, carpet shop, someone's home, an office, a tent – actually, almost anywhere – chances are there will be a boiling kettle nearby. According to the rules of Iranian hospitality, a host is honour-bound to offer a guest at least one cup of tea before considering any sort of business, and the guest is expected to drink it.

Tea is always drunk black and the tea tray is usually set with a bowl of *ghand* (chunks of sugar), often crudely hacked from huge rocks of sugar. It is customary to dip the sugar into the glass of tea, then place it between the front teeth (or on the tongue) before sucking the brew through it.

COFFEE

Traditional Iranian *ghahve* (coffee) is like Turkish coffee, served strong, sweet, black and booby-trapped with a sediment of grounds. However, there's a new urban fashion for coffee-houses that usually double as trendy ice-cream parlours. These places serve a variety of brews made on espresso-style machines. While this sounds hopeful for caffeine addicts, the coffee blends used are often lack-lustre, and the beans pre-ground and somewhat bitter. Usually in rural areas the only option will be instant coffee.

JUICES & SOFT DRINKS

You'll never be too far away from a delicious fresh fruit *ab* (juice) and fruit *shir* (milkshake). Both cost between IR5000 and IR12,000. Depending on the season, you'll find pomegranate (the dark-red *ab anar*), honeydew melon *(ab talebi)*, watermelon *(ab hendune)*, orange *(ab porteghal)*, apple *(ab sib)* and carrot *(ab havij)*. Popular shakes include banana *(shir moz)*, pistachio *(shir peste)* and strawberry *(shir tut farangi)*. Shakes are often loaded with sugar.

Also widely available, *dugh* (churned sour milk or yogurt mixed with water) is a sour but highly refreshing drink. The best *dugh* is usually found in restaurants, comes with chopped herbs and is uncarbonated, unlike most prepacked bottles found in stores.

Tap water is drinkable almost everywhere, though Rasht and Zahedan are notable exceptions. Bottled water is widely available in cities. Despite the US embargo, Coca-Cola is still bottled under licence at a Mashhad plant, though it's worth asking for Zam Zam (cola), Parsi Cola or some other black or orange soft drink. Canned drinks can cost around five times more than the same drinks sold in reusable bottles.

WHERE TO EAT & DRINK

If anyone asks you to their home for dinner, accept the invitation! Eating in an Iranian home is where you're most likely to experience the real joys of Persian cuisine mixed with unbridled hospitality. At other times, your options will be fast-food/pizza joints, *kababis* (kabab shops), traditional restaurants and teahouses, hotel restaurants and the occasional place serving foreign slow food.

Many traditional restaurants are buried below street level and can be hard to find. Even if there is an English sign there's no guarantee there will be a menu in English. Fast-food joints and *kababis*, on the other hand, tend to be at street level near main squares and along main roads.

Quick Eats

The most ubiquitous fast-food joints are shops selling a range of bread-roll 'sandwiches' topped off with tomatoes and pickles for around IR5000. The most common fillings are frankfurter-style sausage *(sausis)*, liver *(jegar)*, hamburger-meat ('hamburger'), felafel, tongue *(zaban)* or brain *(maghz)*.

Puffing on a qalyan (water pipe) over tea is an Iranian tradition that is now banned in several provinces, including Yazd and Esfahan, it's because it's unhealthy. When you do find a qalyan, know that flavoured tobacco is more deadly *and* more expensive than plain tobacco.

The Art of Persian Cooking, by Forough Hekmat, is the only English-language cookbook you'll find in bookstores in Iran. It's not the most complete book, but there are some good recipes and descriptions of the ceremonial role of food.

ISLAMIC BEER BUT NO SHIRAZ

Try to think of your trip to Iran as a cleansing experience, where your body can recover from all that overexposure to alcoholic toxins. Okay, so this might not work, but at least you'll feel better about not being able to get a drink. While alcohol is quietly tolerated in Christian communities, such as the Armenian areas of Tehran and Esfahan, it is strictly forbidden to Iranian Muslims. There is, of course, a black market – oddly enough often operated by green grocers – and you'll occasionally hear a man whisper 'whiskey' as you go by. But, believe us, the sickly sweet clear spirit you'll likely be sold is rocket fuel by any other name.

If you're desperate for a beer, there's always *ma'-osh-sha'ir* ('Islamic beer'). Actually, there are several brands of locally produced and imported beer proudly declaring '0.0% alcohol'. Russian-made Baltika tastes the most like beer. Delster, which comes in several fruit 'flavours', is the most popular local variety, mainly because it doesn't even pretend that it's trying to taste like beer. The lemon version is pleasantly refreshing.

Sadly, the chance of finding a glass of Shiraz (aka Syrah wine) in Shiraz is only marginally greater than seeing swimsuit models at Persepolis. There are various theories on the origin of this grape varietal, most involving cuttings being taken from vineyards in Shiraz back to the Rhone valley in France during the Crusades. Iranian vines were either ripped up after the 1979 revolution or now produce raisins. Today there are no (legal) wineries.

Simple *kababis* selling kababs and cold drinks are popular, particularly around major *meydans* (squares); just follow your nose. These places are usually fairly clean, but remember that the popularity of the eatery is inversely proportional to your chances of spending the next 24 hours on the porcelain throne, so eat where the locals eat.

Some no-frills places serve *ash-e sabzi* (thick, green vegetable soup) all day. It makes a delicious, cheap breakfast or lunch; just look for the huge metal dish and mountains of bread.

The Iranian infatuation with 'pizza' seems to be out of control. In many cities it will be easier to find pizzas and burgers than kabab. Beware that Iranian pizza is rarely to Western tastes with a flabby base, tasteless cheese and a thick layer of anaemic (porkless) sausage. Tomato paste isn't part of the recipe, though locals slosh on tomatoe sauce (ketchup) to taste.

VEGETARIANS & VEGANS

Vegetarianism is foreign to most Iranians. Sure, there are a lot of good vegetarian dishes in Iranian cuisine, but most restaurants don't make them. Even if there is an ostensibly meat-free dish on the menu, such as *ash-e reshte* (noodle soup with beans and vegetables), it will often come with 'bonus' pieces of mutton. Tehran was the only place we found dedicated vegetarian restaurants (two of them, see p119), but more should open in coming years, with the help of the Iranian Society of Vegetarians (www.iranvege tarians.com).

The *anar* (pomegranate) is native to the region around Iran and is eaten fresh and incorporated in a range of Persian dishes most famously in *fesenjun*, but also in *ash-e anar* (pomegranate soup) and in rich red *ab anar* (pomegranate juice).

Solace can be found, however, in the felafels, samosas and potatoes sold in street stalls, and in the Persian mastery of all things *bademjan*. In our opinion one of the highlights of Iranian cuisine is the meatless Caspian dish *mirza ghasemi* (see Cut the Caviar – Gilan Cuisine, p170). Meanwhile, the various *kuku* (thick omelette dishes) make great snacks, served hot or cold. Varieties include *kuku-ye sabzi* (with mixed herbs), *kuku-e ye bademjan* (with eggplant) and *kuku-e-ye gol-e kalam* (with cauliflower).

Vegans will have a hard time finding anything completely free from animal products; even rice is often served with butter. Fortunately, fresh and dried fruit and varieties of nut and vegetables are widely available and are very good. Cheaper hotels will sometimes let you use their kitchen.

HABITS & CUSTOMS

In most Iranian homes and many hotels, breakfast is a simple affair, consisting of endless tea served with leftover (ie rather crisp) *lavash*, feta-style cheese and jam – often carrot-flavoured, which is better than it sounds. Most hotels usually throw in an egg. Lunch is the main meal of the day for Iranians and is generally eaten with mountains of rice between noon and 2pm. Dinner is from about 7pm onwards. Most restaurants, except those in hotels, close earlier on Friday. On religious holidays, almost everywhere selling food will shut, markets and bazaars included, for the morning at least. During Ramazan (p384) the majority of eateries will be closed from dawn until dusk. Some won't open at all during the month and many of those that open after dusk are full with pre-booked parties and then close early. However, because travellers don't have to fast, most hotel and bus terminal restaurants stay open throughout Ramazan, albeit hidden discreetly behind heavy blinds (and thus might look shut). Eating, drinking or smoking in public is bad form during Ramazan.

While your mother would probably have a heart attack if you sat down to lunch on her Persian rug, eating on the floor, or on a *takht* (a sort of day bed), is normal here. Remember to always remove your shoes before sitting around the plastic sheet that acts as the 'Iranian table'. Cutlery normally consists of a fork and spoon. If you need to eat with your hands, avoid putting your left hand into a communal dish; the left hand is used for something else altogether. Once the meal has arrived, conversation often dies as diners work through their meal in silence. Tea and conversation flow freely after dinner.

> Fancy trying some food in an Iranian restaurant before leaving home (or upon your return)? Check the growing list at www.farsieats.com.

EAT YOUR WORDS

You've read about Iranian food, now it's time to eat it. To make that easier, we've included the dishes you'll commonly see while on the road plus some of our favourites. It's worth asking for dishes specifically as menus are typically all in Farsi and are not necessarily comprehensive anyway. This being Iran, even if a restaurant doesn't have what you want, you'll probably be directed (maybe even escorted) to your food of choice. For pronunciation guidelines, see p423; for more Farsi food phraseology, get Lonely Planet's *Farsi Phrasebook*.

IRANIANS: WORLD CHAMPIONS OF PICNIC   *Andrew Burke*

It's official. After an admittedly unscientific survey conducted during years of travel and more than 15 months in Iran, Mark and I have concluded that Iranians are in fact the world champions of picnicking. The evidence is overwhelming. Almost every Iranian vehicle with more than two wheels has a plastic basket in the boot filled with most or all of the following: a carpet or woven plastic sheet for sitting on, plastic 'Iranian table' for eating from, a thermos of hot water, tea, sugar, cutlery, a qalyan (water pipe), tobacco, lighter fluid, coals and a portable grill. And they are just the basics. Iranians who really take their picnicking seriously might add a large, collapsible tent and/or beach umbrella to the mix, plus a football, skipping rope and camera to record the fun.

So where do these picnics happen? The answer is anywhere a car can go (not much further, though, as no-one wants to carry all that gear too far). You'll often see picnickers camped out in places non-Iranians find, well, odd. Like beside motorways. Or even on the median strip of a motorway. For me, my oddest Iranian picnicking experience was on board a car ferry to Kish Island, when high winds and rough seas saw dozens of families haul out their tents to set up camp on the passenger deck. Tea was only minutes behind.

Probably the best time to see Iranian picnicking in full swing is during the No Ruz holiday period; in particular, the ancient tradition of Sizdah be Dar (p385) on the 13th day after No Ruz.

Useful Phrases

I'm a vegetarian.
من سبزیخوارم
man sabzi khar am

Does this dish have meat?
این غذا گوشت داره؟
in ghaza gusht dare?

I can't eat dairy products.
من نمیتونم لبنیات بخورم
man nemintunam labaniyyat bekhoram

What do you recommend?
شما چی پیشنهاد می کنین؟
shoma chi pishnahad mikonin?

I'll try what s/he's having.
من از غذایی که اون می خوره می خوام
man az ghazayi ke un mikhore mikham

Food Glossary
SOUPS & STARTERS

ash-e jo	آش جو	Very common pearl barley soup with cream, butter, parsley and pepper.
ash-e mast	آش ماست	hot yogurt soup with beans, lentils and vegetables
ash-e sabzi	آش سیزی	thick, dark green vegetable soup, sometimes with meat
ash-e reshte	آش رشته	noodle soup with beans and vegetables
kashk-e bademjan	کشک باد مجان	eggplant fried and mashed and served with *kashk* (thick whey) and mint
kuku-ye sabzi	کوکوی سیزی	thick vegetable omelette (with mixed herbs)
mast-o khiyar	ماست و خیار	yogurt dip with cucumber, onion, mint, salt and pepper
nun-o panir	نون و پنیر	thin bread and cheese; common for breakfast

MAIN COURSES
Kabab first, then everything else – like an Iranian menu.

Kabab

bakhtiyari kabab	کباب بختیاری	lamb and chicken
chelo kabab	چلو کباب	any kind of kabab in this list served with *chelo* (boiled or steamed rice); the default option will be *kubide* if you don't specify
file kebab	فیله کباب	meat strips
kubide kabab	کباب کوبیده	mince, breadcrumbs and onion ground together and grilled
juje kabab	جوجه کباب	grilled chicken pieces with *somaq* (sumac)

Other dishes

abgusht	گوشت	see *dizi*
baghali polo	باقالی پلو	chicken with broad beans, steamed rice and vegetables
chelo mahi	چلو ماهی	fried fish served with steamed rice and vegetables
chelo morgh	چلو مرغ	chicken and rice, served with a light tomato sauce
dizi	دیزی	lamb stew made with lentils, potatoes and tomato paste, served with bread; see Getting Dizi (p79) for eating instructions
dolme bademjan	دلمه بادمجان	eggplant stuffed with meat, rice and (sometimes) raisins
fesenjun	فسنجان	sauce of grated pomegranate, walnuts, eggplant and cardamom served over roast chicken and rice

ghorme sabzi	قرمه سبزی	a green mix of diced meat, beans and vegetables, served with rice
khoresht	خورشت	any kind of meaty stew, usually made with lentils, dried lemon and served with rice and/or French fries
khoresht-e bademjan	خورشت باد مجان	stew of chicken or meat, eggplant and tomato paste, served with rice or bread
mirza ghasemi	میرزا قاسمی	mashed eggplant, tomato, egg and garlic, served with bread or rice
tahchin	ته چین	chicken or meat baked in rice with yogurt and eggs
zereshk polo ba morgh	زرشک پلو با مرغ	roast chicken served with rice and barberry

SWEETS & DESSERTS

baghlava	باقلوا	layers of pastry and crushed nuts soaked in syrup
bastani	بستنی	ice cream
fereni	فرنی	looks like yogurt but made with rice flour, sugar and rose water
halva	حلوا	various forms of wickedly delicious, gooey confectionery made of sesame flour and honey

ENGLISH-FARSI GLOSSARY

apple	*sib*	سیب
banana	*moz*	موز
beans	*lubiya*	لوبیا
beef	*gusht e goosale*	گوشت گوساله
bread	*nun*	نان
butter	*kare*	کره
cheese	*panir*	پنیر
chicken	*morgh*	مرغ
eggplant	*bademjan*	باد مجان
egg	*tokhm e morgh*	تخم مرغ
fish	*mahi*	ماهی
fruit	*mive*	میوه
kabab shop	*kababi*	کبابی
mandarin	*narengi*	نارنگی
meat	*gusht*	گوشت
milk	*shir*	شیر
orange	*portegal*	پرتقال
pomegranate	*anar*	انار
potato	*sib zamini*	سیب زمینی
prawns	*meygu*	میگو
rice	*berenj*	برنج
rice (boiled or steamed)	*chelo*	چلو
salt	*namak*	نمک
sugar	*shekar*	شکر
tea	*chay*	چای
teahouse	*chaykhaneh*	چایخانه
tongue	*zaban*	زبان
vegetables	*sabzijat*	سبزیجات
water	*ab*	آب
yogurt	*mast*	ماست

Environment

THE LAND

If you're flying into Iran, be sure to ask for a window seat – you might be surprised by what you see. Rather than the featureless desert wasteland many perceive, Iran is a diverse land where starkly beautiful mountains border vast desert plateaus and mountain villages contrast with tiny oases.

More than half of Iran is covered by mountains and in the vast majority of places there will be a peak of some size looming at the end of the street. Four ranges are most prominent. The smaller, volcanic Sabalan and Talesh Ranges in the northwestern Azeri provinces provide fertile pastures for nomads. Nearby, the majestic Alborz Mountains skirt the Caspian Sea from the border of Azerbaijan as far as Turkmenistan, and are home to forests, ski fields and the snowcapped Mt Damavand (5671m; p131), the Middle East's tallest mountain. Sitting on the world's second-largest known reserve of natural gas, the immense Zagros Mountains stretch about 1500km from Turkey to the Persian Gulf, rising and falling like the ridged back of a great crocodile. There are several peaks reaching more than 4000m, though heights fall to an average of 1500m in the southern parts of the range.

All these mountains exist because Iran sits at the junction of three major tectonic plates – the Arabian, Eurasian and Indian – making the country highly susceptible to earthquakes (see Shaking Iran's Confidence, below).

East of the Zagros Mountains is the central plateau and its two vast deserts, the Dasht-e Kavir (more than 200,000 sq km) in the north and the Dasht-e Lut (more than 166,000 sq km) in the southeast. The deserts include occasional salt lakes and, in total, account for almost 25% of the country.

Think of Iran's mountain ranges as being the foundations and support for a vast central plateau. Everything but the narrow coastal regions of the Persian Gulf and the Caspian Sea, and the Khuzestan plain near southern Iraq, is about 1000m above sea level or higher. This elevation, combined with the prevalence of mountains and the complete lack of major rivers, has had a huge effect on the development of Persian culture (see p45).

> With an area of 1,648,000 sq km, Iran is more than three times larger than France; nearly one-fifth the size of the USA; and nearly as big as Queensland, Australia. Iran shares borders with seven countries: Iraq, Turkey, Armenia, Azerbaijan, Turkmenistan, Afghanistan and Pakistan.

SHAKING IRAN'S CONFIDENCE

To say that Iranians are anxious about earthquakes is quite the understatement. The country sits on dozens of seismic fault lines and every year scores of tremors of varying size rattle homes and gnaw away at nerves. When a major quake strikes, as it did in Bam in 2003 at a cost of more than 31,000 lives (see the boxed text, p323), Iranians everywhere start speculating about who will be next.

Iran has had more than 20 major earthquakes (above 6 on the Richter scale) in the past century, and seismologists estimate that a large population centre will be hit by one every eight years. While the vast majority of seismic activity occurs along the Zagros Mountains, where the Eurasian and Arabian tectonic plates meet, it is in the desert regions of central Iran that the biggest movements are felt: Ferdows (1968; 7.3 on the Richter scale; up to 20,000 dead), Tabas (1978; 7.8; more than 1500 dead) and Bam (6.6) are all in this area.

However, the mountainous regions in the north are also susceptible, and Tehran reportedly has two major faults running directly beneath it. In the wake of the Bam disaster there was much speculation in Tehran about what kind of hell would be unleashed if – or as many people feel, when – a large quake rocks the capital. The citizenry are right to worry. Building standards in Iran are poor, and corruption among inspectors ensures even these standards are seldom met. A government report in 2004 stated that of the 15 million homes in Iran, 7.2 million are vulnerable to a major earthquake. As a visitor, all you can do is hope you don't get unlucky. See p377 for tips in case you do.

Unlike many ancient civilisations, such as those in Egypt and Meso-potamia, Persian settlements did not develop around major rivers. The longest and sole navigable river is the Karun (890km) in the southwest, and it's no Nile. Rather, settled areas are almost entirely confined to the foothills of mountains, where natural springs and melting snow provide sufficient water, with the melted snow often channelled through ingenious underground canals called *qanats* (p260).

Without river connections, and prior to modern transport, these communities lived in relative isolation. In many cases a large town would be the focus of trade for hundreds of surrounding villages otherwise hemmed in by mountains or desert. Almost all further trade and communication was done by camel caravans, which linked these population basins to each other and the rest of the known world via the silk routes and the coasts.

In the north Iran's coast borders the Caspian Sea (Darya-ye Khazar), which, at 370,000 sq km, is the world's largest lake. (Or is it? See p174.) To the southeast, the coast along the Persian Gulf is 965km long. The Persian Gulf becomes the Gulf of Oman east of the strategic Strait of Hormuz. The gulf contains dozens of tiny islands, most of them uninhabited. Those that are, notably Qeshm (p303) and Kish (p292), are being developed, attracting investors and tourists from the Gulf States. Other islands are used as bases for oil prospecting.

Iran boasts an abundance of *cheshmeh* (hot- and cold-water mineral springs), usually found in mountainous regions and much loved by Iranians as picnic venues. The most developed is Sara'eyn (p163), near Ardabil, which is now a full-blown spa resort. In the desert more modest springs are the lifeblood of tiny oasis villages like Garmeh (p254).

> Only about 11% of Iran is arable land: 8% is forest, 47% is natural (ie nonarable) pastures; and the remaining 34% is infertile land, including desert.

WILDLIFE

Iran's diverse landscapes are home to a fascinating and sometimes exhilarating mix of wildlife. Seeing this fauna is not easy but with planning, patience and good guiding, you might get lucky.

Mammals

Iran is home to 158 species of mammal, about one-fifth of which are endemic. Large cats, including the Persian leopard and Asiatic cheetah (see p88), are the most glamorous, but a range of wild sheep, deer, gazelle and bears are just as interesting.

Indeed, Iran's seven species of wild sheep might well be the progenitors of the modern, garden variety sheep and goat. They include species such as the Transcaspian oreal, Laristan mouflon and Alborz red sheep, an ibex with a long black beard and curved horns.

THROUGH MARTIAN EYES

Iran's mountain and desert landscapes are often as spectacular to look at from space as they are in person. So if you have a couple of hours to kill, get on Google Earth and check out the following:

- The Kaluts (p321) N 30°38'34.63", E 58° 0'58.48"
- Qeshm Geological Park (p303) N 26°37'0.46", E 55°29'29.43"
- Zagros Mountains (p252) N 30°15'4.30", E 51°57'21.35"
- Dasht-e Kavir mountains N 33°50'47.00", E 52°34'53.26"
- Dasht-e Lut sand dunes N 30° 5'50.34", E 59°16'48.39"

THE ASIATIC CHEETAH

The Asiatic cheetah is one of the most endangered cats on earth. The 50 to 100 living on the edges of Iran's Dasht-e Kavir are all that remain of a population that once ranged from India to the Mediterranean. Cheetahs were prized by ancient Persian royalty, who trained them to hunt gazelles. It is this long history, and that Iran's population of Asiatic lion and Caspian tiger has been hunted into extinction, that has made the cheetah the poster-cat of the country's conservation movement.

With the support of the UN and the World Conservation Society, the government has designated land, mainly in Yazd and Semnan provinces, as parks and reserves, and has increased punishments for poaching. Tracking studies have been ongoing since 2001 and since early 2007 cheetahs and Persian leopards have been fitted with GPS collars. The Asiatic cheetah requires vast tracts of land to survive so the plan is to identify exactly where the cheetah roam and try to link the existing reserves to form a safe haven for the few remaining populations.

Unfortunately, severe habitat loss during the 1980s and the resultant loss of cheetah prey, traditionally jebeer and goitered gazelles, as well as wild sheep and goats, have forced the cats deeper into mountainous areas in search of more modest meals – such as hare and even lizards. In late 2007 one of the first two cheetahs fitted with a GPS collar was found dead in a mountain valley, killed by a Persian leopard as they hunted the same meal.

On the positive side, education programs have significantly reduced poaching and the creation of protected areas is expected to help other native species to recover. For more information visit www.wcs.org and go to the Iran Cheetah Project, or see www.iraniancheetah.org.

Notable other species of mammal include the spectacular Persian wild ass, goitered and Jebeer gazelles, maral, Asian black bear and brown bear. Wild dogs include wolves, jackals and hyenas, while Iran's unusually large wild boars are often targeted by hunters. The majority of these larger mammals are primarily found in the forests of the Alborz Mountains although large cats, wild dogs and gazelle are also found in the arid lands around the two major deserts.

Camels still roam the deserts of the eastern provinces of Kerman, Sistan va Baluchestan and Khorasan, and while they might look wild they almost certainly belong to nomadic or seminomadic communities.

Birds

About 500 species of bird have been sighted in Iran, but only one – Pleske's ground jay – is unique to the country. However, a small but growing number of birders are coming to Iran in search of montane or arid-land Middle East species that are hard or dangerous to find elsewhere. These include the Caucasian black grouse, Caspian snowcock, Radde's accentor and several species of wheatear.

Birds of the Middle East, by RF Porter, S Christensen and P Schiermacker-Hansen is the best book to buy if you're serious about birding in Iran.

Iran is home to 22 wetlands that are protected under the Ramsar Convention. These are ideal places to see migrating land and water birds in their natural habitat, while en route between Europe and Africa. The range of water birds, ducks in particular, is impressive. While the numbers are far fewer than reported a few decades ago, there are still thought to be more than one million resident (for at least part of the year) in Iran. Migratory water birds include the greater flamingo, once found in their thousands on Lake Orumiyeh in spring but less common now due to rising salination, as well as the glossy ibis and the Smyrna kingfisher.

Other relatively common species include black-and-white magpies, blue rollers, brown-and-green bee-eaters, and black-and-grey hooded crows. Less common are the golden eagle, found in the Caspian provinces; the tiny jiroft, found in Kerman province and along the Persian Gulf; the red-wattled lapwing; the yellow partridge; the delijeh and balaban falcon, found mainly in Hamadan province; and the black vulture and black kite, which live in the central plateau and deserts.

Marine Life

The Persian Gulf is home to a wide range of tropical fish, as well as swordfish, porpoises and sharks. The Caspian Sea has the Caspian seal, whose origin remains a mystery to science as it exists so far from the open sea. The Caspian also has large shoals of sturgeon (producing the world-famous caviar). Sturgeon numbers have fallen by 90% since the '70s due to pollution and overfishing, and in 2006 a UN body banned the export of caviar from four of the Caspian's five littoral states. The exception was Iran, which received an export quota for the caviar of only one species of sturgeon. For more on the Caspian, see p174.

Ancient Greek playwright Aechylus was killed when a tortoise landed on his bald head. This story was thought to be a myth until a bearded vulture was seen dropping a tortoise onto rocks to crack it open. It now seems a bearded vulture confused poor Aechylus' head for a stone.

Endangered Species

According to a 2007 World Bank report, 21 mammals, 18 birds and one major plant species are highly endangered in Iran. Habitat loss is the main threat but the one million hunting licenses (each with free bullets from the state) issued each year do not help. As well as the high-profile Asiatic cheetah, the Persian fallow deer remains vulnerable but is nonetheless a rare Iranian conservation success story. Once common in light woodlands across the Middle East, hunting decimated the population so badly that by the 1950s the Persian fallow dear was thought to be extinct. However a small population was discovered in Khuzestan Province, and intensive breeding efforts saw numbers rise throughout the '60s and '70s. Today populations exist in Khuzestan, Mazandaran, the Arjan Protected Area and on an island in Lake Orumiyeh. In the mountains of northwestern Iran, the lammergeier (bearded vulture) has been shot and poisoned to the brink of extinction due to a misconception among farmers that they attack sheep. In fact, this fascinating bird usually eats only what other vultures have left behind, and often breaks bones by dropping them onto rocks from a great height. They apply the same method to the unfortunate Greek spur-thighed tortoises in the area. The Siberian white crane is another high-profile but endangered bird in Iran.

Plants

Despite its extensive deserts and unrestrained urban development, Iran harbours more than 8200 species of plants, about 2000 of them endemic. The northern slopes of the Alborz Mountains are densely covered to about 2500m with broad-leaved deciduous forest, which forms the largest area of vegetation in the country. Here you will find species similar to those in many European forests (oak, ash, pine, poplar, willow, walnut, maple and elm) and the less common Caucasian wing nut. The loveliest pockets of forest are around Masuleh (p171), in the Golestan National Park east of Minudasht, and, more accessibly, at Nahar Khoran (p338), just south of Gorgan.

WEBSITES FOR BIRDERS

Birding Pal (www.birdingpal.org/Iran) A list of professional and enthusiast birding guides in Iran.
Birdquest (www.birdquest.co.uk)
Oriental Bird Images (www.orientalbirdimages.org)
Ornithological Society of the Middle East (www.osme.org)
Wetlands (www.wetlands.org/RSOB/default.htm) List of 22 protected Iranian wetlands.

There are smaller, less dense forests of oak and juniper on the higher slopes of the central and northwest Zagros Mountains. By contrast, southern and eastern Iran are almost – but not entirely – bare. Particularly during spring, vibrant dashes of green, such as the 20km long 'walnut jungle' at Bavanat (p285), can be found hidden in valleys between barren brown hills. Palm trees grow on the southern coastal lowland, especially near the Strait of Hormuz, and nomadic herders travel up and down between the warmer coast and cooler mountains in search of seasonal pastures.

But it is the luxuriant oases dotted around the bone-dry barrenness of Iran's deserts that are most amazing. Here, where temperatures regularly top 50°C in summer, dozens of subtly different date palms thrive, often sharing space with hardy pomegranate trees and modest fields of cucumber and melon; Garmeh (p254) is a classic example.

> More than a thousand wetland sites around the world are protected under the framework of an agreement signed in 1971 in Ramsar, on the Caspian Sea coast. Known as the Ramsar Convention, birds and their wetland habitats are the greatest beneficiaries.

NATIONAL PARKS & RESERVES

National parks, and the wildlife they are designed to protect, are luxuries that most Iranians don't have the time or money to be concerned with. As a result, most national parks are terribly underfunded and understaffed, and the most accessible zones tend to be rubbish-strewn picnic sites. Unauthorised hunting is an ongoing problem, as is illegal cultivation of protected areas. Attitudes are slowly changing in cities such as Tehran and Shiraz, but realistically, it could be decades before Iran's nature reserves have anything like the status of their Western counterparts.

So what does this mean for the visitor? About 5% of Iran is protected. But in the 16 officially mandated national parks and 137 other protected areas there are few fences, few, if any, rangers, no maps, no guides and no facilities. Even finding certain parks can be difficult, as they don't appear on maps, and there is no public transport and few signs. Other parks such as Sisingan on the Caspian suffer the opposite problem: they are small, overused and all too quickly overrun by weekenders.

Hardy souls might choose to strike out on their own, but unless time is no problem and you have at least basic Farsi, it will probably be a pretty frustrating experience. Your best bet is to employ a travel agency close to the park you want to visit; at least they should know how to get you there. Alternatively, use one of the specialist mountaineering and outdoor agencies, see the boxed text (p373) for details.

A selection of Iran's more accessible national parks and protected areas are listed below. Due to the limited facilities, there is little or no extra detail in the destination chapters.

But if you're keen, these are a start.

Arjan Protected Area Lake and wetland area near Shiraz. Home to masked tits, waterfowl and seasonal migratory birds, plus mammals including Persian fallow deer.

Bakhtegan National Park Incorporating Lakes Bakhtegan and Tashk, this park is about 80km east of Shiraz. Flamingos and other migratory birds loiter here during winter.

Bijar Protected Area About 15km north of Bijar town in Kordestan. Home to Alborz red sheep, hyenas and jackals. Best visited in spring and autumn.

Golestan National Park Forested mountains between Gorgan and the Caspian Sea. Home to wild boars, oreal rams, brown bears, wolves, leopards, goitered gazelles and assorted bird life. Best visited in spring. Permits are required. See also p343.

Lake Orumiyeh National Park An important wetland reserve, this park is home to rare deer and a multitude of birds migrating between Europe and Africa. Relatively accessible (from Tabriz, p146), though increasingly threatened.

Tandoureh National Park Rocky, mountainous terrain favoured by oreal rams, ibex and leopard, near Daragaz on the border with Turkmenistan.

ENVIRONMENTAL ISSUES

Iran faces several serious environmental challenges, most of which can be summed up as habitat loss and desertification and pollution.

But it's not all bad news. Public awareness of the environment has risen significantly in recent years. While most attention has been focused on the nuclear power program, Iran has also opened two wind farms and is building a major solar power plant, due to begin operating in 2010.

Habitat Loss

When environmental historians look back at Iran, the 1980s will be seen as a disastrous decade. Upheaval following the revolution and during the Iran–Iraq War prompted rapid, uncontrolled expansion of grazing lands, often into sensitive semidesert areas, leading to overgrazing and, in some areas, desertification. Massive population growth during this time didn't help: with an extra 20 to 30 million people needing to be fed, crops were soon being sewn in areas unsuitable for intensive agriculture. The impacts have been dire. Estimates suggest that as much as 80% of the forest that existed in Iran during the 1970s is now gone, resulting in flooding, erosion and desertification. Wildlife has been pushed into ever-decreasing areas and, as numbers have fallen, competition for prey has become critical. These problems have been exacerbated by a land tenure act passed in the 1980s that changed millennia of land-use practice. Traditionally rangelands were grazed seasonally by nomadic tribes, but tenure over rangelands is now obtained by regular cultivation of land, regardless of its suitability. The government is aware of the problem and school children have planted millions of trees in a high-profile campaign in recent years. This explains the neat rows of spindly eucalypts emerging from the desert that you might see as you race by in your bus.

Following a disastrous drought in the late 1990s, Iran has built dozens of new dams, for both water storage and hydroelectricity.

Pollution

Chronic air pollution is the environmental problem you're most likely to notice while travelling in Iran. Tehran is one of the most polluted cities on earth (p99) and as industry and car ownership expand in regional cities, the air is becoming more poisonous across the country. In Tehran in 2005–06, as many as 10,000 people are thought to have died from illnesses relating to chronic pollution, which one senior official described as 'a collective suicide'. Iran's pollution problem is worse for having been ignored until it reached crisis point. Much of the air pollution is eminently preventable, with about 70% being emitted from vehicles, including millions of frighteningly inefficient Paykans (p414). The good news is that the Iranian government has taken several dramatic steps to force its people into realising the impact of this culture. The most important, and controversial, has been raising fuel prices (though whether the motivation was environmental or geopolitical is debatable). Iranians tend to believe that cheap fuel is their birthright, however raising the petrol price by 25% – to a whopping IR1000 a litre (or €0.08) – and rationing consumption has resulted in some Iranians taking their cars off the road. However, you do get the feeling that prices will need to rise further to persuade Iranians that there is value in pursuing efficiency. The same applies to natural gas, which Iran possesses in vast quantities – it's not uncommon to find gas burning under samovars all day. There are other problems. The Persian Gulf has been repeatedly contaminated by leaks from oil rigs and tankers, untreated sewage and overly rapid development on the islands of Kish (p292) and Qeshm (p303). Pollution in the Caspian Sea is a problem that now threatens the internationally recognised wetlands of the Anzali Lagoon (p171) at Bandar-e Anzali.

Tehran تهران

With its relatively short history, ugly masks of concrete and smog, and manic streets flowing hot with machines, many travellers and no small number of Tehranis will tell you there's no reason to hang around in the capital. But to take their advice is to miss out. For while Esfahan or Persepolis could mount a convincing case for being the soul of Iran, Tehran is indisputably its big, loud, chaotic, dynamic and ugly beating heart.

This tightly packed city of about 15 million is where change happens first. Politically and socially it's Iran's cutting edge, and from the relatively bold fashion statements of its youth to the range of restaurants, cafés and art galleries, as a visitor you can't help but notice.

However, Tehran is also a city of contrasts that play out on geographic lines. It is modern and traditional, secular and religious, rich and poor – north and south. Most of the spark comes from the affluent north, but wander through southern Tehran and you'll see a contrastingly conservative, religious and poor city with little of the north's brashness.

At a practical level, Tehran has a decent choice of hotels and the best range of restaurants in Iran. There are enough museums to keep you interested, and compared with residents of many capitals, Tehranis are surprisingly welcoming. Certainly, some travellers will find Tehran's traffic, smog and uncontrolled urban sprawl overwhelming. But persist – or better, make short repeat visits – and you'll find it opening up to you in ever more-rewarding ways.

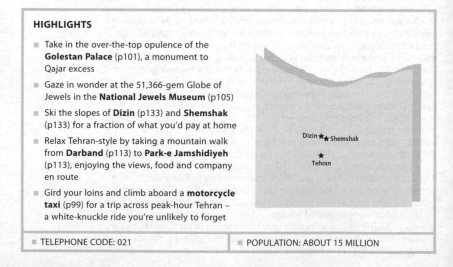

HIGHLIGHTS

- Take in the over-the-top opulence of the **Golestan Palace** (p101), a monument to Qajar excess
- Gaze in wonder at the 51,366-gem Globe of Jewels in the **National Jewels Museum** (p105)
- Ski the slopes of **Dizin** (p133) and **Shemshak** (p133) for a fraction of what you'd pay at home
- Relax Tehran-style by taking a mountain walk from **Darband** (p113) to **Park-e Jamshidiyeh** (p113), enjoying the views, food and company en route
- Gird your loins and climb aboard a **motorcycle taxi** (p99) for a trip across peak-hour Tehran – a white-knuckle ride you're unlikely to forget

Dizin ★★ Shemshak

★
Tehran

■ TELEPHONE CODE: 021 　　　　　■ POPULATION: ABOUT 15 MILLION

HISTORY

Archaeologists believe people have lived in this area since Neolithic times, but apart from 11th-century AD records suggesting the village produced high-quality pomegranates, little was written about Tehran until the 13th century. In his book *Mo'jamol Boldan,* writer Yaqoot Hamavi described Tehran as a village of Rey, then the major urban centre in the region, where 'rebellious inhabitants' lived in underground dwellings. He went on: 'They not only disregard their governors, but are in constant clashes among themselves, to the extent that the inhabitants of its 12 quarters cannot visit each other'.

In 1220 the Mongols sacked Rey as they swept across Persia (see p32), executing thousands in the process. Most of those who escaped wound up in Tehran and the future capital's first ever population explosion turned the village into a small, moderately prosperous trading centre.

In the mid-16th century Tehran's natural setting, many trees, clear rivers and good hunting brought it to the attention of the early Safavid king, Tahmasb I. Under his patronage, gardens were laid out, brick houses and caravanserais built and a wall with 114 towers erected to protect the town and its merchants. As it continued to grow under later Safavid kings, European visitors wrote of Tehran's many enchanting vineyards and gardens.

Threatened by the encroaching Qajars, regent Karim Khan Zand moved his army to Tehran in 1758. At the same time he refortified the city and began constructing a royal residence. Perhaps he had intended to move his capital here, but when Qajar chieftain Mohammed Hasan Khan was killed and his young son Agha Mohammed Khan taken hostage, Karim Khan decided the threat was over and abandoned the unfinished palace to return to Shiraz.

But things didn't work out quite as Karim Khan would have liked. By 1795 he was long dead and his one-time prisoner, Agha Mohammed Khan, declared this dusty town of around 15,000 souls his capital.

As the centre of Qajar Persia, Tehran steadily expanded. By 1900 it had grown to 250,000 people, and in the 20th century into one of the most-populous cities on earth. With this growth has come an influence far greater than most people realise. The capital has fomented and hosted two revolutions, two coups d'etat and much intrigue. As the setting for the CIA's first coup in 1953 (p37), it had a profound impact on post-WWII world politics; and as pronouncements from Tehran have been the driving force behind the growth of radical Islam since 1979, that influence has not waned.

Today it is fascinating to walk in the footsteps of that modern history: you can see the White Palace at Sa'd Abad (p109), where the last shah hosted the CIA's Kermit Roosevelt as they plotted the overthrow of Prime Minister Mohammad Mossadegh; visit the former US embassy now called the US Den of Espionage (p107); gaze up at the Azadi Tower (p114), where hundreds of thousands of people gathered to mark the 1979 revolution; or visit the haunting Behesht-e Zahra cemetery (p131), where the faces of soldiers who died in the Iran–Iraq War stare out from endless fields of glass boxes.

ORIENTATION

Tehran is so vast and so congested that getting lost here is inevitable. Thankfully, most of the streets you're likely to visit have signs in English, though there are still some areas without signs in any language.

As you move through the city the huge social and economic gaps between northern and southern Tehran are plain to see. The south is older, cheaper, more congested and generally less appealing. However, it has almost all the budget hotels, especially around Imam Khomeini Sq, which also hosts the main station on the growing Tehran Metro and has a local bus terminal nearby. The north is more inviting, more expensive, has cleaner air and a range of better hotels and more exotic restaurants.

The main street and top shopping strip is Valiasr Ave, which runs from Rah-Ahan Sq and the train station in poorer southern Tehran all the way to Tajrish Sq in the foothills of the Alborz Mountains in the north – a distance of more than 20km. It's a great street to find when you're lost. One of the main east–west thoroughfares is Azadi Ave, which starts at the Azadi Tower, near the Mehrabad International Airport, and becomes Enqelab Ave east of Enqelab Sq.

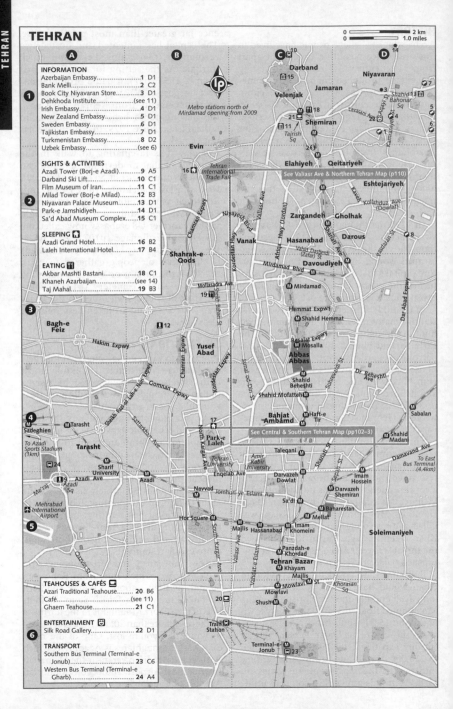

TEHRAN

0 — 2 km
0 — 1.0 miles

INFORMATION
Azerbaijan Embassy.....................1 D1
Bank Melli..................................2 C2
Book City Niyavaran Store............3 D1
Dehkhoda Institute...................(see 11)
Irish Embassy..............................4 D1
New Zealand Embassy..................5 D1
Sweden Embassy..........................6 D1
Tajikistan Embassy.......................7 D1
Turkmenistan Embassy.................8 D2
Uzbek Embassy...........................(see 6)

SIGHTS & ACTIVITIES
Azadi Tower (Borj-e Azadi)..........9 A5
Darband Ski Lift........................10 C1
Film Museum of Iran.................11 C1
Milad Tower (Borj-e Milad).........12 B3
Niyavaran Palace Museum..........13 D1
Park-e Jamshidiyeh....................14 D1
Sa'd Abad Museum Complex......15 C1

SLEEPING
Azadi Grand Hotel.....................16 B2
Laleh International Hotel............17 B4

EATING
Akbar Mashti Bastani.................18 C1
Khaneh Azarbaijan...................(see 14)
Taj Mahal.................................19 B3

TEAHOUSES & CAFÉS
Azari Traditional Teahouse........20 B6
Café..(see 11)
Ghaem Teahouse......................21 C1

ENTERTAINMENT
Silk Road Gallery......................22 D1

TRANSPORT
Southern Bus Terminal (Terminal-e
Jonub)....................................23 C6
Western Bus Terminal (Terminal-e
Gharb)...................................24 A4

Metro stations north of
Mirdamad opening from 2009

See Valiasr Ave & Northern Tehran Map (p110)

See Central & Southern Tehran Map (pp102–3)

It's handy to remember that the Alborz Mountains are known locally as the North Star of Tehran for a reason – yes, they're in the north. And as the whole city slopes down from these mountains, if you're walking uphill that usually means you're going north.

If you plan to use public transport – or any transport – it helps to learn the names and locations of the main squares as soon as you can; see Getting Around (p126) for transport options.

Tehran has two international airports (p123): the older Mehrabad airport on the western edge of the city near Azadi Sq; and the new Imam Khomeini International Airport 35km south of the city. If you're coming or going by bus, you'll need to use one of four bus terminals (p124). The western terminal, adjacent to Azadi Sq, and the southern terminal, near the train station, are the largest. The central (Arzhantin) terminal in the city centre and the eastern terminal have fewer services and serve fewer destinations. All are connected to the rest of Tehran by bus, taxi, shuttle taxi and, increasingly, Metro.

Maps

If you're only stopping in Tehran for a few days and seeing the major sights, the maps in this chapter – redrawn from aerial photographs – should be adequate. You'll need a more detailed map if you want to visit remote suburbs, or – if you have an uncontrollable yearning for danger – drive. Your best bet is to get the latest Tehran map from **Gita Shenasi** (Map pp102-3; ☎ 6670 9335; www.gita shenasi.com; 15 Ostad Shahrivar St, Razi St, Valiasr Crossroads, Enqelab-e Eslami Ave; ☑ 8am-6pm Sat-Wed & 8am-1pm Thu). It will be big and comprehensive, and is updated most years – push the buzzer to be let in.

INFORMATION
Bookshops

For English-language books, the Book City chain is your best option. Elsewhere, the dozens of bookshops on Enqelab Ave opposite Tehran University – one of the longest stretches of bookshops on earth – have a few English titles among their mainly Farsi stock. Most top-end hotels sell books (mainly pictorials) about Iran, as do the

---

A REVOLUTION IN STREET NAMES

Across Iran you'll find streets named after the same few martyrs of the revolution, historical figures and revolutionary buzzwords. In many places the government has conveniently painted a huge mural or erected a mosaic likeness of the person beside the street that bears his (it's almost always a man) name. So who are these dead men?

Ayatollah Beheshti Founded the Islamic Republic Party (IRP) in 1979. He took part in the negotiations over the US embassy hostages but was killed a year later by a bomb planted in IRP headquarters by the Mojahedin Khalq Organisation (MKO).

Ayatollah Taleqani A much-admired cleric who was repeatedly exiled and later tortured by the last shah. He led the first Friday prayers after the revolution but died soon afterwards.

Amir Kabir This was the nickname of Mirza Taghi Khan, a reformist prime minister (1848–1851) who was put to death at the command of Nasser al-Din Shah in Fin Gardens near Kashan.

Dr Ali Shariati Returned to Iran from France in 1964 with a doctorate in sociology from the Sorbonne. He combined radical political thought with socially conscious traditionalism and became an inspiration to many women. Barred from teaching, he went to England in 1977, but was found dead in his apartment three weeks later – apparently a victim of the shah's secret police.

Ayatollah Morteza Motahhari Was a close confidant of Ayatollah Khomeini who railed against communism and the effect it would have on Islam. He became president of the Constitutional Council after the revolution, but was assassinated by a rival Islamic group in May 1979.

Streets are also named after buzzwords of the revolution and key Islamic phrases. These include Valiasr, which means 'Prince of this Time' and is a nickname for Mahdi, the 12th imam, who will one day return as the messiah; Azadi, which translates to 'freedom'; Jomhuri-ye Eslami, which means 'Islamic Republic'; and Enqelab, which means 'revolution'. For more on these and other Iranian personalities, see www.iranchamber.com/personalities.

TEHRAN IN...

Two Days

Start early in the **Tehran Bazar** (p100) watching the hustling, bustling and haggling of the country's biggest market. Stop in **Imam Khomeini Mosque** (p100) at prayer time for a taste of Islam in action, then walk up to **Park-e Shahr** (p104) for some head space and lunch at the **Sofre Khane Sonnati Sangalag** (p121). Spend the afternoon looking at the ancient wonders of the **National Museum of Iran** (p104), then take a shuttle taxi down to Rah Ahan Sq and the **Azari Traditional Teahouse** (p120) for some well-earned *chay* (tea) and a special meal. On day two, check out the **Golestan Palace** (p101), then after a coffee with the paper at **Cafe Naderi** (p121), head down for the 2pm viewing of the **National Jewels Museum** (p105). Round the day out with some alternative cuisine in northern Tehran.

Four Days

Follow the two-day plan, then head north to check out the **Sa'd Abad Museum Complex** (p109) before hiking from **Darband** (p113) across to **Park-e Jamshidiyeh** (p113). Use your last day to take in the relaxed **Tehran Museum of Contemporary Art** (p108) and **Park-e Laleh** (p107), perhaps take in an **art gallery** (p122) to meet young Tehranis and chill out in the cafés of **Gandhi Ave** (p121).

National Museum of Iran and Sa'd Abad Museum Complex.

Book City Hafez Store (Map p110; ☎ 8880 5735; 743 Nth Hafez St) The biggest store of the best chain of bookshops. A decent range of fiction and nonfiction in English (mostly on the 3rd floor), and plenty of pictorials on Iran (1st floor).

Book City Niyavaran Store (Map p94; ☎ 2228 5969; Shahid Bahonar St, near Kamranieh Crossing) Some people like this store even more than the Hafez store, though the fun police have closed the attached café.

Di Rouz Em Rouz Ancien Livres (Map p110; ☎ 8888 8844; Khoddami St, off Valiasr Ave; ☿ by appointment or by chance) Old books in English, French, German and Italian. Some rare works on Iran. Mr Afshar is stimulating conversation.

Jahanelm Institute (Map pp102-3; ☎ 6695 0324; Enqelab Ave) Magazines ranging from the *Economist* to *Vogue*. It's on the floor below ground level in a large arcade with red-painted trim.

Emergency

If your emergency is not life threatening, your embassy or your hotel's front desk should be able to send you to the most appropriate hospital or police station and perhaps help with translation. If that is impossible, call one of these numbers:

Ambulance (☎ 115)
Fire Brigade (☎ 125)
Police (☎ 110)

Internet Access

Internet cafés, or *coffeenets* as they're called here, open and close at a remarkable rate in Tehran – and that's even before the government steps in with regular crackdowns. However, the following places have been around for years and hopefully will not have disappeared into cyberspace by the time you arrive. They have webcams, burning facilities and headphones. For other *coffeenets* look around major squares, usually upstairs, where the rent is cheaper.

Ferdowsi Coffeenet (Map pp102-3; Ferdosi Sq, Enqelab Ave; per hr IR10,000; ☿ 9am-9.30pm) Upstairs past the fruit seller on the southeastern corner of the square; good connections and plenty of software.

Pars Internet (Map pp102-3; ☎ 3392 4173; 369 Ferdosi St; per hr IR9000; ☿ 9am-9.30pm Sat-Thu) Opposite the British embassy, these guys have relatively fast machines; they sell phonecards and offer cheap international calls at IR1500 a minute.

Rahyabnet Cafenet (Map pp102-3; ☎ 8880 1316; 4th fl, 40 Keshavarz Blvd; per hr IR10,000; ☿ 8.30am-8pm Sat-Thu) Near the Iranian Traditional Restaurant.

Valiasr Commercial Centre (Map p110; Valiasr Sq; per hr IR10,000; ☿ 9am-9pm) Several small, fast and busy *coffeenets* on the ground floor.

Vanak Coffeenet (Map p110; ☎ 8878 5192; Vanak Sq; per hr IR15,000; ☿ 9am-midnight) On the 1st floor, southeast corner of Vanak Sq.

Internet Resources

There are few English-language websites devoted to Tehran.

Payvand (www.payvand.com) Hard to navigate, but has some good restaurant reviews.

Tehran 24 (www.tehran24.com) Regularly updated photographs of Tehran.

Tehran Avenue (www.tehranavenue.com) Well-written café, restaurant, film, music, theatre and art reviews. Unfortnuately, though, there is often no address for the places reviewed.

Tehran Metro (www.tehranmetro.com) Everything underground; includes connecting bus routes and numbers.

Laundry

The city is not overrun with laundries and dry-cleaning services, although your hotel should be able to arrange something for you.

Left Luggage

Most hotels are happy to hold luggage, usually at no cost. Alternatively, there are reasonably priced left-luggage offices at Mehrabad and Imam Khomeini International Airports (about IR15,000 to IR20,000 a day).

Medical Services

DENTISTS

Dentists regularly advertise in the *Tehran Times* and are very inexpensive by Western standards.

HOSPITALS

Tehran has by far the largest concentration of doctors and hospitals in all of the country, and the quality of medical care is reasonably high by international standards. Many of the doctors have Western training, and it shouldn't be too difficult finding one who speaks English (or French or German).

Your embassy will usually recommend a doctor or hospital. Alternatively, the following hospitals are accessible, clean and reputable:

Day Hospital (Map p110; ☎ 8879 7111; cnr Valiasr Ave & Tavanir St)

Mehrad Hospital (Map p110; ☎ 8874 7401; Miremad St, off Motahhari Ave)

Tehran Clinic (Map p110; ☎ 8871 2931; Farahani St)

PHARMACIES

Tehran is well stocked with pharmacies, and medications (often generic brands) are cheap. For a 24-hour pharmacy ask your hotel reception to phone the **pharmacy line** (☎ 191) to find the nearest one, or head for **Ramin Drug Store** (Map pp102-3; ☎ 6670 5301; southeast cnr Ferdosi Sq).

Money

Tehran has perhaps the greatest concentration of bank branches of any city on earth; along or just off a 1.5km stretch of Enqelab Ave there are more than 20 branches! Unfortunately, few of these can change your money and none deal with credit cards or travellers cheques (see also Banks, p388).

Instead, the easiest and most common way of changing money is in an official moneychanging shop around Ferdosi Sq or on Ferdosi St south of there. They won't smile, but neither (usually) will they rip you off and it's all done in about 30 seconds.

Chances are you'll be asked to 'change' on the street before you ever reach an official shop. If you're desperate, this is convenient. But if not, the street changers are best avoided unless you know the rates and count your money carefully – both their rates and their mathematical skills are dodgy.

If you must use a bank, the following branches will help, or look for an 'exchange' sign in the window of any other branch. Banks open from 7.30am to 1.30pm but don't change before 9am; the process is tedious (don't forget your passport).

As usual, hotels and their diabolical rates will be your last resort, though some top-end places have attached bank branches; Homa Hotel is one, and they *might* be able to change travellers cheques if you're desperate.

Bank Melli (Map p110; Shariati St, Elahiyeh) If you're in the far north.

Bank Melli Central Branch (Bank Melli Markazi; Map pp102-3; Ferdosi St) If you've run out of cash, speak to these people about getting a transfer from home; see p389 for details.

Bank Tejarat (Map pp102-3; Nejatollahi St) Handy to Iran Air and the travel agencies.

Melli Iran Exchange (Map pp102-3; ☎ 6670 0924; Ferdosi St) Beside Bank Melli Markazi (Central Branch), the most official of the exchange shops.

Newsstands

Pavement newsstands can be found all over Tehran, selling an ever-changing selection of Farsi newspapers (they're only one critical story away from being closed down) and, in some, the four English-language dailies. The following two also stock a random selection of ageing secondhand books.

Enqelab Newsstand (Map pp102-3; Enqelab Ave)

Ferdosi Newsstand (Map pp102-3; Ferdosi St) Just north of Manucheri St.

TEHRAN

Post

DHL (Map p110; ☎ 8871 5906-9; 353 Dr Beheshti Ave; ✆ 5.30am-9pm Sat-Thu & 9am-2pm Fri)

Main post office (Map pp102-3; Sa'di St; ✆ 8am-7pm) About 100m south of Amir Kabir St; come here to post packages.

Post office (Map p110; Valiasr Sq) Northwest corner of Valiasr Sq; for ordinary mail.

Telephone

Telephone cards for local calls can be bought at most newsstands, as can some cards for international calls. Public telephones are plentiful and conveniently dotted along the main streets where traffic noise is loudest. It's quieter, and usually easier, to use an internet café (many have Skype) or a telephone office, though these are surprisingly hard to find in Tehran. See p391 for more on telephones.

Pars Internet (Map pp102-3; ☎ 3392 4173; 369 Ferdosi St; international calls per min IR1500; ✆ 9am-9.30pm Sat-Thu)

Telephone office (Map pp102-3; Ban Hamayoon St, off Imam Khomeini Sq; per min IR1700; ✆ 8am-5pm Sat-Thu) Convenient to the cheap accommodation. It's 10m down an alley.

Toilets

Almost all museums, palaces and other buildings open to the public have clean toilets, as do all but the smallest restaurants. In an emergency, duck into the grounds of the nearest mosque or into a park, where the state of cleanliness or otherwise will depend upon the local caretaker. And remember that old maxim of Iranian travel: 'The wise traveller carries an emergency stash of paper; the unwise can use this page'.

Tourist Information

Incredibly, the capital of Iran – a country that wants to attract 20 million tourists by 2020 – has no tourist information office. Ask your hotel instead.

Tours

For personalised tours or advice from private operators, the following are recommended:

Houman Najafi (☎ 0912 202 3017; houman.najafi@ gmail.com) Specialises in advice on ecotourism around Iran.

Leily Lankarani (☎ 0912 150 8519; llankarani@yahoo .co.uk) Experienced and interesting guide and fixer with extensive media experience.

Travel Agencies

Travel agencies abound in Tehran but for choice and quality the best place to look is along Nejatollahi St in central Tehran. Most agencies sell tickets for domestic and international flights and seats on trains. For local tour operators, see p415.

Asia2000 Travel Agency (Map pp102-3; ☎ 8889 6949; asia2000@samapardaz.com; Nejatollahi St) This professionally run place has English-speaking staff and, in our experience, has been consistently good.

Simorgh Travel Agency (Map pp102-3; ☎ 3397 1525; Baharestan Sq) On the north side of Baharestan Sq, handy to the budget accommodation.

Universities

At the centre of political change in Iran, **Tehran University** (Map pp102-3; Enqelab Ave) is a fascinating place to wander around. There is, however, a ban on foreign nonstudents entering but its enforcement is haphazard. If you're worried, just hang around the front gate (the entrance is on Enqelab Ave) for a few minutes and you'll be 'adopted' by someone keen to practise their English.

Visa Extensions

Extending tourist visas in Tehran is much easier than it used to be, but it still takes a whole frustrating week! The **Foreign Aliens office** (Map pp102-3; Sepah St, off Sepah Sq; ✆ 7.45am-1.30pm Sat-Wed, 7.45am-noon Thu) is walking distance from Taleqani Metro station. The best option is to stop at the nominated **Bank Melli** (Map pp102-3; Sepah Sq) on the way, tell the teller 'visa' and hand over your IR100,000. He'll do the paperwork and in a couple of minutes hand you the all-important deposit slip. Continue to Sepah Sq, turn right (downhill) and enter the green-glass building on your right, about 150m along (look for the uniforms). The visa extension office is on the 1st floor. When we extended here the whole process only took a few minutes, but even after the 30-day extension was approved we had to wait seven days to collect the passport. Yes, annoying. For more on extending, see p395.

DANGERS & ANNOYANCES
Traffic

Even for the experienced Asia hand, the chaotic traffic in Tehran is likely to come as quite a shock. Almost anything goes on these roads and often does. It's not unusual to see

---

BAD DRIVING? IT'S ALL IN YOUR HEAD

The physical danger notwithstanding, the main problem you face as a visitor on Tehran's streets is mental: how to deal with this manic mass of metal. After much testing, we believe the following attitudinal adjustments will not only free you of some of the traffic-induced anxiety, but make your Tehran experience all the more memorable.

Try not to think of Tehrani drivers as 'hopeless', 'crazy' or 'stupid'; it will just make you more scared.

Instead, look at all the tiny gaps your taxi driver is negotiating without recourse to the brakes, the countless sticky situations from which he extricates himself, and you start to realise these guys are actually *good* drivers.

Watch your driver closely: he almost never uses his mirrors (if he has any); he drapes his seatbelt across his chest only when driving onto an expressway, where he can be fined; he rarely indicates; and he happily makes U-turns in the middle of major roads – all without raising his heartbeat.

Then think of how well you'd have to drive to get through this nightmarish traffic without being involved in an accident. That's right, don't fight it, you know these guys are actually *very good!*

Finally, embrace the chaos! Head to the corner of Jomhuri-ye Eslami Ave and Ferdosi St and engage a motorbike taxi for a trip across town. Tell him you're in a hurry, and hold on. At Disneyland you'd pay good money for this kind of white-knuckle ride; in Tehran it's just part of life.

---

motorcycles weaving between pedestrians on the footpath in an attempt to escape the gridlock; Paykans reversing at speed along an expressway to reach that missed exit; and all manner of cars and buses hurtling towards each other in a Darwinian game of chicken where, however, the biggest and fastest don't always survive.

The sheer volume of traffic can be overwhelming and makes crossing the street seem like a game of Russian roulette, only in this game there are fewer empty chambers. Indeed, it is hard to overestimate the risk of an accident, whether you're in a vehicle or on foot.

However, after the initial shock, visitors are often surprised there are not more accidents. You might feel as if you've had three near-death experiences in the course of a single cab ride, but in reality drivers are adept at getting you near to death without actually killing you (see the boxed text, above). As a pedestrian, the best way to ensure a safe negotiation of Tehran's streets is to do what the locals do. Safety in numbers is the usual tactic – wait for one or two other road-crossers to appear and, with them between you and the traffic, step boldly out into the flow. Be aware of contra-flow bus lanes, which turn relatively harmless one-way streets into a far more dangerous street-crossing challenge.

But perhaps the most reassuring thing of all is to remember that no matter how 'crazy' a driver appears to be, he will do everything he can to avoid running you over simply because doing so is just too much hassle. For more on Iran's traffic, see p380.

Pollution

Tehran is one of the most polluted cities on earth. And according to the government, more than 70% of the smog that covers Tehran for about 200 days a year comes straight out of the exhaust pipes of the city's 3 million cars, trucks and motorbikes, with the ultra-inefficient Paykans more culpable than most (see the boxed text, p414). When pollution levels reach crisis point – often during winter – schools are closed and radio warns the old and unwell to stay indoors. Reports say almost 10,000 people die every year as a result of the atrocious air quality.

However, there is some light filtering through from the end of this foggy tunnel. By 2008 Tehran was halfway through a 10-year plan to try and curb pollution. Paykan numbers were falling, and petrol rationing has reduced (slightly) vehicle emissions. Clean air, however, remains a long way off. If the pollution really starts to hurt your throat, or you have asthma, head for the hills and relative purity of Darband or Park-e Jamshidiyeh.

Scams

There are many more dangerous places in the world than Tehran, where crime against foreigners (especially violent crime) is rare.

There is, however, the odd bag snatch, pick-pocketing and scam, most notably the bogus police scam – see p378 for details.

SIGHTS

It's not that long ago that southern Tehran was the centre of the city. Today, the area south of Jomhuri-ye Eslami Ave is the oldest and poorest part of town and is home to many of Tehran's best museums, including the National Museum of Iran and the glittering National Jewels Museum, as well as the Golestan Palace complex and the Tehran Bazar. A little north of here is the area loosely referred to as central Tehran, on the edge of which is Park-e Laleh – home to the Carpet Museum and the Museum of Contemporary Art.

Most locals refer to anywhere north of Valiasr Sq as northern Tehran. Much of this area was semirural until about 35 years ago, but frenetic expansion has spread apartment buildings all the way to the foothills of the Alborz Mountains, engulfing the last shah's opulent Sa'd-Abad and Niyavaran Palaces in the process.

In this guide we have included central and southern Tehran on one map (pp102–3); the area either side of Valiasr Ave heading north of Valiasr Sq on the Valiasr Ave & North Tehran map (p110); while places that don't fall in these two areas can be found on the Tehran map (p94). Places are listed starting at the Tehran Bazar in the south and heading north from there.

Central & Southern Tehran

TEHRAN BAZAR   بازار تهران

The maze of bustling alleys and the *bazaris* that fill them make **Tehran Bazar** (Map pp102–3; main entrance, 15 Khordad Ave; ☽ 7am-5pm Sat-Wed, 7am-noon Thu) a fascinating, if somewhat daunting, place to explore. Traders have been hawking their wares on this site for nearly a thousand years, but most of what you see today is less than 200 years old; it's no architectural jewel. The *bazaris* are a conservative bunch (see the boxed text, opposite) and there will be far more chadors than bleached hair.

The bazaar encompasses more than 10km of covered stores and has several entrances, but it's worth using the main entrance, in a square opposite Bank Melli. The warren of people and goods is a city within a city and includes several mosques,

guesthouses, banks, a church and even a fire station. Most lanes specialise in a particular commodity: copper, paper, gold, spices and carpets, among others.

You'll also find tobacconists, shoemakers, tailors, broadcloth sellers, bookbinders, flag sellers, haberdashers, saddlers, tinsmiths, knife-makers and carpenters. The carpet, nut and spice bazaars might be the most photogenic, but the lane of stores selling fake designer labels also catches the eye.

In our experience there are two ways to visit the bazaar, a place that cartographers seem never to have fully conquered. One is to simply wander the labyrinth of streets and alleys, taking whichever direction you fancy and just going with the flow. You'll almost certainly get lost but will soon enough be found and directed by any number of helpful Iranians.

The other is to allow yourself to be befriended by one of the carpet salesmen – don't worry, they will find you near the front entrance. Tell them what sections of the bazaar you'd like to see (the gold bazaar, spices bazaar, the mosque etc), and they will take you there. When you're done, they will expect you to visit their carpet shop, drink some tea and view a few rugs – which in itself is often quite fun, and prices here are probably the best in Iran. If you do choose to buy a carpet, even better, but no-one is forcing you.

Try and visit in the morning, when business is brisk but not yet frantic, as it becomes at lunchtime and between about 5pm and 7pm. During these times, the chances of being mowed down by some piece of fast-moving haulage equipment are high.

IMAM KHOMEINI MOSQUE مسجد امام خمینی
Tehran has surprisingly few interesting mosques and mausoleums but one that's well worth visiting is the **Imam Khomeini Mosque** (Shah Mosque; Map pp102–3), right inside the bazaar. This is very much a working mosque and one of the largest and busiest in Tehran. The building itself dates from the early 18th century but the real reason you come here is to see Islam in action. The courtyard is accessed from several parts of the bazaar and hundreds of people pass through here, so it's usually possible for non-Muslims to stand and watch the faithful performing their ablutions and praying, though photography is less welcome.

THE BAZARIS

In Iran a bazaar is much more than just a place to stock up on a few essential shopping items. The *bazaris*, the men who run the stalls in the bazaar, are frequently very wealthy and wield enormous political power. They are usually conservative, religious people who have a long history of standing against authority. In an attempt to weaken their power the last shah bulldozed new roads through parts of the bazaar, gave subsidised credit to competing supermarkets and set up state purchasing bodies to handle sugar, meat and wheat. Not surprisingly, the Tehran *bazaris* hit back during the Islamic Revolution when the closure of the bazaar wrought havoc on the economy. They were equally influential in the 1906 Constitutional Revolution and the coup that ousted Prime Minister Mohammad Mossadegh in 1953 (for details, see p37).

It has been estimated that Tehran Bazaar controls a third of Iran's entire retail and trade sector. Prices here set the standard for prices across the country, and the carpet dealers and other merchants can supply loans almost as readily as the banks. However, the power of the *bazaris* is waning. Competition from new supermarkets and the time it takes for most Tehranis to reach the bazaar has slowly bled money away from this traditional market, and with it the power of its merchants.

GOLESTAN PALACE   کاخ گلستان

In what was once the heart of Tehran is this monument to the glories and excesses of the Qajar rulers. A short walk south from Imam Khomeini Sq, the **Golestan Palace complex** (Map pp102-3; ☎ 3311 3335-8; www.golestanpalace.ir; Ark Sq; admissino several tickets; ☯ 9am-3.30pm Fri, Sat & Mon-Wed) is made up of several grand buildings set around a carefully manicured garden. Admission isn't expensive but, annoyingly, you must buy a separate ticket for each building, and all at the front gate. If you ask, they might also give you an informative printed guide.

Although there was a Safavid-era citadel on this site, it was the Qajar ruler Nasser al-Din Shah (r 1848–96), impressed by what he'd seen of European palaces, who built it into the fine complex you see today. Originally it would have been much bigger, with inner and outer sections to encompass offices, ministries and private living quarters, but several surrounding buildings were pulled down under the Pahlavis.

The following description assumes you start your visit at the Ivan-e Takht-e Marmar, then continue in a clockwise direction around the courtyard.

Walk straight ahead from the entrance to the **Ivan-e Takht-e Marmar** (Marble Throne Veranda; admission IR3000), a mirrored, open-fronted audience hall dominated by a magnificent throne. The throne is supported by human figures and constructed from 65 pieces of yellow alabaster from mines in Yazd. It was made in the early 1800s for Fath Ali Shah, a monarch who managed a staggering (and quite likely very tiring) 200-odd wives and 170 offspring. This hall was used on ceremonial occasions, including the Napoleon-style self-coronation of Reza Shah in 1925.

A narrow corridor leads off to a side room covered with murals of the fictional kings described in Ferdosi's *Shahnamah* – look for Zahhak, the king with a snake on his shoulder that had to be fed with human brains. Don't miss the painting of Fath Ali Shah above the fireplace – he's the one with the beard so thick you'd swear it was a falsie!

Leaving the Ivan-e Takht-e Marmar, turn left and you'll come to the **Negar Khane** (Art Gallery; admission IR4000), which displays a fine collection of Qajar-era art. It was the brainchild of Nasser al-Din Shah, who'd been particularly captivated by European museums. Especially interesting are the portraits of the shahs wearing the jewels and crowns you can see in the National Jewels Museum, and pictures of everyday life in 19th-century Iran by Kamal ol-Molk and Mehdi. Women were certainly wearing chadors back then, too. The difference is that the men were also swaddled in three layers of clothing. Well worth a look.

Continue in a clockwise direction around the courtyard and you'll come to the **Howze Khaneh** (Pool Room; admission IR3000), named for the small pool and fountain in the centre of the room. It houses a collection of

TEHRAN

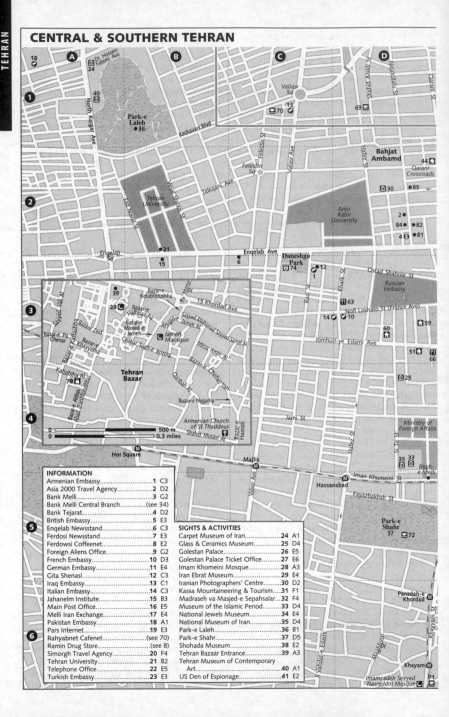

CENTRAL & SOUTHERN TEHRAN

INFORMATION

SIGHTS & ACTIVITIES

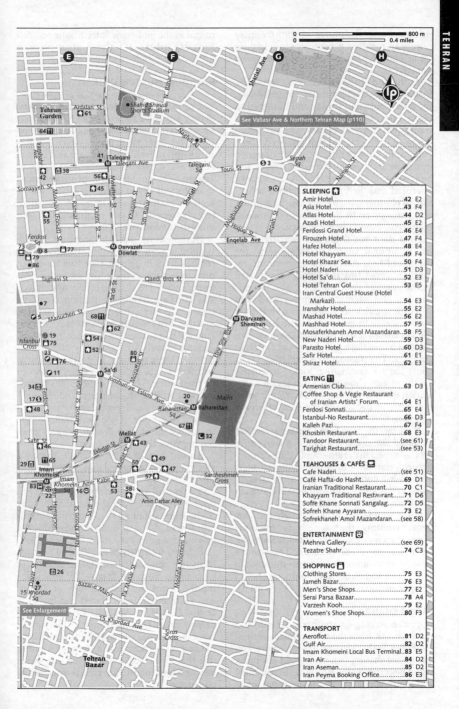

0   800 m
0   0.4 miles

See Valiasr Ave & Northern Tehran Map (p110)

SLEEPING 🏠
Amir Hotel.................................**42** E2
Asia Hotel.................................**43** F4
Atlas Hotel................................**44** D2
Azadi Hotel...............................**45** E2
Ferdossi Grand Hotel..............**46** F4
Firouzeh Hotel.........................**47** F4
Hafez Hotel..............................**48** E4
Hotel Khayyam........................**49** F4
Hotel Khazar Sea.....................**50** F4
Hotel Naderi............................**51** D3
Hotel Sa'di...............................**52** E3
Hotel Tehran Gol.....................**53** E5
Iran Central Guest House (Hotel
   Markazi)..............................**54** E3
Iranshahr Hotel........................**55** E2
Mashad Hotel...........................**56** E2
Mashhad Hotel.........................**57** F5
Mosaferkhaneh Amol Mazandaran..**58** F5
New Naderi Hotel.....................**59** D3
Parasto Hotel............................**60** D3
Safir Hotel................................**61** E1
Shiraz Hotel..............................**62** E3

EATING 🍴
Armenian Club..........................**63** D3
Coffee Shop & Vegie Restaurant
  of Iranian Artists' Forum......**64** E1
Ferdosi Sonnati.........................**65** E4
Istanbul-No Restaurant............**66** D3
Kalleh Pazi................................**67** F4
Khosbin Restaurant...................**68** E3
Tandoor Restaurant................(see 61)
Tarighat Restaurant...............(see 53)

TEAHOUSES & CAFÉS 🍵
Cafe Naderi............................(see 51)
Café Hafta-do Hasht.................**69** D1
Iranian Traditional Restaurant..**70** C1
Khayyam Traditional Restaurant..**71** D6
Sofre Khane Sonnati Sangalag...**72** D5
Sofreh Khane Ayyaran...............**73** E2
Sofrekhaneh Amol Mazandaran...(see 58)

ENTERTAINMENT 🎭
Mehrva Gallery......................(see 69)
Tezatre Shahr...........................**74** C3

SHOPPING 🛍
Clothing Stores.........................**75** E3
Jameh Bazar.............................**76** E3
Men's Shoe Shops....................**77** E2
Serai Parsa Bazaar....................**78** A4
Varzesh Kooh...........................**79** E2
Women's Shoe Shops................**80** F3

TRANSPORT
Aeroflot....................................**81** D2
Gulf Air.....................................**82** D2
Imam Khomeini Local Bus Terminal..**83** E5
Iran Air.....................................**84** D2
Iran Aseman.............................**85** D2
Iran Peyma Booking Office........**86** E3

paintings and sculptures of 19th-century European royalty – generously given to their Qajar counterparts by the same European monarchs.

At the end of the garden is the imposing **Shams-Al Emarat** (Edifice of the Sun; admission IR4000), the tallest palace of its day and designed to blend European and Persian architectural traditions. Born of Nasser al-Din Shah's desire to have a palace that afforded him a panoramic view of the city, it was designed by master architect Moayer al-Mamalek and built between 1865 and 1867. A sequence of mirrored and tiled rooms display a collection of photographs, together with furniture and vases given to the shahs by European monarchs, especially the French.

Next door you'll see four soaring *badgirs* (traditional air-conditioning units; see the boxed text, p257), rising above the recently restored **Emarat-e Badgir**, first erected in the reign of Fath Ali Shah. The interior has typically ostentatious mirror work and is worth a quick look, though upstairs no longer seems to be open. In the basement the **Aks Khaneh** (Historic Photograph Gallery; admission IR3000) is one of the highlights of the Golestan complex. The photographs depicting Qajar court life are fascinating; look particularly for the picture showing the inside of a Zoroastrian tower of silence, with bodies in varying states of decay, and the shot of 'freaks and dwarfs'.

Next up, the tiny **Talar-e Almas** (Diamond Hall; admission IR3000) displays a range of decorative arts – especially 18th- and 19th-century French ceramics – in a room with red walls and a tiled floor. It's not the most riveting room in the palace. The teahouse underneath was closed when we visited.

After wandering back through the gardens, avoiding the sometimes fractious swans, you'll come to the **Ethnographical Museum** near the main entrance. The world's slowest renovation has lasted more than three years so far, but staff told us it should be open in 2009, *insh'Allah* (if God wills it).

PARK-E SHAHR   پارک شهر

If you're staying in southern Tehran and need a break from the traffic, head straight for **Park-e Shahr** (Map pp102–3) where you can go ice skating (when it's cold enough), take a boat trip on the tiny lake (in summer) and enjoy tea or qalyan (water pipe) year-round at the laid-back Sofre Khane Sonnati Sangalag (p121). It's also a great place to just sit and watch Tehranis relaxing.

NATIONAL MUSEUM OF IRAN

(موزه ملي ايران (موزه ايران باستان

The modest **National Museum of Iran** (Iran Bastan Museum; Map pp102-3; ☎ 6670 2061-6; www.national museumofiran.ir; Si Tir St; admission IR5000; ⏱ 9am-5pm Tue-Sun, to 5.45pm summer) is no Louvre, but it is chock-full of Iran's rich history and should be on every visitor's list of things to see in Tehran. The contents will probably mean more to you if you come here after you've seen the main archaeological sites, particularly Persepolis, so you might want to wait until the end of your trip.

Designed by French architect André Godard, it's one of the more attractive modern buildings in Tehran, blending Sassanian principles such as the grand *iwan*-style entrance, with Deco-style brickwork. Inside you'll find a marvellous collection, including ceramics, pottery, stone figures and carvings, mostly taken from excavations at Persepolis, Ismail Abad (near Qazvin), Shush, Rey and Turang Tappeh. Unfortunately, the presentation of these treasures is less than inspired and the lack of thorough explanations can be frustrating. There is some English labelling and an English-speaking guide is available, though you'll probably have to wait around to get one. If you can't wait, be sure to ask for the informative 'brochure' when buying your ticket.

Among the finds from **Shush**, there's a stone capital of a winged lion, some delightful pitchers and vessels in animal shapes, and colourful glazed bricks decorated with double-winged mythical creatures. A copy of the stone detailing the Code of Hammurabi found at Shush is also displayed – the original being in Paris.

Exhibits from **Persepolis** include a magnificent human-headed capital; a cuneiform inscription from the Talar-e Bar proclaiming the might and godly affinity of Xerxes; and a striking frieze of glazed tiles from the central hall of the Apadana Palace. Also on display are a famous trilingual inscription from the time of Darius I; a bull-headed capital and carved staircase; a statue of a sitting dog that looks like it was carved just weeks ago; and four foundation tablets inscribed in cuneiform.

One of the more startling exhibits is the **Salt Man** from Zanjan. He's thought to have been a miner who died in the 3rd or 4th century AD, but whose white-bearded head, leg in a leather boot and tools were also preserved by the salt in which he was buried. Rather more comical is a **bronze statue of a prince**, perhaps Parthian, whose huge bristling moustache looks out from a head obviously made separately from the body and better suited to a smaller monument. Look also for the impressive selection of **Lorestan bronzes** (see the boxed text, p207), dating back to the 8th century BC.

Entry is from Si Tir St – it's behind the small park on the corner of Imam Khomeini Ave. There's a small **coffee shop** (✆ 9am-6pm) in a courtyard behind the National Museum of Iran.

MUSEUM OF THE ISLAMIC PERIOD
موزه دوره اسلامی

Next door to the National Museum and part of the same complex, this **museum** (Map pp102-3; ☎ 6670 2061; Si Tir St; admission IR5000; ✆ 9am-5pm Tue-Sun, to 5.45pm summer) had been closed for some time when we passed, but staff assured us it was due to reopen in 2008. When it does, you'll find a modern building containing two floors of exhibits from a selection of Islamic arts, including calligraphy, carpets, ceramics, woodcarving, stone carving, miniatures, brickwork and textiles. Don't miss the silks and stuccowork from Rey, portraits from the Mongol period, a collection of Sassanian coins and gorgeous 14th-century wooden doors and windows. Look also for the beautiful **Paradise Door**, a 14th-century lustre-painted mihrab (niche in a mosque indicating the direction of Mecca) from Qom, and a 19th-century inlaid door from Esfahan.

Captions should be in English, and – in theory – English-speaking guides will be there to show you around. In the past there was no printed guide, but a plastic-coated page of explanations was available if you asked.

To see both museums you should probably allow two to three hours.

IRAN EBRAT MUSEUM   موزه عبرت ایران
There is nothing subtle about the **Iran Ebrat Museum** (Map pp102-3; www.ebratmuseum.ir; off Sabt St; negotiable admission IR50,000; ✆ tours starting 10am & 2pm Wed-Mon), a one-time prison of the shah's brutal secret police that now exhibits that brutality with an equal measure of pro-revolution propaganda. The prison is an incongruously attractive building, with wings radiating from a circular centre. But what went on here was not attractive at all.

During the 1970s, hundreds of political prisoners – including several prominent clerics and postrevolutionary figures whose names you will recognise from street signs – were held in tiny cells and, in many cases, tortured by the Anti Sabotage Joint Committee, a branch of the despised Savak internal security agency. The various functions of the prison are dramatically recreated with waxwork dummies and liberal doses of red paint. The shah's henchmen are invariably depicted wearing neckties (a pro-Western symbol in modern Iran) and looking cruel and brutish (check out the eyebrows). The propaganda element is emphasised by the photos of members of the former royal family prominently displayed throughout – just in case you forgot who was responsible.

Propaganda aside, this prison was undoubtedly a very bad place to end up and the people running it guilty of some heinous crimes. It's just a pity that the abhorrence of torture and politically motivated incarceration expressed here are not shared by the ruling regime; stories from Tehran's notorious Evin Prison are just as horrifying.

All visitors must follow the one-hour, 45-minute tour, conducted in Farsi by a former prisoner. Some exhibits have brief explanations in English, though little interpretation is required. The tour includes a film that might not be suitable for young children.

NATIONAL JEWELS MUSEUM
موزه جواهرات ملی

Through a large iron gate at the northern end of Bank Melli, past a couple of well-armed guards, you'll find the cavernous vault that is the **National Jewels Museum** (Map pp102-3; ☎ 6646 3785; Ferdosi St; admission IR30,000, child under 12 yr not permitted; ✆ 2-4.30pm Sat-Tue). Owned by the Central Bank but actually housed underneath the central branch of Bank Melli, this museum is probably *the* biggest tourist drawcard in Tehran. If you've already visited the art gallery at the Golestan Palace, you will have seen the incredible

TEHRAN

jewellery with which the Safavid and Qajar monarchs adorned themselves. Come here to gawp at the real things.

Believe it or not, at least one war has been fought over these jewels. Most of the collection dates back to Safavid times, when the shahs scoured Europe, India and the lands of the Ottoman Empire for booty with which to decorate the then capital, Esfahan. However, when Mahmud Afghan invaded Iran in 1722, he plundered the treasury and sent its contents to India. On ascending the throne in 1736, Nader Shah Afshar despatched courtiers to ask for the return of the jewels. When their powers of persuasion proved unequal to the task, he sent an army to prove that he was serious. To get the soldiers off his back, Mohammed Shah of India was forced to hand over the Darya-ye Nur and Kuh-e Nur diamonds, a Peacock Throne (though not the one you'll see here) and other assorted treasures. After Nader Shah's murder in 1747, Ahmed Beg plundered the treasury and dispersed the jewels. The Kuh-e Nur diamond found its way into the sticky fingers of the colonial British and has been locked up in the Tower of London since.

You can pick up a guidebook for IR6000 at the shop as you enter, or take one of the regular and professional tours in English, French, German, Arabic or Turkish – it's included in the ticket price, and worth waiting for, as there are no descriptions in English. Make sure you don't miss the **Darya-ye Nur** (Sea of Light), a pink diamond weighing 182 carats and said to be the largest uncut diamond in the world; the **Peacock (Naderi) Throne** outside the vault door (see the boxed text, below); the tall **Kiani Crown** made for Fath Ali Shah in 1797; the crowns worn by the last shah and his wife, Farah; and the incredible 34kg **Globe of Jewels**, made in 1869 using 51,366 precious stones – the seas are made from emeralds and the land from rubies (with Iran, England and France set in diamonds).

Not surprisingly, cameras and bags must be left at reception and, unless you can hide it under your *manteau* (overcoat), you'll be forced to leave this book outside too. Be careful not to touch *anything* or you'll set off ear-piercing alarms.

GLASS & CERAMICS MUSEUM

موزه آبگینه و سرامیک

North of the National Museum of Iran is the impressive **Glass & Ceramics Museum** (Map pp102-3; ☎ 6670 8153; Si Tir St; admission IR5000; ♥ 9am-4.30pm Tue-Sun, to 6pm summer), housed in a beautiful Qajar-era building. Built as a private residence for a prominent Persian family, it later housed the Egyptian embassy and was converted into a museum in 1976.

The building marks a move away from purely Persian traditions, successfully blending features of both Eastern and Western styles. The graceful wooden staircase and the classical stucco mouldings on the walls and ceilings are particularly delightful, and there are many delicate carvings and other decorations.

The museum itself is probably the best-designed in Iran. It has hundreds of exhibits,

---

THE PEACOCK THRONE

There has long been confusion about the origins of the Peacock Throne that now sits at the entrance to the National Jewels Museum. The real story is this: In 1798 Fath Ali Shah ordered a new throne to be built. His artists made quite a job of it, encrusting the vast throne that looks more like a bed with 26,733 gems. Set into its top was a carved sun, studded with precious stones, so the throne became known as the Sun Throne. Later Fath Ali married Tavous Tajodoleh, nicknamed Tavous Khanoum or Lady Peacock, and the throne became known as the Peacock Throne in her honour.

Fath Ali certainly had a taste for gems, but one of his predecessors, Nader Shah, liked the finer things too. So much, in fact, that he invaded India in order to recover the Kuh-e Nur diamond. During the expedition he also bagged the Moghuls' famous Peacock Throne. But during the haul back to Persia, this piece of booty fell into the hands of rebellious soldiers, who hacked it up to spread the wealth among themselves. In the intervening years the stories of the Peacock Thrones have become muddled, so you might still hear people say (erroneously) that this Peacock Throne originally came from India.

mainly from Neishabur, Kashan, Rey and Gorgan, dating from the 2nd millennium BC. They're organised chronologically into galleries, with explanations of the periods in English, plus other relevant details such as the Persian glass-blowing tradition. The pieces are all lovingly displayed and it's easy to spend an hour or more reading and looking your way through the museum. The ground floor shop sells an English guidebook to the museum.

MADRASEH VA MASJED-E SEPAHSALAR
مدرسه و مسجد سپهسالار

The **Madraseh va Masjed-e Sepahsalar** (Masjed-e Motahari; Map pp102-3; Mostafa Khomeini St, off Baharestan Sq; ◷ Fri only), at the eastern end of Jomhuri-ye Eslami Ave, is one of the most noteworthy examples of Persian architecture of its period, as well as one of the largest. Built between 1878 and 1890, it's famous for its multiple minarets and poetry inscribed in several ancient scripts in the tiling. It still operates as an Islamic college and is usually open to male members of the public on Fridays only. Photography is not encouraged, especially outside where the Majlis building is just to the north.

IRANIAN PHOTOGRAPHERS' CENTRE
کانون عکاسان ایرانی

The **Iranian Photographers' Centre** (Map pp102-3; ☎ 8889 5054; Somayyeh St; admission free; ◷ 9am-7pm Sat-Thu) has rolling exhibits of the work of local and, occasionally, international photographers. The adjoining shop sells and processes slide film and sells pro equipment. Not surprisingly, it's a good place to meet Iranian photographers.

US DEN OF ESPIONAGE لانه جاسوسی آمریکا
More than any other single building in Iran, the former US embassy in Tehran (and the events emanating from it) have had a dramatic and profound influence on the recent history of this country and, indeed, the whole Middle East. From a bunker beneath the embassy building at the junction of Taleqani Ave and Mofatteh St, CIA operatives orchestrated a coup d'etat in 1953 that brought down the government of Mohammad Mossadegh (see the boxed text, p37).

For the next 25 years, US support for and influence over Shah Mohammad Reza was implemented largely from this build-ing. When the shah was finally pushed out, students who feared a repeat of the 1953 coup stormed the embassy and held 52 diplomats hostage for 444 days (see p39). The rest – the birth of the Islamic Republic and the rise of fundamentalism throughout the region – is history.

Today, the former embassy is known as the **US Den of Espionage** (Map pp102-3; Taleqani Ave) and is used by the Sepah militia, a hardline group dedicated to defending the revolution. The interior of the chancery is preserved as a museum, with incriminating documents that had been pieced together after being shredded among the exhibits. Unfortunately, it's rarely open to the public – usually only from 1 to 10 February.

Despite this, the embassy's colourful history and more colourful murals along the Taleqani Ave wall mean most travellers come for a look. The murals pronounce the evil of the 'Great Satan' (the USA) and Israel, including one in which the face of the Statue of Liberty is rendered as a skull. There's no sign saying you can't take pictures of these highly photogenic murals but try to be discreet. We've had reports of travellers asking and being allowed, while others have been told not to take photos. We've photographed the wall several times without trouble, but on the last visit we were briefly apprehended and led away before persuading our half-hearted captors that we hadn't, in fact, taken any photos at all and were just dumb tourists.

Diagonally opposite the US Den of Espionage is the **Shohada Museum** (Martyrs' Museum; Map pp102-3; cnr Taleqani Ave & Forsat St; ◷ 8.30am-3.30pm Sat-Thu), which has rolling exhibitions of photographs, usually from the Iran–Iraq War or the 1979 revolution.

PARK-E LALEH پارک لاله
Near the centre of Tehran, **Park-e Laleh** (Map pp102-3; Keshavarz Blvd) is one of those places that is more than the sum of its parts. Certainly, it is a well-designed green space, but its location amid so much traffic makes the park a real oasis. As you wander through, perhaps on your way to the adjoining Carpet Museum or Tehran Museum of Contemporary Art, you'll notice plenty of young Tehranis refining their flirting techniques over soft-serve ice creams. It's a great place for people-watching.

TEHRAN MUSEUM OF CONTEMPORARY ART

موزه هنرهای معاصر تهران

On the western side of Park-e Laleh, the **Tehran Museum of Contemporary Art** (Map pp102-3; ☎ 8896 5411; www.tehranmoca.com; Kargar Ave; admission IR4000; ☒ 9am-6pm Sat-Thu & 2-6pm Fri, to 7pm summer) is in a striking concrete modernist building constructed during the shah's rush to build modern landmarks in the 1970s. Contrary to preconceptions of Iran, here's a collection of art (not always modern and rarely contemporary) by Iranian artists and some of the biggest names of the last century. Established during the '70s under the direction of the progressive Queen Farah Diba, the museum holds arguably the greatest collection of Western art in Asia – worth between US$2 billion and US$5 billion. It includes works by Picasso, Matisse, Van Gogh, Miró, Dali, Bacon, Pollock, Monet and Warhol, among others.

During the Ahmadinejad years, however, this collection has been locked away in the museum vaults, deemed to be symbolic of a Western liberalism that is decidedly out of favour among the ruling classes. While this is disappointing, it does put a lot more Iranian art on display and it's still well worth visiting. Part of the museum's charm is its distinctively modern design, with gallery after gallery appearing in an ever-descending and circling pattern, with plenty of comfy seats from which to take it all in. It's a good place to meet arty Tehranis, especially in the café (which serves real coffee!).

CARPET MUSEUM OF IRAN موزه فرش ایران

Just north of the Museum of Contemporary Art, the two floors of the **Carpet Museum** (Map pp102-3; ☎ 8896 7707; http://carpetmuseum.ir; cnr Fatemi Ave & Kargar Ave; admission IR5000; ☒ 9am-4.30pm Tue-Sun, to 6pm summer) house more than a hundred pieces from all over Iran, dating from the 17th century to the present day; the older carpets are mostly upstairs. The museum itself was designed by Queen Farah Diba and mixes '70s style with carpet-inspired function – the exterior is meant to resemble threads on a loom, which cool down the main building by casting shadows on its walls. You will often see weavers working on a loom on the ground floor and questions are welcome. Inside, a shop sells postcards and books and there's a pleasant café. Flash photography is not allowed.

Valiasr Ave & North Tehran

Almost everything along Valiasr Ave and the surrounding parts of northern Tehran has been built in the last 50 years, so there aren't many actual 'sights'. Instead, this is modern Tehran, home to hip coffee shops, fancy restaurants and embassies.

To get here, shuttle taxis head north from Valiasr Sq so it's probably simplest to just jump in and out as you need. If you're heading somewhere near to or north of Mirdamad Blvd, however, consider taking the Metro to Mirdamad station and a shuttle taxi the short hop across to Vanak Sq or up to Tajrish.

SARKIS CATHEDRAL کلیسای سرکیس

In case you assume that Islam has a monopoly on Iranian life, visit **Sarkis Cathedral** (Map p110; ☎ 8889 7980; cnr Nejatollahi & Karim Khan-e Zand Sts; ☒ 8am-noon & 1-5pm Mon-Sat). Built between 1964 and 1970, it's interesting not so much for its beauty but because of what it is and where it is. Sarkis Cathedral is by far the most visible and important non-Islamic religious building in Tehran. The area immediately to the south is the Armenian quarter, the centre of a still-thriving community.

Although most of the Christians in Iran are Armenians, there's also a sprinkling of Protestants, Assyrians, Catholics and Orthodox Christians, all of whom have churches in Tehran, most behind large walls in the same district as the Sarkis Cathedral.

PARK-E MELLAT پارک ملت

Many Tehranis say **Park-e Mellat** (Mellat Park; Map p110; Valiasr Ave) is their favourite in-town getaway, and if you're here around dusk on any spring or summer afternoon you'll find plenty of people enjoying the shaded areas around a small lake. On weekend nights you'll find just as many young people cruising up and down Valiasr Ave, several to a car, showing off their new noses as they flirt and swap phone numbers through car windows.

Greater Tehran

This section covers those places that don't appear on our larger scale maps. For sights in the far north, head first to Tajrish Sq, from where shuttle taxis leave almost continuously for the Sa'd Abad and Niyavaran Palaces; the popular walking trails at Dar-

NATION OF NOSE JOBS   *Andrew Burke*

I was at dinner in Esfahan when the conversation turned to nose jobs. After prattling on about how many people I'd seen in Tehran wearing a tell-tale plaster across the bridge of their nose, I asked my friend Behzad whether he knew anyone who had actually had a nose job.

When he looked at me like I had, well, two noses, I should have known. 'She has,' he said, pointing across the table to his sister.

'Oh. Right,' said I, embarrassed that I hadn't noticed the change, before desperately trying to recover with: 'I never would have known.' Mahnaz, to her credit, dealt with it like someone who has had the nose job conversation a thousand times before. Barely skipping a beat, she began explaining that while I might never have known, she didn't really like her new nose. She was hoping to get it done again.

'It's not a big deal,' she explained. Plenty of people have nose jobs in Iran.

But I had to know: 'How much does it cost?' Well, the cheapest nose jobs could be had for less than US$1000, she said, but that was a bit risky because it might turn out badly. A decent surgeon would cost more, but they were cheaper in Esfahan than in Tehran. 'But the best surgeons are in Tehran, and they cost about US$4000.'

Despite Iran being a country where the average yearly wage is far less than that, Tehran is the plastic surgery capital of the universe. Surgeons report that more than 90,000 noses are remodelled in Iran every year. Tehran alone has about 3000 plastic surgeons, and their clients are not just women looking for a cutesy ski jump. A growing number of men are also spending big on taking the bump out of their proboscis.

The contrast with the West, where people disappear on 'holidays' for weeks so they can be remodelled without anyone knowing, is stark. In Tehran, the nose job has become such a status symbol that some people have taken to wearing plasters on their noses just so they can look like they've had the job done. Which might be taking it just a little too far…

band and Darakeh; the cable car to Tochal at Velenjak; and Park-e Jamshidiyeh.

FILM MUSEUM OF IRAN   موزه فيلم ايران

Housed in a Qajar-era mansion built by Shah Nasir od-Din for his daughter, the **Film Museum** (Map p94; ☎ 2271 9001; www.film museum.ir; Bagh-e Ferdows, off Valiasr Ave; admission IR10,000; ⏰ 10am-5pm Tue-Thu, Sat & Sun, 2-5pm Fri) has well-displayed exhibits of equipment, photos and posters from Iran's century-old movie industry. It's interesting, even if you are not well-versed in Iranian film, and the building is fascinating.

The highlight is a sublime 121-seat cinema with moulded plaster ceilings. New and classic Iranian films are screened here at 3pm, 5pm, 7pm and 9pm daily. Seats are IR15,000 and if you ask nicely they will turn on subtitles in the language of your choice (assuming languages are available); call ☎ 2272 3535 to see what's on. A shop also sells hard-to-find Iranian films on DVD (IR40,000), and the chic café (p120) is the ideal place for post-film contemplation.

Look for the street with a garden down the middle and a sign to Bahoner Library.

SA'D ABAD MUSEUM COMPLEX

مجموعه موزه سعد آباد

Set on 104 hectares of spectacular mountainside parkland, the **Sa'd Abad Museum Complex** (Map p94; ☎ 2228 2031; www.saadabadpalace.org; Valiasr Ave, Taheri St; several tickets required; ⏰ 8.30am-4pm, to 5pm summer) was once the royal summer home. There are more than 10 buildings scattered around the site and to see them all you'll need at least three hours; combining a visit here with lunch in nearby Darband is a good idea.

Today, most of the buildings at Sa'd Abad house museums. Some musums are more interesting than others but the individual tickets are only sold at the front gate, so you'll need to decide where to go in advance. For example, be sure to buy a ticket for the Nation's Art Museum, or you won't be able to see the basement of the White Palace. The ticket sellers should give you a map-cum-guide to the site – in barely intelligible English – though you might need to ask. Note too that it's well worth taking the free minibus from outside the White Palace up to the Green Palace, then walking down.

VALIASR AVE & NORTHERN TEHRAN

0 ———— 1 km
0 ———— 0.5 miles

See Central & Southern Tehran Map (pp102–3)

What is now called the **White Palace** (Palace of the Nation; admission IR5000) was built between 1931 and 1936 and served as the Pahlavi summer residence. The two bronze boots outside are all that remain of a giant statue of Reza Shah – he got the chop after the revolution. The 5000-sq-metre, 54-room palace is no Versailles. Instead it's a modern building filled with a hodge-podge of extravagant furnishings, paintings and vast made-to-measure carpets. The tiger pelt in the office, among other things, reveals the shah as a man of dubious taste, though in fairness pelts were more in vogue in the 1950s.

Whatever you think of the furnishings, the White Palace was the height of luxury in its day. Look for the discreet air-conditioning units that fold away into the walls; or the shah's 20 cues in the billiards room – little has changed since the revolution. In the upstairs Ceremony Hall is a 143-sq-metre carpet that is said to be one of the largest ever woven in Iran. The nearby Dining Hall contains a similar carpet, and it is here that the shah, convinced the palace was bugged, dragged a table into the middle of the room and insisted both he and the American general he was entertaining climb on top of it before they spoke. Don't miss the trippy stainless steel staircases at the back of the ground floor, which spiral down to the **Nation's Art Museum** (admission IR3000) in the basement.

At the uphill end of the complex, the more classical-looking **Green Palace** (Shahvand Palace; admission IR5000) was built at the end of the Qajar era and extensively remodelled by the Pahlavis. Shah Reza lived here for only a year and apparently found the bed, if not the mirror stalactites on the ceiling, a little too soft. It was later used as a private reception hall (upstairs) and residence (downstairs) for special guests. The design is over-the-top opulent, with wall-to-wall mirrors in the appropriately named Mirror Hall, and the bedroom. Be sure to go around the back to take in the view.

There are several other small, specialist museums in the complex, including the **Abkar Miniature Museum** (admission IR3000), displaying miniatures by the artist Clara Abkar; the **Farshchian Museum** (admission IR3000), with works by Mahmoud Farshchian; the **Bihzad Museum** (admission IR3000), containing paintings by the artist Bihzad; the **Museum of Ethnological Research** (admission IR3000) with a few waxworks and ethnological artefacts; and the **Mir Emad Calligraphy Museum** (admission IR3000), with samples of Iranian calligraphy from different periods.

The **Museum of Fine Arts** (admission IR3000) is in one of the more impressive buildings and houses some charming Persian oil paintings dating back to the 18th century and some beautiful inlaid furniture. The **Military Museum** (admission IR3000) is inside and around another palace that belonged to the shah's nephew Shahram; just look for the helicopter.

If pushed for time, the White and Green Palaces are the most highly recommended. The **bookshop** (☎ 2794 0373; 🕙 8am-5pm) at the entrance boasts a good range of tourist-oriented and English-language books about Iran.

Getting There & Away

To get to the museum complex, either walk or take a taxi (IR6000 *dar baste* – closed door) the 1.5km northwest from Tajrish Sq, beginning on Ja'fari St and turning left and right (ask anyone for 'Musee Sa'd Abad').

NIYAVARAN PALACE MUSEUM

موزه کاخ نیاوران

About 6km east of the Sa'd Abad Museum complex is the **Niyavaran Palace Museum** (Map p94; ☎ 2228 2050; www.niavaranpalace.ir; Niyavaran Ave, off Shahid Bahonar Sq; individual tickets required; 🕙 8am-4pm winter, 9am-5pm summer), the complex where Shah Mohammad Reza Pahlavi and his family spent most of the last 10 years of royal rule. It's set in five hectares of land-scaped gardens and has four separate museums – tickets must be bought individually at the main gate.

After entering and buying tickets to the various museums, we recommend going straight through to **Sahebqaranieh** (King's Special Office; admission IR5000), which was built at the end of the Qajar period but extensively remodelled by the last shah's wife, Farah Diba, and used as his office. It contains a very fine collection of paintings and other furnishings, including several colourful Qajar-era works that Farah rescued from Shiraz and now adorn the ceilings.

But it is the insight into the shah's daily life that makes it most fascinating. Some of the very attractive rooms include a private basement teahouse, private dental surgery and a bar decorated with Shirazi painted beams. Keep an eye out for the shah's golden phone and gold-coloured pistols, and for photos displayed in the Ambassador's Waiting Room; the mixed bunch sees Mao Zedong share space with Pope Paul VI, while Hitler, Queen Elizabeth II, Richard Nixon, Kemal Ataturk and Dwight Eisenhower (who was a guest at the shah's last wedding), stare out from the past nearby.

The custodians will make you join a guided tour, which on our most recent visit was conducted by a wonderfully well-informed, English-speaking woman.

Adjoining Sahebqaranieh is the **Jahan-Nama Museum & Gallery** (Queen's Private Museum; admission IR3000). Two main rooms here are filled with a small but well-displayed example of the eclectic collection of modern and ancient art gathered by Farah Diba, mainly during the 1970s. Works by Warhol, Picasso and Joan Miró share space with Iranian archaeological artefacts and finds from sites in Mexico and Egypt, and rotating exhibits of modern Iranian art.

Head up the hill to the actual **Niyavaran Palace**, which has been closed since 2004 but, our guide told us, should reopen sometime in 2008, *insh'Allah*. It was built between 1958 and 1968 and has a decidedly '60s look – clean-lined functionality on the outside contrasting with elaborate furniture and carpets inside. The jarring styles, over-the-top opulence and plethora of royal junk are almost a caricature of the classic royal palace and leaves you wondering whether the shah felt his position brought with it a need to be surrounded by the trappings of European palaces, or whether it was, as the guide explained, just 'normal for royals at that time'. If you manage to get inside, don't miss the magnificent Kerman carpet showing Iranian kings right back to the Achaemenids, as well as some European sovereigns, including Napoleon Bonaparte. Adjoining to the east is a private cinema and tennis courts, and in front of the palace, the modest family swimming pool.

To the west of Niyavaran Palace is the **Ahmad Shahi Pavilion** (admission IR3000), an attractive two-storey kiosk dating from the late Qajar period (early 20th century), which was last used as the residence of the crown prince Reza. When we visited the upstairs was closed, but downstairs the prince's white leather–themed living quarters are on display. It's a fascinating display of the prince's belongings, from childhood drawings to model planes (he was a pilot), a rock collection (with a moon rock gifted by Richard Nixon) and a polar bear skin (a gift of the Canadian government), among others.

In front of the Ahmad Shahi Pavilion is the pleasant **Coffee Palace** (🕙 9am-9pm), which serves pastries and very drinkable coffee.

Getting There & Away

Take a shuttle taxi east of Tajrish Sq (IR2500), and ask to be dropped off at Shahid Bahonar Sq, near the museum entrance.

DARAKEH & DARBAND   درکه و دربند

On a sunny day few things could be nicer than fleeing the traffic fumes for the foothills of the Alborz Mountains and the **walking trails** of Darakeh and Darband. Both the trails strike north, passing waterfalls and crossing streams. They are crowded on Thursday afternoon and Friday and make a great place to meet Tehranis in a relaxed, social atmosphere.

The lower reaches of both trails are lined with teahouses and stalls selling food and drinks, which are hugely popular in the evenings – some close mid-week and in winter. A dish of *dizi* (stew), a kabab or two, a cold drink or a huff and a puff on a qalyan by the stream will soon help you forget the Tehran traffic. Among other tasty treats to sample on the way up are dates, apricots, pickled walnuts, *lavashak* (sheets of pressed dried fruit), fresh mulberries and steamed lima beans.

Darband also has a **ski lift** (Map p94; 6am-5pm Sat-Thu, to 7.30pm summer), with tickets costing IR6000/12,000 one way/return to the only station.

Getting There & Away

The starting point for getting to either trail is the northern side of Tajrish Sq. For Darband, either walk 2.5km uphill along Fana Khosrov St (or take a shuttle taxi), or leave the grounds of Sa'd Abad Palace from the rear, cross Meydan-e Darband and continue uphill to where you see the ski lift on the left. The walking trail starts at the end. A visit to Darband can easily be combined with a visit to Sa'd Abad, or you can walk all the way to Jamshidiyeh Park from a trail starting further ahead.

To get to Darakeh take a shuttle taxi from Tajrish Sq. At the end of Darakeh St you'll be dropped in a square; the trail leads off from the northeastern corner. A private taxi costs about IR15,000.

PARK-E JAMSHIDIYEH   پارک جمشیدیه

Meaning Stone Garden, **Park-e Jamshidiyeh** (Map p94; 7am-midnight) climbs steeply up the lower reaches of the Alborz Mountains and offers a clean and relatively quiet atmosphere in which to enjoy the views and escape the smog. It's the sort of place you could happily while away an entire afternoon sipping tea and watching the lights of this huge city slowly come to life – though the prices of food might give you indigestion.

If you're feeling energetic, a steep trail leads from the northwest corner of the park (beyond the Turkomen restaurant) along the side of the mountain for about 5km to Darband, making a pleasant, relatively pollution-free hike.

TOCHAL TELECABIN   تله کابین توچال

Tehran's popular **Tochal Telecabin** (Velenjak Telecabin; Map p130; 2240 4001-5; www.tochal.org; Velenjak Ave; full journey IR90,000; going up 8am-1pm, coming back 2-3.30pm Wed-Fri, closed Sat-Tue) runs 7.5km up Mt Tochal (3957m), stopping twice along the way. It's a popular and easily accessible ski-field that has snow for between six and eight months a year (due to its height, it's the fourth-highest ski field on earth).

The telecabin is busy on Friday but can be virtually empty other days. You can buy one-way/return tickets to whichever station you want. The first stop is **Station 2** (IR15,000/30,000, 12 minutes one way), then **Station 5** (IR30,000/45,000, 25 minutes), where there is an easy ski run, and it finishes at freezing **Station 7** (IR55,000/80,000, 25 minutes), from where a Poma chairlift links to Tochal Hotel. From there, a T-bar works the short runs and a Doppel Mayr lift goes to the mountain summit. It's possible to ski down from Station 7 to Station 5, assuming there is enough snow. Skis can be rented at Station 7. Prices here are for weekends; it's IR5000 or more cheaper each way on weekdays. Ski passes are IR60,000/80,000 per weekday/weekend, sold at Station 1.

While the telecabin runs fairly limited hours, you can choose to torture your thighs and climb the mountain at any time, as locals like to do on Fridays. Teahouses at the stations will help to ease your recovery.

Getting There & Away

From the northern side of Tajrish Sq, ask for a shuttle taxi (IR2000) to Tochal Telecabin. From the entrance you can walk (10 minutes) or catch a bus (IR1000) to the telecabin ticket office.

REZA ABBASI MUSEUM موزه رضا عباسی
Named after one of the great artists of the
Safavid period, the **Reza Abbasi Museum** (Map
p110; ☎ 8851 3002; www.rezaabbasimuseum.ir; 972
Shariati Ave; admission IR5000; ⓨ 9am-4.45pm Tue-Sat)
showcases Iranian art from ancient times
and the Safavid-era paintings of Abbasi
himself. If you like Iranian art, it's one of
the best and most professionally run museums in the country. The museum is organised chronologically starting with the
top-floor Pre-Islamic Gallery, where you'll
find **Achaemenid gold** bowls, drinking vessels,
armlets and decorative pieces, often with exquisite carvings of bulls and rams. Here, too,
you'll find fine examples of **Lorestan bronzes**
(see the boxed text, p207). The middle-floor
Islamic Gallery exhibits ceramics, fabrics
and brassware, while the ground-floor
Painting Gallery shows samples of fine
calligraphy from ancient Qurans and illustrated manuscripts, particularly copies of
Ferdosi's *Shahnamah* and Sa'di's *Golestan*.

To reach the museum you can take a
shuttle taxi from the junction of Shariati
and Enqelab Aves, but not all of them continue as far north as this so you might be
better going by private taxi. Alternatively,
take Metro Line 1 to Mosalla and then a
shuttle taxi down the Resalat Expressway
to Shariati Ave.

AZADI TOWER (BORJ-E AZADI) برج آزادی
Way out west at the end of Azadi Ave is
the inverted Y-shaped **Azadi Tower** (Borj-e Azadi
or Freedom Tower; Map p94; Azadi Sq; admission IR6000;
ⓨ 8am-noon & 2-6pm Sun-Fri), built to commemorate the 2500th anniversary of the Persian Empire in 1971. After being closed for
years the underground gallery, Quran museum, cinema and, best of all, the viewing
platform finally reopened in 2006.

Like the City Theatre, Carpet Museum
and Tehran Museum of Contemporary
Art, the 50m-high structure is a mix of '60s
modern architecture with traditional Iranian influences, such as the *iwan*-style of
the arch. The exterior is clad with more
than 8000 cut stones, while inside you can
see architect Hossein Amanat's complex
structural engineering in concrete. The
park surrounding the monument is a relative oasis compared with the surrounding
maelstrom of traffic. It was the scene of
much protest during the 1979 revolution

and remains a focal point for (progovern-
ment) demonstrations today.

You can reach the top by stairs or lift, and
will probably be accompanied. To get here,
take a bus or shuttle taxi west and ask for
'Azadi' or take Metro line 2 (dark blue) to
Azadi and walk from there.

MILAD TOWER (BORJ-E MILAD) برج میلاد
Ten years in the making, **Milad Tower** (Borj-e
Milad; Map p94; www.miladskytower.com/en/) is the
fourth tallest tower and (in early 2008)
12th-tallest freestanding structure in the
world. Standing 435m high, including
120m of antenna, the tower bears a striking
resemblance to Toronto's CN Tower, with
the octagonal concrete shaft tapering from
the base to a pod with 12 floors. The pod
was due to open in 2008 and will be home to
an observation deck, a revolving restaurant,
a 'sky dome' and various TV, radio and
traffic control functions.

The tower forms part of the Tehran International Trade and Convention Centre,
a vast expanse of ground that includes the
500-room Yadman Hotel, though when it
will open is unknown.

SLEEPING

Tehran's accommodation largely follows the
city's social breakdown, so budget places
are in the poorer south, and the options
get more expensive as you go north. Capi-
tal-city syndrome means room rates are
generally higher than elsewhere in Iran.

The business district is between Enqelab
Ave and Keshavarz Blvd, where you'll also
find several three-star standard business
hotels. Tehran's pre-Revolution era 'five-
star' hotels are most interesting for the
disco-era décor and ornamental outdoor
swimming pools. Service and everything
else isn't great. The best top-end places
are boutique-sized affairs on Valiasr Ave,
Tehran's main north–south artery, in the
north of the city. They are not exactly Ritz
standards, but they're good value.

If you don't have a booking, try telephon-
ing your chosen hotel when you arrive and
bargaining, then taking a taxi to check it
out. Your taxi will usually wait until you're
satisfied, and if you're not, will take you to
the next place on your list. Listings here are
ordered by price, from cheapest to most
expensive.

Budget

Mashhad Hotel (Map pp102-3; ☎ 3313062; www.mash hadhotel.homestead.com; 416Amir Kabir St; dm/s/tw IR40,000/60,000/80,000; ▣) The rooms and shared bathrooms are tiny, but the mainly helpful management have long made it the choice for those on the tightest budgets. There's only one shower, however, and front rooms are horrendously noisy. Don't confuse this Mashhad with the midrange Mashad Hotel, near the former US embassy.

Mosaferkhaneh Amol Mazandaran (Map pp102-3; ☎ 3394 1630; www.amolmazandaran.com; Amin Darbar Alley, off Amir Kabir St; s/tw/tr IR60,000/80,000/120,000; ✖) Set around a small courtyard away from the noise of Amir Kabir St, this 22-room place is one of the best deals in the area for its price, friendly managers and location above a very local *chaykhaneh* (teahouse). Rooms are simple, but clean, as are the shared bathrooms. It's about 150m south of Amir Kabir St, on the right. There's no English sign.

Hotel Khazar Sea (Map pp102-3; ☎ 3311 3860; Ohadi Alley, off Amir Kabir St; s/tw IR65,000/80,000) If you don't mind a bit of peeling paint and a walk to the bathroom, this no-frills place set around a courtyard is welcoming, quiet and good value. The manager speaks some English. It's in the second lane on the left as you head east of the intersection of Amir Kabir and Mellat Sts.

Hotel Tehran Gol (Map pp102-3; ☎ 3311 3477; Amir Kabir St; s/tw IR70,000/100,000) The basic rooms here have a basin inside and are marginally more spacious than the hotel's neighbours, though front rooms are still very noisy. There's not much English. Bathrooms are shared.

our pick **Firouzeh Hotel** (Map pp102-3; ☎ 3311 3508; www.firouzehhotel.com; Dowlat Abad Alley, off Amir Kabir St; s/tw with breakfast IR110,000/160,000; ✖ ▣) If ever there was a hotel whose atmosphere revolved around one man, this is it. Mr Mousavi is the very personification of Persian hospitality, and his enthusiasm, useful information, help with bookings (including day trips to the ski fields) and wonderful guest book make an otherwise unremarkable little hotel in cheap southern Tehran worth the stay. The smallish rooms come with cable TV, fridge and bathrooms with shower and basin; toilets are shared. The best budget option.

Iran Central Guest House (Hotel Markazi; Map pp102-3; ☎ 3391 4798; cnr Zavareian & Lalehzar Sts; s/tw IR100,000/160,000, with bathroom IR180,000/225,000) The small, recently renovated rooms are clean and the welcome is friendly enough. Toilets are squats and some rooms don't have bathrooms.

Hafez Hotel (Map pp102-3; ☎ 6670 9063; hafez hotel@yahoo.com; Bank Alley, off Ferdosi St; s/d with breakfast US$20/27; ✖) In a lane beside the big Bank Melli, the modern rooms here are quiet, clean and have fridge, fan and pokey bathroom. It's conveniently located and fair value.

Hotel Naderi (Map pp102-3; ☎ 6670 1872; Jomhuri-ye Eslami Ave; s/d/tr US$15/30/45; ✖) If service and fastidious cleanliness are important to you, stop reading now. But if you fancy '50s-era bakelite telephones, a manual switchboard, decades-old furnishings and the bohemian Cafe Naderi (Map pp102–3) downstairs, read on. The history is certainly unusual and maybe even unique in Tehran. But this is not a renovated faux-historic hotel (though it could be!); it's just old. So the attractions of the big rooms with their high ceilings are somewhat tempered by broken beds, leaky plumbing, grubby floors, mosquitoes and no toilet paper. And apart from Davoud, the service is mainly unsmiling. Still, we quite like it, and the price is fair, especially for single travellers, and location good. If you do stay, be sure to ask for a rear room (room numbers 107 to 112 or 207 to 212), because the front rooms are frightfully noisy.

If the others are full:

Asia Hotel (Map pp102–3; ☎ 3311 8320; Mellat St; s/tw with breakfast & bathroom IR150,000/200,000; ✖) Metres from Metro Mellat.

Hotel Khayyam (Map pp102-3; ☎ 3311 3757; www .hotelkhayyam.com; 3 Navidy Alley, Amir Kabir St; s/tw/tr US$22/37/46; ℗ ✖) Quiet place with helpful, engaging service but worn, overpriced rooms and squat toilets. Long-discussed renovation can't come soon enough.

Midrange

Most of the midrange hotels are in central and northern Tehran. You'll have to walk further or take a taxi to most of the museums in the south, but will be closer to decent restaurants, parks and cafés. Prices in this range start at about US$30 for a twin or double room. All rooms have a fridge, TV and air-con, and bathrooms with thrones. Reception staff should speak English and there will be a restaurant.

Parasto Hotel (Map pp102-3; ☎ 66720839; hotel_parasto@yahoo.com; Mohammad Buyk Alley, off Jomhuri-ye Eslami Ave; s/d with breakfast US$25/39; P ⊠ 🖵) Style? Ahm, no. The Parasto is as no-frills as it gets but the rooms are spotlessly clean and staff welcoming, making it a reliable lower-midrange choice. There is also a reasonably priced restaurant.

Shiraz Hotel (Map pp102-3; ☎ 3392 5342; www.shiraz-hotel.com; cnr Jaber Zadeh Alley & Sa'di St; s/d with breakfast US$35/52; ⊠ 🖵) The Shiraz offers clean, compact but comfortable and well-equipped rooms with double-glazing to keep out the noise. Good value; shame about the hectic location.

New Naderi Hotel (Map pp102-3; ☎ 6670 9530; new_naderihotel@hotmail.com; Jomhuri-ye Eslami Ave, 53 Gohar Shad Alley; s/d US$35/55; P ⊠) If the 'old' Naderi (p115) is a product of the '50s, this place is certainly a '70s child. The rooms aren't quite as vast as the lobby, but they're cleaner than those in the Naderi and come with breakfast. The restaurant is good value but service can be disinterested.

Atlas Hotel (Map pp102-3; ☎ 8890 6058; www.atlas-hotel.com; 206 Taleqani Ave, near Qarani Crossroads; s/d US$38/58; ⊠ 🖵) Right in the heart of Tehran, the spacious, comfortable, well-maintained and quiet rooms in the Atlas's main building (out the back away from the street) are excellent value. Some overlook a colourful courtyard and the combination of decent service, space and facilities makes it a real oasis. The Indian-Pakistani-Iranian restaurant is reasonably good. Recommended.

Safir Hotel (Map pp102-3; ☎ 8830 0873; www.indianhotelsafir.com; 10 Ardalan St, off Mofatteh Ave; s/tw with breakfast US$39/60; ⊠) Located behind the old US embassy grounds, the Safir is probably better known for its subterranean Indian restaurant. But the three-star standard rooms in this long-running little hotel won't disappoint and nor will the service.

Iranshahr Hotel (Map pp102-3; ☎ 8883 4976; www.hotel-iranshahr.com; Iranshahr Ave; s/d with breakfast US$47/72; P ⊠) Reliable. That pretty much sums up the Iranshahr, where the rooms are reliably clean and the service is reliably well-disposed. Solid.

Mashad Hotel (Map pp102-3; ☎ 8883 5120; 190 Mofatteh St, near Taleqani Ave; s/d with breakfast US$55/65; ⊠) A recent facelift has transformed the Mashad into a good-value, well-located mid-range option. Rooms are smallish but attractively furnished, and those on the 4th floor and above have some views into the old US Embassy compound. Service is so so.

ourpick Ferdossi Grand Hotel (Map pp102-3; ☎ 6671 9991-3; www.ferdossigrandhotel.com; 24 Sabt St, off Ferdosi St; s/d US$65/85; ⊠ 🖵 🕿) Within an easy walk of the museums, Golestan Palace and bazaar, the Ferdossi is the best midrange choice in this part of Tehran. The whole place has recently been renovated, there's professional service and facilities, and the quiet, spacious rooms are fairly priced. The restaurant and coffee shop aren't bad, either.

Amir Hotel (Map pp102-3; ☎ 8830 4066; www.amirhotel.ir; Taleqani Ave, near Iranshahr Ave: d/ste with breakfast US$83/93; ⊠ 🖵) In the midst of the business district, the Amir is a modern business hotel with 70 reasonably sized, clean rooms boasting wood-panelling, soft beds and satellite TV. Service is professional and prompt, and the foyer coffee shop serves real coffee! In-room internet is planned.

These hotels in central Tehran share a pre-revolution heritage and everything about them screams 'make me over, now'.

Azadi Hotel (Map pp102-3; ☎ 8884 2479; info@azadihotel.net; Somayyeh St; r US$48) Rooms at the back are best.

Bolour Hotel (Map p110; ☎ 8882 3080; 191 Qarani St; r with breakfast US$52; ⊠) Large rooms, larger bathrooms but little atmosphere; ask for a room away from the road.

Top End

Tehran has a few 'five-star' hotels, most of them built in the '70s by big chains and renamed after the revolution. Those places have experienced a supernova or two (that is, the stars have burst), but a couple of boutique-sized hotels offer the sort of service and comfort more familiar elsewhere. Following is a selection of places that are comparatively central and reasonable value.

ourpick Raamtin Residence Hotel (Map p110; ☎ 8872 2786; www.raamtinhotel.com; 1081 Valiasr Ave; d with breakfast from US$140; ⊠ 🖵) White leather couches might not be your thing, but the Raamtin's 50 spacious rooms are otherwise very well-equipped. There's free wi-fi internet, DVD players and double-glazing, which keeps out the noise of Tehran's main commercial strip. Service is efficient and professional, the location ideal for business and the classy Bistango restaurant downstairs a centre of lunchtime deal-making.

Simorgh Hotel (Map p110; ☎ 8871 9911; www.simorghhotel.com; 1069 Valiasr Ave; r with breakfast from US$170; ⊠ 🖵 🕿) Virtually next door to the

VOICES OF IRAN: FARAHNAZ TAHERI

Age: 44
Lives in: Western Tehran
Occupation: Housewife

'My husband is a driver and sometimes he brings his foreign passengers home. We Iranians don't see many foreigners so it's very interesting when they come to visit. Some of our customs are unusual for them and we get to see some of their culture, too.

For example, when we eat we sit on the floor – on the carpet – but some foreigners can't sit that way and it's funny to see them with their legs stuck out. Some foreigners forget to take their shoes off, but it's not a problem for us as we understand that they have different customs.

If they come for dinner, the foreigners eat what we normally eat, though I might go to some extra effort to make sure they have good memories of our house. I am from the Caspian Sea region so I like to cook dishes from that area, such as *mirza ghasemi, fesenjun, khashke bademjan*, fish and *gheyme*. Among the foreigners, *fesenjun, ghorme sabzi* and fish are probably the favourites – I think because they are sick of eating kababs all the time!

The men and women who come here always ask how to cook the dishes and I'm happy to tell them. This is funny, too, because Iranian men never cook…although, to be fair, [my husband] Ali has recently been learning how to make an omelette. But that's normal in Iran. I don't know any husbands who can cook, and my two sons aren't much better. Iran is a man's country and a man who cooks is a 'lady man', so I'm not expecting things to change anytime soon. For sure I think it would be good if the men cooked…but we'd all be waiting a long time for dinner.'

Raamtin, this modern-looking 69-room hotel is also popular with business visitors for its stylish, well-fitted rooms (free wi-fi internet throughout) and well-trained staff to go with facilities including gym, Jacuzzi and pool.

Melal Apartment Hotel (Map p110; ☎ 8879 0543; www.melal.com; 68 Naseri St, off Valiasr Ave; s with breakfast US$190-290, d US$225-325; ✗ 🖳 🛋) The Melal's luxurious apartments are a taste of how the wealthy live in Tehran. For your bundles of cash (just imagine the rials!) you get large spaces with two or three bedrooms, all decorated with Persian motifs, such as copper fireplaces adorned with Achaemenid soldiers. Facilities include a terrace swimming pool (men only, summer only), gym, café (yes, with real coffee) and two classy restaurants. All rooms have ADSL internet. Melal Group has three other apartment hotels in Tehran, all of a similar standard if slightly different in style; see them on the website.

If ever there was an argument for the management of an international chain, the following three orphans of the '70s are it. Service can be a bit public service, and prices reflect glories past rather than the wrinkled present. Fortunately, very reasonable rates can be had online.

Azadi Grand Hotel (Map p94; ☎ 2207 3021; www.azadigrandhotel.com; Chamran Expressway, near Evin Crossing; s/d US$120/145; P ✗ 🖳) The Hyatt in its previous life; location in far north Tehran is a long way from anywhere except the International Trade Fair Ground.

Laleh International Hotel (Map p94; ☎ 8896 5021; www.lalehhotel.com; cnr Dr Hossein Fatemi Ave & Hejab St; s/d/ste with breakfast US$130/145/254; P ✗ 🖳 🛋) North of Park-e Laleh, the ex-Inter-Continental is ideally located and rooms have fine views.

Homa Hotel (Map p110; ☎ 8877 3021; www.homahotels.com; 51 Khoddami St; d/ste with breakfast US$183/245; P ✗ 🖳 🛋) Former Sheraton that's almost, but not quite, worth it for the *Saturday Night Fever* flashbacks. Tired, overpriced rooms, though all have free internet.

EATING

Tehran is a long way from being one of the world's culinary capitals, but its range of foreign cuisines make a refreshing change from the Iranian staples. Like the city itself, Tehran's food scene draws on a broad selection of cultural influences and caters to both ends of the budget spectrum. Sleek modern restaurants take a more Western approach to presentation and price, but even something as exotic as Thai curry will probably cost less than you'd pay for a couple of beers back home.

Not surprisingly, Iranian food is available all over Tehran, but for non-Iranian food you'll almost certainly have to head to the wealthier north. Note that most of the places listed under Teahouses & Cafés (p120) also serve excellent Iranian food. All listings here are ordered by price, from cheapest to most expensive. For more on Iranian food, see Food & Drink (p78).

Restaurants

Many Iranian restaurants are hidden away underground, so be on the lookout for anonymous-looking stairwells.

IRANIAN RESTAURANTS

The most atmospheric Iranian restaurants are actually teahouses (see p120).

Istanbul-No Restaurant (Map pp102-3; off Jomhuri-ye Eslami Ave; meals IR20,000-30,000; ☼ 11am-5pm) Tucked away 20m down a lane near the Hotel Naderi, this hole-in-the-wall serves a surprising range of lunchtime dishes, with the usual kababs sharing space with huge pots of *khoresht* (any kind of meaty stew), *ghorme sabzi* (stewed beans, greens and mince) and *mirza ghasemi* (mashed eggplant, squash, garlic, tomato and egg). Recommended particularly for budgeteers.

Ferdosi Sonnati (Map pp102-3; ☎ 6671 4503; Ferdosi St; meals IR15,000-30,000; ☼ 11am-9pm) The Ferdosi is a popular place that is especially busy at lunchtime, when its well-priced classic Persian dishes attract traffic from busy Imam Khomeini Sq.

Tarighat Restaurant (Map pp102-3; ☎ 3391 3097; Amir Kabir St; meals IR35,000; ☼ noon-4pm Sat-Thu) Handy to the budget accommodation, this lunchtime place serves reliably good interpretations of the standard kababs and *zereshk polo ba morgh* (roast chicken served with rice and barberry).

our pick Khosbin Restaurant (Map pp102-3; ☎ 3390 2194; 406 Sa'di St; meals IR15,000-35,000; ☼ 11.30am-3pm & 7.30-10.30pm) If you can't face another kabab – or are looking for some vegetarian (not vegan) fare – the no-frills Khosbin serves a refreshing range of Gilani food. Vegetarians should ask for the delicious *mirza ghasemi* or *baghli* (a broad bean dish), or perhaps the *zeytoun parvardeh* (olives marinated in pomegranate juice with crushed walnuts). There's no English sign; look for the red writing on the front window.

Sofre-Khaneh Sonatee Ali Ghapoo (Map p110; ☎ 8877 7803; Gandhi Ave; meals about IR85,000; ☼ noon-3pm & 7.30-11pm) This big, noisy subterranean restaurant is where Iranians go for a boisterous group meal. Waiters in traditional dress set the tone and the atmosphere is as enjoyable as the Iranian food. The fun is expensive by Tehran standards and gets more so after the traditional band starts at 9pm.

our pick Gilac (Map p110; ☎ 8804 8291; 15 Park des Prices, off Kordestan Hwy; meals IR70,000-130,000; ☼ noon-4pm & 7pm-midnight Sun-Fri) The ambience, décor, music and food presentation at Gilac are more reminiscent of Europe than Iran. But the delicious food is wonderfully Caspian. It's a favourite of vegetarians, with the *mirza ghasemi* (IR22,000), *borani bademjan* (IR25,000) and *dokhtar-e luce* ('spoilt girl', IR27,000) starters all delicious; in combination, they'd happily make a meal on their own. The fish and veal dishes are also excellent. To find it, get to Vanak Sq, walk about five minutes west on Molla Sodra St, under the expressway, then take the first right, go one block north and it's in what looks like a housing estate on your left.

Armenian Club (Map pp102-3; ☎ 670 0521-2; 68 Khark St, cnr France Ave; meals IR80,000-150,000; ☼ 8pm-midnight daily & noon-3pm Fri) The Armenian Club is almost a one-off in Tehran. Because it's a Christian establishment, women can legally eat or just hang out sans hejab, and if you can get your hands on something harder than Fanta, it's fine to BYO and drink it with your meal (sorry, no advice on where to find it). The barbecued sturgeon (IR100,000) and beef stroganoff (IR50,000) are both winners, and the range of kababs goes all the way to 'Mexican'. The club doesn't advertise its existence – look for a yellow awning and a tiny buzzer – but welcomes guests. Note that Muslims (at the government's direction) cannot enter.

Literally on the side of a mountain, **Park-e Jamshidiyeh** (Stone Park; Map p94; Feizieh Ave, Niyavaran St, Tajrish; ☼ all restaurants about 10am-midnight) is home to four restaurants perching on the slope. The first one you'll see is **Khaneh Azarbaijan** (☎ 2282 0114), which is also the best value, with *ash-e reshte* (IR10,000), *dizi* and *kofte Tabriz* (both IR35,000) fair value if you don't add too many extras. Unfortunately, the other three seem to take pride in overcharging tourists, with the Iranian food, which has barely discernible Kurdish and Turkmen influences, overpriced (more than IR100,000 a meal) and extra costs soon inflating the bill to twice what you anticipated – you'll be charged for everything they put on the table. The park is worth a visit, but think about bringing a picnic lunch – even the tea costs IR45,000.

On balmy evenings in summer, Tehranis head for Darband and Darakeh, where the walking trails are lined with cafés and restaurants serving everything from full kabab meals to generous helpings of *dizi*, *ash* (yogurt and barley soup) or just snacks.

OTHER CUISINES

By the time you get to Tehran you might be desperate for something a little more exotic than kababs – even a little spicy! Fortunately, Tehran has it. Foreign food is expensive by Iranian standards, but you'd probably pay much more for far less at home. See the English-language newspapers for other foreign restaurants. It pays to book on weekend nights.

Market (Map p110; ☎ 8879 1959; Gandhi Shopping Centre, Gandhi Ave; sandwiches IR40,000-50,000; ☼ noon-11pm Sat-Thu & 6-11pm Fri) Part café, part gourmet sandwich shop, part delicatessen and salad farm, Market and its fare would be common in Western cities but is new to Tehran. The food is fresh and filling.

Jaam-e Jam Food Court (Map p110; Jaam-e Jam Shopping Centre, cnr Valiasr Ave & Taheri St) You don't come here for the fast food, though the coffee isn't bad. You come to see the closest thing to a Western-style pick-up bar in Iran, complete with designer clothing and inches of make-up.

Taj Mahal (Map p94; ☎ 8803 5444; Vanak Sq, Mollasadra Ave, 29 Sheikh Bahaei St; meals IR55,000) In the hotel of the same name, the Taj has a reputation for serving the best Indian food in Iran. The curries here are mouth-watering and there is a good range of vegetarian options. Pity about the location.

Monsoon (Map p110; ☎ 8879 1982; Gandhi Shopping Centre, Gandhi Ave; meals IR80,000; ☼ closed Fri) Monsoon has been around for several years now and has a reputation for the best Asian food in Tehran. The fare ranges from Thai curries to sushi, served in an intimate setting and complemented by exceptional service.

It's smart, sophisticated, relatively expensive and very new Tehran – menus only come in English.

Tandoor Restaurant (Map pp102-3; ☎ 8830 0873; Ardalan St; meals IR80,000; ☼ noon-3pm & 7-11pm) Under the Safir Hotel, the Tandoor has been popular in Tehran since before the revolution and is the most convenient place in the south to find a decent curry (when we ate, the lamb was far superior to the chicken), though if you want it hot, ask. There are a few vegetarian dishes for about IR35,000 each.

Bix (Map p110; ☎ 8878 8272; Gandhi Shopping Centre, Gandhi Ave; meals IR70,000-100,000; ☼ 12.30-4.30pm & 7pm-midnight Sat-Thu, 7pm-midnight Fri) Bix calls itself a Californian-Italian pizzeria, and that's not far from the truth. The indoor-outdoor setting, well-trained waiters and limited menu of gourmet pizzas and well-presented pastas, salads and meat dishes draw plenty of north Tehran's young and well-heeled.

Bistango (Map p110; ☎ 8855 4409; www.bistangorestaurant.com; Raamtin Residence Hotel, 1081 Valiasr Ave; meals about IR200,000; ☼ noon-3pm & 7-11pm) Arguably Tehran's best restaurant, Bistango's air of sophistication, refined service and relatively adventurous international cuisine keep Tehranis coming despite the wads of rial it costs them. For food, think honey Dijon salmon with garlic roasted potato and ratatouille (IR170,000). Lunchtime specials are just IR110,000.

VEGETARIAN RESTAURANTS

Some Tehranis have just said 'no' to kabab. Check out the www.iranvegetarians.com site for any new options.

Coffee Shop & Vegie Restaurant of Iranian Artists' Forum (Map pp102-3; ☎ 8831 0462; Batulshan St, off Iranshahr Ave; meals IR15,000-35,000; ☼ 11am-10pm) This dedicated vegetarian restaurant is excellent value and a good place to meet young, educated and artistic Tehranis. It's in a brick building at the southern edge of Park-e Tehran, and has an informal, busy ambience with young people coming and going. Owner Aman promised there would be no mystery meat in the salads (less than IR10,000), sandwiches (IR20,000), pizzas (IR25,000) or *khoresht* (IR18,000), among others.

ourpick Ananda Vegetarian Restaurant & Coffee Shop (Map p110; ☎ 2255 6767; South Ekhtiyarieh St, off 10th Behestan St, off Pasdaran St; meals IR35,000-60,000; ☼ 12.30-10.30pm) Way up in north Tehran the Ananda is a gem if you're a vegetarian, and delightful even if you're not. Run in association with the **Iranian Society of Vegetarians** (www.iranvegetarians.com), there's no chance of finding rogue bits of meat here and the food is both delicious and cheap. We can recommend the Ananda lasagne (IR35,000) and Ananda calzone (IR33,000), the freshly made salad (no plastic wrap!) and the service and setting. Come by taxi and ask for Pasdaran PTT – it's just next door.

Quick Eats

The *kababi* (kabab shop) might be under pressure from such foreign influences as the burger joint (Boof is the big Iranian chain) and pizzeria, but head to almost any major square and you'll find both a *kababi* and, usually, at least one fast food joint selling burgers, pizza and meat sandwiches. The area around Tehran Bazar also has felafel places.

Akbar Mashti Bastani (Map p94; Shahid Bahonar Ave; 10am-midnight) Akbar Mashti became famous for his ice cream in the 1950s and today his son continues to sell what he modestly describes as 'the most famous ice cream in Iran and the world'. Try the pistachio bastani (IR7000) and you'll probably agree. It's next to Bank Melli, about 150m east of Tajrish Sq.

For breakfast, you'll notice some low-key looking places selling big boiling pots full of *kalleh pache* (sheep brain and other offal). One such **kalleh pazi** (Map pp102-3; Mostafa Khomeini St) worth checking out is conveniently near to Amir Kabir St, off Baharestan Sq.

Self-Catering

No matter where you are, fresh fruit and vegetables and various types of flat bread won't be far away (see p79 for different types of bread). Small grocery stores stocking food such as tinned fish, Iranian fetta cheese, yogurt, fruit juices, cold meat, pasta, rice and shelves stacked with other staples are also common, except around Amir Kabir St. If you're in southern Tehran, head for the bazaar and Jomhuri-ye Eslami Ave, east of Ferdosi St.

More extravagant options exist in northern Tehran, including the luxury foods underneath the **Jaam-e Jam Shopping Centre** (Map p110; Valiasr Ave) and the tiny **Sanaee Coffee Shop** (Map p110; St 13, off Sanaee St) for a huge range of imported coffee.

Hiland Supermarket (Map p110; 8850 5701; Ahmed Qasir St, off Arzhantin Sq; 10am-10pm) This place is full of hard-to-find Western goods, such as coffee, baby products, pads and tampons, condoms, magazines and plenty of baby products. Look for the green façade just south of Arzhantin Sq.

Teahouses & Cafés

Almost all Iranian teahouses (*chaykhaneh*) also serve food, and in Tehran several of the best restaurants are actually teahouses. Tehran's café scene is also improving, with no shortage of trendy places attracting the Tehrani youth, mainly in the northern suburbs. In contrast to the traditional ambience of the *chaykhaneh*, most of Tehran's cafés are modern places serving an educated, relatively sophisticated youth who look for their influences in Europe more so than the Middle East. Which makes them fun places to hang out, meet people (many of whom will speak English) and get under the skin of modern Iran. Gandhi Ave is probably the café capital of Tehran, thanks in no small part to one complex full of cafés…

Sofrekhaneh Amol Mazandaran (Map pp102-3; 3394 1630; Amin Darbar Alley, off Amir Kabir St; 9am-10.30pm) Under the *mosaferkhaneh* of the same name, this underground place is the classic south Tehran local, with men eating cheap *dizi* (IR13,000), drinking tea (IR500) and smoking qalyan (IR10,000). A genuine working-class Tehran experience.

Ghaem Teahouse (Map p94; 0912 320 0113; Tajrish Sq; meals IR35,00-65,000; noon-midnight) Behind a curtain and up an unmarked stairwell on the southeastern corner of Tajrish Sq, this is an ideal, if somewhat pricey, place from which to watch the people and traffic carnage over tea, qalyan and dates (IR40,000, 4pm to midnight only). It also does the usual range of kababs.

our pick **Azari Traditional Teahouse** (Azari Coffeehouse; Map p94; 5537 6702; Valiasr Ave, near Rah-Ahan Sq; meals IR30,000-65,000; 7am-4.30pm & 8pm-midnight) About 250m north of Rah-Ahan Sq, this restored 'coffeehouse' in south Tehran is wonderfully atmospheric because it remains popular with locals, who use it as an unofficial community centre. The *dizi* and chicken kababs are rightly popular. A traditional band plays most evenings when the boisterous atmosphere is best enjoyed with a group, and bookings are recommended.

ourpick **Iranian Traditional Restaurant** (Agha Bozorg; Map pp102-3; ☎ 8890 0522; 28 Keshavarz Blvd; meals IR45,000; ☾ noon-midnight) This underground place is modern Iranian social interaction in microcosm, and full of young Iranians flirting, smoking and eating (in that order) under attractive vaulted and tiled ceilings. The *dizi* (IR24,000) and kababs are reliably good and well-priced for this location, though at busy times you won't be allowed to linger. It's tucked away down an ornately tiled staircase, just east of the Canon/Konica shop.

Sofre Khane Sonnati Sangalag (Map pp102-3; ☎ 6673 1075; Park-e Shahr; meals IR40,000-60,000; ☾ 9am-11pm) If you're visiting the museums or Golestan Palace, this is the place to stop for lunch (or tea). The green setting in Park-e Shahr, coupled with the relatively quiet space embellished with antique photographs, set the tone. *Dizi* and the *bademjan* (eggplant) dishes are recommended. Musicians sometimes play between noon and 3pm.

Sofreh Khane Ayyaran (Map pp102-3; ☎ 6676 0376; Enqelab Ave, off Ferdosi Sq; meals IR60,000; ☾ 11.30am-midnight) This subterranean *chaykhaneh* makes an attractive escape from the fumes of Ferdosi Sq, though prices are aimed at tour groups (ie, high). However, the large Iranian menu has some hard-to-find dishes and a couple that you might not expect in your standard Tehran basement, such as 'Submissive: IR25,000'. Apparently it's eggplant, master.

Khayyam Traditional Restaurant (Map pp102-3; ☎ 5580 0760; Khayyam St; meals IR60,000; ☾ lunch & dinner) About 200m south of the Khayyam Metro station and opposite the Imamzadeh Seyyed Nasreddin Mosque (look for the dome), this beautifully decorated restaurant is an oasis amid the chaos of the bazaar area. Originally part of the mosque, the 300-year-old building was separated when Khayyam St intervened. It was restored in 2002. The typically Iranian food (mainly kabab, chicken and fish) is well prepared and plentiful. But on this visit we felt service had dropped and the 15% service charge on top of all the extras you have to pay for is irritating. Still, for tea, qalyan and sweets (IR25,000) after an outing in the bazaar, it's hard to beat.

Gandhi Shopping Centre (Map p110; cnr Gandhi Ave & 4th St; ☾ 10am-11pm) Home to several cool little cafés peopled largely by young and fairly liberal Tehranis, this is your one-stop café-society stop. It's a fun place to hang out in the afternoon and evening; just choose a café you like, settle in and then perhaps eat in one of the centre's upscale restaurants.

Gandi 35 (Map (Map p110; ☎ 8878 1646; Gandhi Ave; ☾ 11am-11pm Sat-Thu, 5-11pm Fri) A few blocks north of the shopping centre, this hip café is equally popular and serves tasty and fair-value light meals with its range of coffee.

Cafe Naderi (Map pp102-3; ☎ 6670 1872; ☾ 10am-7.30pm Sat-Thu) Underneath the Hotel Naderi, this café has long been a favourite of intellectuals and artists. One traveller said the Naderi managed to perfectly create a bustling. yet disinterested, atmosphere, well suited to reading alone, people-watching and lingering over coffee. The décor is circa 1940s Paris. The fare is limited to Turkish and French coffee and perhaps a pastry or two. Don't expect any change from the grumpy-grandad waiters.

ourpick **Café Hafta-do Hasht** (78; Map pp102-3; ☎ 8891 9862-3; www.cafe78.com; 78 South Aban St [Shahid Azodi St], off Karim Khan Zand Ave; ☾ 4-11pm) One of the best places to get in touch with Tehran's hip young artistic community is this café. The coffee, wide range of teas and snacks are all good, and the downstairs Mehrva Gallery (p122) has regular exhibitions of Iranian contemporary art.

Café (Map p94; Bagh-e Ferdows, off Valiasr Ave; ☾ 2-11pm) In the lovely gardens of the Film Museum of Iran (p109), this chic café serves a wide range of expensive but very drinkable Italian coffees and light meals. It's an artsy, international scene.

Sanaee Coffee Shop (Map p110; St 13, off Sanaee St) Around the corner from Ikea, Sanaee makes and sells all manner of imported bean, and some of the richest and best chocolate milkshakes on earth (you be the judge).

ENTERTAINMENT

Although Iran has loosened up considerably since 1997, no-one's singing 'Tehran, Tehran…a city that never sleeps' just yet. All those nightclubs and discos lovingly described in guidebooks published before the revolution have long-since disappeared, and are unlikely to reappear anytime soon.

The one time when there is quite a lot of organised entertainment is over the 10 Days of Dawn (1 to 11 February), when you will be able to attend plays, films and concerts of traditional Iranian music as well as music from around the world.

At other times, keep your eyes on www .tehranavenue.com for upcoming theatre, cinema and arts events.

Cinema

For cinema Iranian-style, head for one of the old movie halls along southern Lalehzar St or eastern Jomhuri-ye Eslami Ave, in southern Tehran, or around Valiasr Sq, where films are shown about every two hours between 10am and 8.30pm for about IR5000 a show. All films will be in Farsi or dubbed into Farsi, and forget about seeing anything Kiarostami, Makhmalbaf or anything else remotely controversial.

You can see Iranian classics (with subtitles) at the Film Museum of Iran (p109). See www.tehranavenue.com for news on recent releases and p75 for more on Iranian film.

Galleries

The following are some of the most respected galleries in Tehran, with a rotating roster of mainly contemporary artists that reflects the growing local and international profile of Iranian contemporary art. Check the websites for the latest exhibitions.

Seyhoun Art Gallery (Map p110; ☎ 8871 1305; www .seyhounartgallery.com; No 6, 4th St, off Khaled Eslamboli; ⊙ 10am-6pm) In its 4th decade as a sponsor of young Iranian contemporary artists, Seyhoun has regular exhibitions of painting, photography, sculpture and graphic art in its distinctive, black-fronted gallery.

Mehrva Gallery (Map pp102-3; ☎ 8893 9046; www .mehrvagallery.com; 78 Shahid Azodi St, off Karim Khan Zand Ave; ⊙ 5-9pm) Below the popular Café Hafta-do Hasht (p121), English-speaking Mehrva's gallery exhibits contemporary art in a mix of media, but primarily painting and photography.

Silk Road Gallery (Map p94; ☎ 2272 7010; www .silkroadphoto.com; 112 Lavasani Ave, Farmanieh; ⊙ 11am-7pm Sat-Wed, 5-8pm Thu) Silk Road's primary focus is photographic art, but it also delves into other media. It's professionally run and a pleasure to visit.

Music

There is still much debate in Iran about the religious eligibility of organised public performances of modern music, so getting approval for a rock concert, for example, is prohibitively hard. They do sometimes happen but it's tough to find out where or when. Traditional and classical music is easier to find, though again dates are infrequent and not widely advertised in the English media. Your best bet is to call **Tezatre Shahr** (City Theatre; Map pp102-3; ☎ 6646 0595) and keep your eye on trusty www.tehranavenue.com.

For a guaranteed performance, head to a traditional restaurant or teahouse (see p117 for possibilities).

Nightclubs
Dream on.

Theatre

Tezatre Shahr (City Theatre; Map pp102-3; ☎ 6646 0595; cnr Valiasr & Enqelab Aves) The huge, circular Tezatre Shahr is Tehran's biggest and most impressive theatre and the place you're most likely to see Iranian stage actors at work – performing in Farsi, of course. The booking staff speak English so call them to find out what's coming up. Performances are normally at 6.30pm or 7.30pm and cost about IR25,000.

Sports

Iran's favourite sport is football (soccer), which is played at several smaller stadiums and the giant-sized, 100,000-capacity **Azadi Sports Stadium** (off Map p94; Karaj Hwy). Matches are normally played on Thursday and Friday but to find out where, your best bet is to ask a man working in your hotel. If you can make it to the big Tehran derby between Esteqlal and Persepolis, then do (see p50) – assuming you are not a woman, that is.

The Azadi complex also stages wrestling and even motor racing – though for the latter you could save your time and money and just sit in the middle of any Tehran traffic circle. Most other sports are played behind high walls in small stadia around the city.

SHOPPING

Souvenir shopping in Tehran is not as enjoyable as working your way through the atmospheric bazaars of Esfahan and Shiraz. However, the range in Tehran is bigger and the prices usually smaller. It's well worth giving yourself a half-day to wander through the Tehran bazar (p100), where if you can't find what you're looking for, a carpet salesman will almost certainly find it for you – after you've stopped for tea, of course.

The bazaar is an excellent place to shop for carpets, in particular, and buying here usually means you won't have to carry it around. Qalyans are also a good buy in the bazaar, where you'll get the genuine working article rather than the more elaborately decorated and expensive souvenir shop variety.

Souvenir shops, of course, can be found near or inside most midrange and top-end hotels. Other souvenir shop strips include Ferdosi St around Ferdosi Sq and Taleqani Ave (opposite the US Den of Espionage). Prices are 'fixed' but fall fast if you show any bargaining form.

Locals claim that Valiasr Ave is the world's longest thoroughfare and it's one of Tehran's major shopping districts. Ladies, this is also a good place to start looking for a *manteau* (overcoat). Stores around Valiasr Sq and Vanak Sq sell a decent selection, both in the long, conservative style and more trendy, shorter modes. You can expect to pay about IR150,000 for a standard *manteau*, up to IR2,000,000 for something 'sexier' in the boutiques of Afriqa Hwy, near Vanak Sq. Further south, both sides of Dr Labafinezhad St, just west of Valiasr Ave, are lined with women's clothing stores.

It might be surprising, but Tehran is a good place to shop for European-style clothes and shoes, which sell for a fraction of their cost back home. For shoes, women should head for the boutiques along Mozaffari St (Map pp102–3) in southern Tehran, while men can see the head-spinning choice on Enqelab Ave (Map pp102–3), east of Ferdosi Sq. For threads, see the stores on the corner of Jomhuri-ye Eslami Ave and Ferdosi St (Map pp102–3).

Hossein Hosseiny (☎ 0912 388 5994; trible_carpet _hosseiny@yahoo.com) If you can, catch Hossein Hosseiny between buying missions; we found this young man from a family of carpet *bazaris* to be straight up and offering fair prices on his mainly nomadic carpets. His small store is in the interesting little Serai Parsa bazaar (Map pp102–3), off Kababihah Alley, with merchants who usually supply to larger shops, so prices can be good – ask for directions.

Dusto-e (Map p110; ☎ 2205 0071; cnr Valiasr Ave & Saveh St; ☾ 9am-1.30pm & 3-9pm) The mother of all souvenir stores is Dusto-e, where the range is huge, prices high and quality probably better than average.

A car park near the corner of Jomhuri-ye Eslami Ave and Ferdosi St is also the location for the **Jameh Bazar** (Map pp102–3; Jomhuri-ye Eslami Ave; ☾ mornings Fri), where hawkers from across Central Asia lay out their rugs and sell whatever they can on Friday mornings. Be sure to go up to the higher floors, in the carpark itself, where some bargains can be found.

For modern Iranian music, the small store upstairs in the Gandhi Shopping Centre (p121) has a good range, and you can combine a trip with a coffee or meal.

GETTING THERE & AWAY

Tehran is the hub of almost all bus, train and air services. Every town and city of any size is directly linked to Tehran – always by bus, usually by air and increasingly by train too. Tickets from Tehran can sell fast so book as soon as you know when you're leaving.

Air

Tehran is Iran's main international hub. For information about routes and carriers, see p400. Every day there are flights between Tehran and almost every provincial capital in Iran. Iran Air flies most routes, with Iran's growing number of smaller airlines flying fewer routes, less often.

Almost all international services use **Imam Khomeini International Airport** (IKIA; Map p130; www.ikia.ir), 35km south of Tehran, the exceptions (for now) being flights from Damascus and some Saudi Arabian cities. Domestic flights use the old **Mehrabad International Airport** (Map p94; http://mehrabadairport.ir) on the western edge of the city. Taxi is the only link.

Routes and prices change regularly so check online before making firm plans. If you're in Iran, you're strongly advised to use a travel agency (p98) rather than an airline office.

AIRLINE OFFICES

Airline offices are generally open from about 9am to 4pm, Saturday to Wednesday, and Thursday morning.
Aeroflot (Map pp102–3; ☎ 8880 8480; 23 Nejatollahi St)
Air France (Map p110; ☎ 2204 4498; 12th fl, Sayyeh Bldg, cnr Valiasr Ave & Sayyeh St)

Air India (Map p110; ☎ 8873 9762; Sarafraz St)
Ariana Afghan Airlines (Map p110; ☎ 8855 0156; 1st fl, 29 Khaled Eslamboli St) Next door to Coco Restaurant.
Azerbaijan Airlines (Map p110; ☎ 8855 3335; Khaled Eslamboli St)
British Airways (Map p110; ☎ 2204 4552; 10th fl, Sayyeh Tower, cnr Valiasr Ave & Sayyeh St)
Emirates (Map p110; ☎ 8134 1480; 1211 Valiasr Ave)
Gulf Air (Map pp102-3; ☎ 2225 3284-7; Nejatollahi St)
Iran Air (Map pp102-3; ☎ 8880 8472; Nejatollahi St) Sells only international tickets; use a travel agent for domestic flights.
Iran Aseman (Map pp102-3; ☎ 8889 5568; www.iaa .com; Nejatollahi St)
KLM (Map p110; ☎ 2204 4757; 12th fl, Sayyeh Bldg, cnr Valiasr Ave & Sayyeh St)
Lufthansa & Austrian Airlines (Map p110; ☎ 8873 8701; 2 Sarafraz St, off Dr Beheshti Ave)
Qatar Airways (Map p110; ☎ 2201 5217-18; 2nd fl, Sayyeh Bldg, cnr Valiasr Ave & Sayyeh St)
Turkish Airlines (Map p110; ☎ 8874 8450; 239 Motahhari Ave)

INTERNATIONAL ARRIVALS
Customs and immigration procedures at IKIA are slow but generally hassle-free. Bags are usually X-rayed as you leave the baggage hall, but tourists are seldom hassled. Two banks in the arrivals hall can change money at good rates, which you'll need to do to pay for your taxi – there is no public transport from IKIA. The ladies at tourist information have simple maps but little else.

INTERNATIONAL DEPARTURES
The hardest part about leaving Tehran is getting to the airport on time. Unless your flight is very early or very late, give yourself well over an hour to get through the traffic from central Tehran, then at least 90 minutes to get through customs and immigration. Be sure to tell your taxi driver the correct airport (most likely IKIA). If you have changed money legally at a bank, and have a receipt to prove it, you can convert unused rials into cash euros.

Bus
Masses of buses link Tehran to just about every city and town in the country. Tehran has four bus terminals so you need to work out which station is best for your trip. For more general advice on bus travel, see p127.

Tickets are usually bought at the bus terminal, and with services to major destina-

tions leaving so frequently you don't usually need to book ahead. However, Iran's largest bus company **Iran Peyma** (Taavoni 1; Map pp102-3; ☎ 6671 9857; Ferdosi St; ⏰ 8.30am-4.30pm Sat-Wed, 8.30am-noon Thu) does have a conveniently central office near Ferdosi Sq that sells tickets.

The following tables show services to major destinations on direct buses from Tehran. Where only one price is listed it will be for a Volvo bus or similar; two prices are for *mahmooly*/Volvo.

CENTRAL TERMINAL (TERMINAL-E ARZHANTIN)
The **central terminal** (Arzhantin, Sayro Safar or Beyhaqi terminal; Map p110; ☎ 8873 2535; Arzhantin Sq) is accessible by taxis, shuttle taxis and local buses from around Tehran. All buses from this terminal are Volvos and prices are usually a little higher than other terminals. This list includes some departure times, though in most cases there will be more.

Destination	Fare	Duration	Departures
Bushehr	IR108,000	18-21hr	1.30pm
Esfahan	IR50,000	5-7hr	hourly
Kerman	IR74,000	15hr	3-8pm
Mashhad	IR71,000	14hr	4.30-7.30pm
Shiraz	IR75,000	13-15hr	2.45-8pm
Tabriz	IR60,000	9-10hr	9am, 8.30-10pm
Yazd	IR55,000	10hr	9pm

EASTERN TERMINAL (TERMINAL-E SHARGH)
The compact **eastern terminal** (off Map p94; ☎ 7786 8080) has buses to Khorasan province and the Caspian region. Hopefully Metro Line 2 will soon reach the terminal; otherwise, take a shuttle taxi to Imam Hossein Sq, and then another shuttle taxi, or try the trolleybus directly to the terminal. A private taxi will cost about IR40,000 from central Tehran. Iran Peyma and Taavoni 14 have the most services from this terminal. Prices here are for *mahmooly*/Volvo buses.

Destination	Fare	Duration	Departures
Gonbad-e	IR24,000/ 55,000	9hr	frequent Kavus 5am-noon; 5pm, 9pm & 11pm
Gorgan	IR22,000/ 50,000	7-8hr	3 per day
Mashhad	IR40,000/ 70,000	13-14hr	hourly 7am-noon; 2pm & 6pm
Sari	IR21,000/ 40,000	5hr	5.30am, 1-6pm

SOUTHERN TERMINAL (TERMINAL-E JONUB)

The huge, round **southern terminal** (terminal-e jonub; Map p94) has buses heading to the south and southeast of the city.

To get to the southern terminal take Metro Line 1 to Terminal-e Jonub (then walk about 300m) or grab a shuttle taxi south. Coming from here by taxi, prepare to spend some time negotiating a decent fare.

Departure times in the following table are the minimum you can expect, and where only one price is quoted it is for a Volvo or similar bus. Otherwise, prices are for *mahmooly*/Volvo buses.

Destination	Fare	Duration	Departures
Ahvaz	IR95,000	15hr	6pm (Iran Peyma)
Bandar Abbas	IR120,000	14-18hr	every 2hr 7.30am-6pm
Bushehr	IR120,000	18-21hr	10.30am, 2pm (Iran Peyma & T14)
Esfahan	IR26,000/ 50,000	7hr	hourly 6am-10pm
Kashan	IR15,000/ 25,000	3½hr	hourly
Kerman	IR90,000	14-16hr	6pm, 9pm 3pm, 4pm,
Qom	IR6000/ 10,000	1½hr	hourly
Shiraz	IR37,000/ 85,000	13-16hr	hourly 3-9pm
Yazd	IR33,000/ 45,000	10hr	several 4-10pm
Zahedan	IR120,000	19-23hr	every 2hr 8am-6pm

WESTERN TERMINAL (TERMINAL-E GHARB OR TERMINAL-E AZADI)

The **western terminal** (terminal-e gharb; Map p94; ☎ 4465 9695 ext 233) is the city's busiest terminal, catering for the Caspian region and western Iran, as well as international destinations including Ankara and İstanbul (in Turkey), Baku (in Azerbaijan) and Damascus (Syria).

To get here ask any westbound shuttle taxi 'Azadi?', then walk north to the huge terminal. Or take Metro Line 2 to Azadi and walk further from there. The terminal closes at 11pm.

Prices indicated in the following table are for *mahmooly*/Volvo buses.

Destination	Fare	Duration	Departures
Ardabil	IR38,000/ 69,000	10hr	hourly 6am-10.30pm
Astara	IR26,500/ 60,000	9hr	Ardabil bus
Chalus	IR18,500/ 40,000	6hr	every 15min
Hamadan	IR16,500/ 40,000	6hr	every 15-30min 6am-10.30pm
Kermanshah	IR27,000/ 60,000	9hr	every 30min 6am-8pm
Orumiyeh	IR39,500/ 80,000	12hr	hourly 4-9pm
Qazvin	IR6500/ 12,000	2-2½hr	every 15min
Rasht	IR15,500/ 35,000	5hr	every 30min 6am-10pm
Sanandaj	IR27,000/ 60,000	6-8hr	hourly 7am-10.30pm
Tabriz	IR26,500/ 60,000	9-11hr	hourly 6.30am-10.30pm

Minibus

A few towns in central Iran and nearby Caspian towns are linked to Tehran by minibus. Minibuses are about the same price as a bus and slower, but depart more frequently. They leave from designated sections within the eastern, southern and western terminals, depending on the destination.

Savari

Most towns within about three hours' drive of Tehran are linked by savari, including Amol, Sari, Kashan, Qom, Qazvin, Zanjan, Rasht and anywhere along the way. Prices are two to three times higher than the cheapest bus tickets, but are often worth paying so you can leave almost immediately (only four seats need to fill) and get there quickly; an excellent option for day trips. Savaris leave from designated sections usually just outside the appropriate bus terminals. For example, for Kashan they leave from the northeast corner of the southern terminal, savaris to Sari and Amol leave from outside the eastern terminal, and anything west to Qazvin or Zanjan from the Azadi terminal. Just say your destination and 'savari' and you'll soon be pointed in the right direction.

Train

Tehran is Iran's rail hub and many services start and finish at the impressive **train station** (Map p94; Rah-Ahan Sq) at the south end of Valiasr

Ave. Destinations and arrival and departure times are listed in English, and staff at **tourist information** (☎ 139) are walking timetables. For planning, use the excellent www.rajatrains .com website, which has up-to-date schedules and prices. Departures are punctual.

The train station is easy to reach in a shuttle taxi heading west from Imam Khomeini Sq; just ask for 'Rah Ahan'.

SCHEDULES

The prices and days of departure in the timetable listed here are liable to change; in particular, daily services in summer may well become much less frequent in winter.

Note that trains to Mashhad vary considerably in speed, comfort and price. The Ghazal train (IR198,000, three daily at 5pm, 7.50pm and 8.45pm, 11 hours) is best, followed by the oddly named Train Set (IR197,000, daily at 7am, allegedly taking only 7½ hours), Sabz (Green, IR179,000, daily at 6.55pm, 11½ hours), Simorgh (IR179,000, daily at 6pm, 11 hours), Turbo Train (IR148,000/128,000, daily at 8.25am, 8½ hours), Delijan (IR145,000, daily at 9.30pm, 11 hours), down through a range of sleepers to the all-seat service (IR26,150) at 10.45am, which doesn't arrive until 1am.

Prices shown are for 1st/2nd class unless stated on dedicated services only; it might also be possible to buy tickets to Yazd, for example, on the Bandar Abbas or Kerman trains – speak to the travel agent for details. For services to İstanbul and Ankara, see p404.

Destination	Fare	Duration	Departures
Ahvaz	IR104,600/ 23,400	15/17hr	5.15pm/ 10.40am
Bandar Abbas	IR88,700/ 215,000*	19hr	2.40pm/ 3.40pm
Esfahan	IR35,150	7½hr	11pm
Gorgan	IR39,750/ 26,500	10½hr	8.15pm
Kerman	IR63,150/ 158,000*	13hr	4.45pm, 3.40pm
Mashhad	see Schedules (above)		
Qom	IR4200	2½hr	3 daily
Sari	IR13,750	7hr	9.20am
Tabriz	IR139,000*/ 57,750/27,200	12hr	5.40pm, 7pm
Yazd	IR44,150	8hr	9pm, 10pm
Zanjan	IR14,500	4hr	4.40pm

*Ghazal six-berth couchette, 2nd-class seats only

BUYING TICKETS

You can buy tickets a month in advance at a travel agency – those on Nejatollahi St, among others, can sort you out. At the station you can only buy tickets for travel on the same day.

GETTING AROUND
To/From the Airport

Tehran's two airports have vastly differing transport infrastructures.

IMAM KHOMEINI INTERNATIONAL AIRPORT (IKIA)

After almost three years of operations, public transport remains a stranger to IKIA. You'll need to take a taxi. The price from the airport is a standard IR100,000, though hard bargainers might get it for a Khomeini (IR10,000) less. Going to IKIA the price depends on where you're coming from. From north Tehran, for example, you'll probably pay the full IR100,000, but from the south it should cost less. There are plans to extend Metro Line 1 (red) all the way to IKIA, but for now they remain just that – plans.

MEHRABAD INTERNATIONAL AIRPORT

The main domestic airport is nearer to town and better served by public transport. If you're confident, public buses (IR500) leave every 15 to 20 minutes from immediately outside the domestic terminal for Enqelab and Vanak Sqs.

Unless you're travelling light and know Tehran, however, it's wise to bite the bullet and pay for a private taxi. Fares are fixed but it's still best to use the taxi dispatcher, where they can tell you exactly how much you should pay.

A taxi to southern or central Tehran should cost about IR50,000, and up to IR80,000 to northern and eastern Tehran. If it's peak hour, the price will be higher, which is fair considering the trip will probably take twice as long.

If you want a shuttle taxi (about IR12,000 from the airport to the city centre), ask around or tell a taxi driver *na dar baste* (no closed door), and he will look for other passengers going the same way; it costs more for door-to-door.

A final option is to take a taxi (about IR15,000) to Azadi Metro station and go underground from there.

Car & Motorcycle

If you're driving in Tehran, try to put out of your mind everything you've ever learned about road rules – none of it applies here. Out of a basic instinct for survival you'll soon assimilate to the lawless aggression of the locals and be driving with 100% attention – and 180-degree vision – at all times; see p380 for details.

One adrenalin-inducing way to get across town in a hurry is on a motorcycle taxi. You'll see them loitering on corners all over town, though the corner of Jomhuri-ye Eslami Ave and Ferdosi St is a good place to look for one going north. They cost as much as taxis but take half the time. Good luck!

CAR RENTAL

It's not only difficult to find a car without a driver, but usually unnecessary too. There is little incentive when you can get a car and English-speaking driver for less than a car alone. Any of the travel agencies listed under Tours (p415) will be able to lease you a car with a driver. If you really must drive yourself, **Europcar** (☎ 5567 8316) at IKIA rents out cars from IR440,000 a day.

For private hire the cost depends on many variables, not least whether you want an English-speaking driver who can double as a guide – but reckon on paying between US$50 and US$80 a day.

One highly recommended driver-cum-translator is **Ali Taheri** (☎ 4443 1105, 0912-134 9345; service_taheri@yahoo.com). Ali speaks English and knows Tehran (and much of its history) well. He and his air-con Peugeot will cost you €50 a day, and he can also arrange tours to other parts of Iran, in his or larger vehicles.

Just about any taxi (indeed, any car) in Tehran is available for hire (known locally as taxi service, agence or dar baste). To charter a newish Peugeot for the day would probably cost about US$40 to $50; to charter a Paykan in worse condition costs from about US$25 to $30 – it all depends on your bargaining skills, and how far you plan to go.

Public Transport

BUS

Buses cover virtually all of Tehran, but as they're often crowded and slow, most travellers end up using taxis. Buses run from roughly 6am until 10pm or 11pm, finishing earlier on Friday and public holidays. Tickets cost slightly more than nothing – IR200. You buy them from ticket booths near bus stops or at bus terminals, and then give them to the driver when you board the bus; see the boxed text (p413) for bus travel etiquette.

Buses normally travel from one local bus terminal to another, so you may need to take more than one. Major bus departure points you might use include Imam Khomeini Sq, from where buses go in all directions; the terminal on the opposite side of Imam Khomeini Ave from the National Museum of Iran, for the west (Map pp102–3); Arzhantin, Vanak and Valiasr Sqs, for the north; Azadi Sq, for further west; and Rah-Ahan Sq, for the far south.

Buses never show their destinations in English and numbering is inconsistent. However, if you ask at the station or bus stop, you'll be pointed to the right bus. Some handy routes going north–south include Arzhantin Sq to Tajrish Sq; Imam Khomeini Sq to Arzhantin Sq; Imam Khomeini Sq to Tajrish Sq; and Valiasr Sq to Tajrish Sq.

Private bus companies began operating in 2006, with newer, more comfortable and faster buses for a flat IR1000 cash fare. Azadi Sq to Tajrish was the first route, and expect more.

METRO

Tehran's ambitious underground railway network, the **Tehran Metro** (www.tehranmetro.com), will eventually service much of the city (see the boxed text, p128). However, at the time of writing only sections of Line 1 (or the red line), Line 2 (navy blue) and all of Line 5 (green) were operating,

Tickets cost IR1000 per journey and slightly more on Line 5. Tickets have magnetic strips and are valid for a single journey, 10 journeys (probably the best for travellers), one day, three days or seven days; longer stored-value cards are also available. Trains start at about 6am and stop around 10pm or 10.30pm, running most frequently at peak hours. Station announcements are in Farsi only, so keep an eye on the English maps inside the trains.

The Metro website has extensive information about bus links to its various stations around town.

TEHRAN

Line 1 (Red)

For now, the red line is by far the most useful for travellers. It runs from Haram-e Motahar (Imam Khomeini's tomb) in the south to Mirdamad in the north, via the main junction of Imam Khomeini Sq. More importantly, the Metro PR people assured us the northern extension to Tajrish Sq would be completed in 2009, so getting up to the northern palaces and Darband will be much, much easier, cheaper and faster.

Heading south, Line 1 stops at Terminal-e Jonub, Rey and Shohada, for the Behesht-e Zahra martyrs cemetery, but not yet Imam Khomeini International Airport.

Line 2 (Dark Blue)

Line 2 runs from Tehran (Sadeghieh) in the west, where it connects with Line 5 to Karaj, to Dardasht in the east. It connects to Line 1 at Imam Khomeini Sq, and is handy to the Amir Kabir St cheap hotels (Mellat Metro station). The eastern extension should be completed by the time you read this, meaning it will run all the way to Terminal-e Gharme (the western bus terminal), providing a fast link to Imam Khomeini Sq and western Tehran, where Azadi station is within walking distance of Azadi Sq.

Line 3 (Light Blue)

Line 3 is the one Tehranis are praying for. Running from satellite town Islamsharh in the south to the far northeastern suburbs, Line 3 will be most useful for both Tehranis and travellers because it includes a section from the train station (Rah Ahan) north along mega-crowded Valiasr Ave before veering east underneath Dr Beheshti Ave. It will connect with Line 2, Line 4 and Line 1 (at Shahid Beheshti), and hopefully take thousands of cars off Valiasr Ave.

Line 4 (Yellow)

Work for Line 4 began in 2005 and the first stations are scheduled to open in 2008, with the whole line completed by 2013. This east–west line will eventually run from the western terminal (Azadi terminal) underneath Enqelab Ave to Tehran's eastern suburbs. The western leg will be most useful to travellers, with a spur running to Mehrabad airport.

TEHRAN METRO: A CITY'S SAVIOUR

It's no overstatement to say the Tehran Metro is the only hope of salvation for a city literally choking to death on chronic pollution and endless traffic jams.

Tehran's Metro was first proposed in 1974 and French companies had begun work when the revolutionary government cancelled the contracts in 1981, with just 2km of tunnel completed. It wasn't until 1999 that the first line (Line 5) was eventually opened. By then everyone agreed Tehran's congestion problems had become critical and, in some ways, even life-threatening. With four-hour commutes for trips of less than 20km not uncommon, traffic had begun to affect all aspects of Tehran life. By the early 2000s almost US$600 million a year was being spent on new tunnels and stations.

In 2000 the first sections of Line 2 were opened, followed by sections of Line 1 in 2001 and 2002. Tehranis flocked to the Metro and a shortage of carriages meant that during peak hours just getting on was a test of strength (it's only marginally better today). Inside the carriages became a frotteur's paradise. But while women are free to ride in any carriage, the front carriage of every train is women only, allowing them to avoid groping men.

Despite the money and collective willpower of 15 million desperate Tehranis, progress has been slow. By 2008 Lines 1 and 2 had still not been completed, and work on Lines 3 and 4 had only just begun. The grand plan calls for more than 10 lines to eventually criss-cross the city.

When we dropped in for tea the urbane Metro guys explained that the full network would probably not be completed for another 20 years. But even at this relatively early stage, the benefits of the Metro are plain to see. Already more than 1 million people are using the Metro every day, saving countless millions on fuel, productivity and health costs, not to mention the reduced pollution and stress born of not being stuck in Tehran traffic. The Metro is expected to account for half of all journeys in metropolitan Tehran by 2015 and the plan is to have a staggering 370km of tunnel completed by 2020 – longer than the New York subway.

TEHRAN

Line 5 (Green)
The completed Line 5 is largely above ground and is, in effect, an extension of Line 2. It runs from Tehran (Sadeghieh) out past Karaj to Golshahr.

MINIBUS
Crowded public minibuses are found in the suburbs and most travellers are unlikely to need them. If you do, finding the right minibus is not easy, so ask, ask and ask again. The place you're most likely to need one is going north of Tajrish Sq; for an idea of prices, the trip from Tajrish to Darakeh or Tochal costs IR1000.

TROLLEYBUS
An electric trolleybus runs between the eastern bus terminal and Khorasan Sq.

Taxi
Tehran taxis come in a variety of colours that, in theory, govern what services they can offer. In practice, however, it's anything goes. The vast majority of taxis are Paykans, many of them shitboxes of the first order. Then there is every other car on Tehran's roads, almost all of which have the potential to be a taxi if the driver needs the rial.

PRIVATE TAXI
Yellow taxis are supposed to be private taxis, but any empty car will usually take you *dar baste* if you ask; just say, for example, 'Meydan Azadi *dar baste*'. The alternative is to get your hotel to call a 'wireless taxi' (☎ 133), which cost a little more. You could also call the **Women's Taxi Company** (☎ 1821), whose green taxis are driven by women, for women passengers only, and when you call to book you'll speak only to women then, too.

Unless you're familiar with the going rates, agree on a price before setting out. In Tehran most drivers won't go anywhere for less than IR10,000, and will push prices up in lots of IR5000 or IR10,000 for longer trips. Negotiation is encouraged.

Sample fares include the following: Imam Khomeini Sq to Valiasr Sq for about IR15,000/25,000 in off-peak/peak hour; and Imam Khomeini Sq to Tajrish Sq about IR40,000/60,000. To hire a taxi for an hour or so to visit several sites should cost about IR50,000, so long as they're not too distant.

To get from southern Tehran to the north, even in a private taxi, takes a minimum of half an hour, much longer in peak hour when prices rise accordingly.

Meter taxis do exist, but we've yet to see a meter actually working.

SHUTTLE TAXI
Taxi fares in Tehran are higher than elsewhere in Iran. The minimum fare is IR1000 for one or two *meydans* (squares) of travel, climbing to about IR7000 for the longest trips. Watch what other passengers are paying and you'll soon get an idea of the going rate.

Shuttle taxis ply main thoroughfares between major *meydans* and the best way to use them is to learn the names of the *meydans* and know which one you want to go to. *Meydans* such as Imam Khomeini, Vanak, Valiasr, Tajrish, Arzhantin, Azadi, Ferdosi, Enqelab, Haft-e Tir, Rah-Ahan and Imam Hossein are major shuttle-taxi hubs. However, even these *meydans* may have several ministations for shuttle taxis heading in different directions. You might be lucky and get a shuttle taxi all the way from, say, Valiasr Sq to Tajrish Sq (IR6000), but often you will have to change at Vanak Sq. Metro stations also have plenty of loitering shuttle taxis.

When trying to hail a shuttle taxi, don't bother with anything in any language along the lines of 'Iran Hotel, on the corner of…': the driver will have lost interest after the word 'hotel', picked up someone else and be halfway there before you know it. Use a major landmark or a town square as a destination, even if you are getting off before then. Shout it quickly and loudly: 'FeDOSe!' will do for Ferdosi St or Sq; similarly, 'eHESHTe!' for Beheshti St or Sq; and so on. The driver will either ignore you, or give you a quick beep on the horn and pull over for half a second while you leap in. For more on shuttle taxis and where to sit, see p413.

AROUND TEHRAN

Away from the hyperactive streets of the capital are several easily accessible day trips and ski slopes, and the highest mountain in the Middle East.

HOLY SHRINE OF IMAM KHOMEINI

حرم امام خميني

When future generations look back on the historical periods of Iran, the early years of the Islamic Republic will be remembered as a time of great endeavour on the building front. This, the resting place of His Holiness Imam Khomeini, is the grandest of those endeavours. But while the scale of the **Holy Shrine of Imam Khomeini** (Map p130; ⏲ 24hr) is quite enormous, for the time being it looks more like a shoddily built and empty aircraft hangar than one of Iran's holiest sites.

The shrine is located between Tehran, the town that launched the 1979 revolution, and Qom, where the great man underwent his theological training. It's enormous and flanked by four 91m-high towers symbolising Khomeini's age when he died. The huge gold central dome is adorned with 72 tulips, which symbolise the 72 martyrs who fought and died with Imam Hossein in Karbala.

The shrine itself is inside a stainless steel *zarih*, a cage-like casing through which pilgrims pay their respects and no small number of bank notes. Men and women must approach from different sides. It's surrounded by a vast empty expanse of concrete, that's often covered with large carpets, and where families have picnics, kids roll coins along the floor and homeless men sleep. The ayatollah wanted his shrine to be a public place where people could enjoy themselves, rather than a mosque where they must behave with reverence, and but for the megalomaniacal architecture, his wishes have largely been met.

Outside the shrine are a few shops selling simple food and souvenirs and an adjoining Islamic university.

Getting There & Away

The last stop on Tehran Metro Line 1 (red) is Haram-e Motahar, the holy shrine, and at just IR1000 it is by far the best way to get here. Shuttle taxis and buses do make the trip, but why would you bother? The second last stop is Shohada, for the Behesht-e Zahra martyr's cemetery, and most people see both on one trip.

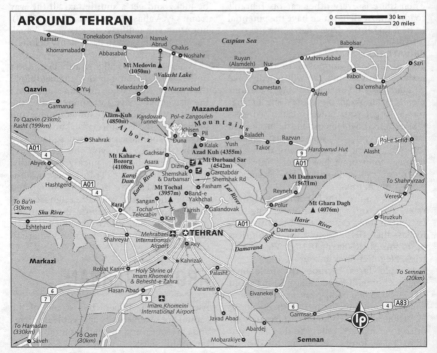

AROUND TEHRAN

TEHRAN

THE FUNERAL OF AYATOLLAH KHOMEINI

In 1989, the Islamic Republic's final send-off for its founder and inspiration, Ayatollah Khomeini, culminated in the largest funeral ever held in the world – a crush of 10 million inconsolable mourners. It was a chaotic scene. As the hearse tried to move through the crowd towards the cemetery it was stopped repeatedly before the crowd eventually took the coffin and started passing it over their heads. By the time a helicopter was summoned it was too late and even the armed Komiteh guards couldn't stop the body falling out of the coffin, and the crowd trying to tear pieces off the shroud to keep as holy relics.

Unless you thrive on chaos, you're advised not to come here on or around 4 June, the anniversary of the ayatollah's death, when hundreds of thousands of mourners visit the shrine.

BEHESHT-E ZAHRA   بهشت زهرا

Behesht-e Zahra is the main resting place for those who died in the Iran–Iraq War (1980–88). It is the sheer scale of the death represented here that is most moving. For some visitors, the roughly 200,000 glass boxes will be familiar from the TV and newspaper images from the '80s depicting hysterical mourners surrounded by countless portraits of the dead. Like windows into another time, these small, glass boxes on stilts contain a watch, a knife, maybe a letter that belonged to the lost father/son/husband staring out from a yellowed photograph. The pine trees have grown since then, but the faces remain. It's a haunting experience that brings home some of the horrific cost of war.

Right at the heart of the cemetery is a shrine to Iranian pilgrims killed during the annual haj (pilgrimage to Mecca), when Saudi Arabian soldiers opened fire on a crowd during the mid-1980s. Elsewhere, the graves of ordinary people stretch on for kilometres.

A visit here is usually combined with a trip to the Holy Shrine of Imam Khomeini. Behesht-e Zahra is packed on mourning days but is eerily empty at other times.

REY   ری

One of the most historically important places in Tehran province is Rey. In the 11th and 12th centuries Rey was a major centre that was much larger than Tehran, but it was devastated when the Mongols swept through. These days it has been swallowed up by the urban sprawl of the capital, but retains enough history to give it a different sensibility – one best experienced by just wandering around on foot.

The main attraction is the **Imamzadeh Shah-e Abdal-Azim**, built for a descendant of Imam Hossein. This mausoleum has elaborate tilework, a golden dome, a pool in the courtyard, a 14th-century sarcophagus with intricate carvings, constructed from betel wood, and enough mirror tiles to make you dizzy. In the same complex is a shrine to Imam Hamzeh (brother of Imam Reza). Women need to wear a chador, which are available at the entrance.

Rey's other attractions include the remains of the Sassanid **Qal'-e Tabarak**, a fortress on a nearby hill; the 12th-century **Gonbad-e Toghoral**, the 20m-high tomb tower of a Seljuk king in the town centre; and the **Cheshmeh Ali** mineral springs, with some Qajar-period **carvings** nearby.

Getting There & Away

Shahr-e Rey (City of Rey) station is easily reached heading south on Metro Line 1. Taxis can be hired in Rey for a negotiable IR30,000 per hour, or take a tour organised by your hotel.

MT DAMAVAND   کوه دماوند

Shaped like Mt Fuji, **Mt Damavand** (5671m) is the highest mountain in the Middle East. It's easily accessible from Tehran, although it is actually in Mazandaran province. Damavand has many mythological tales associated with it but in reality it is a dormant volcano that still belches out sulphuric fumes strong enough to kill unfortunate stray sheep. Its image is one of the most recognisable icons in Iran, appearing on the IR10,000 note, on bottles of Damarvand spring water and numerous other commercial items.

Most people who go to Damavand do so to climb the peak, and start by heading to Reyneh. The climbing season is from June to September, or May and October for experienced climbers.

Reyneh   رینه

The pretty village of Reyneh offers fine views of villages on the far side of the valley and makes a jumping-off point for local walking trails, even if you don't want to climb the mountain. There is no hotel, but if you ask around someone will put you up in their home for about IR65,000 per person and put you in touch with a local guide.

The best place to get information about routes and guides is the **Reyneh Mountain Federation Hut**, on the right (northeastern) side of the main road as you drive into town.

The excellent blog at http://damavand mt.blogspot.com blog has more recent detail than we can include here because it is run by the Azad Group of Iranian mountaineers. It might have details of a new camp and jumping-off point planned for Polur, nearer to Tehran. It has maps, GPS points and links to tours.

Climbing the Mountain

This section describes the classic southern route. From a technical point of view, Damavand is basically a walk-up. Climbing so far so quickly is the most dangerous aspect of this climb. As you ascend be sure to watch out for signs of altitude sickness – dizziness, headaches, nausea and swollen fingers – which kills people here every year. Most first-timers use a guide. One Reyneh-based guide recommended by readers is **Reza Faramarzpour** (☎ 0122-325 2270), who has climbed the mountain countless times and, while he speaks limited English, has a network of people to get you to the mountain and upwards. He charges about US$200 for an all-inclusive two-day tour, excluding the US$50 mountain fee foreigners must pay, during summer, at Gusfand Sara or Base Camp. See p372 for other reliable guides and companies.

Damavand can be climbed in two or three days, though readers report the three-day option is preferable as it allows more time for acclimatisation, and means fewer headaches.

Starting at Reyneh, you can walk (four or five hours) or take a pickup to 'Camp 2', aka Gusfand Sara or Base Camp (about IR25,000), where you can sleep in the Saheb Azaman Mosque. On a two-day itinerary, you'd drive here, then walk about four hours to Barghah-e-Sevvom (4250m), bet-

ter known as 'Camp 3'. Camp 3 has a mountaineers' hut and clean water is available. There's no water en route so you should bring some up with you. There's no way of booking the hut, and on Thursday nights and holidays it is packed with students from Tehran. Bringing a tent, sleeping bag and perhaps a stove (and leaving it there during the final ascent) is strongly recommended, though one reader reported hiring a tent at the shelter. Even in July, nights are freezing and it can be -10°C at the summit. A reader recommends filling water bottles in the evening since the water will be frozen when you get up.

In August you should be able to climb to the peak without special equipment. It's another four to five hours back to the hut from the peak. The summit doesn't require any technical gear but it does require fitness, warm clothes and good-quality hiking boots for the treacherously loose rocks. Bear in mind that the weather can change suddenly and snowfalls are a possibility, even in high summer. Most people return from the summit to Tehran, via a taxi from Reyneh, in one day.

Hot Springs

After expending all that energy climbing Mt Damavand, you'll be pleased to know that just 4km east of Reyneh, at **Ab Karm**, several hotels have been built around hot springs. You can rent a room for the night for around US$15, including breakfast, tea and a dip in one of the baths.

Getting There & Away

The easiest way to get to Reyneh is by taxi *dar baste* for about IR165,000. Alternatively, take a savari or minibus from Tehran's eastern bus terminal towards Amol and get off at the junction to Reyneh (tell the driver 'Reyneh'). From the junction, where there is a decent restaurant, take a shuttle taxi to Reyneh.

ALBORZ SKI RESORTS

Skiing in the Alborz Mountains above Tehran can be one of the most unexpected pleasures of a trip to Iran. There are four resorts within day-trip distance, all of which have equipment for hire and are extraordinarily cheap for a day on the slopes.
Darbansar (day pass IR60,000; ☼ 8.30am-3.30pm Jan-Mar),

near Shemshak, has three easy slopes and is best for beginners; while the slopes and resort at **Tochal** (☎ 021-2240 4001-5; www.tochal.org; day pass weekday/weekend IR60,000/80,000; r US$40-120; ☯ 8.30am-3.30pm) are accessed via the Tochal Telecabin (p113) in northern Tehran. The pick of the bunch, however, are Shemshak and Dizin.

Shemshak شمشک

☎ 0221 / elev 2450m

Just up the valley from Darbansar, **Shemshak Resort** (day pass IR140,000; ☯ 8.30am-3.30pm Jan-Mar) has the slopes that will get hardcore skiers most excited. There are six lifts, the longest being about 1450m with a vertical descent of about 500m (some of it at an adrenalin-inducing 45-degree angle) and plenty of moguls. Snowboards are welcome. Boots, skis and poles can be hired for IR100,000 a day.

The après-ski scene here has been described as 'out-of-control and mind-boggling', but this is Iran so you'll need to know someone, or meet someone on the slopes, to be invited to these private parties.

Shemshak is, in effect, a series of villages in a steep-sided valley. It has a lively café scene and lodging is usually in an apartment, which can be rented from local agents for about IR500,000/600,000 a night in summer/winter, or for more from agents in Tehran. Mid-week is cheaper.

Dizin دیزین

☎ 0262 / elev 2700m

The largest field in Iran and home to Iranian skiing, **Dizin Resort** (day pass IR150,000-400,000; ☯ 8.30am-3.30pm Dec-Apr) has more lifts than Shemshak but the runs aren't as difficult. Still, with a vertical drop of about 900m it should appeal to anyone feeling the need for speed. With base camp at about 2700m and the upper slopes about 3500m, skiing is usually possible from December until April. From the base, you take an antique-looking gondola to the mid-station, and another to the top. A third gondola ferries you to the eastern slopes. There are also six Poma lifts, two chairlifts and a T-bar around the mountain.

Pistes are sometimes groomed and there is plenty of scope for off-piste if you get a fresh snowfall. Apart from Friday, waiting for lifts is not really an issue. Hiring skis can be a lottery, starting at about IR80,000 and climbing as high as IR250,000. If you do hire a guide, they will ensure you get decent skis.

Dizin boasts summer activities such as grass-skiing, hiking, horse riding and tennis, mainly on weekends.

SLEEPING & EATING

Dizin Tourist Hotel (Hotel Jahangardi; ☎ 0262-521 2978; d/tr/5-bed r US$53/71/119; P 🖳) This is one of only two hotels in Dizin itself – right at the bottom of the hill. The recently renovated rooms aren't bad and those in the main building have better views. Four-/five-bed villas are also available for US$230/264.

Gajereh Resort (☎ 0261-521 2232; www.gajereh -hotel.com; r US$60; P 🖳) About 2km down the road to Tehran, the Gajereh Resort is one of several unstylish resort-style places serving Dizin.

Getting There & Away

Local travel agencies sell one- and two-day trips that include transport, accommodation and lift passes for reasonable prices (tours booked through foreign agencies are ludicrously expensive considering the costs). Look for trips advertised in English-language newspapers, or ask at your hotel; Hamid at the Firouzeh Hotel (p115) can help with budget trips.

Shemshak and Dizin are linked by an unsealed mountain road but it's closed for most of the time between late November and May. Instead, you'll need to take the Chalus road to get to Dizin, which is then 123km or roughly 2½ hours' drive from Tehran. In winter you'll need chains or a 4WD for the last 10km or so.

Shemshak and Darbansar are about 55km north of Tehran on much more direct Shemshak Rd, which links to Dizin via the aforementioned summer road. Getting to Shemshak by taxi should cost between IR80,000 and IR120,000, depending on how far away you are. Getting back to Tehran should be cheaper.

Shuttle taxis or minibuses also serve Shemshak from Tehran's eastern bus terminal.

Western Iran
ایران غربی

WESTERN IRAN

From paddy fields to blizzards to the original Garden of Eden, this region will shatter your preconceptions of Iran. Standing at the frontiers with Mesopotamia and Turkey, western Iran has witnessed many of civilisation's great empires, fortunes oscillating between trading glories and military decimation. The deeply hospitable region lacks the iconic gem-city sites of central Iran so it's often skipped by first-time Western visitors. But that makes it all the more appealing for those who relish delving a little deeper and being the 'only tourist'.

Western Iran is a linguistic and cultural patchwork: Kurds predominate in Kordestan and Kermanshah provinces; Lors in Ilam and Lorestan; Arabs inhabit southern Khuzestan; Talesh and Gilaki are the traditional languages of Gilan (the southwest Caspian hinterland); and Azaris whose language is more Turkish than Persian, predominate in the rest of the northwest. In the most remote regions, and more generally in Kurdish towns, traditional dress is still worn.

The chapter starts by the Turkish border. It loops around Lake Orumiyeh to Tabriz, continues through the Azari heartlands to Ardabil and down the Caspian coast via Rasht to Chalus. After Qazvin, Soltaniyeh and Zanjan we consider the central mountains, Kordestan and the historical cities of Kermanshah and Hamadan before descending the former 'Royal Road' towards ancient Shush, Shushtar and Choqa Zanbil.

HIGHLIGHTS

- Hike between flower-filled valleys and snowcapped peaks amid the ruined 12th-century **Castles of the Assassins** (p182)
- Challenge Iran's desert image in the paddy fields and forests of Gilan that lead to the delightful stepped village of **Masuleh** (p171)
- From **Jolfa** (p156) explore ancient churches, mud-walled castles and grand canyons along the biblical **Aras River Valley** (p157)
- Stagger up to **Babak Castle** (p159), the dramatic emotional heart of Azarbayjan
- Venture into **Howraman** (p194), a magical, rarely visited valley of traditional Kurdish villages
- Be awed by lonely **Choqa Zanbil's** (p215) massive, brick ziggurat which somehow managed to get 'lost' for 2500 years
- Cross sparsely populated mountainscapes from Zanjan to reach the ruins of **Takht-e Soleiman** (p187), history's foremost Zoroastrian temple complex
- Potter about between the fairy-chimney homes of **Kandovan** (p155), Iran's mini-Cappadocia

★ Jolfa
★ Aras River Valley
★ Babak Castle
★ Kandovan
Masuleh ★
Takht-e ★ Soleiman
★ Castles of the Assassins
★ Howraman
★ Choqa Zanbil

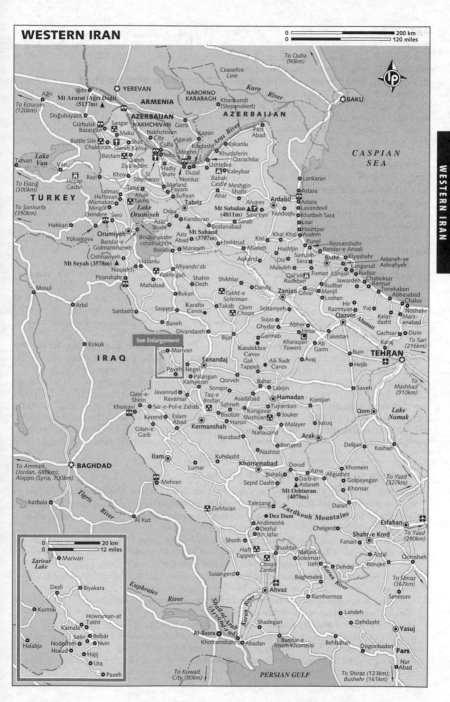

WESTERN IRAN

BAZARGAN

بازرگان

☎ 0462

Car repair yards, shops and nine cheap hotels line Bazargan's Imam St, a gun-barrel straight strip fired towards the striking silhouette of Mt Ararat. About 2km short of the immigration posts, the village ends at the outer border gate. Here the taxi/savari stand faces the basic **Hotel Jafapoor** (☎ 337 2058; Imam St; dm/tw IR20,000/40,000) whose owner is excited to show off his modest English skills and changes money. **Hotel Hamid** (☎ 337 2435; Imam St; tw IR130,000), 300m further east, is somewhat better and has bathrooms with squat toilets.

Locals pay IR10,000 to Maku but taxis ask way more from foreigners.

Ten kilometres along the Bazargan–Maku road, a muddy 2km track leads north towards Sangar past **Farhad Dameh**, a passingly interesting Urartian cave-dwelling with church-like niches and fine views of Ararat.

MAKU

ماکو

☎ 0462 / pop 39,600

Boxed into a soaring rocky canyon, central Maku has a handful of minor sights and makes a sensible base for visiting the old Armenian church of Qareh Kalisa. Long a key fortress and citadel guarding the Ottoman-Persian frontier, Maku was one of many Azerbaijani khanates that gained semi-independence in the chaotic period following the death of Nadir Shah

in 1749. Although rejoining Iran in 1829, the khanate was only finally abolished a century later.

Orientation & Information

Shops and all hotels are within 500m of little Chahara Sq on central Imam St. **Coffeenet Dade Pardazan** (Imam St; internet per hr IR8000; ☯ 10am-last customer) is almost opposite the Tourist Inn, 400m west. The bus terminal is 3km southeast.

Sights

The sad, crumbling remnants of Old Maku's former **citadel** lead up to the **Abu Fazl Mosque** and a series of degraded brick **fortifications** cupped beneath an impressively huge cliff overhang. Fine views justify the sweaty 25-minute hike on steps and footpaths directly north from Chahara Sq.

The celebrated but empty **Kola Ferangi** is a century-old mansion with filigree wrap-around balconies, hidden away in a ruined garden accessed through the unmarked grey gates of a clinic on Taleqani St, just north of Chahara Sq.

The attractive **Baqcheh Juq Palace Museum** (☎ 324 3719; admission IR4000; ☯ 9am-1pm & 3-5pm Tue-Sun) was originally built for the *sardar* (military governor) of Qajar Shah Muzaffar al-Din (1896–1907). Eclectically furnished rooms with colourful, quaintly tacky fruit murals are set around a wonderfully over-the-top mirror-tiled atrium. It's set in a walled orchard at the base of

---

CROSSING THE TURKISH BORDER AT BAZARGAN

Travelling solo, crossing here usually takes under an hour. The hill-top **immigration posts** (☯ 24hr) are 2km above Bazargan village, IR2000/1000 (plus IR1000 for bags) by shared taxi/minibus. They're just 600m from **Gürbulak** in Turkey (no facilities). The nearest Turkish-side accommodation is 40km east in Doğubayazıt famous for its 1784 Işak Paşa palace.

Eastbound from Doğubayazıt to Gürbulak take a dolmuş (minibus; 3YTL, 25 minutes, last 5pm) from the junction of Ağrı and Sehiltik Sts, 100m east of the Karahan Petrol Ofisi station (where Ağrı dolmuşlar wait). That's about five minutes' walk from Doğubayazıt's little bus terminal and cheap hotels. Westbound buses from Doğubayazıt to Erzerum (17YTL, four hours) via Ağrı (5YTL, one hour, 20 minutes) leave at 12.30am, 3pm and 4.30pm.

Arriving in Iran during office hours you're likely to be welcomed by a charming Iranian tourist officer. The bank within the Iran-side customs building offers full rial rates for US dollars and euros. They won't change UK pounds nor Turkish lira for which you'll have to risk the scam-a-lot freelance tricksters outside or more safely ask hoteliers in Bazargan village. Beware that anywhere else in Iran except Orumiyeh, Turkish lira are effectively worthless.

Well-connected Tabriz guide-fixer **Hossein Ravaniyar** (www.iranoverland.com; p149) is experienced at sorting out motorists' border formality problems.

appealing, tree-dappled Baqcheh Juq village whose timeless hay-topped mud houses are backed by a rugged chasm. It's 2km off the main Bazargan road, about 7km west of Chahara Sq from which yellow savaris charge IR1500.

Sleeping & Eating

Hotel Alvand (☎ 322 3491; Imam St; s/tw IR45,000/ 60,000) Just west of Chahara Sq, the Alvand is the most inviting of Maku's several cheap offerings. Rooms are well kept and management understands a little English, but the one shower has limited availability and upstairs shared toilets are out of action.

Makoo Tourist Inn (Mehmansara Jahangardi; ☎ 322 3212; fax 322 3184; tw/ste US$20/30, winter US$16/24; **P**) Appealingly quiet, the Tourist Inn is a green three-storey block set well back off Imam St. Despite a little peeling paint the rooms are by far Maku's classiest option, with hot shower, squat toilet and towels. Decent if haphazard restaurant.

Getting There & Away

From the main terminal buses run to Tehran (IR65,000, three daily), Tabriz (IR12,000, four hours, six daily, last at 1.30pm), and Orumiyeh (IR12,000, 4½ hours), hourly via Khoy (IR8000) and Qareh Ziya'eddin (IR5000). Rare savaris to Bazargan (IR2500) depart from Taleqani St at Chahara Sq.

AROUND MAKU

To conveniently visit Qareh Kalisa, Chaldoran and Bastam, consider chartering a taxi from Maku then jumping out at Qareh Ziya'eddin for public transport to Khoy.

Qareh Kalisa   قره کلیسا

Splendid outside, though plain within, **Qareh Kalisa** (Black Church; admission IR3000; ⏱ 24hr) is the best maintained of all Iran's medieval churches. It's alternatively known as Kalisa-ye Tadi (Church of St Thaddaeus) for St Thaddaeus (aka Tatavoos) who supposedly founded a church here in AD 43. Some say he came with apostle St Bartholomew, others that he *was* St Bartholomew. Whatever the case, Thaddaeus' preaching proved a little too successful and the jealous Armenian king reacted by killing him and massacring his 3000 converts in AD 66. In a curious twist, Armenia later became the world's first Christian nation (AD 301). Thaddaeus'

memory was revived with a chapel built here at his supposed grave in AD 371.

Mostly rebuilt after an earthquake, the smaller black-and-white-striped chapel section dates from 1319–29. The church was much restored and enlarged in 1810 when the main beige-white stone section was added. This is richly carved with saints, angels, kings and crosses, best observed from the chunky fortress-style walls that surround the church site. Ring the bell to the left of the main door if it's locked. The only Christian services are held during a brilliant three-day summer pilgrimage; dates vary and are announced shortly beforehand through the **Armenian Prelacy Office** (☎ 0411-555 3532; archtab@itm.co.ir) in Tabriz.

Qareh Kalisa is tucked behind a photogenically low-rise Kurdish village, 8km off the quiet Shot–Chaldoran road. This crosses rolling arid hills that turn into bright green flower-filled meadows in spring. There's no public transport. Taxis from Maku ask IR120,000 return from Maku via Shot including waiting time.

Chaldoran   چالدوران

In 1514 the Ottoman forces of Selim the Grim devastatingly defeated Safavid Shah Ismail's formerly invincible Persian-Azari army at Chaldoran (Chaldiran, Chaldran). Of 27,000 Iranian soldiers a phenomenal 26,000 died, cut down by Selim's newfangled secret weapon, the cannon. The pivotal battle was followed by a scorched-earth policy that devastated agricultural settlements across much of west Azarbayjan and Kordestan, leaving the emptied land to grazing nomads for centuries to come.

Chaldoran Changi, the lonely battlefield, is commemorated by an impressive brick-domed tomb tower built in 2003. In front stands a statue of Seyid Sadraddin, the Persian army's hapless commander. It's beyond quaint Jala Ashaqi village. That's around 6km (IR10,000 by taxi) from **Siyah Cheshmeh**, a scraggy little market town, itself now officially renamed **Chaldoran**, where a predictable statue of Shah Ismail rides a rearing horse.

Savaris run infrequently between Siyah Cheshmeh and Qareh Ziya'eddin. It's better to combine Chaldoran with a taxi charter from Maku to Qareh Kalisa. Maps show a Bazargan–Chaldoran road via Kalisa Kandi, but it's slow and painfully potholed.

Bastam & Qareh Ziya'eddin

قره ضياء الدين و بسطام

pop 24,000

Of Iran's many Urartian sites, Bastam (aka Rusai-Urutur) is probably the most impressive. That's not saying much. It's simply a steep unfenced rocky hill, but if sheer age excites you, reflect that the occasionally visible, eroded steps were probably carved into the rock around 685–645 BC. Along with slithering sheep-paths, these teeter up the edge of a precipice forming a veritable stairway to heaven. After a 30-minute scramble, the summit reveals what looks like a Bronze-Age helipad. There are lovely views into the valley beyond. Note that the most obvious rock-block 'walls' near the tiny settlement at the hill's base are from a 2004 reconstruction by the archaeology department.

From unexciting low-rise Qareh Ziya'-eddin taxis want IR30,000 each way (15 minutes). Arrange a return ride or pay IR15,000 per hour waiting time (you'll need around 1½ hours to explore). If driving take the Chaldoran road then at the Qareh Ziya'eddin city limits turn west and continue about 6km (though the signpost says '7.5km').

Buses (IR5000) and savaris (IR12,000, 50 minutes) to Khoy are frequent from central Qareh Ziya'eddin. For Maku and Tabriz, passing transport picks up on the main Bazargan road, 3km northeast of Qareh Ziya'eddin.

KHOY

خوى

☎ 0461 / pop 179,000

Occupied since Median times, Khoy (Salt) was named for the salt mines that made it an important spur of the silk route. While not worth a lengthy detour, Khoy is more appealing than much bigger Orumiyeh, with which it shares a long history as an important Christian centre.

Orientation & Information

At central Imam Khomeini Sq, Enqelab (east), Shari'ati (north) and Taleqani (south) Sts all intersect with commercial Imam St. This runs west to Basij Sq then continues as dreary Kuchari St to Gumsal (Keshavarz) Sq passing several internet cafés. Unsigned but more central **Eyvan Coffeenet** (Taleqani St; internet per hr IR6000; ⏰ 10am-midnight) is approximately opposite the conspicuous blue-and-white

Bank Sadarat building. Taleqani St continues south of Imam Khomeini Sq passing Valiasr Sq and the Salmas bus terminal, 2km beyond. **Bank Melli** (Enqelab St) changes money.

Sights

The huge **Motalleb Khan Mosque** (Taleqani St; admission by request) is a roofless 13th-century Ilkhanid edifice of unadorned brickwork. It claims to have the world's largest mihrab. Ask nicely and you might be shown up through passages in the super-thick walls. The entrance is hidden behind street-vendors' stalls just metres from Imam Khomeini Sq. The long **vaulted bazaar** parallels Taleqani St a short block east. It emerges into Perastori Park at the **Darvazeh Sangi**, a black-and-white stone arch with two carved lions that constitutes the last remnant of Khoy's former city wall.

The squat, stone-based cube of **St Sarkis Church** (Kalisa Sorop Serkis; Gumsal Sq) is curious if not especially beautiful, with narrow slit windows suggesting a fortified past. It supposedly dates from the 4th century, though upper brick sections were rebuilt in the 1730s. Notice carved motifs over the western door (usually locked).

The 300-year-old **Shams Tabrizi Minaret** is unique for being encrusted with protruding animal horns, though many are missing or hanging like deflated old party balloons. Named for a celebrated 13th-century dervish (see boxed text, below), it's hidden away in unpromising back alleys off 22 Bahman St, a short taxi hop northeast of Gumsal Sq.

SHAMS TABRIZI

If you find Khomeini-style Islam a little stony faced, don't be put off. Iran has produced other inspirational Muslim thinkers. One such was dervish-philosopher Shams Tabrizi whose brief relationship (1244–46) with Rumi was arguably as significant to Sufi history as Jesus' encounter with John the Baptist was to Christianity. Bravely and often with humour Shams was keen to point out that religion is not an end in itself, merely the first step in a personal journey of spiritual discovery. His *Khatesevom* is generally translated as *The Third Line*. But *The Third Path* might be more accurate, echoing the middle way of the Buddha.

Sleeping & Eating

Hotel Sepid (☎ 222 4234; Taleqani St; dm/tr IR20,000/ 60,000) Women will feel out of place in the decent-enough three- and five-bed dorms with shared clean squats. A single shared hot shower is accessed through the central kitchen.

Hotel Amir (☎ 222 3839; Valiasr St; tr IR63,000) Plants and creepers on upper stairs somewhat humanise this basic crash-pad. One shared squat toilet is designated for women. Traffic noise can be disturbing. It's halfway between the Orumiyeh terminal and Valiasr Sq.

Khoy Tourist Inn (Mehmansara Jahangardi; ☎ 244 0351; fax 244 0352; Enqelab St; s/tw US$23/35) Modern yet cosy, this super-clean place has unusually well equipped rooms including minibar, excellent hot showers and even provides toilet paper. OK restaurant.

Azarbayjan (☎ 222 9800; kababs IR4000, qalyan IR5000; ☽ 8am-9pm) One of three simple *kababis* (kabab shops) on Shahid Samadzade St (parallel to Shari'ati, one block east), the Azarbayjan has a rather appealing teahouse section upstairs through unmarked rear curtains.

There are several central patisseries (Imam St) and juice bars (Shari'ati St).

Getting There & Away

Tehran–Khoy flights (IR306,000) operate on Monday, Wednesday and Saturday. From 5.15am to 4.30pm Orumiyeh-bound buses (IR7000) leave the **Salmas terminal** (Taleqani St) with Salmas savaris (IR9000, 45 minutes) departing from across the road. Use the little **Tabriz terminal** (Nasrolahi Sq), 2km northeast of centre, for Tabriz (bus/savari IR7100/30,000), Marand (savari IR15,000) and Qareh Ziya'eddin (savari IR12,000).

SALMAS سلماس

☎ 0443 / pop 75,000

Archaeologists suggest that **Gül Tappeh** (Ash Hill) once housed one of the world's first settled civilisations (7th millennium BC). Today the site is a mere muddy mound in a field 5km from Salmas accessed by a 600m-long orchard track off the lane to Keleshan village.

Known to the Medes as Zarvand, Salmas was founded as a bulwark against Babylonian incursions under Assyrian king Salmansar (Shalmanseer) III (r 859–824 BC).

Sassanid Persians staked a claim with the **Khan Takhti** royal inscription carved into a cliff 14km south of the city (facing the Sero turning on the Salmas–Orumiyeh road).

Influenced by Armenia and Caucasian Albania, Salmas later became a major Christian centre. Although ravaged by the Turkish invasion of 1915, nearby **Haftevan** (4km south) remains a Chaldean (ie Assyrian Catholic) spiritual centre. Its archetypal 17th-century **church** is a stone cube with wobbly polygonal tower locked in a fenced garden. Ibrahim Abdinzade has the key: ask at the green-trimmed shop-house one small block further south along the main road (towards the space-ship-style silver domes of Haftevan's new mosque).

Known as Shahpur under the Pahlavis, central Salmas lost most visible remnants of its history to a massive 1930 earthquake. Today it's an unremarkable apple- and pumpkin-processing town. Mild curiosities include the 1957 **Imam Hassan Mosque** with oddly bulbous-shaped brick minarets (visible approaching the bus terminal) and a kitschy **giant teapot** in Mellat Park (en route to Haftevan).

Hotel Noor (☎ 524 5070; Imam St; tw IR120,000) has clean, acceptable rooms with shower and toilet above an old-fashioned dining room. Enter beside the pizzeria between Ferdosi and Allah Sqs. No English sign.

Long-distance services plus occasional minibuses to Khoy and Orumiyeh use the **terminal** (Basij Mustazafin St). However, savaris to Khoy (IR9000, 45 minutes), Tabriz (IR25,000, 2½ hours) and Orumiyeh (IR10,000, 1 hour) use relevant roundabouts on the new bypass road *(kamer-bandi)* where passengers also jump aboard passing through-buses.

Glimpsed from the Salmas–Tabriz road, Lake Orumiyeh appears like a distant mirage while inland arid mountains blush with minerals. Bypassed **Tasuj**, hidden amid mud-walled orchards, has an historic Jameh Mosque.

SERO سرو

Minuscule Sero village has a terrific backdrop of mountains but is mostly handy for its border-crossing towards Van in Turkey. From the border gate, taxis to Orumiyeh (45 minutes) should cost IR10,000/40,000 per person/car but even locals battle with bolshie drivers who want double. Walking

WESTERN IRAN

CROSSING THE TURKISH BORDER AT SERO

This **border post** (☺ 8am-10.30pm, Iran time), called **Esendere** in Turkey, consists of just a few lonely buildings on a pretty mountain road. Procedures are relatively easy for individuals but it's wise to cross early to ensure transport connections. Freelance moneychangers offer poor rates for Turkish lira (IR6300) and worse ones for US dollars (IR8000). Get better rates in Orumiyeh or (for euros-dollars) at the bank within the Iran-side customs building. The nearest Turkish-side accommodation is 40km away in Yüksekova. **Van Erçiş** (☎ 0438-351 4193) operates a regular Yüksekova–Esendere dolmuş (minibus; YTL5, 45 minutes) till around 6pm: ignore blatantly lying denials of taxi drivers. Vangölü Turizm run Yüksekova–Van buses (YTL10, 3½ hours) approximately hourly passing the magnificent ruins of Hoşap Castle in Güzelsu village (64km before Van). In central Van, **Vangölü Turizm** (☎ 0432-216 3073; cnr Maraş & Cumhuriyet Sts) also offers a 9.30am direct bus to Orumiyeh. Turkish time is 1½ hours earlier than Iran's, half an hour in summer.

---

away is a risky ruse as the nearest place to get a minibus is 6km east where the scenic, if somewhat degraded road to Salmas branches north via the picturesque upper **Gonbadchay Valley**, **Mingöl** and **Mamakan**.

ORUMIYEH   ارومیه
☎ 0441 / pop 623,000
Known as Rezayeh during the Pahlavi era, Orumiyeh (Urmia, Urumiyeh) is a logical stop en route to southeastern Turkey. It's a large, deeply historic city but offers no must-see sights.

History
Bountiful orchards made Orumiyeh the historically prosperous 'Garden of Persia'. For centuries various Christian groups (Chaldeans, Armenians, Assyrians and Nestorians) lived harmoniously here alongside local Azari Muslims and a thriving Jewish community. However, in the 19th century overzealous Protestant and Catholic foreign missionary activities resulted in a harsh backlash against all non-Muslims. This was initially led by Kurdish groups fearing the possible loss of territory should a Christian-Armenian state be declared. In 1880 the Persian army stormed Orumiyeh to counterattack Kurdish nationalist leader Sheikh Ubayd Allah. Christians were massacred by both sides and orchards were devastated. In 1918 most of the Christian population fled from Orumiyeh, Salmas and Khoy, wisely fearing that invading Ottoman Turks could repeat the butchery that they had perpetrated on the Armenians of eastern Turkey. Most of those who stayed were slaughtered. Some escapee Christians returned when the Turks retreated and today six different Christian faiths remain active. However, with a continual exodus of emigrants to the US and Scandinavia, the total non-Muslim population has dwindled to an estimated 4000 (excluding clandestine converts from Islam).

Orientation
The main commercial streets Imam Ave and Kashani St form a T at attractive Enqelab Sq. Beheshti St, unanimously known as Daneshkadeh St, continues west to Pol-e-Qoyum junction around 3km beyond the museum. Part way Ostadan St doubles back to the north through the city's most upmarket quarter.

Information
Aynet (Tarzi St; internet per hr IR6000; ☺ 9am-9pm Sat-Thu, 10am-1pm & 4.30-8pm Fri) Good internet connection here, some English spoken.
Bank Melli (Kashani St)
Jahan Moneychanger (☎ 222 2255; Ataee St; ☺ 9.30am-1pm & 4-7pm Sun-Thu) Instant exchange for many currencies including Turkish lira.
Miras Ferhangi (☎ 340 7040; Daneshkadeh St; ☺ 8am-2pm Sat-Thu) West Azarbayjan's keen English-speaking tourist information office is beside the museum.
Nashreruz (Tarzi St; ☺ 8am-noon & 4-7.30pm Sat-Thu, 8.30am-noon Fri) Small bookshop stocking excellent city maps (IR7000).
Talanet (Danesh [Kashtghar] St; per hr IR6000; ☺ 8am-11pm Sat-Thu, 10am-10pm Fri)
Telephone office (Imam Ave; ☺ 7am-7pm)
Turkish Consulate (☎ 222 8970; Daneshkadeh St; ☺ 9am-noon Sun-Thu) Very security-conscious.

Sights
CHURCHES
According to local Assyrian Orthodox Christians, **St Mary's** (Kalisa Neneh Mariyam; off Kalisa

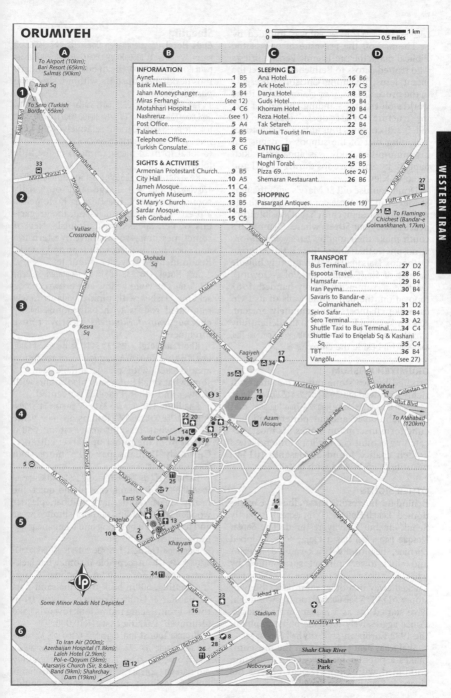

ORUMIYEH

INFORMATION
Aynet..............................1 B5
Bank Melli.......................2 B5
Jahan Moneychanger.........3 B4
Miras Ferhangi...............(see 12)
Motahhari Hospital...........4 C6
Nashreruz......................(see 1)
Post Office.....................5 A4
Talanet..........................6 B5
Telephone Office..............7 B5
Turkish Consulate.............8 C6

SIGHTS & ACTIVITIES
Armenian Protestant Church..9 B5
City Hall........................10 A5
Jameh Mosque................11 C4
Orumiyeh Museum............12 B6
St Mary's Church..............13 B5
Sardar Mosque................14 B4
Seh Gonbad....................15 C5

SLEEPING
Ana Hotel......................16 B6
Ark Hotel.......................17 C3
Darya Hotel....................18 B5
Guds Hotel.....................19 B4
Khorram Hotel.................20 B4
Reza Hotel......................21 C4
Tak Setareh....................22 B4
Urumia Tourist Inn............23 C6

EATING
Flamingo........................24 B5
Noghl Torabi...................25 B5
Pizza 69......................(see 24)
Shemaran Restaurant.........26 B6

SHOPPING
Pasargad Antiques.........(see 19)

TRANSPORT
Bus Terminal...................27 D2
Espoota Travel.................28 B6
Hamsafar.......................29 B4
Iran Peyma.....................30 B4
Savaris to Bandar-e
  Golmankhaneh...............31 D2
Seiro Safar.....................32 B4
Sero Terminal..................33 A2
Shuttle Taxi to Bus Terminal...34 C4
Shuttle Taxi to Enqelab Sq & Kashani
  Sq.............................35 C4
TBT.............................36 B4
Vangölu.......................(see 27)

WESTERN IRAN

Lane; 8am-4pm or on request) was founded by St Thomas on the gravesite of one of the Biblical magi, the pre-Islamic Persian priests who trotted across to Bethlehem to greet the infant Jesus, inventing Christmas presents in the process. This, they claim, makes it the world's oldest still-standing church. In fact the structure you'll see doesn't really feel that old. It still contains four antique tombstones including that of the supposed magus but his mummified body was apparently 'kidnapped' by Soviet troops during WWII and taken to Kiev.

Don't confuse old St Mary's with the new St Mary's in the same courtyard or with the Assyrian Protestant church that's visible from nearby **Khayyam Street** where Orumiyeh's youth make their nightly *passeggiata*. More atmospheric than any of these is the Assyrian Orthodox **Marsarjis Church** in the tiny hillside hamlet of **Sir** (5.6km from Pol-e-Qoyum). Despite a somewhat heavy-handed 1987 renovation, the bare stone walls of its twin cave-like chambers feel genuinely ancient. Ask for key-holder Wilson at the delightfully simple **shop-teahouse** (tea IR2000; 4-8pm Sun-Thu, 8am-8pm Fri) beside the church.

ORUMIYEH MUSEUM

Fronted by two stone rams, this small but richly endowed **museum** (224 6520; Beheshti St; admission IR3000; 9am-1pm & 4-7pm Tue-Sun) displays fabulously ancient pottery and fine cuneiform inscription stones. Its most eye-catching exhibit is a replica of the priceless golden chalice found at Hasanlu (p144), beautifully embossed with charioteers.

OTHER SIGHTS

Behind the interesting **bazaar**, the large brick-domed **Jameh Mosque** (by request) is partly Seljuk-era but heavily restored. The **Sardar Mosque** (Imam Ave) has a Qajar-style tri-lobed cornice, beautifully brick-vaulted interior and clock-tower minaret surmounted by what looks like a giant perfume bottle-stopper. Tucked away in a quiet mini-park, the two-storey AD 1115 **Seh Gonbad** tomb tower might have started life as a Sassanian fire temple. Police aggressively dissuade photography of the 1932 European-style **city hall** (Enqelab Sq).

Shahrchay Dam (19km from the museum) makes a popular local weekend excursion combined with *chay* (tea) at one of the riverside teahouses in **Band** (9km).

Sleeping

Guds Hotel (Mosaferkhaneh Qods; 222 2596; off Imam Ave; s/tw/tr IR60,000/90,000/120,000, with toilet tw/tr IR120,000/170,000) Clean but fairly standard mosaferkhaneh upstairs within a shopping *pasazh* (arcade).

Tak Setareh (223 1861; Sardar Camii Lane; s/tw IR85,000/125,000, with TV s/tw IR100,000/150,000, with toilet tr IR175,000) Quiet, relatively well-kept *mosaferkhaneh* where you can play *nard* (a local form of backgammon) in the little lobby area.

Reza Hotel (222 6580; Besat St; s/tw/tr IR120,000/170,000/220,000; P) Large and outwardly somewhat dowdy, the Reza is nonetheless a pretty good deal and Karim, the gregarious owner, speaks great English. Neat if sometimes noisy rooms have Western loo and good hot showers with soap and towels. Recommended traveller favourite.

Ark Hotel (235 6051; off Montazeri St; s/tw US$15/30) The vivid yellow and brown colour scheme clashes with pink towels in newly renovated rooms with bathrooms. Many cheaper *mosaferkhanehs* nearby refuse foreigners.

Khorram Hotel (222 5444; Sardar Camii Lane; s/tw IR150,000/200,000) A vaguely cosy reception area decked with plastic foliage leads to somewhat small but neatly tiled rooms with shower and toilet. Peaceful yet central.

Ana Hotel (/fax 345 3314; 77 Kashani St; s/d/tw IR180,000/280,000/380,000) Rooms are fair value if somewhat less attractive than you'd expect from the rather upmarket entrance. Curiously Iranians pay 20% more than foreign tourists.

Darya Hotel (222 9562; fax 222 3451; Tarzi [Chamran] St; s/d US$30/40) Pleasant, central and quiet, the nearly smart rooms have minibar, plastic-wooden wall-cladding and only limited wear and tear. There's birdsong and a banana palm in the welcoming foyer.

Flamingo-Chichest (436 2012; tr/apt IR300,000/450,000; P) Acceptable if somewhat lacklustre accommodation in a holiday-camp-style setting, 500m back from the sand-flats of Bandar-e Golmankhaneh, 17km from town. Front-facing rooms look towards Lake Orumiyeh. Parking costs IR10,000.

Urumia Tourist Inn (Orumiyeh Grand Inn, Mehman-sara Jahangardi; 222 3080; fax 222 3202; Kashani St; s/d US$55/80;) The Tourist Inn successfully emulates a typical midrange European chain-hotel in facilities, price and anodyne could-be-anywhere atmosphere. Comes complete with annoying Muzak in the irreproachably clean, utterly bland coffee shop.

A new five-star Laleh Hotel is currently under construction.

Eating

Flamingo (☎ 346 1177; Kashani St; meals IR40,000-75,000; ☺ noon-3pm & 7-10pm) Justifiably considered the best city-centre restaurant, the kababs here are succulent and the salad bar is well stocked if a little pricey (IR10,000 per plateful). Décor is restrained, with solid wooden benches, lanterns and flower arrangements. Head downstairs two doors away from excellent, co-owned Pizza 69, which has a sign in English.

Shemaran Restaurant (☎ 345 9956; Parhizkar St; ☺ 8am-11pm) Predominantly for tea and qalyan (water pipe; IR10,000), this gently atmospheric sonati-style traditional restaurant is immensely popular for great lunchtime *dizi* (see boxed text, p79) and also serves limited dinners (8pm). Next door is a slightly more upmarket equivalent (Heydarbaba) and a pizzeria.

Noghl, West Azarbayjan's speciality confectionery, is made by laboriously coating nuts or fruits in layers of icing sugar using a vessel looking like a copper cement mixer. Buy it from **Noghl Torabi** (Imam Ave; ☺ 8am-10pm),which also sells fabulous carrot-and-walnut halva.

Baked potatoes (IR2000) are sold from carts around the bazaar's northeast entrance. Cake, sandwich and juice shops are dotted along Imam Ave.

Shopping

Pasargad Antiques (☎ 223 1860; ☺ 8am-2pm & 4-8pm Sat-Thu) This shop is the most intriguing of three curio shops along Imam Ave.

Getting There & Away

AIR

Iran Air (☎ 3440520; Daneshkadeh St) flies four times daily to Tehran (IR351,000) and twice weekly to Mashhad (IR690,000). **Espoota Travel** (☎ 345 5555; espoota@espootatravel.com; Daneshkadeh St; ☺ 8am-8pm Sat-Thu, 9am-noon Fri) sells air and train tickets ex-Tabriz.

BUS, MINIBUS & SAVARI

All long-distance buses leave from the **terminal** (Haft-e Tir Blvd). **TBT** (☎ 222 2844), **Seiro Safar**

(☎ 222 8399), **Hamsafar** (☎ 224 4562) and **Iran Peyma** (☎ 222 2954) have central booking offices on Imam Ave. Hamsafar and **Vangölu** (☎ 233 1333) both operate 9am services to Van, Turkey (IR120,000) taking around eight hours (expect long border waits).

Other useful domestic services :

Destination	Fare	Duration	Departures
Ahvaz	IR100,000	19hr	11am, 3pm TBT
Ardabil	IR11,500	4hr	twice hourly, 5am-6pm
Esfahan	IR95,000	19hr	3.30pm, Iran Peyma
Kermanshah	IR30,000	11hr	6pm, 7pm TBT
	IR60,000	11hr	8pm TBT
Khoy	IR7000	2hr	hourly till 6pm Taavoni 16
Maku	IR12,000	4½hr	several Taavoni 9
Maraqeh	IR10,000	4hr	hourly till 4.30pm Taavoni 11 or 8
Sanandaj	IR25,400	10hr	7pm, Seiro Safar
Tehran (west terminal)	IR80,000	12hr	10am, 6-9pm several
Tehran (Arzhantin Sq)	IR85,000	12hr	6-9pm Taavoni 6 or 8

Causeways almost cross Lake Orumiyeh's narrow waist. When linked by a new bridge (nearing completion), Orumiyeh–Tabriz bus travel times will radically reduce. Already Tabriz-bound savaris (IR40,000) use this short cut taking a small ferry (15 minutes, no buses) across the last unbridged section. As vehicle queues can be long, it's faster to take a savari/taxi to the *eskele* (ferry pier; IR8000/24,000, one hour), nip onto the ferry (open 7am to 10pm) as a passenger (free) and continue to Tabriz by a different savari from the far dock (IR20,000, 1½ hours). Ferry services reduce or get cancelled in windy weather.

From the **Sero terminal** (Mirza Shirazi St) minibuses run to villages of the Gonbadchay Valley, turning north 6km before the border. Taxis to Sero cost IR40,000 from outside.

Getting Around

The airport is 13km up the Salmas highway (taxi IR20,000, 20 minutes). The most useful shuttle-taxi routes run from Faqiyeh Sq, either along Imam Ave then down Kashani St or up Taleqani St to the terminal. Savaris to Bandar-e Golmankhaneh lakeside

(IR5000, 20 minutes) leave from the corner of Valiasr and Haft-e Tir Blvds on summer weekends.

AROUND ORUMIYEH
Hasanlu   حسنلو
☎ 0443 / pop 400

The muddy hillock rising behind Hasanlu village was once an important Iron Age settlement that gradually developed into a fortified citadel over 4000 years. Mutilated skeletons found here suggest that the population met a barbaric end at the hands of the Urartians in the 9th century BC. Archaeologists also unearthed a famous 11th-century BC golden chalice here. But all you'll see today at the unfenced site are the wall stumps of former dwellings and storehouses (plastered for protection with straw-flecked adobe) along with a few standing stones that were probably gateways. The wide peaceful panoramas of fields and hay-topped village roofs are pleasant, but 20 minutes here is ample for most non-specialists.

The site is 7km from Naqadeh (IR20,000 return by taxi) to which minibuses run when full from Orumiyeh and Mahabad. Alternatively, if driving the Orumiyeh–Mahabad road via Mohammad Yar it's an 8km detour, the last 2km unsurfaced after Shonagar.

CROSSING THE IRAN–IRAQ BORDER

Much of Iraq is verging on civil war, with visitors risking kidnap or worse. However, conditions are less dire in the northernmost area of Iraqi Kurdistan, which has been virtually independent from Baghdad since the early 1990s. The Haj Omran border post near **Piranshahr**, southwest of Naqadeh, has twice been declared open (and later closed), but in principle you can currently get a visa on arrival here for Iraqi-Kurdistan (NOT valid for Baghdad or south Iraq). However, nothing can be taken for granted. Check the latest situation on Lonely Planet's Thorn Tree forum (www.lonelyplanet.com).

Borders at **Mehran** (accessed via Ilam) and **Khosravi** (via the oasis town of Qasr-e-Shirin) remain popular with bomb-dodging Iranian pilgrim buses heading for the great Shiite shrine cities of Karbala and Najaf. However, both have reportedly been down-graded to 'locals-only' crossings.

Mahabad   مهاباد
☎ 0442 / pop 168,000

Incredibly, this unassuming market city was once the capital of its own mini-country. The Mahabad Republic was a Soviet-inspired independent Kurdish state, but it survived only one year (1946), collapsing once the USSR patched things up with Tehran. In the 17th century, as Savajbulaq Mokri, Mahabad had been the regional capital. Kurdish cummerbunds and baggy trousers tell you this is somewhere different but the only 'sight' is a fine if over-restored **Jameh Mosque** in the ramshackle bazaar.

Extensively refurbished in 2006, the comfortable **Hotel Kohestan** (Koystan; ☎ 233 5738; Shahid Kandi; s/tw IR140,000/175,000) is halfway between the bazaar and bus terminal (900m). Minibuses and savaris leave frequently to Miyando'ab (30 minutes) and Orumiyeh (two hours). The road to Saqqez via Bukan has some great views and passes close to the Ali Sadr–style **Sahulan Water Caves** some 40km from Mahabad.

LAKE ORUMIYEH

Like the Dead Sea, huge Lake Orumiyeh (6000 sq km) is so super-salty that you just can't sink. A Unesco Biosphere Reserve since 1976, it's becoming increasingly shallow (maximum seasonal depth 16m) now that the Zarinarud, a major feeder river, has been diverted to slake Tabriz's growing thirst. Some worry that the lake will soon be as dead as the Aral Sea. Currently the only life-form it supports directly is the very primitive, virtually transparent artimesia worm. But that's enough to attract plenty of seasonal migratory birds, notably flamingos (spring). And the worms are commercially harvested for fish-meal.

Hulagu Khan, grandson of Genghis Khan and founder of Iran's Ilkhanid Mongol dynasty, had his treasury on **Kabudi Island** in the middle of the lake. His burial there in 1265 was accompanied by the wholesale sacrifice of virgins, as demanded by the custom of the day. Tourist access is limited to occasional one-off Friday excursions organised by ALP Tours in Tabriz (p149).

The lake's hard-to-access **eastern coastline** is starkly barren; the vivid blue waters contrast with jagged, sun-blasted rocks and parched mud-flat islands. The western coast is greener but orchards stop well short of the shore.

Of a few lakeside 'resorts', the most up-market is stylishly modern **Bari** (☎ 0433-322 2960; www.bari.ir; s/d US$110/160; **P** ⊠ ⊠), where water is deep enough for floating. Boat rides cost from IR80,000. It's 2km from Qush-chu village. More accessible **Bandar-e Gol-mankhaneh** is a 2km strip of mud flats 17km from Orumiyeh where local boy-racers burn Paykan rubber showing off to a crowd of summer weekenders. It's eerily lonely and atmospheric on a stormy winter's day.

MARAQEH مراغه
☎ 0421 / pop 173,000

While briefly capital of Ilkhanid Iran (from 1255), Maraqeh (Maragheh, Maraga) boasted the medieval world's greatest observatory. Here brilliant mathematician Nasruddin Tusi (Nasir al-Tusi) accurately calculated the diameter of the earth, centuries before the Western world even guessed it was round. On a windswept hill 3km northwest of town, a modern **observatory** (rasad-khana; ⊙ closed to public) occupies the site where the original was destroyed during Tamerlane's ravages.

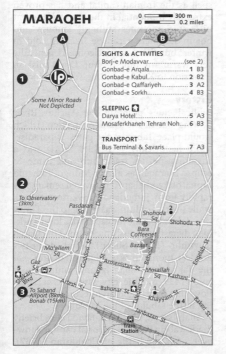

MARAQEH

0 ——— 300 m
0 ——— 0.2 miles

SIGHTS & ACTIVITIES
Borj-e Modavvar............(see 2)
Gonbad-e Arqala.....................**1** B3
Gonbad-e Kabul......................**2** B2
Gonbad-e Qaffariyeh.............**3** A2
Gonbad-e Sorkh.....................**4** B3

SLEEPING 🏠
Darya Hotel...........................**5** A3
Mosaferkhaneh Tehran Noh...**6** B3

TRANSPORT
Bus Terminal & Savaris...........**7** A3

Of several fine tomb towers scattered round town, most interesting is the square-plan **Gonbad-e Sorkh** topped by a squinch-pinched octagon. An upper window-hole is positioned such that sunlight shines directly onto the inner doorway at spring equinox. In nearby gardens, **Gonbad-e Arqala** (Arg-tomb; Khayyam St; admission free; ⊙ 8am-2pm & 4-6pm, till 7.30pm summer) is an attractive, domed, stone building housing a fine collection of gravestones and pre-Islamic totems.

The lovely **Gonbad-e Kabul** (Dark Dome) is thought to be the tomb of Hulagu Khan's mum. It's attractively dotted with blue-tiled inlay but let down by its backdrop of school buildings and a shopping complex.

The squat **Gonbad-e Qaffariyeh** (Dezhban St) sits forlornly in a riverside garden with a tacky trio of concrete dolphins.

Mosaferkhaneh Tehran Noh (☎ 222 7368; Taleqani St; dm/tw/tr IR20,000/50,000/70,000, showers IR5000) is basic but survivable with hospital-style beds and bare light bulbs.

Great free maps are available to guests at the comfortable if outwardly very 1970s **Darya Hotel** (☎ 325 0304; www.darya-hotel.com, in Farsi; Shekari Blvd; s/d/ste US$35/45/65), two minutes' walk west of the bus terminal.

To reach Tabriz choose from savari (IR25,000, 1¾ hours), bus (IR6000, 2½ hours, twice hourly) or train. For Takht-e Soleiman savari-hop via Bonab (IR2000, 25 minutes) or Miyando'ab (IR15,000, 1½ hours).

AROUND MARAQEH
Bonab بناب
☎ 0412 / pop 72,000

Bonab is known for bicycles and atomic research (don't go snooping around its northern 'nuclear' suburbs). For tourists the main attraction is Bonab's active **Mehrabad Mosque** (Motahhari St; ⊙ dawn-9pm) near the junction of Bahonar and Ghom Sts. The exterior is modest but inside are splendid wooden support columns sporting coloured, faceted capitals dated 1083. Just behind, an attractive former *hammam* (bathhouse) houses the appealing **Museum of Anthropology** (☎ 723 1033; admission free; ⊙ 8am-2pm & 4-6pm, till 8pm summer) with some engaging mannequin representations of Azari life.

The surprisingly comfortable **Laleh Hotel** (☎ 726 0386; ring road; s/d/tr US$30/35/40) has a façade like an upmarket Chinese restaurant. Rooms have leather seats, mirror-fronted desks and

WESTERN IRAN

AZARIS, AZERIS, AZERBAIJAN & AZƏRBAYCAN

Although there's an independent republic of Azerbaijan (Azərbaycan), the majority of Azerbaijanis actually live in Iran, where they make up at least 25% of the population. Iranian Azerbaijanis (Azaris) live mostly in the northwest where two provinces use the name Azarbayjan. Commonly called 'Turks' because of their Turkic dialect, Azaris are Shiite unlike the (predominantly Sunni) Turks of neighbouring Turkey. Despite spoil-sport attempts of Western intelligence agencies to stir up Azari separatist feelings, Azaris are very well integrated into Iranian society. Many Azari Iranians are prominent in Farsi literature, politics and the clerical world. The Safavid shahs were Azaris from Ardabil and supreme leader Ali Khamenei is himself ethnic Azari. Although mostly concentrated in northwest Iran, Azaris are famously active in commerce, so bazaars nationwide ring with their voluble voices. Iranian taxi drivers are often Azari so it's always worth having an Azari greeting (*kefez yakhtsede?* or *nijasan?*) up your sleeve to impress. Answer *yakhtse* (good) in Tabriz, *yakhshi* in Ardabil. Thank you (very much) is *(chokh) saghol*.

---

plenty of marble. But the highlight is a basement **bath complex** (admission IR10,000; ☻ 3-9pm for men) of saunas, drop pools and two 10m swimming pools. Open daytime for women by negotiation.

Savaris to Miyando'ab and Maraqeh leave from Mo'allem Sq, almost outside: marked by a conspicuous copper-coloured statue of Ohadie-e Maraqehi, that's where the Maraqeh road meets the ring road 900m east of the Mehrabad Mosque.

Miyando'ab مياندوآب

☎ 0481 / pop 138,000

Miyando'ab is a potentially useful overnight stop en route to Takht-e Soleiman (via Shahin Dezh then Takab). The historic **Mirza Rasoul Bridge** sits at the southern city limits and is visible if you drive into town from Mahabad. The oldest mosque is **Masjid Tag** (alley off Shahrivar St). In the one-room **museum** (☎ 222 4917; Imam St Park; admission IR2000; ☻ 7.30am-3pm Sat-Thu, 9.30am-1pm Fri), look for the ancient little fertility goddess fondling her own breasts. Nearby **Hotel Berenjian** (☎ 222 4975; fax 222 7870; Imam St; s/tw/tr US$25/35/45) is well equipped and very central above a decent restaurant with English menus. Walk five minutes left then around the corner to find the appealing teahouse **Molana** (Shohoda St; qalyan IR7000; ☻ 9am-8.30pm) and helpful internet café **AsooNet** (Shohoda St; per hr IR6000; ☻ 10am-10.30pm).

Minibuses for Shahin Dezh (IR3000, 1¼ hours), Mahabad (IR1500, 35 minutes) and Maraqeh (IR3000, one hour) use the new terminal out in the northeastern city limits. Savaris to Maraqeh (IR15,000) use a more central departure point beside the bright-green 'pincer' clock tower, 1km up Imam St from Hotel Berenjian. Shuttle taxis to the terminal cost IR1500 from that clock tower.

TABRIZ تبريز

☎ 0411 / pop 1,461,000

A fascinating bazaar, a deeply human heart and passionately helpful freelance guides make this gigantic, sprawling city a surprisingly positive introduction to Iran. It had a spell as the Iranian capital and has proven extremely influential in the country's recent history. Sometimes stiflingly smoggy and hot in summer, it can be freezing cold in winter, but the Azari welcome is generally very warm any time of year. Don't miss an excursion to Kandovan, Iran's 'Cappadocia'.

History

Biblical clues point to the Ajichay River flowing out of the Garden of Eden, which would place Tabriz at the gates of paradise! More historically verifiable, Tabriz was a Sassanian-period trade hub and came to eclipse Maraqeh as a later Mongol Ilkhanid capital of Azerbaijan. It recovered remarkably rapidly from Tamerlane's 1392 ravages and, while the rest of Iran was vassal to the Timurids, Tabriz became the capital of a local Turkmen dynasty curiously nicknamed the Qareh Koyunlu (Black Sheep). That dynasty's greatest monarch was Jahan Shah (no, *not* the Taj Mahal's Shah Jahan), under whose rule (1439–67) the city saw a remarkable flowering of arts and architecture culminating in the fabulous Blue Mosque.

Shah Ismail, the first Safavid ruler, briefly made Tabriz Persia's national capital. However, after the battle of Chaldoran (p137),

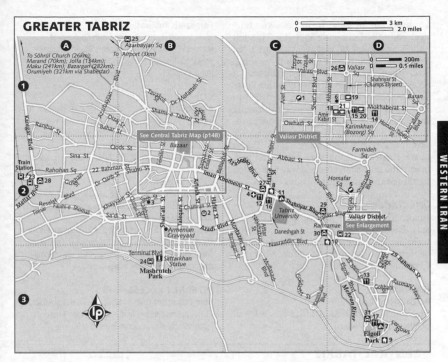

See Central Tabriz Map (p148)

WESTERN IRAN

INFORMATION		EATING 🍴		TRANSPORT	
Azerbaijan Consulate	**1** D2	Abdi	**12** C2	Ahar Terminal	**22** D2
Blue Coffeenet	(see 16)	Baliq	**13** D3	Late Night Buses to Tehran	**23** A2
Main Post Office	**2** B2	Pars Restaurant	**14** D2	Main Bus Terminal	**24** B3
Passport Office		Pizza Fanoos	**15** D2	Marand Terminal	**25** B1
(Visa Extensions)	**3** B2	Revolving Restaurant	(see 9)	Shuttle Taxis to Abarresan	
Pastor Clinic	**4** C2	Sadaf	**16** C2	Crossing	**26** D2
Turkish Consulate	**5** D2	Talar Bozorg Elgoli	**17** D3	Shuttle Taxis to City Centre	**27** C2
				Shuttle Taxis to City Centre	**28** A2
SIGHTS & ACTIVITIES		TEAHOUSES & CAFÉS ☕		Shuttle Taxis to City Centre via	
ALP Tours & Travel Agency	**6** D2	Al Mahdi Teahouse	**18** D2	Bazaar	**29** C2
		Mosbat Cafe	**19** D2	Shuttle Taxis to Elgoli and	
SLEEPING 🛏		Orkideh	**20** D2	Golshahr	**30** C2
Elgoli Camp	**7** D3			Shuttle Taxis to Rahnamae	**31** D3
Ghostaresh Hotel	**8** C2	Sharshab	**21** D2		
Hotel Elgoli	**9** D3				
Shahriyar Hotel	**10** D2				
Summer Camping	**11** C2				

Tabriz suddenly seemed far too vulnerable to Ottoman attack, so Ismail's successor, Tahmasp (1524–75), moved his capital to safer Qazvin. Fought over by Persians, Ottomans and (later) Russians, Tabriz went into a lengthy decline exacerbated by disease and one of the world's worst-ever earthquakes that killed a phenomenal 77,000 Tabrizis in November 1727.

The city recovered its prosperity during the 19th century. Shahgoli (now Elgoli) on Tabriz' southeast outskirts became the resi-dence of the Qajar crown prince, but heavy-handed Qajar attempts to Persianise the Azari region caused resentment. The 1906 constitutional revolution briefly allowed Azari Turkish speakers to regain their lin-guistic rights (schools, newspapers etc) and Tabriz held out most valiantly in 1908 when the liberal constitution was promptly re-voked again. For its pains it was brutally besieged by Russian troops.

Russians popped up again during both world wars and had time to build themselves a railway line to Jolfa (then the Soviet border) before withdrawing in 1945. This left Tabriz as capital of Pishaveri's short-lived Provincial Government (autonomous south Azerbaijan) which tried to barter threats of secession for better Azari rights within Iran. The Provincial Government was crushed in December 1946 and far from encouraging the Azaris, the shah did the opposite, restricting the use of their mother tongue. Reaction against this discrimination put Tabriz in the forefront of the 1979 revolution well before the anti-shah struggle was railroaded by more fundamentalist Muslim clerics.

Orientation

Imam Khomeini St, the central east–west axis, becomes 22 Bahman St towards the train station. Confusingly, its eastern end becomes 29 Bahman St after Abaresan Crossing.

Information
BOOKSHOPS

The tourist information office has a small book-swap cupboard.

Forouzesh Publications (Map p148; ☎ 555 6733; www.forouzesh.com, in Farsi; Imam Khomeini St, upstairs; ⊙ 9am-9pm) Sells some English-language books, guides, dictionaries and a good map of Iran (IR10,000).

CONSULATES

Azerbaijan (Map p147; ☎ 333 4802; Mokhaberat St, Valiasr; ⊙ 9am-noon Sun-Thu) Tourist visas available in five days without invitation or hotel booking. Bring two photocopies of passport and two photos.
Turkey (Map p147; ☎ 330 0958; Homafar Sq, Valiasr)

EMERGENCY

Pardis Clinic (Map p148; ☎ 526 2307; Jomhuri-e Eslami St) Blue building accessed up stairway beside sign saying 'Kalagostare Nazary'.
Pastor Clinic (Map p147; ☎ 334 0104; Imam Khomeini St; ⊙ 24hr) Three blocks west of Abaresan Crossing, downstairs beneath Melli Bank, opposite the strikingly modernist Sarmaye Bank tower.

INTERNET ACCESS

Blue Coffeenet (Map p147; above Sadaf Restaurant, Abaresan Crossing; per hr IR8000; ⊙ 8am-11pm) Astonishingly elegant for an internet café.

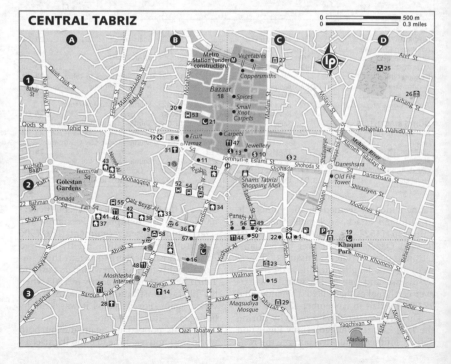

CENTRAL TABRIZ

Caffenet Village (Map p148; basement fl, Ashraf Shopping Centre, Shari'ati St; per hr IR3900; ⏱ 9am-9pm Sat-Thu, 9am-2pm Fri) Cheap with bearable connection speeds.

Deniz Coffeenet (Map p148; Maghazeh Haye Sanqi Alley off Shari'ati St; per hr IR6000; ⏱ 9am-10pm) New computers, fast connection, speech facilities and traditional Azarbayjani mugam music.

LAUNDRY
Iran Express (Map p148; ☎ 525 1627; Shari'ati St; shirts IR6000, socks IR2000; ⏱ 9am-10pm Sat-Thu)

MONEY
Bank Melli (Map p148; Shohoda Sq; ⏱ 9.15am-1pm Sat-Thu) Upstairs for exchange. Allow half an hour.

Mahmud Abidan Exchange (Map p148; ☎ 523 1077; Saraye Amir, Timche Amirno 11; ⏱ 9am-6pm Sat-Wed, 9am-3pm Thu) This exchange has good rates and there's no queue, but it's unsigned and hard to find in a mini mall off the southeast corner of the bazaar's largest caravanserai courtyard. The tourist information office (right) can show you its location.

POST
Main Post Office (Map p147; Artesh St) Helpful for shipping parcels.

TELEPHONE
International telephone office (Map p148; east Miyar Miyar Alley; ⏱ 8am-9pm) There's another branch opposite Deniz Coffeenet.

TOURIST INFORMATION
Tourist information office (Map p148; ☎ 525 2501; off Jomhuri-e Eslami St; ⏱ 9am-2pm & 4-7pm Sat-Thu) Excellent free maps, lots of help with organising trips around Azarbayjan, and a mine of information that will transform your appreciation of this city. It's upstairs in a curious building that straddles the main bazaar entrance.

TOURS
ALP Tours & Travel Agency (Map p147; ☎ 331 0340; fax 331 0825; Karimkhan Sq) Offers a varying choice of Friday trips (from IR60,000) whether sightseeing (Jolfa, Kaleybar or Kabudi Island) or winter sports.

The following are private individuals with other occupations so they're not always available at short notice.

Davoud Faraji (☎ 0914-414 7955; www.alb.ir) Great value driving tours around Azarbayjan. Davoud is lively, energetic and very sensitive to tourists' varying tastes.

Hossein Ravaniyar (☎ 385 9776, 0914 413 8096; www.iranoverland.com) Hossein is captivatingly eccentric. His mind-blowing mixture of outrageous commentary, jokes and conspiracy theories compensate for his driving style and he has a wealth of experience in helping overlanders with their vehicle paperwork.

Mansur Khan (☎ 334 9038) Nasser's charming brother offers driving tours; around town (per hour IR20,000), Kandovan (IR100,000), Maraqeh (IR250,000), Jolfa (IR350,000) or nomad spotting around Kaleybar. Add around IR15,000 per hour visiting time, in situ.

WESTERN IRAN

Nasser Khan (☎ 553 6594, 0914 116 0149; amicodel mondo@yahoo.com) Legendary multilingual pillar of the tourist information office, Nasser often takes small groups on people-watching trips and cultural experiences. He can often get you into officially closed buildings (churches, zurkhaneh etc).

TRAVEL AGENCIES

The following have English-speaking staff and offer train and plane bookings:

Afagh Gasht Travel (Map p148; ☎ 555 2250; Imam Khomeini St; 🕓 8.30am-8.30pm Sat-Thu)

Jahan Seyer Travel Agency (Map p148; ☎ 555 6004; fax 553 2331; Imam Khomeini St)

Mahnavand Travel (Map p148; ☎ 553 9444; Tarbiat St; 🕓 8.30am-6.30pm Sat-Wed, 8.30am-4.40pm Thu) Efficient, well-staffed, new travel and tour agency.

VISA EXTENSIONS

Passport Office (Map p147; ☎ 477 6666; Saeb St; 🕓 7.30am-1.30pm Sat-Wed, 7.30am-11.30pm Thu) Helpful for visa extensions.

Sights

BAZAAR

The magnificent, labyrinthine **covered bazaar** (Map p148) covers some 7 sq km with 24 separate caravanserais and 22 impressive *timches* (domed halls). Construction began over a millennium ago, though much of the fine brick vaulting is 15th century. Upon entering one feels like a launched pinball, bouncing around through an extraordinary colourful maze, only emerging when chance or carelessness dictates.

There are several **carpet** sections, according to knot-size and type. The spice bazaar has a few shops still selling **herbal remedies** and **natural perfumes**. A couple of **hat shops** (Bazaar Kolahdozan) sell traditional *papakh* (Azari hats, from IR100,000) made of tight-curled astrakhan wool. The better the quality, the younger the lamb sacrificed to the milliner's art. Other quarters specialise in gold, shoes and general household goods.

For such a huge construction, the bazaar is surprisingly easy to miss. A useful entrance is the second narrow passage east of the tourist information office. This takes you into the jewellery section.

AROUND THE BAZAAR

At the bazaar's western end an exit passage hidden by a curtain leads to Tabriz's **Jameh Mosque** (Map p148) with a magnificent brick-vaulted interior. Beyond, an alley between two multi-stage new minarets emerges at Motahhari St opposite the heavy wooden door (no English sign) of the 1868 **Constitution House** (Mashrutiyat Museum; Map p148; ☎ 521 6454; Motahhari St; admission IR3000; 🕓 8am-5pm Sat-Thu, 9am-1pm Fri). This charming Qajar-era courtyard house is historically significant as a headquarters during the 1906–11 constitutional revolution, but although many labels are in English the numerous photos and documents are unlikely to excite non-specialist tourists.

At the bazaar's northeast corner, the well-proportioned former Saheb Ul-Amr Mosque now houses a **Quran Museum** (Map p148; ☎ 527 2733; Madani St; admission IR3000; 🕓 8am-6.30pm Sat-Thu, 8am-1pm Fri). Its most intriguing exhibit is the scripture-covered under-shirt worn by Qajar monarchs during coronations.

BLUE (KABUD) MOSQUE   مسجد کبود

Constructed in 1465, the **Blue Mosque** (Map p148; Imam Khomeini St; admission IR2000; 🕓 9am-7pm Sat-Thu, 9am-1pm Fri, earlier in winter) was among the most glorious buildings of its era. Once built, artists took a further 25 years to cover every surface with the blue majolica tiles and intricate calligraphy for which it's nicknamed. It survived one of history's worst-ever earthquakes (1727), but collapsed in a later quake (1773). Devastated Tabriz had better things to do than mend it and it lay as a pile of rubble till 1951, when reconstruction finally started. The brick superstructure is now complete, but only on the rear (main) entrance portal (which survived 1773) is there any hint of the original blue exterior. Inside is more blue with missing patterns laboriously painted onto many lower sections around the few remaining patches of original tiles.

A smaller domed chamber further from the entrance once served as a private mosque for the Qareh Koyunlu shahs. Steps lead down towards Jahan Shah's tomb chamber but access would require some minor gymnastics.

The Khaqani garden outside, honouring 12th-century Azari-Persian poet Shirvani Khaqani, is a good place to meet English-speaking students.

AZARBAYJAN MUSEUM

The **Azarbayjan Museum** (Map p148; Imam Khomeini St; admission IR2000; 🕓 8am-2pm & 4-8pm Sat-Thu summer, 8am-12.30pm Fri, 8am-5pm winter) is 50m west of the Blue Mosque. Enter through a great brick portal with big wooden doors guarded by two stone rams. Ground-floor exhibits include finds from Hasanlu (p144), a superb 3000-year-old copper helmet and curious stone 'handbags' from the 3rd millennium BC. Found near Kerman these were supposedly symbols of wealth once carried by provincial treasurers. The basement features Ahad Hossein's powerful if disturbing sculptural allegories of life and war. The top floor displays a re-weave of the famous Chelsea carpet, reckoned to be one of the best ever made. The original is so-called because it was last sold on King's Rd, Chelsea, some 50 years ago, ending up in London's Victoria & Albert Museum.

ARG-E TABRIZ   ارگ تبریز

This huge brick **edifice** (Map p148; off Imam Khomeini St), an unmissable landmark, is a chunky remnant of Tabriz's early-14th-century citadel (known as 'the Ark'). Criminals were once executed by being hurled from the top of the citadel walls. Far-fetched local legend tells of one woman so punished who was miraculously saved by the parachute-like effect of her chador.

Ongoing construction of a stadium-sized **Mosallah Mosque** next door is reportedly undermining the Ark's foundations and access is usually impossible.

CHURCHES

Tabriz has had a Christian community almost as long as there've been Christians. Near the bazaar, **St Mary's** (Kalisa-ye Maryam-e Moqaddas; Map p148) is a 12th-century church mentioned by Marco Polo and once the seat of the regional archbishop. Behind high gates, the curious **Anglican Church** (Map p148; Walman St) has a tower of four diminishing cylinders. The relatively central **Sarkis Church** (Kalisa-ye Sarkis-e Moqaddas; Map p148; Kalisa Alley) serves the Armenian community. It's hidden in a basketball court behind high white gates.

OTHER ATTRACTIONS
Central Tabriz

The 19th-century bathhouse, **Nobar Hamam** (Map p148; Imam Khomeini St), is usually locked but worth double-checking. Almost opposite, the German-designed **Municipal Hall** (Map p148; Shahrdari Sq) is a century-old Tabriz

icon. It's only open to the public during occasional exhibitions. Follow Tabazan St down its western flank then take the second lane to the left to find the **Measurement Museum** (Sanjesh Muze; Map p148; ☎ 554 2459; admission IR2000; ◷ 8am-6pm Sat-Thu, 9am-1pm Fri) hidden amid very ordinary apartment blocks. The brilliantly restored 160-year-old Qajar mansion is more interesting than its display of rococo German clocks and commercial scales. Two blocks further south a trio of impressive 230-year-old mansions with two-story colonnades and decorative ponds now comprise the Architecture Faculty of the **Islamic Arts University**. Two more blocks further is the **house museum** of much-loved Tabrizi poet Ostad Shahriyar exhibiting the loveably ordinary settee and TV set that he used till his death in 1987. Shahriyar is now commemorated much more ostentatiously with the strikingly modernist **Poets' Mausoleum** (Maghbarat al-Shoara, Maqbar al-Shoara; Map p148; Seyid Hamzeh St). Its angular interlocking concrete arches are best viewed across the reflecting pool from the south. The complex also commemorates over 400 other scholars whose tombs have been lost in the city's various earthquakes. Take bus 116.

Around 350m southeast of the Poets' Monument (but with no direct road between them) is the elegant **Qajar Museum** (Amir Nezam House; Map p148; ☎ 523 6568; Farhang St, Sheshgelan; admission IR3000; ◷ 8am-6pm Sat-Thu, 9am-1pm Fri) within the palatial 1881 Amir Nezam House, Tabriz's most impressive Qajar mansion with a split-level façade. It's oddly hidden between a school and a children's hospital.

Outer Tabriz

About 4km east of Abaresan Crossing is the wealthy if architecturally neutral **Valiasr District**. While hardly SoHo, it's the nearest Tabriz comes to an entertainment district. The city's gilded youth sip espressos around Valiasr's Karimkhan (Bozorg) Sq and make a nightly *passeggiata* along pedestrianised Shahriyar St, misleadingly nicknamed Champs Elysées. In just a few minutes here we met Iranian punks, tuft-bearded Metallica fans and even spotted a transvestite waggling his/her hips far more provocatively than any woman could dare to.

Elgoli (Shahgoli) Park, 8km southeast of the centre, is popular with summer strollers and courting couples. Its fairground surrounds an artificial lake, in the middle of which a photogenic restaurant-pavilion occupies the reconstruction of a Qajar-era palace.

Activities

When there are sufficiently large groups, **ALP Tours & Travel Agency** (Map p147; ☎ 331 0340; fax 331 0825; Karimkhan Sq; ☯ Dec-Apr) can organise Friday skiing excursions to Mt Sahand. The cost for transport is IR50,000, lift pass (IR40,000) and ski rental (IR50,000 to IR160,000) are extra. ALP can also arrange climbing guides for Mt Sabalan (p160).

Sleeping

Summer camping is possible at designated sites, such as in Elgoli Park and near Tabriz University.

BUDGET

All rooms share communal squat toilets unless otherwise indicated.

Darya Guesthouse (Map p148; ☎ 554 0008; Mohaqqeqi St; s/tw from IR4000/6000, with bathroom IR120,000/150,000) This friendly family guesthouse has well-tended rooms in a sensibly graded variety of qualities. The tirelessly helpful owner looks uncannily like Louis de Funes and delights in retelling tales of his 1970s trips to Europe. There's a useful travellers' tip book.

Bagh Guesthouse (Map p148; ☎ 555 2762; Ferdosi St; s/d/tr IR47,000/70,000/90,000) Brighter and cleaner than most *mosaferkhanehs*, rooms here are fairly small but five of the 12 have double beds, unusual at this price range.

Mahmoodi Mehmanpazir (Map p148; ☎ 554 1744; Imam Khomeini St; s/tw/tr from IR50,000/70,000/90,000) The cheaper rooms are simple but quiet off a rear courtyard mini-garden with free communal shower. Rooms with private shower are better-painted but poorer value and suffer from road noise. Handy for the museum.

Park Hotel (Map p148; ☎ 555 1852; Imam Khomeini St; s/tw/tr IR70,000/90,000/120,000) This offers slight olde-worlde charm and there's a vine-trained rear courtyard garden. Large rooms have washbasins but somewhat tatty carpets.

Many basic *mosaferkhanehs* along Ferdosi St and near Terminal Sq cater predominantly to petty traders from the ex-Soviet Caucasus. Not ideal for women travellers: **Mashhad Hotel** (Map p148; ☎ 555 8255; Ferdosi St; dm/s/tw/tr/q IR20,000/43,000/59,700/81,000/92,000; shower IR5000) Possibly the only mosaferkhaneh allowing foreigners to use (five-bed) dormitories.

Masoud Guesthouse (Map p148; ☎ 556 6828; Mohaqqeqi St; s/tw IR40,000/56,000) Newly repainted rooms, shared squats a little whiffy. Marked 'Heloo Welcom Youth Hostel'.

Hotel Delgoshay Salmas (Map p148; ☎ 554 3362; Ferdosi St; s/tw/tr from IR43,360/59,708/70,334; shower IR6000) Some rooms have washing facilities.

MIDRANGE

Morvarid Hotel (Map p148; ☎ 553 3336; Fajr Sq; s/tw IR116,130/160,341) This long-term favourite remains OK value though some of the freshly painted rooms smell a tad damp and their taste in art is a little garish. Decent bathrooms. Jebel speaks good English and doubles as driver-guide.

Qods Hotel (Map p148; ☎ 555 0898; Terminal Sq; s/tw IR130,000/200,000) Acceptable rooms with hot showers and Western loos off spanking clean but ill-lit corridors that feel soulless and slightly eerie.

Ark Hotel (Map p148; ☎ 555 1277; Ark St; s/tw with breakfast IR150,000/200,000) The are sheets on aging mattresses and there's no lift. It's named after the citadel nearby, not Noah.

Kosar Hotel (Map p148; ☎ 553 7691; fax 554 1570; info@kosarhotel.com; Imam Khomeini St; d IR160,000; ⬚) Professionally upgraded historic building with well-furnished, tile-floored rooms that include satellite TV (Euronews) and fridge. Some have Western toilets and double beds. Traffic rumbles all night.

Azarbayjan Hotel (Map p148; ☎ 555 9051; fax 553 7477; Shari'ati St; s/d/tr IR170,000/242,000/302,000; ⬚) A fine, central option with consistently friendly service and unpretentious but regularly renovated rooms with excellent hot showers and towels. Double-glazing reduces traffic noise.

Hotel Sina (Map p148; ☎ 556 6211; Fajr Sq; s/tw IR200,000/300,000; P ⬚) Calm yet central, this relatively plush midrange option has bright corridors with strip carpets over clean tiled floors. Rooms are neat and fully equipped. Enter from Felestin St. Parking is limited.

TOP END

Gostaresh Hotel (Map p147; ☎ 334 5021; fax 334 6778; Abaresan Crossing; s/tw/tr/ste US$54/67/87/108; ⬚) 'Standard' rooms are stylishly redesigned semi-suites with breast-height dividing walls between the bed and a slightly sparse sitting area. Most have kitchenette. Although several kilometres from the bazaar, the location is handy for public transport to both Valiasr and the centre.

Hotel Elgoli (Tabriz Pars; Map p147; ☎ 380 7820; fax 380 8555; www.parshotels.com; Elgoli Park; s/d/ste US$73/106/202; P ⌘) Three convex walls of gleaming blue glass overlook the city's favourite park, 8km from the centre. It has everything you'd expect from a top business hotel except for alcohol in the minibar beers. The atrium is airy and there's a revolving restaurant on top.

The new, five-star **Shahriyar Hotel** (Map p147; www.shahryarinternationalhotel.com; Elgoli Blvd; s/d from US$120/150) opened shortly after we had finished our research.

Eating

On winter evenings, *labu* (beets) are sold roasted or boiled from carts along Imam Khomeini St. Or try *baghla* (boiled broad beans) eaten as a snack with vinegar and paprika at open-air cafés around Elgoli Park.

CENTRAL AREA

There are several decent dining options around Coffeenet Deniz and nearby Shari'ati St has good juice bars. The tourist information office folks like to show you cheap local eateries nearby including part-vegetarian Arzhentin Restaurant (open for lunch only) and the delightful little Ferdosi Restaurant, a subterranean one-room vaulted cavern that's great for *dizi* (see p79) or a puff on the qalyan.

Rahnama Dairy (Map p148; Ferdosi St; snacks IR6500; ⏱ 7am-9pm Sat-Thu, 7am-2pm Fri) This simple dairy-café serves unbeatable breakfasts of *must-asal* (yogurt and honey) or *khame-asal* (cream and honeycomb).

Restaurant Tatly (☎ 555 0505; Shari'ati St; pizzas IR13,000-30,000; ⏱ noon-11pm) Ceilings soar to five-pointed star lamps in this renovated older building. Pizzas are typically Iranian but the *ash* (thick vegetable and noodle soup) is most hearty and excellent value (IR5000).

Honarmandan (Place of Artists; Map p148; ☎ 553 4594; Imam Khomeini St; meals IR15,000-45,000; ⏱ 8am-10pm) Vaulted underground eatery with an amusing if tacky 'sculpted' centrepiece water-feature and a choice of tables or carpeted sitting platforms. Decent kababs and rich *dizi* (IR15,000).

Linette (Map p148; ☎ 555 6483; Baroun Avak St; meals IR21,000-38,000, pizzas IR13,000-27,000, coffee

IR8000-12,000; ⏱ 12.30-4pm & 6.30-11pm Sat-Thu) Warm wood tones, a pseudo-Swiss wooden chimney-breast and glass-topped inset-tables create a congenial atmosphere despite the slightly cutesy Christmas theme. Try the creamy mushroom stroganoff.

Modern Tabriz Restaurant (Map p148; Imam Khomeini St; meals IR30,000-45,000; ⏱ 11am-11pm) This good-value favourite serves great kababs and excellent fried trout in a large, basement dining hall that somehow finds a successful blend of olde-worlde charm, 1960s retro and idiosyncratic kitsch. Meal prices include 'service', ie salad, soft drink and delicious barley-and-barberry soup.

Kahveteria Sonati Tarbiat (Map p148; ☎ 554 8819; Tarbiat St; coffee IR5000-10,000; ⏱ 9am-9pm) Cosy, gently romantic brick-vaulted café for tea and dates (IR10,000) served on porcelain featuring Qajar royalty. Women can smoke a qalyan here without incurring the stares of 40 bemused grey-beards.

VALIASR AREA

Although there's the functional **Al Mahdi teahouse** (Map p147; Amir Kabir St) and the relatively upmarket **Pars Restaurant** (Map p147; ☎ 333 0048; Homam-Tabrizi St; kabab meals IR35,000-60,000; ⏱ noon-4pm & 6.30-10pm) Valiasr's speciality is pizza and people-watching from coffee shops around Karimkhan Sq.

Pizza Fanoos (Map p147; ☎ 332 4700; Karimkhan Sq; pizzas IR25,000; ⏱ 11am-midnight) Typically small but with attractive framed glass-art and a good view-window upstairs.

Mosbat Cafe (Map p147; ☎ 330 2977; Karimkhan Sq; espresso IR10,000; ⏱ 9am-midnight) Marginally the best of Valiasr's trendy coffee shops thanks to its stylish downstairs triangular tables and wooden 'bar' seating. Upstairs is less appealing. Look for the big red-on-yellow 'Café' sign beside Haida Sandwich.

Good, similar alternatives to Mosbat include **Sharshab** (Map p147; ☎ 330 7741; espresso IR7000) just south of Karimkhan Sq and **Orkideh** (Map p147; ☎ 331 1146; Mokhaberat St; coffee IR5000) a block east.

ABARESAN CROSSING

En route to Valiasr or Elgoli you'll usually need to change shared taxi here, but there are several fairly nice little pizza parlours of which **Abdi** (Map p147; ☎ 336 6245; 29 Bahman St; pizza IR25,000-30,000; ⏱ 5-10.30pm) remains the most noteworthy, with black décor and real flames over the doorway. Across the busy junction, **Sadaf** (Map p147; ☎ 334 5346; 29 Bahman St; meals IR22,000-45,000; ⊙ noon-10pm) is an elegant family kabab restaurant serving decent *chelo morq*.

ELGOLI

our pick **Baliq** (Map p147; ☎ 385 9294; Golshahr St; meals IR20,000-50,000) Fish, fish, fish. Fresh whole fish, fish kababs, fish köfte balls in the IR20,000 salad bar, fishing nets on the ceiling, little aquariums between the tables and even fish-shaped souvenir pens. Standards are excellent, the enticing décor includes log-and-rope chairs and a cave-wall trickling with water. Get off a Rahnamae-Golshahr savari (IR1000) on 35m Sina St.

Talar Bozorg Elgoli (Map p147; ☎ 380 5263; Elgoli Park; meals IR30,000) Within Elgoli's mock Qajar palace, this busy, surprisingly unpretentious family restaurant serves *Tabrizi köfte*, a local home-cooking speciality like a giant Scotch egg. Order ahead in winter.

Revolving Restaurant (Map p147; ☎ 380 7820; Hotel Elgoli, 11th fl, Elgoli Park; meals IR50,000-140,000; ⊙ 7.30-11pm) A Plexiglas elevator fires you through the Hotel Elgoli's atrium like Charlie in Willy Wonka's chocolate factory for predictably great views. The basic charge of IR50,000 entitles you to raid the soup-n-salad bar. Then add main courses including steaks, sturgeon kababs and fried shrimp.

Getting There & Away

AIR

Iran Air (☎ 334 9038) has direct flights twice weekly to İstanbul (one way/return IR2,080,000/2,480,000). Kish Air and Caspian Airlines both fly weekly to Dubai (IR1,140,000). Six weekly flights weekly to Mashhad (IR638,000) use Eram Air (Sunday, Wednesday), Caspian (Monday, Thursday) and Iran Air (Tuesday, Friday). For other domestic destinations connect via Tehran (IR322,000, several daily).

BUS, MINIBUS & SAVARI

A couple of bus companies including **Seiro Safar** (Map p148; ☎ 555 7797; ⊙ 8.30am-midnight) have offices on Imam Khomeini St. Agency **Mihan Safar** (Map p148; ☎ 555 4908; Imam Khomeini St; ⊙ 9am-2pm & 4-8pm Sat-Thu, 9am-noon Fri) pre-sells tickets for many domestic long-distance bus companies.

Main Terminal

Most long-distance buses depart from the huge, modern **main bus terminal** (Map p147; ☎ 479 6091), 3km south of centre. Between the bus lanes there's a handy **information office** (⊙ 7am-8pm). Services include the following (prices are for Volvo-class except where marked *):

Destination	Fare	Duration	Departures
Ahvaz	IR65,000	15hr	1.30pm, 4pm Kejave
Ardabil	IR11,500*	4hr	twice hourly, 5am-6pm
Esfahan	IR70,000	17hr	4-5.30pm
Kermanshah	IR65,000	12hr	6pm
Maku	IR12,900	4hr	daily
Maraqeh	IR7400	2½hr	up to four hourly
Mashhad	IR100,000	24hr	2pm, 3pm & 5pm
Qazvin	IR40,000	8hr	use Tehran bus
Rasht	IR40,000	8hr	8.30pm Gilan Tabar
Sanandaj	IR40,000	9hr	8-11am, 7pm
Shiraz	IR105,000	24hr	1.30-2pm
Tehran (west)	IR60,000	9hr	frequent till 10pm
Tehran (south)	IR60,000	9hr	Taavoni 9
Zanjan	IR18,000*	5hr	3pm Seiro Safar

Between 10pm and midnight cheaper buses to Tehran (IR50,000) leave from near the train station.

Savaris to most destinations (but not Ahar or Marand) depart from the terminal's northwest corner. Prepay at one of two ticket booths. For Orumiyeh use savari–ferry–savari hops across Lake Orumiyeh (see p143) until the new bridge is finished (due 2008).

Other Terminals

Use the **Khosrowshahr terminal** (Map p148; off Felestin St) for Osku and thence Kandovan. Out towards the airport, the **Marand terminal** (Azerbaijan Sq) serves Marand and Hadiyshahr (for Jolfa). Buses to Ahar (IR68000, 1½ hours) and Kaleybar (rare) use the **Ahar terminal** (Map p147; 29 Bahman St) with savaris (IR12,000 to IR14,000) waiting across the road.

INTERNATIONAL BUSES

Bus services to Yerevan, Armenia (IR350,000, 20 hours), İstanbul (IR300,000, 30 hours) and Baku, Azerbaijan (IR160,000, 13–17 hours) all typically leave around 10pm from outside the relevant ticket offices on Imam Khomeini Ave (Map p148).
Aram Safar (☎ 556 0597) For Baku.
Khoshrah (☎ 556 4451)
Seiro Safar (☎ 555 7797)

However, services sometimes leave from the train station concourse, so double check.

TRAIN
Overnight trains to Tehran (13 hours) depart 5.30pm (from IR140,000) and 7.30pm (from IR52,000) running via Maraqeh (2¼ hours), Zanjan (nine hours, arriving antisocially early) and Qazvin. The **train station** (Map p147; ☎ 444 4419; Rahohan Sq) is 5km west of central Tabriz. Shuttle taxis and city bus 111 drop off at the junction of Mellat Blvd and 22 Bahman St.

The 9am local train to Jolfa (IR5000, 3½ hours) operates Tuesday, Thursday and Sunday only.

Weekly international trains run to:
- Damascus (from IR420,000, 60 hours) 7.30am Monday; change trains in Tatvan
- İstanbul (from IR380,000, three days) 8.30am Friday
- Van, Turkey (IR124,000, nine hours) 8.30pm Wednesday, returns from Van 9.30pm Thursday

Getting Around
TO/FROM THE AIRPORT
Airport bus 136 runs from Motahhari St every 40 minutes. Taxis (with blue stripe) should cost IR15,000.

BUS & MINIBUS
City buses are relatively infrequent. Pre-buy IR250 tickets. Useful routes from the major city-bus terminal include bus 160 to the bus terminal and bus 110 to Valiasr. Several services run the length of 22 Bahman St (for the train station) including bus 111. Buses 136 (airport) and 115 (Marand terminal) leave from the west side of the bazaar. Bus 101 runs to Elgoli from near Saat Sq.

SHUTTLE TAXI
A key route runs along Imam Khomeini St from Fajr Sq to Abaresan Crossing (IR1000), but on returning diverts onto Jomhuri-e Eslami St passing the bazaar. At Abaresan Crossing, walk under the flyover to continue to Valiasr district (IR1000) or to Rahnamae (IR1000) where you'll change again for Elgoli (IR1000). For the train station start from Qonaga Sq (IR1000). To the bus terminal, shuttle taxis take Shari'ati St southbound returning via Taleqani St.

TRAM/METRO
A tram-metro system is under construction between Elgoli Park and the train station.

AROUND TABRIZ
Kandovan كندوان
☎ 0412 / pop 680
Reminiscent of Cappadocia (Turkey), remarkable **Kandovan** (Chandovan; village admission IR2500) is a photogenic settlement of troglodyte homes and storage barns carved out of curiously eroded rocks. These sit above a newer lower village like a conference of stone ice-cream cones. Scrambling along steep, narrow paths between them gives you ample idea of the place within a few minutes. However, staying overnight allows you to 'feel' the village without its crowds of local tourists.

Beyond Kandovan, smooth steep foothills mask a full view of **Mt Sahand** whose hidden volcanic summit rises to 3707m. David Rohl's book *Legend* suggests that Sahand was the Bible's 'Mountain of God'. If true that would place Kandovan slap bang in the original Garden of Eden. But today it's honey rather than apples that tempt a tasting.

OSKU اسکو
☎ 0412 / pop 24,000
En route to Kandovan you'll pass through **Osku**, famous for silk-weaving, walnuts and tight-fisted residents. In the book *In Xanadu*, William Dalrymple finally achieved his quest for an Iranian silk farm here. But while silk *kalagechi* scarves hang to dry from rooflines above Osku's weaving workshops and are hand-stamped at the town's yellow-brick **Handicraft Cooperative** (☎ 322 0511; Farmandari St), today the raw silk is produced at **Siyah Rud** (see p157).

Osku has two old brick **mosques** and an ancient, *chinar* (giant plane tree) that divides the narrow lane leading towards Kandovan. That road weaves through walnut groves to **Ispanjan village**, where two mosques share three fine minarets. The road then continues over arid rolling hills that turn attractively grassy in spring, bypassing the silk-spinning village of **Khanemu**. Donkey traffic is as common as cars, men wear crumpled *papakh* and women appear to be wrapped in curtains.

SLEEPING & EATING
In Kandovan, several of the discordantly ordinary homes and shops at the village base

offer very basic rooms to rent (mostly May to September only). You'll usually get an unfurnished room with carpeted floor, so consider bringing a sleeping bag. All charge IR40,000 per room but standards vary. Kafe Gazakhuri Daiya is easiest to find (across the bridge from the Dairyman four-table shop-restaurant), but like most it has outside toilets and no real shower. Homestay **Jamshid** (☎ 3230016; r IR40,000) has slightly tattier rooms, but offers hot-water shower and indoor squat toilet.

Kandovan Laleh Rock Hotel (☎ 323 0191; fax 323 0190; tw/tr/ste US$300/370/400) Like traditional Kandovan homes, the Laleh's 10 remarkable rooms have been carved out of 'fairy chimney' rock knolls. But inside they are luxurious affairs with stylish lighting, oriental-style futon-beds, underfloor heating and (in many) deep-stepped Jacuzzis as well as fully equipped bathrooms.

GETTING THERE & AWAY
Minibuses from central Tabriz run regularly to Osku (IR2500, 50 minutes) till around 6pm. From Osku to Kandovan (25km) taxis cost IR40,000 return plus IR15,000 per hour waiting. Minibuses are extremely rare. Direct car-tours from Tabriz (see p149) to Kandovan cost from around IR100,000 return.

Tabriz to Jolfa
SÖHRÜUL CHURCH
Although smaller and less significant than Qareh Kalisa (see p137) the intriguing Söhrüul Church (Söhrül Kalisa) has a unique star-hexagonal bell tower and a picturesque setting on a steep little hillock just above mud-walled Söhrül village. First built in the 6th century AD, the current brick structure is the result of a Franco-Russian rebuild in 1840, very heavily restored in 2006. Söhrül is 25km northwest of Tabriz airport. Turn off the main Tabriz–Sufiyan road beside Golzar Restaurant following the sign for Zabarlu. The last 12km is unasphalted.

PAYAM
An attractive section of the busy Marand highway 50km northwest of Tabriz passes right beside the beautiful **Abbasi Caravanserai**, slated for conversion to an inn. About 3.5km beyond is the turn-off for **Payam (Yam) ski area**.

MARAND   مرند
☎ 0491 / pop 129,000
Traditionally believed to be the burial place of Noah's mother, Marand is mostly useful as a connection point for reaching Jolfa. Transport from Tabriz and Khoy arrives at the main terminal, 1km off the southern ring road. You can continue north from there using minibuses to Hadiyshahr. But direct Jolfa savaris use Istgah Jolfa, a tiny unmarked side street, 700m north of the city centre, around 3km from the terminal. While crossing town you could visit the very historic (if heavily renovated) **Jameh Mosque** (Kashani St; ☯ 11am-5pm) and explore the curious muddy mounds and shattered spires of **Qala**, the ancient citadel.

JOLFA   جلفا
☎ 0492 / pop 14,000
The original Jolfa was once a major Armenian settlement famous for its skilled artisans. So skilled, in fact, that in 1604 Shah Abbas kidnapped the entire population, whisking them off to build a new capital at Esfahan where their descendants still live. Original Jolfa is now a busy little border town focused on Ashura Sq, a sizable roundabout directly south of the Azerbaijan immigration post. Nearby you'll find freelance moneychangers and **No Avaran Internet Club** (Vilaee-Fagih St off Ashura Sq; per hr IR6000; ☯ 9am-2pm & 4-8pm Sat-Thu). The town has little to see in itself, but makes a good low-budget base for visiting the Church of St Stephanos (opposite), exploring the fascinating Aras River Valley or crossing into Nakhchivan or Armenia.

Sleeping & Eating
Yemekhana Hatäm (☎ 302 2828; Ashura Sq; s/tw IR30,000/50,000, tw with shower IR60,000) Survivable rooms available at the back of a popular, recently redecorated restaurant, which serves a splendid *zereshk polo ba morgh* (chicken with rice and barberries) dinner for IR20,000, including soup and drink.

Hotel Durna (☎ 302 3812; Vilaee-Fagih St; tw/tr/q IR65,900/77,900/88,000) Unsophisticated but neat, well-kept and spotlessly clean rooms share decent squat toilets and hot showers. Signed in Cyrillic, 400m east of Ashura Sq, it's a step up in quality from the similarly priced Hotel Azerbaijan almost next door.

Jolfa Tourist Inn (Mehmansara Jahangardi; ☎ 302 4824; fax 302 4825; Eslam St; tw with/without bathroom

US$30/20) Jolfa's smartest option is 1km from the centre. Walk a block south from Ashura Sq then 10 minutes diagonally right at the T-junction, passing the train station en route. Some English is spoken.

Getting There & Away

Savaris gather just north of Ashura Sq for Marand (IR12,000, one hour), Hadiyshahr (Alamdar; IR1500, 15 minutes) and occasionally Tabriz (IR35,000, 2½ hours). Minibuses to Marand (IR4000, 1½ hours) run from Hadiyshahr, but not from Jolfa itself. The road to Khoy, shown on most maps, is partly mud track across almost uninhabited wilderness. It can be very hard to follow in places, but it's possible in a Paykan (IR200,000, 2¼ hours). You'll need a full-day taxi charter to do justice to the scenic Aras River road to Kaleybar.

AROUND JOLFA
West of Jolfa

Jolfa's main tourist drawcard is the very attractive Armenian **Church of St Stephanos** (Kalisa Darreh Sham; admission IR3000; ☽ dawn-dusk). The earliest surviving part of the building is 14th century. However, St Bartholomew first founded a church on the site around AD 62, a single generation after Christ. The well-preserved exterior reliefs include Armenian crosses, saints and angels. The bell tower is under reconstruction.

Tucked into a wooded glade, access is five minutes' stroll from the car park passing an ancient stone arch and 'mill' cascade. The church is 17km west of central Jolfa along the Aras valley. It's a wonderfully scenic drive especially in the golden pre-sunset light, but be careful with your camera as the river constitutes a potentially sensitive international border. On the Azerbaijani riverbank 7km west of Jolfa, a truncated **tomb stub** and **broken bridge** are all that mark the original site of ancient Jolfa (view across the Aras from near a police 'fort'). About 1km further west, as you enter a spectacular **red-rock canyon**, there's a ruined **caravanserai** (north of the road) and, 400m beyond, a cute, minuscule **Shepherd's Chapel** (south).

GETTING THERE & AWAY

A taxi from Jolfa (25 minutes each way) costs around IR60,000 return with stops. A car with an English-speaking driver from Tabriz costs around IR350,000 return (p149).

CROSSING THE AZERBAIJAN (NAKHCHIVAN) BORDER AT JOLFA

Culfa, in Azerbaijan's disconnected Nakhchivan enclave, is a short walk across the Aras River from central Jolfa. Use up your rials or exchange them for Azerbaijani Manats (AZN1=US$1.19) before leaving Iran. Note that in Azerbaijan 'one Shirvan' confusingly means AZN2.

Beware that Culfa's paranoid police assume that all foreigners are spies. Jump quickly into a taxi (AZN5, 35 minutes) or minibus (AZN1) to Nakhchivan city, which is contrastingly relaxed and cosmopolitan. From Nakhchivan city there are direct buses to İstanbul (AZN30 plus border bribes, five daily) taking around 30 hours via Iğdır (AZN7).

However the enclave is separated from the rest of Azerbaijan by aggressively closed Armenian borders. You'd have to fly to reach Baku (US$100, six daily) or Gəncə (US$50, four weekly) but air tickets often sell out a week ahead.

East of Jolfa

The **Aras River** is the Bible's River Gihon. For millennia its valley formed a major thoroughfare for traders, armies and holy men. Only with the treaties of 1813 and 1828 did Russia and Persia turn it into a border line. Several mud fortifications remain from the 18th-century conflicts that led to its division. But today the tension is east–west, not north–south. Clearly visible on the Aras' north bank are ruined villages, sad signs of the still unresolved 1989–94 Armenia-Azerbaijan war. What a difference 50m makes. It's fine to drive along the south (ie Iranian) riverbank as a casual tourist (though taking photos isn't advised). Yet travelling the parallel north bank's now-severed train line would be unthinkable folly. That crosses two globally forgotten 'front lines': from Nakhchivan (Azerbaijan) to mortal enemy Armenia, on through Karabagh (Armenian-occupied Azeri territory), then back through minefields to Azerbaijan again. There's not been active fighting for over a decade, but the guard posts, bombed-out trains and barricaded tunnels add a

CROSSING THE ARMENIAN BORDER AT NORDUZ

On the Iran side, the Norduz customs yards occupy an otherwise unpopulated sweep of rural valley. Walking-distance away on the Armenian side is Agarak village. Armenian 14-day tourist visas (US$30) or three-day transit visas (US$20) are available at the border, but the application might take a while – annoying if you're on one of the through buses (Yerevan–Tehran via Tabriz). Hopefully, they'll wait for you. Moneychangers on the Iran side buy and sell Armenian dram (US$1 = 307 dram) as well as dollars and rials for around 5% below bank rates. One or two taxis usually wait outside the Iranian border compound asking IR60,000 to Jolfa. From within the compound you'd pay IR20,000 more. On the Armenian side Aries Travel (☎ 374-1-220138; www.bedandbreakfast.am) coordinates pleasant homestays from 5000 dram in both Agarak and in bigger Meghri, a 15-minute, 2000-dram taxi ride away. From the Hotel Meghri near central Meghr there's a 9am minibus to Yerevan (7000 dram, nine to 11 hours) and a 7.30am bus to Kapan (1000 dram, two hours).

considerable geopolitical frisson to the Aras River Valley's great natural beauty.

Leaving Jolfa, the horizon is a gateau of red-and-white cliffs backed by snow-streaked Armenian peaks. In the middle distance is the cleft rocky beak of Nakhchivan's abrupt **Ilan Dağ** (Snake Mountain), through which Noah's Ark supposedly crashed en route to Ararat. Just beyond attractive **Marazakand**, the sinuous mud wall of **Javer Castle** rises on a rocky shoulder. Four kilometres further, the main road bypasses **Ahmadabad** village: it's worth a five-minute, 500m detour to admire its cubist array of mud-and-stone homes on a small riverside knoll. Another side road 2.5km further east leads steeply up to the popular, if somewhat overrated, **Asiyab Khurabe** spring and picnic area. The side trip is justified mainly by the valley views as you drive back down.

Siyah Rud is hardly attractive, but its farmers produce the raw silk for Khanemu's spinners and Osku's weavers (p155). Locals are happy to show you the cocoon-extraction process if you're passing through during May or June. Further east the road passes through canyons with glimpses of spiky crested ridges leading up to **Kuh-e Kamtal** (Chamtal Dagh, Tiger Mountain). Sixty kilometres from Jolfa, the canyon widens slightly at **Norduz**, the modern Irano-Armenian border terminal (see boxed text, above). Four kilometres further east, picturesque **Duzal** village rises on a hillock dominated by a distinctive **octagonal tomb tower** and Imamzadeh. Behind the next rocky bluff the road passes through the gate towers and sturdy mud-topped stone walls of the once huge **Abu Mirza** fortress (Kordasht Castle). When viewed from the east, they

frame an impressive spire of eroded rock on the Armenian side. One kilometre further east is a large, lovingly renovated **historic hammam** (Kordasht village; ☺ by request) with newly marbled floors and attractive ceiling patterns. Two kilometres further east, at the end of Kordasht village, look west for a particularly inspiring view of saw-toothed craggy ridges.

After another 25km, a side road rises steeply to the south beside a police post. This leads to **Ushtebin** (Oshtabin, Oshtobeyin) village after 5km (the last 2km un-asphalted and muddy when wet). Ushtebin has been touted by local tourist information offices as a 'new Masuleh', but virtually no visitors seem to have come, let alone any rubbish collectors. Despite the trash, the hamlet is a very picturesque huddle of stone and mud homes rising steeply in a fold of 'secret' valley famous for its white pomegranates.

The main road continues via photogenically stepped village of **Qarachilar** (7km from Ushtebin junction) to Eskanlu (88km) where you could cut inland through nomad summer pastures to Kaleybar (opposite).

AHAR   اهر
☎ 0426 / pop 89,000
Set on high, windswept plains, Ahar is worth a 10-minute stop en route to Kaleybar to see the imposing **Sheikh Shahabdin Ahari mausoleum** (☎ 222 4310; Sheikh Shahabdin St; admission IR3000; ☺ 9am-1.30pm & 4pm-5.30pm). Incorporated into its front *iwan* (barrel-vaulted hall opening onto the courtyard), one of two giant exterior columns retains the original blue glaze. Inside, beyond displays of Safavid Qurans, candlesticks and *keshkul* dervish 'coconut

handbags', is an inner courtyard where the sheikh's simple black slab tomb lies behind a carved stone perimeter screen. The mausoleum lies in a park 400m south of central Ragaei (Shahid Bajlari) St. Turn at Police Sq, northeast of which is the renovated 1906 **covered bazaar**. Around 600m east, facing the vegetable market and friendly, four-room crash-pad **Mosaferkhaneh Reza** (☎ 222 4724; Ragaei St; s/tw IR25,000/40,000) is the savari terminal for Kaleybar (IR10,000, one hour), Meshgin Shahr (IR10,000, 1¼ hours) and Tabriz (back/front IR12,000/14,000, 1¼ hours). A block north is the small, simple but relatively comfortable **Hotel Razavi** (☎ 222 2482; Imam Khomeini St; tw IR150,000) and simple teahouse **Azizi** (Imam Khomeini St; qalyan IR1000; ☺ 7am-9pm) where craggy old grey-beards puff on some of Iran's cheapest sheeshas.

The bus terminal is 1.5km southwest of town via Basij Sq with its flag waving soldier monument.

KALEYBAR & BABAK CASTLE

کلیبر و قلعه بابک

☎ 0427 / pop 17,000

Set attractively in a wide, steep-sided mountain valley, unassuming Kaleybar town makes a great starting point for random hikes and visiting nomad camps en route to the upper Aras River Valley. But by far its biggest draw is the extensive crag-top ruin of **Babak Castle** (Qal'eh Babak). Known to some as Bazz Galasi, the castle has a unique emotional resonance for Azari people as the lair of their 9th-century national hero Babak Khorramdin. Occupying a cultural position somewhere between King Arthur, Robin Hood and Yasser Arafat, Babak is celebrated for harrying the anti-Shiite Abbasid-Arab regime between 815 and 837. Beware of visiting Kaleybar during Babak's controversial 'birthday celebrations' (last week of June). While culturally fascinating, all accommodation will be packed full and authorities might suspect you of being involved in stirring up political unrest amongst the high-spirited Azari nationalists.

There are several access paths to the castle. The most popular route starts behind the seasonal Babak Hotel and takes two fairly strenuous hours with part of the route up dizzyingly steep stairways with fabulous views. Stronger vehicles can drive up an unsurfaced

track to a summer nomad camp reducing the walk to under an hour. But in winter and spring, snow and fog can render any route hazardous or completely impossible.

Sleeping & Eating
Araz Hotel (☎ 422 2290; dm/tw IR30,000/60,000; P) Kaleybar's cheapest option has six recently redecorated rooms, mostly stuffed with four or five comfy beds sharing one shower and toilet. To find it take the second alley east of the petrol station, 300m down Mo'allem St from the Kaleybar Grand. It looks like a private house, but hides a long banqueting hall downstairs. Staff seem curiously ill-informed and speak little Azari, let alone English.

Kaleybar Grand Hotel (☎ 422 2048; fax 422 4666; Shahrdari Sq; s/tw/tr/ste IR50,000/100,000/150,000/300,000) Pleasant enough rooms share decent washing facilities and squat toilets, while the comparatively upmarket suites have bathrooms. There's a kitchen and communal sitting area with good views. The friendly manager speaks some English. It's on the top floor of a yellow-brick shopping centre surveying upper Mo'allem St. Use the middle stairway. The right-hand stairs lead up one floor to the unmarked Kabir (Chabizh) Restaurant (☎ 422 4676; meals IR25,000 to IR40,000; open 12.30pm to 4pm).

Sitting on a lonely hill above Shoza-Abad hamlet, 6km from town, the basic summer-only Babak Hotel is ideally located for climbing the castle and has sweeping views from its café-restaurant.

Getting There & Away
Savaris are fairly frequent to Ahar (IR10,000, 60km, one hour). There are direct buses to Tabriz (IR12,000, three hours) at 8am and 11.30pm. Taxis want IR10,000 to IR30,000 to the castle access paths depending on which route you choose. A taxi to Jolfa along the Aras River will cost around IR350,000.

AROUND KALEYBAR
A lonely asphalt road winds 63km from Kaleybar to the tiny junction hamlet of **Eskanlu,** descending through a wonderful variety of landscapes, from bald mountain-passes to semi-desert badlands and green agricultural oases. Some 25km out of Kaleybar it passes the dramatic triple rock-topped ridge where **Avarsian Castle** once stood. This

area is particularly popular with Shahsevan nomad herders who put their tents relatively close to the road in late spring and summer. Nomad women often wear startlingly colourful flowery costumes. See the boxed text (p164) for more information.

Swing west at Eskanlu and follow the Aras River (the Azerbaijan border) for 18km to reach **Khudaferin**. War-gutted since 1994, the wrecked village sits on the Azerbaijan side. Two impressive **Safavid bridges** here have been ruined much longer. Directly behind is a big, contrastingly new dam. An interesting trip continues to Jolfa (95km; p156) via Ushtebin (see p157) and Kordasht's Abu Mirza fortress (p157).

MESHGIN SHAHR مشگین شهر
☎ 0452 / pop 57,000

Some 80km northwest of Ardabil, Meshgin Shahr is a busy market town set at the foot of Mt Sabalan's craggy north face. Climbers generally access the mountain using a 4WD as far as **Shavil** (Shabil), hiking to a shelter at around 3500m then summitting next day. ALP Tours & Travel Agency (p149) can arrange guides. If you just want mountain views, take a taxi 16km to the archaic-looking brick-box foothill village of **Mo-il** (pronounced 'meurl') for around IR50,000 return. Behind Mo-il mosque, where the road ends, very tatty hot spring pools (IR4000) are used as communal village baths. For more salubrious hot springs (IR15,000) backtrack 3km then fork west 4km to **Qeynarzheh** (Qinarjeh), a relatively modern complex in a lonely steep-cut glen. Bathing sessions alternate every 90 minutes for men (first 8.30am, last 7.30pm) and women (first 10am, last 6pm).

The foremost attraction in Meshgin Shahr itself is the cylindrical brick tomb-tower of **Sheikh Heydar Imamzadeh** (Jonubi St) tucked behind the police station (bring your passport in case of questions). The central, blue-tiled new **Amir al-Mominam Mosque** (Azadi Sq, Imam St) has golden spires like the crows' nests of a medieval galleon. Just 20 seconds' walk north from here is the town's very basic **Mosaferkhaneh Baharestan** (☎ 522 8101; Ayatollah Meshkineh St; s/tw IR30,000/45,000).

Savaris to Ardabil (IR15,000, 1¼ hours) depart from **Istgah Ardabil** (☎ 522 2425; Imam St), a yard that's 300m beyond Imam Sq with its 'Allah' calligraphic centrepiece. Savaris

to Ahar (IR12,000, 1¼ hours) leave from Razmandagan Sq at the westernmost end of Imam Khomeini St, along which shuttle taxis cost IR500 per hop.

ARDABIL اردبیل
☎ 0451 / pop 421,000

Ardabil is a logical stopping point between Tabriz and the upper Caspian coast. Ardabil's magnificent Sheikh Safi-od-Din Mausoleum is by far its greatest attraction but there's a fair scattering of other minor sights and a truly superb teahouse restaurant. When the chilly smog clears, Mt Sabalan's snow-topped peak is dramatically visible from Ardabil's Shurabil Lake. Driving to Alvares ski-slope from the nearby hot-springs resort of Sara'eyn gets you well up Sabalan's slopes for some lovely summer trekking.

Ardabil sits on a high plateau. The weather is pleasantly cool in summer, but terrifies brass monkeys in winter. Snow is probable from November.

History
A military outpost for millennia, Ardabil was declared a city around AD 470. It was capital of the Sajid dynasty Azarbayjan from AD 871 to 929, and saw independence as a khanate from 1747 to 1808. However, Ardabil is best remembered for spawning two great leaders: the Safavid patriarch and great dervish-Sufi mystic Sheikh Safi-od-Din (1253–1354), plus his later descendant Ismail Safavi. The latter expanded the clan domains so successfully that by 1502 Ismail had become Shah of all Persia. His glorious Safavid dynasty was to rule Iran for over two centuries.

Orientation
The central triangle formed by Imam Hossein, Imam Khomeini and Ali Qapu Sqs is manageable on foot. Beyond that the city expands in three big concentric hoops.

Information
Aryana Currency Exchange (☎ 223 8747; Sheikh Safi St; ⏲ 9am-2pm & 4-8pm) Changes many currencies including Azerbaijani manats.

Coffeenet Mohsen (Imam Khomeini Sq; per hr IR4000; ⏲ 8am-midnight) Downstairs. The best connection of five internet places within 50m.

Miras Ferhangi (☎ 225 2708; Khane Ershadeh St; ⏲ 7.30am-2pm Sat-Thu) Excellent free maps of Ardabil,

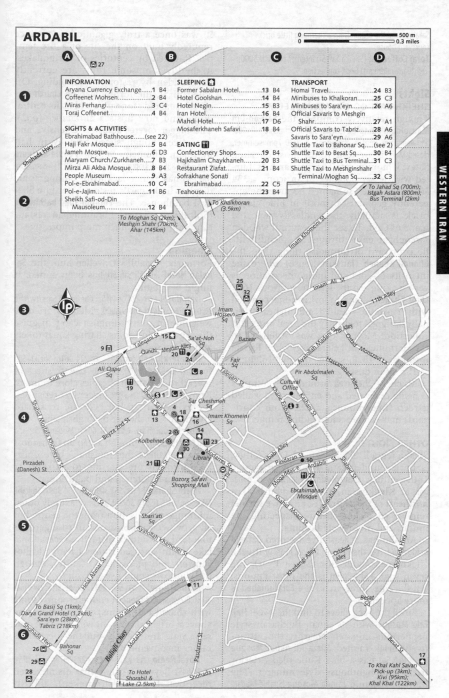

ARDABIL

0 ———————————— 500 m
0 ———————————— 0.3 miles

INFORMATION
Aryana Currency Exchange.....1 B4
Coffeenet Mohsen.................2 B4
Miras Ferhangi......................3 C4
Toraj Coffeenet.....................4 B4

SIGHTS & ACTIVITIES
Ebrahimabad Bathhouse......(see 22)
Haji Fakr Mosque..................5 B4
Jameh Mosque......................6 D3
Maryam Church/Zurkhaneh....7 B3
Mirza Ali Akba Mosque..........8 B4
People Museum.....................9 A3
Pol-e-Ebrahimabad..............10 C4
Pol-e-Jajim...........................11 B6
Sheikh Safi-od-Din
  Mausoleum.......................12 B4

SLEEPING
Former Sabalan Hotel............13 B4
Hotel Goolshan.....................14 B4
Hotel Negin..........................15 B3
Iran Hotel.............................16 B4
Mahdi Hotel..........................17 D6
Mosaferkhaneh Safavi...........18 B4

EATING
Confectionery Shops..............19 B4
Hajkhalim Chaykhaneh..........20 B3
Restaurant Ziafat..................21 B4
Sofrakhane Sonati
  Ebrahimabad.....................22 C5
Teahouse.............................23 B4

TRANSPORT
Homai Travel........................24 B3
Minibuses to Khalkoran.........25 C3
Minibuses to Sara'eyn...........26 A6
Official Savaris to Meshgin
  Shahr..............................27 A1
Official Savaris to Tabriz........28 A6
Savaris to Sara'eyn...............29 A6
Shuttle Taxi to Bahonar Sq.....(see 2)
Shuttle Taxi to Besat Sq.........30 B4
Shuttle Taxi to Bus Terminal...31 C3
Shuttle Taxi to Meshginshahr
  Terminal/Moghan Sq..........32 C3

WESTERN IRAN

To Jahad Sq (700m);
Istgah Astara (800m);
Bus Terminal (2km)

To Khalkhoran
(3.5km)

To Moghan Sq (2km);
Meshgin Shahr (70km);
Ahar (145km)

Shohada Hwy

Beheshti St
Engelab St
Imam Khomeini St
Imam Ali St
11th Alley

25
32
31

7
Imam
Hossein
Sq

6

Bazaar

9
Taleqani St
15
Sa'at-Noh
Sq
Ayatollah Madani St
9th Alley
Ostad Monsavi La

Qeinchi
Meydan Alley
20
24

Fajr
Sq

8

Ali Qapu
Sq
12
19

Taleqani St

Pir Abdolmaleh
Sq

Hassanabad Alley

Sadi St
Sheikh Safi St
1
5
Sar Cheshmeh
Sq

Cultural
Office

Khane Eskhadeh St
Kashan St

3

Shahid Moafari Khomeini St
Beyza 2nd St
4
18
13
16
Imam Khomeini
Sq

2
Kolbehnet
14
30
23

Library
Moqadres St
Arbabi Alley

Pasdaran St
10
Ardabili
St

Pirzadeh
(Danesh) St
21

22
Ebrahimabad
Mosque

Moqadas-e
Ebrahimabad St

Bozorg Safavi
Shopping Mall
Shahid Moadi St

Shari'ati St
Imam Khomeini St

Shari'ati St

Ayatollah Khamenei St

Khadangi Alley
Orfabaz
Alley

11

Besat
Sq

To Basij Sq (1km);
Darya Grand Hotel (1.2km);
Sara'eyn (28km);
Tabriz (218km)

Hefal Annar St
Mo'allem St
Motahhari St
Pasdaran St
Shohada Hwy

Besat St
Shohada Hwy

Baliqli Chay

26
29
Bahonar
Sq
28

17

To Hotel
Shorabil &
Lake (2.5km)

To Khal Kahl Savari
Pick-up (3km);
Kivi (95km);
Khal Khal (122km)

Sara'eyn and the region from a charming little brick courtyard house.

Toraj Coffeenet (Sheikh Safi St; internet per hr IR5000; ☒ 10am-midnight) Good connection.

Sights

SHEIKH SAFI-OD-DIN MAUSOLEUM

Though relatively compact, the **Safi-od-Din Mausoleum Complex** (Sheikh Safi St; admission IR4000; ☒ 8am-5pm winter, 8am-noon & 3.30-7pm summer, closed Mon) is western Iran's most dazzling Safavid monument. The patriarch is buried with lesser notables in an iconic 1334 **Allah-Allah tower**, so named because the apparently geometrical motif in blue-glazed brick is actually the endlessly repeated name of God. To see the beautiful wooden sarcophagi enter through a splendid little courtyard of turquoise tiling then the **Ghandil Khaneh** (lantern house) where the intensity of gold and indigo decoration is very striking. To the left, the glorious 1612 **Chini Khaneh** (china room) is honeycombed with 'stalactite'-vaulted gilt niches originally designed to display the royal porcelain collection. Most of that was carted off to the Hermitage (St Petersburg) when Russia invaded in 1828, saving the mausoleum's staff a lot of dusting.

Much of the area around the complex is being excavated and an attractive walled garden (free entrance, access from courtyard) makes a peaceful reading refuge.

OTHER SIGHTS

Sheikh Jebra'il, Sheikh Safi-od-Din's father, is buried underneath a mildly attractive 16th-century **mausoleum** (admission by donation) at Khalkhoran, a village-suburb 3km northeast of the centre. It's an active shrine; remove your shoes before inspecting the murals and multifaceted ceiling.

Ardabil has at least five restored **Safavid bridges** across the Baliqli Chay (Fishy River). Nicknamed Yeddi Göz (Seven Eyes), the seven-span **Pol-e-Jajim** is the most famous, but the cute, three-arch **Pol-e-Ebrahimabad** is more appealing.

Stroll the back alleys to find the sweet **Haji Fakr Mosque** with its squat, Bukharan-style peppermill minaret. Nearby, the attractively brick-vaulted **Mirza Ali Akbar Mosque** (Sa'at-Noh Sq) has a blue Kufic-tiled exterior frieze and lighthouse-style minaret. The Mongol Ilkhanid **Jameh Mosque** (Shahid Madani

St) was once a truly gigantic brick edifice reputedly built on the site of a fire temple. Ravaged by centuries of earthquakes, its heftily lumpsome ruins are currently part-hidden by restorers' scaffolding. Off Taleqani St, the former **Maryam Church** has an unusual old stone pyramid as its central dome and now hosts a *zurkhaneh* (p52). The bigger **covered bazaar** is extensive and attractive, though sliced brutally in half by Imam Khomeini St. The **People Museum** (☎ 444 5885; Ali Qapu; admission IR3000; ☒ 8am-8pm Thu-Tue) has rather lacklustre ethnographic displays in the partly restored Merdum Shenasi bathhouse. The **Ebrahimabad bathhouse** (Sofrakhane Sonati Ebrahimabad restaurant, opposite) is much more impressive.

Sleeping

Formerly Ardabil's traveller hub, the **Sabalan Hotel** (Sheikh Safi St) has been gutted. It might be rebuilt.

Iran Hotel (☎ 224 6644; Sar Cheshmeh Sq; s/tw/tr/q IR50,000/66,000/81,500/92,000) Mehdi's friendly welcome in partial-English can't disguise the rag-bag old rooms sharing squat toilets and grimy shower.

Mosaferkhaneh Safavi (☎ 224 0616; Sheikh Safi St; s/d/tr IR40,000/80,000/98,000) The freshest of several rock-bottom cheapies close to Imam Khomeini Sq. Some recently repainted rooms have a tap but beds are rock hard and there's no shower or English sign.

Hotel Goolshan (☎ 224 6644; Modarres St; s/tr IR80,000/100,000) Although a step up from most *mosaferkhanehs*, the Goolshan's bare, once-bright rooms are starting to look pretty tired. Shared kitchen and bathrooms.

Hotel Shorabil (☎ 551 3096; fax 551 3097; Shurabil Lakeside; s/d/tr US$18/30/38) This relaxingly quiet, midrange place is 4km from the centre but all a-twitter with birdsong in rose gardens that lead down to an attractive recreational lake. Light-suffused rooms have good hot showers and pleasant red fabrics, though the windows could use a wash.

Mahdi Hotel (☎ 661 4011; Besat St; s/tw from IR230,000/400,000) Decent enough rooms (some with shared bathrooms) suffer road noise above a bright restaurant with striking murals. Staff are friendly but the location is rather inconvenient.

Hotel Negin (☎ 223 5671; fax 223 5674; Taleqani St; tw US$45) Beyond a somewhat disinterested reception (no English spoken), almost-smart corridors lead to very good rooms with full Western facilities.

Darya Grand Hotel (☎ 771 6977; Atayi St; s/d/tr/q/ste US$35/53/66/78/105; **P**) Once considered Ardabil's best, the Darya now feels empty and forlorn. Despite some cracks in the walls it's clean enough, if lacking any real style. It's 200m east of Basij Sq.

If nothing suits in Ardabil, there's loads more accommodation in nearby Sara'eyn (p164).

Eating

Teahouse (Modarres St; ⏱ 7am-3pm) An unnamed, all-male teahouse almost opposite the library does fabulous curds-and-honeycomb breakfasts (IR5000).

Hajkhalim Chaykhaneh (Qunchi Meydan Alley; tea IR500, dizi IR8000, qalyan from IR2000; ⏱ 6.30am-11pm) Equally daunting for women, this place offers a very cheap, thoroughly 'real' local teahouse experience. Expect stares.

Restaurant Ziafat (☎ 224 4985; mains IR17,000-38,000; ⏱ 7.30am-10.30pm) Several unexotic places for standard Iranian fare, pizzas and roast chicken are clustered along Imam Khomeini St. Of these, Ziafat is comparatively spacious with a very 1980s interior and glass-sided kitchen so you can watch chefs burning your rubbery kababs.

our pick **Sofrakhane Sonati Ebrahimabad** (☎ 224 9588; Moadi St; mains IR25,000-60,000; tea IR3500, qalyan IR10,000) This hidden, fabulously renovated 640-year-old former *hammam* oozes atmosphere with three domed chambers each more magnificent than the last. Local speciality *pichag qeimeh* (tender lamb, diced almonds, caramelised onions and soft-boiled egg stranded with saffron) is cooked with finesse and packed with flavour, albeit in small portions. After dining retire to the central tea-chamber. Manager Sheikhlovand speaks English.

Numerous shops facing the Safi-od-Din Mausoleum sell *helva siyah* (black halva or 'pest'), a rich local speciality vaguely reminiscent of Christmas pudding. It costs around IR30,000 per kilogram but a small plateful sprinkled with coconut, grated nuts and cinnamon is plenty (IR1000). Ardabil's famous honey is sold throughout the city.

Getting There & Away

Flights to Tehran (IR315,000) leave three times daily with **Iran Air** (☎ 223 8600) and

daily with Iran Aseman. Helpful **Homai Travel** (☎ 223 3233; Sa'at-Noh Sq; ⏱ 8.30am-7.30pm Sat-Thu, 9am-1pm Fri) sells air tickets and train tickets ex-Tabriz.

BUS, MINIBUS & SAVARI

From the **main terminal** (Moqaddas-e-Ardabili St), Tehran buses (IR38,000 to IR60,000, 10 hours) leave hourly (7am to 11pm) via Astara (IR6000 to IR10,000, two hours), Rasht (IR17,000 to IR25,000, five hours) and Qazvin (IR38,000 to IR60,000, eight hours). Buses run to Tabriz (IR17,000 to IR25,000, four hours) via Sarab hourly till 3.30pm.

For Ahar make savari hops via Meshgin Shahr. Either start from **Istgah Meshgin** (☎ 333 1855; RTA Sabalan, Beheshti St), a hidden yard 200m northwest of Shohoda St, or risk casual drivers from Moghan Sq.

From different points near Bahonar Sq savaris run to Tabriz (IR50,000) and Sara'eyn (IR5000).

Savaris to Astara (back/front/whole car IR13,000/15,000/60,000, 1½ hours) use **Istgah Astara** (☎ 882 0876; Jam'e-Jam St), a small yard with a green sign 100m northeast of Jahad Sq.

Khal Khal savaris (IR12,000, 1½ hours) and rare buses depart from huge Isar Sq, 3km southeast of Besat Sq.

Getting Around

The airport is 1km off the Astara road, 11km northeast of Ardabil (IR25,000 by taxi). From Imam Khomeini Sq shuttle taxis run to Bahonar Sq (for Sara'eyn minibuses) and to Besat Sq. Khalkhoran minibuses start near Imam Hossein Sq.

AROUND ARDABIL
Sara'eyn   سرعین
☎ 0452 / pop 12,000

On otherwise-lonely plains sloping gently towards mighty Mt Sabalan (4811m) sits this brash little hot-springs resort. Its mineral waters are said to cure anything from baldness to syphilis, and tacky souvenir stores overflow with Iranian miracle seekers in summer, making for great people-watching opportunities. Bathing in outdoor hot pools like **Gavmish-Goli** (admission IR6000; ⏱ women 6am-1pm, men 2pm-late) is amusing in winter snow.

The modest **Alvares chair-lift** (telecabine; ☎ 222 0222; per ride IR15,000), 21km from Sara'eyn, only operates in the ski season. But in summer Alvares still makes a great, accessible starting point for higher altitude hikes. Scenery is bracing and en route you'll probably pass Shahsevan nomads (see boxed text, right), whose flocks graze close to Sara'eyn in June, their womenfolk often dressed in pink dresses and patterned white shawls.

SLEEPING

Hotels sprout like mushrooms in Sara'eyn but many are jerry-built and decay quickly. Cheaper rooms are available above shops. Touts around the central Hydrotherapy Centre can find you a place in virtually any price range. Bargains are possible off-season.

Motel Kaveh (☎ 222 2447; Valiasr St 671; q IR100,000; P) Arched windows and a two-tiered terrace give the Kaveh a vaguely colonial look. Neat rooms with kitchen, shower and Western loo are excellent-value year round. It's very central in an overgrown garden (marked '096'). Owners speak German and English.

Hotel Amin (☎ 222 4290; d low/high season IR290,000/500,000) At the north edge of town, north-facing rooms have an unparalleled view towards Mt Sabalan. However, while the semi-smart tower is almost new, it's already showing signs of wear.

Laleh International (☎ 222 2750; s/d/ste with breakfast US$80/122/256; P ✷) This long-established resort hotel has neat, motel-style rooms and English-speaking staff who can arrange mountain guides for climbing the mighty Mt Sabalan.

EATING

A local speciality served from steaming cauldrons all around town is *nokhut sabzijak* (*ash-e dugh*, IR3500 per bowl). It tastes like a sort of hot tangy rice pudding with hints of rhubarb and the odd chickpea. *Fatir* (gingerbread) is also popular and honey sellers are ubiquitous.

GETTING THERE & AWAY

Grindingly slow minibuses (IR2000, 40 minutes) and more frequent savaris (IR5000, 25 minutes) to Ardabil's Bahonar Sq depart from the corner of Valiasr and Imam Khomeini Sts. That's 400m west of the Hydrotherapy Centre, outside which drivers offer rides all the way to Tabriz in season. **Taxis**

(☎ 222 4888) want IR60,000 plus waiting time for a Sara'eyn–Alvares return.

Fandoqlu فندقلو

Turn off the hectic, but patchily beautiful Ardabil–Astara road near Namin and follow country lanes south for 10km through fields thickly carpeted with spring flowers to reach this over-popular 'recreation zone'. If the thick mists deign to clear there should be magnificently panoramic views down towards the Caspian. No public transport.

Khal Khal خلخال

☎ 0452 / pop 41,000

A scenic alternative route from Ardabil to Rasht follows a broad valley of sparsely populated nomad territory through the almost-attractive stepped town of **Kivi** (Chivi, Giwi, Kosar) then climbs a steep-cut rocky valley to **Khal Khal**. Though rather characterless, this 4km strip-town could make a great trekking base. East of Khal Khal the road wheels through high grassy hills before tumbling down through deciduous forests to Asalem on the Caspian coast with some brilliant glimpsed views en route.

SHAHSEVAN (ELSEVAN) NOMADS

From the 17th century, various Turkic nomad tribes of Eastern Azerbaijan formed a pro-regime bulwark against foreign invaders, earning them the loose, collective name *Shahsevan* ('Shah-lovers'). However, after painful 19th-century treaties divided their traditional grazing lands between Russia and Persia, some turned to brigandry. In 1909, following the Constitutional Revolution, Shahsevan fighters sacked Ardabil – a vicious attack that eyewitnesses remembered as being far crueller than the later Soviet invasion. The Shahsevan continued their revolt until 'tamed' in 1923 by Reza Shah who bribed them with offers of considerable autonomy.

During the 20th century most Shahsevans became sedentary farmers, but some semi-nomadic groups (now officially renamed 'Elsevan') are still to be found, wintering around Parsabad then moving flocks up to summer pastures around Kaleybar and the slopes of Mt Sabalan.

A lovely if tough road from Khal Khal to Aqkand zigzags across the Qizil Owzan valley where incredibly isolated, inaccessible villages cling valiantly to the distant canyon sides.

SLEEPING

Mosaferkhaneh Bastan (☎ 422 3884; dm/q IR20,000/70,000) Ultra-basic unmarked crash pad with no shower. There's no receptionist: ask for keys at the pharmacy beside Bank Tejarat opposite Coffeenet Novin, 1km west of the bus terminal.

Khal Khal Tourist Inn (Mehmansara Jahangardi; ☎ 425 3991; s/tw/tr US$17/20/26) Acceptable rooms with clean squat toilets have been recently redecorated, though some furniture remains ropy. Walk five minutes east of the terminal then two minutes up an unlikely mud track where the dual carriageway ends.

GETTING THERE & AWAY

The terminal is beside an amusingly purposeless pedestrian overpass. TBT buses run to Ardabil (IR6500, two hours) at 6am, 7am and 4pm and to Rasht (IR20,000) at 8am and 5.30pm. From outside, savaris run to Ardabil (back/front IR20,000/23,000, 1½ hours) and to Asalem (IR17,000, 1¼ hours) for Rasht connections. There's a handy taxi **agency** (☎ 425 3070) beside the terminal.

ASTARA　　　　　　　　　آستارا
☎ 0182 / pop 35,000

Astara has a wide but litter-strewn **beach** (Sahel Darya) and could make a base to visit the forested Talesh mountain hinterlands, but most travellers head straight on to Ardabil, Rasht or Azerbaijan.

If arriving from Azerbaijan walk directly south (150m) from the border post to find Hakim Nezami St for midrange accommodation, such as **Belal Hotel** (☎ 521 5586; Mo'allem Sq; s/d/tr IR148,000/218,000/270,000) with an English-speaking manager and relatively pleasant en suite rooms off somewhat scrappy corridors. Or walk 400m west to Shahrdari Sq for **Mehmanpazir Aseman** (☎ 522 2300; off Shahrdari Sq; tw with/without shower IR60,000/50,000), a bearable if typically male-dominated *mosaferkhaneh* with shared toilets. It's marked 'Asiman Mehmanxanasi' and accessed via a clothing *passaj* beside Bank Melli (no exchange). The international-standard **Espinas**

Hotel (☎ 525 2700; www.espinashotel.com; Rasht Hwy; s/d/ste US$90/110/160; P ✗), 8km south of here, sits beside an attractive mountainbacked **lake** where you can rent jet skis. That's 5km beyond the **terminal** (Imam Khomeini St) with buses to Tehran (IR50,000), Tabriz (IR30,000, six hours, 3pm), Rasht (IR30,000, 10am and 1pm) and Qazvin (IR50,000, 4pm). More frequent through buses plus convenient savaris to Rasht (IR40,000, 2½ hours) and Ardabil (IR15,000, 1½ hours) pick up around massive Laleh (Shohoda Qomran) Sq, 200m further south.

ASTARA TO RASHT

Between Astara and Rezvanshahr several relatively unspoilt sections of Caspian hinterland offer attractive views of rice paddies (notably at **Lavandevil**, **Khotbeh Sara** and **Sust**). There's some lovely woodland behind **Asalem** (change savaris here for Khal Khal). Most accessible of the region's castle ruins is the cute little **Dezhe Sasal Fortress** (Qal'eh Lisar; Salsal St), which crowns a petite wooded knoll at the southern end of **Lisar** town, just five minutes' walk off the main highway. Its gate arch is intact and offers sea views, though the rest of the site is fenced off.

Little **Hashtpar** is often referred to as 'Talesh', somewhat confusing as Talesh is also the name of the region and its people. Behind Hashtpar's charioteer statue in the central square is an attractive Qajar-era octagonal pavilion, but since it's used by revolutionary guards, photography is unwise.

RASHT　　　　　　　　　رشت
☎ 0131 / pop 618,000

Rapidly expanding Rasht is the capital of Gilan province and by far the largest city of the Shomal (Caspian littoral) region. Gilan has had extended periods of independence and the lispy local Gilaki dialect remains noticeably distinct from Farsi, its reversed adjective–noun order causing much amusement for other Iranians.

Although 15km inland, Rasht is a popular weekend and holiday destination for Tehranis, for whom the greatest attraction is its 'refreshing' climate (ie lots of rain). It's mildly amusing to watch local tourists driving with arms outstretched to feel the drops. But year-round downpours and steaming summer humidity don't otherwise appeal to most foreign tourists.

CROSSING THE AZERBAIJAN BORDER AT ASTARA

A narrow river divides Astara (Iran) from Astara (Azerbaijan). By Caucasus standards the pedestrian border here is quick and straightforward with neither fees nor bribes to pay. Things are contrastingly slow for vehicles. International Baku–Tehran buses wait between three and seven hours while the whole bus is checked. Visas are *not* available on arrival. The pedestrian **crossing point** (Mosaferi Gümrük; 7.30am-noon & 1.30-4.30pm) is easy to miss up a small lane north of Hakim Nezami St. On the Azerbaijan side, the unmarked metal border gate is 500m along Heydar Əliyev küçasi from the excellent-value Hotel Şindan.

Freelance moneychangers at the Iran-side border-gate offer passable rates. Get rid of rials here if heading north. Leave bigger exchanges till Ardabil or Rasht if heading south. Near Hotel Şindan on the Azerbaijan side, Kapital Bank has an ATM cash machine.

Confusingly many Azeris count in 'Shirvans' rather than New Azeri Manats (AZN, US$1=0.84AZN). One Shirvan means AZN2.

Decrepit night buses to Baku (AZN5) and daytime minivans to Lənkəran (AZN1) start 100m north of Hotel Şindan.

An overnight sleeper train to Baku (AZN2.70, 11 hours) leaves Astara around 7pm, but the station is 3km from the border and tickets often sell out.

The city has precious little in the way of historical buildings, but Rasht is a useful transport hub from which to visit the lush mountain forests, rice paddies and thatched-house villages of the emerald-green Gilan hinterland, most famously at Masuleh. It's also a great place to taste the garlic-stoked, vegetable-rich Gilan cuisine (p170).

History

Historically Lahijan and Fuman were Gilan's main centres. Rasht (previously Resht) developed in the 14th century, but the population was massacred in 1668 by the forces of Cossack brigand Stepan 'Stenka' Razin who also sank Persia's entire Caspian navy. The Russians, a constant factor in the region thereafter, were back in 1723 clearing spaces in the then-impenetrable forest to allow Resht's growth. In 1899 a Russian company cut the road to Qazvin, diminishing Gilan's isolation from the rest of Iran. By WWI the town boasted 60,000 inhabitants and four international consulates. From 1917 it was the centre of Kuchuk Khan's Jangali ('Forest') Movement, an Islamic, Robin Hood–style rebellion. Among their grievances with collapsing Qajar Iran was the shah's perceived sell-out to oil-hungry Britain. Courting the Bolsheviks who'd just taken control of Russia, Kuchuk Khan joined forces with communist-agitators and, on 4 June 1920, set up Gilan as the 'Soviet Socialist Republic of Iran'. However, radical-leftists and land-owning Muslim nationalists

made very prickly bedfellows. Once Kuchuk Khan had ejected the infidel communists from his 'government', his Russian backers slipped away leaving Gilan prey to the efficient new regime of Reza Khan (later Shah Reza Pahlavi) who'd taken over Persia in a February 1921 coup. Reza Khan first dealt with Azadistan (temporarily independent Tabriz/Azarbayjan) then attacked Gilan. Most of Rasht's pretty wooden houses were burnt, Kuchuk Khan was executed and his severed head was brought to Tehran for public display.

These days any enemy of the Pahlavis has become a friend of the current Islamic Republic. Thus Kuchuk Khan has ridden back into favour on many a horseback statue across Gilan.

Orientation

The three main thoroughfares, Shari'ati St, Sa'di St and Imam Khomeini Blvd, converge at pleasantly palm-filled Shahrdari Sq (maps call it Shohada Sq). Traffic can be nightmarish but budget accommodation is conveniently close. Golsar in the north is comparatively chic and middle class.

Information

BOOKSHOPS

Barg Bookshop (222 5718; Sabz Sq; 8.30am-1.30pm & 4-9pm Sat-Thu) Stocks Farsi phrase books and some English-language magazines.

Ta'ati Bookshop (222 2627; A'lam-ol Hoda St; 9am-1.30pm & 4-9pm) Sells brilliant city maps (IR10,000).

RASHT

0 _____ 2 km
0 _____ 1.0 miles

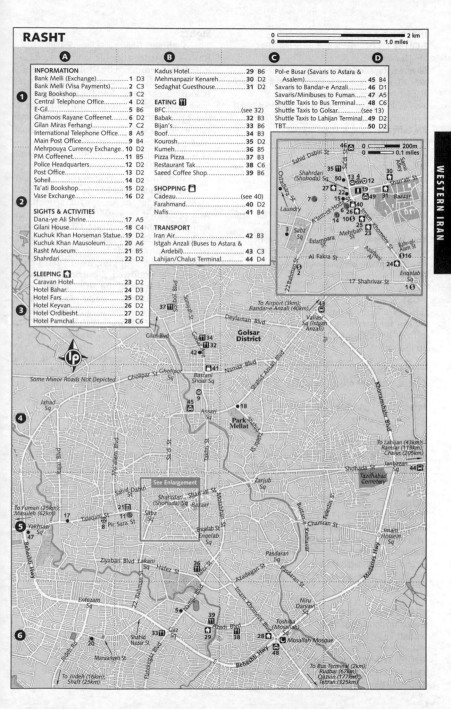

❶

INFORMATION
Bank Melli (Exchange)....................**1** D3
Bank Melli (Visa Payments).............**2** C3
Barg Bookshop.............................**3** C2
Central Telephone Office................**4** D2
E-Gil..**5** B6
Ghamoos Rayane Coffeenet............**6** D2
Gilan Miras Ferhangi.....................**7** C2
International Telephone Office........**8** A5
Main Post Office...........................**9** B4
Mehrpouya Currency Exchange.....**10** D2
PM Coffeenet..............................**11** B5
Police Headquarters.....................**12** D2
Post Office..................................**13** D2
Soheil..**14** D2
Ta'ati Bookshop...........................**15** D2
Vase Exchange............................**16** D2

❷

SIGHTS & ACTIVITIES
Dana-ye Ali Shrine.......................**17** A5
Gilani House................................**18** C4
Kuchuk Khan Horseman Statue.....**19** D2
Kuchuk Khan Mausoleum.............**20** A6
Rasht Museum.............................**21** B5
Shahrdari....................................**22** D2

❸

SLEEPING 🛏
Caravan Hotel..............................**23** D2
Hotel Bahar.................................**24** D3
Hotel Fars...................................**25** D2
Hotel Keyvan...............................**26** D2
Hotel Ordibesht...........................**27** D2
Hotel Pamchal.............................**28** C6

Kadus Hotel................................**29** B6
Mehmanpazir Kenareh...................**30** D2
Sedaghat Guesthouse...................**31** D2

EATING 🍴
BFC.....................................(see 32)
Babak...**32** B3
Bijan's..**33** B6
Boof...**34** B3
Kourosh......................................**35** D2
Kumeh..**36** B5
Pizza Pizza..................................**37** B3
Restaurant Tak............................**38** C6
Saeed Coffee Shop.......................**39** B6

SHOPPING 🛍
Cadeau................................(see 40)
Farahmand..................................**40** D2
Nafis..**41** B4

TRANSPORT
Iran Air.......................................**42** B3
Istgah Anzali (Buses to Astara &
    Ardebil)..................................**43** C3
Lahijan/Chalus Terminal...............**44** D4

Pol-e Busar (Savaris to Astara &
    Asalem)..................................**45** B4
Savaris to Bandar-e Anzali............**46** D1
Savaris/Minibuses to Fuman..........**47** A5
Shuttle Taxis to Bus Terminal........**48** C6
Shuttle Taxis to Golsar...........(see 13)
Shuttle Taxis to Lahijan Terminal...**49** D2
TBT..**50** D2

WESTERN IRAN

0 _____ 200m
0 _____ 0.1 miles

**Golsar
District**

To Airport (3km);
Bandar-e Anzali (40km)

Valiasr
Sq (Istgah
Anzali)

Deylaman Blvd

Gilan Blvd

Some Minor Roads Not Depicted   Cholipar St   Gholipar
St

Bastani
Shoar Sq

Namaz Blvd

Ittihad
Sq

Ansari
Sq

**Park
Mellat**

To Lahijan (43km);
Ramsar (119km);
Chalus (205km)

Zarjub Blvd

Shahrdari
(Shohoda) Sq

See Enlargement

Sabz
Sq

To Fuman (25km);
Masuleh (62km)

Yakhsazi
Sq

Enqelab St

Enqelab
Sq

Shohada St

Tazehabad
Cemetery

Imam
Hossein
Sq

Ziyabari Blvd

Lakani
Sq

Hafez St

Pasdaran
Sq

Entezam
Sq

Gaz
Sq

Azadi Blvd

Niru
Daryavi
Sq

Toshiba
(Mosallah)
Sq

Mosallah Mosque

Shahid
Nazar St

To Jirdeh (16km);
Shaft (25km)

To Bus Terminal (2km);
Rudbar (67km);
Qazvin (177km);
Tehran (325km)

Sahid Dabiri St

Shahrdari
(Shohoda) Sq

Shari'ati
St

Bazaar

Laundry

A'lam-ol-Hoda
St

Imam Khomeini St

Mehrban
St

Eslampara

Azadhol

Bahr-ol-
Alam St

Al Fakra St

Eslampara

17 Shahrivar St

Enqelab
Sq

INTERNET ACCESS

E-Gil (☎ 323 1306; Namju Blvd; per hr IR6000; ☉ 10am-9pm)

Ghamoos Rayane Coffeenet (☎ 2235970; Passaj Nefis, A'lam-ol Hoda St; per hr IR4500; ☉ 9am-9pm Sat-Thu) Fast connection, friendly people but hidden away on the 4th floor (take the lift from the *pasazh* beside Bank Tejarat).

PM Coffeenet (Taleqani St; per hr IR6000; ☉ 10am-9pm) Graffiti-cool interior with separate women's room.

Soheil (A'lam-ol Hoda St; per hr IR5000; ☉ 10am-10pm) Enter from alley behind.

MONEY

Mehrpouya Currency Exchange (☎ 222 7826; Sa'di Ally; ☉ 9am-1.30pm & 4.30-8pm Sat-Thu)

Vase Exchange (☎ 224 0597; Moravid Close, 1st fl; ☉ 9.30am-1.30pm & 5-8pm Sat-Wed, 9.30am-1.30pm Thu) Free chockies while you change money. Good rates.

POST

There's a central post office on Shahrdari Sq but for parcel service use the main post office (Bentolhoda St) just off Golsar Ave in Golsar.

TELEPHONE

Central telephone office (Shahrdari Sq; ☉ 8am-8pm) Domestic calls only.

International telephone office (Taleqani St; ☉ 8am-9pm Sat-Thu)

TOURIST INFORMATION

Gilan Miras Ferhangi (☎ 775 4664; Ehtesab Alley off Sabz Sq; ☉ 8am-2pm Sat-Thu) Historic brick building and attractive garden hosts the tourist information office.

TOURS

Hassan Mohit (☎ 0911 136 7796; www.aryantour.com) This delightfully personable English-speaking driver-guide has a refreshingly easy-going manner. Daily rates range from US$130/50 with/without car. Hassan can provide scrumptious family meals and homestay beds at Titi ('blossom') Cottage in the semi-rural village of Ebrahim Sara (25km east of Rasht).

VISA EXTENSIONS

Police headquarters (☎ 218 3481; room 8, 1st fl, Shohada Sq; ☉ 8am-1.30pm Sat-Thu) To extend your visa, apply before 10am. Pay IR100,000 to the specific Bank Melli (cnr 22 Bahman and 17 Shahrivar Sts), return with the receipt and pay a further IR2500 to a uniformed officer. Processing takes about three hours.

Sights

The **Shahrdari** (Municipality Bldg; Shahrdari Sq) is Rasht's most identifiable landmark, its colonial style tempered by a token mini-dome topping a distinctive whitewashed tower. It looks great when floodlit at night. Palm trees admire the interplay of fountains in the square opposite. The central **horseman statue** (Shohada Sq) is Kuchuk Khan, the Jangali leader of 'Soviet Iran' (p166). A steady flow of well-wishers visit his **mausoleum** (Manzariyeh St), sheltered by a contemporary brick gazebo with intricate wooden roof.

Rasht Museum (Taleqani St; admission IR3000; ☉ 8am-5.30pm Tue-Sun, 9am-1pm Fri) is small, but well presented in a 1930s house. Its mannequin displays illustrate Gilaki lifestyle, amid a selection of 3000-year-old terracotta *riton* drinking horns in the shape of bulls, rams and deer. Supping from such vessels supposedly endowed the drinker with the powers and skills of the animal depicted.

Cute little **Dana-ye Ali Shrine** (middle of Taleqani St) is topped with a faceted pyramid of blue tiling.

Supposedly 'typical' thatched-roof **Gilani cottages** with upper wooden balustrades are shown in many brochures, but are very rare in situ. One such has been dismantled and moved to a traffic island in Shahid Ansari Blvd (behind a drive-in burger takeaway) and is now used as a tourist information outpost. Many more are being reassembled in the excellent **Gilan Rural Heritage Museum** (☎ 323 9490; admission IR3000; ☉ 9am-dusk Thu-Fri) 18km south of Rasht (2km off the Qazvin highway). Six full homesteads complete with rice barns are already 'active' in 150 hectares of woodland. On open days, local crafts (thatching, mat-making, cloth-weaving) are displayed and there are tight-rope walking mini-shows. Houses display local tools left lying around as though the owners had just nipped out to the pub.

Sleeping

There are many options, but occupancy is high in peak summer season (May to September) when overwhelming humidity makes air-con virtually essential.

BUDGET

Sedaghat Guesthouse (☎ 223 6088; Shari'ati St, upstairs; s/tw/tr IR47,000/62,500/75,000) Rooms are better than the grimy entrance stairs suggest. Singles are claustrophobically small, but worn twins are passable.

Hotel Fars (☎ 222 5257; Sa'di Lane; tw/tr/q IR70,000/80,000/90,000) Set back from the main road, the basic Fars is quieter and marginally cleaner than the average *mehmanpazir*, but charges double if you check in before 2pm.

Caravan Hotel (☎ 222 2612; Shahid Mehrban Lane; s/d/tr IR80,000/90,000/100,000) and **Hotel Bahar** (☎ / fax 222 1350; Imam Khomeini Blvd; tw/tr IR75,000/90,000) both occupy once-attractive but now slightly ragged buildings with high ceilings. Readers report spotting wildlife in the shared bathrooms.

Mehmanpazir Kenareh (☎ 222 2412; Ferdosi Alley off Shari'ati St; s/tw/tr IR70,000/100,000/120,000) By far the most appealing of the central cheapies, this relatively new place has sparkling white-tiled floors, reliably changed sheets and its off-road location means it's reasonably quiet. No English sign.

MIDRANGE & TOP END
Hotel Keyvan (☎ 222 2979; Imam Khomeini Blvd; tw with breakfast IR180,000; 🗙) Choose your room carefully. Some are good value: well air-conditioned and recently redecorated, albeit with a few rough edges. Others (same price!) are very ragged fan-only boxes, albeit with toilet and hot shower.

Hotel Ordibesht (☎ 222 9210; fax 222 2221; tw US$30; P 🗙) Delightful staff and loveably dated décor behind concrete Corinthian columns make up for a slight mustiness in some of the rooms. Set well back off Shahrdari Sq, it manages to be splendidly central yet very quiet.

Hotel Pamchal (☎ 660 3031; 15 Khordat St; d/ste IR540,000/700,000; 🗙) Attractively rebuilt rooms with designer armchairs and pot plants. The orange globe-lamps are stylish if somewhat too dim. Good big bathrooms have Western toilets.

Kadus Hotel (☎ 322 3075; cadus_hotel@yahoo .com; Azadi Blvd; s/d/tr/ste US$60/80/90/120; P 🗙 🗙) A full-blown refit has cleverly used contemporary-retro touches to bring alive the Kadus' 1970s architecture. Rooms have trendy faux-antique basins, Western loos and brightly tasteful décor.

Eating
For cheap desserts, nuts and snacks there are stalls around the bazaar. Many cheap kabab barbecues appear at night on Imam Khomeini St and Toshiba Sq.

Kumeh (☎ 322 6579; Hafez St; kababs IR10,000-22,000; 🕑 11am-2pm & 5.30-11pm) The most interesting of a huddle of restaurants in the Park-e-Shahr area, Kumeh has Irano-Hawaiian covered dining platforms outside. Inside is more standard but sharing a post-prandial qalyan here is an ideal way to meet friendly regulars.

Saeed Coffee Shop (☎ 323 4298; Azadi Blvd; coffees IR10,000-17,000, sandwiches IR20,000-25,000; 🕑 11am-11pm) Gently stylish café serving good strong espressos. There's a billiard hall and decent pizzeria in the same block.

Kourosh (☎ 222 8299; Gilantur Lane; meals IR30,000-50,000; 🕑 11am-4pm & 6.30-11pm) Kourosh wins no prizes for décor but offers numerous typical Gilani dishes including dill-rich *bagilah qotoq* (p170), *zeitun parvarden* (olives in walnut paste) and garlic mast. On a good day the *mirza ghasemi* (mashed eggplant, squash, garlic, tomato and egg, served with bread or rice) can be superb but the *fesenjun* (chicken with walnuts) is rather tart.

our pick Bijan's (☎ 424 5260, 0911-131 2588; bijan nabi@yahoo.com; Gaz Sq, Namju Blvd; meals IR40,000-70,000; 🕑 dusk-11pm Sat-Thu) Soft Mediterranean music, sepia photos and displays of olive-oil bottles create a delightful atmosphere in this very un-Iranian Italian bistro where talented chef Bijan (trained in Sheffield rather than Sorrento) turns out scrumptious pastas served with huge bowls of Parmesan.

Restaurant Tak (☎ 323 2147; Azadi Blvd; meals IR45,000-90,000; 🕑 11.30am-4pm & 7-10.30pm) Three floors of comparatively upmarket dining with Gilani options including *torshe tareh*, a citrusy dish of local sorrel and egg.

GOLSAR DISTRICT
BFC (Golsar Ave at 100th St; chicken dinner IR17,000; 🕑 10am-3pm & 5.30pm-midnight) An amusingly blatant Kentucky takeoff.

Babak (Golsar Ave at 102nd St; cappuccino IR20,000; 🕑 10am-midnight) A stylish green, cream and chrome coffee-bar serving sundaes and shakes.

Boof (Golsar Ave at 104th St; burgers IR20,000-28,000; 🕑 noon-3pm & 5.30-11.30pm) This big, fast-food outlet has a grey-and-neon battleship interior and is worth visiting if only for the futuristic titanium column sinks in the toilets.

Pizza Pizza (Gilan Blvd at 149th St; pizzas IR40,000-70,000; 🕑 6.30-midnight) Comparatively pricey but unusual in having female wait-staff and a children's play area. Order downstairs; menu in English.

Shopping

Farahmand (Imam Khomeini Blvd; 9.30am-9pm Sat-Thu) Souvenirs ranging from Gilaki wooden spoons to amusing wicker frogs are sold at Farahmand.

Cadeau (Imam Khomeini Blvd; 10am-12.30pm & 6.30-9.30pm Sat-Thu) Nearby Cadeau sells plenty of canework and the odd briar pipe.

Nafis (772 7308; Bastani Shoar Sq; 9am-1.30pm & 4-10pm) If you're looking for more upmarket inlay boxes, this is the place.

Getting There & Away

AIR

Iran Air (772 4444; Golsar Ave; 7.30am-7pm Sat-Thu, 9am-1pm Fri) flies twice weekly to Mashhad (IR497,000). **Iran Aseman** (775 9594; Rasht airport) flies to Shiraz (IR501,000, Saturday) and Bandar Abbas (IR682,000, twice weekly). Both airlines fly at least daily to Tehran (IR315,000).

BUS, MINIBUS & SAVARI

The main bus terminal is 300m northeast of Gil Sq, itself 2km south of 'Toshiba' (Mosallah) Sq. Several bus companies have handy central booking offices. **TBT** (222 3520; Sa'di St) serves most destinations (prices are for *mahmooly*/Volvo):

Destination	Fare	Duration	Departures
Ahvaz	IR42,000	18hr	11am, 2.30pm
Esfahan	IR60,000	12hr	6pm
Gorgan	IR22,000/40,000	8hr	hourly 7am-2pm & 7-10pm
Hamadan	IR19,000 (Merc)	9hr	9am, 11am, 6pm
Mashhad	IR47,000/80,000	16hr	2.30pm
Tabriz	IR40,000	10hr	4-8pm
Tehran	IR30,000	5hr	frequent

Savaris to Tehran leave from five different points along Imam Khomeini St. Informal Tehran and Qazvin savaris pick up at Toshiba and Gil Sqs.

Many buses to Ardabil (IR25,000 to IR40,000, five hours) via Astara start from Tehran and pick up at **Istgah Anzali** (Valiasr Sq).

Savaris to Astara (IR40,000, 2½ hours) and Asalem (change for Khal Khal) start at **Pol-e Busar** (Sa'di St).

For Bandar-e Anzali, savaris pick up on a lane off Sa'di St behind the Armenian church.

CUT THE CAVIAR – GILAN CUISINE

The Caspian Sea produces 95% of the world's caviar. But don't count on seeing any. Iran's caviar is virtually all for export. In fact, Gilan's cuisine largely ignores the sea and focuses on the local wealth of fruit, nuts, olives and vegetables. Typical dishes are packed with garlic and turmeric, rather shocking for the sensitive taste buds of central Iranian tourists. *Sirabi* is essentially fried garlic leaves with egg, *shami Rashti* are deep-fried lentil-and-meat patties, *baghilah qotoq* are dill-and-garlic-flavoured broad beans, while *anarbij* (meatballs in walnut and pomegranate sauce) is a variant of *fesenjun*. Easier to find than any of the above is *mirza ghasemi*, a vegetarian marvel of mashed aubergine, squash, garlic and egg. Although often listed as a starter it makes a delicious meal of its own when served with rice.

Informal Lahijan savaris pick up on Shari'ati St, but the official Lahijan terminal is 500m east of Janbazan Sq hidden opposite a Saipa showroom. Durations will vary widely according to traffic conditions, but prices for minibuses/savaris are Lahijan IR2000/6000, Ramsar IR6000/25,000 and Chalus IR11,500/35,000.

For Fuman, and thence Masuleh, savaris/minibuses (IR1500/5000) depart from Yakhsazi Sq (Shohaday Gomnam Sq).

Getting Around

Many shuttle-taxi routes run the length of Imam Khomeini Blvd from Shohada Sq, or along Shohada St to the Lahijan terminal. Northbound, many shuttle taxis go up Sa'di St via Shahid Ansari Sq, where some swing left up to Golsar, others continuing to Valiasr Sq (Istgah Anzali). These return southbound down Takhti St.

AROUND RASHT
Bandar-e Anzali   بندر انزلی
 0181 / pop 113,000

Now Iran's foremost Caspian port city, Bandar-e Anzali's development began in the late 19th century when Enzeli village was selected as a harbour for the Russian Caspian & Mercury Mail-Steamship Company. In 1918 this 'infamous malarial hellhole of barely 4000 souls' was the launching pad for 'Dunsterforce', Britain's secret WWI army that launched a futile attempt to prevent Baku's Azerbaijani oilfields from falling to the Turks.

Amid modern Anzali's 10km-long sprawl, just two short, ragged blocks around central Imam Khomeini Sq retain any of the once-beautiful **Russian house façades**. A block east then north of Khomeini Sq is a leafy waterside promenade lined with teahouses. From here it's possible to rent scarily fast speedboats (around IR400,000 per hour) to go bird-watching amid the reeds and waterlilies *(nenufar)* of the world's largest fresh(ish), water **lagoon**. The historic lighthouse, converted into a **clocktower**, looks good when floodlit at night.

About 900m south of Khomeini Sq, don't miss the **Martial Museum** (Kakh Moze; ☎ 421 0067; admission Iranian/foreigner IR3000/10,000; ⏰ 8am-12.30pm & 3-6pm). It exhibits guns, model ships and the conjectured uniform of a Persepolis-era soldier (looking more like the costume for a hippy toga party). But the real fascination is the splendid setting, a classically styled mansion-palace with sweeping stairways that was once Reza Shah's Caspian getaway. The surrounding garden, full of armoured vehicles, backs onto the harbour area.

Bandar-e Anzali's most appealing hotel, the **Ancient Golsang** (☎ 424 5256; Imam Khomeini Sq; s/tw/tr IR80,000/150,000/200,000), is a 1912 brick building in the form of stepped triangle. Paint is chipping off the antique wooden-framed windows, but rooms are clean and have bathrooms. Staff are friendly if a little eccentric and the restaurant serves a heavenly *mirza ghasemi* (opposite).

Direct savaris (IR5000, 30 minutes) link Imam Khomeini Sq with central Rasht (Sa'di St or Shahrdari Sq). Don't bother with inconvenient minibuses.

Fuman   فومن
☎ 0132 / pop 36,000
Gilan's main attractions are wooded hinterland villages accessed via Fuman. Formerly known as Dar-al-Emareh, and once capital of Gilan, Fuman itself is a leafy junction town 25km west of Rasht, its boulevards lined with date palms, plane trees and numerous rather tacky plaster-cast statues. The mountains on its southwest horizon stay snow-topped well into April, though

it's often too hazy to see them. Fuman is the most famous place to buy *klucheh fuman,* typical Gilan cookies filled with walnut paste, available hot from the oven at several bakeries around town. Savaris to Rasht leave from a bizarrely hidden yard at the northeastern edge of town. West of the bazaar at Velayet Faghi Sq, the roads to Masuleh (Blvd Imamzadeh Mirza) and to Qal'eh Rudkhan divide; savaris to either leave from 400m up each respective road.

Masuleh   ماسوله
☎ 0132 / pop 1500
At least a millennium old, Masuleh is one of Iran's most beautiful villages. Rising through mist-draped forests, earth-coloured houses climb a cupped mountainside so steeply that the roof of one forms the pathway for the next. In summer, day-tripping local tourists merrily fill its appealing tea-terraces, seek out its two minuscule museums and peruse the tiny bazaar's trinket and halva shops. To avoid the coach-tour hordes, stay overnight, hike the surrounding mountains or visit in winter when cold and snow mean you'll often get the place virtually to yourself.

SLEEPING & EATING
Many villagers rent out rooms (double from IR80,000), which makes for a great way to experience a taste of rural Gilan.

Mehran Hotel (Mehran Suites; ☎ 757 2096; apt IR100,000-200,000) At the back of the village, rooms here are great value with bathrooms, kitchenettes, up to six beds and terraces with photo-perfect village views.

Mehmanpazir Navid (☎ 757 2288, 0911-239 6459; apt IR150,000-250,000) Nearer the bazaar, this place also has surprisingly sizable rooms with fold-out couches and kitchenette.

Monfared Hotel (☎ 7572050; s/d IR150,000/250,000) At the base of the village where savaris arrive, this older hotel has 26 timber-walled rooms with bathroom and newly tiled floors, but some peeling paint on ceilings. Mr Nabizadeh speaks some English.

On sunny days, the best places for delicious *mirza ghasemi* are the terraces at **Khaneh Mo'allem Restaurant** (☎ 757 2122; meals IR30,000-45,000; ⏰ 12.30-3.30pm & 7.30-9.30pm), behind the Monfared Hotel, and especially the Mehran Hotel's superbly situated café balcony.

GETTING THERE & AWAY

From Fuman minibuses/savaris (IR2000/6000, 45 minutes) are regular in summer, but rare in winter. The forest scenery en route is charming and around halfway there's a brilliant traditional thatched Gilani house at the western edge of Makhlavan (Makelun) village, now the backdrop for a roadside teahouse.

Qal'eh Rudkhan   قلعه رودخان

This very impressive Seljuk-era **mountain fortress** (admission IR3000; 8am-5pm) covers the top of an idyllic wooded butte ringed by a curl of forested mountain. The brick rampart-ruins are relatively complete, with many photogenic towers, arches and wall sections calcified white with age or tufted with wild flowers. Access requires a steep, sweaty but gorgeous 50-minute walk starting out along a streamside full of mossy rocks then climbing pebble-studded concrete steps to the chorus of birdsong and tapping woodpeckers. The trailhead is beyond a pair of teahouses at **Qal'eh Daneh** hamlet. That's 7km (IR5000) by motorbike taxi) from Qal'eh Rudkhan village to which five-in-a-Paykan savaris from Fuman cost IR2000 per person. Even if you don't make the climb, the 25-minute drive from Fuman to Qal'eh Daneh is delightful, crossing rice paddies and skirting hills with neat green-tea haircuts. If cloud and rain make climbing impractical, a scale model of the castle in Rasht Museum (p168) shows what you missed.

Rasht to Qazvin

The Rasht–Qazvin highway is a frightening deathtrap with a few minor sights. About 33km out of Rasht the much-revered **Imamzadeh Hashem** is plonked on a wooded knoll by the roadside. Almost all public transport halts in **Rudbar** for passengers to buy nationally famous olives and pickled garlic. Olive groves and conifers grace the grassy, rocky valley walls above town, offering attractive random rambles. Climbing steeply towards breezy **Manjil**, famous for its huge wind turbines, the highway passes the **Sefidrud dam** and lake, at whose far, inaccessible western end lies the isolated ruin of **Shemiran Castle** a former Assassins' lair (see p180 for more famous Assassins' castles). Passing through **Loshan** look north to glimpse a sloping

Safavid bridge. Greenery gives way to long rocky defiles for the final stretch towards Qazvin.

Lahijan & Around   لاهیجان و اطراف

 0141 / pop 61,000

Famed for its tea, Lahijan is one of Gilan's oldest towns with some tree-lined charm to its main streets.

Several minor sights are ranged around central Vahdat Sq. These include the **Jameh Mosque** (pierced by a blue-tipped brick minaret) and a charmingly run-down old men-only domed **bathhouse** (shower/massage IR5000/15,000; 6am-7pm) that will eventually host a traditional teahouse. Across the square is the tile-roofed **Chahar Padeshah Mosque**. Some of its famed carved wooden doors have been removed to Tehran's National Museum of Iran, but there are attractive pseudo-medieval-styled murals on the front wall.

Alleyways around Vahdat Sq hide a few old buildings with mossy, tiled roofs, notably the intriguing **Akbariyeh Mosque** (4th West Kashef Alley).

A kilometre further east, the austere, grey **Mausoleum of Kashef-ol-Saltaneh** (224 1003; East Kashef St; admission IR4000; 8am-6pm Tue-Sun) entombs the man who is credited with introducing tea cultivation to Iran (see boxed text, below). It houses an underwhelming museum of tea paraphernalia.

The easternmost 800m of Kashef St climbs **Sheitan Kuh** (Satan's Mountain), a tree-covered ridge fringed with tea gardens. It's crowded on Friday with local tourists enjoying fine views down over Lahijan's rectangular lake. A new **cable-car** (10 min ride return

---

ROOTS OF THAT CUPPA

Gilan province produces 90% of Iran's tea. The deep green, manicured tea-bushes are now so emblematic that it's hard to believe they were introduced only a century ago. In fact, tea didn't reach Persia at all until the 17th century, when it became an expensive luxury. Qajar-period attempts to grow the stuff were unsuccessful until Kashef-ol-Saltaneh, an Iranian consul in India, managed to learn the secret art. Around 1900 he slipped home to Lahijan with some 4000 tea plants and the rest is history.

IR30,000; 9am-dusk) whisks sightseers across to another neighbouring hilltop that's only slightly higher.

The blue, pyramidal roof of the distinctive wooden **Sheikh Zahed Mausoleum** (Boq'eh Sheikh Zahed; admission by donation) is Lahijan's architectural icon. The holy man buried here supposedly lived to the ripe old age of 116 (1218–1334). That's longer than the present mausoleum, which was rebuilt after a devastating 1913 fire. It's in a quiet, rural setting 2.3km east of the artificial lakeside cascade at the base of Sheitan Kuh. Take the small tea-field lane that parallels the main Ramsar road (from which the mausoleum can also be glimpsed east of the bypass).

Of several attractive villages in the appealing semi-alpine mountain hinterland, the best known is **Deilaman** (60km).

SLEEPING & EATING
Chaharfasl Mehmankhaneh (222 3222; Shohada Sq; tw/tr IR80,000/95,000;) Well-kept if basic rooms with fridge and TV share separate bathrooms up steps marked 'Drawing Room'. Some rooms are windowless.

Tourist Inn (Mehmansara Jahangardi; 223 3051; off Sepah Sq; tw US$45; P) Comfortable, well-equipped rooms with a perfect central location and a restaurant that overlooks the western edge of the lake.

Several snack bars and *kababis* lie along Karimi St that links Shohada and Vahdat Sqs perpendicular to Kashef St (400m).

GETTING THERE & AWAY
Savaris from Rasht (IR6000, 45 minutes) arrive at Vahdat Sq and leave (unofficially) from near Shohoda Sq. Minibuses (IR2000) and official savaris use Entezam Sq about 1.5km further west. For Ramsar and Chalus transport leaves from near Basij Sq, a junction 200m northeast of the Tourist Inn.

Astaneh-ye Ashrafiyeh   آستانه اشرفیه
Die-hard Imam Reza fans add **Astaneh**, near Lahijan, to their busy pilgrimage schedules. That's to visit the **mausoleum** (dawn-midnight) of Reza's brother Seyid Jalal od-Din Ashraf, a remarkably modest shrine compared to equivalent Reza siblings' tombs in Qom, Shiraz and Nardaran (Azerbaijan). Some 22km north, 2km beyond **Kiyashahr**, a wooden walkway allows bathers and bird-

watchers access to a predictably rubbish-marred beach across a vaguely attractive reed-choked lagoon.

RAMSAR   رامسر
The tiresome Caspian coast road offers barely a glimpse of beach, but at **Ramsar** mountains and sea conjoin fairly attractively. A grand avenue of palmyra palms sweeps up from the tatty seafront to the wonderful **Ramsar Grand Hotel** (522 3592; old wing s/d/ste US$40/57/76; P). Its 'old wing' lobby oozes neo-colonial charm and the manicured rear gardens are impressive. Rooms are somewhat less luxurious but fair value, especially if you opt for a more spacious suite. Avoid the new wing, a drearily ordinary 1970s concrete-box appendage (20% cheaper). Just five minutes' walk west, the **Caspian Museum** (522 5374; Motahhari St; admission IR40000; 8am-3pm winter, 8am-1pm & 4-8pm summer) is housed in the 1937 summer palace of Reza Shah. In between a (male-only) bathhouse is ideal for relaxing the muscles after the trek from Alamut (p183).

Westbound savaris use Imam Khomeini Sq. Eastbound (from Basij Sq) you'll usually have to change savaris in Tonekabon (aka Shahsavar) for Chalus via Abbasabad where a forest road short-cuts to Kelardasht (p175).

CHALUS & NOSHAHR   چالوس و نوشهر
0191 / pop 83,000
Of these twin towns, Noshahr (Nowshahr) is the more attractive, with palm trees, manicured gardens and a neat little bazaar around central Azadi Sq. The main reason to come is to use the spectacular Chalus–Karaj road that starts at Mo'allem Sq in Chalus (marked by a tall telephone mast). From this square, 17 Shahrivar St leads west across a bridge into central Chalus while Noshahr Blvd leads east passing the Malek and Kourosh Hotels (2km) and airport (4km) before reaching central Noshahr (6km) at Jame Mosque Sq. Azadi Sq is a block further.

Sleeping & Eating
Mosaferkhaneh Tavakol (222 2157; central Chalus; d IR70,000) The Tavakol has basic rooms, shared toilet, no showers and a strict 10am

THE MIGHTY CASPIAN SEA

At 370,000 sq km the Caspian (Darya-ye Khazar) is five times the size of Lake Superior. That makes it by far the world's largest lake. Or does it? Its littoral states (Iran, Russia, Turkmenistan, Azerbaijan and Kazakhstan) can't decide if the Caspian's a lake at all. Perhaps it's a 'sea'. That's more than petty semantics. In international legal terms, each nation deserves its own territorial slice of any 'sea' it borders. But with a 'lake', resources below must be shared equally among all littoral states. So the exact definition has vast economic implications given the Caspian's immensely valuable offshore oilfields. The debate continues.

The Caspian has many environmental worries (see www.caspianenvironment.org). Under-sea mud volcanoes and oil vents add to the murk of industrial effluent flowing in through its tributary rivers, notably the Volga. And at 26.5m below sea level, there's no outlet from which pollution can escape. Pollution along with climate change are probably to blame for increasingly severe algal bloom, the vast annual growths of surface water-weeds which, in summer 2005, covered an astonishing 20,000 sq km of the Caspian. Scientists are also worried by the appearance of *Mnemiopsis Leydiyi* (a comb jellyfish) whose explosive 1990's reproduction in the Black Sea had threatened fish stocks there. All this along with heavy over-fishing is a particular worry for the slow-growing Caspian sturgeon, which produces 95% of the world's caviar, but is now facing possible extinction.

To Westerners brought up reading CS Lewis novels, the name 'Caspian' sounds romantic. Sadly the reality isn't very beautiful. Between 1977 and 1994 Caspian Sea levels rose an astonishing 15cm to 20cm per year. Those beaches that survived are mostly grey and ugly, but local holiday-makers don't seem to mind too much. After all, swimming in full chador isn't much fun. When Iranians tell you how wonderful the coast is, they might mean because of all the lovely rain. Rasht incorporates rain drops into the calligraphy of its welcome sign. There are even seaside restaurants named Barun (Rain). For people from the desert plateau, the Caspian coast's regular downpours must seem exotic. But few foreigners have ever shared their enthusiasm.

check-out time. It's a short stroll from Mo'allem Sq in a lane off 17 Shahrivar St: turn beside Tejarat Bank.

Shahlizar Hotel (☎ 325 0001; fax 323 2090; Azadi Sq, Noshahr; tw IR150,000-250,000; 🞩) Comfortable, cosy rooms have cutesy straw bows decorating their doors. Manager Maziyar speaks some English and is keen to show guests the beautiful views (to mountains and port) from the fifth-floor rooftop (no lift). It's conveniently positioned right at the heart of Noshahr.

Hotel Malek (☎ 222 4107; www.hotelmalek.com; Noshahr Blvd; s/d/tr/ste IR180,000/250,000/350,000/600,000; P 🞩 ▯ 🞩) Stylish rooms have pleasing décor, bathrooms and good-sized double beds. Suites have playful modernist furniture. The outdoor swimming pool operates summer only. The hip restaurant (open noon to 3.30pm and 8pm to 11pm) has a fine menu (in English) ranging from steaks and fish dishes (IR41,000 to IR67,000) to chicken Kiev and *mirza ghasemi* (IR21,000).

Kourosh Hotel (☎ 222 3940; fax 222 4174; Noshahr Blvd; tw IR200,000-450,000; P 🞩 🞩) Across the

road from the Malek, rooms here have pine-fresh interiors, there's a courtyard café, trendy coffee shop, fitness room, sauna and small pool.

Getting There & Around

Iran Aseman (☎ 322 5217; Karimi St, Noshahr; 🕘 7am-4pm) has twice weekly flights to both Tehran (IR195,000) and Mashhad (IR329,000).

To Tehran, buses (IR40,000) and more frequent savaris (IR60,000) leave from a small terminal on the Karaj road, 1.5km south of Mo'allem Sq. Savaris to Kelardasht (IR10,000, one hour) leave from an adjacent yard. Eastbound minibuses/savaris to Nur (IR2200/5000) and Amol (IR6500/20,000) start a block east of Azadi Sq in Noshahr. Westbound minibuses to Ramsar, Lahijan and Rasht use an inconvenient terminal off Chalus' southwestern bypass. Shuttle taxis (IR1000) drive here from Mo'allem Sq. Shuttle taxis from Mo'allem Sq to Jameh Mosque Sq, Noshahr (IR1500, 15 minutes) operate until late evening.

AROUND CHALUS

Namak Abrud نمك آبرود

For extraordinary Caspian views take the long **Namak Abrud cable car** (telecabine; ☎ 0192-246 2012; admission IR50,000; ☺ 10am-3pm), up 1050m Mt Medovin. The ropeway station is 2km off the main Rasht highway, 14km west of Chalus. Dress up warmly and expect the unexpected from notoriously antisocial clouds.

Kelardasht كلاردشت

☎ 0192 / pop 23,100

Cupped between towering, broad-shouldered peaks, Kelardasht is nicknamed the 'Paradise of Iran'. It's probably the most popular Caspian-area getaway for nature-loving Tehranis. Surrounding areas offer trout fishing, cross-country skiing, trekking, mountain climbing and plenty of cool fresh summer air. The mountain panorama approaching Kelardasht from Marzanabad is particularly impressive with several spectacular views of snow-toothed Alam Kuh soaring behind the town. At **Kaleno** an 11km part-paved road leads up to much-vaunted **Valasht Mountain Lake**.

Kelardasht's commercial centre is **Hasankeif** where most of the shops, banks and an internet café are clustered close to Hasankeif Sq. More traditional **Rudbarak** starts around 5km south of Hasankeif. It's closer to the mountains and the starting point for most hikes, though with fewer direct views. Here, amid the holiday homes, you can still find a few old **log-framed barns** and houses with slate or wood-slat roofs anchored down with rocks.

ACTIVITIES

The Alborz offers climbers a selection of 4000m peaks, including **Alam Kuh** (Mt Alam), which at 4850m is Iran's third tallest and most technical. An 800m near-vertical granite **wall** makes the mountain's north face a special challenge for climbers, though there are much easier alternative routes to the top. Ascents start 20km from Rudbarak. Before starting you should sign in (and pay US$20 peak fees) at the **Mountaineering Federation** (Federasion-e-Kuh Navardi; ☎ 264 2626; Tohid St, Rudbarak; ☺ call ahead), 7.4km from Hasankeif Sq. Staff here can help arrange mules and guides, can show you climbing maps and sell a great set of postcards with suggested climbing routes marked onto photos of various peaks.

For Alam Kuh it takes at least a day to trek to one of two base-camp huts. Hesarchal offers the easier summit approach. For the wall use the climbers' hut at Sarchal (3900m) and continue to a cwm called Alamchal (4150m). Climbing the wall itself is a very serious undertaking even for highly experienced mountaineers.

From Sarchal it's also possible to climb **Mt Takht-e Soleiman**, at the other end of the main knife-edge ridge, but there's a lot of bolder-jumping on the glacier and plenty of slippery scree. NB: this *is* the peak that Freya Stark wandered up almost by mistake in her book *Castles of the Assassins*. However, it is *not* the Takht-e Soleiman citadel near Takab (p187).

SLEEPING & EATING

Hotel Azarbayjan (☎ 262 2678; Mahestan 3rd lane off Nasiri St, Hasankeif; tr IR200,000-450,000) Cheap by Kelardasht standards, this overgrown homestay is just 500m from Hasankeif Sq via Modarres St (fork left then right). Rooms have gas stove, fridge, bathroom and three squeezed-in beds. Those with sitting rooms cost IR100,000 extra. The communal dining terrace is good for meeting other guests.

Hotel Park Chaman (☎ 264 3159; Park Chaman, Rudbarak; small/big ste IR250,000/500,000, bungalows IR500,000) Almost 7km from Hasankeif Sq, 700m before the Mountaineering Federation, look for the obvious blue-roofed modernist restaurant across the river. While not entirely tasteful, the suites are well-equipped with bathtub, choice of toilets and a balcony (no mountain views). The peaceful location is a good starting point for hikes.

Maral Hotel (☎ 262 6726; Pasdaran Blvd; ste IR400,000-800,000) Full-blown suites are comfortable though oddly the kitchenettes are much bigger than the cramped bathrooms. A big new extension should soon offer swimming pool, Jacuzzi and billiard room. It's 1.3km south of Hasankeif Sq.

Arash Restaurant (☎ 262 8312; Hasankeif Sq; meals IR25,000-55,000; ☺ 11am-3.30pm & 7.30-10pm) Bright, clean pine-ceilinged restaurant offering Iranian and Caspian favourites right on Hasankeif Sq.

GETTING THERE & AROUND

Rare savaris to Abbasabad (IR10,000, one hour) take an attractive forest lane and depart from Hasankeif Sq near Melli Bank.

Savaris to Chalus (IR10,000, one hour) and Tehran (back/front IR60,000/80,000, 3½ hours) and Karaj (IR50,000/70,000, 2¾ hours) leave from a stand 400m north of the square. Buses (IR30,000, five hours) to Tehran's west terminal leave from the tiny Rahat Safar/Talayi Safar office in Zibardast, 3km east of Hasankeif departing at 8am and 2pm in either direction.

Transport within Kelardasht usually requires chartering a **taxi** (☎ 262 9191; per hr IR50,000).

Karaj–Chalus Road

Were it not for the terrifying traffic, this fabulously scenic trans-Alborz road would easily justify a visit to Chalus/Noshahr. Unlike the Haraz (Amol–Tehran) road, landscapes are beautiful almost immediately. Soaring surrounding peaks remain **snow-topped** late into the season and as you slither inexorably down through steep-cut forest valleys the engineering feat of the road's construction remains striking. However, stopping en route can be perilous and, especially in icy conditions, it's hard to focus on the scenery given the suicidal driving style of the speeding maniacs. On a few key holidays the road becomes one-way, which can mess up your plans. Massive engineering works currently deface some of the upper sections and a new expressway will eventually bypass the southern half of the road via an entirely different route. If driving, consider the contrastingly quiet side trip to Baladeh (p334).

KARAJ
کرج

☎ 0191 / pop 2,594,000

When the Shah's sister had Frank Lloyd Wright design her a spiral-roofed palace here (1966), Karaj was a peaceful escape from Tehran. Today it's a vast, sprawling commuter dormitory-town. For most travellers, the only conceivable reason to stop is to transfer between Qazvin and the beautiful Chalus mountain road without getting ensnared in the Tehran traffic. Karaj's gridlock is plenty bad enough! Chalus-bound savaris depart from Hafez Sq right at the northern fringe of town. For destinations west use the main terminal (7km away by a double-back loop of motorway) or the expressway lay-by outside where passing buses and car drivers fill up their vehicles en route for virtually anywhere in western Iran.

QAZVIN
قزوین

☎ 0281 / pop 342,000

Qazvin is famed for carpets and seedless grapes. The city was once capital of all Iran and has a considerable sprinkling of minor sights, but for most Western travellers its foremost role is as a launch point for excursions to the famous Castles of the Assassins in the marvellous Alamut Valley.

History

Founded by the Sassanian king Shapur I in the 3rd century AD, Qazvin prospered under the Seljuk rulers, who erected many fine buildings. It had a second, much later burst of prominence when the second Safavid shah, Tahmasp I (r 1524–76), transferred the Persian capital here from Tabriz. A great patron of the arts, his ambitious architectural plan for Qazvin proved to be only a dress rehearsal for Esfahan, where his successor, Shah Abbas I, set up court in 1598.

Orientation

The city centre is Azadi Sq, widely known as Sabz Meydan. The bazaar and alleys to its southeast are the most atmospheric areas for random strolling.

Information

INTERNET ACCESS

All charge IR6000 per hour.

Coffeenet Setayesh (☎ 332 0571; Ayatollah Khamenei Blvd)

Coffeenet Yahoo (Khayyam St; ⏲ 9am-11pm Sat-Thu, 11am-11pm Fri)

Parsee Coffeenet (☎ 223 0119; Tous Deadend, off Khayyam St; ⏲ 9am-midnight)

Shahbda Coffeenet (☎ 223 9093; Modarres Blvd; ⏲ 9.30am-10pm Sat-Thu, 10am-11pm Fri)

MONEY

Sharifi Exchange (Ferdosi St; ⏲ 9am-1pm & 5-8pm Sat-Thu)

TOURIST INFORMATION

Tourist information booth (☎ 335 4708; www.qazvin tourism.com; Naderi St; ⏲ 8am-12.30pm & 5-7pm Sat-Thu) Facing the historic Rah Kushk Gate, this is one of Iran's most professional tourist information offices, offering great free maps and useful brochures (partly in English). It can arrange guides to get you into normally closed architectural curiosities and has masses more detailed information available, if you ask the right questions.

Sights

CHEHEL SOTUN چهلستون

When Qazvin took its turn as Iran's capital, this attractive, colonnaded cube was Shah Tahmasp's **royal palace**. Built in 1510, it was greatly remodelled in the Qajar era. Set in the town's little central park it looks especially photogenic at night, with its delicate balustrades floodlit and its back-lit coloured-glass windows glowing through the foliage. Inside is a new **calligraphy museum** (☎ 223 3320; admission IR2000; ⊙ 9am-1pm & 5-8.30pm).

QAZVIN MUSEUM

This spacious modern **museum** (☎ 223 4935; Helel-e-Ahmar St; admission IR3000; ⊙ 9am-12.30pm & 4-6.30pm winter, 9am-12.30pm & 5-7.30pm summer, closed Mon) predominantly features 19th-century decorative arts but the bottom floor has some 3000-year-old bronzes and ceramics from the Alamut Valley.

MOSQUES

Built in 1115, but extensively remodelled in the early 17th century, the **Jameh Mosque** has huge *iwans* and a fine marble mihrab. The very appealing Qajar-era **Nabi (Shah) Mosque** with its Mogul-style topknots also has an impressively expansive courtyard.

AMINIHA HOSSEINIYEH حسینیه امینها

Tucked away in a walled rose garden is the well-preserved 1773 **Aminiha Hosseiniyeh** (Molavi St at Amin Deadend; admission IR5000; ⊙ 9am-1pm & 5-8pm). It's a private mansion that doesn't look much from outside, but has a splendidly gaudy wood, glass and mirror interior and a refreshingly cool, brick vaulted basement. A great place to unwind and write up your diary in peace.

IMAMZADEH-YE HOSSEIN امامزاده حسین

This large, well-proportioned **shrine** has a Qajar façade, a 16th-century blue dome and plenty of new mirror tiling. It commemorates a son of Imam Reza and is convivially set in a big fountain courtyard surrounded by coloured-brick alcoves. Behind is a martyrs' graveyard and an aged fighter plane on a stick.

BAZAAR & CRAFT WORKSHOPS

The fascinating covered bazaar amply repays idle wandering. At the east end of the fine Bazaar-e Vazim, **Saroye Vazir** is stacked high with bundled old carpets. It's one of several wonderfully down-at-heel caravanserais between which you'll still find the odd door-maker and metal workshop. A **cushion maker** reveals his craft in an alley off Molavi St and there's a **traditional shoemaker** near Shohada Sq.

CISTERNS

Qazvin has some of Iran's best-preserved domed cisterns where water was stored underground and cooled by wind towers. Sadly getting in is rarely possible so don't make a special trip, but if you're passing the most impressive from outside are the **Sardar cisterns** and the **Haji Kazem Cistern** with its well-preserved wind tower.

GATES

Tehran Gate (Darvazeh-e-Qadim-e-Tehran) and **Rah Kushk Gate** (Darbe Kousht; Naderi St) are two dinky little Qajar decorative remnants of Qazvin's once-vast city walls. The much more massive **Ali Qapu** (Helel-e-Ahmar St) was originally a 16th-century gateway to the royal precinct, a kind of forbidden inner city. Today it's a police post so don't take photographs.

OTHER SIGHTS

Tourist maps mark dozens of other historic buildings, but few are at all visually exciting. Even the colourfully domed 14th-century **Amineh Khatun shrine** with fine blue conical spire and Kufic script seems forlornly lost in the warren of banal modern backstreets.

The cute, 20th-century **Kantur Church** (Borj-e-Naghus) has a blue-brick belfry dome and sits in a tiny Russian graveyard.

Safa Hammam (Molavi St at Taqavi Alley; bath IR5000; ⊙ 7am-7pm Sat-Thu, 7am-2pm Fri) is the best known of Qazvin's traditional subterranean bathhouses to remain active. The domed central rest area is attractive. Men only.

Activities

Qazvin is a good place to prepare for Alamut-area hikes. **Nakhajir Camping Shop** (☎ 222 4551; Ferdosi St; ⊙ 8am-1pm & 4-9pm Sat-Thu) sells great-value camping gear including head torches (IR30,000 to IR50,000), sprung hiking sticks (IR70,000) and 1:300,000 Farsi maps of the Alborz (IR15,000).

Mehdi Babayi (☎ 0912-682 3228) is an experienced trekking and climbing guide who pays

WESTERN IRAN

QAZVIN

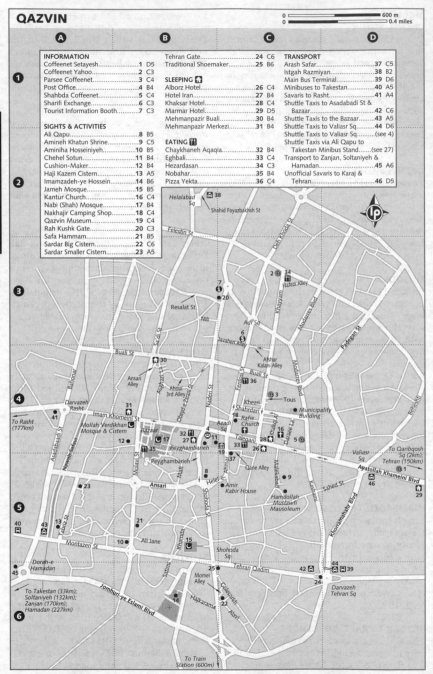

attention to key safety details, even though his organisation can seem somewhat haphazard. He's a surreal Iranian Shane Warne lookalike with a comically dextrous 200-word English vocabulary; a character you'll remember long after any trek.

Sleeping

Mehmanpazir Buali (☎ 222 3329; Buali St; s/d/tr IR80,000/90,000/120,000) Repapered rooms (some windowless) have TVs and top-sheets and share faultlessly clean bathrooms, though the whole place has a slightly musty smell.

Khaksar Hotel (☎ 222 4239; Khaleqi Alley; s/d/tr IR80,000/100,000/120,000) Neat, spacious recently redecorated rooms with shared bathrooms. Better than most other Qazvin *mosaferkhanehs*.

Mehmanpazir Merkezi (☎ 2226279; Imam Khomeini St; d/tr IR100,000/150,000) Fairly sweet little rooms with top-sheets, rug, fan and central air-conditioning share very clean showers and squat toilets. Road noise can be disturbing.

Hotel Iran (☎ 222 8877; Peyghambarieh St; s/tw IR120,000/160,000) This popular traveller favourite manages to be simultaneously quiet yet eminently central. The pleasant, decently furnished rooms are great value with good bathrooms and central air-conditioning – if they turn it on! Owner Karim Noruzi speaks good English, but compare options before signing up to his Alamut trips.

Alborz Hotel (☎ /fax 222 6631; hotel_alborz_q@yahoo.com; Taleqani Blvd; s/tw US$25/40; 🍴 🖳) This appealing midrange option has small but fully equipped modern rooms with added bedcovers, towels and BBC World TV. Staff are very helpful and the lobby coffee shop makes a pleasantly low-key meeting point.

Marmar Hotel (☎ 255 5771; www.marmarhotel.com, in Farsi; Ayatollah Khamenei Blvd; s/d IR400,000/540,000) The Marmar is a festival of nouveau-riche kitsch, overloaded with mouldings and chandeliers. Little armour-clad knights guard the soapstone marble stairs. Comfortable rooms are graciously less lurid, but with some wear to the furniture. Bring earplugs for the road rumble.

Eating

Qazvin's local speciality is *qimeh nasar* (also spelt *gheymeh nasser*), a tangy lamb stew made with diced pistachios.

Nobahar (☎ 222 2451; Bazar Dimaj; mains IR13,000-30,000; 🕙 10am-4pm Sat-Thu) This is a fairly large, comparatively low-stress bazaar eatery that serves stews (including *qimeh nasar*), which you can choose by pointing at the relevant kitchen cauldron.

Pizza Yekta (☎ 222 2407; Ferdosi St; pizzas IR16,000-35,000; 🕙 11am-3pm & 6-11pm Sat-Thu, 6-11pm Fri) Designer off-line windows add a little architectural smile to this popular air-conditioned fast-food place. There is a bit more seating upstairs.

Hezardasan (☎ 335 0100; Hafezi Alley, off Khayyam St; meals IR20,000-40,000; 🕙 11.30am-3.30pm & 7-11pm) At the upmarket northern end of Khayyam St, Hezardasan makes a valiant attempt at giving its cellar room that *sofrakhane sonati* feel, but the overall effect is a little too neat to be memorable. Its delicious *qimeh nasar* comes mounded into barberry rice.

Eghbali (☎ 223 3347; Taleqani St; mains IR20,000-83,000; 🕙 11am-4pm & 7-10pm) Prices are high and despite the odd fake stone frieze there isn't much atmosphere. Nonetheless it's popular with travellers for its English menu and reliable food.

The convivially crowded Yas, in a dead-end alley opposite Hotel Alborz, is cheaper. There are several similar restaurants on Ayatollah Khamenei Blvd east of Valiasr Sq.

Chaykhaneh Aqaqia (off Imam St; tea IR1000; 🕙 8am-10pm Sat-Thu) This wonderfully unpretentious, cheap and down-market all-male teahouse has chess and *nard* to play. Easily missed, the entrance is on the left off a covered access-way to the workaday Sadd Sultani caravanserai.

Getting There & Away

BUS, MINIBUS & SAVARI

Handy bus services from the main terminal include the following:

Destination	Fare	Duration	Departures
Esfahan	IR65,000	6hr	1pm Talayi, Taavoni 6
Hamadan	IR12,000	3½hr	7am Seiro Safar
	IR25,000	3½hr	2pm Seiro Safar
Kermanshah	IR40,000	7hr	7.45am, 2.30pm Seiro Safar
Mashhad	IR80,000	18hr	2pm, 2.30pm Talayi
Rasht	IR12,000	3hr	7.45am, 2.45pm Alborz 7.30am, 3pm TBT
Tehran	IR6500-12,000	2½hr	frequent

Official Tehran and Karaj savaris leave from outside (IR30,000). Unofficial ones pick up at Valiasr Sq.

Cranky buses run to Hir (via Razmiyan) around 11am and to Mo'allem Kalayeh (IR10,000, 2½ hours) around 1.30pm (not Friday). However, for these Alamut Valley destinations savaris are vastly better. Mo'allem Kalayeh savaris (IR25,000, 1¾ hours) depart from gigantic Qaribqosh Sq, 2km east of Valiasr Sq. Razmiyan savaris (per person/car IR18,000/70,000, 1¼ hours) depart very occasionally from **Istgah Razmiyan** (Helalabad Sq off Sa'di St): to get there take a shuttle taxi up Naderi St to Sardaran Sq, walk a block west along Beheshti St then 300m southwest down Shahid Fayazbakhsh St.

Some buses en route to Zanjan, Tabriz and Hamadan stop momentarily at the busy Dorah-e Hamadan junction. Minibuses to Takestan congregate nearby.

For Rasht, savaris depart from **Darvazeh Rasht** (Enqelab Sq) where some through buses also pick up/drop off.

TRAIN
The best-timed trains to Tehran (IR5900, two hours) depart at 8.30am and 10.35am. For Zanjan (2½ hours) handy trains leave at 8am and 5.40pm. There are useful sleeper trains to Tabriz at 9.10pm (IR39,350, 11 hours) and to Mashhad at 8.45pm, but tickets can be in short supply. **Arash Safar Travel** (☎ 222 2260; Helel-e-Ahmar St; ◷ 8am-1pm & 4-8pm Sat-Thu) can book for you and sells air tickets ex-Tehran.

Getting Around
City buses run both ways along the main drag (Imam Khomeini St/Taleqani Blvd), but cars and shuttle taxis can only use it eastbound, returning from Valiasr Sq to central Azadi Sq (Sabz Meydan) via Shahrdari or Buali Sts. From the centre to the bus terminal change at Valiasr Sq. From the terminal to Azadi Sq loop round via the bazaar.

ALAMUT VALLEY   الموت
Few places in Iran offer a more tempting invitation to hike, explore and reflect than the fabled Alamut and Shahrud Valleys. Beneath soaring Alborz peaks, the landscapes are inspirational and delightfully varied, with scenic suggestions of Patagonia, Switzerland, central Australia and Syria all

spiced by a uniquely fascinating medieval history. Nestled almost invisibly on widely spread rocky knolls and pinnacles lie the shattered remnants of over 50 ruined fortresses. Shrouded in fabulous myths, they were the heavily fortified lairs of the medieval world's most feared religious cult and are collectively known as the **Castles of the Assassins** (see boxed text, p182). The most interesting are at Gazor Khan (Alamut Castle, p182) and Razmiyan (Lamiasar Castle, below). Beware that Alamut Castle is NOT in Alamut town (aka Mo'allem Kalayeh, p182).

Using a mix of savaris and taxis it's possible to visit both Razmiyan (65km) and Gazor Khan (110km) in a long day trip from Qazvin. But it's much more fun to take your time, sleeping a night or three at Gazor Khan to do some trekking. If you can manage enough Farsi to charter a taxi there's no real reason to take a guide, though a knowledgeable historian could help bring to life the castles' bare stones.

A guide (or at least a bag-carrying mule and mule-driver) is wise, however, if you're planning a multi-day, cross-Alborz trek into the Caspian hinterland (p183).

Razmiyan & Lamiasar Castle
رازميان و كاخ لامياسر
☎ 0272 / pop 1800
The winding descent into Razmiyan from Qazvin passes some timeless mud hamlets and gives wonderful views over the Shahrud Valley's rice terraces. Central Razmiyan itself is a strangely soulless place but a handily central **taxi agency** (☎ 322 2828) makes it easy to arrange onward transport if you've arrived by savari. A taxi costs IR20,000 up to the Lamiasar Castle access path (2.5km towards Hir). From there it's an obvious 20-minute stroll to the top edge of the castle where a remnant hint of round bastion and some other wall chunks remain. The castle site sweeps down from here to outer-wall remnants that drop vertically into the valley below. Allow at least an hour to seek out the various degraded fortifications, enjoy the birdsong and meet the lizards. Bring a hat and sunscreen as there's minimal shade.

There's no formal accommodation in Razmiyan. A taxi to Mo'allem Kalayeh costs IR80,000, or IR100,000 if you tack on an 8km detour to **Evan Lake** en route. With its powerful

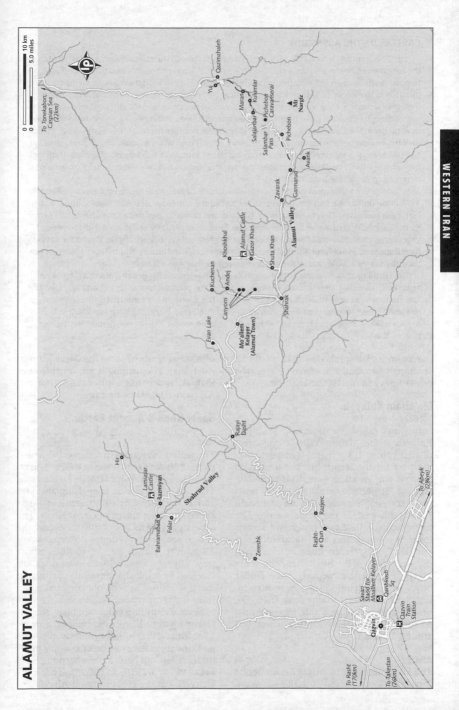

ALAMUT VALLEY

WESTERN IRAN

CASTLES OF THE ASSASSINS

In the 12th century, a network of incredibly well fortified Alborz mountain castles sheltered the followers of Hasan-e Sabbah (1070–1124), spiritual leader of Islam's heretical Ismaili sect. In popular myth, Sabbah led a bizarre, much-feared mercenary organisation whose members were dispatched to murder or kidnap leading political and religious figures of the day. They believed that their actions would transport them to paradise. Supposedly Sabbah cunningly cultivated such beliefs by showing them beautiful secret gardens filled with enticing young maidens while unwittingly stoned on hashish. This gave them their popular name 'Hashish-iyun', root of the modern English term 'assassin'. Or so the story goes. Peter Willey's book, *Eagle's Nest,* gives an altogether more sympathetic version portraying Hasan Sabbah as a champion of the free-thinking, pro-science Islamic tradition and suggesting that the hashish tales were fabricated exaggerations designed to denigrate Ismaili Islam.

Whatever the truth, most of the impregnable Ismaili castles were captured by Hulagu Khan in 1256 using diplomatic trickery, having earlier forced the surrender of the Ismailis' spiritual leader (Sabbah's successor). Only two fortresses, Girdkuh and Lamiasar, decided to put up a fight. Thanks to their sophisticated water cisterns and vast food reserves they could hold out for years, 17 years in the case of Girdkuh! Before moving on, the Mongols systematically destroyed the castles' fortifications to avoid future difficulties. That means today it's history and brilliant scenery more than the scanty rubble that draws the few travellers that make it here.

The crushing of Alamut was effectively the end of the Ismailis for generations though believers resurfaced centuries later and now Ismaili Islam is the predominant faith in parts of Tajikistan and northern Pakistan (though not at all in Iran). The castles were forgotten and only returned to public consciousness with the publication of Dame Freya Stark's 1930s travel diary *Valleys of the Assassins*. A copy of that recently reprinted volume makes a great companion for the trip.

mountain backdrop, the tiny lake would be stunningly beautiful if it weren't for nearby power lines and muddy car-washing spots.

Mo'allem Kalayeh   معلم کلایه
☎ 0282 / pop 4700

Sometimes called Alamut town, Mo'allem Kalayeh is the Alamut Valley's one-street district centre. It's a useful transport staging post for the region but not a sight in itself. If you get stuck here, **Haddodi Restaurant** (☎ 321 6362; tw/6-bed IR80,000/140,000) rents two very simple rooms. It's on the main street 50m east of the eagle statue. The town centre, where rare buses and savaris loiter, is 600m further east. Savaris to Qazvin (IR25,000) are an hour quicker than the dreadfully slow bus (IR15,000, daily except Friday) that departs once feeder buses from outlying villages have arrived. For Gazor Khan taxi charters cost IR40,000, or IR80,000 including a side trip to Andej en route. Or take the returning school bus around 11.45am.

ANDEJ   اندج
The 8km road-spur to Andej passes beside three truly awesome red-rock side-canyons,

somewhat reminiscent of the Olgas (central Australia). The turning is just northwest of **Shahrak,** which has a prominent (but not Assassin-related) castle ruin.

Gazor Khan & Alamut Castle
گازرخان و قلعه الموت
☎ 0282

The region's greatest attraction is the fabled ruin of **Alamut Castle** (admission IR4000; ☉ dawn-dusk), Hasan-e Sabbah's famous fortress site. The site is a dramatic crag rising abruptly above the pleasant, unpretentious little cherry-growing village of Gazor Khan. The access path starts about 700m beyond the village square and requires a steep, sweaty 25-minute climb via an obvious stairway. On top, archaeological workings are shielded by somewhat unsightly corrugated metal sheeting. But the phenomenal views from the ramparts are unmissable.

Several tempting mountain hikes start in Gazor Khan or Khoshkchal village, a steep, 15-minute 4WD ride beyond. Route suggestions are extensively described in a helpful travellers' tip book at the charming **Hotel Koosaran** (☎ 377 3377; dm IR30,000). That's effectively just the guest room in Ali Samie's family home. It can sleep up to five, curled up on cotton mattresses on the floor. Simple but tasty meals are available (IR15,000) if you ask ahead and the flat roof facing Gazor Khan's village square makes a great people-watching perch.

Managed by a Grimm's fairy-tale crone, the **Golestan Inn** (☎ 3773312; room/'suite' IR120,000/150,000) offers rather tatty accommodation amid trees on the slight rise that directly overlooks the stairway to Alamut Rock. The 'rooms' share a decent kitchen and a grotty squat toilet. The 'suites' are a pair of semi-detached concrete houselets with run-down balcony seats amid overgrown foliage. Kabab meals cost IR30,000 (by pre-arrangement).

Hotel Farhangian (☎ 377 3446; tr IR160,000) is a converted former school whose ex-classrooms now form reasonably well equipped though not luxurious 'suites' with kitchen and bathroom. Beware that the place gets locked up when the receptionist (a small boy) goes home for his meals! Bring your own food. There's no English sign, but it's tucked behind the Alamut Research Centre, up a short driveway that heads south from, castle trailhead. Don't rush to believe locals who tell you it's closed.

Savaris usually run to Qazvin at around 7am (IR30,000, 2½ hours). At the same time there's a bus to Mo'allem Kalayeh (school days, IR3000, 45 minutes). Both leave from the village square outside Hotel Koosaran.

Trekking Towards the Caspian: Garmarud to Yuj

Crossing the Alborz on foot from the Alamut Valley to the Caspian hinterland is geographically compelling, scenically stunning and culturally fascinating. You'll be one of just a handful of foreigners since Freya Stark (1930s) to make such a trip, but hurry: road builders are slowly extending tracks further and further into the isolated mountain villages and a whole way of life revolving around donkey transport will soon be a thing of the past.

The route described here isn't especially arduous, though a guide and/or mule-driver is recommended to avoid difficulties at a few awkward spots, especially if you attempt the walk before June, when you'll be tramping through treacherous snows on the highest sections. It's most pleasant to allow three days, though two days or even less is

quite possible if you're in some inexplicable hurry. (In midsummer you could shorten the walk by arranging a 4WD to take you as far as **Salajanbar.**)

The hike starts in pretty, canyon-framed **Garmarud** village, 18km east of the Gazor Khan turning, where the Alamut Valley road's asphalt ends. Whether you walk or drive, the route goes via picturesque **Pichebon hamlet** and across the 3200m **Salambar Pass** beside the small, partly renovated (but deserted) **Pichebon Caravanserai**. Fabulous views. On foot from Garmarud it took us 5½ hours to that caravanserai (with a guide, short-cutting through flower-filled meadows and beneath a waterfall). From the caravanserai it's another three hours to Salajanbar, descending very slowly through pretty thorn shrubs and fields of yellow iris. If you follow the jeep track instead of the walking path, take the right-hand fork an hour beyond the pass.

Wonderfully picturesque **Maran** is the last village en route with no semblance of a road. Walking there from Salajambar takes three hours and requires fording a stream twice. While not that hard, it's potentially dangerous when the water's high: slip and you'll be washed over a waterfall to certain doom.

Another three hours' downhill hike from Maran brings you to an un-asphalted road below pretty **Yuj** village set in flower-filled meadows.

SLEEPING

In Garmarud a hotel is under construction: if completed that will make the village a great base for shorter hikes. Mr Sardeghi's tiny **Grocery Shop** (☎ 379 4008, 0912-682 8991) sells biscuits and might help you arrange *qotr* (mules) to carry your bags.

At Pichebon, grassy meadows are great for camping – ask permission in the village.

In Maran village, **Nematullah Mansukia** (☎ 0192-282140) can provide a simple homestay with great home-cooked meals (around IR40,000 per person). By pre-arrangement he can also organise mules from Yuj (around IR120,000) or even Garmarud (around IR300,000). The village has a tiny, super-rustic *hammam*.

GETTING THERE & AWAY

To reach Garmarud, a *dar baste* (closed door) savari costs IR100,000 from Qazvin or

IR50,000 from Mo'allem Kelayeh. From the end of the hike in Yuj, a savari to Tonekabon supposedly departs at 8am (IR25,000, two hours). Otherwise get someone to phone the savari driver **Shabani** (0911-394836) from Yuj's village telephone. Hopefully he'll arrive to pick you up within a few hours. Yuj has an informal baker but no shops so keep some snacks in reserve for the wait.

SOLTANIYEH   سلطانيه
 0242 / pop 8700

Little Soltaniyeh ('Town of the Sultans') was purpose-built by the Ilkhanid Mongols as their Persian capital from 1302. But less than a century later in 1384 it was largely destroyed by Tamerlane. Fortunately three fine monuments survived. By far the most dramatic of these is the magnificent **Oljeitu Mausoleum** (Gonbad-e Soltaniyeh; www.sultanieh.ir, in Farsi; admission IR5000; 8am-5pm), now a Unesco World Heritage site. Almost 25m in diameter and 48m high it's the world's tallest brick dome. Inside, renovators' scaffolding can't hide the enormity of the enclosed space. A ground-floor exhibition illustrates the ongoing restoration process. Spiral stairs within the hugely thick walls lead up two floors to a terrace with panoramic views and fine stucco-work vaulting.

The building is named for its sponsor, Mongol sultan Oljeitu Khodabandeh. Oljeitu changed religions as often as a film star changes wives. During his Shiite phase, egged on by a favourite concubine, he had planned for the mausoleum to re-house the remains of Imam Ali, son-in-law of the Prophet Mohammed. That would have made it Shiite Islam's holiest pilgrimage site outside Mecca (instead of Najaf, Iraq). However, Oljeitu couldn't persuade the Najaf ulema to give him Ali's relics and eventually he was buried here himself in 1317.

The mausoleum approach crosses partly rebuilt stubs of Soltaniyeh's **citadel wall** and some **archaeological excavations** (admission free) of the Mongol-era townscape.

Some 500m southwest of the main complex, the 1330 **Khanegah Dervish Monastery** (Hamadan highway; admission free; 8am-5pm) has restored cells around a courtyard leading to the **Boq'eh Chelabi-oglu Mausoleum** behind the mihrab of a shattered-sided former mosque.

From the Oljeitu Mausoleum's upper terrace, it's easy to spot the lonely blue-domed **Mullah Hasan Kashi tomb** (admission free) in semi-desert, 1.5km south towards the mountain skyline. It was built by Safavid Shah Tahmasp to honour Hasan Kashi, a 14th-century mystic whose recasting of Islam's historical sagas as Persian-language poetic epics unwittingly had a vast influence over Shia Islam's future direction.

GETTING THERE & AWAY
Soltaniyeh is 5km south of the old Zanjan–Qazvin road, but *not* accessible from the parallel motorway. By public transport it's easiest to visit as a day trip from Zanjan. Direct savaris (IR5000, 30 minutes) and very irregular minibuses (IR1500, 50 minutes) from Zanjan's Honarestan Sq drop you an obvious 10-minute walk north of the mausoleum.

AROUND SOLTANIYEH
The extensive **Katalekhor Caves** (0242-482 2188; admission IR15,000; 8am-7.30pm, last entry 6pm, closed after heavy rain) are 130km southwest of Soltaniyeh via the quiet if slightly monotonous Soltaniyeh–Hamadan road. The visit involves around 1¼ hours underground walking up and back in small guided groups. The experience isn't unduly claustrophobic and it culminates in several vistas of fine stalactite formations that are much more impressive that those at better-known Ali Sadr (p206). There's no public transport. We paid IR100,000 return by taxi from **Ghydar** (aka Qeydar or Khodabandeh) whose quaint **Ghydar Nabi madraseh** (off Imam Khomeini St) sits where a prominent cockscomb of rocky outcrop descends to the town's original heart. Savaris run semiregularly from Ghydar to Soltaniyeh and Zanjan. En route consider making a 15-minute detour to the celebrated but tumble-down little **Sojas Jameh Mosque** (Dr Chamran St). Its ornate interior stuccowork is just visible through all the restorer's scaffolding. It's amid collapsing mud houses at the western end of Sojas town.

By car it's feasible to visit Soltaniyeh and all the above in a long day trip from Zanjan or while driving between Zanjan and Hamadan.

ZANJAN   زنجان
 0241 / pop 367,000
Hidden in tiny alleys behind its modern façade, Zanjan retains some attractive mosques, a fantastic bazaar, a plethora of

knife-grinders and some delightful teahouse restaurants. The city is a logical base for visiting the impressive Soltaniyeh mausoleum and a good staging point to reach Takht-e Soleiman via the scenic Dandy road.

Zanjan city's moment of infamy came in 1851 with a bloody siege ordered by Persian prime minister Amir Kabir. The resulting massacre was part of the relatively successful campaign to crush the nascent Baha'i religion. Baha'i-ism had only broken away from Islam three years before, but was spreading much too rapidly for Tehran's liking.

Orientation & Information

The main commercial centre is Enqelab Sq. **Export Development Bank** (Ferdosi St; ☺ 9am-noon) changes money. **Rayanet** (Sa'di St; per hr IR5000; ☺ 8am-midnight) has excellent internet connection and (over) friendly staff. Farsi-only city maps are sometimes sold from bookshops opposite the **telephone office** (Sa'di St; ☺ 7am-10.30pm) and are available free from room 25, **Miras Ferhangi** (☎ 323 9007; miras_zanjan@hotmail.com; Khayyam St; ☺ 8am-2pm).

Sights

Built in 1926 but looking considerably older, the unique, unmarked **Rakhatshor-Khaneh** (Rakhatshorkhaneh Alley; admission IR4000; ☺ 8am-5.30pm Tue-Sun) is a dome-and-column subterranean hall whose water channels were originally constructed as a public laundry-place. It's dotted with wax washerwomen to remind you how life was before Electrolux and Zanussi. There's also a calm garden courtyard.

The long, narrow, mostly brick-vaulted **bazaar** is inspiring and surrounding alleys hide half-a-dozen historic mosques. Entered between copper shops off Enqelab St at the bazaar's ungentrified eastern end is the delightfully decrepit yet still-active **Dokhtar Caravanserai**. Grandly tiled, the dome and minarets of the **Rasul-Ullah (Sai-ini) Mosque** peep above central Enqelab Sq. Madraseh cells line the inner courtyard of the sizable 1826 **Jameh Mosque**, accessed through a spired portal on Imam St. **Seyid Ibrahim (Imamzadeh) Mosque** is similarly extensive. The dinky **Khanum (Women's) Mosque** has a commonly photographed pair of squat pepper-pot minarets but its 1940s architecture is of little artistic merit.

The 1851 Baha'i massacres were perpetrated in lanes behind where you now see philosopher **Soravardi's bust** (Sa'di St) on a library wall. **Pol-e-Sardar**, an attractive Safavid bridge, is visible west of the Bijar road.

Sleeping

Hotel Sa'di (☎ 322 2528; Imam St; s/tw/tr IR40,000/55,000/70,000) This sensibly priced *mosaferkhaneh* is relatively well kept but the windowless singles are truly minuscule.

Hotel Hafez (☎ 322 2740; Enqelab Sq; s/tw/tr IR80,000/150,000/220,000) Peeling paint, window bars and the odd cockroach might make prison inmates feel at home here. Still, it's perfectly central and rooms do have basic shower and squat toilet attached.

Park Hotel (☎ 332 2228; fax 332 6798; Imam St; s/tw IR192,000/288,000; ✿) Upgrades are ongoing at this reliable midrange option near Azadi Sq. The manager speaks some English.

Sepid Hotel (☎ 322 6882; Imam St; s/tw IR250,000/320,000; ✿) An inviting foyer leads to wood-effect walled corridors and pleasant-enough rooms with glittery floral bedspreads and curtains. Metal gauze lamps cast curious patterns at night, but the somewhat ragged bathrooms are a let down.

Zanjan Grand Hotel (Hotel Bozorg Zanjan; ☎ 728 8190; Basij Sq; s/tw/ste US$92/104/139; ☑ ✿ ▯) By far Zanjan's top option, the stylishly sparse, international-standard rooms are spacious, with impeccable bathrooms, a slight niggle being the ill-conceived light-switching system. Staff try hard to please. However, the noisy location is inconvenient if you're not driving.

Eating

In addition to the traditionally styled places listed below there are numerous standard *kababis* along Imam St.

Sofrakhane Sonati Abache (Bostani Bashkah; ☎ 323 7250; Bashkah Alley; dizi IR15,000, qalyan IR12,000; ☺ 8.30am-10pm) Good for bread-and-honey breakfasts, this former *zurkhaneh* chamber is an octagonal domed cellar eccentrically decorated with old samovars, portraits and peacock feathers. Tea (IR3500) comes with dates and a swizzle-stick of crystal sugar. At night it's popular with (male) university students. Look for the black door with brass knobs and knockers.

Haji Dadash (☎ 322 2020; bazaar; meals IR15,000-30,000; ☺ 10am-11pm) This family-oriented

WESTERN IRAN

ZANJAN

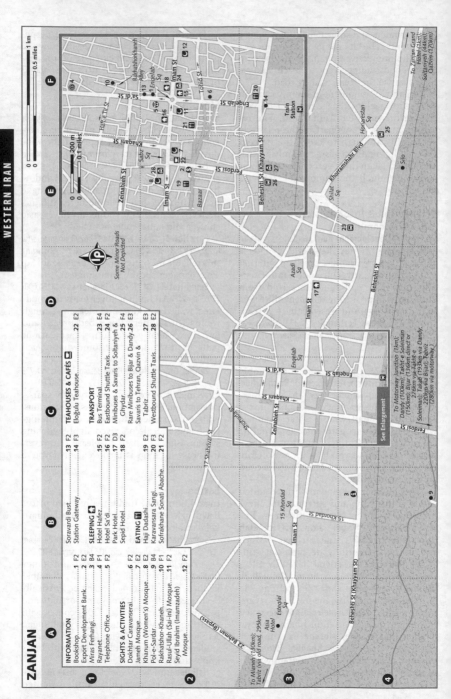

tea-cavern overflows with character, especially in its carpet-draped front cellar. The good *dizi sangi* comes with a plate of fresh herbs to fine-tune the flavour but tea and qalyan for four costs a hefty IR30,000. Enter opposite the portal of Mirza Mehdi mosque within the main bazaar.

Karavansara Sangi (☎ 326 1266; Beheshti St; meals IR20,000-25,000; ☽ 11am-4pm & 6-11pm) Atmospheric if a little over-lit, this 400-year-old stone building is an L-shaped remnant of a caravanserai with 10 carpet-decked vaulted alcoves facing a long row of tables. Try the *kashki bademjun* (eggplant paste, IR17,000).

Eloğlu Teahouse (Ferdosi St; tea IR3000, qalyan IR10,000; ☽ 8am-9.30pm) Yet another appealing subterranean teahouse; the Eloğlu is in a modern basement beautified with Rajasthani textiles.

Getting There & Away

Buses to Esfahan (IR24,000, 6.30pm), Rasht (IR18,500, 8.30am) and Tehran (fairly frequent) use the big but eerily empty terminal, five minutes' walk south of Shilat Sq.

Savaris and some buses for Tehran, Qazvin and Tabriz pick up at the Khayyam/Ferdosi St junction along with very rare Bijar- and Dandy-bound minibuses. If arriving on a Tehran–Tabriz bus that's bypassing Zanjan on the motorway, get off at the junction marked 'Bijar' (an easy, obvious 2km walk from central Zanjan) NOT at the 'Zanjan' exit, which is around 10km out to the east.

Savaris and occasional minibuses to Soltaniyeh (IR5000) and Ghydar (IR17,000) leave from Honarestan Sq.

If you're driving to Tabriz, notice the paws of eroded low cliffs in dramatic tiger-striped pink and white layers after 115km.

The train station is beyond a Dali-esque gateway of winged wheels. Best-timed departures for Tehran (IR9850 to IR14,500, four hours) via Qazvin (two hours) are at 6.14am and 8.24am. Tickets are hard to find for the 9.45pm and 23.10pm sleepers to Tabriz (IR30,000, 8½ hours) via Maraqeh (five hours).

Getting Around

Useful shuttle-taxis run from Enqelab Sq to Honarestan Sq passing near the terminal. Others go from Sabz Sq to Esteqlal Sq.

ZANJAN TO TAKAB & BIJAR

A great way to visit Takht-e Soleiman (see below) is by chartering a taxi for a day from Zanjan (around IR350,000, full day with stops) travelling on afterwards via Takab to be dropped off in Bijar. If you take the daily Zanjan–Dandy minibus (around 9am), use Dandy's taxi stand (☎ 0242-352 2566) to charter a ride for the last 50km to Takht-e Soleiman.

Zanjan to Takht-e Soleiman

The route passes some fabulously timeless villages, particularly once you've passed the un-exotic mining town of Dandy. **Shikhlar**, 20km from Dandy, is dramatically backed by the pyramidal peak of **Tozludagh** (Dusty Mountain). **Qaravolkhana**, 20km further (10km before Takht-e Soleiman), has particularly picturesque mud-block homes rising between spindly trees and a lurid, metallic-green igloo-shaped mini-shrine at its southern end. Bucolic meadowland behind offers great hikes and the possible ascent of **Mt Belqeis**, topped by fragmentary ruins of a Sassanid line-of-sight fortress.

Takht-e Soleiman   تخت سليمان
THE MAIN RUINS

Sitting in a high, lonely bowl of mountains ringed by 1500-year-old fortress walls, this **Unesco World Heritage site** (☎ 0482 563 3311; admission IR5000; ☽ 8am-sunset) is one of the most memorable sights of western Iran. In the 3rd century AD the state religion of Sassanian Persia was Zoroastrianism and Takht-e Soleiman (then called Azergoshnasb) was its spiritual centre. The site was perfect. Zoroastrianism had by this stage incorporated many Magi-inspired elements, including the veneration of earth, wind (plenty here), water and fire. Water (albeit undrinkably poisonous) was provided in abundance by the limpidly beautiful 'bottomless' **crater lake** that still forms the centre of the site. This pours forth 90L per second and would have been channelled through an Anahita-style water temple (see boxed text, p206). The fire was provided thanks to a natural volcanic gas channelled through ceramic pipes to sustain an 'eternal flame' in the *ateshkadeh* (fire temple).

Today only relatively fragmentary ruins remain and you shouldn't expect Persepolis-style carvings. Nonetheless, the sheer age and magnificent setting here are attractions enough.

Takht-e Soleiman's name (Throne of Solomon) is not based on real historical links to Old Testament King Solomon. It was in fact a cunning 7th-century invention by the temple's Persian guardians in the face of the Arab invasion. Realising Islam's reverence for biblical prophets they entirely fabricated a tale of Solomon's one-time residence to avert the site's certain destruction. The ruse worked, the complex survived and the name stuck.

In the 13th century, Takht-e Soleiman became a summer retreat for the Mongol Il-khanid khans. The remnants of their hunting palace is now covered with a discordant modern roof forming a store-room (often locked) for amphora, unlabelled column fragments, photos and a couple of ceramic sections of those ancient gas pipes.

A guide is often available at the site gate and can help you make sense of all the piles of stone if you share enough language. Alternatively, navigate yourself using a glossy bilingual Farsi/English map/brochure (IR3000), which are sold at the ticket booth but not displayed. Ask.

Takht-e Soleiman is 2km from **Nosratabad**. Archaeologists believe that beneath that mud-and-haystack village is the site of Shiz, once a Nestorian-Christian centre of Graeco-Persian learning (not just a 'Land of Oz' fiction). Nosratabad has a minuscule kabab window, but the nearest accommodation is 42km away in Takab.

ZENDAN-E SOLEIMAN

This dramatic 97m conical peak dominates the valley landscape for miles around. Though it's now bare of all construction, the cone was once enclosed by fortified walls and topped by a religious sanctuary that archaeologists suggest dated back to 900 BC. Zendan-e Soleiman means Solomon's Prison, though anyone jailed within the central crater wouldn't have lasted long given the noxious sulphurous fumes. Peering gingerly into its dizzying void can be suffocating enough. Assuming you're reasonably fit, climbing to the crater's edge should take under 15 minutes. The path is muddy but obvious, zig-zagging up from the Takab road about 4km south of the main Takht-e Soleiman ruins.

GETTING THERE & AWAY

Unless you charter a ride from Zanjan or Dandy, the approach is from Takab. From a small taxi stand an the western edge of Takab town taxis ask IR50,000 return including enough time to quickly run around the site and to dash up Zendan-e Soleiman. Add IR15,000 per hour if you hang around. Savaris and minibuses only run to Nosratabad once or twice a day and leave you 2km short of Takht-e Soleiman. Traffic is often very thin making hitch-hiking awkward.

Takab   تكاب

☎ 0482 / pop 50,000

This hilly market town is of interest only as the closest access point for Takht-e Soleiman. Bank Saderat at the crossroads of Imam and Enqelab Sts approximately marks its commercial centre. About 100m southeast of that junction opposite Bank Melli, the extremely basic, showerless **Mehmunpazir Takht-e-Jamshid** (☎ 522 2119; Imam St; tw IR60,000) is signed 'Pensiun'. Rooms have recently been

---

THRONE OF SOLEIMAN – MAKE A DAY OF IT

A great way to visit Takht-e Soleiman (see p187) is by chartering a taxi for a day from Zanjan (around IR350,000, full day with stops) travelling on afterwards via Takab to be dropped off in Bijar. The route passes some fabulously timeless villages, particularly once you've passed the un-exotic mining town of Dandy. **Shikhlar**, 20km from Dandy is dramatically backed by the pyramidal peak of **Tozludagh** (Dusty Mountain). **Qaravolkhana**, 20km further (10km before Takht-e Soleiman), has particularly picturesque mud-block homes rising between spindly trees and a lurid, metallic-green igloo-shaped mini-shrine at its southern end. Bucolic meadowland behind offers great hikes and the possible ascent of **Mt Belqeis**, topped by fragmentary ruins of a Sassanid line-of-sight fortress.

If you take the daily Zanjan–Dandy minibus (around 9am), use Dandy's **taxi stand** (☎ 0242 352 2566) to charter a ride for the last 50km to Takht-e Soleiman.

repainted but conditions remain far from inviting. The owner knows the odd word of English. A kilometre uphill from the Bank Saderat crossroads, passing close to **Coffeenet Yahoo** (☎ 523 2288; Pasdaran St; per hr IR7000; ☺ 10am-8pm) en route, is the comparatively upmarket **Rangi Hotel** (☎ 522 3179; fax 522 4650; Upper Enqelab St; s/tw/tr/q with breakfast US$25/32/40/45). Since a major re-fit and expansion in 2007, the top-floor rooms are now the most comfortable. The restaurant has improved of late and manager Ayub speaks good English.

GETTING THERE & AWAY
Buses and minibuses use a new terminal in the northeast corner of town. Bijar and Shahin Dezh minibuses depart roughly hourly until 1pm. The 5am bus to Zanjan (IR12,000) drives via Bijar.

Savaris to Bijar (IR15,000, one hour) leave from outside **Taavoni 16** (☎ 522 2136; Imam St) just across the bridge from Meh-munpazir Takht-e-Jamshid.

The taxi stand for Takht-e Soleiman is near Galem Sq, 600m further west along Imam St.

For Miyando'ab (and thence Maraqeh or Orumiyeh) start by taking a savari from the western edge of town to Shahin Dezh (IR15,000, 1¼ hours), cross that town by taxi (IR2000, 3km) then continue by savari (IR10,000) or minibus (IR3000).

Around Takab
KARAFTU CAVES
These intriguing four-storey **cliff-caves** (admission IR4000) are normally visited from Di-vandareh (67km to the south), but should soon be accessible via an improved road from Takab. An antique inscription within says in Greek: 'Hercules lives here: no evil may enter'.

Takab to Bijar
The 84km road to Bijar offers some scenic vistas across the high plateaus and towards a variety of dry mountain-tops. It passes two notable villages of mud houses: **Sadbil** (17km from Takab) and **Qizil Belakh** (25km). Some 35km from Takab, an unasphalted side road leads about 10km to **Qom Choqa** (Ghamchoghay). This dramatic nose of cliff overlooks the Shahan River and was the site of a fortress thought to date back to the 8th century, though it is now virtually invisible.

BIJAR　　　　　　　　بيجار
☎ 0872 / pop 51,000

Cradled between arid hills topped in rocky crags, Bijar is a fairly diffuse junction town, but is more scenic and has better trans-port connections than Takab. Tohid St is the main north–south axis. The town centre is where Tohid St meets Taleqani St and almost-parallel Imam St one block further north. A block west of Tohid St is handily central **Click Coffeenet** (Taleqani St; s/tw IR20,000/23,000; ☺ 8am-10pm).

Mosaferkhaneh Moqadam (☎ 422 3260; Shahid Ardalon St; s/tw 40,000/50,000, shower IR5000) has simple, unexciting rooms with big ceil-ing fans, wooden-board beds, maybe-clean sheets and shared squat toilets. It's an Escheresqe maze of stairways reached through a subterranean restaurant on a quiet tree-lined street between Bank Melli and the small brick-vaulted bazaar. That's one block north and west of the Imam/Tohid St junction.

The much smarter **Iran Bam Hotel** (☎ 423 3160; Sanandaj Hwy; tw 300,000) is a modern three-storey circular building of blue glass with a decent restaurant and café. Rooms are fully equipped and have fancy sash curtains but the thick pile carpets are already looking soiled. It's about 3km west of town, 800m beyond the roundabout at which Imam and Taleqani Sts converge.

Near the Taleqani St petrol station (1km west of the Coffeenet) is the kitschily atmos-pheric teahouse **Sofrakhane Ferdin** (Taleqani St; qalyan IR6000; ☺ 8am-11pm).

Getting There & Away
The main terminal, 4km northeast of town handles all minibuses (last at 3pm) and buses plus savaris to Zanjan (IR25,000), which depart regularly till dusk. Minibuses to Hamadan (IR15,000) depart at 7.30am and 8am only.

Savaris for Takab (IR15,000, one hour) and Sanandaj (IR22,500, 1¾ hours) depart until dusk from outside the Iran Bam Hotel. A taxi from the terminal costs IR5000 *dar baste*.

SANANDAJ　　　　　　سنندج
☎ 0871 / pop 358,000

Even by Iran's super-hospitable standards, Sanandaj is a remarkably friendly city. It's the capital of Kordestan province, a good base for visits to Palangan and a great place to learn more about Kurdish history and culture. You'll see plenty of men wearing traditional cummerbunds and baggy Kurdish trousers. Yet it's a modern, noticeably prosperous city with a large, fashionable population of students ever anxious to try out their English. In Sanandaj's Sorani-Kurdish *ju-an* means beautiful and *deso hoshbe* means thank you.

History
Originally known as Senna (as it still is to local Kurds), the city was of major importance in the Middle Ages but withered to nothing in the chaotic post-Chaldoran era. A *dej* (fortress) was built here in the early 18th century and Senna-dej slowly developed into Sanandaj. From here the powerful Ardalan emirs came to rule the last autonomous principality of Iranian Kurdistan up until 1867. Under the Ardalans the town developed many fine 19th-century buildings, though most have since been lost to rapacious 20th-century development.

Orientation & Information
Busily commercial Ferdosi St links the twin centres Enqelab and Azadi Sqs. From the latter, Abidar St slopes up into the folds of a rocky ridge that was the city's historic defence and is today the pleasant **Abidar mountain park**. The delightfully helpful, multilingual **Cultural Heritage Organisation of Kordestan** (☎ 225 5440; www.kurdistanmiras.ir; Habibi Lane; ☼ 8am-2pm Sat-Thu) offers beautiful brochures and basic, up-to-date maps. Its office is an inner section of the lovely mansion that houses the Regional Museum. A little one-window **stationery shop** (Imam St) sells city maps that are very accurate for back alleys but dangerously outdated for main streets (many being newly constructed). To change money use **Bank Melli** (Taleqani St), but not the big branch on Azadi Sq. Internet is available in the plush Tejari Kordestan shopping mall on Pasdaran St and at **Ashyanneh Coffeenet** (☎ 323 6187; Seyid Qotb St; per hr IR7000; ☼ 8am-11pm). The website www.sanandaj.com has city photos to send as e-postcards.

Sights
The well-renovated Lotfolla Sheikh-al-Islam Mansion houses a **Regional Museum** (Habibi Lane; admission IR20,000; ☼ 9am-12.30pm & 3-6.30pm) whose multicoloured windows (*orosi*) were designed for practicality as well as beauty: supposedly they disoriente mosquitoes. Exhibits include some extraordinarily old pottery and metalwork treasures but sadly the acoustically engineered fountain-cellar is generally kept locked.

Another attractively restored Qajar building, the **Asef Mansion** (Asif Diwan; Imam St; admission IR4000; ☼ 8.30am-12.30pm & 2.30-5pm Tue-Sun), is now a museum of Kurdish life. Mannequins are dressed in various distinctive tribal cos-

---

THE KURDS

Just as many Westerners have the misguided impression that Iran is somehow 'dangerous', so Iranians are similarly misinformed about Kurdish areas of their own country. In fact Kurdish hospitality often trumps even that of mainstream Persians.

Kurds comprise nearly 10% of Iran's population. But there are several different Kurdish subgroups speaking languages that are almost mutually unintelligible. Kurds around Howraman and Paveh are the most traditional and speak poetic Hurami. Those in Sanandaj usually speak Sorani. Both groups are typically Sunni. However, some Kurds around Kermanshah are Shiite. Kermanji, the language of most Kurds in Turkey, isn't widely spoken, though Kermanji satellite TV stations, some openly glorifying PKK leader Abdulla Öcalan, are starting to change this. Curiously there are pockets of native Kermanji speakers around Kalat in northeastern Iran. They were originally sent there by the Safavids to defend Iran's 17th-century borders, and never left.

There are variations between tribes, but a common element in traditional dress for most Iranian Kurdish men is the slightly tasselled headscarf (*mezare*) and the distinctive *kawa pantol* suit with heavily pleated baggy trousers. These are typically belted by a wide cummerbund (*biben*) which, when dancing, men pull off and whirl above their heads. Women wear colourful long dresses over baggy trousers and rarely resort to chador. At celebrations the real finery comes out, notably caps covered in gold coins over cascading stitched tulle scarves.

tumes that are still commonly worn in valleys around Kordestan. One room features Sanandaj's speciality wood-inlay crafts. A side courtyard just within the mansion's entrance leads through to a vaulted **gallery** (admission free) that has sporadic art exhibitions.

Several other historic buildings are only partially repaired. The trefoil-topped **Moshir Divan** is a particularly iconic mansion still in dire need of renovation. It's hidden in a walled garden off Shohada St: ring the speaker phone and hope.

The formerly grand **Khosroabad Mansion** (Khosroabad St; admission free; 10am-dusk) has an impressive central courtyard with reflecting pools and was once the palace of Ardalan emir Amonulla Khan but is now in

a fairly parlous state. It's two blocks up a quiet boulevard of plane trees from Sahar Kaveh St.

In 1813, Amonulla Khan sponsored the fine **Jameh Mosque** (Darolesan Mosque; Imam St), with tiled twin minarets and 32 interior domes. He was so pleased with the result that he reputedly had the architect blinded to prevent its repetition for any other patron. The punishment would have been more appropriate for whoever built the ugly new mosque directly behind.

The **fortress site** (Imam St) is firmly closed for military use, though a tea bazaar huddles at its eastern edge. The **covered bazaar** is cruelly bisected by Enqelab St but within is the unusual 1805 **Khan Hamam** (admission IR2000;

SANANDAJ

⏰9am-1pm & 3-7pm Tue-Sun). The interior has considerably restored grey-and-white floral and bird motifs, attractive tiling and remarkably lifelike 'bathers' enjoying the historic bathhouse. The easily missed door has a brass 'fist' knocker: walk one mini-block into the bazaar beside Mehmanpazir Jahan, then one block right and it's on your left.

Sleeping

Mehmanpazir Kaj (☎ 323 1162; Ferdosi St; s/tw from IR60,000/80,000) The Kaj is unusually presentable for a cheap guesthouse with corridors that have renovated old wall-mouldings. The simple rooms have nicely tiled bathrooms with squeaky clean squat toilets and gushingly powerful showers. Unsigned in English, it's four doors along from the bridge that crosses Kordestan Blvd.

Nehro Hotel (☎ 225 5170; Ferdosi St; tw/tr IR70,000/90,000) This great-value place has clean, well-kept rooms above a small shopping centre. All have shower and squat.

Hotel Abidar (☎ 324 1645; Ferdosi St; s/tw with bathroom IR110,000/170,000). Rather ill-maintained, though standards vary somewhat between rooms. It's one of few cheaper places to accept single women travellers.

Shadi Hotel (☎ 662 5112; Pasdaran St extension; tw/tr US$35/55; Ⓟ 🛇) By far the best accommodation in Sanandaj, this very professional hotel deserves at least three of its four self-awarded stars. A choice of restaurants lead off a spacious lobby that wraps around a big copper fireplace. Staff speak English. The hotel's main drawback is its out-of-town position beyond Mellat Park but shuttle taxis from Azadi Sq pass outside (very fast!).

Other options if the above are full:
Hotel Jabar (☎ 323 6584; Enqelab Sq; tw with/without bathroom IR118,000/82,500, tr IR100,000) Very central.
Hotel Hedayat (☎ 226 7117; Ferdosi St; s/tw IR91,100/127,600, without bathroom IR80,200/106,350)

Eating

Typical *kababis* and fruit-juice squeezers are scattered along Ferdosi St, especially around Enqelab and Azadi Sqs where **Shahreqashang** (☎ 322 7706; ⏰7.30-2.30am) serves ice creams and snacks till very late. An unnamed, unexotic teahouse beside the Hotel Hedayat is good for fried egg breakfasts or *dizi*.

JimJim (☎ 356 4213; Abidar St; coffee IR6000-9000, Pizzas from IR18,000; ⏰10am-2pm & 4pm-midnight) Gold tables, swirly wrought-iron seats and very friendly staff make this little café a pleasant place for refreshment if walking between Abidar Park and the Khosroabad Building. In Abidar Park itself and beyond Kuhnavar Sq there several places for ice cream, kababs and snacks.

Khansalar (☎ 662 351; Pasdaran St; meals IR20,000-45,000; ⏰11.30am-3pm & 5.30-10pm) Sanandaj's most interesting restaurant has waiters in Kurdish costume, plays Kurdish music and has some Kurdish menu options including *dokhwa* (tinglingly tart barley soup) and various types of *köfte* (meatballs). There's *kashka bademjun* (mashed eggplant with yoghurt) for vegetarians (IR10,000). Take a shuttle taxi from Azadi Sq, alighting opposite the university just before EN Bank.

Jahannama (☎ 226 4212; Taleqani St; meals IR25,000-50,000; ⏰8am-4pm & 7-10pm) Descend a glittery stairway into a weird stylistic mish-mash of OTT opulence, middle-class kitsch and genuine local artefacts including antique qalyans and samovars. Food is excellent and sensibly priced. Try the delicately flavoured *khoresht sabzi* (vegetable, meat and bean stew), succulent *juje pofaki* (marinated chicken morsels) or curious *tahchin agusht* (meat, raisins and barberries arranged like a gateau between layers of saffron rice).

Shobo (☎ 324 1179; Shahid Namaki St; meals IR30,000-50,000; ⏰noon-10pm) The service is off-hand and our *chelo mahi* (fried fish on rice) was rather underwhelming, but the downstairs section has a fairly pleasant atmosphere with bed-seats and a central fountain pool. The menu has vague English translations.

Shopping

Several workshops around the Asef Mansion create and sell Sanandaj's famous woodcrafts, notably inlaid *nard* sets.

Khaledi (☎ 225 5680; Shohoda St; ⏰8am-1pm & 3-8pm) This shop sells traditional musical instruments including beautiful *setars* (long-necked local lutes).

Getting There & Away

Travel agency **Kia Parvaz** (☎ 222 7770; alley off Imam St) sells tickets for Iran Aseman's daily Sanandaj–Tehran flight on a Fokker 100.

Savaris to Kamyaran (IR16,000, one hour), Kermanshah (IR35,000, two hours), Qorveh

(IR20,000) and Hamadan (IR35,000) wait in neat, well-organised queues in the main terminal area, 4km east of centre. Minibuses leave from behind and long-distance buses from a half-hidden section to the left. Several bus companies have handy central ticket offices around Enqelab Sq.

Destination	Fare	Duration	Departures
Ahvaz	IR60,000	13hr	6pm Seiro Safar, Taavoni 7
Esfahan	IR36,000	9hr	8pm Taavoni 5
Orumiyeh	IR35,000	9hr	9am Taavoni 5, 7.45pm Taavoni 15
Rasht	IR34,000	7hr	6pm Taavoni 15
Tabriz	IR32,700	9hr	8pm Taavoni 5
Tehran	IR29,600-60,000	6hr	various

To Bijar, Saqqez and Marivan, savaris and rare minibuses leave from the far northern edge of town, but inbound often drop passengers 1km further south at Taleqani (Sohrevardi) Sq at the northern end of Taleqani St.

Getting Around
Fast-filling shuttle taxis (IR1000 per standard hop) from Enqelab Sq run east to the main terminal and north along Taleqani Sq to the Marivan terminal. From Azadi Sq they run down Pasdaran St to the Shadi Hotel and up Abidar St. For Abidar mountain park things are complicated by the one-way system: some cars up Keshavarz St divert and continue up Abidar St past JimJim leaving you to walk the last 15 minutes or so. A taxi *dar baste* to the upper hairpin sections of Abidar Park costs around IR10,000.

AROUND SANANDAJ
Palangan   پلنگان
pop 850
Brilliant Palangan is one of Iran's most picturesque villages. Its earth-coloured stone houses climb steeply up both sides of a rocky chasm while traditionally dressed villagers shoe horses in the narrow pathways or simply stand gazing from their flat rooftops. Wobbly old bridges cross the gushing river at either end of town. Unlike Howraman this is not an 'undiscovered' gem. Local tourists come in considerable numbers at weekends to picnic in the local

orchards. However, as many come dressed up in Kurdish Friday-best costumes this adds further photogenic colour to the scene. Access is relatively easy. Start in dreary Kamyaran, halfway between Hamadan and Sanandaj. Savaris for Palangan start from Salahaddin St (2km southeast of Kamyaran's main terminal), but you'll probably need to pay *dar baste* (IR60,000 return plus waiting time). The asphalted road (45km) passes some other interesting mud-and-stone Kurdish villages en route. Vehicles arrive at a car park outside Palangan's big, rather ugly fish farm. Don't be dismayed. The old village is hidden around the corner, a 15-minute stroll along a covered watercourse.

Marivan   مریوان
☎ 0875 / pop 123,000
The main tourist draw of this bustling Kurdish market town is **Zarivar Lake**, 3km to the west. Backed by low, rolling mountains and fronted by marshlands the lake is invaded by pleasure boats during summer weekends, but is idyllically peaceful at other times. Marivan has several very decent hotels of which the finest is the new six-storey **Hotel Zarivar** (☎ 34 0777; s/d/ste IR230,000/350,000/600,000). Fully equipped international-style rooms with fresh pine décor overlook the lake's marshy eastern end (albeit from the wrong side of the road), and there's an excellent top-floor-view restaurant. The **ITTIC Tourist Inn** (Mehmansara Jahangardi; ☎ 322 1626; tr IR315,000) has 10 contrastingly dowdy old bungalows but all have bathrooms and the location is an ideal perch overlooking the lake, high above the boating jetty.

The Marivan–Sanandaj road has some very attractive stretches and passes through the mid-sized stepped village of **Negel**. This is incongruously dominated by a modernist mosque that houses the priceless **Negel Quran**. It's reputedly one of only four Qurans to survive from the time of the third caliph, Osman (ie barely a generation after Mohammad PBUH). Although it's been stolen three times, each time it has been recovered and has only a single page missing.

Sanandaj-bound transport uses Marivan's terminal, 2km east of the centre with occasional minibuses (IR8000, 2¼ hours) and regular savaris (IR30,000, 1¾ hours). Shared 4WDs into Howraman are sometimes available from Jomhuri St, but there's a better chance of finding a shared ride from **Biyakara**, a roadside junction market 17km towards Sanandaj.

HOWRAMAN هورامان

Caught at the intersection of powerful empires, the Kurds had their homes destroyed so regularly in medieval history that, by the 18th century, a sizable part of society had foregone villages altogether and resorted to nomadism and brigandry. An important exception, thanks to its impenetrable mountain-hemmed position, was the Howraman (Orumanat) valley. This remains one of Iran's least known and most spectacular areas. In colder months you'll still see Howraman men wearing *kolobal*, brown-felt jackets with distinctive shoulder 'horns'. There is plenty of age-old stone terracing and the villages are stacked Masuleh-style, one house's roof forming the next one's yard. The Hurami Kurdish language is quite distinct from Sorani Kurdish, which replaced it in Sanandaj, though Hurami was once the dialect of choice for regional Kurdish poets. Knowing even a few words will flabbergast and delight locals you meet. *Fere-washa* and *zarif* mean beautiful, *wazh-maze* means delicious, *deset wazhbu* (literally 'hand good') means thank you to which one replies *sarat wazhbu* ('head good' ie you're welcome).

From **Biyakara**, 17km east of Marivan, an asphalted road leads up through a narrow canyon, transits the extensive village of **Dezli**, and climbs a high pass where it divides. Two roads from here lead to Paveh, both breathtakingly beautiful. What appears to be the smaller branch wiggles along the Iraqi borderline at **Dalani** (don't take photos there), bypasses **Nodesheh** and continues via **Nosud**. This is now asphalted so much easier than the alternative, but classic, route via picturesque **Kamala** (basic kabab shops) and austere **Howraman-at-Takht** (Oruman-Takht) where the asphalt ends. Howraman-at-Takht is a particularly impressive and steep array of rock-and-mud bungalows viewed most photogenically from the diminutive **Pir Shaliar shrine**, 600m beyond. Although there's now a green-domed Muslim prayer-room here, that shrine's real interest lies in the animistic rocks and trees, behind, which are draped with votive rag-strips Buddhist-style. A Mithraic midwinter festival is reportedly still held here on the Friday nearest to 4 February. Some suggest that this is a cultural relic from pre-Zoroastrian 'angel' worship, albeit with an Islamic overlay.

The slippery mud road from Howraman-at-Takht onwards to Paveh (72km, 4½ hours) is 90% hairpins: marvellously scenic but spine-jarringly exhausting, and impossible if wet or snowy (ie most of the winter). The most appealing villages en-route are **Belbär**, cupped in a deep mountain hollow, and **Selin** where brightly attired women sit at the roadside crocheting classic Howraman slippers (*giveh*). The best views are around **Hawasawa** (visible but inaccessible from the 'road') with grandeur reminiscent of the Karakoram Highway. Asphalt returns at Ura, 21km from Paveh.

Sleeping
There's no formal accommodation en route, but if you are invited to stay you might find hospitality so overwhelming that a polite quick 'escape' is hard to arrange.

Getting There & Away
Snow allowing, Howraman-at-Takht makes a relatively easy taxi day-trip from Marivan (or even Sanandaj). There are also shared 4WDs between Biya Kaya and Howraman-at-Takht (IR20,000, 1¾ hours, 50km), but you can't be sure of finding a ride back again the same day. A great idea is to engage a taxi or 4WD at Biya Kaya or Marivan and continue all the way to Paveh. *Dar baste* expect to pay IR250,000 via Nosud, or IR500,000 via Belbär. Sharing a ride, prices will vary enormously according to vehicle, driver and what other co-passengers you can find for intermediate points.

PAVEH پاوه
☎ 0832 / pop 13,700
The rapidly developing Hurami-speaking town of Paveh (sometimes pronounced 'Pawa') makes an accessible introduction and gateway to Howraman. It's a phenomenally hospitable place with a fine setting, high up a fold of mountainside valley. Views

of Paveh's most characteristic stepped area are best from the Ferris wheel in Kazemi Park. At the back of the park you'll find the **Ateshgah Suites** (☎ /fax 722 1732, 0918 888 3059; r IR150,000), where six concrete box-rooms with bathroom and unfinished kitchenette are carpeted and have blankets but no beds. It's named Ateshgah for what was once Sassanian Persia's second-greatest Zoroastrian temple complex (after Takht-e Soleiman) on a pronounced rocky knob on the mountaintop opposite. The site is very distantly visible from rooms 1 and 2 across a deep valley. Locals claim somewhat optimistically that they can walk there and back in a long day.

There's cheaper accommodation, in little dormitories at the **Ostad Khanim Mo'allem** (Female-teachers' Hostel; ☎ 722 5574; dm IR15,000) if they allow you to stay. It's supposedly for women only, but the caretaker (who speaks no English) might accept foreign men if they're suitably polite. Access is down steps marked with a restaurant sign featuring a chicken (beside the Piraysh-foad barber shop). By far the nicest dining option in Paveh is **Kapr** (☎ 722 1112; Shohoda Sq; meals IR12,000-30,000; ☯ 8am-10pm) at the top of the town's little blue-glass shopping centre.

Getting There & Away

From the main terminal 3km east of central Paveh, Kermanshah minibuses (IR5500) and savaris (IR20,000, 1¾ hours) fill slowly. It might prove quicker to go in hops via Javanrud (IR3000, 45 minutes) or Ravansar (IR3500, one hour). En route you'll pass the slippery-floored **Ghuri Gahleh Cave** (Goori Gala Qar; admission IR4000; ☯ 9.30am-5pm), which claims to be Asia's longest, but what you see is very disappointing and somewhat claustrophobic.

For Marivan and Howraman shared Toyota (pronounced 'tweeter') pick-ups gather outside a trio of orange container huts, 1km west of Shohoda Sq. Departure times are highly unpredictable, typically before dawn to Howraman-at-Takht (IR70,000, five hours) if at all. To allow plenty of photo stops consider renting a taxi *dar baste* to Marivan from the delightful folks at **Kurd Taxi Agency** (☎ 722 777; Blvd Janbazan) either via Nosud (IR250,000) or in perfect dry weather via Howraman-at-Takht (IR500,000, very rough road).

KERMANSHAH
کرمانشاه
☎ 0831 / pop 765,000

By far the largest and busiest city in central west Iran, Kermanshah developed in the 4th century AD astride the Royal Road to Baghdad. Its strategic position has brought both prosperity and attack. Most recently it suffered missile damage during the Iran-Iraq War. Briefly renamed Bakhtaran in the 1980s, the city is a melting pot of Kurds, Lori and other Iranians. Though not a major tourist draw, its backdrop of glowing red-rock mountains is impressive and, if you're passing through, don't miss Taq-e Bostan.

Orientation

Kermanshah is bewilderingly vast. The main street changes names (Kashani-Modarres-Beheshti-Sheikh Shiroodi) as it stretches over 10km from the busy commercial centre (the southern third) to the foot of the magnificent rocky Parom Mountain massif. Here the Taq-e Bostan carvings, ringed by parks and outdoor restaurants, form the city's foremost attraction. Cheap accommodation is found south of the mammoth Azadi Sq, which has a mini Dome-of-the-Rock in its midst. Another key junction is 15 Khordat Sq, nicknamed Meydan Labab, actually a daunting high-speed flyover rather than a square.

Information

INTERNET ACCESS

Emperator (Modarres St; per hr IR6000; ☯ 8am-8pm) Upstairs. Fairly good connection.

Hesabgarnet (☎ 723 1309; Shari'ati St; per hr IR6000; ☯ 10am-9pm)

MONEY

Sepehr Exchange Co (Bank Sepah Bldg, Kashani Sq) Changes money, unlike the big Bank Melli on Azadi Sq.

TOURIST INFORMATION

Cultural Heritage Office of Kermanshah (☎ 836 7403; off Beheshti St; ☯ 7.30am-2.30pm Sun-Wed, 7.30am-1pm Thu) Lavish free brochures and decent if undetailed map.

Khadivi House (☎ 721 2696; Ma'adem St; ☯ 8am-3pm Sat-Thu) The Cultural Heritage Office operates a more convenient tourist information outlet at a beautifully restored Qajar mansion and garden used as occasional exhibition space.

Shapur Ataee (☎ 0918 856 6220; shapurataee@yahoo .com; per day plus tips IR200,000) Extremely learned

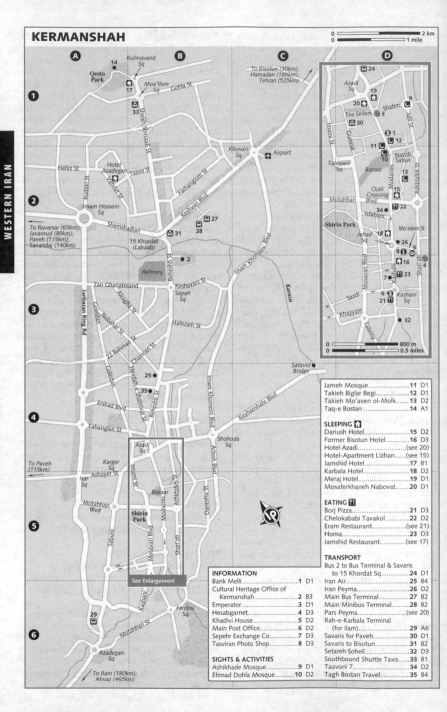

KERMANSHAH

WESTERN IRAN

INFORMATION

Bank Melli	**1** D1
Cultural Heritage Office of Kermanshah	**2** B3
Emperator	**3** D1
Hesabgarnet	**4** D3
Khadivi House	**5** D2
Main Post Office	**6** D2
Sepehr Exchange Co	**7** D3
Tasviran Photo Shop	**8** D3

SIGHTS & ACTIVITIES

Ashikhade Mosque	**9** D1
Ehmad Dohla Mosque	**10** D2

Jameh Mosque	**11** D1
Takieh Biglar Begi	**12** D1
Takieh Mo'aven ol-Molk	**13** D2
Taq-e Bostan	**14** A1

SLEEPING

Dariush Hotel	**15** D2
Former Bisotun Hotel	**16** D3
Hotel Azadi	(see 20)
Hotel-Apartment Lizhan	(see 15)
Jamshid Hotel	**17** B1
Karbala Hotel	**18** D2
Meraj Hotel	**19** D1
Mosaferkhaneh Nabovat	**20** D1

EATING

Borj Pizza	**21** D3
Chelokababi Tavakol	**22** D2
Eram Restaurant	(see 21)
Homa	**23** D3
Jamshid Restaurant	(see 17)

TRANSPORT

Bus 2 to Bus Terminal & Savaris to 15 Khordat Sq	**24** D1
Iran Air	**25** B4
Iran Peyma	**26** D2
Main Bus Terminal	**27** B2
Main Minibus Terminal	**28** B2
Pars Peyma	(see 20)
Rah-e-Karbala Terminal (for Ilam)	**29** A6
Savaris for Paveh	**30** D1
Savaris to Bisotun	**31** B2
Setareh Soheil	**32** D3
Southbound Shuttle Taxis	**33** B1
Taavoni 7	**34** D2
Tagh Bostan Travel	**35** B4

and interesting tour-guide with good English and decent spoken French.

Tasviran Photo Shop (☎ 722 8560; Kashani St; ☺ 8am-9pm) Develops film and prints digital pictures. English spoken, no slides.

Sights

TAQ-E BOSTAN تاق بستان

At the city's northern edge, Kermanshah's star attraction is **Taq-e Bostan** (admission IR5000; ☺ 8am-9pm), a towering cliff inscribed with some extraordinary **Sassanian bas-reliefs**. They are set in and around a pair of **carved alcoves**. The biggest and newest alcove features elephant-backed hunting scenes on the side walls and highlights the coronation of Khosrow II (AD 590–628) beneath which the king rides off in full armour and chain mail looking like the Black Prince (albeit half a millennium before European knights had 'invented' such armour). The second niche shows kings Shapur II and Shapur III twiddling their sword handles and enjoying a relaxed chat apparently oblivious to the footballs that have landed on their heads. To the right of the niches is the finest and oldest tableau showing Shah Ardashir II (r AD 379–383) trampling on the defeated Roman Emperor Julian the Apostate (who he'd beaten in AD 363 when Shapur II's commander). He receives a crown of blessing from Zoroastrian god Ahura Mazda, or perhaps from Shapur II – experts disagree. Meanwhile Mithras sneaks up behind pretending to be Luke Skywalker with a light sabre.

Surrounding open-air restaurants remain popular late into the evening. Even after the reliefs-complex closes, sympathetic lighting means that a golden glow emanates warmly from the alcoves, making the reliefs attractively half-visible through trees across a boating pond.

HOSSEINIEHS

Distinctively Shiite, Hosseiniehs are shrines where plays are acted out during the Islamic month of Moharram, commemorating the martyrdom of Imam Hossein at Karbala (AD 680). The finest in Kermanshah is the 1913 **Takieh Mo'aven ol-Molk** (Hadad Abil St; admission IR4000; ☺ 10am-noon & 4-7.30pm Sat-Thu). Enter down stairs, through a courtyard and domed central chamber decorated with grizzly scenes from the great Karbala battle. The shrine remains very much active, pilgrims kissing the doors and looking genuinely moved by the 'footprint of Ali' on the wall of the second courtyard. This is set amid tiles depicting a wacky gamut of images from Quranic scenes, to pre-Islamic gods including Shahnameh kings, European villages and local notables in 19th-century costumes. A lovely building to the right is now an ethnographic museum displaying regional costumes and tools.

The lesser known **Takieh Biglar Begi** (☎ 827 6597; admission free; ☺ 8am-7pm Sat-Thu) now houses a fairly cursory calligraphy museum, but is worth visiting for its dazzling mirror-tiled central dome-room. To find it take the lane opposite the fine **Jameh Mosque** (Modarres St), which has a beautiful Yazd-styled twin minaret. Then take the first alley left.

OTHER SIGHTS

The extensive, much restored **covered bazaar** slopes up from Modarres St. It's well worth exploring with a couple of dilapidated old caravanserai courtyards at the western end. Within the bazaar, **Ehmad Dohla Mosque** (Jewellery Bazaar), entered through an attractive tiled portal, has a Qajar-era clock tower.

The once interesting area of older houses around the blue-domed, 20th-century **Ashikhade Mosque** (Jalil St) has now been largely bulldozed, but some curiosities remain if you poke about in the back alleys.

Sleeping

BUDGET

A gaggle of cheapies lie handily close to Azadi Sq, many marked only in Farsi and almost all above shop fronts via stairways that are sometimes hard to spot.

Mosaferkhaneh Nabovat (☎ 823 1018; Modarres St; s/tw/tr IR60,000/105,000/140,000, without shower IR50,000/80,000/140,000) The friendly Nabovat has sensibly priced, no-frills rooms whose sheets are clean if cigarette-burnt and whose showers are powerful and stay hot for a reasonable while.

Hotel Azadi (☎ 823 3076; Modarres St; s/tw with private bathroom IR174,000/200,000, with shared bathroom IR108,000/123,000) Somewhat worn furniture in newly painted rooms, some with a tap, others with aging bathrooms. The hearty teacher-manager looks like an Iranian Richard Branson and enterprisingly tends to add around 35% to the bill for foreigners.

WESTERN IRAN (side tab)

Meraj Hotel (☎ 823 3288; Modarres St; s/tw IR150,000/250,000) *Mosaferkhaneh*-style rooms albeit with small shower booths and squat toilets. Access up stairs guarded by a stuffed goat.

MIDRANGE & TOP END
Karbala Hotel (☎ 727 3665; fax 727 5999; Parking Shahrderi; s/d with breakfast US$25/37; ⊠) There are some attractive mouldings in the foyer, but the recently redecorated rooms at Karbala remain fairly characterless with war-torn bathrooms.

Dariush Hotel (☎ 722 7001; Motahhari Blvd; s/d IR300,000/350,000; ⊠) Partial redecoration has failed to rid the Dariush of its 1970's atmosphere, typified by the Blue Peter DIY look of the corridor ceilings. Room décor now uses a pleasant coffee-and-cream colour scheme, but bathrooms (with Western toilet) are distinctly aging.

Bisotun Hotel (Kashani St) Kermanshah's most delightful old hotel is sadly closed for now while the owner (wanting to demolish it) battles with the government (trying to protect the lovely building).

Jamshid Hotel (☎ 429 9666; fax 429 6002; Kuhnavand Sq, Taq-e Bostan; d/tw/tr/ste US$58/87/112/136) Easily the best of Kermanshah's top-end hotels the new Jamshid Hotel has an eccentric white-stone 'castle' façade, but interior décor and service are elegantly international and restrained. Rooms have all the usual extras down to minibar, kettle and logo-ed slippers.

Hotel-Apartment Lizhan (☎ 721 0102; fax 727 6666; Motahhari Blvd; apt IR600,000; ⊠) Self-contained apartments with full kitchens sleep up to six in two bedrooms, which might have a 1970's Cindy Doll feel but are 110% clean, comfy and new. The perfumed entranceway features Leonardo's 'Last Supper'; well, not the original obviously.

Eating
Around Azadi Sq and on Motahhari Blvd near Ojak Crossing there are snack stalls and confectioners selling Kermanshah's archetypal Nan Berenji cookies (literally 'bread-rice'; a round semi-sweet confection that's usually yellow and flavoured with saffron). There's a great concentration of kabab cafés and open-air teahouses near the Taq-e Bostan carvings and several restaurants around Kashani Sq.

ourpick Chelokababi Tavakol (☎ 722 7184; Modarres St; meals IR18,000-25,000; ⊠ 11.30am-3pm & 5.30-9pm) This would be the backpacker meeting place, if there were any backpackers. Excellent value Iranian food is served in an atmospheric once-grand old bathhouse that's slightly gone-to-seed. Charming owner Ali Rahban looks somewhat like Dudley Moore, speaks good English and can rustle up eggplant delights for vegetarians. Head downstairs through white-framed doors with coloured glass panels.

Borj Pizza (☎ 728 9741; Shahid Ashrafi St; medium pizzas IR21,000-26,000; ⊠ 10am-2.30pm & 5-10pm) Though not quite as swish as nearby Zagros Pizza, its unusually good Borj Special Pizza (IR26,000) has enough flavour that you don't need to reach immediately for the ketchup. Rare indeed in Iran.

Eram Restaurant (☎ 727 8506; Bahmany Bldg, Shahid Ashrafi St; meals IR22,000-50,000; ⊠ 9am-3pm & 6-10.30pm) Beneath the same fake 1920's-style tower building as Borj Pizza, Eram's staff are as eccentric as its wavy brickwork interior, which culminates in green-bronze framed copies of the Bisotun reliefs. It serves mainly kababs, but does fesenjun at lunchtime.

Homa (☎ 723 4246; Kashani/Dabir Azam Sts; meals IR30,000-55,000; ⊠ noon-3pm & 7-11pm) Combining the atmosphere of a teahouse with the calm elegance of an upmarket restaurant, Homa has embroidered tablecloths and blue-brick dining niches ranged around a gently trickling fountain. Though not a patch on homemade equivalents, the semi-sweet *fesenjun* (IR30,000) is ideally complemented by their acidic *dugh* (churned sour milk or yogurt mixed with water).

Jamshid Restaurant (☎ 424 4185; basement, Jamshid Hotel; meals IR45,000-85,000; ⊠ noon-3pm & 8-9.30pm, longer in summer) Surveyed by a gigantic bronze eagle and huge samovar, this unusual dining room is cut in two by an artificial 'stream'. Try the local speciality *khoresht khalol* (lamb stewed with almonds) rather than the three-skewer *dandeh kabab* (IR65,000), which is famous more for its excessive size than for its flavour.

Getting There & Away
AIR
Flights to Tehran (IR315,000) leave thrice daily on **Iran Air** (☎ 824 8610; Beheshti St; ⊠ 7.30am-2.30pm Sat-Thu, 7.30am-1pm Fri), plus four times weekly on Iran Aseman. Tickets

are sold by **Tagh Bostan Travel** (☎ 824 6222; Vila St; ☼ 8am-6pm Sat-Thu, 10am-1pm Fri), **Setareh Soheil** (☎ 727 1115; fax 727 1116; Kashani St; ☼ 9.30am-7pm Sat-Thu) and other travel agencies.

BUS, MINIBUS & SAVARI
The huge main bus and minibus terminals are side by side about 8km northeast of Azadi Sq. Use savaris or bus 2 from Azadi Sq. Several offices sell advance tickets including **Iran Peyma** (Javad Sq), **Taavoni 7** (Modarres St) and very handy **Pars Peyma** (Modarres St) beside the Hotel Nobovat, which offers tickets to almost anywhere. Useful options:

Destination	Fare	Duration	Departures
Ahvaz	IR60,000	9hr	8am, 9pm via Andimeshk
Esfahan	IR60,000	9hr	5pm Pars Peyma
Orumiyeh	IR70,000	12hr	5pm Iran Peyma
Tabriz	IR45,000-75,000	8hr	6am, 6pm-10pm
Tehran (west)	IR29,000 IR60,000	9hr 9hr	Taavoni 13, TBT frequent

For Khorramabad, Taavoni 7 has an 8.30am bus via Eslamabad (IR35,000, 4½ hours), but it's generally much quicker in hops. Start with a minibus to Harsin (IR3800, 45 minutes), a sizeable town in an agricultural valley surrounded by moorland bluffs reminiscent of a drought-stricken Scotland. Cross town by shuttle taxi (IR2000, 3.5km) and continue by savari to Nurabad (per person/car IR10,000/50,000, 40 minutes) from which there are minibuses/savaris (IR4500/15,000, 1¼ hours) to Khorramabad.

For Hamadan there are direct minibuses (IR10,000, 2½ hours) and savaris (IR40,000).

For Sanandaj, savaris cost IR35,000 (two hours), but strangely it can prove cheaper to break the savari journey in Kamyaran (IR12,000, one hour), which works well for visiting Palangan.

Transport to Ilam and Qasr-e-Shirin (for the Iraq borders) uses the quite separate **Rah-e-Karbala terminal** (Sabuni St) in the southwest corner of Kermanshah.

Savaris to Paveh (back/front IR20,000/25,000) depart from Gumruk St close to Azadi Sq.

Savaris to Bisotun (IR5000, 25 minutes) start from the southeast slip-road of the intimidating 15 Khordat (Labab) overpass.

TRAIN
A new railway is planned linking Tehran to Baghdad (Iraq) via Kermanshah and Qasr-e-Shirin, but construction will probably take years.

Getting Around
Bisotun-bound shuttle taxis from 15 Khordat Sq pass the airport gates. Shuttle taxis from Azadi Sq head in all directions, most usefully to the terminals and to Mo'allem Sq for Taq-e Bostan. On Modarres St, city buses usefully drive the 'wrong way' (northbound), but northbound shuttle taxis have to wind around the one-way system until 8.30pm.

AROUND KERMANSHAH
Bisotun   بیستون
☎ 0832

Awesome dry cliffs line the north flank of the busy, partly industrialised Kermanshah–Hamadan road, looking especially majestic when approaching Bisotun from Sahneh. At Bisotun these cliffs are inscribed with a series of world-famous **bas-relief carvings** dating from 521 BC. They were awarded Unesco recognition in 2006. The key feature is a well-preserved Darius receiving chained supplicants while a *farohar* (winged Zoroastrian 'angel' denoting purity) hovers overhead. Though hard to make out from ground level, the scene is surrounded by cuneiform inscriptions expounding upon Darius' greatness in three 'lost' languages (Elamite, Akkadian and Old Persian). In 1835, eccentric British army officer Henry Rawlinson bemused locals by dangling for months over the abyss to make papier-mâché casts of these texts. It's hard to know how his superiors gave him the time off to attempt so life-threatening an eccentricity, nor why Rawlinson didn't just tootle up to Ganjnameh (p205) and copy those inscriptions instead. Nonetheless, his transcriptions later allowed the deciphering of the cuneiform scripts, a thrilling breakthrough that renders Bisotun as significant to Persia-philes as the Rosetta Stone is to Egyptologists.

To reach the carvings jump out of a savari from Kermanshah where the road entering Bisotun's swings 90° right (east). Then walk through a large car park following the mighty cliffs west. You'll pass a club-wielding little **Hercules statue** from 148 BC (albeit with recently replaced head) sitting on a rocky ledge. A little further is a very eroded **Parthian relief of Mithrades II**, partly overwritten by a 17th-century Arabic inscription by Sheikh Alikhan. The main reliefs face east, high above this, requiring a good zoom lens and early-morning sunlight for decent photos.

Some 200m beyond the main site is the huge, smooth **Farhad Tarash** rock face, popular with climbers who consider it among Iran's greatest challenges. In fact it was artificially smoothed in the 7th century AD for an inscription that Khosrow II never got around to scribbling. Walk 10 minutes' further west, crossing some lumpy archaeological diggings, to find a well-restored but unused 1685 caravanserai.

GETTING THERE & AWAY
The savari stop for Kermanshah and for Sahneh (and thence Kangavar and Hamadan) is a 10-minute walk east through Bisotun town, just beyond Bank Keshvari.

HAMADAN   همدان
☎ 0811 / pop 528,000
Known in classical times as Ecbatana, Hamadan was once one of the ancient world's greatest cities. Pitifully little of antiquity remains, but significant parts of the city centre are given over to excavations and there is a scattering of historical curiosities. Sitting on a high plain, Hamadan is graciously cool in August, but snow-prone and freezing cold from December to March. In the summer the air is often hazy, but on a rare, clear spring day there are impressive glimpses of snow-capped Mt Alvand (3580m) preening itself above the ragged neo-colonial cupolas of Imam Khomeini Sq. A popular summer retreat, Hamadan's main draw card for Iranian visitors is its proximity to the Ali Sadr Caves (p206), but these are vastly over-rated.

History
According to ancient Greek historians, Median king Deiokes fortified a palace here in 728 BC, and over succeeding decades the Median capital of Ecbatana grew into an opulent city. Its massive walls were said to have had seven layers, the inner two coated in gold and silver, the outer one as long as that of classical Athens. By 550 BC it had fallen to the Achaemenid Persians, and King Cyrus was using it for his summer court.

The Medes retook the city in 521 BC but were kicked out again within six months by Darius who was so pleased with himself that he recorded his achievements in stone beside the Royal Road at Bisotun (p199).

After centuries of wealth and pre-eminence under Parthian and Sassanian dynasties alike, Ecbatana/Hamadan faded somewhat after the Arab conquest in the mid-7th century AD, but it became the regional capital under the Seljuks for some 60 years in the late 12th century. Known as Hegmataneh (Meeting Place of Sufis) in Old Persian, Hamadan suffered the usual devastations by Mongols (1220) and Tamerlane (1386), but only hit a major decline in the 18th century following a Turkish invasion. It began to recover in the mid-19th century and was totally redesigned to a modern city plan in 1929 by German engineer Karl Frisch.

Orientation
Frisch's master plan is a cartwheel design with six avenues radiating from the circular hub of Imam Khomeini Sq, widely referred to simply as 'meydan'. The wheel distorts to the northeast around the lumpy hill of Tappeh-ye Mosallah and the excavation site of Hegmataneh Hill. Distances between blocks are deceptively long if you're walking.

Information
INTERNET ACCESS
Coffeenet Arshia (Imamzadeh Sq; per hr IR7000; ☽ 8am-10pm) Slower connection.
Coffeenet Rozhan (Takhti St; per hr IR8000; ☽ 9am-2pm & 4-9pm) Handy for the Arian Hotel.
Sib Coffeenet (Khaje Rashid Blvd; per hr IR8000; ☽ 9am-10pm) Good connection and decorated with lots of smiley-faces, hearts and ceiling netting. Three other coffeenets are within a block.

POST
Main Post Office (off Buali St)
Sub Post Office (Khaje Rashid Blvd)

TELEPHONE
Telephone office (Mahdiyeh St) Take a shuttle taxi down Shari'ati St.

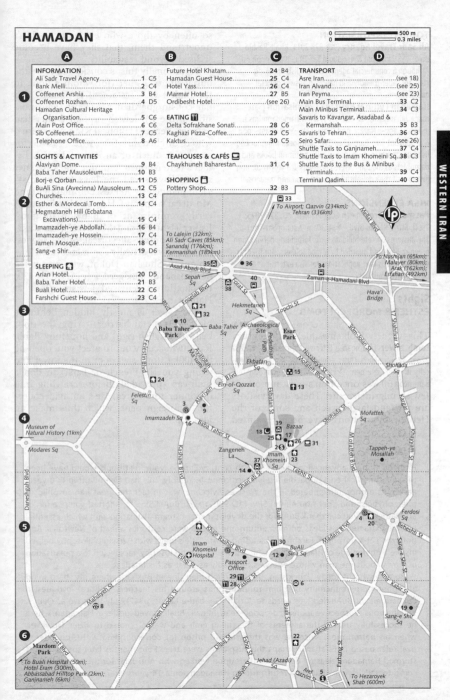

HAMADAN

WESTERN IRAN

TOURIST INFORMATION

Ali Sadr Travel Agency (☎ 828 2011; Khaje Rashid Blvd; ☺ 9am-1pm & 4-7.30pm Sat-Thu, 10am-noon Fri) Although a commercial agency, the English-speaking staff are super-friendly and happy to answer general questions.

Hamadan Cultural Heritage Organisation (Sazemane Jahangardi; ☎ 827 4771; www.hamedanmiras.ir, in Farsi; Gagh-e Nazari, Aref Qazvini St; ☺ 8.30am-noon & 2-5pm Sat-Thu, 8am-11am Fri) Staff speak minimal English but merrily load up visitors with beautiful books and pamphlets as though it were Christmas. It's worth coming just to visit their delightful Qajar mansion and gardens.

VISA EXTENSIONS

Passport Office (Edareh Gozannameh; ☎ 826 2025; 1st fl, Khaje Rashid Blvd; ☺ 8.30am-2.30pm Sat-Thu) The austere concrete building looks forbidding behind high green railings and guarded by armed soldiers. But friendly staff assured us that applications for visa extensions are now granted routinely.

Sights

ESTHER & MORDECAI TOMB

بقعه استر و مردخای

This vaguely Tolkeinesque, 14th-century **tomb tower** (Aramgah-e Ester va Mordekhay; ☎ 252 2285; 12 Zangeneh Lane; admission by donation, typically IR10,000 & a pen; ☺ 8am-noon & 3-6pm Sun-Thu, 8am-noon Fri) was once Iran's most important Jewish pilgrimage site. These days visitors are few and far between and some of the Hebrew inscriptions have been repainted so often by those who evidently couldn't understand them, that they have become stylised beyond readability.

Traditionally this is considered to be the burial site of Esther (for whom a book in the Bible's Old Testament is named) and her cousin/guardian Mordecai (who possibly wrote it). Jewish orphan Esther had married Xerxes I (Biblical King Ahasuerus) who'd ditched his first wife, Vashti, for being too much of an early feminist. Esther's better-honed feminine wiles are later said to have saved the Jews from a massacre planned by Xerxes' commander (and Mordecai's enemy) Haman. With names eerily reminiscent of Babylonian gods, Esther (Ishtar?) and Mordecai (Morduk?) might be purely allegorical. Some suggest that the tower actually commemorated Jewish queen, Shushan-Dokht, who persuaded her husband, Yazdgerd I (r AD 399–420) to sanction a renewed Jewish colony at Hamadan.

The tower is mostly hidden behind a high grey metal barrier – ring the door bell (no English sign) and hopefully Rabbi Rajad will scurry out to greet you, opening the 400kg stone-slab door to the tower and telling you (in French or Farsi) to don a scull-cap (provided) before crawling into the inner tomb area. He's an avid collector of foreign pens, which thus make an ideal tip.

BUALI SINA

Had you studied advanced medicine in 17th-century Europe, your 'text book' would have been the great medical encyclopaedia, *Canon Medicinae*. Incredibly, this had been written 600 years earlier. Its author, remembered in the West as Avicenna, was in fact the great Iranian philosopher, physicist and poet Abu Ali Ibn Sina (AD 980–1037), 'BuAli' Sina for short. If you're a fan of aromatherapy you can thank BuAli for the development of steam distillation with which essential oils are extracted. His ideas on momentum and inertia were centuries ahead of Newton's. And (following al-Kindi and al-Farabi), his blending of Aristotle's ideas with Persian philosophy helped inspire a golden age of Islamic scholarship. However, this philosophy, rapidly led to a polarisation of views about the man whose ego was reputedly as great as his intellect.

Born in what is today Uzbekistan, BuAli studied medicine in Bukhara where his sharp mind and photographic memory had him running rings around his teachers. Political intrigues in Bukhara meant BuAli fled westwards to Jorjan (Gonbad-e Kavus, p342) only to arrive as Qabus, his illustrious prospective sponsor, dropped dead. Initially Buali proved luckier in Hamadan, where he successfully treated the ailments of the ruling emir and was promoted to vizier. However, when his patron died, Avicenna was thrown into prison for corresponding with Abu Jafar, a rival ruler based in Esfahan. Perhaps the suspicions were true. Four months later the Esfahanis stormed Hamadan releasing BuAli who thereupon worked with Abu Jafar for the rest of his life, coincidentally dying while on a return trip to Hamadan some 14 years later.

OTHER MAUSOLEA & TOMB TOWERS

Hamadan's icon is the **BuAli Sina (Avicenna) Mausoleum** (Aramgah-e Buali Sina; ☎ 826 1008; admission IR4000; ☺ 8am-6pm summer, 8am-4pm winter) a 1954 tower that looks something like a vast, unfinished concrete missile. It is loosely modelled on Qabus's 1000-year-old tower in Gonbad-e Kavus (p342), which Buali probably saw inaugurated. Paying the entry fee (entry from west) allows you to see the single-room **museum** of Avicenna memorabilia, his tombstone, a small library and a display on medicinal herbs. But the tower itself is better observed from a distance.

Of a similar era but architecturally less successful is the heavily buttressed **Baba Taher Mausoleum** (Aramgah-e Baba Taher; admission IR3000; ☺ 8am-5.30pm). It looks like a failed prototype for Thunderbird 3. There's little reason to go inside unless you enjoy Persian calligraphy, inscribed here on some gently opalescent stone wall-slabs.

The **Alaviyan Dome** (Gonbad-e Alaviyan; Shahdad Lane; admission IR3000; ☺ 8am-7pm) is now a misnomer, as the 12th-century green dome, immortalised in a Khaqani reference, has long since been removed. The dome-less brick tower remains famous for the whirling floral stucco added in the Ilkhanid era. This ornamentation enraptured Robert Byron in *Road to Oxiana*, but frankly it's ugly. In the crypt (narrow steps down from the interior at the back) is the plain-blue tiled Alaviyan family tomb covered with votive Islamic embroidery.

A useful landmark is the golden dome of the unfinished **Imamzadeh-ye Abdollah** (Imamzadeh Sq). More appealing is the 1883 **Imamzadeh-ye Hossein**, tucked behind the Hotel Yass in a little courtyard with an ancient mulberry tree. The 13th-century **Borj-e Qorban** is a classic 12-sided, pointy-roofed tower tomb, but it looks sadly out of place in its dowdy housing-estate setting.

HEGMATANEH HILL تپه هگمتانه

In the mud beneath this scraggy low hill lies Hamadan's ancient Median and Achaemenid **city site** (☎ 822 4005; admission IR4000; ☺ 8am-4pm Tue-Sun, 8am-noon Mon). Small sections of the total area have been fitfully excavated by several teams over the last century, most extensively in the 1990s. The most interesting of several shed-covered 'trenches' allows you to walk above the excavations of earthen walls using plank walkways on wobbly scaffolding. The walls' gold and silver coatings are long gone of course and it's hard to envisage the lumpy remnants as having once constituted one of the world's great cities. A nicely presented museum tries to fill the mental gap, showing some of the archaeological finds including large amphorae, Seljuk fountains, Achaemenid pillar-bases and Parthian coffins.

A few decades ago when the government relocated inhabitants from the hill and demolished their homes in the name of archaeology, they spared a pair of 19th-century **churches**, which remain at the southern edge of the site.

OTHER ATTRACTIONS

A vaulted passage of the bazaar leads into the courtyard of the large Qajar-era **Jameh Mosque** (admission free). The off-line south *iwan* leads into a hall (currently under restoration) over which there's an impressively large brick dome. The new north *iwan* is lavished with patterned blue tilework that continues on four of the mosque's six minarets. Some areas are restricted to men only.

Sang-e Shir is a walrus-sized lump of rock eroded beyond recognition by the rubbing of hands over 2300 years. Supposedly once a lion, you'd never look twice at were it not the only surviving 'monument' from the ancient city of Ecbatana whose gates it once guarded. Some claim it was carved at the behest of Alexander the Great.

Sleeping

BUDGET

These three cheap *mosaferkhanehs* are conveniently located close to central Imam Khomeini Sq.

Farshchi Guest House (Mosaferkhaneh-ye Farsi; ☎ 252 4895; Shohada St; tw/tr/q/5-bed IR60,000/ 80,000/100,000/130,000, showers IR5000) By *mosaferkhaneh* standards the Farshchi is a cosy, friendly place with something of a family atmosphere, plastic flowers and samovars giving vague touches of humanity to the area of shared squat toilets and washbasins. Most rooms are four-bedded.

Hamadan Guest House (☎ 252 7577; Ekbatan St; bed IR60,000; Ⓟ) This large, confusing and male-dominated place has four- and six-bed dorms for which locals pay around IR20,000 per person. Foreigners pay IR60,000 per person, but will usually get the whole room between them. It's a fairly long walk to the shared toilets whose doors don't lock. There's no English sign: take the green-framed stairway beyond the first alley-yard as you walk down Ekbatan St from the *meydan*. Ask for help as there's no reception desk.

Ordibesht Hotel (☎ 252 2056; Shohada St; s/tw/ tr/q IR100,000/150,000/180,000/200,000) Bright and unusually airy, this no-nonsense *mosaferkhaneh* is compulsively cleaned and Ali speaks some English. There are separate toilet facilities for men and women and 'free showers for foreigners'. Most rooms are quads (IR150,000 for single occupancy).

MIDRANGE & TOP END

Except for the Arian, Hamadan's better accommodation is lacklustre and charges 'foreigner rates' in US$ that are around 70% higher than local rial prices. However, discounts of 30% are not uncommon if you ask. The new Hotel Khatam at Felestin Sq should be complete by the time this book goes to print.

Hotel Yass (☎ 252 3464; fax 251 2680; Shohada St; s/tw US$20/25) With an excellent location and some early 20th-century features, the Yass could be a pleasant choice given some TLC. But for now the rooms are dreary with institutional beds, aging showers and feeble-flush Western toilets. The building is marked in Latin letters but no English is spoken. Reception is on the 3rd floor.

Marmar Hotel (☎ 827 1840; Shari'ati St; tw IR300,000) In Japanese, mar-mar would translate as 'so-so'. Very apt. A creaky glass elevator takes you to rooms where crimson curtains and bedspreads are lit by bright unshaded lamps. The bathrooms could be cleaner and there's no shower curtain. No English (spoken or signage) except to state the misleading foreigner rack-rate of US$50: that's baldly ignored should you ask in Farsi.

Arian Hotel (☎ 826 1266; www.arianhotel.com; Takhti St; s/tw/tr US$40/50/60) At this inviting midrange hotel, each floor has a different, gently appealing style of décor with modernist lamps on the 3rd floor and a more opulent period look on the 4th. Check out the 2nd floor to see what they consider 'British style'. The lobby has a couple of gratuitous Persepolis-aping columns. Some English is spoken.

Hotel Eram (☎ 825 2001; Eram Blvd; d US$75; P 🗙) Behind a swishly upgraded lobby, rooms are less impressively renovated with aging bed-boxes and half-length baths. It's at the southwest edge of town. Some English spoken.

Buali Hotel (☎ 825 0856; Buali St; tw/ste US$87/138; 🗙 💻 🗙) The standard rooms have fridge, BBC World TV and floral pseudo-silk fabrics, but the bathrooms are rather outdated. Suites are a considerable step up.

Baba Taher Hotel (☎ 422 6517; fax 422 5098; Baba Taher Sq; s/tw/ste US$103/134/161; P 🗙) The mirror-tiled lobby and restaurant offer a dazzlingly garish festival of Las Vegas kitsch while corridors test out the full palate of pastel colours. The reasonably well-appointed rooms are thankfully somewhat more subdued, but barely justify the discounted price (from US$70) let alone rack-rates. English spoken.

Eating

Apart from Hezaroyek Shab, none of the following have menus in English. For that you'll have to resort to hotel restaurants of which the BuAli's (meals IR40,000 to IR70,000) is about the best.

Chaykhuneh Baharestan (☎ 254 2777; Shohada St; dizi IR7000; 🕑 6am-7pm) This atmospheric, if decidedly down-market 100% male teahouse is charmingly adorned with metalwork, sepia photos and Quranic murals. It's ideal for a greasy fried-egg breakfast, cheap *abgusht* (aka *dizi*) lunch or a puff on the qalyan, and is populated by photogenically haggard old white-beards. To find it, head upstairs through a partly illustrated doorway opposite a small branch of Bank Maskan.

Kaghazi Pizza-Coffee (☎ 825 3870; Pastor St; coffee IR5000-12,000, snack meals IR16,000-24,000) Pine furniture and a few African masks bring some character to this gently stylish two-room café whose pizzas are refreshingly crispy and thin-crusted.

ourpick Delta Sofrakhane Sonati (☎ 826 1813; basement, Eshqi St; qalyan IR10,000, meals IR20,000-50,000; 🕑 6am-7pm) This delightful neo-traditional retreat lies beneath the unremarkable Delta restaurant using separate stairs from outside. Tea (IR5000) comes in ceramic Lalejin pots, women can smoke qalyan on carpeted bed-seats without undue attention and the chicken 'biriyani' comes on a flaming plate. Don't miss the scrumptious *kashka bademjan* (IR12,000), eggplant paste with yoghurt, mint and roasted red peppers.

Hezaroyek Shab (1001 Nights; ☎ 824 5217; Farhang St; local mains IR15,000-35,000, European dishes IR35,000-50,000; ☺ noon-3pm & 7.30-11pm) This cosy if slightly garish restaurant is quite a trek from the centre (IR5000 *dar baste* taxi) but there's a wide Irano-European menu and owner Pari Bakhtiyari speaks fluent English. Call ahead.

Kaktus (Buali Sq; meals IR30,000-70,000; ☺ noon-3pm & 7-10.30pm) Down easy-to-miss stairs, Kaktus remains one of Hamadan's most popular middle-class kabab restaurants. It's tastefully lit if not imaginatively decorated.

Shopping

Hamadan region is famous for its leatherwork, wooden inlay, ceramics and carpets. Try contacting the **Union of Carpet Co-operatives** (☎ 252 8622) if you can't find what you want in the rather tatty carpet bazaar. Several **pottery shops** (Baba Taher Sq) sell colourful, locally famous pottery from Lalejin, 32km away.

Getting There & Away

AIR

Kish Air flies to Tehran (IR195,000, twice weekly). Tickets are sold by Ali Sadr Travel Agency (p202).

BUS

All long-distance bus services start from the new **Tehran terminal** (Enqelab Blvd), but most companies have city centre **ticket offices** (☺ 7am-noon & 3-7pm) near Imam Khomeini Sq. **Seiro Safar** (☎ 252 2860) and **Iran Peyma** (☎ 252 1213; ☺ 7am-noon & 2-7pm) are either side of the Ordibesht Hotel. **Asre Iran** (☎ 252 5376) and **Iran Alvand** (☎ 252 5763) face each other across Ekbatan St.

Useful bus departures:

Destination	Fare	Duration	Departures
Ahvaz	IR70,000	11hr	6-7pm Seiro Safar, Asre Iran
Esfahan	IR38,500	8hr	8am, 10.30am, 9pm, 10pm Alvand
Mashhad	IR120,000	21hr	9.30am Asre Iran
Qazvin	IR14,000	3½hr	2.30pm Seiro Safar
Orumiyeh	IR34,900	9hr	1.30pm Iran Peyma
Rasht	IR21,500	6hr	9.15 Iran Peyma
Tehran	IR40,000	6hr	7-10.30am, 2-4pm and 11.30pm
Zanjan	IR18,000	4hr	Taavoni 5, 3.30pm

Tehran buses take either the expressway via Takestan or the more direct road via Saveh, but few go via Qazvin. Expect delays after fresh snow.

MINIBUS & SAVARI

There are two minibus terminals. Use the **Main Minibus Terminal** (Zaman-e Hamadani Blvd) for Kermanshah, Sanandaj (maybe changing in Qorveh), Bijar (at 11am and noon via Qorveh) and Ali Sadr (several daily). Use **Terminal Qadim** (Ekbatan St) for hourly minibuses to Tuyserkan, more frequent services to Malayer (and thence Nahavand or Borujerd and on to Khorramabad), and to Asadabad (for Kangavar). Savaris to Malayer wait outside.

Savaris to Kermanshah (IR40,000), Kangavar (IR15,000), Sanandaj (IR35,000) and Tehran (IR120,000) leave from relevant points near Sepah Sq. The Tehran savaris are well-organised with a sign-up **booth** (☎ 423 8669).

Getting Around

Shuttle taxis run along the spokes of Hamadan's cartographic wheel for IR500 (one block), IR1000 (longer hop) or IR5000 (*dar baste*). Shuttle taxis to the bus and minibus terminals leave from Ekbatan St.

AROUND HAMADAN
Ganjnameh   گنج نامه

Literally translated as 'Treasure Book', Ganjnameh is so named because for years its **cuneiform rock carvings** were thought to be cryptic clues to help find caches of mythical Median treasure. Belatedly translated, the texts turn out instead to be a rather immodest thank you to the Zoroastrian god Ahura Mazda from the Achaemenid monarch Xerxes (486–466 BC) for making him such a very, very good king. To emphasise the point the message is repeated in three languages (Old Persian, Elamite and neo-Babylonian) on rock faces some 2m high. A second panel similarly commemorates his dad, Darius.

The site is in a rural mountain valley at Hamadan's westernmost extremity, some 8km from the centre. From the parking area the carvings are a very obvious two-minute stroll passing a row of tatty teahouses, souvenir stalls and snack bars. Just beyond is a 9m-high waterfall that becomes a popular ice-climbing spot when frozen in winter. At weekends the site can get crowded and messy with rubbish but several long-distance paths lead directly up the peaceful fore-slopes of Mt Alvand making for relatively convenient yet bracing **hikes**.

A narrow lane continues 4km to the Tarik Dare **ski slopes** (☼ Thu & Fri winter) and in summer a road winds on very attractively right across Mt Alvand's lower slopes to Oshtoran near Tuyserkan (opposite).

GETTING THERE & AWAY

Shared taxis (IR2000) take approximately 20 minutes departing from Shari'ati St near the Esther & Mordecai Tomb. They're fairly frequent at weekends, but midweek you'll probably have to charter (from IR10,000 each way). Finding a ride back can take a while.

Ali Sadr Caves ٠ غار عليصدر

☎ 0812

For most Iranians these highly commercialised **caves** (Qar Ali Sadr; ☎ 553 3440; locals/foreigners IR5000/150,000; ☼ 8am-4pm winter, 8am-9pm summer) constitute quite simply western Iran's greatest tourist attraction. You might not agree. Indeed if you have visited vastly more impressive equivalents in France or Lebanon, you are best to be prepared for a major disappointment.

The caves rise to a maximum internal height of 40m, with a river (up to 14m deep) flowing through the middle. Visits through the caves take about two hours with no 'escape' possible once you've begun. You start and end with a 20-minute trip on the underground river in roped-together paddle-boats. The boat route is colourfully lit, though the big central cavern has many more steps than geological superlatives. In summer the caves feel cool, so bring a sweater. In winter it's refreshingly warm compared with the snow-bound exterior.

Close to the cave entrance **Ali Sadr Hotel** (Mehmansara; ☎ /fax 553 3312; tent/tw/bungalow IR50,000/250,000/200,000; P ☒) has a decent restaurant and reasonable rooms with bathrooms. Out of season prices are negotiable and the location would make it a delightfully peaceful getaway and possible trekking base. **Stalls** around the cave entrance sell drinks and there's even a **teahouse** within the cave.

GETTING THERE & AWAY

From Hamadan, minibuses run to Ali Sadr village several times daily (IR7000, 1½ hours). Taxis want around IR200,000 return with waiting time: consider stopping briefly en route to admire the remarkable mud walls of fortified farm village **Mihamlar Ohlea** at the roadside. Tours by Hamadan's Ali Sadr Travel Agency in Hamadan (p202) cost IR4500 per person including return transport and snacks but not entrance fees.

Malayer ملاير

☎ 0851 / pop 181,000

Taking public transport between Hamadan and Borujerd or Nahavand you'll probably have to change in Malayer (pronounced ma-*loy*-ya). If so, look out for the ancient beehive-domed **Yakhchad-e Mirfattah** (usually locked). This was the medieval equivalent of a deep freezer: ice put inside in winter would stay frozen well into summer. It's amid trees and suburban fields, visible from Tusi Blvd (the ring road), less than 1km southwest of Taavon Sq from which savaris leave to Borujerd and Nahavand. Savaris for Hamadan leave from Revolution Sq (Meydan Enqelab) 2km northeast, IR1000 by shared taxi.

Around Malayer

NUSHIJAN (TAPPEH NUSH-E JAN) نوشيجان

Sitting on an abrupt pimple of hill amid flat, comparatively fertile plains this unique **Median Citadel** (☎ 225 1225; admission IR4000; ☼ 8am-5pm) originally hosted the fortified grain

---

ANAHITA

Zoroastrianism had always venerated the four elements but it was fundamentally a monotheistic faith worshiping Ahura Mazda. So when Achaemenian king Artaxerxes II (404–359 BC) starting wall-papering Kangavar's temple in solid gold to honour Anahita (أناهيتا) as an anthropomorphic 'water goddess', he seems to have been acting under the heavy cultural influence of his Greek wife. Not that that stopped Persia warring with Greece: the temple's incredible wealth was eventually seized and plundered by Alexander the Great's Greek forces around 331 BC.

THE LORS OF LORESTAN

Call them Lurish, Lori or Lor, these proud people (around 2% of Iran's population) are best known to Westerners for the magnificent bronze-crafts of their hazily documented Kassite forebears. Around 1800 BC, these polytheistic horse-breeding warriors were pushing forward the boundaries of metallurgical technology, casting exquisite bronzes whose fine decoration belies their often mundane purposes. The Lurish golden age was destroyed by centuries of medieval wars that wiped out virtually all settled agriculture. Lorestan lapsed into lawless nomadic 'backwardness' such that the Lors, like many Kurds, remained predominantly semi-independent nomads until well into the 20th century. In 1931 the valiant Freya Stark considered Lorestan to be the 'wastes of civilisation' as she risked brigands, bandits and police ire seeking ancient gravesites from which to procure Lurish bronzes. Today admiring such bronzes is much easier thanks to Khorramabad's Falak-ol-Aflak (p209) or Tehran's National Museum of Iran (p104) and Reza Abbasi Museum (p114).

The Lori language is a dialect based on Old Persian with additions from Arabic and modern Farsi. A handy greeting is *damaqechaqı* (are you well?); 'delicious' is *tomdara*.

stores and temples of a 7th-century BC settlement. It's relatively small and shaded by steel-girders with ugly shed-roofing, but nonetheless makes a worthwhile 3km diversion from the Malayer–Hamadan road. Before climbing the hill, stop at the sparse exhibition centre where friendly staff use models and pictures to make sense of the mud-daub walls, arches and tunnels that you'll see up top. Then drive on 600m to a second car park part-way up the hillock from which climbing to the site entrance takes just three minutes. However, you'll need a certain level of athleticism to reach the rear *apadana* (audience hall) behind which are the (rather plain) remnants of what archaeologists have dubbed Iran's earliest fire temple.

Tuyserkan (Towiserkan) تو یسر کان
☎ 0852 / pop 39,000

This ancient city has a covered bazaar and a 17th-century **madraseh** (totally rebuilt in 1991); but the main tourist attraction is **Gonbad-e-Hayaquq-Nabi**. Try saying that with your mouth full of Tuyserkan's famous walnuts. It's an eight-sided brick tower with clamshell-grooved conical roof sitting in a garden on the west edge of town, 500m off Shahid Ashraf Esfahani Blvd. The tower is considered to be the tomb of Jewish prophet Habakkuk, whose book within the Bible's Old Testament is mostly a vitriolic rant against the Chaldeans. Possibly a guardian of the temple of Solomon, Habakkuk was probably amongst the Jews who had been exiled to Babylon. Maybe he

'retired' to the Hamadan area after Darius released them in 538 BC.

In the hills above town (passing close to a golden domed mosque en route), is **Mir Razi Mausoleum** (☎ 4228420; admission free) a 1975 memorial to Safavid sufi poet Mir Razi-ed-Din-e-Artisani (died 1627). The architecture is along the lumpsome lines of Hamadan's Baber Taher tower but the site is peaceful and attractive.

Becoming one of the first foreigners ever to stay at the unsuspecting **Mosaferkhaneh Tadayon** (☎ 422 0006; Bahonar St; s IR41,500, d & tr IR80,000, tw with/without bathroom IR70,000/60,000) is a great way to immerse yourself in rural Iranian life. Rooms aren't fancy but they're better value than anything in Hamadan and just getting in is quite an adventure. The sign (in Farsi) leads into a shopping passage halfway between the bazaar and Farshid Sq. There's no reception: just ask someone to find the elderly gentleman who runs the place.

Minibuses (IR6500) and savaris (IR20,000) to Hamadan loop right around via Joukar, departing from a point some 3km east of the bazaar in Tuyserkan's Sarabi suburb. For the very scenic mountain road via Oshtoran and Ganjnameh (p205) you will need to charter a taxi (during summer-only).

If you're heading for Kermanshah, a direct bus service departs at 8am from Basij Sq. Alternatively you could change in Kangavar (45km) to which minibuses (IR2700) and savaris (IR7000) depart from further up Ashrafi Blvd.

WESTERN IRAN

Around Tuyserkan
OSHTORAN   اشتران

On a grassy knoll above the low-rise, mountain-backed village of **Oshtoran** are the extensive ruins of **Qal'eh Hamza Khan**. This mud-walled fortress is comparatively intact with all four corner-towers well-preserved and much of the interior looking as though it had been lived in till relatively recently. The 20km road from Tuyserkan passes through walnut groves then crosses a low pass with great views across broad valleys to an array of mountains. These look superb when snowcapped, but too much snow can block the road's continuation across Mt Alvand's foothills from Shahrestan to Ganjnameh (p205).

FARASVAJ   فرسوج

A 5km side trip off the Tuyserkan–Kangavar road, **Farasvaj** has a modest **Safavid bridge** and an impressively restored (but currently unused) 17th-century **caravanserai** at the top of Chamran St. Returning to the main road there are excellent views towards the rugged bulk of **Mt Khan Gormaz** (2863m) whose slopes form a nature reserve protecting ibex and wild goats.

Kangavar   کنگاور
☎ 0837 / pop 58,000

A chaos of rocky lumps, dressed-stones and ancient column-bases tumble down a grassy hillside in the middle of Kangavar town. That's virtually all that remains of Kangavar's famous 2300-year-old **Anahita Temple** (admission IR4000; ☼ 8am-sunset). While not really warranting a long detour, it's conveniently on the Kermanshah–Hamadan road so worth stopping en route. Marvel at the workmanship that created such perfect stone columns, a massive 4ft in diameter. And at the force of all the earthquakes that toppled them. An impressive section of 5m-tall stone wall topped with stubby columns is easily viewed for free as you walk up Raja'i St from Araqi St (the main Hamadan road). Raja'i St culminates in a quietly attractive bazaar area where there's a basic *mosaferkhaneh*.

The savari terminal for Hamadan is 2km east of the ruins. It might prove quicker to change cars halfway in Asadabad (easy as there's a single departure point for Hamadan and Kangavar there). For Kermanshah, flag down a passing bus or use the Nahavand ter-

minal at the western end of town and make savari hops via Sahneh and/or Bisotun.

Nahavand   نهاوند
☎ 0852 / pop 67,000

Nahavand was founded by Alexander the Great's general Seleucus Nicator well over 2000 years ago. It was also the site of a pivotal battle in AD 642 that effectively sealed Arab-Muslim victory over Sassanid Persia. However, the town has little to show for all that history. Apart from a couple of column fragments plonked in the Nikanjam Passaj shopping centre (Abuzar Sq), there's no sign of the 193 BC Seleucid temple that once graced a local hill. And the historic Jameh Mosque took a direct bomb hit during the Iran–Iraq War.

Minor attractions if you're passing through include the mural-filled 1852 **Hamam-e Haji Agha Torab** (former bathhouse), and the central, eye-catching if architecturally unremarkable **Nabi-e Sardab Mosque**. Its gilt-tipped, octagonal, blue minaret is visible as you shuttle between the Borujerd terminal (south) and the main northern bus terminal (for Kangavar, and for Hamadan via Malayer).

KHORRAMABAD   خرم آباد
☎ 0661 / pop 339,000

Little visited by foreigners, Khorramabad is nonetheless scenically appealing and a possible base from which to discover Lorestan province, the glorious Zagros Mountains and the Lori (Lurish) people.

Khorramabad lies in a long, wide gorge sandwiched by dry, impressive crags in which have been found at least five Palaeolithic cave-dwelling sites. Historians disagree whether Khorramabad was the site of Shapurkhast or of Samha. Both are ancient 'lost' cities that had advanced irrigation and milling systems over 1500 years ago, judging from archaeological clues like the Gerdab-e-Sangi cistern.

In the Middle Ages a fortified central citadel was built here by the Atabegs, the powerful clan who ruled Lorestan from the 12th century until subjugated by Shah Abbas around AD 1600. The citadel later became the residence of Persian governors who developed it into a classical fortress that soared so impressively that it became known as Falak-ol-Aflak (Heaven of Heavens). In the 1830s, the governors moved into a mansion at the castle's base (now a military academy) and the fortress became a prison. It's now an interesting museum.

Orientation

Around the fortress, narrow central streets are attractively lined with *chinar* (plane) trees, but driving is awkward thanks to an infuriating one-way system. Bypassing the melee, busy Shari'ati St (the main Ahvaz–Hamadan highway) hosts the bus offices and several hotels.

Information

INTERNET ACCESS

AryaNet (Motahhari St; per hr IR7000; ⊗ 9am-9pm) The best of several grindingly slow coffeenets around Motahhari/Enqelab Sts.
Shaba-key Sabz Coffeenet (Imam Khomeini St; per hr IR6000; ⊗ 8am-8pm) Reasonable connection, easy to miss up two floors near Shohoda Sq.

MONEY

Export Development Bank of Iran (Bank Tose-shadarat; Alavi St; ⊗ 9.30am-3.30pm Sat-Wed, 9.30am-12.30pm Thu) Changes money relatively painlessly (10 minutes) for a flat US$1 commission. Take an Alavi taxi from beside Bank Melli (no exchange).

POLICE REGISTRATION

Police Station No 5 (☎ 218 2864; Valiasr Ave) For registration (necessary to stay in cheap guesthouses in Khorramabad) ask for 'Amaken', present passport or passport/visa copy and fill a form stating where you'll stay. The office is around 800m from Kyo Sq, entered from an alley beside Ghavamin Finance.

POST

Post office In a yard off the castle access lane.

TOURIST INFORMATION

Hassan Niknam (☎ 0916-361 1135; niknamhassan@ yahoo.com) Dignified and well-informed, Hassan co-manages the Karon Hotel, speaks great English and acts as guide and tourist helper. He can put mountaineers in touch with members of the local climbing federation.
Lorestan Cultural Heritage Organisation (☎ 221 6718; www.lorestanmiras.ir; Lorestan University, Falak-ol-Aflak Lane; ⊗ 7am-2pm Sat-Thu) Nobody in the office speaks English, but their beautiful maps and brochures are given away free by better hotels.

Sights

FALAK-OL-AFLAK　　　　　　قلعه فلك الافلاك

This unmissable eight-towered **castle** (☎ 220 4090; www.lorestanmiras.org, in Farsi; admission IR4000;

⊗ 8am-6pm, 8am-8pm summer) dominates the city centre from a rocky promontory. It looks especially dramatic when floodlit at night and offers extensive city views from the crenellated battlements. The entrance weaves up past sellers of tacky Lurish tourist trinkets into a courtyard where you can dress up in Bakhtiyari tribal garb for a posed photo. Above the inviting **teahouse** (see p211) a grating covers the dizzyingly deep castle **well** (43m), but there are other 'falling danger' spots where a 'disciplinarian' watches out for your safety as well as your behaviour.

The main buildings around the rear courtyard form a very well-presented **ethnographic museum** showing vignettes of Lurish life accompanied by folk music appropriate to each theme. A video-room shows off regional attractions (English version available) and an exhibition culminates with a hoard of Lorestan bronze daggers and axe-heads recently discovered at Sang Tarashan, around 40km away.

OTHER SIGHTS

If you have time to kill there are several minor curiosities, many very historic but none vastly photogenic. Khorramabad's unremarkable bazaar sells a lot of colourful scarves and hosts the modern **Imamzadeh Zaid-ibn-e-Ali** with tiled north façade. The low-key **Tavasuli Mosque** (Shakaster St) was also photogenic till they built a big mobile telephone tower behind it. **Gerdab-e-Sangi** (Takht Sq) is a 1600-year-old Sassanian stone reservoir, 18m in diameter, said to be the world's oldest. Spring water wells up within and once provided the proto-city's water supply. Behind is a steep rocky slope indented with caves said to have been home to early humans around 40,000 years ago.

In a stone-edged circle beside thundering Shari'ati St is an **inscribed stone** (Sang Neveshteh

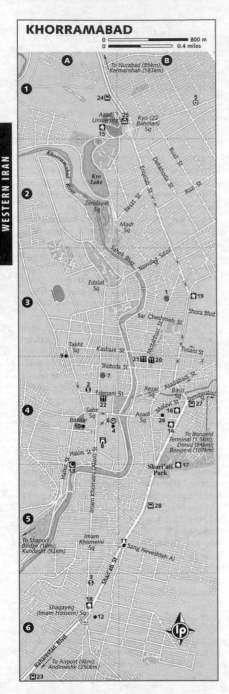

KHORRAMABAD

Alley) from around AD 1150, apparently setting out details of local grazing rights.

The 20m-high pale brick tower called **Minar-e Ajon** (Ajon Minaret; Shaqayeq Sq) might look like a chimney but it was actually a 900-year-old signalling point for caravans. Ruins of the ancient **Shapuri bridge** (Pol-e-Eshkeseh) are stranded in a field off the Khudasht road. Five of the 28 original arches remain intact.

Sleeping

Mehmanpazir Iran (☎ 221 9529; Shari'ati St; s/tw/tr IR70,000/75,000/90,000, no shower) The friendly Iran is the most inviting and best maintained of several cheapies near Basij Sq. But there's a snag. Before you can check in you'll need to register with police across town (p209). Some rooms have new beds, others mattresses on the floor. Light sleepers might be disturbed by road noise and lack of door-curtains.

INFORMATION	
AryaNet.......................................**1** B3
Bank Melli....................................**2** A4
Export Development Bank of Iran..........**3** A6
Lorestan Cultural Heritage Organisation..**4** A4
Police Station No 5 (for registration)......**5** B1
Post Office...................................**6** A4
Shaba-key Sabz Coffeenet..................**7** A4

SIGHTS & ACTIVITIES	
Falak-ol-Aflak...............................**8** A4
Gerdab-e-Sangi..............................**9** A4
Imamzade Zaid-ibn-e-Ali...................**10** A4
Inscribed Stone..............................**11** B5
Minar-e Ajon................................**12** A6
Tavasuli Mosque............................ **13** A5

SLEEPING	
Hotel Karon.................................**14** B4
ITTIC Tourist Inn............................**15** A1
Mehmanpazir Iran...........................**16** B4
Shahrdari Inn................................**17** B5
Shaqayeq Hotel..............................**18** A6
Venon Hotel.................................**19** B3

EATING	
Castle Teahouse.............................(see 8)
Moka..**20** B4
Pizza Park...................................**21** B4
Shem Shad Nemune.......................(see 22)
Yalda.......................................**22** A4

TRANSPORT	
Andimeshk Terminal.........................**23** A6
Minibuses to Nurabad & Alishtar..........**24** A1
Savaris to Nurabad & Alishtar..............**25** B1
Seiro Safar..................................(see 28)
Soleyman Travel............................**26** B4
Taavoni 1...................................(see 16)
Taavoni 17..................................**27** B4
Taavoni 7 & 15.............................**28** B5

Venon Hotel (☎ 323 4076; Enqelab St; s/tw/tr/q IR150,000/360,000/480,000/580,000) Above an expansive restaurant, sparklingly clean, new rooms have tiled floors, displays of plastic flowers and curtained-off shower booths. Toilets are shared. It's bearable value for single travellers but otherwise overpriced.

Hotel Karon (☎ 220 5408; Shari'ati St; s/tw/tr with breakfast US$20/30/37; P 🖵) A major makeover has given the Karon a swish new foyer, lift and cosmetically improved rooms. The wood-effect vinyl floors could use more frequent washing and water supply remains dodgy, but staff are obliging and Hassan speaks excellent English.

Shaqayeq Hotel (☎ 420 3390; Shaqayeq Sq; s/tw US$20/30) Seriously tatty last resort.

Shahrdari Inn (☎ 220 2227; Shari'ati Park; s/tw US$45/60; P 🗙) Clad in multicoloured marble behind the trees of the park, attractive rooms in cream and pastel-blue have bay windows with sitting areas. A few have castle views (eg room 127). Bathrooms are passable if less polished. Some staff speak English.

ITTIC Tourist Inn (☎ 322 5672; Jamejam St; bungalow IR310,000; P 🗙) Semi-detached bungalow units with crazy-paving walls are peacefully perched above the popular Kyo boating lake. They are fully renovated with good bathrooms, wooden floors and velveteen bedspreads.

Eating

Cheap but unexciting *kababis* bracket Mehmanpazir Iran with nicer versions along Motahhari St. Fancier restaurants are often serenaded by caged birds rather than CDs. A Lorestan speciality is *chelo-gusht*: most of a boiled sheep lurking in a mound of rice.

Moka (☎ 221 9760; Motahhari St; coffee IR5000-12,000; 🕙 9am-1pm & 4pm-midnight) Enjoy real espressos (IR10,000) and amusingly creative sundaes in what looks like a sauna-room tucked behind a party supply shop. It's nicer than it sounds!

Shem Shad Nemune (☎ 220 5235; mains IR21,000-35,000; 🕙 8am-3pm & 6-10pm) Almost next door to Yalda, the fried trout (IR26,000) is good but mind those bones.

Yalda (☎ 220 5128; Taleqani St; meals IR27,000-50,000; 🕙 noon-3pm & 6-10pm) Moulded ceilings, pastel-toned wall paintings and a gently upmarket feel make this a congenial place to taste *chelo-*

gusht (IR40,000). Opt for *baqelipulau* (herb pilaf) when selecting the type of rice. *Mast* (yogurt) sets off the flavours perfectly.

Pizza Park (☎ 220 5888; off Motahhari St; pizzas IR21,000-26,000; 🕙 9am-11pm) Across a small triangle of park from Moka this is Khorramabad's nicest central pizzeria.

Castle Teahouse (Falak-ol-Aflak; tea IR2500-5000; 🕙 8am-6pm, 8am-8pm summer) This vaulted stone chamber has the obligatory carpeted bed-seats and serves lovely cinnamon tea in china pots. However, it's a little touristy and the only food, a delicately flavoured *ash* (IR5000), comes disappointingly in disposable plastic bowls.

Getting There & Away

AIR

Taban Air tickets to Tehran (IR250,000, daily) are sold by helpful **Soleyman Travel** (☎ 220 0600; Muhajadine-e Islam St; 🕙 8am-1pm & 3-6pm Sat-Thu). The airport is 5km south of Imam Hossein Sq.

BUS

Long-distance buses leave from the relevant company offices found along Shari'ati St. Most have morning and evening services to Esfahan (IR40,000, eight hours) and Tehran (IR45,500, eight hours via Qom). Taavoni 15 has services to Orumiyeh (normal/Volvo IR52,000/90,000, 17 hours) at 3.30pm and to Sanandaj (IR25,000) at 1.30pm.

Taavoni 1, 7 and 15 have night buses to Ahvaz (IR40,000, six hours) via Andimeshk. However, to see the beautiful canyon-lands south of Pol-e Dokhtar you'd be better off travelling by day to Andimeshk by minibus (IR12,000, 4½ hours) or savari (IR35,000, 3¾ hours) from the small **Andimeshk terminal** (Baharestan Blvd), 800m south of Imam Hossein (Shaqayeq) Sq.

For Kermanshah, Taavoni 17 (Pekesaba) has a direct bus at 2pm (IR25,000, 3½ hours), but if the timing is inconvenient it's easy enough and often faster to do the trips in hops via Nurabad and Harsin (see p199). Savaris to Nurabad (IR12,000, 85km) and Alashtar (IR8000) leave from Kyo Sq, minibuses starting from 200m further up a feeder road.

Incoming minibuses from Borujerd (IR6000, two hours) and Dorud (IR5000, 1¾ hours) might drop you at Basij Sq, but departing they use a terminal 1.5km further

WESTERN IRAN

northeast up Shimsherabad (Daneshju) St. Scarily fast savaris take barely half the time.

Getting Around
Handy shuttle-taxi routes (IR1000) run along Shari'ati St (Shimsherabad–Shaqayeq) and between Basij and 22 Bahman Sqs (Shimsherabad–Kyo) with two diversions northbound due to the one-way system. More centrally, a northbound route runs up Imam Khomeini St to Sabz Sq then up Kashani St to Takht Sq, returning by wiggling through traffic jams around the back of the bazaar.

AROUND KHORRAMABAD
Dorud & Lake Gahar   دورود
☎ 0665 / pop 103,000
Dominated by a huge, satanic cement factory, **Dorud** is useful as a launching point for hiking to beautiful, mountain-ringed **Lake Gahar**, famed for its succulent *qizil arla* fish. The trailhead is **Haft Cheshmeh**, a lonely refuge hut, car park and drinking-water spring 23km from Dorud. In midsummer guides and ponies are usually available here. The trek skirts 4070m **Mt Oshturan** taking around four hours out, less back. Bring your own food and tent. Even if you don't hike, great views justify the car journey as far as **Darb-e-Astaneh**, a mud-house village 18km from Dorud.

Friendly but easy-to-miss, the basic **Mosaferkhaneh-e Baharestan** (☎ 422-2919; Shari'ati St; s IR60,000) is upstairs opposite Dorud's cinema.

The porticoed **Mehmansara Shahrdari** (☎ 422 0020; Beheshti Blvd; tw/tr IR170,000/250,000, summer IR200,000/300,000) has spacious, very comfortable rooms and a decent restaurant featuring great photos of local beauty spots. It's in a park off Dorud's main through-street 1.5km west of the train station, 2.5km east of the bus terminal where minibuses and scorchingly fast savaris run to Khorramabad and Borujerd. Esfahan-bound buses pick up passengers around midnight from taavoni offices on Beheshti Blvd. Incoming trains are met at the station by savaris for both Khorramabad and Borujerd.

THE DORUD-ANDIMESHK RAILWAY
This super-scenic railway trundles through beautiful, remote and virtually roadless valleys skirting Lorestan's pointy peaks and passing through dozens of tunnels. Most trains run in the evenings but there's a day service departing Andimeshk at 5.30am, returning from Dorud at 2pm. It's timetabled to take 5¼ hours but often takes nearer seven. Often overcrowded to the point of sheer mayhem, the journey is a cultural experience but also a test of endurance.

Bisheh Waterfalls   آبشار بیشه
The tiny village of **Bisheh** (Bishehpuran) hides one of Iran's prettiest **waterfalls**. It cascades in 30m chutes off a tree-topped gully then trickles in rivulets into the river below. In summer many local tourists make the scenic day trip from Dorud (train only) or Khorramabad (new road, no public transport). By autumn only their litter remains and you'll have the village to yourself, the entire population of children following you Pied Piper-style. The best waterfall views are from across the river using a new footbridge at the northern edge of the village. From Dorud the day train takes about half an hour to Bisheh with fabulous glimpses of ziggurat-shaped **Mt Parvis** en route. You'll have an ample 4½ hours in Bisheh before the 7pm Tehran-bound train arrives to take you back to Dorud.

Sepid Dasht   سپید دشت
The railway does a switchback at **Sepid Dasht**, the biggest village en route. Sepid Dasht itself isn't architecturally attractive but its mountain backdrop is spectacularly spiky. Rare savaris bump their way to Khorramabad on a scenic road that passes close to the **Gerit Falls**.

Talezang   تله زنگ
Of anywhere along the line, isolated **Talezang** is the most tempting hop-off point for trekking into the mountain wilderness. This place is six stops south of Bisheh, three hours north of Andimeshk. One hiking challenge is to make for **Shevi Waterfall**, which emerges directly as a spring from a cliff then falls around 100m in a wide sweep. The Shevi Waterfall is reportedly around five hours walk from Talezang with some climbing involved. Bring food and tent.

Borujerd بروجرد
☎ 0622 / pop 257,000

In transit between Khorramabad and Hamadan you might need to cross this large, mountain-backed town. Sadly a March 2006 earthquake seriously damaged Borujerd's three remaining historic monuments, strung out over a kilometre off central Jafari St. The Seljuk blue-domed **Jameh Mosque** and fine Qajar-era **Soltani (Imam) Mosque** (Safa St) remain closed as sections are dangerously close to collapse. The celebrated **Imamzadeh Jafar** (Imamzadeh Lane) has reopened but its unusual, conical spire remains scaffolded.

On a pronounced hill 2½km northwest of centre, the upscale **Zagros Hotel** (☎ 350 4901; tw/ste US$95/115) is a local tourist attraction in itself with park-like grounds, a 'geyser' lake and a (currently broken) mini-cable car. The hotel has an impressive three-storey modern atrium, decent restaurant and appealing if pricey pseudo-traditional teahouse section. Rooms have Scandinavian-style pine interiors and vast picture windows, but carpets are starting to look slightly scuffed. For the best mountain views take rooms 202 to 207. Creaky glass elevators.

Savaris leave regularly for Dorud (IR10,000, 45 minutes) and Khorramabad from Dora Sq, around 5km southeast of the centre with most minibuses using the main terminal 600m nearer town. Savaris to Nahavand and Malayer start around 1km northwest of the Zagros Hotel. For Hamadan change in Malayer.

Alashtar Valley

Before Tamerlane's 14th-century ravages, Alashtar had been a major city. However, by the time Freya Stark came tomb-raiding here in the 1930s, all that remained was a nervous garrison of Persians huddled insecurely within a mud-walled fortress, in fear of the 'wild' Lurish tribes beyond. The town briefly made world news in 2005 when an unmanned drone spy-plane (presumed to be American) crashed nearby.

Alashtar's mountain-rimmed setting has a certain grandeur at the end of a long, agricultural valley from Nurabad. The road south passes through a canyon 10km before Khorramabad nicknamed the 'Velvet Mountains' for its eye-catching mossy bluffs. Several grassy areas here make popular picnic sites.

ANDIMESHK اندیمشك
☎ 0642 / pop 174,000

Flat, uninteresting Andimeshk has useful transport connections to Shush, Dezful and Shushtar. You'll need to sleep here if taking the scenic day-train to Dorud. **Hotel Rostan** (☎ 424 1818; Imam St; s/tw/tr IR140,000/170,000/200,000) is handily central between Sa'at and Beheshti Sqs. Rooms have good bathrooms but the curiously patchy décor gives the impression that ambitious redecoration works stopped in mid-flow. Don't assume that the air-conditioners actually cool.

Just east of Azadegan Sq, the relatively up-market **Hotel Bozorg Andimeshk** (Andimeshk Grand; Southern Bypass; ☎ 422 2100; fax 422 9295; s/d US$64/91; ℗ ✖) is out of the centre but handy for the zoo-funfair and bus terminal. Rooms with balconies and decently equipped bathrooms just about justify local prices (single/double IR316,900/479,600), but seem vastly overpriced at foreigner rates.

Many snack bars and small restaurants surround Beheshti Sq offering samosas, falafels, burgers, kababs and some particularly outstanding *dizi*.

Getting There & Away
BUS, MINIBUS & SAVARI

Almost any service from Ahvaz can also be booked ex-Andimeshk at the new **main bus terminal** (Azadegan Sq), 1.5km south of Beheshti Sq on the southern ring road. Iran Peyma runs to Esfahan at 7.45am (IR42,000), 10am (IR32,800) and 8pm (IR70,000, Volvo). They also have overnight Volvos to Tabriz (IR100,000, 2.30pm) and Shiraz (IR75,000, 4pm).

Savaris to Dezful (IR2000, 15 minutes) leave frequently from Sa'at Sq. Savaris for Ahvaz depart from Beheshti Sq. Minibuses for Shush (IR2250, 45 minutes) use a hidden yard off a lane directly west of Beheshti Sq.

For Khorramabad, minibuses (IR12,000, 4½ hours) and more frequent savaris (IR35,000, 3¾ hours) depart from Enqelab St around 2km north of the centre. They travel via **Pol-e-Dokhtar** (Virgin Bridge) a town that's named for a 3rd–10th century brick bridge of which only a single chunky

WESTERN IRAN

brick arch remains, straddling the main road in a canyon further north.

TRAIN

The **train station** (Taleqani St) is handily central, one short block west of Sa'at Sq (two blocks north then one west from Beheshti Sq). Arrive way before the 5.30am departure if you want a seat on the brilliantly scenic but appallingly overcrowded day train to Dorud via Bisheh (see p212). A 9pm train originating in Andimeshk runs overnight to Tehran (14 hours).

SHUSH شوش

☎ 0642 / pop 44,000

Shush (Susa) was once among the greatest cities of ancient Persia. Now it's a pleasantly small, relatively new town with a vast archaeological site, splendid castle, enigmatic Tomb of Daniel and bustling market. Across the square from Hotel Nazr is **Paradise Coffeenet** (☎ 522 0780; Haft-e Tir Sq; per hr IR8000; 10am-midnight).

History

An important Elamite city from about the middle of the 3rd millennium BC, Susa was burnt around 640 BC by the Assyrian king Ashurbanipal, but regained prominence in 521 BC when Darius I set it up as the Achaemenids' fortified winter capital. At that time it was probably similar in grandeur to Persepolis.

The palace survived the city's fall to Alexander the Great in 331 BC, and indeed Alexander married one of Darius III's daughters here. Still prosperous in the Seleucid and Parthian eras, Susa re-emerged as a Sassanian capital. During Shapur II's reign (AD 310–379) it regained renown as a Jewish pilgrimage site and became a centre of Nestorian Christian study. Evacuated in the face of Mongol raids Shush disappeared into the sands of time, only re-emerging after 1852 when the British archaeologist WK Loftus became the first to survey the site. His work was continued by the French Archaeological Service from 1891 more or less continuously until the Islamic Revolution of 1979.

Sights

ANCIENT CITY

Entered from YaZahra Sq on Khomeini Blvd, the **archaeological site** (admission IR4000; 8am-7pm, closes after heavy rain) occupies the whole southern flank of modern Shush. To the right as you enter, the landscape is entirely dominated by the **Chateau de Morgan**. On the site of an Elamite acropolis, this crenellated masterpiece looks like an Omani desert fortress but was in fact built by the French Archaeological Service between 1897 and 1912 to defend researchers from raids by local Arab and Lurish tribesmen. Notice a cuneiform-inscribed brick incorporated into the castle's west doorway.

Turning left at the top of the site's main entry ramp, you can walk through the site of the 521 BC **Palace of Darius**. That is now just a muddy rise on which a 30cm-high labyrinth of brick-and-wattle wall fragments marks the former room layout. At the northern rim are the massive stone bases of what was once an **apadana**, of six by six 22m-high columns topped with animal figures. A couple of double-horse capitals are partly preserved on the paved terrace.

To the east, beyond the partly paved **Royal Gate**, the **Royal City** is a misleading name for barren, lonely undulations stretching to the far horizon. It's more sensible to loop back towards the castle amid muddy gullies, pottery shards and thorn thickets alive with darting desert foxes. At the western side of the castle there's an earthen watchtower above ancient caves and niches.

SHUSH MUSEUM

Some tourists visit this bright new **museum** (Susa Park, Khomeini St; admission IR3000; 7.30am-1pm & 3.30-7pm, Tue-Sun) quite by mistake, thinking that they've actually entered the archaeological site (whose access track is right beside it). The museum's five rooms display seriously ancient stone- and pottery-work from regional archaeological sites. Highlights include a giant bullhead capital from Shush's *apadana*, a lion-hugging Hercules statue from Masjid-i Soleiman (p218) and some spooky clay masks from Haft Tappeh (opposite).

TOMB OF DANIEL

As in a typical imamzadeh, Muslim pilgrims crowd the glittery interior of the **Tomb of Daniel** (Aramgah-e Danyal), kissing the zarih grate around a green-draped grave slab. Here, however, this behaviour is particularly intriguing given that Daniel has at best tangential relevance to Islam. In fact, he's a semi-mythical Jewish figure who supposedly served as a faithful *satarap* (administrator) to Darius I (522–486 BC). Dubiously recorded in the Bible as having 'tender love with the prince of the eunuchs' (Daniel 1, 9) he is best remembered for unenviable ordeals in lions' dens. These exploits were already over 300 years old when recorded in the Old Testament (Daniel 6, 16-23).

Whatever the real provenance of the Daniel relics, they brought Shush an extremely lucrative flow of Jewish pilgrims from right across the Middle East. Great wealth accrued to the townsfolk living nearby, but those living across the river were missing out on the bonanza and wanted a share of the pilgrims' shekels. A compromise was arranged whereby Daniel's bones would spend alternate years on either riverbank, bringing prosperity to both communities. In the 12th century, travellers reported that an even more fanciful arrangement had left the holy remains dangling in a crystal coffin suspended from a metal bridge across the middle of the river.

What happened to them during the Mongol destruction is not recorded, but the present structure with its distinctive, pine-cone faceted spire, so typical of Khuzestan tombs, was only built in 1871.

The tomb complex is easy to find in the bazaar area, two blocks from the museum. It remains open late into the evening.

Sleeping & Eating

Apadana Hotel (☎ /fax 521 3131; s/tw US$22/33; P ✕) Comfortable and central above a good restaurant, the Apadana's rooms are fully equipped, though the wallpaper is starting to look a little tatty and water pressure can be rather low in the upper rooms. Staff are friendly and some speak English.

Hotel Nazr (☎ 522 9611; Haft-e Tir Sq; tw/q IR200,000/250,000; ✕) Rooms have good bathrooms and are newer than the Apadana's, but the place lacks any atmosphere and is about 1km further from the historical sites. From the minibus yards walk 300m up Shari'ati St. Prices are hazily defined so it's worth bargaining.

Plenty of snack bars and *kababis* are scattered near the museum and Haft-e Tir Sq.

Getting There & Away

Long-distance buses en route to Ahvaz can often be persuaded to drop passengers off on the main highway, 2km east of town. Shuttle taxis head from this point into the centre, but not necessarily at 2am when many southbound buses go by. Heading out of Shush, you'll usually need to go first to Andimeshk or Ahvaz.

Minibuses to Ahvaz depart frequently from Khomeini Blvd, 800m northeast of the archaeological site. For Andimeshk (IR2250, 38km) and Dezful they use small, separate yards across the road. The Apadana Hotel can arrange sensibly priced agency taxis for Choqa Zanbil (IR90,000 return) and Shushtar.

CHOQA ZANBIL & HAFT TAPPEH
Haft Tappeh   هفت تپه

Muddy Elamite-era mounds pimple this otherwise-flat oasis area. Several are thought to have been small ziggurats dating from around 1400 BC. None are mind-blowingly exciting, but recent archaeological work has rendered them a little more interesting. Beside the site, a Unesco-sponsored **museum** (admission IR2000; ⏰ 8am-5pm Sat-Thu) is beautifully set amid bougainvillaea and soaring palms. It displays archaeological finds including a curious black sarcophagus. Photo-rich explanations detail the excavation, restoration and partial reconstruction of Choqa Zanbil (25km away).

The Haft Tappeh site is 3km off the Ahvaz–Andimeshk highway. Beyond the museum, after crossing the train tracks there's a 1km unpaved short cut south to the Choqa Zanbil road.

Choqa Zanbil   چغازنبیل

One of Iran's Unesco World Heritage sites, Choqa Zanbil's magnificent brick **ziggurat** (admission IR5000; ⏰ 7am-6pm, guarded 24hr) is the best surviving example of Elamite architecture anywhere. Even if you're not a fan of ancient ruins, the great bulk and splendid semi-desert isolation of Choqa Zanbil can't fail to impress. Although close access is prevented after 6pm, the ziggurat arguably looks most appealing after dusk when the golden floodlighting emphasises

THE ROMAN CONNECTION

Some of Shushtar's then state-of-the-art irrigation systems were built using Roman technology and labour: legionnaires defeated at the AD 259 battle of Edessa (today's Şanlıurfa in Turkey). Their leader, vanquished Valerian, became the only Roman Emperor ever to be captured alive. Sassanian king Shahpur I was so proud of his victory that he recorded the event with boastful carved reliefs at Naqsh-e Rostam (p283) and Bishapur (p286). Stories vary as to Valerian's fate, but Shushtaris insist that he was imprisoned in Qal'eh Salosel (opposite). In some versions he was systematically insulted then brutally killed by being forced-fed a 'soup' of molten gold.

the structure's form better than the hazy desert daylight.

HISTORY

The ancient inhabitants of proto-Iran attached great religious importance to mountains. Where they had no mountains, they made their own. This was the origin of distinctive pyramidal, tiered temples known as ziggurats. Choqa Zanbil's ziggurat was the *raison d'être* of the town of Dur Untash, founded by King Untash Gal in the mid-13th century BC. Dur Untash bloomed especially in the early 12th century BC when it had a large number of temples and priests. The town was eventually sacked by Ashurbanipal around 640 BC and, incredibly, remained 'lost' for more than 2500 years. It was accidentally rediscovered during a 1935 aerial survey by the Anglo-Iranian Oil Company, the forerunner of BP.

THE ZIGGURAT

The ziggurat was dedicated to Inshushinak, the chief god of the Elamite pantheon and patron of Shush. In those days the area was fertile and forested, and the ziggurat was built on a slightly raised base to guard against flooding. It has a square plan with sides measuring 105m. The original five storeys were erected vertically from the foundation level as a series of concentric towers, not one on top of another as was the custom in neighbouring Mesopotamia. At the summit (now lost) was a temple accessi-

ble only to the highest elite of Elamite society. Even now the taboo remains and you're not allowed to climb the remnant stairways that rise on each of the four sides.

The structure is made of red bricks so well-preserved that an observer could believe they're brand new. However, if you look very closely, a brick-wide strip at around eye-level is intricately inscribed in **cuneiform**, the world's spiky first alphabet that looks like a spilt box of tin-tacks. The inscriptions are not easy to make out unless you cross the rope cordon. Permission to do so is the only apparent advantage of tipping the 'guide'. He speaks not a word of English, but gesticulates with gruesome clarity as to the purpose of the **sacrifice stones** (halfway along the northwest side). Easy to spot is an ancient **sun dial** (facing the southwest central stairway) and, beside it, a strangely moving **footprint** of an Elamite child, accidentally preserved for three millennia.

AROUND THE ZIGGURAT

The ziggurat was surrounded by a paved courtyard protected by a wall. At the foot of the northeastern steps would once have been the **Gate of Untash Gal**, two rows of seven columns where supplicants would seek the pleasure of the king. Around the wall was originally a complex of **tomb chambers**, tunnels and **qanat** channels. Once the site's climate became drier, qanats brought water an incredible 45km from ancient rivers. Vestiges are still visible. Outside were the living quarters of the town and 11 temples dedicated to various Elamite gods and goddesses. Little of this remains.

Walk a couple of minutes east of the main asphalt access road towards an isolated lamppost to find some more, excavated **Elamite royal tombs**. There's little to see here, either, though steep ancient steps lead down into (unlabelled) **tomb number five**. Descending is unwise as the pit stinks of toiletry misdemeanours… especially bad when the temperature hits 45°C. Nonetheless, it's still worth strolling up the slight rise nearby to look back at the ziggurat from a particularly photogenic angle.

Getting There & Away

There's no public transport. An ideal way to visit both sites is as side trips on a taxi-charter from Shush to Shushtar (IR130,000). Visit Haft Tappeh first, as its museum is a good primer for Choqa Zanbil. In reverse you'd find Haft Tappeh's lumpy ziggurats somewhat of an anticlimax. Add IR15,000 per hour waiting time.

SHUSHTAR شوشتر

☎ 0612 / pop 66,000

The deeply historic city of Shushtar lies strategically where the last contoured red ridges of the expiring Zagros Mountains fade into the endless flat watermelon fields of southern Khuzestan. Beneath the initially unexciting surface of today's low-rise cityscape, there's lots to discover including a complex of artificial ancient 'watermills' and no less than 14 imamzadehs. The town centre is 17 Shahrivar Sq marked by Bank Melli (no exchange). The very fast-connection **Persian Coffeenet** (17 Shahrivar Sq; per hr IR10,000; ☏ 8am-11pm) is across the square on the second floor of a building that looks like a pair of mini glass Empire State Buildings.

In an alley behind the Shandravan Bridge, the delightful little **Mostofi House** (admission free; ☎ 8am-2pm) hosts a small **tourist information office** (☎ 622 0850; www.shushtarchtb. ir) where you can get useful brochures and maps. While here peruse a small museum in their *shabestun* (a below-ground sitting room typical of traditional Khuzestani houses) and enjoy river views from their palm-tree courtyard.

Sights
WATERMILLS آبشارهای سیکا

Shushtar's *raison d'être* for millennia was controlling the irrigation of the Khuzestan plains, and the town's most famous attraction is a set of ancient '**watermills**' (Abshari Sika; Shari'ati St; admission IR5000; ☏ 8am-10pm). Actually, these aren't buildings at all but a powerful arc of cascading water chutes that are strangely mesmerising, especially when floodlit at night. They're especially impressive considering that the water is fed through ancient man-made feeder tunnels. One mill has been reconstructed so you can observe an old paddle-wheel device turning a millstone. Entrance is down steps beside an attractive blue-façaded building now home to souvenir and pickle shops. You can see the watermills site almost as well by simply peering over

the parapet of the Shari'ati St bridge (one block south of 17 Shahrivar Sq), or even better by climbing the hill behind: follow signs to the attractively renovated **Marashi House** (☎ 622 3484; Abdullah Banu St; admission free; ☏ 8am-9pm, variable).

POL-E SHANDRAVAN پل شاندروان

About 400m west of the bus terminal are substantial ruined sections of this partly Sassanid **bridge** cum weir, also known as Band-i Qaisar or Valerian's Bridge. Along with the **Band-e-Mizan** weir, this raised the river level by 2m, providing the waters necessary for irrigation and mills. Considered a wonder of the world by 7th-century invading Arabs, the workers and architects were Roman captives (see boxed text, opposite). The bridge originally had 45 arches and remained intact, albeit with many a renovation, until around a century ago. According to some Khuzestani historians, it was then deliberately dynamited by British agents. The idea was to break Shushtar's trade connections, thus encouraging locals to seek alternative work at the new (British-owned) oilfields of Masjid-i Soleiman. Less conspiratorial theories blame rebellions and floods for the bridge's deterioration.

Today the Pol-e Shandravan ruins parallel to a newer Dezful Rd bridge. A park is being built to landscape the scene.

QAL'EH SALOSEL قلعه سلاسل

The historic heart of Shushtar was **Salosel Castle**, a prominent cliff-hill overlooking the river. This is where Shapur I is said to have imprisoned Roman Emperor Valerian. It's also here that Persians held out for two years against the invading Arab-Muslim armies until secret tunnels were revealed to the attackers by a traitor. For centuries Khuzestan was governed from a palace ('Kushk') on this site and an impressive three-storey pyramidal building stood here until the 1920s. Sadly, above-ground, only a mound of rubble remains. However, the castle's impressive Sassanian-era subterranean rooms and water channels have been rediscovered. As yet they are only open on special occasions like No Ruz but at such times they are very imaginatively lit.

The site is one long block north of Shahrivar Sq then three minutes' walk to the east.

THE BAKHTIYARI

The nomadic Bakhtiyari's traditional goat-herding migration (around 350km each way between seasonal pastures) inspired feisty writers like Gertrude Bell (in 1902) and Virginia Woolf's Bloomsbury buddy Vita Sackville-West (in 1927) to follow their footsteps. It is also the subject of two inspiring documentary movies including Oscar-nominated *People of the Wind* (1976). Today some migrations continue. Although the predominant use of trucks rather than bare-footed toil to transport the flocks makes for a rather less glamorous image, meeting hospitable Bakhtiyaris in their make-shift tent-camps is still a highlight of travel in northern Khuzestan.

See also Iran's Nomads, p285.

OTHER SIGHTS

Visible from the minibus as you arrive from Ahvaz, **Imamzadeh Abdullah** has a white pinecone of a central tower reminiscent of Daniel's tomb in Shush. A gory local tale records a woman beheading her own son to swap his head for the skull of a long-dead holy man, which is now enshrined here as a sacred relic. Colourfully decked with strings of lights, the building resembles a cruise liner against the evening horizon. At its foot is the small but impressive 11-arched ancient **Lashgar Bridge**.

A short walk south of the bus terminal, the partly 9th-century **Jameh Mosque** (Masjid Jameh Lane) has a truncated, gently leaning minaret and sits in a quiet tree-filled quadrangle of fruit-sellers.

Just beyond the Hotel Jahangardi is a great viewpoint beside the octagonal **Kola Ferangi tower**, which looks like (and probably was) a stone lighthouse, though local lore relates that Shapur's slave driver would watch over the Roman prisoners from here surveying progress on the **Band-e-Mizan** (Sassanid weir) that divided the river to provide water for the watermills. Across the water you'll see the blue-domed **Seyid Mohammad Golabi Shrine** behind which rises an *iwan* of the vast new **Sheikh Alome Shushtari Shrine**. Currently in yellow brick, it entombs the 20th-century philosopher Mohammad Taq Shushtari and should eventually be covered in fabulous blue

tiling, Esfahan style. About 1km further such tiling already graces the brilliant and considerably older **Saheb-al Zaman shrine** at which awed devotees have supposedly made sightings of the Mahdi (last imam), hence the 'empty seat' shrine box.

Sleeping & Eating

Mehmanpazir Shushtar (☎ 622 3288; Sharafat St; s/d/tr IR100,000/120,000/150,000) Recently rebuilt with reasonably neat tiled floors, this upstairs place charges what it feels you'll pay, apparently irrespective of whether you get a room with an OK bathroom or have to share the communal squat toilet. Mattresses and sheets are clean and new.

Hotel Jahangardi (☎ 622 1690, fax 622 1692; Sarafat St; s/tw/tr IR225,000/278,000/331,000; P) Right beside the river you can gaze across to the mausolea from this wonderful location that's peaceful until nocturnal tourists decide to crank up their party music. The clean, reasonably comfortable rooms have bathrooms.

Restaurant Abshar (☎ 622 4805; Shahrivar Sq; meals IR25,000; 7.30am-3pm & 5-10pm). There's a good selection of eateries around Shahrivar Sq of which this deceptively cavernous eatery makes a friendly choice and supplements kababs and *ghorme sabzi* (meat and vegetables with rice) with scrumptious spit-roast chicken (IR50,000 half-bird).

Several shops sell Shushtar's famous pickles and preserved fruits. Local *koluche* (soft-centred biscuits with a hint of caraway) taste best when stuffed with dates.

Getting There & Away

Shushtar's single, handily central bus terminal is a block north and west from Shahriyar Sq, between Almas and Sheikh Sts. Very regular buses run to Ahvaz (IR5000, 1½ hours) and Dezful (IR2000, one hour), where you can transfer for Shush or Andimeshk. There's no public transport to Shush (90km), but a good asphalt road exists passing within 5km of Choqa Zanbil and emerging near Haft Tappeh.

AROUND SHUSHTAR
Masjid-i Soleiman   مسجد سليمان
☎ 0481 / pop 108,000

At 4am on 26 May 1908, British oil-prospectors finally hit a 'gusher' at Masjid-i

Soleiman, nicknamed MiS ('em-ai-ess'). It was the first commercially viable Iranian oil strike and came just in the nick of time for the exploration company, forerunners of BP, who were on the verge of financial collapse. The result was ultimately to transform Iran's history and provide Britain's navy with a crucial edge in looming WWI: having switched their ships to petrol-power, finding a plentiful fuel source had become essential. The whole thrilling history is brilliantly retold in Daniel Yergin's book, *The Prize*. The original first oil well, **Naftom Yek**, is 200m up an alley just east of MiS's central post office, visible through locked railings along with an antiquated steam-engine.

On a hill overlooking town (IR10,000 by taxi), **Sar Masjid** is the stone terrace on which some believe a 6th-century BC fire temple once stood. Others claim this was the birthplace of Cyrus. It seems to have later housed a Seleucid sanctuary: several statues found here and on nearby hills suggest a Hercules cult. Masjid-i Soleiman's apparently ultra-Muslim name (Solomon's Mosque) was probably conceived as a 'cover' to protect the site at the time of the Muslim-Arab invasions as happened at Takht-e Soleiman (p187).

Bardnashandar (Bardneshandeh) is a similarly enigmatic stairway and stone platform close to the Andika road. There's a single, spindly 3.5m-high 'column' but the main attraction is the 40-minute drive from MiS passing through Bakhtiyari spring pasturelands where the nomads' traditional black **tent-camps** are easy to spot in April/May. If invited in, a handy greeting is *che-khoni?* (reply *khubam*). Thank you is *beoumi*.

DEZFUL دزفول

☎ 0641 / **pop 208,000**

Sometimes pronounced dez-*bil*, Dezful makes an interesting brief stop between Shushtar and Andimeshk. Its 12-span **Pol-e Qadim** is supposedly 'the world's oldest bridge still in use'. That's rather misleading. While the bridge's stone foundation pillars date back to the reign of Sassanian king Shapur I (AD 241–272), today's arches are a mix of Safavid brick and modern ferro-concrete. A series of '**grinds**' (rather indistinct ancient 'mill' remnants) stretch along the river towards a newer bridge above

which the historic **Tiznoo House** (☎ 223 1033; ⊗ 7am-2pm) hosts a tourist information centre. Behind this stretches Dezful's extensive 'old' **bazaar**. It's very lively, but after sustaining 900 bomb-hits during the Iran–Iraq War, doesn't really look 'old' any more. Set on a more distant cliff-top, **Pir-e-Ruband** is an attractive 1609 mausoleum with a lop-sided Khuzestani pinecone tower.

Kornasiyun Hamam (admission IR2000; ⊗ 9am-1pm & 3-8pm) houses a museum of local life in an old bathhouse near the somewhat overpriced riverside **Ronash Hotel** (☎ 223 7907; Saheli St; d/ste IR250,000/1,500,000; 🗱).

With three weekly Iran Aseman flights to Tehran (IR255,000), the airport is virtually all that stops Dezful merging with Andimeshk to the northwest. Andimeshk-bound savaris leave from the east end of the new bridge. Minibuses from Shushtar drop off at Moghavemat Yakoub Lays Sq, 600m northwest of the **long-distance bus terminal** (Payam Noor Blvd) at the southeast edge of town.

AHVAZ اهواز

☎ 0611 / **pop 1,005,000**

Abu Nuwas ('Father of Curls') is perhaps the only Muslim poet celebrated for writing homoerotic drinking songs. He was born in AD 756 in Ahvaz, but got out as soon as he could. You'll probably want to do the same. But hopefully not (as Abu was) sold as a sex slave to a Yemeni drug dealer.

Using the well-served airport is the only likely reason you'd choose to transit this vast, featureless, industrial city where summer temperatures regularly top 50°C. Acceptable central accommodation options include the quiet if basic **Mehmanpazir Parknow** (☎ 222 2534; Imam Khomeini St, pedestrianised section; s/d IR84,000/113,500) and the assiduously cleaned **Iran Hotel** (☎ 221 7200; fax 221 7206; Shari'ati St; s/tw IR200,000/300,000; 🗱). Before a flight, congenial modern rooms at the professionally run **Oxim Hotel** (☎ 447 4720; 7200; MiS Highway; s/tw/d US$64/91/91; 🄿 🗱 🖵) are a sensible choice, being just 2km from the airport.

Getting There & Away

Helpful English-speaking **Tayareh Travel Agency** (☎ 222 9849; fax 222 6108; tayareh_travelagency@yahoo.com; Azadegan St; ⊗ 8am-1pm & 5-9pm Sat-Thu) sells air tickets including to Tehran (IR332,000, frequent), Esfahan (IR315,000, daily), Shiraz

(IR315,000, twice weekly), Kuwait (one way/ return IR660,000/1,094,000, weekly) and Dubai (one way/return IR762,000/1,277,500, four weekly).

You can get to Shush (IR6000, two hours) and virtually anywhere else in Iran from the big main **bus terminal** (Andimeshk Rd) 5km west of centre up Enqelab St. Andimeshk savaris/minibuses (IR25,000/7500) depart from a hidden yard 200m further north. Dezful buses (IR15,000, 1¾ hours) use a different yard 100m to the southeast of the main terminal across Enqelab St.

Buses for Shushtar (IR5000, 1½ hours) use **Istgah Shushtar** (Pasdaran Blvd) way across town, 4km northeast of centre (halfway to the airport). Call ☎ 447 2020 for a taxi.

AROUND AHVAZ

From Khorramshahr, 125km south, **Valfarje-8 Shipping** (☎ 336 7116) sails to Kuwait at least weekly. Dusty **Shalamcheh**, west of Khorramshahr, is the official crossing point for Basra in Iraq for those with suicidal self-confidence. Wreckage still litters surrounding tracts of land devastated in the Iran–Iraq War.

Central Iran
ایران مرکزی

Ever since Cyrus the Great's dramatic rise from provincial overlord to ruler of the largest empire on earth, central Iran has been something of a showcase for the region's greatest civilisations. The unrelenting splendour and majesty of Esfahan, the refined elegance of Shiraz and the mud-brick antiquity of Yazd, Abyaneh and Kharanaq are a fascinating contrast, representing the fusion over 2500 years of myriad cultures and starkly different terrains. Then, of course, there's that monumental expression of artistic harmony commissioned by Darius I – Persepolis.

With so much on offer, it's no surprise that the towns of Iran's central provinces are where you'll probably spend the most time. But it's not just about ticking off the popular sights, because central Iran has many an unsung gem. Kashan, with its splendid mosques, gardens and magnificently restored traditional houses, is one. If you want to get off the beaten track there's the desert oasis of Garmeh, the cave village of of Garmeh, caravanserai stops such as Zein-o-din and Toudeshk, or the chance to camp with nomads in the Zagros Mountains.

Central Iran's people are as diverse as the places they live. In Qom they're conservative and religious, Shirazis are laid-back and fun-loving, and the Qashqa'i and Bakhtiari nomads live a lifestyle dictated by nature. Often you will experience the region's cultural richness and physical beauty in combination: sitting in the garden of Hafez's tomb discussing the ways of the world with a Shirazi medical student, perhaps; watching a nomad woman make yogurt by hand; or drinking tea with a carpet salesman in Esfahan's Imam Sq. Whatever it is you happen upon, central Iran is a place you'll remember for a long time.

HIGHLIGHTS

- Watch the sun set over Esfahan's many-splendoured **Imam Square** (p238) from the rooftop **Qeysarieh Tea Shop** (p249)
- Sit on the hill behind the sublime **Persepolis** (p279), just soaking it all up
- Haggle over a carpet or kilim in the vaulted arcades of Esfahan's **Bazar-e Bozorg** (p238) or **Imam Square** (p238)
- Lose yourself in the historic laneways of **Yazd** (p255), and find yourself in a traditional hotel
- Treat yourself to a dose of Safavid-era luxury in the wonderfully restored **Caravanserai Zein-o-din** (p267)
- Experience a real desert oasis at simple, silent **Garmeh** (p254)

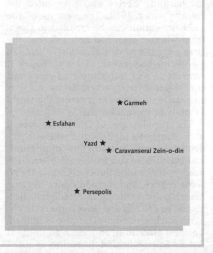

★ Garmeh

★ Esfahan

Yazd ★

★ Caravanserai Zein-o-din

★ Persepolis

CENTRAL IRAN

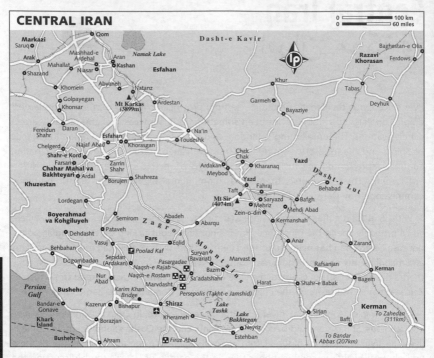

QOM

قم

☎ 0251 / pop 1,070,000 / elev 931m

Iran's second-holiest city after Mashhad, Qom (Ghom) is home to both the magnificent Hazrat-e Masumeh shrine and the hardline clerics who have ruled the country since 1980. The genesis of the 1979 revolution can be credited to Qom, from where clerics had railed against the shah's regime since well before Ayatollah Khomeini was exiled in 1964. Today it remains one of Iran's most religious and conservative cities, where Shiite scholars and students come from across the world to study in the madrasehs.

The 'peoplescape' of Qom is absorbing in its contrasts. Mullahs and religious students mix with a steady flow of pilgrims, and everywhere you look women wear the head-to-toe chador. But even Qom is seeing some change, and the odd figure-hugging manteau and made-up face. Still, travellers should be discreet and dress conservatively, particularly around the Hazrat-e Masumeh. The best place to sit and watch all this is at Astane Square, behind the shrine.

Despite the ever-present scaffolding the shrine is magnificent. And if you are not going to Mashhad and have an interest in the kind of devotion that is a hallmark of Shiism, then Qom is worth a quick visit. Note that little English is spoken in Qom.

Orientation

Hotels, restaurants and countless souvenir shops coalesce around the Hazrat-e Masumeh shrine and neighbouring Qom River. The 'river', however, is so dry that it has been concreted over and is usually used as a car park, market and late-night raceway. Buses stop at Haftdad Sq, 4.5km from the shrine, en route to and from Tehran.

Information

Bank Melli (Mar'ashi Najafi St) Slow as a wet week.
Coffeenet (Mo'allem St; per hr IR6000; ⏰ 10am-10pm)
International Telephone Centre (Mar'ashi Najafi St; ⏰ 7am-11pm)
Money Exchange (Mar'ashi Najafi St; ⏰ 9am-8pm)
SabaCenter Internet (☎ 774 7711; A Khoshraftar Alley, off Mar'ashi Najafi St; per hr IR6000; ⏰ 10am-10pm) Good place to meet young people.

Sights

Pilgrims come to Qom to see the shrine, and that's pretty much it. Southeast of the shrine the unremarkable **Khan-e Khomeini** (Ruhollah Sq), where Ayatollah Khomeini lived before being forced into exile, is of interest if you're staying in the midrange hotels nearby, though it's not open to visitors. It's the single-storey place with rendered mud walls.

HAZRAT-E MASUMEH   حضرت معصومه

At the physical and spiritual centre of Qom is the **Hazrat-e Masumeh** (⊙ 24hr), the burial place of Imam Reza's sister Fatemeh, who died and was interred here in the 9th century AD. It's an impressive sight, with one enormous tiled dome and another golden dome flanked by exquisite minarets. Much of what you see today was built under Shah Abbas I and the other Safavid kings who were anxious to establish their Shiite credentials and provide a counterweight to the sect's shrines at Karbala and Najaf (in modern-day Iraq), then under Ottoman occupation. The magnificent golden cupola was an embellishment built by Qajar ruler Fath Ali Shah, and today's 'shahs', the Ayatollahs of Qom, have embarked on a massive project to expand the complex.

Nonmuslims are allowed into the grounds (women must wear a chador, available at entrance No 3 on Eram St), but not to see the shrine itself. However, several readers report wandering around either with an escort or alone. Cameras are banned unless you can convince the stewards otherwise.

Sleeping

Qom's sleeping options are conveniently gathered by budget range. Most budget places are in or near Haramnema Lane, a small alleyway just north of the Ahanchi Bridge, opposite the shrine. There are also some lower midrange places in the lane, but their foreign prices are so high that they aren't worth it – without a big discount. Shop around. Three new midrange places have opened about 2km southwest of the shrine. During religious festivals Qom is packed, and it's busier most Fridays.

The next two places are about a 2km walk from the shrine. A third, the larger Olympic Hotel, should open in 2008.

Mosaferkhaneh-ye Haram (Haramnema Lane; r per person IR50,000) There's no English spoken,

no English sign, and the rooms and shared bathrooms are uberbasic. But it's the cheapest in town and the welcome is warm. Popular with families, it's a reasonable choice for lone women travellers. Guests can use the utilitarian kitchen.

Etminan Hotel (☎ 660 9640; cnr Haramnema Lane & Imam Musa Sadr Blvd; s/d IR150,000/190,000) Some of the small but functional rooms with bright-pink squat bathrooms offer fine views of the holy shrine, and double-glazing keeps most of the noise out. There's a kitchen, and hefty discounts are possible.

Negin Hotel (☎ 663 0246; neginhotel2006@yahoo.com; Haramnema Lane; s/d/tr IR120,000/150,000/200,000; ✖) The Negin is a step up from its neighbours and fair value.

Aria Hotel (☎ 774 8450; Astane Sq; s/tw/apt IR150,000/200,000/500,000; ✖ ▢) With its front-row spot overlooking Astane Sq, the Aria's rooms, some with six beds, are good value, especially in low season. Popular with Arab pilgrims.

Safa Apartment Hotel (☎ 773 2499; Mo'allem St; r US$49-80; ℗ ✖) It's busy, but the rooms are tired – and when we visited, staff seemed tired of seeing so many guests. Head here only if Ghasr is full. Don't confuse this with the budget Safa on Imam Musa Sadr Blvd.

Ghasr Apartment Hotel (☎ 783 1151; fax 783 1154; Mo'allem St; ste/apt with breakfast US$50/94; ✖) This new, modern-styled hotel has good-sized rooms and facilities at fair prices. Double beds are available; apartments have two bedrooms.

Eating

The dining in Qom is about as diverse as the range of faiths: standard Iranian cuisine with felafel to meet the Arab-pilgrim demand. Not surprisingly, most of the independent eateries are lined up along busy Mar'ashi Najafi St, opposite the shrine and square, and include *kababis* (kabab shops), pizza and barbecued chicken joints, drink shops and a couple of restaurants.

Qom is famous for *sohun*, a sinfully delicious pistachio-and-ginger brittle, which is often sold in attractive tin boxes and makes a good gift.

Restaurant Bihan (☎ 774 3433; Mar'ashi Najafi St; meals IR35,000; ⊙ 11am-3pm & 6.30-11pm) Of the options along this strip the Bihan is consistently good, with tasty kababs and large serves of *zereshk polo ba morgh* (chicken and rice with barberries).

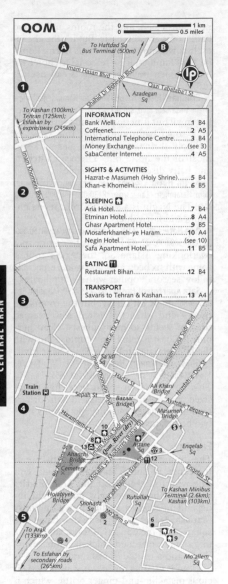

here as they wait for the dozens of buses passing through en route to or from Tehran. Buses to Tehran (IR10,000, 1½ to two hours) stop several times an hour. Southbound services to major destinations are frequent, including Esfahan (IR20,000/30,000, five to six hours), Kermanshah (IR22,500/50,000, seven to eight hours), Yazd (IR22,500/35,000, eight hours) and Shiraz (IR35,000/65,000, 11 to 14 hours). Competition for seats can be positively unholy.

For Kashan, minibuses (IR7000, two hours) leave the Terminal-e Kashan at the eastern end of Enqelab St roughly every hour, or pick up a big bus (IR10,000, 1½ hours), at Haftdad Sq.

Savaris to Tehran and Kashan leave from Haftdad Sq and, more conveniently, from the end of the Ahanchi Bridge opposite the holy shrine.

TRAIN
Trains run from **Qom train station** (☎ 441 7151) to Tehran (2nd class IR4250, 2½ hours) a couple of times a day, but most people opt for a bus.

Getting Around
Most sights are easily reached on foot. To get to or from Haftdad Sq or Terminal-e Kashan, ask for a shuttle taxi (approximately IR1500) near the Ahanchi Bridge or go to the corner of Imam Khomeini Blvd and Hadaf St.

KASHAN   كاشان
☎ 0361 / pop 320,000 / elev 935m
Kashan and its surrounds have been home to human settlements since at least the 4th millennium BC. However, much of what is known of Kashan's history is interwoven with legend (see A Sting in the Tail, opposite). What is certain is that Kashan was twice destroyed by invading armies. The city walls were rebuilt, and during the Seljuk period (AD 1051–1220) it became famous for its textiles, pottery and tiles.

Shah Abbas I was so enamoured with this delightful oasis city on the edge of the Dasht-e Kavir that he insisted on being buried here rather than in Esfahan. Much of Kashan was destroyed by an earthquake in 1779 but the subsequent Qajar period saw building on a lavish scale. The most notable survivors are the fine covered bazaar and

Getting There & Away
Transport to Qom is packed on Fridays and on any religious holiday.

BUS, MINIBUS & SAVARI
Qom's main bus terminal is actually a huge roundabout in the north of town called Haftdad Sq. Touts pester potential passengers

---

A STING IN THE TAIL

While there is no written history of Kashan before the Seljuk period, there is an entertaining oral history. One story has the Bible's 'Three Wise Men' setting out from Kashan to pay their respects to the newborn Christ, an event that is distinctly possible given the 'Wise Men' were magis (Zoroastrian priests), hence the 'Adoration of the Magi'. Nearby Saveh also claims the three.

Another legend tells of Abu Musa al-Ashari's novel method of taking the city during the Arab invasion of the 7th century AD. When the Arab general found the city's walls impregnable, he ordered his men to gather (somehow?) thousands of scorpions from the surrounding deserts. Armed with these stingers, he attacked the city by having them thrown over the walls. According to the tale the poor Kashanis, who could never have expected an attack of such diabolical genius, soon capitulated.

---

several meticulously restored mansions that have become synonymous with the city. The bazaar is deceptively large and has an enchantingly lethargic atmosphere that serves as the perfect counterfoil to the frantic bustle of Tehran and the sightseeing intensity of Esfahan.

Accommodation options might be limited and the populace very conservative, but you'll still need a very good excuse for skipping Kashan – it just might be one of the unexpected highlights of your trip.

Orientation

The centre of town is Kamal-ol-Molk Sq, from where most sites can be reached on foot. For sites along the northeast–southwest main road to Fin Gardens (variously known as Fin Rd and Amir Kabir Rd), you will need a take a taxi or take a bus. The bus terminal is located about 2.5km northeast of the centre but most buses stop instead at Valiasr Sq.

Information

Amir Kabir Exchange (☎ 444 0616; Mir Ahmad St; ☉ 8am-2pm Sat-Thu) Short hours but no paperwork.

Bank Tejarat (Ayatollah Kashani St) Changes money... slowly.

Central City Cafenet (Shahid Mohammad Ali-ye-Raja'i St; per hr IR10,000; ☉ 8am-10pm)

Milad Hospital (Dr Beheshti St) Try here first.

Police (☎ 110)

Safar Doostan Travel Agency (☎ 445 7040; Ayatollah Kashani St; ☉ 8.30am-8pm Sat-Thu)

Sepanta Coffeenet (Ayatollah Kashani St; per hr IR10,000; ☉ 2-9pm Sat-Thu) Run by helpful women; popular with young Kashanis. It's unsigned, downstairs in a green-tiled building.

Telephone office (Abazar St; ☉ 8am-2pm & 4-9pm Sat-Thu, 10am-1pm Fri) International calls at the usual rates.

TOURS

Kashan is full of driver-guides looking to take you to Abyaneh (usually about IR150,000), Abyaneh and Natanz (IR200,000), or those two and on to Esfahan (IR250,000).

Ahmad Pourseyedi (☎ 533 0321, 0913 264 3012; ahmad_pourseyedi@yahoo.com) 'Charming old rogue' Ahmad's septuagenarian legs have seen better days and his history is sometimes awry, but he's delightful company as he recalls anecdotes while driving sedately around the Kashani hinterlands.

Cheap Taxi Reza (☎ 444 9581, 0913 361 1136) Reza Shoghi is a nice guy, a safe driver and has enough English.

Mahdi Galekhah (☎ 0913 261 3530; mgalekhah@yahoo.com) Works in historical houses, generous and engaging.

Mohammad Fatehi (☎ 0913 363 1796; mr_fatehi2006@yahoo.com) Easygoing, very knowledgeable and reliable. Also works in historical houses.

Sights

BAZAAR   بازار

Kashan's **bazaar** (☉ Sat-Thu) is one of the most enjoyable in Iran. Busy but not hectic, traditional but with a wide variety of goods, large enough to surprise but not to get lost in, it is a great place to wander for a couple of hours, especially before lunch and in the late afternoon. The multidomed roof of the bazaar dates from the 19th century, but the site has been the centre of trade in Kashan for much longer. If you step off the main thoroughfare, you'll find yourself in ancient caravanserais, mosques or the refreshingly unrenovated Hammam-e Khan (p230).

The best way to appreciate the extent of the bazaar is to climb to its roof. There are tiny staircases throughout and it's fun to ask a *bazari* (bazaar shopkeeper) to lead you up. If that doesn't work, head to the magnificent **Timche-ye Amin al Dowleh**, a high dome with lavish interior mouldings completed in 1868. Beneath the dome, in a square dominated by carpet shops, ask the guys at the Chaykhaneh Caravan Sara (p230) to show you to the roof (they might ask for a payment, but not if you eat there). You can climb all the way to the top of the dome, from where the views over the brown town and bulbous roofscape of

the bazaar are inspired. Look for the just-dyed wool drying in the sun.

TRADITIONAL HOUSES   خانه های سنتی

Hiding behind the high mud-brick walls of Kashan are hundreds of once-grand traditional houses. Built during the 19th century, most have long-since been carved up

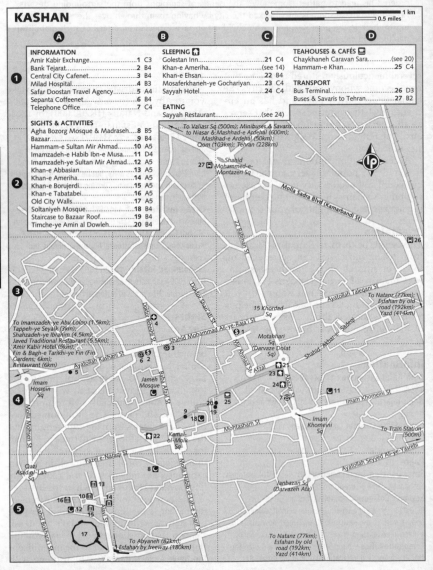

KASHAN

INFORMATION
Amir Kabir Exchange................1 C3
Bank Tejarat................2 B4
Central City Cafenet................3 B4
Milad Hospital................4 B3
Safar Doostan Travel Agency...........5 A4
Sepanta Coffeenet................6 B4
Telephone Office................7 C4

SIGHTS & ACTIVITIES
Agha Bozorg Mosque & Madraseh.....8 B5
Bazaar................9 B4
Hammam-e Sultan Mir Ahmad........10 A5
Imamzadeh-e Habib Ibn-e Musa....11 D4
Imamzadeh-ye Sultan Mir Ahmad...12 A5
Khan-e Abbasian................13 A5
Khan-e Ameriha................14 A5
Khan-e Borujerdi................15 A5
Khan-e Tabatabei................16 A5
Old City Walls................17 A5
Soltaniyeh Mosque................18 B4
Staircase to Bazaar Roof............19 B4
Timche-ye Amin al Dowleh........20 B4

SLEEPING
Golestan Inn................21 C4
Khan-e Ameriha................(see 14)
Khan-e Ehsan................22 B4
Mosaferkhaneh-ye Gochariyan......23 C4
Sayyah Hotel................24 C4

EATING
Sayyah Restaurant................(see 24)

TEAHOUSES & CAFÉS
Chaykhaneh Caravan Sara............(see 20)
Hammam-e Khan................25 C4

TRANSPORT
Bus Terminal................26 D3
Buses & Savaris to Tehran............27 B2

or are literally turning to dust, but several have been restored, and, mercifully for the city, the idea is catching. Those that can be visited are monuments to the importance of Kashan as a Qajar-era commercial hub, embellished with fine stucco panels, ostentatious stained glass and lofty *badgirs* (windtowers), all set around a series of interlinked courtyards.

Khan-e Ameriha   خانه عامری ها
The oldest of Kashan's restored houses, **Khan-e Ameriha** (Alavi St; admission IR3000; ☉ 8am-sunset) is also the most impressive. It was built at the end of the 18th century when Agha Ameri decided his father's house wasn't nearly big enough for one of the country's wealthiest men and needed a little extension. Ameri was Kashan's governor and made his money supplying the shah with war material and providing security along the trade route between Tehran and Kerman. By the time work finished, his was the largest home in Persia, encompassing a staggering seven courtyards over 9000 sq metres.

All this, however, was fast returning to dust by the time restoration work began in 1999. So far more than €2 million has been spent, and one by one the courtyards and surrounding buildings are returning to their extravagant best. Highlights include the two *hammams* (bathhouses), one of which was built specifically for local pregnant women, and the *naghib* (mask room), which leads to a secret escape tunnel. To see it, get chummy with the attendants...and ask to be let onto the roof.

Parts of the home should have been open as a top-end traditional hotel in the next few years.

Khan-e Tabatabei   خانه طباطبایی
Built around 1880 by wealthy carpet merchant Seyyed Ja'far Tabatabei, the **Khan-e Tabatabei** (☎ 422 0032; off Alavi St; admission IR3000; ☉ 8am-sunset) is renowned for its intricate stone reliefs, fine stucco and wonderful mirror and stained-glass work; photographers will love it. Larger than the Borujerdi house, it covers 4730 sq metres, has 40 rooms and more than 200 doors. It consists of three sections: the *andaruni* (internal area), where family members lived; the *biruni* (external area), used for entertaining

guests; and the *khadameh* (servants' quarters). They are set around four courtyards, the largest of which boasts a fountain pool. From mid-afternoon (depending on the month), sunlight and stained glass combine to bathe some rooms in brilliant colour.

To get here, walk south past the Khan-e Borujerdi towards the blue conical tower of the Imamzadeh-ye Sultan Mir Ahmad, turn right and the entrance is on the left. There is a handicraft shop selling locally made silks, but the more alluring courtyard teahouse has been closed down.

Khan-e Borujerdi   خانه بروجردی ها
Legend has it that when Sayyed Jafar Natanzi, a merchant known as Borujerdi, met Sayyed Jafar Tabatabei to discuss taking his daughter's hand in marriage, Agha Tabatabei set one condition: his daughter must be able to live in a home at least as lovely as his own. The result – finished some 18 years later – was the **Khan-e Borujerdi** (off Alavi St; admission IR3000; ☉ 8am-sunset).

The home originally consisted of two sections, an *andaruni* and a *biruni*, but today only the *andaruni* is open to the public. What you see is an ornately decorated courtyard, laid out around a central fountain pool. At its far end is a two-storey reception hall sumptuously decorated with splendid motifs above the *iwan* entrance, intricate stalactite mouldings, fine glass and mirror work and frescoes painted by Kamal ol-Molk, the foremost Iranian artist of the time. In one of the smaller adjoining rooms, a carpet design is carved on the ceiling.

If you ask nicely you might be allowed to climb to the roof for views over the courtyard and the distinctive six-sided, domed *badgirs*, which have become the symbol of Kashan.

Follow the signs from Alavi St up a small incline opposite the Khan-e Ameriha.

Khan-e Abbasian   خانه عباسیان
Famous for its ground-breaking design, the **Khan-e Abbasian** (off Alavi St; admission IR3000; ☉ 8am-sunset) is a bewildering complex of six buildings spread over several levels. Unusually, the numerous courtyards are designed to enhance the sense of space by becoming larger as they step up, culminating in an open courtyard on top. The high porticos and reception halls are decorated as

extravagantly as you'd expect, with the usual plaster reliefs, fine mirror work and exceptionally beautiful and detailed stained-glass windows.

It's down a lane parallel to Alavi St, starting opposite the Sultan Mir Ahmad Hammam.

HAMMAM-E SULTAN MIR AHMAD   حمام سلطان میراحمد

A few metres from the entrance to the Khan-e Borujerdi, **Hammam-e Sultan Mir Ahmad** (☎ 422 0038; off Alavi St; admission IR3000; ☿ 8am-5pm, to 7pm summer) is a superb example of an Iranian bathhouse, built around 450 years ago. A recent restoration has stripped away 17 layers of plaster (look just inside the second room to see them) to reveal the original *sarough,* a type of plaster made of milk, egg white, soy flour and lime, which is said to be stronger than cement. There is usually an English-speaking guide at the door who can show you around. The *hammam* no longer operates as a teahouse.

OLD CITY WALLS   دیوارهای قدیمی شهر

As one of the few remnants of the ancient city of Kashan, this circular **wall** and an attractive park to the southeast are worth a quick look if you're visiting the nearby traditional houses. Enter the interior of the circular walls from the southeast and climb the northeastern part of the wall for some city views.

AGHA BOZORG MOSQUE & MADRASEH
مسجد و مدرسه آقا بزرگ

Arguably the finest Islamic complex in Kashan and one of the best of the mid-19th century, **Agha Bozorg Mosque & Madraseh** (admission IR3000; ☿ 8am-noon & 2-4pm, to 5pm summer) is

---

> **WHO'S THAT KNOCKING AT MY DOOR?**
>
> As you wander around the narrow streets of Kashan look carefully at the doors. Most have two knockers: one round and fat, the other long and thin. These were designed to give off different sounds so that those in the house would be able to tell whether a man or woman was knocking and so decide who should go to the door – vital in a society where women lived in purdah (in seclusion or behind a veil).

---

famous for its precise architecture, including four storeys beginning in a large sunken courtyard, an austere dome and unusual lofty *badgirs* above the entrance. It also has a fine portal and mihrab (niche indicating the direction of Mecca) at the back. The imposing dome is flanked by two minarets adorned with coloured tiles in geometric designs. Quranic inscriptions and mosaics stand out against the mud-brick used for much of the construction. The wooden front door is said to have as many studs as there are verses in the Quran.

IMAMZADEH-E HABIB IBN-E MUSA
امامزاده حبیب ابن موسی

The revered Shah Abbas I might well be turning in his grave at the senseless destruction wrought on what was once a fine Seljuk-era **shrine** (off Imam Khomeini St). Shah Abbas chose to be buried here because he revered the saint Habib Ibn-e Musa. The king's low, black porphyry tombstone is near the shrine's entrance, but almost everything else from the original tomb has been cleared away and replaced by a bigger, uglier concrete monstrosity.

Two of the highlights, a magnificent lustre mihrab and a carpet woven for the shah's tomb, are in the National Museum of Iran (p104).

SOLTANIYEH MOSQUE   مسجد سلطانیه

Lost in the midst of the labyrinthine bazaar is the Seljuk-era **Soltaniyeh Mosque**. The current structure was built in 1808 by Fath Ali Shah and now houses a madraseh, which is not open to women.

ALONG THE FIN ROAD

There are several sights worth a quick look on the road to Fin Garden. If you decide to walk, it's all downhill if you start at Fin. Otherwise, jumping on and off buses is easy enough, or hire a taxi.

Imamzadeh-ye Abu Lolou امامزاده ابو لولو
Off the left of the road as you come from Kashan, the **Imamzadeh-ye Abu Lolou** (Amir Kabir Rd; ☿ 9am-4pm) is the shrine to the man believed to be the assassin of Omar, the second Muslim caliph. It dates to the Seljuk or Mongol periods, though it has been heavily renovated since. The shrine is notable for its fine, slender dome.

Shahzadeh-ye Ibrahim شاهزاده ابراهیم

The delightful **Shahzadeh-ye Ibrahim** (Amir Kabir Rd; ☺ 9am-4pm) shrine was built in 1894 and boasts European-style painted ceilings, colourful tiles, tall minarets and a pretty courtyard. The conical, tiled roof is distinctive to this area and chances are you'll have seen it on posters long before you arrive. It's clearly visible from the main road to Fin.

Tappeh-ye Seyalk (Sialk) تپه سیلک

One of the oldest and richest archaeological sites in central Iran, the **Tappeh-ye Seyalk** (Sialk, Seyalk Mound; off Amir Kabir Rd; ☺ 7.30am-sunset) has given up a plethora of interesting pottery pieces, metal tools and domestic implements made from stone, clay and bone. They date from as early as the 4th millennium BC. More significant, perhaps, is the structure itself – what is emerging from the dust is clearly a ziggurat (stepped pyramidal temple), and some Iranians are claiming this predates those of the Mesopotamians.

It is still a (seasonal) working dig and, while visitors are welcomed, there are few facilities. Most finds have been moved to museums, including the National Museum of Iran in Tehran (p104) and the Louvre in Paris. There's no charge, but if you are shown around, a tip is appreciated.

Seyalk is halfway between Kashan and Fin – that's 4.5km from either – on the north side of the road.

Bagh-e Tarikhi-ye Fin (Fin Garden) باغ تاریخی فین

Designed for Shah Abbas I, **Bagh-e Tarikhi-ye Fin** (Fin Garden; Amir Kabir Rd; admission IR5000; ☺ 8am-sunset) is a classical Persian vision of paradise and is renowned as one of the finest gardens in Iran. It's famous for its spring water, which flows into the garden via the **Lasegah**, an octagonal pool behind the garden. From here the water, which has unusually high levels of mercury, is channelled through several pools and fountains, watering the garden's orchards and tall trees, before continuing on down the road in *jubs* (canals, pronounced 'joobs').

At the centre of the garden is **Shotorgalu-ye Safavi**, Abbas' two-storey pavilion. At the rear is the Shotorgalu-ye Qajari, built by the Qajars, with ornately painted ceilings and walls. Nearby is a delightful **teahouse** (☺ 8am-4pm, to 6pm summer), which sells cheap tea and kababs.

But it is the **bathhouse** that is most historically significant as the place where Iranian nationalist hero Amir Kabir was murdered. Mirza Taqi Khan, known as Amir Kabir, served as prime minister under Nasir od-Din Shah from 1848. He was a moderniser who instituted significant change, especially in the fields of education and administration. But his popularity proved unpopular in the royal court and the shah's mother eventually persuaded her son that he had to go. Amir Kabir was imprisoned in Fin Garden and eventually murdered in the bathhouse, though some say he slashed his own wrists.

The gardens are in the village of Fin, 9km southwest of central Kashan at the end of Amir Kabir St. You can get here by shuttle taxi (IR2000), taxi *dar baste* (closed door; IR10,000) or minibus (IR500) from central Kashan.

Sleeping

Kashan has so few hotels and so little competition that the overall standard is shockingly low and value for money is poor. There is, however, some cause for hope, with the city's first traditional hotel having opened in 2007. The cheapest places can be found around Motahhari Sq (Darvaze Dolat Sq) near the entrance to the bazaar.

Mosaferkhaneh-ye Gochariyan (☎ 444 5495; Abazar St; s/d IR40,000/80,000) This bare-bones *mosaferkhaneh* has small, Spartan rooms with rock-hard beds. The share bathrooms could be cleaner and no English is spoken, but it's cheap.

Golestan Inn (☎ 444 6793; Motahhari Sq; s/d IR100,000/150,000) The friendly owners don't speak much English, but the location and small, primitive, but clean, rooms keep it popular with backpackers, despite the typically hard beds and shared bathrooms. Some rooms have vaulted ceilings and windows looking down on the bazaar.

our pick **Khan-e Ehsan** (☎ /fax 444 6833, 0913 276 2561; www.kajweb.com; off Fazel-e Navaji St; ☐) At long last Kashan has its first traditional hotel, and it was worth the wait. The house is run by friendly Mr Sater, who aims to use money from the rooms to help fund his NGO, which promotes the arts, and is based in the house. There is a small performance space (poetry the night we stayed) and a museum, and staying here is a great way to meet young, educated Iranians. Rooms come in a variety of shapes and sizes, some with raw, arched earthen ceilings, others more modern. We were the very first guests and prices had yet to be set, but expect to pay about €7 to €10 for a dorm bed and €20 to €35 for a room. It's easy to miss, down a small lane opposite the street leading to Agha Bozorg Mosque. All up, *kheyli khub* (very good)!

Sayyah Hotel (☎ 444 4535; www.sayyahhotel.com; Abazar St; s/tw US$27/33, r without shower US$20/27; **P** **✕** **▣**) Sayyah is well located and has small, green, uninspiring rooms, some of which have fine views of the old city. Service varies from friendly and engaging to disinterested, depending on who is working. Prices include breakfast.

Amir Kabir Hotel (☎ 530 4091-95; fax 530 4090; Amir Kabir Rd; s/tw US$35/53; **P** **✕**) Way out near Fin Gardens, the overly large Amir Kabir claims to have had a makeover but if that's true then they should be asking for a refund. The rooms are still tired and overpriced, though discounts are usually possible. Minibuses to town run past the front door, or a taxi will cost IR10,000.

Khan-e Ameriha (Alavi St; **✕**) When completed, parts of this wondrous traditional house will be open as a lavishly furnished and decorated traditional hotel. Expect to pay more than US$100 a night. Also see p227.

Eating
RESTAURANTS
With the much-loved Delpazir recently closed, finding a memorable (for the right reasons) meal in Kashan can be a trial. If something good opens, do let us know.

Sayyah Restaurant (☎ 444 4535; Abazar St; meals IR40,000; **✕** 7am-9pm) Under the hotel of the same name, the standard Iranian fare here gets mixed reviews but none of them has criticised the size of the serves.

The garden restaurants lining the road before Fin Garden are the best places to eat and are hugely popular with Kashanis, especially in the evenings. Most have water running soothingly through the eating area and the whole experience is quite social.

Jawed Traditional Restaurant (☎ 533 7123; Amir Kabir Rd; meals IR35,000-60,000; **✕** 11.30am-3pm & 6-11pm) Arguably the best of the garden restaurants, Jawed serves several varieties of delicious kababs and some less meaty dishes, all washed down with *chay* (tea) and qalyan (water pipe).

TEAHOUSES & CAFÉS
Hammam-e Khan (☎ 445 2572; Bazaar; **✕** 8am-9pm) Down a few stairs from the bazaar (look for the sign), this old bathhouse is now a genuinely local teahouse, complete with tweeting birds, neon lights, disco ball, plastic-covered cushions and…locals (plus the odd Iranian tourist). Be sure to specify if you only want tea, not the accompanying biscuits and dates, which cost extra.

Chaykhaneh Caravan Sara (Timche-ye Amin al Dowleh, in the Bazaar; **✕** 8am-8pm) This tiny place under the cavernous dome is rightly famous for its richly flavoured *dizi* (soup-stew meal) and tea, and you can go onto the roof (buy something first).

Getting There & Away
BUS, MINIBUS & SAVARI
As with Qom, most buses that pass through Kashan are going to or from Tehran. They are supposed to stop at the **bus terminal** (Molla Sadra Blvd) north of the city but often will leave from Montazeri Sq, where an office on the south corner sells tickets. There are regular Volvo services to Esfahan (IR21,000, four hours) and Tehran (IR25,000, 3½ hours) via Qom (IR10,000, one hour), and *mahmooly* (normal, usually old Mercedes) buses leave less frequently for about half the price.

Minibuses to Qom (IR7000, two hours) leave from the southwestern corner of Vali-asr Sq (Madkhal Sq; it's the one with the New Age ziggurat in the middle) about every hour. You might also find savaris to Tehran here.

TRAIN
There are at least three trains a day between Kashan and Tehran (IR16,500, 3½ hours, 217km), but they generally pass in the middle of the night. There are also daily trains to Esfahan (four hours, 270km), and a daily nonluxury service to Kerman (10 hours, 711km), via Yazd (six hours, 475km), which passes Kashan at about 9pm and arrives in Kerman after 7am.

The **train station** (☎ 446 0010; Molla Sodra Blvd) is about 2km north of the city centre.

Getting Around
Taxis, shuttle taxis and buses run regularly between Fin and 15 Khordad Sq, or a taxi within town should cost about IR6000. For longer-term drivers, see Tours (p225).

AROUND KASHAN

Several villages can be visited on day trips from Kashan. The most interesting are detailed in the following sections, though if you want to get off the track, **Niasar** (at 1710m above sea level) is an easy 35km savari or minibus trip away in a picturesque mountain setting. The sights include a well-preserved Sassanian-era fire temple, a unique, Parthian-era cave built as a Mithraist temple, the Niasar waterfall and famous rose fields, which bloom during late spring.

About 50km west of Kashan, **Mashhad-e Ardehal** is home to a once-magnificent Seljuk-era tomb that has suffered badly at the hands of what one reader accurately described as a 'megalomaniac religious building program'. Shame. The tomb is for Sultan Ali ibn Mohammad, the son of the Fifth Imam, who was murdered here. It's only really worth the trip for the carpet-washing ceremony (see below).

Namak Lake (Salt Lake) is about 60km east of Mashhad at the western edge of the Dasht-e Kavir. Guides in Kashan offer desert day trips to sand dunes near **Maranjab** (where there is also a restored caravanserai) and the cracked white surface of the lake.

Abyaneh   ابیانه
☎ 0362 / pop – a few old ladies most of the time / elev 2235m

The ancient village of Abyaneh is the perfect antidote to Iran's bustling, traffic-clogged cities. Serenely situated at the foot of **Mt Karkas** (3899m), Abyaneh's steep, twisting lanes of mud and stone wind through a maze of red mud-brick houses with lattice windows and fragile wooden balconies. It's testament to both the age and isolation of Abyaneh that the elderly residents speak Middle Persian, an earlier incarnation of Farsi that largely disappeared centuries ago.

The village is at least 1500 years old and faces east across a picturesque valley. It was built this way to maximise the sun it receives and minimise the effects of howling gales in winter. And if you come here in winter you'll understand why – it's freezing! In summer, however, it's refreshingly cool and Abyaneh is most lively, filled with residents returning from winter in Tehran and tourists haggling with colourfully clad, toothless old women over the price of dried apples (they take no prisoners).

Abyaneh is best appreciated by just wandering, but do look for the 14th-century **Imamzadeh-ye Yahya** with its conical, blue-tiled roof, and the **Zeyaratgah shrine** with its tiny pool and views. Probably the most beautiful building is the 11th-century **Jameh Mosque** (Masjed-e Jameh), with its walnut-wood mihrab and ancient carvings. Abyaneh's houses are mainly two-storey; people live downstairs in winter and upstairs in summer.

It's fun to cross the river and climb up to the high walls of a **castle**, from where the views (and photos) of the valley and the village are spectacular.

SLEEPING & EATING

Abyaneh Hotel (☎ 436 2223-25; fax 436 2226; s/tw/tr with breakfast IR330,000/550,000/690,000; P) Located on a hill above Abyaneh, this

---

THE CARPET-WASHING CEREMONY OF ARDEHAL

On the second Friday of the Iranian month of Mehr (usually early October, unless there is a clashing religious festival), the *qali shuran* (carpet-washing ceremony) is held at Mashhad-e Ardehal. The ceremony commemorates the assassination of Sultan Ali ibn Mohammad, the son of the Fifth Imam, who had settled in Fin (near Kashan) to bring Shia Islam to the people. After living in Fin and Ardahal (during summer) for several years, jealous officials plotted to assassinate him because he had become too powerful. He was attacked, but with support arriving from Fin was able to hold out for 10 days. Legend has it that it was only concluded after the desperate plotters sent 40 naked women ahead of them. It was too much for the Sultan, who led his men away to begin praying on carpets. They were murdered as they prayed. Later, followers from Fin placed the Sultan's body on a carpet, washed it in accordance with tradition and buried it. They also washed the carpet.

On the anniversary of his murder, thousands of locals, joined by visitors from Kashan, Qom and as far away as Yazd, carry a symbolic carpet from the crypt, beat it to symbolise their hatred of the murderers, and then wash it in a local spring.

multi-storey place is the only hotel and restaurant in town. It's taken years to complete and the finished product is very comfortable. Rooms are modern, well-equipped and some have panoramic views, and the family who runs it are friendly. Rates are high, but given how the place is often empty, negotiation is eminently possible. The huge restaurant (open noon to 4pm and 8pm to 10pm) serves a long menu of generous Persian dishes (IR35,000 to IR70,000).

GETTING THERE & AWAY

Abyaneh is 82km from Kashan and not easy to reach. Minibuses (IR6500) run directly between Abyaneh and Kashan once or twice a day, depending on demand. The bus usually returns to Kashan in the early afternoon, or you could try hitching back. Alternatively, take a minibus from Kashan towards Natanz and tell the driver to let you off at the turn-off. Then wait for a lift from whatever is passing for the remaining 22km. The Natanz nuclear facility is near here; *do not* get caught taking photos of it.

Most people just hire a taxi. See p225 for recommended driver-guides; they charge about IR150,000 for the trip plus two or three hours in Abyaneh.

Natanz   نطنز
☎ 0362 / pop 12,000 / elev 1655m

The old, well-treed village of Natanz, on the lower slopes of Mt Karkas, has two main attractions – neither of which is an underground uranium enrichment plant, which is several kilometres away. The magnificent **Jameh Mosque** (Masjed-e Jameh; ☾ 8am-noon & 2pm-sunset) and **Imamzadeh-ye Abd al-Samad** stand side by side in what was an important early Islamic complex. The tomb belongs to a renowned local Sufi mystic of the 11th century, while the mosque is one of the best-preserved of all Ilkhanid-era buildings. The highlight is a tall, exquisite portal with turquoise, black-and-white tiled calligraphy that is satisfyingly symmetrical without being over the top. The nearby entrance to the mosque has an intricately carved wooden door. It's a good 2km walk (mainly downhill) from where the buses usually stop; walk north, turn east at the roundabout, then north again at the tree-lined avenue; or just ask 'koja imamzadeh?'.

Natanz's two hotels are usually quieter than a small-town mortuary.

Hotel Shahin (☎ 424 2402; s/tw US$15/30; ꩜), in a small square about 300m from the Jameh Mosque, is a modest little place with clean, bright rooms and a welcoming owner.

Hotel Saraban (☎ /fax 424 2603; r US$30; P ꩜), on the main road near where the buses stop, has unexciting but functional rooms, most with a balcony. You'll want to bargain, but it will almost certainly be a futile endeavour. There's a similarly unexciting restaurant in the hotel and *kababis* nearby.

Regular slow buses between Esfahan (IR11,000, two hours) and Kashan (IR6000, one hour) pass through Natanz – wait outside the Saraban.

ESFAHAN   اصفهان
☎ 0311 / pop 1,630,000 / elev 1574m

Esfahan is Iran's masterpiece, the jewel of ancient Persia and one of the finest cities in the Islamic world. The exquisite blue mosaic tiles of Esfahan's Islamic buildings, its expansive bazaar and its gorgeous bridges demand as much of your time as you can spare. It is a city for walking, getting lost in the bazaar, dozing in beautiful gardens, and drinking tea and chatting to locals in the marvellous teahouses. More than anything else, though, Esfahan is a place for savouring the high refinements of Persian culture most evident in and around Imam Sq – the Imam Mosque, Sheikh Lotfollah Mosque, Ali Qapu Palace and Chehel Sotun Palace.

Such is Esfahan's grandeur that it is easy to agree with the famous 16th-century half-rhyme 'Esfahan nesf-e jahan' (Esfahan is half the world). Robert Byron was slightly more geographically specific when he ranked 'Isfahan among those rarer places, like Athens or Rome, which are the common refreshment of humanity'. Today it is a Unesco World Heritage site.

There are, however, some less-than-refreshing elements to the city of Esfahan. This is the country's third-largest city and capital of Esfahan province, and the outskirts are home to plenty of heavy industry, including a much-discussed nuclear facility. So Esfahan has traffic jams and air pollution; the long-awaited underground railway should help – if indeed it is ever finished.

History

Little is known of Esfahan's ancient history, but the Ateshkadeh-ye Esfahan (Esfahan Fire Temple; p244) and pillars of the Shahrestan Bridge (p243), both from the Sassanid period, attest to its longevity. The Buyid period saw an explosion of construction and by the late 10th century the walled city of Esfahan was home to dozens of mosques and hundreds of wealthy homes. In 1047 the Seljuks made Esfahan their capital and during the next 180 years it was adorned with the magnificently geometric Seljuk style of architecture, several prominent parts of which remain.

The Mongols put an end to that, and it wasn't until the glorious reign of the Safavid Shah Abbas I (also revered as Shah Abbas the Great), which began in 1587, that Esfahan was again Iran's premier city. After moving the capital from Qazvin to Esfahan, Abbas set about transforming it into a city worthy of an empire at its peak. His legacy is the incomparable Imam Sq (p238) and artistic advances – particularly in carpet weaving – that were celebrated and envied as far away as Europe. Subsequent Safavid rulers also contributed to Esfahan's skyline, but little more than a century after Abbas' death the dynasty was finished and the capital transferred first to Shiraz and later Tehran.

Orientation

The main street, tree-lined Chahar Bagh (Four Gardens), was built in 1597 and was once lined with many palaces and the four gardens after which it is named. Although it's over 5km long, most travellers base themselves along the middle section of the street, called Chahar Bagh Abbasi St, between Si-o-Seh Bridge (Pol-e Si-o-Seh) and Takhti Junction. Most of the sights, shops, offices and hotels are within easy walking distance from this part of Esfahan. The few outlying attractions are easily visited by shuttle or private taxi.

The Zayandeh River starts in the Zagros Mountains, flows east through the heart of Esfahan and eventually peters out in the Dasht-e Kavir. It separates the older and low-rise northern part of the city from the Armenian quarter in Jolfa, southwest of Si-o-Seh Bridge, and the fast-growing southern part of town where there is no restriction on building heights.

The main Kaveh bus terminal is a few kilometres north of town along Chahar Bagh St; the smaller Soffeh terminal in the south caters to more southerly destinations.

MAPS

Gita Shenasi's *New Map of Esfahan* (IR15,000; 2006) is available in bookstores. There is also a free tourist map available at the tourist information office (see p236) in several languages.

Information

BOOKSHOPS

Bookshops in the complex opposite the Abbasi Hotel also sell a few English-language books on Iran.

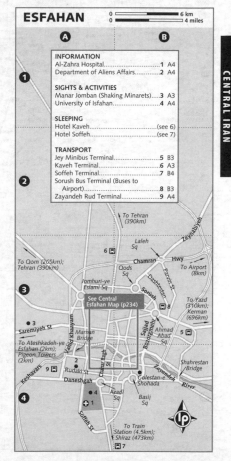

ESFAHAN

INFORMATION	
Al-Zahra Hospital	1 A4
Department of Aliens Affairs	2 A4

SIGHTS & ACTIVITIES	
Manar Jomban (Shaking Minarets)	3 A3
University of Isfahan	4 A4

SLEEPING	
Hotel Kaveh	(see 6)
Hotel Soffeh	(see 7)

TRANSPORT	
Jey Minibus Terminal	5 B3
Kaveh Terminal	6 A3
Soffeh Terminal	7 B4
Sorush Bus Terminal (Buses to Airport)	8 B3
Zayandeh Rud Terminal	9 A4

CENTRAL IRAN

Abbasi Hotel Bookshop (Map p234; ☎ 223 2967; Shahid Medani St; ⏱ 7.30am-10.30pm) Expensive, but has big range, including many out-of-print works on Iran. **Kowsar International Hotel** (Map p234; ☎ 624 0230; Mellat Blvd) On the ground floor.

EMERGENCY
Ambulance (☎ 115)

Tourist police (Map p234; ☎ 221 5953; Chahar Bagh Abbasi St; ⏱ 24hr) Very helpful English-speaking officers can be found at this booth in the middle of the street outside the Madraseh-ye Chahar Bagh.

INTERNET ACCESS
Esfahan's *coffeenets* (internet cafés) seem to open and close faster than the door of a

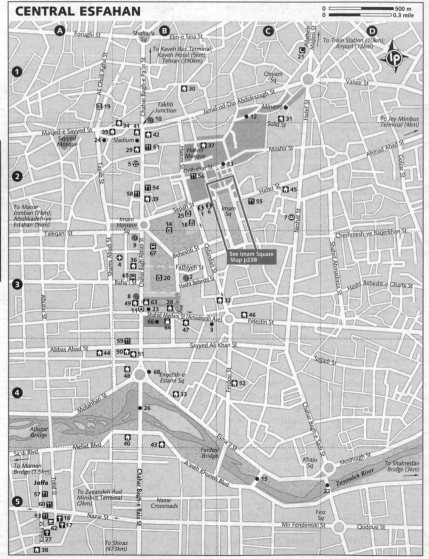

CENTRAL IRAN

filthy squat toilet, but you should always be able to find something along Chahar Bagh Abbasi St. More-established *coffeenets*:

Central Library of Esfahan (Map p234; ☎ 222 3698; Goldasteh Ave; per hr IR5000; ☒ 8am-8pm Sat-Thu) Friendly, English-speaking staff and loads of terminals. Could be faster.

Negareh Internet Café (Map p234; ☎ 220 8645; Chahar Bagh Abbasi St; per hr IR6000; ☒ 7am-11pm) Cheap, very fast, with an associated travel agency for tours and tickets. It's inside an arcade, upstairs on the left. Arctic air-con. Some machines have Skype.

Rose Internet (Map p234; Imam Hossein Sq; per hr IR8000; ☒ 8am-9pm Sat-Thu, 9.30am-7pm Fri) New, fast machines, and ports for laptops.

Sky Net Internet (Map p234; Jamal-od Din Abdolrazagh St, near Takhti Junction; per hr IR8000; ☒ 10.30am-10pm) Near the budget accommodation.

Several carpet shops around Imam Sq let you check email for free in exchange for the opportunity to bend your ear about carpets, including Nomad Carpet Shop (p250) and Aladdin Carpets (p250).

MEDICAL SERVICES
Al-Zahra Hospital (Map p233; ☎ 668 4444; Soffeh St) Best hospital in Esfahan. English-speaking doctors.

Dr Hosseini Pharmacy (Map p234; ☎ 222 3511; Shahid Medani St; ☒ 24hr) Central and well stocked.
Esfahan Hospital (Map p234; ☎ 223 0015; Shams Abadi St) Convenient and recommended.

MONEY
To change, head straight to Sepah St, where the Bank Melli and exchange shops compete for your forex.
Bank Melli Central Branch (Bank Melli Markazi; Map p234; Sepah St) Upstairs. English is spoken.
Jahan-e Arz Money Changer (Map p234; Sepah St; ☒ 9am-4pm Sat-Thu)

POST
DHL (Map p234; ☎ 221 3520; Shahid Medani Ave; ☒ 8am-5pm Sat-Wed, 8am-noon Thu) Upstairs in the complex opposite Abbasi Hotel.
Main post office (Map p234; Neshat St) East of Imam Sq; come here to post anything big – like a carpet. Also has EMS.
Post office (Map p238; Imam Sq) Postcards and letters.

TELEPHONE
International telephone office (Map p234; Chahar Bagh Abbasi St; ☒ 8am-2.15pm & 3.30-7pm Sat-Thu)

ESFAHAN IN...

Two days

Start by taking the **'Half of the World' Walking Tour** (p245), which will take up most of your first day. Dinner at the traditional **Sofreh Khaneh Sonnati** (p248) on the square is a good option. On the second day, head back to **Imam Square** (p238) in the morning for a more leisurely look around and to suss out the **carpet shops** (p250) for something that might look good on your floor. After lunch, wander down to the **Zayandeh River** (p242) for a bridge-appreciation walk, stopping for tea and poetry recitals along the way.

Four days

On the third day, take the bus out to **Manar Jomban** (Shaking Minarets; p244), then walk up to the **Ateshkadeh-ye Esfahan** (p244) for a (hopefully clear) view over Esfahan. Walk back into town along the riverbank, watching the cloth-makers drying their wares on the river-bed and stopping for tea with the locals. Get back to **Jolfa** (p243) in time to see the striking frescoes of **Vank Cathedral** (p244), then spend the evening eating in the relaxed Armenian quarter.

On day four, just chill out in the square, on a bridge, in the garden around the **Hasht Behesht Palace** (p242); or in your favourite teahouse with a book, or renew your visa.

TOURIST INFORMATION

Tourist information office (Map p238; ☎ 221 3840, 221 6831; Imam Sq; ☽ 8.30am-5pm Sat-Thu & 2.30-6pm Fri) Under the Ali Qapu Palace; helpful English-speaking staff have maps and brochures on city and province. The Esfahan Tourist Guides Association operates from here; see Tours (below).

TOURS

Several carpet shops offer trips into the Zagros Mountains to visit nomads. In our experience, however, none is worth recommending specifically. Be very specific about what you want to see and what you're paying for, and don't pay more than half upfront. The following are probably better options:

Azade Kazemi (☎ 0913 327 9626; azadekazemi@ hotmail.com) Highly knowledgeable Spanish- and English-speaking guide.

Esfahan Tourist Guides Association (Map p238; ☎ 221 3840, 221 6831; Imam Sq) Based at the tourist information office; has 150 guides speaking English, Spanish, Arabic, French and German. Guides can lead a variety of trips; contact them a day ahead if you want anything more than a local day trip. Full day's guiding costs IR210,000.

Maryam Shafiei (☎ 0913 326 6127; marie13572002@ yahoo.fr) French- and English-speaking guide with a good reputation; Esfahan and beyond from €20 a day.

TRAVEL AGENCIES

Iran Travel & Tourism Tour (Map p234; ☎ 222 3010; irantravel1964@yahoo.com; Shahid Medani St) Opposite Abbasi Hotel; efficient English-speaking staff book plane, train and even ferry tickets. Car hire and local tours can be arranged (per day with driver and guide IR280,000).

VISA EXTENSIONS

Department of Aliens Affairs (Map p233; ☎ English-speaking officers at Tourist Police 221 5953; Rudaki St; ☽ 7am-1.30pm Sat-Wed, 7am-noon Thu) Esfahan is not the express extension it once was. The Department of Aliens Affairs is in a large, drab-looking government building. Show your passport at the gate, pick up the paperwork at the office in the courtyard and follow pointed fingers from there. It normally takes three days, but several travellers have reported getting same-day service if they arrived by 8am and showed a pre-booked plane/bus ticket. To get here, walk or take a shuttle taxi 1.7km south from the southern end of Si-o-Seh Bridge (IR700) to Shariati St, then take another shuttle taxi (IR1500) 3km west. The building is about 400m after the third major intersection and a slight bend right and left, on the right (north) side of the road. Alternatively, get the Tourist Police on Chahar Bagh Abbasi St to help – they can put you on a bus that stops outside the office or give a taxi directions; very helpful! For more on extending visas, see 'More Time, Please' (p395).

Sights

These sights are listed roughly north to south.

JAMEH MOSQUE   مسجد جامع

The **Jameh Mosque** (Masjed-e Jameh; Map p234; Allameh Majlesi St; admission IR5000; ☽ 8-11am & 1-5pm) is a veritable museum of Islamic architecture and still a working mosque. Within a couple of hours you can see and compare 800 years of Islamic design, with each example near to the pinnacle of its age. The range is quite stunning: from the geometric elegance of the Seljuks, through to the

Mongol period and on to the refinements of the more baroque Safavid style. At more than 20,000 sq metres, it is also the biggest mosque in Iran.

Religious activity on this site is believed to date back to the Sassanid Zoroastrians, and the first sizable mosque was built by the Seljuks in the 11th century. Of this, the two large domes above the north and south *iwans* (rectangular halls opening onto a courtyard) have survived intact, with most of the remainder destroyed by fire in the 12th century. The mosque was rebuilt in 1121, with later rulers making their own enhancements.

In the centre of the main courtyard, which is surrounded by four contrasting *iwans,* is an attractive **ablutions fountain** designed to imitate the Kaaba at Mecca; would-be haji pilgrims would use it to practise the appropriate rituals. The two-storey porches around the courtyard's perimeter were constructed in the late 15th century.

The **south iwan** is the most elaborate, with Mongol-era stalactite mouldings, some splendid 15th-century mosaics on the side

walls, and two minarets. The **north iwan** has a wonderful monumental porch with the Seljuk's customary Kufic inscriptions and austere brick pillars in the sanctuary.

The **west iwan** was originally built by the Seljuks but later decorated by the Safavids. It has mosaics that are more geometric than those of the southern hall. The courtyard is topped by a *maazeneh,* a small raised platform with a conical roof from where the faithful used to be called to prayer.

To fully appreciate this mosque you must go into the fine interior rooms. The **Room of Sultan Uljeitu** (a 14th-century Shiite convert) is home to one of the mosque's greatest treasures – an exquisite stucco mihrab awash with dense Quranic inscriptions and floral designs. Next door is the Timurid-era **Winter Hall** (Beit al-Sheta), built in 1448 and lit by alabaster skylights – ask the caretaker to turn off the neon (or do it yourself) to see the full effect.

The room beneath the grand **Nezam al-Molk Dome** and the Seljuk-era hypostyle **prayer halls** either side just breathe history, while at the other end of the complex the

CENTRAL IRAN

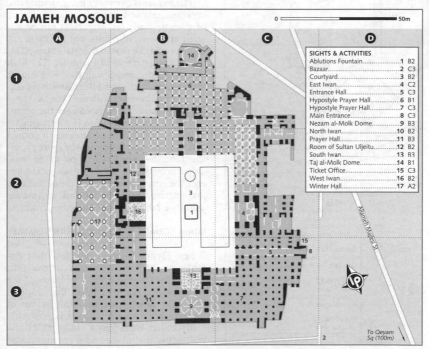

JAMEH MOSQUE

0 ———— 50m

SIGHTS & ACTIVITIES	
Ablutions Fountain	1 B2
Bazaar	2 C3
Courtyard	3 B2
East Iwan	4 C2
Entrance Hall	5 C3
Hypostyle Prayer Hall	6 B1
Hypostyle Prayer Hall	7 C3
Main Entrance	8 C3
Nezam al-Molk Dome	9 B3
North Iwan	10 B2
Prayer Hall	11 B3
Room of Sultan Uljeitu	12 B2
South Iwan	13 B3
Taj al-Molk Dome	14 B1
Ticket Office	15 C3
West Iwan	16 B2
Winter Hall	17 A2

Allameh Majles St

To Qeyam
Sq (100m)

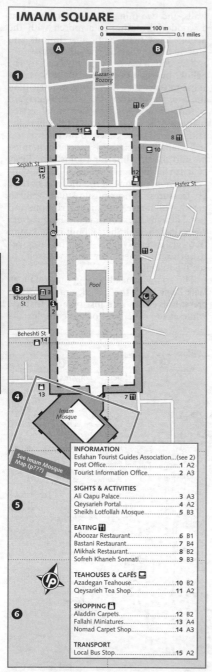

IMAM SQUARE

Taj al-Molk Dome is widely considered to be the finest brick dome ever built. While relatively small, it is said to be mathematically perfect, and has survived dozens of earthquakes with nary a blemish for more than 900 years. To reach it you walk through a forest of imposing pillars. These domes are among the oldest parts of the mosque.

The **ticket office** is at the **main entrance** and once you've paid admission the gatekeeper will summon an English-speaking guide to show you around.

BAZAR-E BOZORG

بازار بزرگ

Esfahan's **Bazar-e Bozorg** (Great Bazaar; Map p234; ⏱ approximately 9am-8pm Sat-Thu) links Imam Sq with the Jameh Mosque, 1.7km northeast. The bazaar's arched passageways are topped by a series of small domes, each with an aperture at its apex spilling shafts of light onto the commerce below. While the oldest parts of the bazaar, around the Jameh Mosque, are more than a thousand years old, most of what you see today was built during Shah Abbas' aggressive expansions in the early 1600s.

The bazaar is a maze of lanes, madrasehs, caravanserais and *timcheh,* arcaded centres of a single trade (eg carpet). It can be entered at dozens of points, but the main entrance is via the **Qeysarieh Portal** (Map p238) at the northern end of Imam Sq. The high gateway is decorated with tiles and, higher up, frescoes by the great Reza Abbasi depicting Shah Abbas' war with the Uzbeks. These paintings have deteriorated over the centuries and a slow restoration is continuing.

Industries tend to congregate in certain areas of the bazaar. Among the more prominent are the carpet sellers, off to the west. Trade is busiest in the mornings. Undoubtedly the best way to discover the bazaar is to just wander; if you get lost, ask anyone for 'Naqsh-e Jahan' or the 'Masjed-e Jameh'.

IMAM SQUARE (NAQSH-E JAHAN SQUARE)

(میدان امام (میدان نقش جهان

When French poet Renier described Esfahan as 'half of the world' in the 16th century, it was the myriad wonders of the square called Naqsh-e Jahan that inspired him. The description wouldn't be out of place today, because while it is now officially called **Imam Square** (Map p238) few people use that name and it remains home to arguably the most majestic collection of buildings in the Islamic world.

Naqsh-e Jahan means 'pattern of the world', and it's a world that owes much to the vision of Shah Abbas the Great. Begun in 1602 as the centrepiece of Abbas' new capital, the square was designed as home to the finest jewels of the Safavid empire – the incomparable Imam Mosque, the supremely elegant Sheikh Lotfollah Mosque and the indulgent and lavishly decorated Ali Qapu Palace and Qeysarieh Portal. At 512m long and 163m wide, this immense space is the second-largest square on earth – only Mao Zedong's severe Tiananmen Sq in Beijing is bigger.

The square has changed little since it was built. The upper level of arched arcades surrounding the square is empty these days, though long-talked-about plans to restore it for use as a museum of Esfahan's history are still being discussed. The open space has been reconstituted several times, most recently by the Pahlavis, who added the fountains. At either end of the square, you can still see the goal posts used in regular polo games 400 years ago. You'll see these polo matches depicted on miniatures for sale around the square.

The square is best visited in the late afternoon and early evening when local families flood in to outnumber the Iranian and foreign tourists. This is also when the fountains are turned on, the light softens and the splendid architecture is illuminated; you can't beat the view from the Qeysarieh Tea Shop (p249).

Imam Mosque   مسجد امام

The **Imam Mosque** (Masjed-e Imam; Map p239; admission IR4000; ☾ 8am-sunset, 8am-11.30am & 12.30pm-sunset summer, closed 11am-1pm Friday) is one of the most beautiful mosques in the world. The richness of its blue-tiled mosaic designs and its perfectly proportioned Safavid-era architecture form a visually stunning monument to the imagination of Shah Abbas I and the ability of his architect. The sumptuous decoration of the mosque perfectly complements the architectural elegance.

Work started on the magnificent entrance portal in 1611, although it took four years to finish – look for mismatches in its apparent symmetry, intended to reflect the artist's humility in the face of Allah. It was

not until 1629, the last year of the reign of Shah Abbas, that the high dome, and therefore the mosque, was completed. Little has changed since.

Although each of the mosque's parts is a masterpiece, it is the unity of the overall design that leaves a lasting impression. The original purpose of the **entrance portal** had more to do with its location on the square than with the mosque's spiritual aims. Its function was primarily ornamental, providing a counterpoint to the Qeysarieh Portal at the entrance to the Bazar-e Bozorg. The foundation stones are of white marble from Ardestan and the portal itself, some 30m tall, is decorated with magnificent *moarraq kashi* (mosaics) featuring geometric designs, floral motifs and calligraphy by the most skilled artists of the age. The splendid niches contain complex stalactite mouldings in a honeycomb pattern, each panel with its own intricate design.

Although the portal was built to face the square, the mosque is oriented towards Mecca and a short, angled corridor neatly connects the square and the **inner courtyard**,

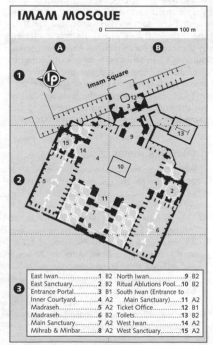

IMAM MOSQUE

0 —————— 100 m

East Iwan.................1 B2	North Iwan.................9 B2
East Sanctuary..........2 B2	Ritual Ablutions Pool...10 B2
Entrance Portal.........3 B1	South Iwan (Entrance to
Inner Courtyard.........4 A2	Main Sanctuary).....11 A2
Madraseh..................5 A2	Ticket Office...........12 B1
Madraseh..................6 B2	Toilets.....................13 B2
Main Sanctuary..........7 A2	West Iwan...............14 A2
Mihrab & Minbar........8 A2	West Sanctuary.........15 A2

with its pool for ritual ablutions and four imposing **iwans**. The walls of the courtyard contain the most exquisite sunken porches, framed by painted tiles known as *haft rangi* (see p66) of deep blue and yellow. Each *iwan* leads into a vaulted sanctuary. The **east** and **west sanctuaries** are covered with particularly fine floral motifs on a blue background.

The **main sanctuary** is entered via the **south iwan**. Find yourself a quiet corner in which to sit and contemplate the richness of the domed ceiling, with its golden rose pattern (the flower basket) surrounded by concentric circles of busy mosaics on a deep blue background. The interior ceiling is 36.3m high, but the exterior reaches up to 51m due to the double-layering used in construction. The hollow space in between is responsible for the loud echoes heard when you stamp your foot on the black paving stones under the centre of the dome. Although scientists have measured up to 49 echoes, only about 12 are audible to the human ear – more than enough for a speaker to be heard throughout the mosque. The marble **mihrab** and **minbar** are also beautifully crafted.

The main sanctuary provides wonderful views back to the two turquoise **minarets** above the entrance portal. Each is encircled by projecting balconies and white geometric calligraphy in which the names of Mohammed and Ali are picked out over and over again. Each is topped by an elegant dome.

To the east and west of the main sanctuary are the courtyards of two madrasehs. Both provide good views of the main **dome** with its tiles every shade of turquoise. Cameras are welcome.

Sheikh Lotfollah Mosque مسجد شیخ لطف الله

A study in harmonious understatement, this mosque is the perfect complement to the overwhelming richness of the larger Imam Mosque, and is arguably the most fabulous mosque in Iran. Built between 1602 and 1619, during the reign of Shah Abbas I, the **Sheikh Lotfollah Mosque** (Masjed-e Sheikh Lotfollah; Map p238; admission IR4000; ☼ 8am-sunset, 8am-11.30am & 12.30pm-sunset summer) is dedicated to the ruler's father-in-law, Sheikh Lotfollah, a revered Lebanese scholar of Islam who was invited to Esfahan to oversee the king's mosque (now the Imam Mosque) and theological school.

The pale dome makes extensive use of delicate cream-coloured tiles that change colour throughout the day from cream to pink (sunset is usually best). The signature blue-and-turquoise tiles of Esfahan are evident only around the dome's summit.

The pale tones of the cupola stand in contrast to those around the **portal**, where you'll find some of the best surviving Safavid-era mosaics. The exterior panels contain wonderful arabesques and other intricate floral designs; those displaying a vase framed by the tails of two peacocks are superb. The portal itself contains some particularly fine stalactite work with rich concentrations of blue and yellow motifs.

The mosque is unusual because it has neither a minaret nor a courtyard, and because steps lead up to the entrance. This

---

SHAH IN A HURRY

When the Imam Mosque was begun, Shah Abbas the Great probably didn't think it would be 25 years before the last of the artisans left the building. He was already 52 when work began, and as he grew older he grew ever-more impatient to see his greatest architectural endeavour completed.

Legend has it Abbas repeatedly demanded that corners be cut to hasten the progress, even insisting work on the walls be started despite the foundations having not yet set. His architect, Ali Akbar Esfahani, was having none of it. He flatly defied his boss before making himself scarce until Abbas calmed down. After all, Abbas was notoriously insecure and had killed two sons and blinded another, so Esfahani was understandably nervous. He eventually returned to the court where, because the wisdom of his decision had been demonstrated, he was welcomed back with a royal pardon.

Some of the time-saving techniques were quite innovative: rather than covering the entire complex with millions of individual mosaic tiles, larger prefabricated patterned tiles called *haft rangi* were created – they've been standard ever since.

was probably because the mosque was never intended for public use, but rather served as the worship place for the women of the shah's harem. The **sanctuary** or prayer hall is reached via a twisting **hallway** where the eyes become accustomed to the darkness as subtle shifts of light play across deep blue tilework. This hallway is integral to both the design and function of the mosque because it takes the worshipper from the grand square outside into a prayer hall facing Mecca, and thus on a completely different axis.

Inside the sanctuary you can marvel at the complexity of the mosaics that adorn the walls and ceiling, which is extraordinarily beautiful with its shrinking, yellow motifs drawing the visitor's eye into the exquisite centre. The shafts of sunlight that filter in through the few high, latticed windows produce a constantly changing interplay of light and shadow.

The mihrab is one of the finest in Iran and has an unusually high niche; look for the calligraphic montage that names the architect and the date 1028 AH.

Photography is allowed but flashes are not.

Ali Qapu Palace   كاخ عالی قاپو

Built at the very end of the 16th century as a residence for Shah Abbas I, the majestic six-storey **Ali Qapu Palace** (Map p238; admission IR4000; ☻ 8am-sunset) also served as a monumental gateway (Ali Qapu means the 'Gate of Ali') to the royal palaces that lay in the parklands beyond. Named for Abbas' hero, the Imam Ali, it was built to make an impression and at six storeys and 48m tall it did. French traveller Sir John Chardin described it as 'the largest palace ever built in any capital'.

The highlight of the palace is arguably the **elevated terrace** with its 18 slender columns. The terrace affords a wonderful perspective over the square and one of the best views of the Imam Mosque. If you look up, you'll see an attractive wooden ceiling with intricate inlay work and exposed beams, reminiscent of the nearby Chehel Sotun Palace.

Many of the valuable paintings and mosaics that once decorated the small rooms, corridors and stairways were destroyed during the Qajar period and since the 1979 revolution. However, some remain in the **throne room**, which leads off the terrace.

On the upper floor, the **music room** is definitely worth the climb. The stucco ceiling is riddled with the shapes of vases and other household utensils cut to enhance the acoustics. This distinctive craftsmanship, considered by some to be one of the finest examples of secular Persian art, extends to the walls.

CHEHEL SOTUN PALACE   كاخ چهلستون

One of the only surviving palaces from the royal parklands between Imam Sq and Chahar Bagh Abbasi St, Safavid-era **Chehel Sotun** (Map p234; Ostandari St; admission IR5000; ☻ 8am-5pm, 8am-noon & 2pm-sunset summer) is today most famous for its frescoes. It was built as a pleasure pavilion and reception hall, using the Achaemenid-inspired *talar* (columnar porch) style. There are historical references to the palace dating from 1614; however, an inscription uncovered in 1949 says it was completed in 1647 under the watch of Shah Abbas II. Either way, what you see today was rebuilt after a fire in 1706.

The palace is entered via the elegant *talar* terrace, which perfectly bridges the transition between the Persian love of gardens and interior splendour. Its 20 slender, ribbed wooden pillars rise to a superb wooden ceiling with crossbeams and exquisite inlay work. Chehel Sotun means '40 pillars' – the number reflected in the long pool in front of the palace.

The Great Hall (Throne Hall) contains a rich array of frescoes, miniatures and ceramics. The upper walls are dominated by historical frescoes on a grand scale, sumptuously portraying court life and some of the great battles of the Safavid era. From right to left, above the entrance door, the armies of Shah Ismail do battle with the Uzbeks; Nader Shah battles Sultan Mahmud (astride a white elephant) on an Indian battleground; and Shah Abbas II welcomes King Nader Khan of Turkestan with musicians and dancing girls.

On the wall opposite the door, also from right to left, Shah Abbas I presides over an ostentatious banquet; Shah Ismail battles the janissaries (infantrymen) of Sultan Suleiman; and Shah Tahmasp receives Humayun, the Indian prince who fled to Persia in 1543. These extraordinary works survived the 18th-century invasion by the Afghans, who whitewashed the paintings to

CENTRAL IRAN

show their disapproval of such extravagance. Other items, including Safavid forebear Safi od-Din's hat, are kept in a small **museum**.

In the garden there is a small teahouse and a bookshop. Early morning is the best time for photos (flash not allowed inside).

MUSEUMS

Near the entrance to the Chehel Sotun Palace are three museums. The **Decorative Arts Museum of Iran** (Map p234; Ostandari St; admission IR3000; 8am-1pm Sat-Wed, 8am-noon Thu) is in a building that once served as stables and warehouse to Safavid kings. Today it contains a fine collection from the Safavid and Qajar periods, including miniatures, glassware, lacquer work, ancient Qurans, calligraphy, ceramics, woodcarvings, traditional costumes, weapons and horse gear.

Just to the north (right) the **Museum of Contemporary Art** (Map p234; Ostandari St; admission IR3000; 9am-noon & 4-7pm Sat-Thu, 5-8pm summer) shows temporary exhibits, mainly of Esfahani artists; while on the corner a large 15th-century building is home to the **Natural History Museum** (Map p234; Ostandari St; admission IR3000; 8am-1pm & 2-5pm, 4-9pm summer), where the fibreglass dinosaurs out front are not that enticing. The exhibits inside are better but won't have you rushing off to write home about them.

HASHT BEHESHT PALACE کاخ هشت بهشت

Once the most luxuriously decorated in Esfahan, the interior of the small **Hasht Behesht Palace** (Map p234; admission IR3000; 8am-8pm) has been extensively damaged over the years. However, it retains a seductive tranquillity, with the soaring wooden columns on its open-sided terrace seeming to mirror the trees in the surrounding park.

Hasht Behesht, meaning 'eight heavens', was built in the 1660s. The interior boasts some impressive mosaics and stalactite mouldings and ceilings cut into a variety of shapes – similar to the music room in the Ali Qapu Palace.

MADRASEH-YE CHAHAR BAGH
مدرسه چهارباغ

The **Madraseh-ye Chahar Bagh** (Madraseh-ye Mazadar-e Shah or Theological School of the Shah's Mother; Map p234; Chahar Bagh Abbasi St; No Ruz only) was built between 1704 and 1714 as part of an expansive complex that included a caravanserai

(now the Abbasi Hotel) and the Bazar-e Honar. Revenues from these buildings paid for the upkeep of the madraseh.

Entry is through an imposing wood-and-silver door but this, unfortunately, is mostly closed to visitors. Apart from the two-week No Ruz period (admission IR30,000), you'll need to befriend a student to get in. If you do, you'll find a tree-filled courtyard surrounded by two-storey porches leading to the students' rooms. Around it are a prayer hall with a superb mihrab, two of the finest Safavid-era minarets in Esfahan, some exquisite mosaics and an attractive dome.

HAMMAM-E ALI GHOLI AGHA حمام علیقلی آقا

In the historic district of Bid Abad, the recently restored **Hammam-e Ali Gholi Agha** (Ali Gholi Agha Bathhouse; Map p234; Ali Gholi Agha Alley, off Masjed-e Sayyed St; admission IR10,000; 8.30am-5pm Sat-Thu, 9am-3pm Fri) is now a well-maintained (but poorly signed) museum to bathhouses. Fortunately there is information at the entrance, explaining the Qajar-era history and uses of the *hammam*. English-speaking guides are also available. It's worth a look, especially if you didn't see Hammam-e Sultan Mir Ahmad in Kashan.

To get there, walk west from Takhti Junction on Masjed-e Sayyed St, and turn right (north) down Ali Gholi Agha St, 50m beyond the junction with Tayab St. Walk about 250m and turn right inside a covered bazaar, then left at the mosque.

ZAYANDEH RIVER BRIDGES پلهای زاینده رود

There are few better ways to spend an afternoon than strolling along the **Zayandeh River** (Map p234), crossing back and forth using the old fairy-tale bridges and listening to Esfahanis reciting poetry and just chilling out. Such a stroll is especially pleasant at sunset and early evening when most of the bridges are illuminated. In total, 11 bridges (six are new) cross the Zayandeh. All but one of the historic Safavid-era crossings lie to the east of Chahar Bagh St – the exception is the shorter **Marnan Bridge** (Pol-e Marnan; Map p233) – but most people satisfy themselves with the walk from Si-o-Seh Bridge to Khaju Bridge, and back.

Si-o-Seh Bridge سی و سه پل

The 298m-long **Si-o-Seh Bridge** (Pol-e Si-o-Seh, Bridge of 33 Arches or Allahverdi

Khan Bridge; Map p234) was built by Allahverdi Khan, a favourite general of Shah Abbas I, between 1599 and 1602 to link the upper and lower halves of Chahar Bagh St. It served as both bridge and dam, and is still used to hold water today. Until recently there were teahouses at either end of the bridge, both accessed through the larger arches underneath, though only the northern one remains (see p249).

Chubi Bridge   پل چوبی
Nearly 150m long, and with 21 arches, **Chubi Bridge** (Map p234) was built by Shah Abbas II in 1665, primarily to help irrigate palace gardens in the area. Chubi and the two parlours within were for the exclusive use of the shah and his courtiers. Until recently one of these parlours was one of the most atmospheric teahouses in Iran; hopefully it will be again.

Khaju Bridge   پل خواجو
Arguably the finest of Esfahan's bridges, the **Khaju Bridge** (Map p234) was built by Shah Abbas II in about 1650 (although a bridge is believed to have crossed the waters here since the time of Tamerlane). It also doubles as a dam, and has always been as much a meeting place as a bearer of traffic.

Its 110m length has two levels of terraced arcades, the lower containing locks regulating water flow. If you look hard, you can still see original paintings and tiles, and

the remains of stone seats built for Shah Abbas II to sit on and admire the views. In the centre, a pavilion was built exclusively for his pleasure. It was a teahouse, but not anymore. Vendors at the end of the bridge sell tea and snacks.

Shahrestan Bridge   پل شهرستان
This is the oldest of Esfahan's bridges (Map p233). Most of the 11-arched stone and brick structure is believed to date from the 12th century, although the pillars themselves remain from a much earlier Sassanian bridge. Although it's almost 4km east of Khaju Bridge, it's a pleasant walk.

JOLFA: THE ARMENIAN QUARTER
کلیسای ارامنه
The Armenian quarter of Esfahan is **Jolfa** (Map p234). It dates from the time of Shah Abbas I, who transported this colony of Christians from the town of Jolfa (now on Iran's northern border; see p156) en masse, and named the village 'New Jolfa'. Abbas sought their skills as merchants, entrepreneurs and artists – a look at the walls of Vank Cathedral reveals what he was after. The Armenian Christians had their religious freedom respected, but they were restricted to this area across the river and kept away from the Islamic centres.

Today there are 13 Armenian churches and an old cemetery scattered around Jolfa, serving a Christian community of about

---

MOURNING ZAYANDEH RIVER TEAHOUSES

One of the great joys of any visit to Esfahan used to be walking along the Zayendeh River and stopping in the atmospheric teahouses in the Khaju, Chubi and Si-o-Seh Bridges. These teahouses were loved by locals and visitors alike, places to socialise over tea and qalyan (water pipe) just as Esfahanis have been doing since the bridges were built more than 300 years ago. But one by one they have been closed and only the teahouse at the northern end of Si-o-Seh Bridge remains (see opposite).

Various reasons have been offered for closing these wonderful teahouses. Some cite the crackdown on the highly unhealthy qalyan. Others say the tobacco smoke was damaging the bridges, though given that people have been smoking in these stone places for centuries this seems unlikely. Others are convinced the rise of religious conservatives in the provincial government is to blame and the antismoking campaign is just a smokescreen – after all, they say, you can still smoke cigarettes almost anywhere. The result is that places where young men and women might get together and do dangerous things – like looking at each other – have been forced to close.

Whatever the reason, the city that likes to think of itself as the 'Venice of the Middle East' and (rightly) thinks it deserves a bigger share of international tourists, has lost some of its best attractions. With luck, the city will see to it that the teahouses are reopened – even without the qalyan.

7000. It's worth heading out here (it's not far) in the afternoon, seeing the sights and staying around for dinner in the relatively liberal village atmosphere.

Vank Cathedral   کلیسای وانک

Built between 1606 and 1655 with the encouragement of the Safavid rulers, **Vank Cathedral** (Kelisa-ye Vank; Map p234; ☎ 624 3471; Kelisa St; adult/student IR30,000/16,000; ⏲ 8am-12.30pm & 2-5.30pm, to 6.30pm summer) is the historic focal point of the Armenian church in Iran. The church's exterior is unexciting, but the interior is richly decorated and shows the curious mixture of styles – Islamic tiles and designs alongside Christian imagery – that characterises most churches in Iran. The frescoes are truly magnificent, and sometimes wonderfully gruesome.

The attached Vank Cathedral **museum** contains, among other things, more than 700 handwritten books and a disturbing display covering the Armenian genocide in Turkey.

Other Churches

Of the other 12 churches in Jolfa only these two are open (sometimes). The frescoes on the walls and ceilings of the **Church of Bethlehem** (Kelisa-ye Bethlehem; Map p234; Nazar St; admission IR10,000), built in 1628, are arguably of a higher quality than those in Vank Cathedral. The interior of the high dome is decorated with swirling black motifs on a golden background, while the base is surrounded by paintings of Biblical scenes. The **Church of St Mary** (Kelisa-ye Maryam; Map p234; Jolfa Sq) is similarly decorated, though with less flair. If the churches are closed, as they often are, and door-knocking doesn't work, ask for help at the cathedral.

MANAR JOMBAN (SHAKING MINARETS)   منار جنبان

The 14th-century tomb of Abu Abdullah, a revered dervish, is 7km west of central Esfahan in Kaladyn. The tomb is popularly known as **Manar Jomban** (Shaking Minarets; Map p233; Saremiyeh St; admission IR5000; ⏲ 8.30am-1pm & 3-5pm, to 6pm summer) because pushing hard against one minaret will start it, and the other minaret, swaying back and forth. The minarets were added during the 17th century. Attendants climb up to shake them once an hour, on the hour. Iranians love this sight, but it's only barely worth the

trip – and on slow days they might not be shaken at all.

Many buses (IR250, 20 minutes) going west along Baha'i St from near the corner of Chahar Bagh Abbasi St run past Manar Jomban; the man in the ticket booth will point you to the right one. Chartering a taxi for an hour to include the nearby Ateshkadeh-ye Esfahan fire temple is another alternative (about IR40,000).

ATESHKADEH-YE ESFAHAN   آتشکده اصفهان

Dating from Sassanian times, the crumbling mud bricks of the **Ateshkadeh-ye Esfahan** (Esfahan Fire Temple; off Map p233; Saremiyeh St; admission IR2000; ⏲ 8.30am-5pm, to 6pm in summer) stare out over the Zayandeh River and the city from a low hill on its outskirts. The 10-minute scramble uphill is worth the effort on a clear day. It's about 2km west from the Manar Jomban, along the same road.

PIGEON TOWERS   کبوتر خانه

For centuries Esfahan relied on pigeons to supply guano as fertiliser for the city's famous fields of watermelons. The guano was collected in almost 3000 squat, circular pigeon towers, each able to house about 14,000 birds. Today they are unused, made

---

A SHAKE TOO FAR?

Ask guides why the shaking minarets shake and they are likely to embark on a lengthy explanation of vibration theory. Some who have studied a bit might even quote a geologists' report suggesting the sandstone used in the minarets contains something called felspar, which dissolves over time, leaving stone flexible and liable to shake. The geologists say their theory is supported by the fact there are no historic references to the minarets shaking. There are, however, conflicting views. Another expert points out that other buildings in Esfahan were constructed from the same sandstone and yet show no propensity to shake.

Then again, there's another theory. As the minarets are made of brick and timber, it seems more feasible that it's the timber that bends and is the connection between the two minarets. It's a theory supported by one traveller, who wrote: 'Flexible stone – pull the other leg.'

redundant by chemical fertiliser, but more than 700 of the mud-brick towers remain in the city's environs.

The best place to see them is dotted along the Zayandeh River south of the Ateshkadeh. The 10km walk back into Esfahan makes a great afternoon, and you're also likely to see locally made cloth being laid out to dry.

'Half of the World' Walking Tour

Esfahan is often described as 'half of the world', and this walking tour takes you through several of the city's highlights. Starting at Imam Hossein Sq, walk north along Chahar Bagh Abbasi St and turn right (east) down quiet Golbahar St. Walk past the Russian Consulate and into a covered bazaar, then turn left (north) when you reach Hakim St, crossing under the bazaar roof. About 150m along you'll come to the **Hakim Mosque (1)** on the right. The western entrance should be open, but if it's not continue north and turn west along Hakim Alley to reach the northern entrance. This is Esfahan's oldest mosque, but only the beautiful portal (beside the northern entrance) has survived from the Buyid-dynasty structure built about 1000 years ago. The dome beneath the southern *iwan* has an impressive echo and, if you climb the stairs in the southeastern corner, you'll enjoy fine views over the rooftops of the bazaar.

Exiting through the northern entrance you'll enter the narrow, attractive lanes around the bazaar. Continuing east on Hakim Lane, you'll pass through the quieter alleys of the **Bazar-e Bozorg (2**; p238) with vendors selling household goods and at least one male-dominated but charismatic little **chaykhaneh (3)**. The bazaar veers northeast and becomes busier, with domestic goods shops, mosques, madrasehs, teahouses, banks, bathhouses and even the occasional garden.

At a fork the main bazaar veers right, but keep straight for about 40m to get to the **Madraseh-ye Nimurvand (4)**, where the students normally welcome visitors (though women shouldn't loiter too long). Rejoin the main bazaar and follow it across Jamal-od-Din Abdolrazagh St to the imposing **Jameh Mosque (5**; p236) – give yourself time here and remember it's closed between about 11am and 1pm.

From the mosque, skirt around Qeyam Sq, stopping for a look at the **bird market (6)**, and head down Haruniyeh St. You'll soon see the

WALKING TOUR

Start Hakim Mosque
Finish Sofreh Khaneh Sonnati
Distance about 7km
Duration four to seven hours, depending on how often you stop and for how long

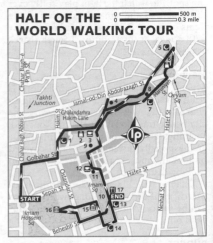

HALF OF THE WORLD WALKING TOUR

attractive, 48m-high **Minaret of the Mosque of Ali (7**; Manar-e Masjed-e Ali). Inside the mosque, which was rebuilt in 1522, are some impressive Safavid paintings that until recently were hidden under Qajar-era decoration. Opposite the mosque and back about 20m is the 16th-century **Mausoleum of Harun Vilayet (8**; Bogh-e Harun Vilayet), an important pilgrimage site containing some high-quality frescoes depicting the son of the 10th, or perhaps the 11th, Shiite Imam (no-one is quite sure). The courtyard also contains big, photogenic mosaics of Khomeini and Khamenei.

Continuing west keep right to rejoin the main bazaar and wander southwest through the shafts of sunlight and spice-filled air towards Imam Sq. En route, the **Madraseh-ye Sadr (9)** has a large, green courtyard that can provide momentary respite from the bustling bazaar. On entering **Imam Square (10**; p238) through the grand **Qeysarieh Portal (11**; p238), go straight upstairs to the delightful **Qeysarieh Tea Shop (12**; p249), overlooking the square. After tea, launch into the square by either following the covered bazaars or by setting off to explore the jewels of Esfahan:

the **Sheikh Lotfollah Mosque** (**13**; p240), **Imam Mosque** (**14**; p239)and the **Ali Qapu Palace** (**15**; p241).

If you still have the energy, exit through the rear of Ali Qapu Palace and cross to the **Chehel Sotun Palace** (**16**; p241) on Ostandari St. If not, just head back up to the Qeysarieh Tea Shop (yes, there's no better viewing spot!) to watch the light play softly over the square as the sun goes down and the lights come up. Sublime! Round off the day with a meal at the traditional **Sofreh Khaneh Sonnati** (**17**; p248).

Sleeping

Much of Esfahan's accommodation is relatively expensive and rather lacking in character. However, in recent years the city's first traditional hotels have opened, so things are improving in the midrange area especially. Esfahan is best discovered on foot and most of these places are within walking distance of Imam Sq.

Esfahan's high season runs from mid-March until the end of June, when rooms can be scarce. At other times, bargain your head off.

BUDGET

Amir Kabir Hostel (Map p234; ☎ 222 7273; mrziaee@ hotmail.com; Chahar Bagh Abbasi St; dm/s/tw/tr IR35,000/ 75,000/120,000/150,000; 💻) For years the Amir Kabir has been Esfahan's backpacker base and, for lack of competition, it still is. The managers, Ziaee brothers, might not like spending money, but they're helpful enough with advice on timetables, booking onward tickets and some reasonably priced tours. Rooms and the dorm are basic, and cleanliness is not as consistent as it could be. Breakfast is served for an extra IR15,000.

Kakh Inn (Map p234; ☎ 222 5650; omid_anvary@ yahoo.com; Chahar Bagh Abbasi St; s/tw/tr with breakfast IR90,000/160,000/180,000) Small rooms here have shortish beds, bathrooms (most of them) and that's it. But manager Omid creates a good feel.

Shad Hostel (Map p234; ☎ 221 8621; fax 220 4264; Chahar Bagh Abbasi St; s/d US$11/18) A good-value, central option, with small, clean two- and three-bed rooms and sometimes-whiffy shared bathrooms. Front rooms are noisy.

Sahel Hotel (Map p234; ☎ 222 1702; www.sahel hotel.com; Chahar Bagh Abbasi St; s US$16-21, tw US$22-29; 🌣) Fresh paint, soft beds and bathrooms

make this central place fair value by Esfahan standards. English-speaking manager is helpful and there's the atmospheric Bame Sahel Teahouse (p250) upstairs. Ask for a quiet room.

Saadi Hotel (Map p234; ☎ 220 3881; saadi_hotel@ yahoo.com; Abbas Abad St; s with breakfast US$15-20, tw US$21-28; 🌣) Quiet location, alright rooms, nice price.

Hotel Totia (Map p234; ☎ 223 7525; Masjed-e Sayyed St; tw/tr with breakfast IR250,000/300,000; 🌣) Another welcoming, family-run place with spotless rooms at fair prices. Adjoining rooms are available and the overhead fans are a bonus if you hate air-con. Discounts for single travellers.

Everything's full? Try these:

Persia Hotel (Map p234; ☎ /fax 220 4062; Chahar Bagh Abbasi St, near Takhti Junction; s/tw US$20/28; 🌣) Family-run; very clean, relatively spacious rooms with bathroom; dubious plumbing.

Tous Hotel (Map p234; ☎ 222 1599; toos@yahoo.com; Chahar Bagh Abbasi St; s/tw/tr IR180,000/260,000/315,000; 🌣 💻) Rooms are bigger than some, and noisier than many.

If you have an early bus, functional **Hotel Kaveh** (Map p233; ☎ /fax 442 5440; s/d US$21/27; 🌣) is at the northern end of Kaveh terminal, and **Hotel Soffeh** (Map p233; ☎ 668 6462; s/d US$21/27; 🌣) is at Soffeh bus terminal.

MIDRANGE

All the rooms in this range have bathrooms, air-con, fridge and TV, though there's no guarantee on English-language channels.

Bekhradi Historical Residence (Map p234; ☎ 448 2072; Sonbolestan Alley, off Ebn-e Sina St; r IR250,000-900,000; 🌣 💻) This quiet, modest-sized *khan-e sonnati* (traditional house) is the real Safavid-style deal; five wonderfully restored rooms, some with bathrooms, some not – like the old days. Set around two garden courtyards, there is also a restaurant. It's beside the Masjed-e Dawazeh-Noh.

our pick **Hasht Behesht Apartment Hotel** (Map p234; ☎ 221 4868/9; hotel8behesht@yahoo.com; Ostandari St; apt from IR350,000; 🌣 💻) The family-run Hasht Behesht offers reliable, comfortable-if-not-desperately-stylish two-, three- and four-bed apartments in a wonderfully central location. English-speaking Mohammad is efficient, engaging and informative, and (don't fall over) charges everyone the same price. Great value!

Iran Hotel (Map p234; ☎ 220 2740; www.iranhotel.biz; off Chahar Bagh Abbasi St; s/d with breakfast US$28/43; 🏶) Not desperately charismatic, but the bright rooms with double-glazed windows are not bad in this price range. Bathrooms have squat toilets.

Pol and Park Hotel (Map p234; ☎ 667 4785-7; park_pol_hotel@yahoo.com; A'ineh Khuneh Blvd; s/d US$34/43; ℗ 🏶) With half the 35 rooms sporting balconies overlooking the Si-o-Seh Bridge and an overall friendly feel, you can forgive the ageing but clean rooms. Excellent value.

Tourist Hotel (Map p234; ☎ 220 4437; www.esfahantouristhotel.com; Abbas Abad St; s/d/ste with breakfast US$30/44/66; 🏶) Helpful English-speaking management has transformed this place into a reliable, if not exciting, lower mid-range place. The suite has a kitchenette.

Hotel Melal (Map p234; ☎ 222 4532-4; Kemal Esma'il St; s/d with breakfast US$41/64; ℗ 🏶) Overlooking the river east of Si-o-Seh Bridge, Melal is so professionally managed that staff refused all our attempts to actually see a room because it was full. However, several readers have reported the three-star standard rooms and top-floor restaurant (with views) are both excellent value.

Zohreh Hotel (Map p234; ☎ 223 1060; www.zohrehhotel.com; Ferdosi St; s/d/tr/ste with breakfast US$46/67/92/150; 🏶 🖳) The new, 50-room Zohreh is a temple to classic Persian kitsch – think lots of odd-shaped mirrors, gold paint, moulded plaster, chandeliers and portraits of colourfully clad maidens. Then there's the Achaemenid motifs. Rooms are more restrained and a fair size. Some have bathtubs, and all have ADSL internet.

Safavi Hotel (Map p234; ☎ 220 8600; Felestin St; s/d from US$49/72; 🏶) Nearer to Imam Sq than the Zohreh, the Safavi seems to have used the same stylists as the Zohreh with the head-spinning basement restaurant the *pièce de résistance*! Rooms are modern and mercifully less psychedelic to look at. Don't miss the views from the rooftop teahouse.

our pick **Dibai House** (Map p234; ☎ 220 9787, 0912 154 6964; www.dibaihouse.com; 1 Masjed Ali Alley, Harunieh; s/tw/tr with breakfast €35/60/75) Dibai House is Esfahan's most atmospheric hotel. Hidden away off a narrow, vaulted alley deep in the Bazar-e Bozorg district, the colourful, painstakingly restored traditional house and the chilled, interesting and arty female owners set a paradoxically modern-yet-

traditional Iranian tone. For pure facilities the 10 rooms are overpriced – bathrooms are outside and there are few modern luxuries – but what you're paying for is the ambience. Children under 14 are not allowed. It's hard to find: from Qeyam Sq, walk southwest towards the tall minaret at the Ali Mosque, take the alley about 10m along on the left, follow this around to the left, take the first right and right again, into a tunnel-like passage. The door is unsigned inside this passage, on the right. Prices are €10 less in low season.

Isfahan Traditional Hotel (Hotel Sonnati Isfahan; Map p234; ☎ 223 6677, 0913 305 1556; www.isfahanhotel.com; Bagh-e Ghalandarha Alley, off Hakim St; s/d/ste with breakfast €32/45/160; 🏶 🖳) Deep in the Bazar-e Bozorg area, this attractive traditional hotel is set around two courtyards in adjoining Safavid- and Qajar-period homes. The 16 rooms are spacious, comfortable and most have attached modern bathrooms. The stunning royal suite would make a memorable splurge. The service, however, was very raw when we stayed. It's about 75m east of the entrance to the Hakim Mosque.

Sadaf Hotel (Map p234; ☎ 220 2988; Hafez St; s/d US$63/90; 🏶 🖳) A super location near Imam Sq, professional management and impressive rooms with satellite TV and fridge make this an excellent choice. The rooftop restaurant is delightful in summer. Discounts are available in the low season. Family rooms available.

The following are 'solid' fall-back options: clean, comfortable enough, fair value but largely devoid of character.

Julfa Hotel (Map p234; ☎ 624 4441; www.julfahotel.com; Hakim Nezami St; s/d US$28/43; ℗ 🏶) A few metres from Vank Cathedral, with 72 small rooms and unhelpful service. Khangostar Restaurant (p248) is downstairs.

Pardis Apartment Hotel (Map p234; ☎ 220 0308; fax 222 7831; Takhti Junction; apt from US$50; 🏶) No frills apartments in two- to five-bed (US$77) varieties. Discounts very possible; good, cheap food in the restaurant.

Safir Hotel (Map p234; ☎ 222 2640; www.safirhotel.com; Shahid Medani St; s/d/ste US$63/87/95; 🏶 🖳) Professionally run place popular with businesspeople. Central location, several languages, tired rooms.

TOP END

There are surprisingly few top-end options in Esfahan considering it is such a tourist drawcard, so it's worth booking ahead.

Kowsar International Hotel (Map p234; ☎ 624 0230-39; www.hotelkowsar.com; Mellat Blvd; tw/d US$108/$158; P 🍴 🖥 🛄) Portraits of Aya-tollahs Khomeini and Khamenei on the wall confirm this one-time Sheraton is now government owned. Mercifully, however, professional management, a recent facelift, exceptional restaurants and facilities, in-cluding wi-fi and a kids playground, have transformed it from state-run disappoint-ment to quality luxury hotel. Ask for a 5th- or 6th-floor front room.

Abbasi Hotel (Map p234; ☎ 222 6010; www .abbasihotel.com; Shahid Medani St; s/d from US$110/165; P 🍴 🖥 🛄) In the remains of a 17th-century caravanserai, the Abbasi has a reputation as one of the best hotels in Iran. Reputations, however, can be misleading. While the central garden courtyard is sub-lime, most of the rooms are plain (neither luxurious nor historic looking), the serv-ice can leave you feeling more like a sheep than a shah, and the prices are double what Iranians pay. If you do stay, 'special' rooms (US$179) are in the original building and have garden views. Anything cheaper is in the drab 'new wing'.

Eating
Esfahan has its fair share of good restaurants and some memorable teahouses, but if it's culinary variety you seek, then prepare for disappointment. Most places listed here are walking distance from the hotels, though it's also worth venturing to relatively relaxed Jolfa one night. Most midrange and top-end hotels have restaurants, and remember that most teahouses (opposite) also serve food.

Esfahan's famous speciality is *gaz*, a deli-cious nougat usually mixed with chopped pistachios or other nuts. It's available pretty much everywhere, but especially in confec-tionery shops along Chahar Bagh Abbasi St and around Imam Sq.

RESTAURANTS
Mikhak Restaurant (Map p238; ☎ 222 3291; meals IR15,000-50,000; ⌚ noon-4pm Sat-Thu) Just off the northeast end of the bazaar, the Mikhak serves quality Iranian comfort food that seems to comfort half of the *bazaris* every day. Vegetarians should look elsewhere.

Aboozar Restaurant (Map p238; ☎ 222 0654; Bazar-e Bozorg; meals IR20,000-35,000; ⌚ 11am-3pm)

The rest of the *bazaris* seem to come here for fast, cheap and tasty meals. Arrive early or the best food will be gone.

Restoran-e Sa'di (Map p234; ☎ 222 0237; Chahar Bagh Abbasi St; meals IR20,000-35,000; ⌚ 10.30am-11pm) Down the mirrored staircase opposite Amir Kabir Hostel, this place is a classic lower middle-class Esfahani restaurant, with a cheapish, not that stylish, small menu with only half the dishes available.

Nobahar Restaurant (Map p234; ☎ 221 0800; Chahar Bagh Abbasi St; meals IR25,000-45,000; ⌚ 11am-3pm & 6-10pm) Nobahar Restaurant has been around forever because it serves reliably good, reasonably priced staples like kababs and *zereshk polo ba morgh*. It's not stylish and service isn't great, but that's not what you're here for.

Sadaf Hotel (Map p234; ☎ 220 2988; Hafez St; meals IR35,000; ⌚ dinner only for rooftop) The Sadaf Hotel's restaurant is especially recom-mended between June and October when you can eat on the rooftop. The food, includ-ing steak with mushroom sauce (IR30,000), and the usual range of tasty kababs, is consistently good and complements the rooftop views (when you stand up) across the Old City. It opens indoors during the rest of the year.

Arabo (Map p234; ☎ 624 7119; Kelisa St, Jolfa; meals IR30,000-45,000; ⌚ noon-4pm & 6-11pm) This popular underground pizza joint–cum-café offers heavily made-up, crimson-clad waitresses and pizza that's tasty despite the usual Iranian-pizza limitations.

our pick **Sofreh Khaneh Sonnati** (Traditional Banquet Hall; Map p238; ☎ 221 9068; Imam Sq; meals IR25,000-50,000; ⌚ noon-3pm & 7-10.30pm) Just off Imam Sq, this restaurant uses stained glass, colourful tiles and *takhts* (day beds) to create a Qajar-era (if slightly touristy) ambience. The food makes it memorable, with Esfahani biryani and *khoresht-e bademjan* (aubergine or eggplant stew) some of the well-prepared and reasonably priced recommendations. To find it, walk out the square north of Lotfol-lah Mosque, turn left, left again, and up the stairs.

Khorshid (Map p234; ☎ 624 7536; Khorshid St , Jolfa; meals IR40,000; ⌚ 6.30-11.30pm) This modern Iranian place appeals to upwardly mobile young Esfahanis with its relaxed atmos-phere and reasonably priced Iranian food.

our pick **Khangostar Restaurant** (Map p234; ☎ 627 8989; Hakim Nezami St , Jolfa; meals IR60,000; ⌚ noon-

3.30pm & 7.30-10.30pm) Located in Julfa Hotel, Khangostar Restaurant offers probably the best food in Esfahan – locals, our own experience and overwhelmingly positive reader feedback can attest to this. Servings are enormous here, (even by Iranian standards!) and the menu large and varied, but mainly Iranian. It's busy rather than romantic, and the salad and dessert bars might seem a bit Sizzler, but hey, you won't complain when you get there.

Bastani Restaurant (Map p238; ☎ 220 0374; Imam Sq; meals IR45,000-80,000; ☽ 11.30am-4.30pm & 6.30-10.30pm) In the shadow of the Imam Mosque, the Bastani is the best-located restaurant in Esfahan. That, however, is where the compliments end. In recent years the quality of the food has been less consistent. Which is a pity, as the menu is full of interesting-sounding dishes. If you do eat here, the billing can be confusing so check it carefully. It's a pity, as the menu is full of interesting-sounding dishes and it used to be good. Hopefully it will pick up.

Restaurant Shahrzad (Map p234; ☎ 220 4490; Abbas Abad St; meals IR50,000-70,000; ☽ 11.30am-10.30pm) The opulent Qajar-style wall-paintings, stained-glass windows and mirror work contribute to the Shahrzad's reputation as the best restaurant in Esfahan. And on a good night, it's excellent – strip lights notwithstanding. Too often, however, it's packed with tour groups and the service (and food) feels factory produced.

Restoran-e Khayyam (Map p234; Nazar St, Jolfa; meals IR25,000) Cheap, popular, very local and justifiably busy little kabab, rice and bread place.

QUICK EATS

The lower end of Chahar Bagh Abbasi St has the greatest concentration of Iranian fast food joints, selling pizza, sandwiches, burgers, ice cream and, occasionally, real kababs. The roads leading into Imam Sq also have a few options, but not the square itself. The small but growing café scene is best in the streets around Vank Cathedral, where several atmospheric little places compete for business.

For genuinely Iranian fast food, try the following places.

Kalleh Pache (Map p234; Bazar-e Bozorg; ☽ 7am-5pm) If you take the 'when in Rome' philosophy seriously, or just like the taste of sheep brains, then this tiny shop is for you. Turn east off Hakim St where the bazaar roof crosses the street, and look for the men about 20m along.

Azam Beryani (Map p234; Chahar Bagh Abbasi St; biryani IR18,000; ☽ 9am-4pm Sat-Thu) Biryani is an Esfahani speciality and this modest little place is a favourite of Esfahanis. Join the queue.

Fereni Hafez (Map p234; Hafez St; ☽ 8am-midnight) For an Iranian breakfast experience (at any time of day) head for where you can enjoy a delicious bowl (or two) of *fereni* (made of rice flour, milk, sugar and rose-water) for IR2000; look for the red sign.

TEAHOUSES & CAFÉS

Sitting in an Esfahani *chaykhaneh* (teahouse), sipping tea through sugar and puffing on a qalyan, is a quintessentially Iranian experience. The Qeysarieh Tea Shop is probably the highlight, and stopping for tea as you wander along the river is something Esfahanis have been doing for centuries (see the boxed text, p243). The bazaar is also a good place to discover tiny local places where grizzled but welcoming old fellas puff away on the qalyan with nary a care for modern antismoking legislation.

Abbasi Hotel Teahouse (Map p234; Shahid Medani St; ☽ 4-11pm) The setting at the back of the hotel's courtyard is a delight, and while you might need to start singing to get a waiter's attention it's worth the effort after 6pm, when you can tuck into the famous *ash-e reshte* (noodle soup with beans and vegetables; IR9000).

our pick Si-o-Seh Bridge (Map p234 Enqelab-e Eslami Sq; ☽ 8am-11pm) This teahouse at the north end of Si-o-Seh Bridge is an Esfahani institution (and it's not touristy) and the last of the bridge *chaykhanehs*; see the boxed text, p243. The teahouse is typically male dominated, but foreign women do get honorary male treatment and it is invariably a boisterous atmosphere, especially under the pylons.

our pick Qeysarieh Tea Shop (Map p238; Imam Sq; ☽ 8.30am-11pm) Sitting at the outdoor tables, sipping tea (IR5000 per person) and puffing qalyan (IR10,000), is the perfect way to soak up this beautiful 'half of the world', especially when the colours and moods of the square change in the late afternoon. And despite its position, the Qeysarieh Tea Shop is often pretty quiet. The tea shop is up a steep staircase to the left of the Qeysarieh Portal.

Azadegan Teahouse (Chaykhaneh-ye Azadegan; Map p238; ☎ 221 1225; off Imam Sq; ☼ 7am-midnight) In a lane off the northeastern corner of Imam Sq, this is the classic old-style teahouse, with an astonishing collection of teahouse-junk hanging from the walls and ceiling and grumpy men lined up opposite each other sipping tea and smoking…ahm, hang on… It's just sipping and eating before 6pm; the qalyans come out after that.

Bame Sahel Teahouse (Map p234; Chahar Bagh Abbasi St; ☼ 7.30am-midnight) On the top of Sahel Hotel, Bame Sahel is a bit rough around the edges and very local, and all the better for it. Escape the traffic for tea, or enjoy a good *dizi* dinner (IR27,000). There's also a breakfast buffet (IR20,000).

Teria Ani (Map p234; Vank Kalisa Alley, near Vank Cathedral; ☼ 9am-midnight) This is allegedly the oldest café in Esfahan and with its dim interior, regular clientele and oddball characters, it feels like an inner-city dive bar.

Shopping

Esfahan has probably the widest selection of handicrafts in Iran. The best buys are carpets, hand-painted miniatures on camel bone (many of the artists run the stores themselves and are happy to give demonstrations), intricate metalwork and lacquerware. Prices can be higher than elsewhere but there's more choice and it's certainly more pleasurable to shop here than in Tehran. For gold, head directly to **Bazar-e Honar** (Map p234; Chahar Bagh Abbasi St; ☼ 8.30am-1pm & 4-9pm Sat-Thu).

The Bazar-e Bozorg (Map p234) and the arcades around Imam Sq (Map p238) are literally full of shops. You will find postcards and junk souvenirs for sale in one store, and expensive works of art in the next. Stores vary by price, quality and honesty, with competition among the carpet dealers particularly fierce (and sometimes nasty), so don't pay too much attention to what one shop owner says about his competitor. For more information, see p64.

Some places do employ high-pressure sales tactics, but most are friendly and willing to chat over a *chay* without twisting your arm too much. It can actually be quite enjoyable as long as you remember that you don't *have* to buy anything. Nevertheless, whatever you're shopping for, check prices in several stores and bargain hard (see What A Bargain, p392).

A few Imam Sq shops recommended by readers:

Aladdin Carpets (Map p238; ☎ 221 1461; aladdin _shop@yahoo.com; Imam Sq) Small shop, interesting range of carpets, experienced salesmen, underwhelming nomad tours.

Fallahi Miniatures Shahid Medani St (Map p234; ☎ 222 4613); Saadi St (Map p238; ☎ 222 6733; off Imam Sq) Charming and internationally renowned Hossein Fallahi's works are excellent.

Nomad Carpet Shop (Map p238; ☎ 221 9275; nomad shop@yahoo.com; Imam Sq) Almost-comatose approach to selling, mainly tribal range of carpets and kilims.

Getting There & Away

AIR

The **Iran Air office** (Map p234; ☎ 222 8200; www .iranair.com; Shahid Medani St) is in the shopping complex opposite the Abbasi Hotel. See the following table of domestic services; Iran Air also flies twice a week to Dubai and three times to Kuwait City. Kish Air flies to Kish and Dubai.

Destination	Fare	Frequency
Ahvaz	IR245,000	5 per week
Bandar Abbas	IR454,000	2 per week
Bushehr	IR283,000	Wed only, via Shiraz
Mashhad	IR476,000	4 per week, via Shiraz
Shiraz	IR246,000	6 per week
Tehran	IR245,000	several daily
Zahedan	IR512,000	Fri only, via Kerman

BUS

Esfahan has two main bus terminals: Kaveh terminal (Map p233) in the north is the busiest and is the terminal you're most likely to use; while Soffeh terminal (Map p233) is in the south. Except at the busiest times it's easiest to just get your tickets at the terminal before you depart. Alternatively, accommodation such as the Amir Kabir Hostel (p246) and the Negareh Internet Café (p235) can book tickets for a small commission.

See the following table for routes from Kaveh; fares are for *mahmooly*/Volvo buses, or just Volvo. As there are no bus offices in town, it's a good idea to ask about departure times of buses when you first arrive in Esfahan.

Destination	Fare	Duration	Departures
Bandar Abbas	IR45,000/ 75,000	14-16hr	frequent
Bushehr	IR30,000/ 55,000	13-16hr	4-7pm (Soffeh)
Hamadan	IR38,500	8hr	7.30am-10am & 9-10pm
Kashan	IR12,000/ 21,000	2½-3½hr	very frequent
Kermanshah	IR60,000	9hr	evenings Pars Peyma
Khorramabad	IR40,000	8hr	7-10am & 7-10pm
Mashhad	IR95,000	17-19hr	1-8pm
Orumiyeh	IR95,000	18-20hr	evenings Iran Peyma
Sanandaj	IR36,000	9hr	evenings
Shiraz	IR20,000/ 38,000	8hr	frequent
Tabriz	IR70,000	17hr	2-5pm
Tehran	IR26,500/ 50,000	5-7hr	very frequent
Yazd	IR12,500/ 30,000	4-5hr	1-2pm Kaveh, or Jey minibus terminal
Zahedan	IR90,000	16-19hr	infrequent, book ahead

For the Kaveh terminal, take a shuttle taxi north along Chahar Bagh St for IR2500; to get to Soffeh, take one from just south of the Si-o-Seh Bridge (IR3000). A private taxi to either terminal will cost between IR10,000 and IR30,000 depending on your bargaining prowess. The Esfahan Metro will (one day) link the two terminals via Chahar Bagh St.

MINIBUS & TAXI
For destinations around Esfahan there are two minibus terminals. The Zayandeh Rud terminal (Map p233) has services to Shahr-e Kord (IR5000, two hours, 107km), with departures every hour or so. To get to Zayandeh Rud terminal, take a shuttle taxi west from just south of the Si-o-Seh Bridge (IR3000).

From the Jey minibus terminal (Map p233), there are at least five departures each day to Yazd (IR10,000, six hours, 316km). Minibuses also go to Na'in (IR5000, three to four hours, 138km) and Ardestan (IR6000, 132km). To get to the Jey minibus terminal, take a shuttle taxi from Takhti Junction (IR1500).

Savaris leave from outside the terminals far more frequently than minibuses but for about three times the price, such as the service to Shahr-e Kord (IR15,000, 80 minutes).

TRAIN
There is a daily train between Esfahan and Tehran (six-berth IR35,15, 7½ hours) that leaves at 11.30pm and stops at Kashan. Trains also run to Mashhad (Ghazal/six-berth IR199,000/92,850, 18½ hours, 5.50pm daily) and Bandar Abbas (six-berth/six-seat IR66,100/41,700, 2.25pm Monday, Wednesday and Friday). The new line to Shiraz will open in 2010 at the earliest.

The **Raja Trains ticket office** (Map p234; ☎ 222 4425; Enqelab-e Eslami Sq; ☻ 8am-4pm Sat-Thu) is on the northeast side of the square. Alternatively, **Iran Travel & Tourism Tour** (Map p234; ☎ 222 3010; irantravel1964@yahoo.com; Shahid Medani St) has a dedicated train ticket desk.

The **train station** (off Map p233; ☎ 668 8001) is way out to the east of the city. To get here, catch a bus from outside Kowsar International Hotel; ask for the 'istgah-e ghatah' and you'll be put on the right bus. Be at the bus stop well over an hour before your train is due to depart. A private taxi (IR45,000) can cost almost as much as the train ticket to Tehran. Alternatively, take a shuttle taxi south from the south end of Si-o-Seh Bridge.

Getting Around
Esfahani taxi drivers have a bad reputation, but in reality they're not much worse than taxi drivers anywhere else in the universe – if they see someone fresh off the plane, train or automobile, they'll try to take you. The cartel at Kaveh terminal will ask IR30,000 for a trip to a central hotel, but you should laugh at this and offer IR10,000. If you're lucky, you might get it for IR15,000. Either way, settle the price before getting in. Alternatively, take a shuttle taxi or bus – traffic passing on the terminal side of the road is heading south into town. Getting from town to Kaveh is cheaper.

TO/FROM THE AIRPORT
The airport (off Map p233) is about 25km northeast of town and there is no airport bus service. To get there, take any bus heading east along Jamal-od-Din Abdolrazagh St from Takhti Junction. Get off the bus at Ahmad Abad Sq where the small Sorush bus terminal (Map p233) has buses to the airport. From the airport, ask around for any shuttle taxis heading into the city, from where you might need to get another to your hotel. A private taxi will cost about IR50,000.

BUS & MINIBUS

Buses and minibuses leave the local bus terminal, near Chehel Sotun Palace, every few minutes. Just ask – and keep asking – for one heading your way. Elsewhere in town ask at a bus stop and you will soon be pointed to the correct conveyance. Rides cost IR200 to IR500 and you buy books of tickets at booths along the routes. One very handy bus links the Kaveh and Soffeh bus terminals (IR500).

TAXI

Depending on the distance – and your negotiating skills – a fare in a private taxi around inner Esfahan costs anything from IR6000 to IR15,000. Luckily there are so many taxis that it's easy to negotiate by threatening to find another one. Avoid the taxi drivers hanging around Imam Sq as they can spot tourists a mile off. To hire a private taxi for an hour costs between IR20,000 and IR40,000, and can be a good way to see the Ateshkadeh-ye Esfahan and Manar Jomban.

The long Chahar Bagh St is the city's main thoroughfare, and every couple of seconds a shuttle taxi goes *mostaghim* (straight ahead) for about IR1000 per kilometre or so. To outlying destinations such as the transport terminals, look for taxis heading in the right direction from the following places: Takhti Junction, Laleh, Qods and Ahmad Abad Sqs (for anywhere to the east); Imam Hossein and Shohada Sqs (for the north); and the southern end of Si-o-Seh Bridge and Azadi Sq (for the south and west); or just ask anywhere.

ESFAHAN TO SHIRAZ VIA THE ZAGROS MOUNTAINS

If the idea of a direct bus or flight between Esfahan and Shiraz sounds like a missed opportunity, then consider an alternative jaunt through the Zagros Mountains, where the sharp folds of barren ridge and flowing valley stretch like a giant crocodile's back for 1500km from the Turkish border in northwestern Iran southeast to the Persian Gulf coast. The population is made up of Persian, Lori, Kurdish and a vast number of nomads, primarily Bakhtiari and Qashqa'i.

As a travelling experience, this trip definitely qualifies as 'off the beaten track'. Few people speak English, transport can be infrequent and accommodation basic. Summers are pleasantly mild but during winter snows often block roads. But tourists are rare, welcomes are warm and the scenery absolutely breathtaking.

Shahr-e Kord   شهر کرد

☎ 0381 / pop 137,000 / elev 2061m

The first leg is from Esfahan to Shahr-e Kord (see p251 for transport details). Nestled between two mountain ranges, the sleepy capital of Chahar Mahal va Bakhtiyari province is a staging post rather than a destination. The main sights are the **Atabakan Mosque** and the **Imamzadeh Khatoon**, near the bazaar, but even the province's own literature doesn't mention them.

For lodgings, the super basic **Hotel Mohammad** (☎ 0912 455 3306; Valiasr St; tw IR60,000), unmarked in English opposite the Imamzadeh, is not the sort of place you'll stay more than one night. Better but overpriced is the government-run **Shahr-e Kord Inn** (Hotel Jahangardi; ☎ 222 1077; Dr Shariati St, north of Basij Sq; r US$40; P ❄); while the best available is the **Shahr-e Kord Azadi Hotel** (☎ 333 0020; r/ste US$49/64; P ❄), a taxi-ride up the hill at the edge of town. The **Ferdosi Soffrekhaneh** (☎ 225 4355; Ferdosi Sq; ☣ 8am-10pm), just west of the bazaar, is one of the most atmospheric, original teahouses in Iran, and serves cheap *dizi* and kababs with its *chay* and qalyan; it's highly recommended.

Transport radiates out from the Terminal-e Azadi, southwest of the Imamzadeh. One minibus departs for Chelgerd (IR6000; two hours) at 8am, returning after lunch. In the late afternoon buses head south to Shiraz (*mahmooly*/Volvo IR22,000/35,000), but it's much easier to take a savari towards Yasuj (IR50,000) and get out wherever takes your fancy.

Chelgerd   چلگرد

Chelgerd is the home of skiing in this part of the Zagros range and is also the ideal base for climbing some of the many surrounding peaks of just less than 4000m. The Kuhrang Ski Resort has a single 800m-long T-bar running up a slope near the Kuhrang Tunnel; the snow is skiable between late December and early March, and you'll often have it to yourself on weekdays. There are a couple of cheaper places, but the **Hotel Kuhrang** (☎ 0832-762 2301; hotelkoohrang@parsonline.net; r US$50) is the place to stay because the English-speaking and statesman-like manager Mr Raisi is an absolute mine of information about the whole region. Alternatively, the guys in the Esfahan office of the **Mountaineering Federation** (Map p234; Shams Abadi St) have climbed most of these peaks and have photo albums to prove it; they can arrange guides, insurance, equipment, transport and permissions. As little English is spoken, they are usually contacted through the Ziaee brothers from Amir Kabir Hostel (p246).

Farsan to Yasuj

There is no tourist infrastructure whatsoever between Farsan and Yasuj, but the road is one of the most spectacular in the country. Winding through villages and gorges and steep-sided valleys hosting fast-flowing rivers, you won't soon forget the trip. The first two hours is most interesting.

Sepidan   سپیدان
pop 15,000

Sepidan is a sort of alpine resort village with rental accommodation and a handy information office on the main road. It's the jumping-off point for Poolad Kaf, a ski slope about 15km uphill from Sepidan. There are four lifts, one being 2100m long and climbing to 3400m. There is no regular transport to Poolad Kaf from Sepidan, but stand around the information office and you'll soon have a ride. From Yasuj, savaris (IR15,000), buses and minibuses (IR5000) run frequently to Sepidan and on to Shiraz.

Activities such as horse riding, cross-country skiing, trekking and rock climbing can also be arranged; Mr Raeesi from **Iran Sightseeing** (☎ 0711-235 5939, 0917 313 2926; www .iransightseeing.com) has had good reports.

There are, of course, several other routes through the Zagros and we don't have space to cover them all. To read about a 2006 bicycle trip from Hamedan to Esfahan, see www.travelblog.org/Middle-East/Iran/Es fahan/blog-76174.html.

INTO THE DESERT

'A great silence overcomes me, and
I wonder why I ever thought to use
language.'

Great Persian poet Rumi may never have been to these towns, but this oft-repeated line could have been written specifically for

them. Dasht-e Kavir, the northern of the two deserts that lay themselves across Iran like slowly dehydrating camels, is a mix of sand and salt that is as blinding in its whiteness as the desert is deafening in its total, unimaginable silence. Within these desolate environs exist oases, and among these oases are some sweet spring villages.

Toudeshk   تودشک
☎ 0312

Most people take a bus or savari straight through to Na'in, but it's well worth stopping in on Mohammad Jalali and the villagers at Toudeshk, 95km – or one day's cycling – from Esfahan. This classic desert village of mud-brick buildings, *badgirs* and hospitable locals has been hosting cyclists for years. And now Mohammad and co are eager to welcome others so they too can experience the real Iran and dispel the stereotypes.

English-speaking Mohammad works for a cultural heritage NGO called Miras-e Yarane Jadeye Abrisham (Heritage of Silk Road Followers). It's hard to summarise exactly what they do, but visitors to Toudeshk will live desert life as it's been lived for centuries. That includes a guided walk through the ancient town, *chay*, eating a local meal, *chay*, bathing *hammam*-style and sleeping desert-style, *chay*, and if you've got more time, visiting the Gavkhuni Wetland 70km away. Oh, and that traditional desert activity – free internet. All this for US$8 a night. Sounds good? Contact **Mohammad Jalali** (☎ 0312-637 2586, 0913 365 4420; silkroadngo@ yahoo.com) for details.

If you're not pedalling, take any bus, minibus or savari from Esfahan or Na'in, and ask to get off at Toudeshk.

Na'in   نائین
☎ 0323 / pop 26,300 / elev 1557m

Slumbering Na'in is an important transit point at the geographical centre of Iran and the start of the desert road to Tabas and Mashhad. The ancient town has long been famous for its carpets and 10th-century **Jameh Mosque**. This mosque has no *iwan* and is especially notable for its fine mihrab and innovative yet simple use of stucco decoration, which is remarkably well preserved. Watch out also for the restored **traditional houses** dotted around town. For local knowledge, seek out enthusiastic computer shop owner–cum–freelance guide **Mahmood Mohammadipour** (☎ 225 7930; greenmemoryna@yahoo .com), who will happily show you around.

There are two sleeping options. Budgeteers should try good-value **Mosaferkhaneh Gholami** (☎ 225 2441, 0913 223 4667; r IR70,000), about 300m east of Imam Sq towards the Imamzadeh; there's no English sign but it's a three-storey place above a bakery. Alternatively, the government-run excellent **Na'in Tourist Inn** (Jahangardi Inn; ☎ 225 3088; fax 225 3665; Shahid Rajaie St; r US$40; P ⊠) has stylish split-level apartment-style rooms, 150m south-west of Imam Sq.

Food and internet cafés are concentrated on or near Imam Sq, including **Keliza Pizza** (Imam Sq; ⊗ 11.30am-10pm) and **Teria Torang Coffee Shop** (Imam Sq; ⊗ 10am-8pm Sat-Thu).

Regular buses run from Esfahan (IR5000, 138km, two hours), Kashan (2½ to three hours) and Yazd (1½ to two hours) to Na'in. There is also a direct minibus from Esfahan's Jey minibus terminal (IR7000, three to 3½ hours). Buses usually stop at the roundabout a few hundred metres from Imamzadeh Soltan Said Ali. For Garmeh, wait here at about 4pm for buses en route to Mashhad, which stop at Khur (IR20,000, four hours).

Garmeh گرمه

☎ 0324 / pop – about 260 people & two camels / elev 857m

The tiny oasis village of Garmeh is everything you'd imagine an oasis village to be. More than 25 varieties of date palm spread out from a small spring, and where the palms finish the 1600-year-old mud-brick village begins. In the midst of this village is **Ateshoni** (☎ 443 2156, 0913 223 0874; www.ateshooni .com; per person IR220,000), where Tehrani artist Maziar Ale Davoud and his family have renovated their 265-year-old home into an oasis of the soul in this oasis in the desert. Rates include all the food (such as wonderful dates, pomegranates and the to-die-for cooking of Hadi and Sarra) you can eat.

Part of the beauty of Garmeh is its total, overwhelming silence. When you're not chilling out in the quiet, for a few extra dollars you can hike to hot-water springs, take a desert mountain walk, visit the salt deserts or go camel riding. Accommodation is in the traditional style, with basic mattresses unfolded on the floor of your room.

Ateshoni's popularity means you should book ahead, especially for weekends. You can stay at any time of year, but during summer it gets ridiculously hot.

GETTING THERE & AWAY

Getting to Garmeh is not easy. From Esfahan take the 1pm bus to Khur, 38km to the north of Garmeh on the Na'in to Tabas road. Or meet the bus in Na'in at about 4pm. From Tehran, buses come direct from Terminal-e Jonub to Khur (14 hours) on Sunday and Wednesday. On other days, the bus to Birjand stops in Khur.

From Tehran, five or six buses (Taavonis 8 and 10) depart every day Terminal-e Jonub for Birjand between 2.30pm and 5pm. All of them stop at Khur about 10 hours later; call Ateshoni to arrange to be met in Khur. From Esfahan, a bus leaves daily at 1pm for Khur, or you could get on any bus to Mashhad (though these usually leave later so arrive at inconvenient times).

A bus leaves Yazd for Khur at 7am Saturday and Monday, and 3pm on Thursday. On other days, take any bus to Na'in and connect with the bus from Esfahan at the big roundabout just outside town (the driver will drop you at the right place).

Khur is pretty quiet, but even at 9.30pm you will probably be able to find someone to drive you out to Garmeh. Just say '*Maziar*'. Expect to pay about IR30,000 for the trip. If you call ahead, Ateshoni will arrange for someone to collect you.

Leaving Garmeh, you'll first need to get a lift to Khur. From there, a daily bus to Na'in and Esfahan at 1pm; link to Yazd from Na'in. There are also buses direct to Yazd via the desert route on Sunday and Wednesday at 7am, and Friday at 3pm. These stop at Kharanaq, if you want to stay there – ask Hadi for all the details.'

Tabas طبس

☎ 0353 / pop 35,000 / elev 678m

Once known as the jewel of the desert, the oasis town of Tabas is the largest in Iran's two vast deserts and, as such, is an important hub. Tabas's palm-lined roads and public gardens in vividly painted colours are in stark contrast to the surrounding sands. But most of the evocative architecture that made the town famous was flattened by a massive earthquake in 1978 that killed 26,000.

Today the highlight is the **Bagh-e Golshan** (Imam Khomeini Sq), with water surging through its lush variety of tropical plants, though the small cages of local fauna will appeal mainly to people who don't like animals. The garden is well signed. The ruined 11th-century citadel, the **Arg-e Tabas**, is also worth a look.

Hotel Bahman (☎ 422 5951; tw/apt IR150,000/300,000; P 🖳), on the street leading east from the enormous new Imamzadeh Hossein Nebn Musa (at the northern entrance to town), has ancient, overpriced and unpleasant rooms.

Imam Khomeini Sq is home to the **Restaurant Khatam** (☯ 7am-midnight), which serves tasty food in large portions and offers the only (uberbasic) budget rooms in town (for about IR60,000).

GETTING THERE & AWAY

Tabas is not exactly a bus hub. Most services are going to or from Mashhad, including to Yazd (IR38,000, eight hours, 419km) at about 11.30pm; Mashhad (IR45,000, 10 hours, 521km) via Ferdows (IR8000 to IR15,000, three hours); Esfahan (IR60,000, nine to 10 hours, several from 8pm to midnight). Try to check departures ahead of time at the traffic circle–cum–bus terminal beside the Imamzadeh Hossein Nebn Musa. Savaris run to Ferdows (IR40,000, two hours) and Khur (IR40,000, two hours), also from near the 'terminal'.

Baghestan-e Olia   باغستان اوليا
☎ 0534 / pop – not many / elev 1594m

Two hours' drive east of Tabas is Ferdows, a largish town at the edge of the desert flanked to the north and east by rocky mountains. Ferdows is of little interest really, but in the garden village of Baghestan-e Olia 15km north, architect Noushin Ghiassi has built two modern homes and has opened them to visitors.

The experience is totally different to Garmeh or Toudeshk. Rather than mud-bricks, the richly decorated contemporary-style **Moonlight House** (☎ 223 3096, 0912 314 5200; in Tehran gnoushina@yahoo.com; per person incl food €45) feels sophisticated but homely. Noushin speaks Italian and English.

The surrounding hills are home to steep-sided valleys, fast-flowing streams and orchards of pomegranate, walnut and almond that are spectacularly green between about April and July, when the valleys are filled with the smell of exotic herbs. Noushin can arrange reasonably priced half- and full-day walks with a guide or just a map, and trips to villages such as tiny Koreshk (see the boxed text, p256). Advance bookings are essential as Noushin is not always there. Moonlight House and a neighbour's home sleep a maximum of 15 people, in beds and on carpets, and the food is absolutely delicious.

From Mashhad, buses (IR25,000, four hours) pass between about 6pm and 10pm en route to Esfahan and Yazd. Ask to be dropped at the police check point in Baghestan; taxis opposite here will take you the last 5km. From points west, buses en route to Mashhad pass late at night. A savari from Tabas to Ferdows (IR40,000, two hours) is easier, then take a taxi. Alternatively, Iran Air flies daily between Tehran and Birjand, from where a taxi service costs about IR170,000 – Noushin can arrange it.

YAZD   يزد
☎ 0351 / pop 533,000 / elev 1213m

With its winding lanes, forest of *badgirs*, mud-brick old town and charismatic accommodation, Yazd is one of the highlights of any trip to Iran. Wedged between the northern Dasht-e Kavir and southern Dasht-e Lut, it doesn't have the big-ticket sights of Esfahan or Persepolis, but as a whole, and in the context of its relationship with the desert, it is at least as enchanting. It is a place to wander and get lost in the maze of historic streets and lanes (and your imagination), before returning to a hotel that is itself a piece of Yazd's history. It's also an ideal base for day trips to several evocative villages and towns.

Yazd has been known for its silks and other fabrics since before Marco Polo passed through. And while weaving remains an important industry, it is tourism on a far grander scale than Polo would have imagined that has been booming since the traditional hotels began opening. While nothing like Qom, Yazd is a fairly conservative town, especially in the older parts. It is also home to Iran's largest population of Zoroastrians (see the boxed text, p261). Yazd can be quite cold in winter and is boiling hot in summer, but not humid.

VOICES OF IRAN: ZOHREH ZAMBE

Age: 15
Lives in: Koreshk, South Khorasan Province, at the edge of the Dasht-e Kavir

'Koreshk is a very small village and there are only about 50 people living here, in 20 families. I am the youngest in my family and I have three sisters and two brothers – for some reason there are always more girls than boys in this village. We're in the mountains and most people farm for fruit, walnuts and almonds. Everyone works here and we daughters help all the time. Last night we were up at 2am to change the water channels.

We also grow roses and sell the petals to be used in rose water and in medicines, though I don't know which ones. Oh, and carpet weaving! It's hard work! And we don't like it, but it's important. All the girls who make carpet have to get eye glasses when they're young because they are always looking so hard! Everyone in the village is related somehow and we all work together. When we don't have enough bread we ask the neighbours, and when they don't have enough, they ask us. That's how it works here.

I like the village, but it gets very cold and icy here in winter. Definitely, in winter the city is better. My brother lives in Tehran and I like to visit him. When I'm there I am with my brother all the time so I don't see so much traffic, but we do visit Qom.

There are no jobs here so most of the young people leave for the city, either to Gonabad or Tehran. I'd like to go but the parents won't allow me to leave until I get married. My mother was married when she was 13! And she had her first baby when she was 14! My father is seven years older. But I don't want that. I want to be 20 or 25 when I get married, and my husband should be not more than four years older. But then, it is hard to find a husband here…'

History

Yazd is said to be the 'oldest living city on Earth'. This might be a difficult claim to verify, but it is widely believed the site has been continually inhabited for about 7000 years. Its position on important trading routes and a tendency towards diplomacy go some way to explaining Yazd's longevity. The fact that commercial prosperity never really translated into real political power is probably another reason. When Marco Polo passed this way in the 13th century, he described Yazd as 'a very fine and splendid city and a centre of commerce'. It was spared destruction by Genghis Khan and Tamerlane, and flourished in the 14th and 15th centuries, with silk, textile and carpet production the main home-grown industry. Like most of Iran, Yazd fell into decline when the Safavids were defeated and remained little more than a provincial outpost until the last shah extended the railway line to Yazd.

Orientation

Yazd is laid out on a very loose northeast–southwest grid, the centre of which is Beheshti Sq. Within this grid, however, lies the mud-brick old city, a warren of *kuches* (lanes) and covered walkways and bazaars. Expect to get lost when walking around the old city – when you want to get out, just ask for directions or orient yourself by climbing until you can see the minarets of the Jameh Mosque.

Most of the hotels listed are in the old city and it's easy enough to explore the town on foot. Imam Khomeini St is the main street, running northeast from Beheshti Sq. It's crossed by Qeyam St, from where the bazaar fans out.

The airport is on the western fringe of the city while the train station and bus terminal are about 2.5km southwest of Beheshti Sq.

Information

EMERGENCY

Dr Mogibiyan Hospital (☎ 624 0061; Kashani St) For urgent problems.
Police headquarters (☎ 110; Azadi Sq)
Tourist police (☎ 621 4444; ⏲ 24hr) Opposite the Heidarzadeh Coin Museum.

INTERNET ACCESS

Both of the following places can burn photos to either CD or DVD.

Friendly Internet (Masjed-e Jameh St; per hr IR8000; ☾ 9am-1pm & 5-10pm) 'Is everything alright?' Eager to please.

Issatis.net (☎ 623 1425; www.issatis.net; Kashani St; per hr IR6000; ☾ 9am-1.30pm & 5-9.30pm Thu) Not so convenient, but the services here include international calls, writing DVDs and the sale of pre-paid internet access and international phonecards.

MEDICAL SERVICES
Chamran 24-hour Pharmacy (☎ 626 6900; Farrokhi St)

MONEY
Banks in Yazd take a commission of about US$2 on exchanges.

Bank Melli Central Branch (Shohada Crossroads) Exchange is upstairs.

Bank Tejarat (Qeyam St) Also upstairs.

Yazd Exchange (☎ 624 7220; www.yazdexchange.com; Kashani St; ☾ 8am-10pm) Opposite the Ateshkadeh, these guys have a good reputation for the best rates; call them and they'll deliver the cash to your hotel. Also has an office at the airport and can safely store luggage.

POST
Main post office (Ghasem Abad St; ☾ 7.30am-2pm) It's out of town but you'll have to come here if you're looking to turn your rug into a flying carpet.

Post office (Imam Khomeini St) Near Bank Melli.

TELEPHONE
Far Away International Telephone (Imam Khomeini St; calls per min IR2500; ☾ 9am-1pm & 4-10pm)

Main telephone office (Motahhari St)

Shohada Telephone Office (Amir Chakhmaq Sq; ☾ 8am-10pm Sat-Thu, 8am-2pm & 5-10pm Fri)

TOURIST INFORMATION
Tourist information office (☎ 621 6542-5; info@caravansalar.ir; Ziaee Sq; ☾ 9am-6pm, to 8pm summer) A few maps and brochures, but mainly about selling tours. There should usually be an English-speaker there.

TOURS
Most hotels can arrange tours but using an independent guide can be more rewarding. The following can lead tours to almost anywhere in Yazd province, and further, and have been recommended. The most common tour is the Kharanaq–Chak Chak–Meybod loop (about US$40 for three or less people, US$55 with breakfast and lunch), which is impossible on public transport. Other options include camel tours (about US$25 per person for a half-day, US$75

overnight, more for groups comprised of fewer than five people) and desert walks (one day and one night about US$20 per person). Old city tours are also popular. Silk Road Travel (p258) also runs these tours.

Hossain Bagharian (☎ 0913 352 0370) Hossain has been guiding for years and is a straight-shooter. He could talk under wet cement, so rest assured he'll tell you everything he knows…and a bit more.

Massoud Jaladat (☎ 0913 352 4752; fravahar_m@yahoo.com) Massoud is the energy behind Fravihar Ecotours, a fledgling group of Yazdis running mainly desert tours. There are all sorts of reasonably priced options, mainly involving desert trekking; email or call for options and ask about the desert guide.

Mohsen Hajisaeed (☎ 0913 351 4460; yazdguide@yahoo.com) Young, highly organised Mohsen speaks excellent English, leads tours in Yazd, Kerman, Fars and Esfahan provinces (including Bavanat), and can arrange hotel discounts.

Keykhosro Lorian (☎ 0913 353 3343; mrlorian_tourdriver@yahoo.com) Mr Lorian is an English-speaking Zoroastrian driver who has excellent access to the Zoroastrian community.

TRAVEL AGENCIES
The following are good for plane and train tickets.

THE BADGIRS OF YAZD

Any summer visitor to Yazd will understand immediately why the city's roofscape is a forest of *badgirs* (windtowers or wind catchers). These ancient systems of natural air-conditioning are designed to catch even the lightest breeze and direct it to the rooms below. To appreciate the effect, just stand beneath one.

Badgirs range from standard two-sided versions to elaborate six-sided models and all but the simplest consist of at least four parts: the body or trunk that contains the shafts; air shelves that are used to catch some of the hot air and stop it entering the house; flaps to redirect the circulation of the wind; and the roof covering. The currents that enter the house often do so above a pool of cool water, thereby cooling the air, while the warm air continues its circular path, redirected upwards and out of the house through a different shaft. Genius! And while not quite as cold as modern air-con, the *badgir* is a whole lot healthier.

Saadat Seyr Travel & Tour Agency (☎ 626 6599; saadatseyr@pishgaman.com; 21/1 Imamzadeh-ye Ja'far St; ⏲ 7.30am-8pm Sat-Thu, 9am-noon Fri)

Silk Road Travel (☎ 626 7783; www.silkroadhotel.ir; 6th Alley, off Masjed-e Jameh St) Located in the Orient Hotel; has day trips and longer that are aimed at independent travellers. Reasonable value and well organised.

VISA EXTENSIONS

When the **Tourist Police** (☎ 621 4444; Heidarzadeh Coin Museum; ⏲ 24hr) heard we were in town they came to tell us that extending visas in Yazd was easy, and promised that 'if tourists have any problems, just call us and we'll solve it'. Promises, promises. In fact, getting your visa extended here can take as long as

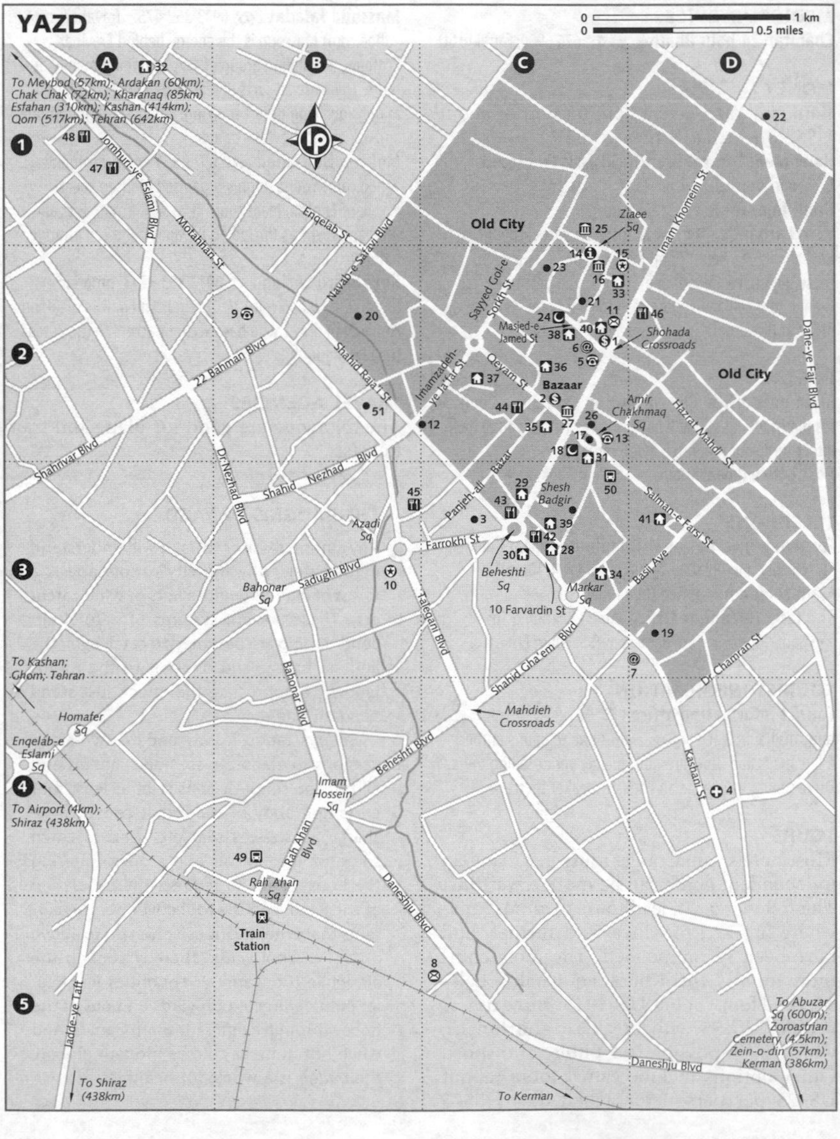

a week. We travelled with one unfortunate guy who, when his passport still hadn't been stamped six days after he submitted it, asked if he could leave town. Of course, they said, if you have any problem 'just call us'. When the two of us were subsequently arrested (my guilt was apparently by association), the Yazd visa guys denied everything, and my travelling companion was put on the first bus back to Yazd. If you can't avoid Yazd, the Tourist Police office deals with extensions (open 7am to noon Saturday to Thursday) and the Bank Melli Central Branch is the place to deposit your cash. They don't promise 30-day extensions, however. See More Time, Please (p395) for details.

Sights

OLD CITY   بافت قديم

With its *badgirs* poking out of a baked-brown labyrinth of lanes, the **old city** of Yazd emerges like a phoenix from the desert – a very old phoenix. Yazd's old city is one of the oldest towns on earth, according to Unesco, and is the perfect place to get a feel for the region's rich history. Just about everything in the old city is made from sun-dried mud bricks, and the resulting brown skyline is dominated by tall *badgirs* on almost every rooftop (see the boxed text The Badgirs of Yazd, p257). The residential quarters appear almost deserted because of the high walls, which shield the houses

from the narrow and labyrinthine *kuches* that crisscross the town.

Follow the walking tour (p262) or just wander around; you'll doubtless discover simple courtyards, ornate wooden doors and some lovely adobe architecture. In the meantime you'll be discovered by countless children who will help lead you out of the maze when you are ready. Be sure to get yourself to the rooftops at some point for fine views over Yazd and into the vast brown expanses of the desert.

Jameh Mosque   مسجد جامع

The magnificent **Jameh Mosque** (Masjed-e Jameh; Masjed-e Jameh St) dominates the old city. Its tiled entrance portal is one of the tallest in Iran, flanked by two magnificent 48m-high minarets and adorned with an inscription from the 15th century. The exquisite mosaics on the dome and mihrab, and the tiles above the main western entrance to the courtyard are particularly stunning.

Built for Sayyed Roknaddin in the 15th century, it's on the site of a 12th-century building believed to have itself replaced an earlier fire temple. In the courtyard of the mosque there is a stairwell leading down to part of the Zarch Qanat, used these days for ritual ablutions. For a small tip, the caretaker will allow you down. The guys at Friendly Internet Café (p256) can arrange access to the roof, usually in the late afternoon.

CENTRAL IRAN

THE QANAT

For at least 2000 years Iranians have been digging *qanats* (underground water channels) to irrigate crops and supply drinking water. To build a *qanat* you first need to find an underground water source. This source could be more than 100m deep, but as the whole system is reliant on gravity the source must be higher than the final destination. Then you dig a tunnel just wide and tall enough to crawl along, so the water can flow across an extremely shallow gradient to its destination. The mounds of soil you'll see in long lines across the desert are the top of wells, dug to dispose of excavated soil and allow ventilation. Because of the hazards and expense of constructing a *qanat*, complex laws govern every aspect of their use and maintenance. Iran is thought to have more than 50,000 *qanats*. While modern irrigation projects now take priority, *qanats* and other traditional methods of supplying water are still very important. And as hundreds of towns and villages – including Bam, Kashan and Mahan – still rely on qanats for water, the highly skilled and well-paid *qanat* builders of Yazd won't be picking up redundancy cheques for many years yet.

For the lowdown on *qanats,* head for the impressive **Yazd Water Museum** (☎ 626 8340; Amir Chakhmaq Sq; admission IR10,000; ☉ 8am-7pm), located in a restored mansion that happens to have a *qanat* or two underneath. The displays are clear and mostly in English.

Bogheh-ye Sayyed Roknaddin

بقعه سید رکن الدین

The beautiful blue-tiled dome of the **Bogheh-ye Sayyed Roknaddin** (Mausolem of Sayyed Roknaddin; off Masjed-e Jameh St; ☉ 8am-1pm & 4-8pm Sat-Thu, 10am-noon Fri), the tomb of local Islamic notable Sayyed Roknaddin Mohammed Qazi, is visible from any elevated point in the city. Built 700 years ago, the dome is notable but the deteriorating interior stucco and other decoration remains impressive. The door is often closed but a knock should bring the caretaker.

Khan-e Lari

خانه لاری

The 150-year-old **Khan-e Lari** (admission IR2000; ☉ 7am-6pm, to 8pm summer) is one of the best-preserved Qajar-era houses in Yazd. The *badgirs*, traditional doors, stained-glass windows, elegant archways and alcoves mark it out as one of the city's grandest homes. The merchant family who built it have long gone, and it's now home to architecture students and cultural heritage officers. It's signposted west of Zaiee Sq; see the walking tour (p262) for directions.

Alexander's Prison

زندان اسکندر

This 15th-century domed school is known as **Alexander's Prison** (Zaiee Sq; admission IR2000; ☉ 8am-sunset, 8am-1pm & 4pm-sunset summer) because of a reference to this apparently dastardly place in a Hafez poem. Whether the deep well in the middle of its courtyard was in fact built by Alexander the Great and used as a dungeon seems doubtful, no matter what your guide tells you. Recently

renovated, the building itself is worth a look for the small display on the old city of Yazd, the clean toilets, the overly fluorescent but mercifully cool subterranean teahouse and the studio-shop of sitar-maker and -player **Moslem Mirzazadeh** (☎ 0913 351 5452; moslemmirzazadeh@yahoo.com; ☉ 9am-2pm & 4-7pm).

The early-11th-century brick **Tomb of the 12 Imams** is almost next door to Alexander's Prison. The once-fine (but now badly deteriorated) inscriptions inside bear the names of the Shiite Imams (see The 12 Imams, p56), though none are actually buried here.

Amir Chakhmaq Complex

مجموعه امیر چخماق

The stunning three-storey façade of the *takieh* (a building used during the rituals to commemorate the death of Imam Hossein) in the **Amir Chakhmaq Complex** (Amir Chakhmaq Sq; admission IR3000; ☉ No Ruz only) is one of the largest Hosseniehs in Iran. Its rows of perfectly proportioned sunken alcoves are at their best, and most photogenic, around sunset when the light softens and the towering exterior is discreetly floodlit. Recent work has added sides, though their exact purpose wasn't clear when we visited (hopefully not shops!). During the No Ruz holiday it's possible to climb up for spectacular views across Yazd, but at most other times it's closed.

Underneath the complex is a lacklustre **bazaar**, where *kababis* and souvenir shops open only when there is sufficient interest. In front of the *takieh*, look out for the huge wooden palm *nakhl*, an important centrepiece for the observance of the Shiites' passionate Ashura commemorations.

Saheb A Zaman Club Zurkhaneh

زور خانه صاحب الزمان

Just off the north side of Amir Chakhmaq Sq is the **Saheb A Zaman Club Zurkhaneh** (admission IR10,000; ⓦ workouts 5pm & 8.30pm Sat-Thu), which is worth seeing both for its Iranian brand of body building and because it's a quite amazing structure. The modern club is inside a cavernous *ab anbar* (water reservoir) built about 1580. Looking like a 29m-high standing egg from the inside, and crowned with five burly *badgirs*, the reservoir stored water for much of the town. The hour-long workouts in the Zurkhaneh are an interesting window on Iranian culture; see (p52).

BAGH-E DOLAT ABAD

باغ دولت آباد

Once a residence of Persian regent Karim Khan Zand, **Bagh-e Dolat Abad** (admission IR30,000; ⓦ 7.30am-5pm, to 6pm summer) was built about 1750 and consists of a small pavilion set amid quiet gardens. The interior of the pavilion is superb, with intricate latticework and exquisite stained-glass windows. It's also renowned for having Iran's loftiest *badgir*, standing over 33m, though this one was rebuilt after it collapsed in the 1960s. The entrance can be reached from the western end of Shahid Raja'i St.

ZOROASTRIAN SITES

اماكن زرتشتى

Yazd is home to the largest and most active Zoroastrian community in Iran; see (below).

Ateshkadeh

آتشكده

Zoroastrians come from around the world to see this **Ateshkadeh** (Sacred Eternal Flame; ⓦ by appointment), often referred to as the Zoroastrian Fire Temple, said to have been burning since about AD 470. Visible through a window from the entrance hall, the flame was transferred to Ardakan in 1174, then to Yazd in 1474 and to its present site in 1940. Above the entrance you can see the Fravahar symbol.

ZOROASTRIANISM

Zoroastrianism was the main religion across the Iranian plateau until the Arab Conquest brought Islam to the fore. Zoroastrians are followers of Zoroaster (Zartosht or Zarathustra), who was probably born between 1000 BC and 1500 BC, possibly near present-day Lake Urimiyeh or further north in Central Asia – no-one is sure. Zoroastrianism was one of the first religions to postulate an omnipotent, invisible god. The supreme being, Ahura Mazda, has no symbol or icon, but he asked that followers pray to him in the direction of light. The only light the ancients controlled was fire, so they created fire temples to keep the flame burning eternally.

Very little of what Zoroaster wrote has survived, though the teachings in the Avesta (sometimes referred to as the Zoroastrian bible) are attributed to him. The core lesson is dualism: the eternal battle of good and evil. Zoroaster believed in two principles – Vohu Mano (Good Mind) and Ahem Nano (Bad Mind), which were responsible for day and night, life and death. These two opposing 'minds' coexisted within the supreme being, Ahura Mazda, and in all living things.

Since Zoroastrians believe in the purity of the elements, they refuse to bury their dead (pollutes the earth) or cremate them (pollutes the atmosphere). Instead, the dead were exposed in 'towers of silence', where their bones were soon cleaned up by the vultures. Nowadays, deceased Zoroastrians are usually buried in graves lined with concrete to prevent 'contamination' of the earth.

Many Zoroastrian temples are adorned with bas-relief winged figures that symbolise Fravahar, the part of the spirit that reaches Ahura Mazda after death. The old man symbolises experience and wisdom, the three layers of feathers on the wings symbolise purity of thought, word and deed, and the semi-long tail in front represents Vohu Mano, while the rear tail is Ahem Nano.

Of the 150,000 or more Zoroastrians in the world, the number in and around Yazd has dwindled to about 5500. Zoroastrian women can be recognised by their patterned headscarves and embroidered dresses with predominant colours of white, cream or red. They never wear chadors, but do follow the strict hejab laws governing women's dress.

Zoroastrianism is also known as Mazdaism from the name of its supreme god, Ahura Mazda, and as Magism from the name of its ancient priests, the magi. The Three Wise Men of the Bible are believed to have been Zoroastrian magi, hence the Adoration of the Magi.

Getting in is difficult as the caretaker is often not around. Try knocking at the small gate in a side alley, but if that doesn't work your best bet is a Zoroastrian guide (p257). In the northeast of Yazd, the **Fortress of Lions** (Ghal'eh-ye Asadan) houses another Zoroastrian eternal flame. It is also usually closed.

Towers of Silence برج خاموشی

Set on two lonely, barren hilltops on the southern outskirts of Yazd are the evocative Zoroastrian **Towers of Silence** (Dakhmeh-ye Zartoshtiyun). In accordance with Zoroastrian beliefs about the purity of the earth, dead bodies were not buried but left in these uncovered stone towers so that vultures could pick the bones clean. Such towers have not been used since the '60s. At the foot of the hills are several other disused Zoroastrian buildings, including a defunct well, a water cistern and two small *badgirs*, a kitchen and a lavatory. The modern **Zoroastrian cemetery** is nearby. The easiest way to get here is by chartering a private taxi for about IR30,000 return, including waiting time of 45 minutes or so. Ask for Dakhmeh-ye Zartoshtiyun.

Get Lost In Yazd Walking Tour

Start at the **Amir Chakhmaq Complex** (**1**; p260), and check out the nearby **Amir Chakhmaq Mosque** (**2**) and, on the opposite corner, the **Yazd Water Museum** (**3**; see The Qanat, p260). From here, head up Imam Khomeini St, take a quick look at the **Hazireh Mosque** (**4**), and turn left up Masjed-e Jameh St. Before you reach the imposing mosque, turn down a lane to the right to see the stunning portal of the turquoise-domed **Bogheh-ye Sayyed Roknaddin** (**5**; p260). If you're hungry, you could now stop at the **Orient Hotel** (**6**; opposite) for lunch and a spectacular view, or continue into the **Jameh Mosque** (**7**, p259). Exit the mosque through the northeastern door (near the *qanat*), turn right, then left, and keep straight for about 75m to a junction with several arches and open ceilings. Turn left here and you'll reach an open space with a playground. Stay on the right (eastern) side and keep heading northeast. After about 250m on Fazel St a small lane leads off to the right, where a **water reservoir** (**8**) surrounded by four *badgirs* stands next to a shaded park. Continue left (northeast), parallel to Fazel St, and you'll pass the Kohan Hotel. Stay straight another

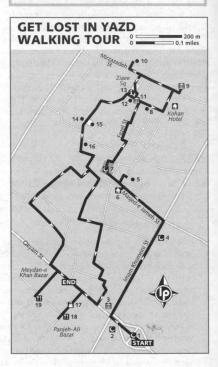

WALKING TOUR

Start Amir Chakhmaq Complex
Finish Hammam-e Khan Restaurant
Distance about 5km
Duration three to five hours, depending on how often you get lost

100m or so and you'll come to Mirzazadeh St. To the right is the **Heidarzadeh Coin Museum** (**9**), which is actually more interesting than it sounds. Heading northwest, walk past Ziaee Sq and keep straight for about 150m. Turn right down a small alley to the **Khan-e Lari** (**10**; p260). Head back to Ziaee Sq and turn right. Ahead is the dome of **Alexander's Prison** (**11**; p260) – which has a clean bathroom – and just beyond is the **Tomb of the 12 Imams** (**12**; p260). You can stop for a drink or directions at the **tourist information office** (**13**; p257) opposite. From the tomb, turn left and follow a sweeping bend until it comes to a dusty space with a concrete table-tennis table. Then head left (southwest) under a domed passage for about 70m until you come to a square with a three-storey white façade *(takieh)* on the left. If you're very lucky, the green-and-white metal door on the right will be unlocked (reach through to try it from the inside), and you'll be able to climb to the domed roof of the **Hosseinieh (14)** for quite splendid views of the old city. If not, you could carefully climb the stairs at the back of the **takieh (15)** for almost-as-good views. Continue southwest for about 150m. On your left is the untiled domed roof of the now-closed **Madraseh-e Kamalieh (16)**. Keep along the same lane and you'll see the minarets of the Jameh Mosque. Using these as a guide, you're now on your own. Wend your way through the old city, heading roughly southwest, until you reach Qeyam St. Cross into the **Panjeh-ali Bazar (17)** and head for either **Malek-o Tojjar (18**; p264) or the **Hammam-e Khan Restaurant (19**; p265) for some well-earned sustenance.

Sleeping

Yazd has quite simply the most charismatic, historic bunch of hotels in Iran, and possibly the entire Middle East. More than 10 *khan-e sonnati* (traditional houses) have now been transformed into hotels. The result is 24-hour cultural immersion; see the sights of this historic city by day, and then sit on the *takhts* (daybeds), sip tea and eat local food as Iranians have for centuries. Compare this with the sense of place you get in the usual cookie-cutter hotels. Even better, your money contributes to the preservation and renaissance of this historic Silk Road city.

Not surprisingly, the old city is the most atmospheric area to stay in. Almost all hotels offer day trips to Chak Chak, Meybod and Kharanaq (see Around Yazd, p266), and prices are in proportion to room rates.

BUDGET

Hotel Amir Chakhmagh (☎ 626 9823; Amir Chakhmaq Sq; s/tw/tr IR50,000/80,000/120,000; ✗ 🖳) The Amir Chakhmagh is not a historic hotel, though at this rate in a few years it will be…very old indeed. It's in a great location beside the Amir Chakhmaq complex, but rooms can be noisy and the shared bathrooms could be cleaner. The dorms listed in any of the following places are probably better.

ourpick Silk Road Hotel (Jada-e Abrisham; ☎ 625 2730; www.silkroadhotel.ir; 5 Tal-e Khakestary Alley, off Masjed-e Jameh Ave; dm €4, s/d/tr with breakfast €14/22/30; 🅿 ✗) Two minutes' walk from the Masjed-

e Jameh, the Silk Road's mix of traditional courtyard setting, delicious food, laid-back vibe and fair price has made it the most talked about travellers' stop in Iran. With 15 simple but attractive rooms (no TVs) and a seven-bed underground dormitory (no bathroom), it caters to backpackers, flashpackers and even the odd ambassador. The buffet breakfast is both delicious and wonderfully social. Owners Ali and Sebastian can offer discounts for longer stays.

Kohan Hotel (Kohan Kashaneh; ☎ 621 2485; www .kohanhotel.com; off Imam Khomeini St; dm IR50,000, s/tw with breakfast IR170,000/250,000; ✗ 🖳) Owner Taslim and his family have renovated the family home and given it a relaxed, welcoming ambience. The 18 traditional but unadorned rooms are set around a lush garden courtyard, while two six-bed dorms (each with bathroom) open off a long stairway to a *qanat*. A restaurant should be open when you arrive. To find it, head northeast on Imam Khomeini St, past Masjed-e Jameh Ave, and follow the stencil signs along a lane on your left. If you get lost, it's near the Coin Museum.

Rose Traditional Hotel (☎ 622 5790-92; Farhang Alley, off Imam Khomeini Ave; s/d IR220,000/300,000; ✗) Deep in the Old City, this unpretentious little place has comfortable and fair-value if not-exactly-inspiring rooms. A restaurant is attached.

If the others are full (or you need the parking), the following two oldies are cheap but uninspiring.

Aria Hotel (☎ 626 0411; 10 Farvardin St; r IR80,000-150,000; ✗) Overpriced rooms, some without bathroom, around a courtyard. Communal kitchen. No English is spoken.

Beheshty Hotel (☎ 626 5517; Imam Khomeini St; s/tw/tr IR60,000/80,000/110,000; ✗ 🅿) Simple, clean rooms. Only the triple has attached bathroom. Secure parking for overlanders.

MIDRANGE

All of the following are traditional hotels in renovated or converted homes in Yazd's old city.

Soroush Guesthouse (☎ 625 5159; off Basij Ave; s/tw/tr US$27/38/50; ✗) The attractive-looking Soroush has rooms on two levels around a sunken courtyard, though for size, cleanliness and value they are not fantastic; try others first.

Orient Hotel (☎ 626 7783; orient_hotel@gmail .com; 6th Alley, off Masjed-e Jameh St; s/d/tr with breakfast €20/30/40; ✗ 🖳) From the same owners as the Silk Road Hotel, the Orient is set around two high-sided courtyards and is a more family-oriented place. The convivial service, comfortable rooms, unbeatable location beside the Masjed-e Jameh and rooftop Marco Polo Restaurant (opposite) make this a top choice. Discounts possible.

Malek-o Tojjar (☎ 622 4060; www.malek-o-tojar .com; Panjeh-ali Bazar, Qeyam St; dm US$5, s US$20-25, tw US$35-40, tr US$45-60, f US$75; ⊠) Down a narrow, lamp-lit passage from the Panjeh-ali Bazar is Yazd's original traditional hotel, where you'll soon be lying around drinking tea, eating fine food and feeling transported to a different time. This Qajar-era home was converted, not completely renovated, which means everything is original. Rooms are cobbled together from odd spaces connected by low doorways and steep stairways, bathrooms are tiny and plumbing can be inconsistent. Still, the atmosphere, delicious food (see right) and homely service make it a good choice. There's also a fine dorm, though it can be cold in winter. Coming from Qeyam St, look for the sign and small doorway on the left.

Yazd Traditional Hotel (☎ 622 8500-09; www .yazdhotel.com; Amir Chakhmaq Sq; s/d/tr/f US$50/70/85/100; ⊠ 🖳) At the top of the midrange, this 215-year-old mansion was recently restored and is run by enthusiastic young Yazdis who deliver above-average service. The 24 attractive rooms retain their odd shapes, stained glass and low doorways, and there's even a sauna and two small Jacuzzis, to be used one-sex-at-a-time, of course.

Mehr Traditional Hotel (☎ 622 7400; www.mehr hotel.ir; Labe Khandaq Alley, off Qeyam St; s/d/tr/ste with breakfast US$35/50/70/95; Ⓟ ⊠ 🖳) The 250-year-old Khan-e Zargar-e Yazdi has been lovingly restored and converted and is an excellent traditional choice. Signposted from Qeyam St, the rooms here are bigger and better equipped than some, the food is delicious, service responsive and rooftop views expansive.

Moshir Caravanserai Yazd Hotel (☎ 622 7050-54; www.caravanseraihotel.com; Imamzadeh-ye Ja'far Blvd; tw/ste IR600,000/1,000,000; ⊠) This Moshir, not to be confused with the Mamalak Moshir, is a good choice deep in the Old City. The 22 mid-sized rooms are set around a two-storey restored caravanserai. It has a welcoming feel, and big low-season discounts make it particularly worthwhile.

Dad Hotel (☎ 622 9444; www.hoteldadint.com; 214 Favardin St; s/d US$30/60, ste US$100-120; Ⓟ ⊠ 🖳 🕱) Dad is not named for anyone's father,

though as the brainchild of an 84-year-old patriarch it could be called 'great granddad'. The 54 spacious, modern and well-equipped rooms are reasonably stylish, though there is not much natural light and, well, they don't feel as real as the genuinely old places. Still, they're good value, especially when you can take a dip in the sparkling underground pool (women AM, men PM).

TOP END

Jumping on the *khan-e sonnati* bandwagon are these two faux-traditional places, purpose built as hotels.

Hotel Mamalak Moshir (Moshir Gardens; ☎ 523 9760-65; www.hotelgardenmoshir.com; Enqelab Ave; s/d/tr/ste with breakfast US$65/85/100/140; ⊠ 🖳) The largest hotel in Yazd, the Mamalak Moshir is a faux-traditional place set around an expansive, attractive garden. Rooms are a mix of subterranean and above-ground affairs, all very attractively decorated with bright colours and stained glass. The restaurant is also quite good. For Iranians, this is *the* place to stay in Yazd, but the location away from the Old City is inconvenient and the service disorganised.

Laleh Hotel (☎ 622 5048; www.yazdlalehhotel.com; opposite Abanbar Golshan, off Basij Ave; s/d US$70/95; Ⓟ ⊠ 🖳) Laleh is undoubtedly one of the most stunning of the restored homes, with 40 luxurious rooms set around three courtyards. It's not, however, the best place to stay. Service, especially in the restaurant, is very one-star, and that's before we even mention the food. Better value elsewhere.

Eating

Most of the traditional hotels use one of their courtyards as a restaurant. We're listing some of the better options here, but rest assured that if you're staying in a traditional hotel, food won't be too far away. Yazd is famous for *baghlava*, which is similar but thicker than classic Turkish baklava, and *pashmak*, a solid type of fairy floss or cotton candy.

RESTAURANTS

our pick **Malek-o Tojjar** (☎ 622 4060; www.malek -o-tojar.com; Panjeh-ali Bazar, off Qeyam St; meals IR35,000) The evocative surrounds and fine Iranian dishes here are complemented with several regional classics, including some delightful soups, *bademjan* and other vegetarian dishes. And it's very reasonably priced considering the surrounds.

our pick **Marco Polo Restaurant** (☎ 626 7783; off Masjed-e Jameh Ave; meals IR35,000-65,000) Set like a crown atop the Orient Hotel, this glass-sided restaurant serves up sumptuous views of the Masjed-e Jameh and surrounding blue-tiled domes and delicious Iranian food that's fit for the setting. Ideal for a romantic dinner.

Silk Road Hotel Restaurant (☎ 625 2730; 5 Tal-e Khakestary Alley, off Masjed-e Jameh Ave; meals IR30,000-65,000) While the Iranian food here is very good, the delicious (if not super-hot) sub-continental curries are the most popular dishes among travellers who can't face another kabab. Relaxed, social atmosphere.

Mozaffar Traditional Restaurant (☎ 622 7664; Khalf Bagh Alley, off Motahari Ave; meals IR35,000-60,000; ☺ noon-3pm & 6-11pm) A recent addition to the *sonnati* scene, the Mozaffar is set in and around a particularly large courtyard, with both private rooms and *takhts*. To the standard Iranian menu, add (brace yourself) pizza. Expected to open rooms by 2009.

Hammam-e Khan Restaurant (Chaykhaneh-ye San'ati; ☎ 627 0366; Meydan-e Khan Bazar, off Qeyam St; meals IR35,000-60,000; ☺ 11.30am-3.30pm & 7.30-11pm) Deep in the heart of the old city, this restored underground *hammam* is one of the original historic restorations in Yazd and deserves its ongoing popularity. The interior is all tranquil pools, arched ceilings and fine tilework, and the food is delicious (as long as it's not too busy). Follow the signs from Qeyam St.

Pizza Gole Sorkh (☎ 725 7519; Jomhuri-ye Eslami Blvd; pizzas IR20,000-50,000; ☺ 6-11pm) After working for almost 30 years as a pizza chef in Australia, the owner returned home to open a modern, busy restaurant serving arguably the best pizzas in Iran and a range of Italian classics. His serve of Aussie slang is pretty good, too.

Baharestan Restaurant (☎ 622 5107; Beheshti Sq; meals IR25,000; ☺ 11.30am-5pm) Forget atmosphere and style, the Baharestan is about tasty staples at tasty prices; the *khoresht* is best.

QUICK EATS

Amiran Paludeh (Favardin St, off Beheshti Sq) This tiny place specialises in delicious *paludeh*, a type of sorbet made of rice flour, grated fruit and rose-water (IR1500 a bowl).

Yazd Traditional Cookie (☎ 525 3673; Jomhuri-ye Eslami Blvd; ☺ 8am-4pm) Sweet shop extraordinaire! A huge array of *shirin* (sweets) is made in front of you by a team of busy men who will happily let you taste a few offerings; the pistachio-flavoured *loz-e peste* is supreme!

Nemoner Sandwich (Imam Khomeini St; camel burgers IR8000; ☺ Sat-Thu) Fancy a camel burger? This modest little place can knock one up in about three minutes. There's no English sign, but it's directly opposite the camel butchery.

Sito Coffee Shop & Pizza (☎ 622 0888; Amir Chakhmaq Sq; pizzas IR30,000; ☺ 11am-11pm) The modern Iranian mix of pizza and miscellaneous other dishes won't have you writing home, but the views from the rooftop (in summer) just might.

Shopping

The old city bazaars are probably the best places in Iran to buy silk (known locally as *tirma*), brocade, glassware and cloth – products that brought the town its prosperity in centuries past. If you have a sweet tooth, don't forget to try *pashmak* (Iranian fairy floss), available in many shops around Beheshti Sq.

Getting There & Away

AIR

Yazd airport (☎ 199) is not the busiest in Iran. **Iran Air** (☎ 622 2080; Motahhari St) flies to Tehran (IR316,000, 70 minutes, twice daily).

BUS & MINIBUS

All buses leave from the **main bus terminal** (Rah Ahan Blvd), about 3km southwest of the centre, and accessible by shuttle taxi from Beheshti and Azadi Sqs.

Fares are for *mahmooly*/Volvo buses, though Volvos are more frequent:

Destination	Fare	Duration	Departures
Bam	IR50,000(V)	7-9hr	4pm service, usually a few others
Bandar Abbas	IR36,000/ 60,000	9-11hr	frequent
Esfahan	IR12,500/ 30,000	4-5hr	frequent
Kerman	IR16,500/ 30,000	4-5hr	frequent
Mashhad	IR42,000/ 80,000	14-16hr	3-6pm
Shiraz	IR18,000/ 45,000	5-7hr	8am, 2pm & 8.30pm
Tabas	IR37,000	8hr	3-6pm
Tehran	IR33,700/ 45,000	10hr	frequent
Zahedan	IR65,000(V)	14hr	4pm service, usually a few others

The 4pm Zahedan service gets you there with time to continue to the border for a morning crossing. Any bus to Zahedan will drop you in Bam. For Garmeh, see p254.

TRAIN

There are three trains daily from Yazd to Tehran (though berths can be hard to come by): two with six-berth couchettes (IR48,550, eight hours), via Kashan and Qom, departing at 9pm and 10.10pm; and a four-berth couchette at about 2am en route from Bandar Abbas. From Tehran, trains leave at 8.35pm and 10.20pm. For Kerman the train from Tehran stops at about 2.20am, but the 2nd-class train (IR15,950, five hours) departing at 6.10am is a better choice. For Bandar Abbas (1st class only, IR53,000, nine hours) there is a daily train at midnight, and on Monday, Wednesday and Friday at 7.10pm. Trains to Mashhad (Ghazal 1st class IR149,000) leave at 4.50pm Monday, Wednesday and Friday, arriving at 6.10am.

The **train station** (☎ 139; ⊙ 8am-1.30pm & 7-11pm) is next to the main bus terminal. Get here by shuttle taxi from Beheshti or Azadi Sqs, or charter a taxi for about IR10,000. Oddly, train tickets are much easier to buy from agencies (p257) than at the station.

Getting Around

To the airport take a shuttle taxi from Enqelab-e Eslami Sq for about IR2000, or a private taxi for IR20,000. Taxis *dar baste* start at about IR6000 for short trips, and cost IR10,000 to the terminals.

AROUND YAZD

Kharanaq, Chak Chak, Meybod and Ardakan are best seen as part of a looping day trip from Yazd. It's a long day (about 7am to 6pm) and you can either hire a taxi from the street (about IR250,000) or take a guided tour (p257), which is much more rewarding but more costly. Minibuses run to Meybod or Ardakan from the main bus terminal in Yazd, but there's no public transport at all to Chak Chak. The irregular bus to Garmeh (p254) passes Kharanaq, and you can sleep there – either en route to/from Garmeh or as a destination in itself.

Kharanaq   خرانق

The virtually deserted and crumbling mud-brick village of Kharanaq, in a valley about 70km north of Yazd, is believed to be more than 1000 years old and the site occupied in some form for more than 4000 years. The Qajar-era **mosque**, 17th-century **shaking minaret** and **caravanserai** on the edge of town have all been restored. You'll need a key to get into these, however, and you'll need a guide (or the folks at Silk Road Kharanaq) to arrange that.

Many of the buildings are falling down and we've seen at least one tourist fall through the roof, so watch your step. Walk into the valley below to see an ancient aqueduct, built to irrigate the surrounding fields. Photographers will love it mid-afternoon. **Silk Road Kharanaq** (dm/s/d €5/10/15) is run by the Silk Road guys in Yazd (p263), and all bookings should be made through them. The modest adobe building has been extensively renovated but remains as simple – and appropriate – as you'd expect in a virtual ghost town. Rates include breakfast and dinner, and guidance for onward transport.

Chak Chak   چک چک

Chak Chak is Iran's most important Zoroastrian pilgrimage. About 72km northwest of Yazd and deep in the desert, legend has it that after the Arab invasion in AD 637 the Sassanian princess Nikbanuh fled to this site. Short of water, she threw her staff at the cliff and water began dripping out – *chak, chak* means 'drip, drip'. The steep, cliff-side location is impressive even if most of the buildings are not. The exception is the **Pir-e-Sabz fire temple**, home to the drip, which has a brass door embossed with the likeness of Zoroaster. The dramatic views make it worth the climb.

Chak Chak attracts thousands of pilgrims for an annual festival held between 14 and 18 June.

Meybod   میبد

About 52km north of Yazd, Meybod is a sprawling mud-brick town that is at least 1800 years old. It has three main sights near each other in the west of town, all open from 9am to 5pm, or 7pm in summer. They include a 300-year-old **post house** (admission IR3000) that served as a relay station on, as it says above the door, the 'King's Road, Rey to Kerman'; a **caravanserai** with a covered *qanat*; and a huge Safavid-era **ice house** *(yakh dan)* across the street. Crumbling **Narein castle** (admission

IR2000; ⊙ 9am-5pm, to 7pm summer), in the centre of town, dates from Sassannian times and affords desert-rooftop views across town.

As you enter town, stop at the circular **pigeon tower** that once housed 4000 pigeons whose guano was collected as fertiliser. The tower has been meticulously restored and today about 100 pigeons swing from strings in a crude celebration of the taxidermist's art. Avoid taking anything mind-altering before coming here… It's on government property so ask at the gate before entering.

Ardakan   اردکان
Now almost merging with Meybod, Ardakan is another ancient desert city and a regional agricultural centre courtesy of its amazing *qanat* irrigation system (see The Qanat, p260). Ardakan's desert setting, rather than specific buildings, makes it worth a detour on the way to or from Chak Chak. There are some attractive old lanes and *badgirs* around the **Jameh Mosque** (Masjed-e Jameh). Ardakan is famous for its camels and you can sample delicious camel kababs in almost any *kababi*.

Saryazd   سریزد
Saryazd means 'head of Yazd' and its two caravanserais were the last stop before Yazd for hauliers heading north. About 6km east of the highway, the sleepy village has zero tourist infrastructure. What it has is the crumbling but still largely intact, Safavid-era **Robat-e Noh** (New Caravanserai), complete with three floors of rooms, some with ancient pots scattered around the dusty floors, and fine rooftop views. And the village is just a fun place in which to wander a bit.

Infrequent minibuses come here from Abuzar Sq in Yazd, though most people come with a taxi *dar baste* (one way IR40,000).

Zein-o-din   زین الدین
Blink and you'd miss Zein-o-din, where the sole structure and *raison d'etre* is a 400-year-old caravanserai built on the orders of Shah Abbas I. Located two days' camel ride south of Yazd (that's 60km) in a vast desert plain flanked by mountains, the caravanserai was part of a network of 999 such hostels built to promote trade. Of those, it's one of only two circular caravanserais (the other, near Esfahan, is largely destroyed).

Thankfully, this one was built to last and today **Caravanserai Zein-o-din** (☎ 0351-824 3338, 0912 306 0441; zeinodin2003@yahoo.com; per person incl two meals €48; **P**) is a serendipitous, romantic taste of a caravan traders' life on the Silk Road. A three-year renovation, during which 13,000 pumice stones were used to scour centuries of grime from the walls, saw the simple accommodation restored to almost its original state: the raised rooms offer mattresses on top of carpets with just a curtain separating you from the corridor. Where it differs is in the stylish and clean communal bathrooms, the service and the delicious food. Zein-o-din's isolation means food and excursions need to be planned ahead, so advance booking is essential. Prices are negotiable in summer and December.

Apart from just chilling out Safavid style, desert walks to a mountain spring can be arranged – with notice.

Take any bus heading south to Kerman (pick one up at Abuzar Sq) and ask to be dropped at Zein-o-din, or take a savari *dar baste* for about IR80,000 one way; add IR30,000 per hour waiting time.

ABARQU   ابرقو
☎ 0352 / elev 1510m
This historic town on the road between Yazd and Shiraz is a good off-the-tourist-trail stop. There are several attractions, including a huge **ice house**, the 11th-century **Gonbad Ali dome**, the Jameh Mosque and a 4000-plus-year-old **cypress tree**. The main draw, however, is the **Khan-e Aghazadeh**, a restored Qajar-era mansion that might one day be a hotel; look for the distinctive two-storey *badgir*.

The **Hotel Pouya Abarkuh** (Mehmansar Jahangardi; ☎ 682 1030; s/d US$36/48; **P** ✗ ⬚), on the left as you come into town from the east, has a decent restaurant and will often charge local rates. Get off any bus between Yazd and Shiraz.

SHIRAZ   شیراز
☎ 0711 / pop 1,750,000 / elev 1531m
Shiraz is a city of sophistication that has been celebrated as the heartland of Persian culture for more than 2000 years. Known as the Dar-ol-Elm (House of Learning), the City of Roses, City of Love and City of Gardens, Shiraz has become synonymous with education, nightingales, poetry and wine.

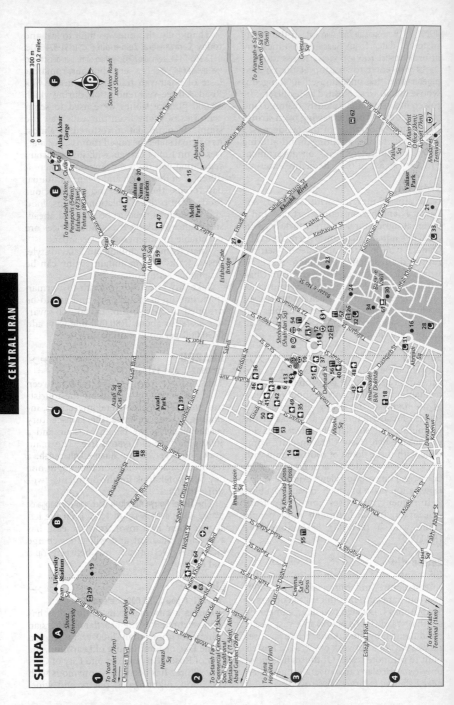

CENTRAL IRAN

SHIRAZ

It was one of the most important cities in the medieval Islamic world and was the Iranian capital during the Zand dynasty (AD 1747–79), when many of its most beautiful buildings were built or restored.

In his 1893 book *A Year Amongst the Persians*, Edward Browne described Shirazis as '…amongst all the Persians, the most subtle, the most ingenious, the most vivacious'. And even in Iran, where regional one-upmanship is common, everyone seems to like Shirazis. This is a city of poets and home to the graves of Hafez and Sa'di, themselves major pilgrimage sites for Iranians. Shiraz is also home to splendid gardens, exquisite mosques and whispered echoes of ancient sophistication that reward those who linger longer than it takes to visit nearby Persepolis (p279).

There are the usual Iranian traffic issues, but Shiraz's agreeable climate, set as it is in a fertile valley once famed for its vineyards, makes it a pleasant place to visit (except at the humid height of summer or the freezing depths of winter).

History

Shiraz is mentioned in Elamite inscriptions from around 2000 BC and it was an important regional centre under the Sassanians. However, Shiraz did not become the provincial capital until about AD 693, following the Arab conquest of Estakhr, the last Sassanian capital (8km northeast of Persepolis, but now completely destroyed). By 1044 Shiraz was said to rival Baghdad in importance and grew further under the Atabaks of Fars in the 12th century, when it became an important artistic centre.

Shiraz was spared destruction by the rampaging Mongols and Tamerlane because the city's rulers wisely decided that paying tribute was preferable to mass slaughter. Having avoided calamity, Shiraz enjoyed the Mongol and Timurid periods, which became eras of development. The encouragement of enlightened rulers, and the presence of Hafez, Sa'di and many other brilliant artists and scholars, helped make it one of the greatest cities in the Islamic world throughout the 13th and 14th centuries.

Shiraz remained a provincial capital during the Safavid period, when European traders settled here to export its famous wine. But by the mid-17th century it had entered a long period of decline. This was worsened by several earthquakes, the

Afghan raids of the early 18th century, and an uprising led by Shiraz's governor in 1744, which was put down in typically ruthless fashion after a siege by Nader Shah.

At the time of Nader Shah's murder in 1747, Shiraz was squalid and its population had fallen to 50,000, a quarter of the number 200 years earlier. But the city soon returned to prosperity. The enlightened Karim Khan, the first ruler of the short-lived Zand dynasty, made Shiraz the national capital in 1750. Despite being master of virtually all of Persia, Karim Khan refused to take any higher title than *vakil* (regent). He was determined to build Shiraz into a worthy capital, the equal of Esfahan under Shah Abbas I.

Karim Khan founded a royal district in the area of the Arg-e Karim Khan and commissioned many fine buildings, including what was the pre-eminent bazaar in Persia. After his death, however, things fell apart. The Qajars, longtime enemies, attacked and destroyed the city's fortifications and by 1789 had moved the national capital – and the remains of Karim Khan – to Tehran.

Shiraz remained prosperous due to its position on the trade route to Bushehr, but this role was greatly diminished with the opening of the trans-Iranian railway in the 1930s. Much of the architectural inheritance of Shiraz, and especially the royal district of the Zands, was either neglected or destroyed as a result of irresponsible town planning under the Pahlavi dynasty. Lacking any great industrial, religious or strategic importance, Shiraz is now largely an administrative centre, though one famous for its universities.

Orientation

The main street of Shiraz is the wide, tree-lined Karim Khan-e Zand Blvd (shortened simply to Zand). This boulevard runs about as far east and west as you would want to go without leaving Shiraz. Most of the things to see, and nearly all the hotels, are on or within walking distance of Zand.

The old city or nearby is where you'll spend most of your time. The city centre is Shohada Sq (still widely known as Shahrdari Sq), within walking distance of most hotels, the bazaar and the major mosques and shrines. To the north is the Khoshk River, and north of that the tombs of Hafez and Sa'di and the major gardens. To the west and northwest of town are the smarter residential areas and, on a hill, many university buildings. The airport and two major bus terminals are short taxi trips from the centre.

Information

BOOKSHOPS
Aramagh-e Hafez Bookshop (☺ 9am-5pm) Wide range of Hafez books at tourist prices.
Persepolis Bookshop (☎ 233 8200; Rudaki St) Opposite the new Shahreraz Hotel, a good range of pictorials and postcards.

EMERGENCY
Shiraz is famous for its medical training so it's a good place to get sick.
Dena Hospital (☎ 628 0411-18; www.denahospital .com; Dena Alley, Motahari Blvd) Best in Shiraz.
Dr Faqihi Hospital (☎ 235 1091; Zand Blvd) The most central hospital; public.
Tourist Police (Karim Khan-e Zand Blvd) Outside the Arg-e Karim Khan. There's rarely anyone here outside peak season.

INTERNET ACCESS
You won't need GPS technology to find one of Shiraz's many *coffeenets*, which include the following:
Maral Coffeenet (Park Hotel Lane; per hr IR8000; ☺ 9am-1pm & 4-9pm)
Paytakht (☎ 222 7989; Sa'di St; per hr IR8000; ☺ 8.30am-2.30pm & 4.30-9pm Sat-Thu, 8.30am-2.30pm Fri) English-speaking and very helpful.

MONEY
The central branches of the major banks have foreign exchange facilities. However, the exchange offices along Zand are simple, safe and your best option.
Bank Melli (Karim Khan-e Zand Blvd) Next to the Arg-e Karim Khan. Exchange on 1st floor.
Zand Exchange (☎ 222 2854; Karim Khan-e Zand Blvd; ☺ 8am-1pm & 4-7pm Sat-Thu) Good rates, no commission, fast, and longer hours.

POST
Main post office (☎ 726 9070; Modarres Blvd) On the road to the airport, for big items only.
Post office (☎ 224 1516; Hejrat St)

TELEPHONE
Local calls are free from public phones in Shiraz. For international calls:
Telephone office Park Hotel Lane (☺ 8am-9pm Sat-Thu); Hejrat St (☺ 8am-8pm Sat-Thu)

TOURIST INFORMATION

Tourist information office (☎ 224 1985; Karim Khan-e Zand Blvd; ⊗ 8am-8pm) Outside the Arg-e Karim Khan. Helpful English-speaking staff will give you a free map and/or directions, and have useful brochures on individual sights.

TOURS

Travellers commonly hire a taxi or driver for trips to Persepolis or other attractions around Shiraz; see p280 for details. Tours can also be arranged through almost every hotel.

Arash Sadeghzadeh (☎ 0917 317 1652; www.trip topersia.com) Young, enthusiastic, knowledgeable and highly organised guide and fixer. Recommended.

Hossein Soltani (☎ 0917 713 1517; h-soltani-n@ hotmail.com) Hossein works in the Shiraz Eram hotel and moonlights as a (safe) driver and fixer.

Kazem Salehi (☎ 0917 113 0858; ilovetourists@yahoo .com) Kazem is not a guide as such, but he's a lovely guy and good fun. He works with Pars Tourist Agency or independently.

Morteza Mehrparvar (☎ 0917 314 6124) More driver than tour guide, Morteza has nonetheless been recommended by several readers who have used him across Iran.

Park Taxi Service (☎ 222 5544; Park Hotel Lane; ⊗ 24hr) Long-running, reliable and recommended taxi service. Note that they're drivers, not guides.

Pars Tourist Agency (☎ 222 3163; www.key2persia .com; Zand Blvd; ⊗ 9am-9pm Sat-Thu, 9am-1pm Fri) Pars runs probably the most diverse, well-organised, good-value and – best of all – enjoyable tours of any Iranian agency. The 100 options include: half-day group trips to Persepolis for US$8 per person, leaving daily at 8am; Pasargadae for US$50 per car; also Firuz Abad, Bishapur, Bavanat, skiing, trekking, climbing and nomad tours. All prices are fixed and listed online. They also rent bikes (US$1 per hour) and on Friday take a bus full of interested Iranians for walking and a picnic lunch (US$10)... it's a great way to meet the locals. Guides cost about US$25 a day, or US$50 a day for overnight trips; several languages can be arranged.

TRAVEL AGENCIES

Pars Tourist Agency (☎ 222 3163; www.key2persia .com; Zand Blvd; ⊗ 9am-9pm Sat-Thu, 9am-1pm Fri; ▣) As well as tours, the multilingual team do the usual travel agency jobs: air, bus and train ticketing, visa extensions etc. In the event of an emergency, owner Masoud Nematollahi can be contacted to help sort things on ☎ 0917 111 8514. Highly recommended.

VISA EXTENSIONS

Police Department of Aliens Affairs (off Valiasr Sq; ⊗ 7.30am-1.30pm Sat-Wed, 7.30am-noon Thu) When we were here, Shiraz was the best place in Iran for visa ex-

tensions. Arrive before 9am and you should be able to pick up a 30-day extension the same day. To get there, take a shuttle taxi (about IR1000) east along Zand Blvd to Valiasr Sq, walk another 300m or so east, then take the third lane heading north at an angle. It's another 70m along, behind the light green door – it's on the 3rd floor. Your cash must be deposited at Bank Melli Markazi (Shohada Sq); ask Pars Tourist Agency (left) for the account number and deposit before going for the extension to save doubling back. For more on extending visas, see More Time, Please (p395).

Sights

ARG-E KARIM KHAN ارگ کریمخان

Dominating the city centre, the burly **Arg-e Karim Khan** (Citadel of Karim Khan; ☎ 224 7646; Shohada Sq; admission IR2000; ⊗ 8am-sunset, to 8pm summer) was built in the early Zand period and formed part of the royal court that Karim Khan had hoped would develop to rival Esfahan. The exterior is fairly mundane, with high walls punctuated by four 14m-high circular towers. The southeastern tower has a noticeable lean, having subsided onto the underground sewerage system that served as the Arg's bathhouse.

Inside the Arg is a large, open courtyard filled with citrus trees and a pool. More interesting are the exhibition of photos taken in Shiraz in the late 19th and early 20th centuries, starting inside the north wall, and the museum of the Zand period, with wax figures in traditional dress. These recent additions mean you might now agree with the sign at the entrance, which has for years been proclaiming: 'The exalted stature of the Karim Khan citadel amuses every new traveller for a long time who arrives in Shiraz'.

BAGH-E NAZAR & PARS MUSEUM

باغ نظر و موزه پارس

Bagh-e Nazar (Eye-catching Garden; Zand Blvd) and the octagonal **Pars Museum** at its centre are other notable Zand-era additions. It's possible to walk around the garden and view the delightfully decorated pavilion where Karim Khan received foreign dignitaries. The interior is stunning, with the stalactite ceiling a particular highlight. Exhibits include Karim Khan Zand's sword and indeed, his grave. Photography is not allowed.

MASJED-E VAKIL مسجد وکیل

The beautiful **Masjed-e Vakil** (Vakil Mosque; admission IR3000; ⊗ 8am-noon & 2-8pm) was begun by

Karim Khan and is the only major mosque surviving from the late Zand period. Beside the entrance to the bazaar, it has two vast *iwans* to the north and south, a magnificent inner courtyard surrounded by beautifully tiled alcoves and porches, and a pleasingly proportioned 75m-by-36m vaulted prayer hall supported by 48 carved columns. Inside the prayer hall are an impressive mihrab and 14-step marble minbar, carved from a monolith carried all the way from Azerbaijan. Much of the tiling, with its predominantly floral motifs and arabesques, was added in the early Qajar era.

HAMMAM-E VAKIL ‎حمام وكيل

After years as one of the most popular traditional restaurants in Iran, the **Hammam-e Vakil** (Taleqani St) was closed because the kitchen was damaging this classic old building. Shame. In early 2008 it reopened as a modest carpet museum, but its future remained uncertain. If it is open in some form, it's worth popping in for a look at the classic old bathhouse.

THE BAZAARS ‎بازار وكيل

Shiraz's ancient trading district is comprised of several bazaars dating from different periods. The finest and most famous is the **Bazar-e Vakil** (Vakil Bazaar; ⊙ dawn-dusk Sat-Thu), a cruciform structure commissioned by Karim Khan as part of his plan to make Shiraz into a great trading centre. The wide vaulted brick avenues are masterpieces of Zand architecture, with the design ensuring the interior remains cool in summer and warm in winter. Today, it's home to almost 200 stores selling carpets, handicrafts, spices and clothes and is one of the most atmospheric bazaars in Iran, especially in the early evening when it is fantastically photogenic. As usual, it's best explored by wandering without concern for time or direction, soaking up the atmosphere in the maze of lanes leading off the main thoroughfares.

Chances are you'll stumble across **Serai Mushir**, off the southern end of the main bazaar lane coming from Zand. This tastefully restored two-storey caravanserai is a pleasant place to gather your breath and do a bit of souvenir shopping.

On the north side of Zand is the less touristy but still pleasingly proportioned **Bazar-e Nou** (New Bazaar), built during the Qajar era.

MARTYR'S MOSQUE ‎مسجد شهدا

One of the largest ancient mosques in Iran, the rectangular courtyard of the **Martyr's Mosque** (Masjed-e Shohada; Ahmadi Sq; ⊙ Fri) covers more than 11,000 sq metres. Founded at the start of the 13th century, the mosque has been partially rebuilt many times and now has very little in the way of tiling or other decorations, though it does boast some impressive barrel vaulting. It lives under acres of unsightly corrugated fibreglass and is only open on Fridays, when it is still used for prayer. Entry is through a gate off Ahmadi Sq.

ARAMGAH-E SHAH-E CHERAGH ‎آرامگاه شاهچراغ

Sayyed Mir Ahmad, one of Imam Reza's 17 brothers, was hunted down and killed by the caliphate on this site in AD 835. His remains are housed at the glittering **Aramgah-e Shah-e Cheragh** (Mausoleum of King of the Light; ☎ 222 2158; Ahmadi Sq; ⊙ variable, often 24hr). A mausoleum was first erected over the grave during the 12th century but most of what you see dates from the late-Qajar period and the Islamic Republic; expansion is ongoing.

The expansive courtyard is a great place to sit and take in the bulbous blue-tiled dome and dazzling gold-topped minarets while discreetly observing the pious at what is one of the holiest Shiite sights in Iran. In the shrine itself, countless minute mirror tiles reflect the passion within.

In theory, however, non-Muslims are not allowed to enter the shrine. Enforcement seems to be mixed, but if you are polite and in a small group you should be fine. Women must wear a chador, which can be borrowed from the entrance. Cameras are forbidden inside the shrine but permitted in the courtyard.

Hidden away in the northwestern corner of the courtyard is a small **museum** housing some highly prized old Qurans that have been on the site for centuries. When we visited, however, it was closed for repairs.

In the southeastern corner is the **Bogh'e-ye Sayyed Mir Mohammad** (Mausoleum of Sayyed Mir Mohammad; ⊙ variable, often 24hr), which houses the tombs of two brothers of Mir Ahmad. The shrine has the typical Shirazi bulbous dome, intricate mirror work and four slender wooden pillars, leading some to describe it as more beautiful than Shah-e Cheragh.

MASJED-E JAMEH-YE ATIGH مسجد جامع عتیق
Walking through the southeastern (back) entrance to the Shah-e Cheragh courtyard and turning right after about 50m leads to the ancient **Jameh-ye Atigh Mosque** (Masjed-e Jameh-ye Atigh; ☻ variable). Dating from 894 this is Shiraz's oldest Islamic structure, though most of what you see is from the late Safavid period onwards.

While the dome of the north *iwan* and the hypostyle columns in the ancient prayer hall in the southeast corner are impressive, the highlight is the rare turreted **Khodakhaneh** (House of God). It was built in the mid-14th century (or perhaps earlier) to preserve valuable Qurans; poet Hafez is believed to have worked here. The Khodakhaneh bears an uncanny likeness to the Kaaba at Mecca, and bears a unique Sassanid-style *Tholth* inscription in raised stone characters on a tiled background.

MADRASEH-YE KHAN مدرسه خان
In 1615, Imam Gholi Khan, governor of Fars, founded the serene **Madraseh-ye Khan** (Dastqeib St; ☻ knock on the door) theological college for about 100 students. The original building has been extensively damaged by earthquakes and only the impressive portal at its entrance has survived; watch for the unusual type of stalactite moulding inside the outer arch and some intricate mosaic tiling with much use of red, in contrast to the tiles used in Yazd and Esfahan. The college (still in use) has a fine stone-walled inner courtyard and garden.

The building can be reached via a lane off Lotfali Khan St. The doors are usually closed but if you get lucky the caretaker will open it; a tip is appreciated. If you get in, ask to be shown to the roof for panoramic views over the bazaar.

NASIR-OL-MOLK MOSQUE مسجد نصیر الملک
Down the road from the Madraseh-ye Khan, **Masjed-e Nasir-ol-Molk** (Nasir-ol-Molk Mosque; off Lotfali Khan St; admission IR15,000; ☻ 8am-1pm & 3.30-5pm, to 6pm summer) is one of the most elegant and photographed mosques in southern Iran. Built at the end of the 19th century, its coloured tiling (an unusually deep shade of blue) is exquisite. There is some particularly fine stalactite moulding in the smallish outer portal and in the northern *iwan*, but it is the stunning stained glass, exquisitely

carved pillars and polychrome faience of the winter prayer hall that are most eye-catching. Photographers should come as early as possible in the morning for shots of the hall lit up through the glass (you might have to tip the caretaker to open the curtains). A museum in the opposite prayer hall opens into the **Gav Cha** (Cow Well), in which cows walked downhill to raise water. The structure has survived numerous earthquakes, due in part to its construction using flexible wood as struts within the walls – look for the wooden bricks in the *iwan* columns.

BAGH-E NARANJESTAN & KHAN-E ZINAT OL-MOLK باغ نارنجستان خانه زینت الملک
Bagh-e Naranjestan (Orange Garden; Lotfali Khan St; admission IR30,000; ☻ 7.30am-6pm, 8am-7.30pm in summer) is Shiraz's smallest garden and is famous as the setting for the opulently decorated **Naranjestan-e Ghavam** pavilion, built between 1879 and 1886, as part of a complex owned by one of Shiraz's wealthiest Qajar-era families. The pavilion's mirrored entrance hall opens onto rooms covered in a breathtaking combination of intricate tiles, inlaid wooden panels and stained-glass windows. Ceilings in the upstairs rooms are particularly interesting, with the beams painted with European-style motifs, including Alpine churches and busty German frauleins.

Down a small lane beside the garden is the **Khan-e Zinat ol-Molk** (Fars History Museum; ☎ 224 0035; ☻ 9am-7pm), which was originally the private, *andaruni* area of the complex and is named after its last owner, the daughter of the builder Qavam. Today most of the finely decorated rooms are stuffed with exhibits in the Fars History Museum, while others serve as galleries for young Shirazi artists. The gardens are in a walled compound 400m south of the Nasir ol-Molk Mosque.

CHURCHES
The **Anglican Church of St Simon the Zealot** (Kelisa-ye Moqaddas-e Sham'un-e Ghayur; کلیسای مقدس شمعون غیور), built by R Norman Sharp in 1938, is very Iranian in character and even contains stone tablets with biblical stories incised on them in cuneiform, probably by Sharp. According to local tradition, St Simon was martyred in Persia together with St Thaddeus, another of the 12 Apostles. The great metal door bearing a Persian cross is usually closed – ring the doorbell.

The 17th-century **Armenian Church** (Kelisaye Aramani; ارامنه کلیسای; Nohahar Alley, off Qa'ani St), is famous for its frescoes and flat, painted ceiling. However, knocking might not be enough to get you in.

IMAMZADEH-YE ALI EBN-E HAMZE
امامزاده علی ابن حمزه

The **Imamzadeh-ye Ali Ebn-e Hamze** (☎ 222 3353; Hafez St, near Hamzeh Bridge; ☾ dawn-dusk) stands as the tomb of Emir Ali, a nephew of Shah Cheragh who also died here while en route to Khorasan to help Imam Reza. The existing shrine was built in the 19th century after earthquakes destroyed previous incarnations. It has an eye-catching bulbous Shirazi dome, dazzling mirror work, stained-glass windows and an intricate, ancient wooden door. The tombstones around the courtyard, for which families of the deceased paid a small fortune, are also interesting. Unlike some other shrines, the caretakers here are very welcoming of foreigners; women are happily handed a chador, and in you go!

ARAMGAH-E HAFEZ
آرامگاه حافظ

Iranians have a saying that every home must have two things: first the Quran, then Hafez (see p74). And many would reverse that order. Hafez the poet is an Iranian folk-hero – loved, revered and as popular as many a modern pop star. Almost every Iranian can quote his work, bending it to whichever social or political persuasion they subscribe to. And there is no better place to try to understand Hafez's eternal hold on Iran than here, at **Aramgah-e Hafez** (Tomb of Hafez; ☎ 228 4552; Golestan Blvd; admission IR3000; ☾ 8am-10pm), his tomb.

Set in a charming garden with its two pools, the whole scene is restful despite the ever-present traffic noise. The marble tombstone, engraved with a long verse from the poet, was placed here, inside a small shrine, by Karim Khan in 1773. In 1935, an octagonal pavilion was put up over it, supported by eight stone columns beneath a tiled dome. Plan to spend a couple of hours sitting in a discreet corner of the grounds, at sunset if possible, to watch the way Iranians react to what is, for many, a pilgrimage to his tomb.

You might see people performing the *faale Hafez*, a popular ritual in which you seek insight into your future by opening a volume of Hafez – the future is apparent in his words. After sunset, with the tomb floodlit and sung

poetry piped over the public address system, it is difficult not to feel transported back to the magic of ancient Persia. The charming teahouse in the walled garden at the back of the grounds was closed when we passed, but should be open by the time you arrive.

To get here from the centre of town you can walk (about 2km); take a shuttle taxi from Shohada Sq to Ghaem Sq, then walk; or take a private taxi (about IR7000).

ARAMGAH-E SA'DI
آرامگاه سعدی

While not as popular as Hafez's tomb, the **Aramgah-e Sa'di** (Tomb of Sa'di; ☎ 730 1300; Bustan Blvd; admission IR3000; ☾ 7.30am-9pm, to 10pm summer) and its generous surrounding gardens are appropriate for a man who wrote so extensively about gardens and roses. It's a tranquil place, with the tombstone housed in an opensided stone colonnade, inscribed with various verses from Sa'di and supporting a tiled dome (see p74 for more on Sa'di). Nearby is an underground teahouse (p278) set around a fish pond that is fed by a *qanat*.

It's easy to visit the tombs of both Hafez and Sa'di in a single afternoon. From Golestan Blvd (outside Hafez's tomb), take a shuttle taxi three squares southwest (IR1000) to Sa'di Sq, then walk about 800m uphill to the tomb. Food and drink is available near the entrance.

BAGH-E ERAM
باغ ارم

Famous for its tall cypress trees, the delightful **Bagh-e Eram** (Garden of Paradise; ☎ 627 3647; Eram Blvd; admission IR40,000; ☾ 8am-noon & 2-7pm, to 7pm summer) will impress budding botanists and social anthropologists – the many hidden corners of the gardens are popular with young Shirazis. The gardens are centred around a pretty pool beside a Qajar-era palace, the **Kakh-e Eram** (Eram Palace), which is not open to the public. The gardens are managed by Shiraz University, which chooses to charge foreigners 10 times the local price. The gardens are easy enough to reach by taking any shuttle taxi going along Zand towards the university.

BAGH-E JAHAN NAMA
باغ جهان نما

After being closed for years, the lovely **Bagh-e Jahan Nama** (Jahan Nama Garden; Hafez St; admission IR1500; ☾ 8am-noon & 2-5pm, to 7pm summer) was reopened in 2005. It doesn't have the reputation of Bagh-e Eram, but if you just want

VOICES OF IRAN: MAJID PIROOZMAND

Age: 28
Lives in: Shiraz
Occupation: Architect, consultant to Miras Feranghi
(Cultural Heritage Organisation)

'I like Shiraz more than anywhere in the world. My childhood was here in these *kuches* (lanes) and the city has a very rich history. Until now it still doesn't have the terrible traffic you have in other cities, people are especially friendly and the weather is perfect – not too hot and not too cold.

I work with Miras Ferhangi and we want to preserve the cultural heritage. Now Shiraz is ready to grow and advance, but we are still working to preserve the history. There are many threats; we have to pay attention to every detail and if a plan threatens the heritage, we reject it. To keep the old city alive we have programs to help the old places pay for themselves. The traditional hotels in Yazd are a good example, and we know how important tourism is in making this endeavour a success. When tourists spend money in historic buildings it helps to keep that building alive, and that's important. In Shiraz, I love the gardens the most. We have some of the most famous gardens in Iran. Shirazis specialise in going out and we love to go out on the weekend, find some spare grass and sit, especially in summer.

The gardens are important for another reason, too. Usually, a girlfriend and boyfriend have a problem because they want to go somewhere to enjoy themselves – nothing illegal, just to be together – but there is nowhere to go. The garden is a great place for this, much better than restaurants or cafés. I used to go with my girlfriend and now we are married we still go.

I love to travel and with my work I travel about one week every two months, to Esfahan, Yazd, Kashan, Kerman, Mahan or Bam. Maybe it's because I'm an architect, but Kashan is my favourite; I love the old houses and Madraseh-ye Khan.'

to hang out in the greenery, don't want to spend IR30,000 for the privilege and want it to be within walking distance of your hotel, come on down.

DARVAZEH-YE QURAN   دروازه قرآن

At the northern and main entrance to Shiraz is a ravine known as the Allah Akbar Gorge because people would praise Allah when they looked from here down to Shiraz below. This is also home to the **Darvazeh-ye Quran** (Quran Gateway; Quran Sq), a modern and not desperately impressive structure built in 1949 to replace two earlier gateways. The gateway holds a Quran and travellers have traditionally passed underneath it before undertaking any journey. The fine original Quran, installed during the Zand period, was stolen from the Pars Museum in 2003.

Those with good leg muscles might want to climb up Mt Baba Kuhi in search of two more tombs and some **bas-reliefs**, from where the views of Shiraz are breathtaking. There are three teahouses here that are popular with young people hanging, especially at sunset. To get here, take a shuttle taxi to Quran Sq or walk

up from either the Aramgah-e Hafez (opposite) or the Bagh-e Jahan Nama (opposite).

Sleeping

Shiraz has probably the best range of hotels, in the most confined space, of all Iranian cities. Unless otherwise stated, they are located in streets leading off Zand Ave and are a short walk to the main sights. They tend to be clustered by price range, making comparisons a breeze. The main downside is that hotels on Zand can be noisy – ask for a room away from the street. Competition is keen so most managers will be happy to knock a few rial off the price out of season. And if you're arriving by plane, the reservation desk at the airport offers discounts of up to 20% on many hotels. Almost every hotel in Shiraz can arrange trips to Persepolis and Pasargadae.

BUDGET

The cheapest places are mainly concentrated in neighbouring Dehnadi and Pirouzi Sts; a couple of better budget options are on Anvari St.

Mehmunsara Fadagh (☎ 222 5135; Kuche Mohan-dase; dm/tw IR20,000/60,000) Deep in the old city, this mehmunsara in a 200-year-old building is the cheapest, most interesting hotel in town; note we didn't say atmospheric. It's owned by the Sepah militia and mainly used by male pilgrims (not great for solo women), who like the enormous dorm. But the small, clean twins are good value and the court-yard, with its underground teahouse (open 8am to 8pm), is good for chilling. There's no sign in English and it's hard to find; walk past the Imamzadeh Bibi Dokhtar, turn right and follow the signs to the Meshkin-fam Museum of Art – it's about 15m before the museum.

Zand Hotel (☎ 222 2949; alvanch@yahoo.com; Dehnadi St; tw with/without shower IR100,000/80,000; P   ) Zand has ultra-basic, reasonably clean rooms with or without showers (toilets are shared). It's popular with overlanders because it has (limited) courtyard parking, a kitchen for guests and a free washing machine.

Esteghlal Hotel (☎ 222 7728; Dehnadi St; tw with/without bathroom IR140,000/115,000;) Opposite the Zand Hotel, the Esteghlal has long been popular with budgeteers but not, it must be said, for the quality of the small, boxy rooms. They're adequate, but note that while all rooms with 'bathrooms' cost the same, some don't have a toilet – look at several. English-speaking manager Reza can advise on transport and flogs the usual day trips.

our pick Anvari Hotel (☎ 233 7591; Anvari St; tw IR160,000;) There's nothing fancy about the modest, four-storey Anvari, but almost all like the place. It's clean, comfortable enough for the money and, most importantly, has a consistently convivial atmosphere. Ideal for solo women travellers and the place you're most likely to meet other travellers.

Sasan Hotel (☎ 233 7830; sasanhotel@shirazsport .com; Anvari St; s/d/tr US$15/20/24;   ) Next door to the Anvari, Sasan has slightly better rooms, with softer beds and more furniture, for slightly more money. The manager is a friendly old guy who could, as one reader reported, talk 'all four legs' off a billiard table. Good upper budget choice.

If the other places are full, no-frills hotels line noisy Piruzi St (ask for a back room): **Saadi Hotel** (☎ 222 5126; s/tw/tr IR70,000/110,000/13 0,000) Boxy, noisy but clean rooms and shared bathrooms, lumpy beds.

Hotel Sina (☎ 222 5665; Piruzi St; tw with/without bathroom IR180,000/150,000;) Good beds, fridge and squat toilets; clean relatively large rooms.

MIDRANGE
Rudaki Ave and the adjoining Eizedi St are the places to look for midrange options. Rates include breakfast and, at most, bargaining is worthwhile.

our pick Shiraz Eram Hotel (☎ 230 0814-16; www .eramhotel.com; Karim Khan-e Zand Blvd; s/d US$45/55; P   ) For years we've been getting let-ters and emails complimenting the Eram's relaxed but professional service, and it's the guys at reception who set the tone. Rooms in the new wing (specify them) are big, quiet and reasonably well-equipped with phone, minibar and satellite TV. Buffet breakfast in the Sarve Naz Restaurant (meals IR35,000 to IR70,000; open breakfast, lunch and din-ner) is refreshingly varied, and the mains here are also good. In short, the Eram is comfortable, dependable, friendly, central and good value – and has embraced some energy-saving measures.

our pick Aryo Barzan Hotel (☎ 224 7182-4; www .aryohotel.com; Rudaki Ave; s/d/ste US$45/65/97;   ) The Aryo is a favourite among readers for its intelligent, smiling and extravagantly coiffed service, fair prices and modern rooms. The small but tastefully furnished rooms are set around an atrium and have correspond-ingly small and spotlessly clean bathrooms, with Mini Me–sized bathtubs. Significant discounts are possible off season.

Park Saadi Hotel (☎ 227 4901-19; parksaadi_hotel@ yahoo.com; Hafez St, s/d/ste/apt US$45/65/110/150; P   ) The Saadi's 52 newly refurbished rooms are in a quiet location opposite lovely Bagh-e Jahan Nama. It's solid three-star through and through, with large, bright rooms (some with wi-fi), a decent restaurant and experienced management.

Jaam-e-Jam Apartment Hotel (☎ 230 4002; www .jaamejamhotel.com; Eizedi St; 1-/2-bed apt from US$60;   ) Choose between the sprawling apart-ments in the four-year-old 'old' wing and smaller rooms in the Persepolis-inspired new wing, opened in 2007. The location is quiet, and management and service are professional. Be nice and a big discount might come your way; we were offered an apartment for US$40. Great value.

Persepolis Hotel (☎ 229 5370-73; www.persepolis hotel.com; Azadi Blvd, off Ghaem Sq; s/d US$65/95;

🅧 🅠 🅡) Opened in 2006, this has modern-looking and well-equipped, if not huge, rooms. Service is enthusiastic and the pool can be 'booked' after 11pm. Discounts are available; if not, try Aryo Barzan first.

If those are full:

Kowsar Hotel (☎ 230 0207; kowsarhotel@yahoo.com; Zand Blvd; s/d US$27/40; 🅧 🅠) Old but reasonable value. Discounts are possible.

Parsian Hotel (☎ 233 0000; www.parsian-hotel.com; Rudaki Ave; r/ste US$66/100; 🅟 🅧 🅠) Compact rooms, good beds, decent service.

TOP END

Hadish Apartment Hotel (☎ 235 1988; www.hadishhotel .com; Rudaki Ave; 1/2-bed apt US$100/150; 🅟 🅧 🅠) The big apartments here are a bit austere but have fully equipped kitchens. They're most appealing for the value and friendly staff, who at most times are happy to discount (rates were halved after about 10 seconds' bargaining).

Pars International Hotel (☎ 233 2255; www.pars-international-hotel.com; Zand Blvd; s/d/ste with breakfast US$81/117/186; 🅟 🅧 🅠 🅡) This four-star business hotel is probably the best in town. Rooms are well equipped (though there's no internet; it's only available in the lobby) and those upper floors offer panoramic views.

Homa Hotel (☎ 222 8000-09; www.homahotelgroup .com; Meshkin Fam St; s/d/ste with breakfast US$90/120/175; 🅟 🅧 🅠 🅡) The '70s-era Homa is showing its age and the rooms – and indeed some of the staff – look tired. But the location, restaurants, front-desk service and views over the city, and Park-e Azadi in particular, make it a decent choice. The pool is men-only.

Eating

Shiraz is noted as a culinary capital but Shirazis have embraced Western-style fast food with an almost embarrassing relish. We've listed the best places and will mostly leave you to find the pizza and burger joints on your own. Sadly the world-famous Shiraz (Syrah) grape is no longer made into the wine that inspired Hafez to poetry.

RESTAURANTS

There are some excellent Iranian restaurants.

Gavara Restaurant (☎ 222 7211; Piruzi St; meals IR20,000-40,000; 🕙 11am-10pm) The subterranean Gavara is an old-style local – an unpretentious, neon-lit hall divided into sections for men, and women and families. The menu is big and the food unsophisticated but very tasty; kababs, *khoreshts,* fish (sometimes) and a decent *ghorme sabzi.* Look for the Achaemenid-style staircase beneath the Saadi Hotel.

Haji Baba Restaurant (☎ 233 2563; Zand Blvd; meals IR25,000-50,000; 🕙 7am-11pm) Not exactly atmospheric, but the food is delicious, location and opening hours convenient and prices reasonable.

Yavar Restaurant (☎ 228 7728; Ghaem Sq; meals IR30,000; 🕙 11.30am-3.30pm & 6.30-11pm) For traditional Shirazi food, local prices and character, the Yavar is excellent. The *eslamboli* (rice and tomato) and *khoresht bademjan* (eggplant stew) make a refreshing alternative to kababs (which it also has). There's no English sign; look for Hossein riding a white horse across the front wall.

Restaurant Hatam (☎ 222 1709; Piruzi St; meals IR35,000; 🕙 11am-9pm Sat-Thu) No frills, soulless cheapie with a limited range of decent Iranian food.

our pick Yord Cultural Complex (☎ 625 6774, 0917 715 2059; Mansour Abad, Dinakan St, after Maliabad bridge; meals IR55,000; 🕙 lunch & dinner, dinner only in winter) In an enormous colourful *yord* (tent) about 8km northwest of town, this complex not only offers the chance to enjoy some fine Iranian-nomad food, but also to experience the Qashqa'i culture. The warm atmosphere, colourful costumes, live music and delicious food afford a dreamy escape from modern life into a Qashqa'i tented embrace. Yord is almost impossible to reach by public transport, so ask your hotel to write the name in Farsi and get a taxi (about IR25,000); it is also worth paying the taxi to wait for you (about IR70,000 total) as taxis out here are rare indeed. We heard a second Yord has opened, and that both are periodically closed because of licensing issues, so always call ahead and get the address sorted.

our pick Sharzeh Traditional Restaurant (☎ 224 1963; Vakil St, off Zand Ave; meals IR65,000; 🕙 11am-3pm & 8-11pm) Talk about atmosphere! The night we ate at the Sharzeh it was going off like the proverbial frog in a sock, with diners singing and clapping along with musicians playing traditional music in the centre of the two-level space. Great fun! The Iranian food was well-prepared, tasty and plentiful. It's diagonally opposite the entrance to the Vakil Bazaar. There's no English sign; look for the man in costume outside an arcade.

Shater Abbas Restaurant 1 (☎ 229 1440; Khakshenasi St, off Azadi Blvd; meals IR80,000; 🕙 11am-4pm & 6-11.30pm)

The low light, open kitchen, bustling staff and modern design touches create an atmosphere that is hugely popular with middle-class Shirazis. The menu mixes the classic range of kababs with some less familiar dishes – turkey kabab and mushroom steak, for example. Prices seem to have climbed with demand, sharply. Look for the flame torches outside.

Other recommendations:

Soofi Traditional Restaurant 2 (☎ 626 1573; Afif Abad St; meals IR50,000-80,000; ☾ noon-3.15pm & 7-11.15pm) Beside the Setareh Fars shopping centre; popular with young, wealthy Shirazis; live music at night.

Pat Traditional Restaurant (☎ 235 4186; Paramount Cross; meals IR55,000; ☾ lunch & dinner) Subterranean, traditional place with live music.

QUICK EATS

Shiraz might just be the pizza capital of the world. Dozens of new pizza joints have opened here serving the usual array of thick-crusted, tomato-less pies topped with too much tasteless sausage. Zand is packed with places selling pizzas, burgers, hot dogs, *saucis* (sausage) sandwiches, soft-serve ice cream and other such delicacies.

110 Hamburgers (Anvari St; meals IR25,000; ☾ 11am-midnight) The best, however, is this place to which Shirazis come like moths to a neon flame (two glowing palm trees). Their version of the *shwarma*, with meat sliced off a spit and shovelled into a bread roll with healthy bits like tomato and pickle (IR18,000), is good.

Mahdi Faludeh (Naser Khosrow St; ☾ 2-10pm) The most famous faludeh (IR3000 a cup) shop in Shiraz that does a good line in *bastani*, too. It's opposite the Arg and beside the mosque entrance.

TEAHOUSES & CAFÉS

There are some cracking teahouses in Shiraz, and a few decent cafés too. Unfortunately, the historic and popular Hammam-e Vakil has closed as a teahouse.

Aroosh Khorshid (Dehnadi St; meals IR25,000-45,000; ☾ 8am-10pm Sat-Thu) Convenient to the cheap accommodation, the Aroosh has plenty of old paraphernalia hanging about and the big space can have a decent atmosphere when it's busy. The food is decent if unadventurous; check the bill carefully.

our pick **Seray-e Mehr Teahouse** (☎ 222 9572; Seray-e Mehr, Bazar-e Vakil; meals IR35,000-50,000; ☾ 9am-9pm Sat-Thu) This is a serendipitous place to find after wandering through the Bazar-e Vakil.

Hidden away through a small door behind the Serai Mushir Bazar, the split-level teahouse has a small menu of tasty favourites (think *dizi, kubideh, zereshk polo*) and a delightfully relaxed atmosphere in which to sit, sip tea and puff on qalyan.

Khajo Teahouse (Darvazeh-ye Quran; ☾ 11am-10pm) One of three little places selling tea and qalyan on the side of the rocky slope above the Quran Gate. Panoramic city views at sunset.

Aramgah-e Hafez Teahouse (☎ 228 4552; Golestan Blvd) Set at the back of the ground of Hafez's tomb, this teahouse is a great place to chill out with some live traditional music and a cup of *chay*, though the man himself might have preferred a glass of Shiraz. At the time of writing the teahouse was closed, but should be back by the time you arrive.

Sa'adi Teahouse (☎ 727 2300; Aramgah-e Sa'di) This subterranean *chaykhaneh* isn't quite as atmospheric as the Hafez version, but it's still plenty of fun.

Shopping

Good buys in the Bazar-e Vakil include metalwork and printed cottons, especially tablecloths and rugs woven by Fars nomads. Shiraz can be a good place to buy kilims and *gabbehs* (traditional rugs), though the selection is not as great as in Esfahan. For handicrafts, head to Serai Mushir in the Bazar-e Vakil, where you'll find some excellent shops and a great atmosphere. For a taste of modern Iran, head for the Setareh Fars Commercial Mall, a shopping mall (lots of labels), games complex (10-pin bowling IR40,000 a game!) and top-floor food court (Mexican and Chinese, open 4pm to midnight) where the young and hip hang out. Come in the evening for a taste of modern, consumer Iran.

Getting There & Away

AIR

It's easy to start or finish a trip to Iran in Shiraz because several airlines operate between Shiraz and gulf cities. **Iran Aseman** (☎ 230 8841; Zand Blvd; ☾ 8am-8pm Sat-Thu) flies between Shiraz and Dubai (one way IR820,000, daily) and Kuwait (IR882,000, daily), while other Gulf cities are served by Gulf Air (Bahrain) and Iran Air (Bahrain, Doha).

Shiraz International Airport (☎ 722 5020; http://shirazairport.ir) has a handy **flight information number** (☎ 199; ☾ 8am-9pm) and a hotel booking counter offering hefty discounts.

Iran Air (☎ 233 0041; cnr Zand Blvd & Felestin St; ☽ 8am-3.30pm) flies the following domestic routes.

Destination	Fare	Flights
Bandar Abbas	IR289,000	5 weekly
Bandar-e Lengeh	IR244,000	4 weekly
Esfahan	IR246,000	daily
Kish	IR253,000	5 weekly
Mashhad	IR540,000	6 weekly
Tehran	IR395,000	several daily

Iran Aseman, Mahan Air, Kish Airlines and other domestic carriers serve a mix of the same destinations, for the same prices; see a travel agency (p271) for tickets.

BUS & MINIBUS

Most long-distance buses operate from busy **Carandish bus terminal** (Terminal-e Bozorg; Salman-e Farsi Blvd). Prices are for *mahmooly*/Volvo buses (or just Volvo), and the main (but usually not the only) departure times are noted.

Destination	Fare	Duration	Departures
Ahvaz	IR25,000/ 55,000	8-9hr	7pm-9.30pm
Bam	IR65,000	7-10hr	Zahedan buses
Bandar Abbas	IR26,500/ 55,000	10hr	5-9pm
Esfahan	IR20,000/ 38,000	8hr	regular
Hamadan	IR34,500/ 60,000	15hr	1.30pm (Fars Mihan)
Kerman	IR45,000	8hr	7.30am, 9.30am (T8); 1.30-10pm
Kermanshah	IR85,000	18hr	2.30pm (Fars Mihan)
Sanandaj	IR90,000		1.30pm (Fars Mihan)
Tabriz	IR115,000	20hr	1.30pm (Fars Mihan)
Tehran	IR37,000/ 75,000	13-18hr	hourly 4-11pm
Yazd	IR18,000/ 45,000	5-7hr	7.30am, (T8), 5-8pm 2pm, 3pm (Seiro Safar Jonub)
Zahedan	IR85,000	13-17hr	7am, 1pm, 6pm (T8)

If you're on a tight schedule it's worth booking ahead at the **Iran Peyma** (Taavoni 1; ☎ 222 3888; Zand Blvd; ☽ 7am-8pm Sat-Thu, 8am-noon Fri) office near the corner of Sa'di St, or nearby Pars Tourist Agency (p271).

Buses to towns west and southwest of Shiraz leave from Amir Kabir Terminal on the southern outskirts. Buses for Kazerun (IR10,000, two to three hours) and Bushehr (IR13,000/30,000, five hours) depart at least every hour; arriving from Bushehr, you'll probably be dropped here.

SAVARI

Savaris for regional towns such as Bishapur, Firuz Abad and Marvdasht (for Persepolis) go from the southern edge of Carandish Terminal, near the river, on a semiregular basis.

Getting Around

TO/FROM THE AIRPORT

A private taxi to or from the city centre should cost about IR15,000. Ask at the airport information desk if the public bus has resumed, and if it runs all the way into town.

METRO

The **Shiraz Urban Railway** (www.shirazmetro.ir) is being built and will eventually include three lines, with 40 stations on 47km of track, including a link to the new Esfahan–Shiraz mainline station. Line 1 will open in 2010 at the earliest, and will run from southeast to northwest, including a stretch along Zand Ave between Valiasr Sq (good for visa extensions) and Imam Hossein Sq.

TAXI

Shiraz's fleet of old, green-and-white Paykan taxis, known locally as *mas' khiyari* (yogurt cucumber) is slowly being phased out in favour of shiny yellow Prides. Shuttle taxis ply the streets for IR1000 to IR2000 per trip. Chartering starts at IR5000.

PERSEPOLIS   پرسپولیس

☎ 0728 / elev 1630m

Magnificent **Persepolis** (Takht-e Jamshid; admission IR5000; ☽ 7.30am-5pm Nov-Mar, 8am-6pm summer) embodies the greatest successes of the ancient Achaemenid Empire...and its final demise (see History, p27). The monumental staircases, exquisite reliefs and imposing gateways leave you in no doubt how grand this city was and how totally dominant the empire that built it. Equally, the broken and fallen columns attest that the end of empire was emphatic. Persepolis is a result of the vast body of skill and knowledge gathered from throughout the Achaemenids' empire.

CENTRAL IRAN

It is Persian in ideology and design, but truly international in its superb architecture and artistic execution.

This multicultural concoction is alone in the ancient world, and while largely ruined it remains the greatest surviving masterpiece of the ancient Near Eastern civilisations. Respected scholar Arthur Upham Pope ably summed up the philosophy behind Persepolis in *Introducing Persian Architecture* (published by Tuttle in 1982):

> Humane sentiments found expression in the nobility and sheer beauty of the building: more rational and gracious than the work of the Assyrians or Hittites, more lucid and humane than that of the Egyptians. The beauty of Persepolis is not the accidental counterpart of mere size and costly display; it is the result of beauty being specifically recognised as sovereign value.

Some historians believe the site of Persepolis was chosen by Cambyses II, son of Cyrus the Great, but work did not begin until after Darius I (the Great) took the throne in 518 BC. It was added to by a host of subsequent kings, including Xerxes I and II, and Artaxerxes I, II and III, over a period of more than 150 years.

The ruins you see today are a mere shadow of Persepolis' former glory. But their very existence is due in part to the fact the ancient city was lost for centuries, totally covered by dust and sand. It wasn't until the 1930s that extensive excavations revealed its glories once again.

Note that there is little shade at Persepolis and from May until early October it can be sweltering, so bring a hat and water. For computer illustrations of Persepolis in all its glory, see www.persepolis3D.com.

Tours

Just about every hotel in Shiraz organises 'tours', with prices proportional to room rates; be sure about whether you'll have an actual guide who speaks your language (more expensive) or just a driver. For a list of reputable tour guides, see p271.

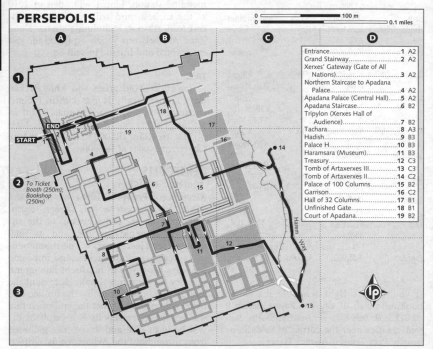

PERSEPOLIS

Entrance	1 A2
Grand Stairway	2 A2
Xerxes' Gateway (Gate of All Nations)	3 A2
Northern Staircase to Apadana Palace	4 A2
Apadana Palace (Central Hall)	5 A2
Apadana Staircase	6 B2
Tripylon (Xerxes Hall of Audience)	7 B2
Tachara	8 A3
Hadish	9 B3
Palace H	10 B3
Haramsara (Museum)	11 B3
Treasury	12 C3
Tomb of Artaxerxes III	13 C3
Tomb of Artaxerxes II	14 C2
Palace of 100 Columns	15 B2
Garrison	16 C2
Hall of 32 Columns	17 B1
Unfinished Gate	18 B1
Court of Apadana	19 B2

Many travellers opt for an English-speaking driver to ferry them around for a half or full day. The driver usually won't enter the site with you, so you'll have to rely on this book, or if you're lucky, a brochure from Persepolis. To Persepolis, Naqsh-e Rostam and Naqsh-e Rajab, it usually costs from about IR200,000 to IR250,000, while the full day to Pasargadae costs IR300,000 to IR350,000. For the best of these drivers, see our list (p271).

The Persepolis Complex
The following descriptions are set out like a walking tour in the order suggested on the map. This route is different to that taken by many guides, meaning you can avoid the throngs.

ENTERING THE CITY
As it always has been, entry to Persepolis is via the monumental **Grand Stairway (2)** at the northwest corner of the site. The stairs were carved from massive blocks of stone, but each step was shallow so Persians in long elegant robes could walk gracefully up into the palace.

Whenever important foreign delegations arrived, their presence was heralded by trumpeters at the top of the staircase; fragments of one of these bronze trumpets are on display in the museum. Acolytes then led the dignitaries through **Xerxes' Gateway** (3; also known as the Gate of All Nations),

which is still a wonderfully impressive monument.

The gateway was built during the time of Xerxes I and is guarded by bull-like figures that have a strong Assyrian character. Above these, look for a cuneiform inscription in Old Persian, Neo-Babylonian and Elamite languages. It declares, among other things, that 'King Xerxes says: by the favour of Ahuramazda this Gate of All Nations I built. Much else that is beautiful was built in this Parsa, which I built and my father built.' Centuries of graffitists have also left their mark; look for explorer Henry Morton Stanley.

APADANA PALACE & STAIRCASE
Important Persian and Median notables were probably ushered to the **Apadana Palace (5)** to the south. Constructed on a terrace of stone by Xerxes I, the palace was reached via another staircase. Although it can be difficult to picture the grandeur of the palace from what remains, the bas-reliefs along the northern wall evocatively depict the scenes of splendour that must have accompanied the arrival of delegations to meet with the king.

Most impressive of all, however, and among the most impressive historical sights in all of Iran, are the bas-reliefs of the **Apadana Staircase (6)** on the eastern wall, which can also be reached from the Palace of 100 Columns. The northern panels recount the reception of the Persians in long robes and the Medes

---

PERSEPOLIS UNDER THE ACHAEMENIANS

In its heyday Persepolis spread over about 125,000 sq metres and was one of four cities at the heart of an empire that spread from the Indus River to Ethiopia. Its original name was Parsa and the first known reference to it by its Greek name of Persepolis – meaning both City of Parsa (City of Persia) and Destroyer of Cities – came after its sacking by Alexander the Great's army in 330 BC. Oddly, however, Persepolis is rarely mentioned by any name in foreign records, fuelling speculation among some archaeologists that the existence of the city was kept a secret from the outside world. The few remaining records focus instead on other Achaemenid capitals, including Babylon, Ecbatana (modern Hamadan) and Shush.

More certain is that Persepolis was built on the slopes of Mt Rahmat (the Mount of Mercy) as a showcase for the empire, designed to awe visitors with its scale and beauty. It served this purpose during the annual No Ruz (New Year) celebration, when subjects came from across the empire to climb up from the level of the surrounding plain and pay homage – and tribute – to their kings. It's quite possible that at other times the business of the empire returned to Shush.

Persepolis was burned to the ground during Alexander's visit in 330 BC. If you're wondering how a palace built almost entirely of stone could be burned to the ground, the explanation lies in the roof. The ceilings of most buildings are believed to have been made from huge timber beams, and as these burned they heated, then melted, the iron and lead clamps that held it all together.

in shorter dress. The three tiers of figures are amazingly well preserved. Each tier contains representations of the most elite of the Achaemenid soldiers, the Imperial Guard and the Immortals. On the upper tier, they are followed by the royal procession, the royal valets and the horses of the Elamite king of chariots, while on the lower two tiers they precede the Persians with their feather headdresses and the Medes in their round caps. The stairs themselves are guarded by Persian soldiers. The central panel of the staircase is dedicated to symbols of the Zoroastrian deity Ahura Mazda, symbolised by a ring with wings, flanked by two winged lions with human heads and guarded by four Persian and Median soldiers; the Persians are the ones carrying the indented shields. An inscription announces that the palace was started by Darius and completed by Xerxes and implores God to protect it from 'famine, lies and earthquakes'. The panels at the southern end are the most interesting, showing 23 delegations bringing their tributes to the Achaemenid king. This rich record of the nations of the time ranges from the Ethiopians in the bottom left corner, through a climbing pantheon of, among various other peoples, Arabs, Thracians, Indians, Parthians and Cappadocians, up to the Elamites and Medians at the top right.

Today, the staircase is covered by a permanent shelter and the only direct sunlight is early in the morning; it's worth heading straight here when the site opens.

TRIPYLON (XERXES' HALL OF AUDIENCE)
This small but handsomely decorated palace is known as both the **Tripylon (7)** and Xerxes' Hall of Audience. It stands at the heart of the city but what its exact function was remains unknown. One of the more widely accepted theories is that the king used it to receive notables and courtiers in a private area, possibly to make important political decisions. On the columns of the eastern doorway are reliefs showing Darius on his throne, borne by the representatives of 28 countries; the crown prince Xerxes stands behind his father. The 28 have their arms interlinked, representing a union of nations.

ROYAL PALACES
The southwestern corner of the site is dominated by palaces believed to have been

constructed during the reigns of Darius and Xerxes. The **Tachara (8**; or Winter Palace) is easily the most striking, with many of its monolithic doorjambs still standing and covered in bas-reliefs and cuneiform inscriptions. The stairs on the southern side bear highly skilled reliefs and are some of the most photogenic. The palace opens onto a royal courtyard flanked by two palaces. To the east is the **Hadish (9)**, a palace completed by Xerxes and reached via another monumental staircase. Some scholars speculate that its wooden columns on stone bases might have served as kindling for Alexander's great fire – especially as it had been Xerxes who had put Athens to the torch. To the south of the square are the remains of an unfinished palace known as **Palace H (10)**.

HAREMSARA (MUSEUM)
Accessed via stairs east of the Tripylon, the **Haremsara (11**; admission IR5000; ⏱ 8am-5pm) is the most argued about building at Persepolis. Despite the depictions around the door of the king defeating evil, scholars argue that is was either a harem for the king's consorts and concubines or a residence for visiting ambassadors (it has the same number of rooms as the number of subject nations). Restored in the 1930s, today it houses a museum and administrative offices. The museum contains a stone foundation tablet and a range of artefacts discovered during excavations: alabaster vessels, cedar wood, lances and arrow tips. Note the highly polished walls; almost every wall in Persepolis was finished in this expensive, labour-intensive fashion.

TREASURY & TOMBS
The southeastern corner of the site is dominated by Darius' **Treasury (12)**, one of the earliest structures at Persepolis. Archaeologists have found stone tablets in Elamite and Akkadian detailing the wages of thousands of labourers. When Alexander looted the Treasury it's reported he needed 3000 camels to cart off the contents. The foundations of walls and bases of more than 300 columns are all that remain. On the hill above the Treasury are the rock-hewn tombs of **Artaxerxes II (13)** and **Artaxerxes III (14)**. It's worth sitting on the hill for a while to get a feel for the enormous scale of Persepolis.

THE LAST SHAH'S TENT CITY

Outside the entrance to Persepolis, through the pine trees behind the toilets, are the remains of a luxurious tent city built by Shah Mohammad Reza Pahlavi to celebrate the 2500th anniversary of the Persian monarchy in 1971. The tents played host to a lavish and incredibly expensive party, attended by dignitaries including 60 monarchs or heads of state, but few Iranians. Food was flown in from Maxims in Paris, and many of the VIPs were put up in luxury tented apartments, complete with marble bathrooms. They were arranged on five streets, each representing a geographical area (Europe, Oceania, Asia, Africa and America), which came together to form a five-pointed star.

The celebration had two main objectives: to promote Iran to the rest of the world, and nurture Iranian nationalistic pride and love of their monarch. The first was a huge success, but the second was a public relations disaster. Opponents quickly pointed to the unnecessary extravagance, and some believe the party was a turning point from which the shah never recovered. It has stood rusting, with canvas slowly decaying, ever since.

In late 2007 it seemed the tent city, so long portrayed as a symbol of wasteful monarchy, would be rehabilitated through the uncomfortable mix of politics, pragmatism and ideology that is Iranian life. Reports suggested the city would be restored to its original luxury to house wealthy tourists. Talk about ironic…

PALACE OF 100 COLUMNS

With an extravagant square hall measuring almost 70m square and supported by 100 stone columns, the **Palace of 100 Columns (15)** was the second-largest building at Persepolis, built during the reigns of Xerxes and Artaxerxes I. Some scholars believe it was used to receive the military elite upon whom the empire's security rested. An impressive array of broken columns remain, and reliefs on the doorjambs at the back (south) of the building show a king, soldiers and representatives of 28 subject nations. Little remains of the **Hall of 32 Columns (17)**, built at the end of the Achaemenid period. The arrival of Alexander and his armies stopped work on a larger version of the Gate of All Lands, in the wide courtyard in front of the Palace of 100 Columns, now aptly called the **Unfinished Gate (18)**.

SOUND & LIGHT SHOW

On summer Thursday and Friday nights a sound and light show (IR5000; usually in Farsi) lights up Persepolis at 8.30pm. You must enter the site by 6pm. Check that it's on at the Tourist Information in Shiraz (p271).

Sleeping & Eating

Camping in the parking lot at Persepolis is allowed, but otherwise the only sleeping option is **Persepolis Tourist Complex** (Hotel Jahangardi; ☎ 447 4001; Takht-e Jamshid Blvd; r/ste US$24/50; ❄), about 1.5km west of Persepolis, where recently restored bungalows are fair value and the open-air teahouse is attractive.

Nearby, the best restaurant is the faux-grotto **Parsian Restaurant** (☎ 447 3555; Takht-e Jamshid Blvd; meals IR30,000-50,000; ✺ lunch & dinner). At Persepolis itself, snacks, drinks and ice creams can be bought near the ticket office.

Getting There & Away

Many travellers take tours or hire taxis (see Tours, p271), but it's not difficult to get to Persepolis by a combination of bus and local taxi from Shiraz. Take a minibus (IR4000, 42km, hourly) or savari (IR8000, or IR40,000 for the whole car to Persepolis) from the southern edge of Carandish Terminal to Marvdasht, where they stop at Basij Sq. From here you should be able to find a shuttle taxi (IR3000, 12km) or private taxi (IR15,000) to Persepolis. Alternatively, drivers in Marvdasht told us they would go *dar baste* to Persepolis and Naqshe-e Rostam, then back to Shiraz for IR120,000, including a couple of hours waiting time. Returning from the site, there are always plenty of vehicles lurking outside the entrance (about IR80,000 per car to Shiraz), or try hitching.

NAQSH-E ROSTAM & NAQSH-E RAJAB

نقش رستم و نقش رجب

Definitely worth visiting as part of a trip to Persepolis are these sites The rock tombs of **Naqsh-e Rostam** (admission IR3000; ✺ 8am-5pm winter, 7.30am-5.30pm summer) are magnificent. Hewn out of a cliff high above the ground, the four tombs are believed to be those of Darius II, Artaxerxes I, Darius I and Xerxes I (from left to right as you look at the cliff) although historians are still debating this. The tombs of the later Artaxerxes above Persepolis were modelled on these. The openings lead to funerary chambers, where bones were stored after the vultures had picked them clean. The reliefs above the openings are similar to those at Persepolis, with the kings standing at fire altars supported by figures representing the subject nations below. The cruciform design of the tombs supposedly represents the cardinal points, but some historians wonder whether this religious symbol has any relationship to the Christian cross.

The eight Sassanian **stone reliefs** cut into the cliff depict scenes of imperial conquests and royal ceremonies; there are detailed descriptions in front of the tombs and reliefs.

Facing the cliff is the **Kaba Zartosht**. It was long thought to be an Achaemenid fire temple, but scholars now argue that it might have been an ancient calendar, or perhaps a treasury. The walls are marked with inscriptions cataloguing later Sassanian victories.

Naqsh-e Rajab (admission IR2000; 🕑 8am-5pm winter, 7.30am-5.30pm summer) is directly opposite the turn-off to Naqsh-e Rostam on the old Shiraz–Esfahan road and is worth a quick look. Four fine Sassanian bas-reliefs are hidden from the road by the folds of a rocky hill and depict various scenes from the reigns of Ardashir I and Shapur the Great. A man called Rajab once had a teahouse here, hence the name.

Getting There & Away

Most private taxi trips to Persepolis also stop at Naqsh-e Rostam and Naqsh-e Rajab. If you don't have a vehicle and it's winter, you could walk the 6km from Persepolis to Naqsh-e Rostam, stopping off at Naqsh-e Rajab en route. In summer, this would be idiotic. Alternatively, negotiate with a taxi driver to take you to these places, perhaps en route back to Marvdasht.

PASARGADAE پاسارگاد

elevation 1847m

Begun under Cyrus the Great in about 546 BC, the city of Pasargadae was quickly superseded by Darius I's magnificent palace at Persepolis. **Pasargadae** (admission IR3000; 🕑 8am-5pm, 7.30am-5.30pm summer) is about 50km north of Persepolis and some travellers have questioned whether it's worth the effort of getting there. The site is not nearly as well preserved as Persepolis, but is beautiful in a lonely, windswept way.

The austere and awesomely simple **Tomb of Cyrus** stands proudly on the Morghab Plain. It consists of six stone tiers with a modest rectangular burial chamber above, and its unique architecture combines elements of all the major civilisations Cyrus had conquered. During the Achaemenid period it was surrounded by gardens and protected, but was plundered by the armies of Alexander the Great, an act that greatly distressed the Macedonian conqueror.

About 1km north of the tomb begin the insubstantial remains of the early Achaemenid empire. **Cyrus's Private Palace** is first, notable for its unusual H-shaped plan, central hall of 30 columns (the stumps of which remain), and wide verandahs front and back. About 250m southeast is the rectangular **Audience Palace**, which once had an 18m-high hypostyle hall surrounded by smaller balconies. Incredibly, one of the eight white limestone columns remains standing on its uncommon black limestone plinth. In both the Audience Palace and in Cyrus' Private Palace there is a cuneiform inscription that reads: 'I am Cyrus, the Achaemenid King'.

Another 500m north of Cyrus's Private Palace are the remains of the **Prison of Solomon** (Zendan-e Soleiman), variously thought to be a fire temple, tomb, sun dial or store. On the hill beyond is the **Throne of the Mother of Solomon** (Takht-e Madar-e Soleiman), which was actually a monumental 6000-sq-metre citadel used from Cyrus's time until the late Sassanian period. Local historians believe the references to Solomon date from the Arab conquest, when the inhabitants of Pasargadae renamed the sites with Islamic names to prevent their destruction.

By far the easiest way to get here is to charter a taxi from Shiraz; see p271 for options. Some travellers take a driver to/from Yazd, stopping here and at Persepolis.

By public transport, follow the instructions for Persepolis (p283), then walk another 1.5km and ask for the Sadahan Asenjan (taxi station), from where you take another savari to Sa'adatshahr (also known as Sa'adat Abad; IR10,000, 45 minutes), and then another to Pasargadae (IR5000). Alternatively, take a bus (IR11,000) from Carandish terminal in Shiraz to Sa'adatshahr, and a (very rare) taxi

---

IRAN'S NOMADS

The 20th century saw the Iranian government try repeatedly to settle Iran's many nomadic tribes. For all their efforts, however, there are still about a million people living as nomads in Iran. They are mostly Turkic Qashqa'i and Bakhtiyari, but there are also nomadic Kurds, Lors, Baluchis and smaller groups such as the Khamseh of Bavanat.

The Bakhtiyari are concentrated in an area extending southward from Lorestan province to Khuzestan province and westward from Esfahan to near the Iraqi border, moving their herds of sheep and goats between summer and winter pastures. They speak a dialect of Lori.

The Qashqa'i are based in central Iran where they move between summer and winter pastures in Fars Province. Their migration routes are among the longest and most difficult of all of Iran's pastoral tribes, as they are often on the road for 45 days. They have become famous for their production of simple rugs – the *gabbeh* – which have proved very popular with Westerners (Iranians are rather snobbish about *gabbeh*). You can usually spot Qashqa'i women in the Shiraz bazaar.

Nomadic women wear long, colourfully layered dresses with much jewellery and no chadors. The men sometimes wear tall hats with a rounded crown. To see them it's best to go with a guide, who can translate and just find them. Pars Tourist Agency (p271) in Shiraz has several nomad tour options, or try Bavanat Tours (below). Also see The Bakhtiyari, p218.

---

or (rare) minibus the remaining 30km. Easier is taking any bus towards Yazd or Esfahan (you may have to pay full fare), getting out at the turn-off to Pasargadae and walking or hitching the last 8km. Leave plenty of time to hitch/bus/whatever back to Shiraz or on to Abarqu/Yazd.

BAVANAT   بوانات

In a quiet valley 230km northeast of Shiraz, the Bavanat region is a 20km-long walnut forest in a lush valley between the Zagros Mountains in the south and deserts to the north.

The main town is Suryan, aka Bavanat, but the real destination here is the village of Shah Hamzeh Bazm (or just Bazm) 18km further east. The mountains near Bazm are home to Khamseh nomads, a confederation of five groups of Arabic, Turkish and Farsi-speaking people. From about April until October they pitch their tents in the hills and survive with few of the 'luxuries' you might see in the tents of Qashqa'i nomads north of Shiraz.

Abbas Barzegar, himself part Khamseh, opens his family home in Bazm to visitors and runs one- and two-day **Bavanat Tours** (☎ 0752-326 2357, 0917 317 3957) tours to stay with the nomads (in summer, of course). He's a lovely guy, though his very basic English is a problem. Alternatively, you could just hang out in his place (price negotiable). Tours cost US$40 for one person, US$35 for two to five, and US$30 each beyond that, including the

delicious food – his wife is an award-winning cook – and transport.

To get to Bazm, first come to Suryan. One bus leaves Abuzar Sq in Yazd (IR12,000, three hours) at 1pm, returning at 7.30am. From Shiraz (IR12,000, three hours), buses leave Carandish Terminal at 7.30am and 12.30pm, returning at the same times next day. There are no regular savaris to Suryan, but you can go *dar baste* to Shahr-e Babak (IR200,000 one way) if you're continuing to Meymand (see p311). From Suryan, you'll have to hire a taxi or hitch.

FIRUZ ABAD   فیروز آباد
☎ 0712 / pop 70,000 / elev 1330m

The monumental Sassanian-era remains around modern Firuz Abad are often missed by those in a rush to get to Persepolis. The palaces and city were built by the founder of the Sassanian empire, Ardashir Babakan, in the 3rd century BC. Firuz Abad was once an important stop on the Sassanid Roadway between Shiraz and the ancient port of Shiraf. Today, it's mainly a Qashqai farming town. Coming from Shiraz, the first site is **Qal'eh-e Doktar** (Maiden's Palace), sitting atop a steep hill with commanding views into the valley below. You'll know you're there when you see a footbridge crossing the road. Take the bridge and it's a 10- or 15-minute climb. This three-tiered palace made of rock and gypsum was Ardashir's first, and its position and fortification reflect the lingering Parthian threat of the time. While crumbling, it's not difficult to imagine the palace's original layout, and the views from the top are magnificent.

About 2km towards Firuz Abad, a signed dirt road fords the Tang Ab river to reach **Ardashir's Palace** (admission IR3000; ☼ 7.30am-sunset), a much grander structure built beside a wonderfully refreshing spring once Ardashir felt more secure. Given it is almost 1800 years old, its domes, high *iwans* and clean, stable lines – which set the tone for all Sassanian architecture – remain hugely impressive. The *iwans* and domes, with their accompanying squinches, are some of the earliest surviving examples. In winter, the Tang Ab is impassable so you'll need to take a lengthy detour through Firuz Abad by taxi.

Beyond Ardashir's Palace is his city, **Gur** (N 28°51'2.66", E 52°31'58.52"), which in its current form is an archaeologist's dream, but requires plenty of imagination. With its perfectly circular plan, divided into equal sectors and separated by high walls, Gur was a hugely ambitious town-planning feat. The only existing building is the 30m-high 'minaret' that marked the centre of the circle. Gur is about 3km along the sealed road between Firuz Abad and Ardashir's Palace.

Sleeping

The only place to stay in Firuz is the over-priced **Firooz Abad Tourist Inn** (Mehmunsara Jahangardi; ☎ 622 3699; s/d US$25/35; P ⌘); most people wisely take a day trip from Shiraz.

Getting There & Away

Minibuses run from Shiraz's Carandish terminal to Firuz Abad (IR10,000, 2½ hours) several times a day, or take a savari (IR18,000, 80 minutes). Returning, the last savari leaves about 7pm. For Qal'eh-e Doktar, ask to get off when you see the overhead footbridge. Returning by savari you'll need to go to Firuz Abad, as they will be full when they pass Qal'eh-e Doktar. Or you could hitch. Alternatively, take a tour or driver (p271).

KAZERUN & BISHAPUR

کازرون و بیشاپور

Just off the ancient royal road between Shiraz and Bushehr are the small but fascinating ruins of another two ancient cities: Kazerun and, about 25km to the west, Bishapur. At

Kazerun (the name comes from an ancient word meaning 'people who wash cotton clothes') there are several Sassanian-era **bas-reliefs** most interesting to archaeologists for their unique inscriptions.

Bishapur (admission IR3000; ☼ 8am-4pm, to 5pm summer), or 'Shapur's City', is better. It was the grand capital of possibly the greatest of the Sassannian kings, Shapur I. Shapur and his armies defeated the Romans three times, and much of Bishapur was built by Romans taken captive after their Emperor Valerian was defeated in AD 260; he lived his final years a captive at Bishapur. The site has been partly excavated, revealing the enormous **Palace of Shapur** and nearby **Anahita's Temple**, where a stairway leads underground to a pool around which the faithful once walked and prayed. Some fine Irano-Roman mosaics remain, but the best are now in the Louvre.

The city was originally approached along the Shapur River in the steep-sided Chogan Gorge. A short walk from Bishapur, its rocky walls bear six large **bas-reliefs** commemorating, among other historical moments, Shapur's investiture as king and his victory over Roman invaders. The deep groove running through the reliefs was caused by a powerful flood in the 1960s; the groove marks the high-water mark.

About 4km along the gorge is the **Tang-e Chogan** (Shapur Cave) and its awesome 7m-high **Statue of Shapur I**, one of the most impressive archaeological sites in Iran. Getting to the cave is easiest on a taxi tour, but you could walk the 5km or so from Shapur. Take the road along the river for about 4km to a village on your left, where one of the villagers will probably offer to lead you up the steep ascent to the cave (start very early in summer). A tip is appreciated.

Getting to Bishapur is easiest by charter taxi (at least IR200,000 from Shiraz), but public transport is viable with an early start. Take the bus to Kazerun from the Amir Kabir terminal in Shiraz (IR10,000, 2½ hours) or from Bushehr, or a savari. From Shiraz, keep an eye out en route for the 15-arch **Karim Khan Bridge**, a Zand-era bridge about 40km west of Shiraz.

Alternatively, take a guided tour; see p271 for guides and drivers.

Persian Gulf
خليج فارس

Whether you're watching the sun set over the Gulf, scrambling over the ruins of the Portuguese castle at Hormoz, or just dropping down several gears to the ultra-relaxed pace this region operates, you can't escape the fact that the Persian Gulf offers a different experience to the rest of Iran. There's the geographical contrast – the coast and islands of the Gulf itself – but the major difference comes from the variety of people and how they live.

The history of the Gulf is tied inextricably to trade. Africans, Arabs, Indians and Europeans as far back as Alexander the Great have passed by this way, some finding business so good they've set up shop and stayed. The result is a rich hybrid of ancient Persia and Arabia that is best seen in Bandari communities, such as Bushehr, Hormoz and Minab. These communities are unusual in Iran, with most Bandaris being Sunni Muslims, speaking Arabic at home and wearing more colourful clothes. They're known as Bandaris because they live in *bandars* (ports). Qeshm Island is probably the highlight of the Gulf, and its tiny village of Laft is the jewel in its sun-scorched crown. Sitting with the locals as the sun sets over the forest of *badgirs* (windtowers) and *lenges* (traditional wooden boats) is almost worth the trip to the coast by itself.

Unfortunately, most travellers avoid the coast because of inconvenient transport times, relatively expensive accommodation, the distance from Iran's mainstream destinations and the enervating heat. Winter days often enjoy clear skies and 25°C, but it's hot by March and diabolically hot – like, 50°C – in summer.

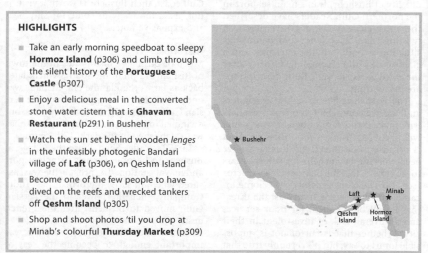

HIGHLIGHTS

- Take an early morning speedboat to sleepy **Hormoz Island** (p306) and climb through the silent history of the **Portuguese Castle** (p307)

- Enjoy a delicious meal in the converted stone water cistern that is **Ghavam Restaurant** (p291) in Bushehr

- Watch the sun set behind wooden *lenges* in the unfeasibly photogenic Bandari village of **Laft** (p306), on Qeshm Island

- Become one of the few people to have dived on the reefs and wrecked tankers off **Qeshm Island** (p305)

- Shop and shoot photos 'til you drop at Minab's colourful **Thursday Market** (p309)

★ Bushehr

Laft ★ ★ Minab
★
Qeshm   Hormoz
Island   Island

PERSIAN GULF

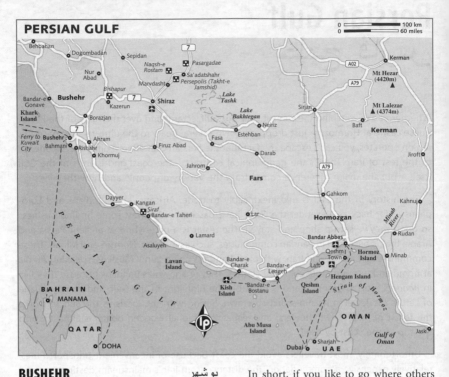

PERSIAN GULF

BUSHEHR   بوشهر

☎ 0771 / pop 176,000

Visitors tend to rave about or revile the old city of Bushehr, Iran's main seaport in the northern Gulf. Readers have described the once-elegant Bandari architecture, twisting mud-brick lanes and peninsular situation as both 'a living museum' and a clapped-out ruin resembling 'Grozny after the third Russian war'. Both descriptions are partly right.

The Bushehris like to talk to foreigners and are welcoming of the few travellers who make it this far, though anyone white will likely be mistaken for a Russian. That is because more than 1000 Russians have been working in Bushehr for several years to complete the Bushehr nuclear reactor (see also The Nuclear Issue, p42). Some locals blame the reactor, or at least the threat that it will be bombed, for poor services and an overall lack of investment in their city. Whether that is fair or not is impossible for us to say, but it's certainly true that almost nothing is being done to maintain or restore Bushehr's crumbling heritage.

In short, if you like to go where others don't, have an interest in Bandari culture or plan on working your way along the Persian Gulf coast, then Bushehr is worth a visit. If not, it's a long way to come for silly heat and expensive hotels.

History

Much of Bushehr's history lies in the town of Rishahr, 12km to the south, which dates back as far as the Elamite era. Rishahr was one of the chief trading centres of the Persian Gulf from the 7th to 16th centuries, but dwindled in importance after Bandar Abbas was established in the early 17th century.

In 1734 Nader Shah chose the village of Bushehr to become Persia's principal port and naval station. Its prosperity was assured when, in 1759, the British East India Company, then the power in the Persian Gulf, moved to Bushehr after the French destroyed its factory at Bandar Abbas.

In the mid-19th century Bushehr was important enough to become the seat of the British political residency on the Persian Gulf. However, Bushehr's long, slow decline began in the 1930s when it was bypassed by the trans-Iranian railway in favour of the ports in Khuzestan province. The British closed their consulate in 1951. Bushehr was an important naval base during the Iran–Iraq War, but most of its commercial activities were relocated to the less-exposed Bandar Abbas.

Orientation

Bushehr is built on a peninsular jutting into the Persian Gulf. The Old City is at the northern tip and the town centre is En-qelab Sq. The interesting parts of Bushehr are easy enough to explore on foot. Most attractions, hotels and restaurants are in the northern part of Bushehr, which is circled by Khalij-e Fars St (the esplanade). The new bus terminal is about 6km southeast of town.

Information

Amaken (Leyan St; 🕙 6am-9pm)
Bank Melli (Leyan St) Exchange on the first floor.
Coffeenet (Leyan St; internet per hr IR10,000; 🕙 8.30am-1.30pm & 4-11pm Sat-Thu)
International telephone office (Imam Khomeini St; 🕙 7.30am-2pm & 3-11pm)
Main hospital (☎ 252 6591; Siraf St) Not the best hospital in Iran.
Money exchange (Leyan St; 🕙 8am-1pm & 5-8pm Sat-Thu) Better hours, less paperwork.
Police headquarters (☎ 253 0027/0799; Qods Sq; 🕙 8am-2pm) The English-speaking major on the ground floor is a pleasant enough chap and will extend your visa

without too much hassle. It takes one or two days, and 30-day extensions are common. For more on extending visas, see 'More Time, Please' (p395).
Post office (Valiasr St)
Setar-e Bandar Travel Agency (☎ 252 8878; Imam Khomeini St) Handles domestic and international air tickets, in English.

Sights

Whether or not you are enchanted by decaying Bandari buildings and winding *kuches* (alleys), Bushehr's **Old City** is a rarity among the ports of the region in that it offers glimpses of a fast-disappearing way of life. There is little of the traffic and noise found in Bandar Abbas, for example, and as we found it's easy to lose yourself in the Old City only to end up drinking *chay* (tea) and eating oranges in the home of a local family.

The densely packed wooden struts that overhang some of the narrow lanes are unique to Bushehr. Of particular interest are the door-knockers shaped like human hands in the northwestern quarter of town. Also check out the pillars and white façade of the **Amirieh Edifice** (Khalij-e Fars St), which was once home to a rich merchant and more recently a museum.

The crumbling seaside ruins of the **British consulate** (Khalij-e Fars St) are worth a look for a hint of Bushehr's former grandeur.

Sleeping

Bushehr has a chronic shortage of decent accommodation. Making things worse,

---

KHALIJ-E FARS

The body of water dividing Iran and the Arabian Peninsula has been known as the Persian Gulf, or Khalij-e Fars in Farsi, since the Greeks called it this more than 2000 years ago. But the rise of Arab nationalism during the 1960s saw that begin to change. Governments and map-makers in Arab countries started referring to the Arabian Gulf, and slowly the name has gained traction.

For Iranians, it's an outrage. When the Louvre in Paris started referring to the Arabian Gulf a few years ago, and America's National Geographic Society included Arabian Gulf as an alternative name in its 2004 atlas, Iran responded with a high-level campaign to have them changed back. Historians were wheeled out, ancient maps reproduced and conferences held to support the 'Persian Gulf' case. But with Iran not exactly topping any international popularity contests, and the Arab states sitting on much of the world's oil supply, winning support was not easy. At home it became a nationalist issue and politicians of all stripes railed against the historical injustice. To press home the point they renamed almost every intercity road in the country Khalij-e Fars Hwy. Ordinary Iranians were right behind them.

Eventually, the campaign paid off. While the Arab states will continue to refer to it as the Arabian Gulf, at least independent institutions, including the Louvre and National Geographic relented. The success was celebrated as a national victory in Iran.

PERSIAN GULF

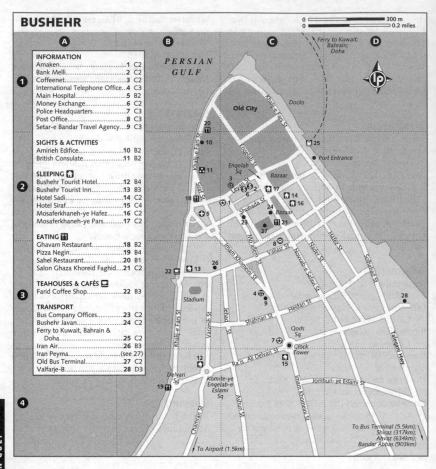

BUSHEHR

0 ——————— 300 m
0 ——————— 0.2 miles

PERSIAN GULF

Old City

Docks

Ferry to Kuwait;
Bahrain;
Doha

Port Entrance

Bazaar

Enqelab Sq

Stadium

Qods Sq

Clock Tower

Komite-ye Enqelab-e Eslami Sq

Delvari Sq

To Bus Terminal (5.5km);
Shiraz (317km);
Ahvaz (634km);
Bandar Abbas (903km)

To Airport (1.5km)

Jomhuri-ye Eslami St

PERSIAN GULF

Bushehr's police still insist that foreigners wanting to stay in a *mosaferkhaneh* (lodging house) first get a letter of permission from the police. Thankfully it's a fairly painless process. Go to the Amaken (p289) where, if your experience is anything like ours, you'll shake several hands, drink some tea, be asked how you like Iran and after about 10 minutes be issued with a stamped slip of paper, *kheyli mamnun*. The bad news (which we can also report first-hand) is that buses to Bushehr have an unhappy habit of arriving in the middle of the night. For us, no amount of pleading at *mosaferkhanehs* or at the Amaken worked. Our taxi driver even suggested we sleep in his car until 6am! Nice offer, but we grudgingly forked

out for the grossly overpriced midrange option instead…The three cheap options are near Enqelab Sq; go to the Amaken first.

Mosaferkhaneh-ye Pars (☎ 252 2479; Enqelab Sq; dm/s/tw IR20,000/60,000/70,000) This ultra-basic place has small, clean rooms and shared bathrooms and a rooftop dorm overlooking the old town. The dorm is big, bright and noisy, but cheap – not great for women. Welcoming manager, but no English.

Mosaferkhaneh-ye Hafez (☎ 252 5783; Nader St; r IR60,000) Two-storey place with rainbow-coloured sign in Farsi; no-frills rooms (some with four beds) and shared bathrooms.

Hotel Sadi (☎ 252 2605; Nader St; r IR200,000-300,000; ❄) More comfortable than the first two, but the foreign price (IR200,000 without a bathroom!) is ridiculous; a bathroom costs another IR100,000.

Hotel Siraf (Hotel Reza; ☎ 252 7171; Imam Khomeini St; s/d with breakfast US$40/50; ✖) The large, tired rooms need an overhaul and could be much cleaner. They're not worth the money, but are better than the Bushehr Tourist Inn. Bargain as hard as you can.

Bushehr Tourist Inn (Sadra Inn; ☎ 252 2346; cnr Valiasr & Khalij-e Fars Sts; r US$42; P ✖) Great location, pity about the rooms/price ratio. Your last resort.

Bushehr Tourist Hotel (Delvar Hotel; ☎ 284 0910; delvar@ittic.com; Komite-ye Enqelab-e Eslami Sq; tw/ste with breakfast US$70/119; P ✖ 💻) Rising like a modern-day ziggurat out of central Bushehr, this is easily the best place in town. Most of the semi-luxurious rooms have Gulf views, the restaurant is reasonable and rooms on the second floor have wifi.

Eating

You can usually find simple, cheap food along the Bushehr waterfront, particularly near the seafront building housing the **Farid Coffee Shop** (Khalij-e Fars St; ☽ noon-2.30pm & 5-10pm), where the view is better than the coffee, and in the park near the Ghavam Restaurant. This is a great area for people-watching, especially on Thursday or Friday evenings when the whole of Bushehr seems to be promenading along the esplanade with the cool sea breezes.

Salon Ghaza Khoreid Faghid (☎ 252 5755; Novvab-e Safavi St; meals IR15,000-30,000; ☽ 7.30am-8pm) There isn't an English sign and there's nothing fancy about this little place near the bazaar, but the local speciality *ghalye mahi* (a richly flavoured fish stew) is delicious.

Sahel Restaurant (☎ 252 1279; Khalij-e Fars St; meals IR20,000-45,000; ☽ 11.30am-2pm & 7-10.30pm; ✖) The Gulf-side location makes Sahel a good place to interrupt your Old City wanderings. And the kababs, fish and *ghorme sabzi* (stewed beans, greens and mince, served with rice) are pretty tasty.

Pizza Negin (☎ 258 0079; Delvari Sq; large pizzas IR35,000; ☽ 11am-11pm; ✖) This trendy place, inside a concrete boat 'sailing' along the seaside esplanade, is super popular and the pizzas are relatively good.

ourpick Ghavam Restaurant (☎ 252 1790; Khalij-e Fars St; meals IR35,000-65,000; ☽ noon-3pm & 7-11pm) Once a cistern used to store Bushehr's water, Ghavam is now one of the best restaurants on the Persian Gulf coast. The underground

---

ARABS

About 3% of Iranians are Arab and most of these live in Khuzestan, Bushehr and Hormozgan provinces, near or on the Persian Gulf coast. They have traditionally lived in the Gulf ports (known as *bandars*) and are often called *bandari*. Arabs in Khuzestan are mostly Shiite, many having arrived from Iraq during the Iran–Iraq War, while those along the Persian Gulf are mainly Sunni.

Arabs are different enough that they are considered exotic by many Iranians. They speak a dialect of Arabic, usually have darker skin, include a significant number of black-skinned people with forebears from Africa, and dress differently. Women's clothes are refreshingly colourful (see Bandari Burqas, p297), while men wear the *abba*, a long sleeveless tunic, usually in white, with sandals and perhaps an Arabic turban. Elsewhere you will see men in *dishdasha*, the traditional floor-length shirt-dress, with the long headscarf known as *gutra*.

Iranian Arabs have their own music, characterised by the *ney ammbooni* (a sort of bagpipe) and a strong, faster beat often accompanied by a shimmying dance similar to belly dancing.

---

location offers relief from the heat, and the vaulted ceilings, antique photographs and live traditional music (dinner only) create a warm, convivial, enjoyable atmosphere. The menu includes a range of local specialities, including boiled rice with broadbeans and fish.

Getting There & Away

AIR

Iran Air (☎ 252 3925; Valiasr St) has flights between Bushehr and Tehran (one way IR433,000, 90 minutes, twice daily), Shiraz (IR245,000, one hour, weekly) and Esfahan (IR283,000, 70 minutes, weekly). **Iran Aseman** (www.iaa.ir) flies to/from Dubai (one way IR1,265,000, one hour, three days weekly). Setar-e Bandar Travel Agency (p289) sells tickets.

BOAT

Apart from enterprising fishermen, there are no domestic boat services from Bushehr. However, the Valfajre-8 shipping company operates (in theory, though not always in practice) to Qatar (one way US$50, Mondays), Bahrain (US$45, seven to eight hours, Mondays) and Kuwait (US$70, seven to eight hours, Wednesdays).

For information on impending departures go to the **Valfajre-8 office** (☎ 253 0246/7; Solhabad St; ⏱ 7am-5pm).

BUS

Bushehr's big new bus terminal is about 6km southeast of town near Meydan-e Borj. It's a private taxi (about IR20,000) or shuttle taxi (IR3000) ride away, but most bus companies maintain offices at or nearby the old bus terminal in town, including **Iran Peyma** (☎ 252 4575). For Kazerun (IR10,000) take any bus heading to Shiraz; for Kangan, **Bushehr Javan** (☎ 253 0930; Novvab-e Safavi St) has a dedicated bus daily at 10.30am. Prices in the table here are for Volvo buses except Esfahan and Shiraz (where fares indicate *mahmooly*/Volvo).

Destination	Fare	Duration	Departures
Ahvaz	IR55,000	7hr	6am, 7am, 2pm, 2.30pm
Bandar Abbas	IR85,000	13-15hr	3am, 3.30pm
Bandar-e Lengeh	IR60,000	9-11hr	5pm
Esfahan	IR30,000/ 55,000	13-16hr	3.30-6pm
Kermanshah	IR95,000	14hr	4.30pm
Shiraz	IR14,500/ 30,000	5hr	regular
Tehran	IR108,000	18-21hr	10.30am, 1-5pm

Getting Around

A private taxi between Bushehr airport and town costs about IR10,000 (you'll undoubtedly be asked for more). Alternatively, take a shuttle taxi from Komite-ye Enqelab-e Eslami Sq for about IR2000.

Shuttle taxis around town cost IR500 to IR2000; trips *dar baste* (closed door) cost about IR5000, except to the airport or new bus terminal (IR20,000).

FROM BUSHEHR TO BANDAR-E LENGEH

There are some charming towns dotted along the long, quiet road that skirts the Persian Gulf coastline. About 250km southeast of Bushehr, **Kangan** is a pretty fishing village that's well worth exploring. **Bandar-e**

Taheri, a little further southeast, boasts the ruins of an 18th-century sheikh's fortress; the views from the *badgir* over the Gulf are superb and the town itself is quite picturesque. Nearby on the rocky coastline are the ruins of the ancient town of **Siraf** and some well-preserved stone graves. **Bandar-e Bostanu**, 18km west of Bandar-e Lengeh, has some great *badgirs*.

Without a vehicle this area is difficult to fully explore. Most traffic just races by and there are no hotels. However, unless you arrive during the long summer siesta you'll probably get a warm welcome from the locals, who are unlikely to have seen another tourist for quite some time. If you are not found by someone who insists on putting you up for the night (probable if your bus passes at 3am), then your best bet is the local town mosque (which will usually have a room with a roll-out bed on the floor).

KISH ISLAND   جزیره کیش
☎ 0764 / pop 20,000

'Oh, but have you been to Kish? You absolutely must go.' Travelling in Iran you'll likely hear this more than once. And when you ask what is so special about Kish, you're told: 'But Kish is wonderful; everything works there. It is clean, shopping is cheap, you can swim…and there are no Paykans!'

Yes, all of this is true. Kish, the desert island that the last shah started transforming into a playground for the rich and famous during the 1960s, is now seen by Iranians the way Americans view Hawaii. The island is both a novelty – for most Iranians this is the only beach resort they'll ever be able to visit – and more liberated than the rest of Iran. Kish is a free-trade zone and, as one islander told us, many Iranians understand the 'free' to apply to social activities as well.

Kish is booming. Hotels, shopping centres and theme parks are emerging from the sand to cater to migrant workers on 'change visa' runs and more than one million Iranians a year. But for foreigners, used to swimming and sunbathing with their partners and with no interest in duty-free DVD players, the appeal isn't so great. And it's expensive.

However, there are reasons to visit Kish. The resort water-sports make a pleasant diversion, there are a few ancient sights and cycling around the island on the coastal bike path is fun. More than anything else, though, it's the relaxed atmosphere that appeals to Iranians, many of whom treat the island as something of a mental-health break – it's not a bad approach.

Arriving after 2009 you should see the distinctive tower of the Flower of the East Hotel (www.floweroftheeast.com), part of an enormous resort being built on Kish's northeast corner; and the 500-room Cyrus Hotel, said to be both 'seven-star' and the world's first fully solar-powered hotel.

History
Kish Island is first recorded in the memoirs of Nearchus, the Greek sailor commissioned by Alexander the Great to explore the Persian Gulf in 325 BC. In the Middle Ages Kish became an important trading centre under its own powerful Arab dynasty and at one time supported a population of 40,000. The main town was Harireh, which is believed to be the town referred to by poet Sa'di in his famous work, *Golestan* (Rose Garden).

Kish was known for the quality of its pearls; when Marco Polo was visiting the imperial court in China, he remarked on the beauty of the pearls worn by one of the emperor's wives and was told they had come from Kish. In the 14th century Kish fell into decline and remained obscure until the 1970s, when it was developed as a semi-private retreat for the shah and his guests – complete with international airport, luxury hotels and even a grand casino.

GULF TIME

Most of the Persian Gulf coastline is hotter than Hades between about mid-April and late October and, not surprisingly, life adjusts accordingly. No-one wants to work in the scorching early-afternoon heat so you'll find most businesses start early and then shut up shop from about noon to 5pm – including air-conditioned *coffeenets* (internet cafés) and shopping malls. Air-conditioned government offices work regular hours, and transport still operates, though less frequently. The best part of the day is invariably the evening, when temperatures drop and everyone sits outside drinking tea and thanking Allah for sea breezes.

Orientation
Kish is 15km long, 8km wide and rises just 45m at its highest point. You'll find many of the offices, banks, shops and hotels between Sanaee and Siri Sqs along the eastern coast, which also has the best beaches. Most residents live in this area or in the Arab settlements of Saffein, on the northern coast, and tiny Baghu, in the southwest.

Information
Most government offices work from 8am until 1.30pm or 2pm Saturday to Thursday. There are busy *coffeenets* attached to the Farabi and Salar Kish Hotels, catering to visa runners.

Bank Melli (Sanaee St; ☉ 7.30am-1.30pm) Changes money with less paperwork than normal.

Customs (☎ 452 2578) Buying duty-free goods can be more trouble than it's worth as the customs paperwork can be tedious in the extreme. Call for the latest rules before deciding to buy.

Kish Hospital (☎ 442 3711; Hormuz Sq)

Kish Tourism Organisation (☎ 442 2434; www.kto.ir; Kish Tourism Organisation Bldg, Sanaee Sq; ☉ 7.30am-2.30pm Sat-Thu) Maps and brochures in English and French; English-speaking staff are on the 2nd floor.

Ministry of Foreign Affairs Kish office (☎ 4442 0734; 1st fl, Kish Tourism Organisation Bldg, Sanaee Sq; ☉ 8am-2.30pm) Kish is the only place in Iran that foreigners can visit without needing a visa. If you're arriving by air or boat from outside Iran, you get a free 14-day 'Kish visa' on arrival. Once on Kish, the ministry can issue normal tourist visas and you can continue into Iran, making this a handy back door. We know of several travellers who have come in this way and when we asked in the office this time they told us 'yes, no problem'. Visa fees vary by nationality and take four to five days to issue, or two days if you pay a reasonable 'urgent' fee.

Paniz Coffeenet (Paniz Bazar; internet per hr IR12,000; ☉ 9.15am-1pm & 5-11.30pm)

Police headquarters (☎ 442 2143; Khatam Blvd)

Post office (Khajoo Sq)

Sights & Activities
Between November and March the best way to see Kish's sights is by bicycle (see p295). The most interesting is the restored and mercifully cool underground water reservoir called the **Payab** (off Olympic Sq; admission IR20,000, including guided tour; ☉ 10am-6pm). Worth a quick look are the crumbling remains of ancient **Harireh** (☉ 24hr). Otherwise, the **Greek ship** that ran aground here on a clear night in 1966 lures photographers at sunset.

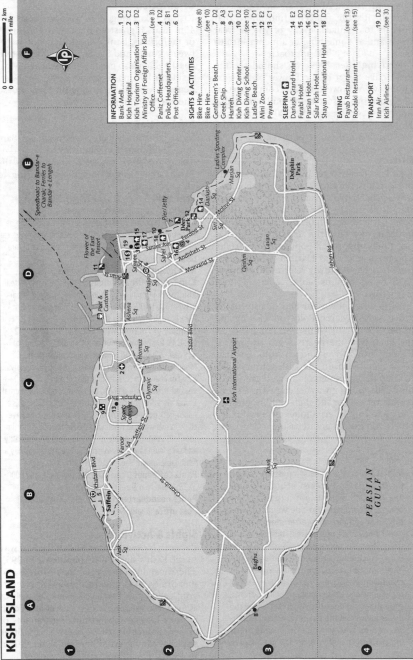

KISH ISLAND

INFORMATION
Bank Melli	1 D2
Kish Hospital	2 C2
Kish Tourism Organisation	3 D2
Ministry of Foreign Affairs Kish Office	(see 3)
Paniz Coffeenet	4 D2
Police Headquarters	5 B1
Post Office	6 D2

SIGHTS & ACTIVITIES
Bike Hire	(see 8)
Bike Hire	(see 10)
Gentlemen's Beach	7 D2
Greek Ship	8 A3
Harireh	9 C1
Kish Diving Center	10 D2
Kish Diving School	(see 10)
Ladies' Beach	11 D1
Mini Zoo	12 E2
Payab	13 C1

SLEEPING
Darush Grand Hotel	14 E2
Farabi Hotel	15 D2
Parsian Hotel	16 D2
Salar Kish Hotel	17 D2
Shayan International Hotel	18 D2

EATING
Payab Restaurant	(see 13)
Roodaki Restaurant	(see 15)

TRANSPORT
Iran Air	19 D2
Kish Airlines	(see 3)

Kish is one of the very few places in Iran where swimming is actively encouraged. There are sandy, uncrowded beaches around most of the coast, but women must use the **Ladies' Beach** (admission IR25,000; Arian St, off Sanaee Ave; ☺ 8am-6pm). For now this remains hidden away east of the port, but a 25,000-sq-metre **Ladies Sporting Complex** on the east coast might be finished by the time you arrive. There's also a **Gentlemen's Beach** on the east coast near the hotels, tho+ugh men can in theory swim anywhere (except the Ladies' Beach, of course). Other activities include diving, horseback riding, glass-bottomed boats and several 'themed' parks, including **Deer Park** (Park-e Ahovan; Ferdosi St; admission IR20,000; ☺ 9am-1pm & 4-9pm), a **mini zoo** and **Dolphin Park** (www.dolphinparkkish.com; admission US$30, ☺ 9am-8pm). Jet-skiing (IR200,000 for 15 minutes) and snorkelling (IR200,000 per trip) are also available; both these activities are run by the diving schools (see below).

CYCLING
Cycling the flat, approximately 40km-long Special Bicycle Route around Kish is a great way to spend a day. Bikes can be hired (for about IR15,000 an hour) from outside the dive shops near the Shayan International Hotel and at the Greek ship.

DIVING
Kish has a fairly well-developed diving scene, with nearby reefs and islands well-stocked with fish. However, prices have sharply increased recently and winds often mean the choice of dive site can be limited. One unimpressed reader told us his three-day diving trip saw him dive the same spot each day. Qeshm might be better (see p305).

Kish Diving Center (☎ 442 2757; www.kishdivingcenter.com; ☺ 7am-sunset), and **Kish Diving School** (☎ 442 4355; ☺ 7am-sunset), both found on the beach outside Shayan International Hotel, charge about IR350,000 for a one-hour dive with equipment. A four-day PADI open-water course costs IR3,500,000 – and would make you one of a very small group who could say: 'Where did I learn to dive? Iran!'

Sleeping & Eating
Kish has 46 hotels (and counting) and prices are significantly higher than elsewhere in Iran, though still reasonable by Western standards. Prices do vary by season – these are mid-season rates – and top out during No Ruz (Iranian New Year) when the island is totally mental. At non-peak times the hotel desk at the airport offers good midrange deals.

There are no *mosaferkhanehs* on Kish. The only cheap beds are in apartment hotels packed full of migrant workers renewing their visas. Farabi and Salar Kish Hotels serve this market, as do cheap restaurants in the area.

Farabi Hotel (☎ 442 3417; Sanaee Sq; bed IR70,000; ✖ 🖳) Sprawling, busy place beside Kish Airlines. Apartments are a bit worn but fine.

Salar Kish Hotel (☎ 442 0111; Sanaee Sq; per bed/s IR70,000/500,000; ✖) Smaller than Farabi but with bigger apartments; usually four or five beds in each.

Parsian Hotel (☎ 442 4991; Ferdosi St, off Sahel Sq; tw/tr/ste with breakfast US$63/74/125; P ✖ 🖳) One of the many new, three-star options. Well-located, spacious rooms that are more like mini apartments. Discounts possible.

ourpick Shayan International Hotel (☎ 442 2771; Sahel Sq; r/ste with breakfast US$110/280, cabana US$75; P ✖ 🖳) Shayan means 'gorgeous' and when it opened as the Shah's beachfront hotel in 1973 it was the best on the Gulf. It hasn't changed much and the angular architecture and sea of sprayed concrete have acquired a bit of retro cool. Rooms, most with balcony, are holding up fairly well.

Dariush Grand Hotel (☎ 444 4900-95; www.dariushgrandhotel.com; Dariush Sq; r from US$145; P ✖ 🖳 🕾) This ostentatious, Achaemenid-style monument in marble is arguably Iran's best hotel, though if don't fancy Vegas-like theme places it might feel over the top. The service, 192 rooms and suites, restaurants and facilities are all very good.

Roodaki Restaurant (off Sanaee Sq; meals from IR15,000; ☺ 11am-2.30pm & 6-10.30pm) Between the cheap apartment hotels and the beach, the Roodaki serves cheap, pre-prepared curries and Philippine cuisine.

ourpick Payab Restaurant (☎ 0934 769 1213; Olympic Blvd; meals IR45,000-70,000; ☺ 8pm-1am) Above the underground water reservoir, the Payab is cool and romantic in the evenings and the food is delicious. It offers fresh bread, big serves or fish, kabab or *dizi* (soup-stew). Extras (like *chay*) are expensive.

Getting There & Away
Most people fly into Kish, but you can get there by boat from Bandar-e Charak

or Bandar-e Lengeh; see Boat (below) for details.

AIR

Several airlines fly to/from Kish. Book ahead and reserve your onward ticket before you arrive.

Kish Airlines (☎ 442 3922; Sanaee Sq; ☺ 8am-8.30pm Sat-Thu & 9am-12.30pm Fri) flies to Bandar Abbas (IR245,000; 40 minutes, six times weekly); Tehran (one way IR567,000, 90 minutes, at least twice daily); Esfahan (IR417,000, one hour, daily) and Shiraz (IR253,000, 45 minutes, three weekly) and has occasional flights to Mashhad. It also flies six times daily to Dubai (one way US$80, 30 minutes), plus regular flights to Abu Dhabi and Sharjah.

Iran Air (☎ 442 2274; Sanaee Sq) has less-frequent flights to Shiraz, Esfahan and Tehran, and **Mahan Airlines** (www.mahan.aero) flies twice weekly to Kerman.

BOAT

Leaving Kish by boat is ridiculously bureaucratic. On this trip it took us 30 minutes to get questioned at passport control, get the paperwork allowing us to leave, have it photocopied three times in the restaurant, then go outside to the car park to buy a ticket on the speedboat to Bandar-e Charak. And we didn't even have any goods to declare.

Valfajre-8 shipping links Kish with Bandar-e Lengeh (one way IR120,000) – when Kish is busy enough to warrant it. As we have discovered, this means there are as many as six packed boats (with families in tents on deck) during No Ruz, but just a few weeks later no services at all. When they run, catamarans make the trip in about two hours, but the bigger Ro Ro ferries take about five hours. Catamarans usually leave about 10am, *insh'Allah* (if God wills it). Buy tickets at the port or a travel agency.

The alternative, often the only alternative, is the open speedboat to/from Bandar-e Charak (IR40,000, 45 minutes). For details of the Charak end, see p298. From Kish, they leave from sunrise until about 4pm, though most are in the mornings when conditions are usually better.

Getting Around

You will probably need to charter a taxi from the airport for about IR15,000.

Excellent air-con minibuses (IR1000) cruise the northern and eastern roads. (Buses are for seated passengers only, ie standing is not allowed.) From the boat terminal, you can crowd onto a local minibus or take a private taxi. Chartering a taxi costs about IR60,000 per hour.

BANDAR-E LENGEH   بندر لنگه

☎ 0762 / pop 23,000

Bandar-e Lengeh (or 'Lengeh') to the locals) is a lethargic place and most travellers stop only long enough to get the boat to Kish. It is typical of the mixed Arab and Persian communities of the southern Persian Gulf, with Sunnis and Shiites speaking Arabic, Farsi and often both. This diversity is reflected in the

BANDAR-E LENGEH

0 ━━━━━ 300 m
0 ━━━━━ 0.2 miles

INFORMATION	
Bank Saderat...........................1	A4
Money Exchange.......................2	A3
Morvarid Gasht Travel Agency.........3	A4
Valiasr International Telephone Centre...............................4	A4

SLEEPING 🛏	
Hotel Amir 🛏........................5	A4

EATING 🍴	
Amir Restaurant....................(see 5)	
Flowers Restaurant...................6	A4
Ice-Cream Shop......................7	A3
Minimarket..........................8	A4

TRANSPORT	
Boats to Kish Island.................9	A4
Iran Air...........................10	B4
Valfarje-8.........................11	B4

To Main Post Office (500m)

22 Bahman Sq

To Bus Terminal (1km); Bandar Abbas (254km)

Engelab St

Shahrivar St

Pharmacy

Shahrdari St

Engelab St

Bazaar

Shahrdari St

Imam Khomeini Blvd

Imam Khomeini St

To Bus Terminal (1.2km); Bandar Abbas (254km)

To Shahid Doktor Beheshti Hospital (1km); Savaris to Bandar-e Charak (1.5km); Bandar Lengeh Inn (1.8km); Airport (6km); Bandar-e Charak (89km); Bushehr (557km)

PERSIAN GULF

PERSIAN GULF

BANDARI BURQAS

In the Persian Gulf provinces, and particularly in Bandar-e Lengeh, Bandar Abbas and Minab, you will see Bandari women wearing the burqa. This inflexible mask differs depending on the region; in Lengeh it is usually a metal frame jutting from the face but hiding very little of the face itself – vaguely reminiscent of the structure of Darth Vader's mask. In Minab it is often bright red with multicoloured stitching along the border, covering all of the face that's not already hidden by the chador (except for two tiny slits for the eyes). Ethnologists do not believe these masks have any religious links, but were a fashion accessory introduced during the period of Portuguese rule.

Bandari women have traditionally worn tattoos on their faces and, sometimes, their hands, though these are becoming less common. They wear eye-catchingly colourful pants, often in red or green, which are worn tight around the ankle and usually have elaborate gold patterns stitched above the hem. Some Bandari women wear the shamat, a finely patterned, gauze-like chador that comes in pale colours; usually blue, orange, cream, beige and pink. It's draped Indian-style around the body and head. Others wear chadors that look more like those found in other Arab parts of the Gulf, with several fine cloths in black, one folded over to hang down from the head with another fastened above the ears, meaning their eyes can be uncovered or, with a flick of the cloth, the woman can disappear completely behind this black curtain.

If you think your mother-in-law might look good in a burqa, head for the market in Minab and ask around. The locals will think you're mad, but a burqa could make a, well, provocative gift.

hybrid architecture and clothing of the locals (for more information, see above).

The main streets are Imam Khomeini Blvd (the coastal road and esplanade) and Enqelab St, opposite the port. This is not a town where foreigners are expected; few signs are in English, but it would be hard to get lost.

Information

Pretty much everything shuts down between about 12.30pm and 5pm or 6pm. To change money, head to **Bank Saderat** (Shahrdari St) or the **Money Exchange** (☎ 224 4373; 17 Shahrivar St; ☽ 8am-1pm & 5-8pm Sat-Thu). Make phone calls from **Valiasr International Telephone Centre** (Enqelab St; ☽ 7.30am-1pm & 4-9pm).

Sights

During the day, especially in summer, there's little to do except observe the obligatory five- or six-hour siesta. By late afternoon it's a lovely place to wander when the setting sun turns the town a soft shade of yellow. Sights include several pale-stone **mosques**, with single minarets decorated in the Arab style, and a few old and largely derelict **Bandari buildings** made of mud brick with squat badgirs.

Sleeping & Eating

There's a total of two hotels in Lengeh. Lengeh's eating scene has improved since we first came here, but you'll still have the typical Iranian options – kabab, burger, pizza and, thankfully, fish. Enqelab St is home to the fast-food places, a well-stocked minimarket and an oh-so-welcome ice-cream shop.

Hotel Amir (☎ 224 2311; Enqelab St; r IR70,000; ☒) A short walk from the port, the Amir has simple but clean rooms and shared bathrooms; and some staff are helpful. Guests can use the kitchen.

Bandar Lengeh Inn (Mehmar Sara Jahangardi; ☎ 222 2566; d with breakfast US$35; ☒ ℗) Most of the plain but clean rooms have Gulf views though you'll need big biceps to get the windows open. It's 1.8km west of town down a lonely side road but the position, literally on the water's edge, justifies the trip.

Flowers Restaurant (☎ 224 0421; Imam Khomeini Blvd; meals IR25,000-40,000; ☽ 11am-4pm & 6-11pm Sat-Thu) Opposite the port, Flowers serves a reasonable selection of Iranian fare in a surprisingly inviting little restaurant; good value.

Amir Restaurant (☎ 224 1370; Enqelab St; meals IR40,000-60,000; ☽ 12-4pm & 6-11pm) Underneath the hotel of the same name, this no-frills restaurant and teahouse serves delicious Iranian fare. We can vouch for both the khoresht (stew; IR25,000) and chicken kabab (IR50,000). A cosy teahouse adjoins and it will store bags if you're waiting for a boat.

Getting There & Away

For air and boat tickets and local information in English, see **Morvarid Gasht Travel Agency** (☎ 224 0026; Enqelab St).

PERSIAN GULF

AIR

Looking at the size of the huge office of **Iran Air** (☎ 2222799; Imam Khomeini Blvd; ☼ 7.30am-1.30pm & 5.30-8.30pm Sat-Thu, 8am-noon Fri) you'd think you were in Tehran or Esfahan, but a total of four flights a week to Tehran (IR522,000, 2½ hours) via Shiraz (IR256,000, 30 minutes) puts paid to that idea.

BOAT

Catamaran and ferry services run to Kish (IR120,000, catamaran/Ro Ro ferries two/ five hours) in season, though departure times are elastic and services often cancelled due to lack of interest or rough seas. Tickets can be bought at the ticket office of **Valfajre-8** (☎ 222 0252; Imam Khomeini Blvd; ☼ 7am-2pm & 3-6pm Sat-Thu, 7.30am-1.30pm Fri, when boats are running).

Assuming the seas aren't too rough, it's quicker to take an open speedboat (IR40,000, 45 minutes) from Bandar-e Charak (89km west of Lengeh). To do this, take a savari (IR25,000, one hour) from Lengeh to Charak, where it will drop you at the beach from which the boats leave when full (10 passengers). Most people travel this route between about 6am and 10am.

If you want to get an early start on the trip to Kish (perhaps make a day-trip of it), head to Charak (see Bus & Savari, below) the night before and stay at the **Hotel Khorshid Jonub** (Southern Sun; ☎ 0764-422 2369; r IR85,000; ✖), a simple but clean family-run place about a 10-minute walk east of where the speedboats leave. Do check the sea conditions before heading to Charak, lest you get there and find the boats are not running.

Valfajre-8 also runs a passenger-only catamaran to Dubai (IR450,000 one way, three to four hours) most Saturdays and Wednesdays.

BUS & SAVARI

Lengeh's bus terminal, about 2km east of town on the right (south) just before a large square, is not our favourite place. In four visits over the years, we've been misled each time about when the bus would leave, how long it would take and where it would stop. Savaris are a better option. If you must use the bus, they leave regularly to Bandar Abbas (IR20,000, three to four hours, 255km) and much less often

to Bushehr (IR70,000, eight to 10 hours, 656km), usually at about 10am and 4.30pm. There are a couple of buses a day to Shiraz (IR33,000/70,000 *mahmooly*/Volvo).

Savaris (IR40,000, three hours) to Bandar Abbas leave regularly between 6am and 8pm from outside the bus terminal. Savaris to Charak leave from outside the NIOPC petrol station, about 1.5km east of the port.

Buses from Bushehr often arrive in the middle of the night. If you're staying in the Hotel Amir (p297) ask to be dropped at the port entrance (other locals will get out here), or near Bandar Lengeh Inn (p297) if you're staying there.

BANDAR ABBAS   بندر عباس
☎ 0761 / pop 365,000

For a city founded by one of Persia's greatest kings, Shah Abbas I, and named in his honour, the bustling 'Port of Abbas' is less charismatic than you might expect. Strategically positioned overlooking the Strait of Hormoz and the entrance to the Persian Gulf, the city, known to most Iranians simply as 'Bandar', is home to Iran's busiest port. Smuggling is big business – everything from cars to carpets circumnavigate the customs inspectors in these parts. Needless to say, if you're walking along the seafront at night and notice boxes being hurriedly unloaded from a dark-coloured speedboat, resist the temptation to offer to help with the haulage.

Bandar's fast-growing population is a mix of Persians, Bandaris, Arabs and Africans, with a large Sunni minority and a long-established Hindu community. Depending on your perspective, Bandar Abbas is either delightfully seedy with the audible whisper of smugglers, or an uninspiring and overpriced stepping-off point for the more languid nearby islands.

History

The rise, fall and rise again of Bandar Abbas over the last five centuries has been directly linked to the role of meddling European powers. Once a tiny fishing village called Gamerun, it was chosen as Persia's main southern port and naval dockyard after Shah Abbas I defeated the Portuguese on nearby Hormoz Island in 1622 (see The Portuguese on Hormoz, p307). The British East India Company was granted a trading concession,

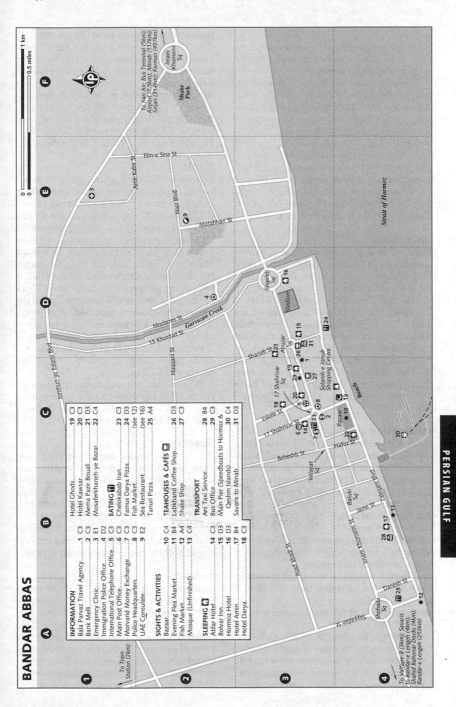

BANDAR ABBAS

INFORMATION
Bala Parvaz Travel Agency	1 C3
Bank Melli	2 C3
Emergency Clinic	3 E1
Immigration Police Office	4 D2
International Telephone Office	5 C3
Main Post Office	6 C3
Morvarid Money Exchange	7 C3
Police Headquarters	8 C3
UAE Consulate	9 E2

SIGHTS & ACTIVITIES
Bazaar	10 C4
Evening Flea Market	11 B4
Fish Market	12 A4
Mosque (Unfinished)	13 C4

SLEEPING
Atlar Hotel	14 C3
Bolvar Inn	15 D3
Hormoz Hotel	16 D3
Hotel Amin	17 B4
Hotel Darya	18 C3

Hotel Ghods	19 C3
Hotel Kawsar	20 C3
Merna Pazir Bouali	21 D3
Mosaferkhaneh-ye Bazar	22 C4

EATING
Chelokabab Iran	23 C3
Famus Darya Pizza	24 D3
Fish Market	(see 16)
Sea Restaurant	(see 16)
Tanuri Pizza	25 A4

TEAHOUSES & CAFÉS
Labkhand Coffee Shop	26 D3
Shake Shop	27 C3

TRANSPORT
Ani Taxi Service	28 B4
Bus Office	29 C3
Main Pier (Speedboats to Hormoz &Qeshm Islands)	30 C4
Savaris to Minab	31 D3

Strait of Hormoz

Shahr Park

To Iran Air; Bus Terminal (5km); Airport (7.5km); Minab (117km); Sirjan (314km); Kerman (497km)

To Train Station (2km)

To Valfajre-8 (3km); Savaris to Bandar-e Lengeh (4km); Shahid Bahonar Docks (4km); Bandar-e Lengeh (253km)

as were Dutch and French traders, and by the 18th century Bandar had become the chief Persian port and main outlet for the trade in Kermani carpets.

The port went into decline following the end of the Safavid dynasty and the withdrawal in 1759 of the British East India Company. The Sultan of Oman took control of Bandar in 1793 and held sway until 1868. Its role remained peripheral until the Iran–Iraq War, when Iran's established ports at Bushehr, Bandar-e Imam Khomeini and Khorramshahr were either captured or became too dangerous for regular shipping. With the help of road and railway links to Tehran and Central Asia, it hasn't looked back.

Orientation

Bandar Abbas is stretched along a narrow coastal strip. The main east–west thoroughfare changes its name from Beheshti Blvd (in the eastern suburbs) to Imam Khomeini St (through the centre of town), ending as Pasdaran Blvd (towards the docks to the west). The city is well signposted in English. Apart from the top-end options, most accommodation is on or just off Imam Khomeini St, between Velayat Sq and Abuzar Sq – all within an easy walk of the bazaar, the old quarter to the north and the boats to Hormoz and Qeshm. The airport is about 8km east of the bazaar.

Information

Imam Khomeini St has several internet cafés, and the arcade in the Setareh-e Jonub Shopping Centre, on the seafront Taleqani Blvd, has several more. The bazaar has a black market in UAE dirhams and other Gulf State currencies.

Bala Parvaz Travel Agency (☎ 222 4500; moridiprz@yahoo.com; Imam Khomeini St; ☾ 7am-8.30pm Sat-Thu, 8am-1pm Fri) Don't go anywhere else. Helpful, English-speaking staff – especially the delightful Ms Marjan Naemi – book air, train and ferry tickets.
Bank Melli (17 Shahrivar Sq) The only bank to change money officially, and only between 10am and 12.30pm. It's a nightmare at lunchtime.
Emergency Clinic (☎ 553 1001; cnr Jomhuri-ye Eslami Blvd & Amir Kabir St)
Immigration police office (☎ 218 2620; Modarres St) Visa extensions are possible, if not encouraged at this office. The officers here don't see too many tourists, and didn't exactly welcome us with open arms, so choosing another city is a good idea. See p393 for details on extending your visa.

International telephone office (☎ 224 8350; Mahan Alley; ☾ 7am-10pm winter, 8am-1pm & 4-10pm summer) Down an alley about 30m east of 17 Shahrivar Sq.
Main post office (Shahrivar St) About 50m north of 17 Shahrivar Sq.
Morvarid Money Exchange (☎ 222 7446; Imam Khomeini St; ☾ 7.30am-1pm & 4.30-8.30pm Sat-Thu) Much, much easier than changing money at Bank Melli. Good rates and no hassle. In an arcade just west of 17 Shahrivar Sq.
Police headquarters (☎ 222 7676; 17 Shahrivar Sq)

Sights

Bandar isn't blessed with a lot of must-see sights – actually, none – but it's not totally devoid of flavour. The lively **bazaar** (Taleqani Blvd) rambles its way across two blocks just back from the seafront, and is probably the most colourful part of town. A seafront promenade leads east and has an **evening flea market**. At its end, the busy **fish market** (p302) is full of charismatic old salts happy to pose for pictures with their catch. Work on the huge **mosque** a few metres east of the bazaar seems to have restarted despite local concerns that the engineering is not good enough for a major earthquake zone. If it is ever finished it will have one of the tallest *iwan*s (rectangular hall opening onto a courtyard) in Iran.

If you fancy just wandering about, walk north from downtown to the older part of town, which has more of a Bandari feel with its old buildings and narrow lanes.

Sleeping

Accommodation in Bandar isn't the best value in Iran, and for the third trip in a row we found bargaining here about as effective as looking for a stiff drink in a mosque. Most accommodation is centrally located, an easy walk from 17 Shahrivar Sq. In summer air-con is a very good idea – without it you run the risk of melting, to be discovered the next day as nothing more than a grease spot.

BUDGET

Mosaferkhaneh-ye Bazar (☎ 222 2303; cnr Taleqani Blvd & Hafez St; dm/s/tw/tr IR25,000/51,000/69,300/82,100) If you're on a budget, this busy, clean but ultra-simple place above the bazaar is the cheapest in town. In summer, beds on the covered rooftop (just IR15,000) afford wonderful views of the smugglers and sunset over the Persian Gulf. It's social, male-dominated and unashamedly downmarket, with shared bathrooms. Relaxed security and lots of glass walls mean it's not great for women.

Mema Pazir Bouali (☎ 222 2516; Shariati St, near Abuzar Sq; tw/tr IR70,000/80,000) The faded-yellow awning and anonymous staircase don't promise much, and the noisy, no-frills rooms and shared bathrooms don't deliver much. But the welcoming mother and daughter, who will practise their English with you – and the price – make it worth a look.

Bolvar Inn (☎ 222 2625; Abuzar St; r IR105,000; 🖭) We liked the atmosphere in this unpretentious, family-run place set around a courtyard filled with the din of air-conditioners. Rooms and toilets are clean, but there's only one shower.

The next two places are tricky to find. It's best to get a taxi to 17 Shahrivar Sq, then walk east about 40m from the square, turn left down an alley beside a multi-storey building (look for the wooden beams protruding from the wall), past the international telephone office and turn right. The Kawsar is there, and the Darya another 150m down the street opposite Kawsar.

Hotel Kawsar (☎ 224 2389; Eskele St; s/tw IR150,000/200,000; 🖭) The big, clean rooms and shared bathrooms (all rooms) are aging, but acceptable. Staff don't speak English.

Hotel Darya (☎ /fax 224 1942-49; Eskele St; s/tw/apt IR160,000/220,000/600,000; 🖭) Recently refurbished, the Hotel Darya is probably the pick of the half-decent budget places. Rooms here are clean and pleasant enough, with good beds, fridge and Iranian TV, but if you're in a single you'll have to share a bathroom. The seven flights of stairs can get tedious.

To check out these and a couple of other budget options not listed here, you should start at Abuzar Sq (Meydan-e Abuzar) and walk.

MIDRANGE

Hotel Amin (☎ /fax 224 4305; Taleqani Blvd; s/tw/tr with breakfast IR280,000/350,000/500,000; 🖭 🖳) On the seafront west of the bazaar, the glass-fronted Amin is a good-value midrange hotel that has been praised by readers. The refurbished rooms are small but well-equipped (with overhead fans!), and the management has some concept of service.

Hotel Ghods (☎ /fax 222 2344; Imam Khomeini St, cnr Haleh Alley; s/d IR450,000/500,000; 🖭 🖳) The

Ghods has the size and fittings you'd expect in a midrange hotel, but little of the personal charm you might like. Rooms are big and you can choose to squat or sit in the bathroom. The upper floors have city views, but the restaurant is overpriced.

Atilar Hotel (☎ 222 7420-25; 17 Shahrivar St; s/d/tr US$45/65/80 with breakfast; 🖭) Dominating the centre of town, this brand new multi-storey hotel has modern-looking, big and fairly stylish rooms; upper levels have views across town or to the Gulf. Staff speak English. Atilar is a good choice.

TOP END

Hormoz Hotel (☎ 334 2201-5; www.hormoz-hotel.com; Enqelab Sq; s/d/ste US$88/123/193; 🅿 🖭 🖳 🖳) Clearly the pick of Bandar's lodgings, the enormous Hormoz is an international standard hotel with the look, facilities and most of the service that entails. Rooms are luxurious and most have a balcony – with either views or glimpses of the Gulf. There are four restaurants (for details of one option, see Sea Restaurant, p302) and cafés, and an indoor pool.

Eating

Bandar is not noted as one of Iran's culinary capitals, though the seafood is reasonably good. The local speciality is *chelo meigu* (battered prawns or shrimps with boiled rice), and the deep-fried theme extends to fish, too.

Fast food and *kababis* (kabab shops) can be found around Abuzar Sq on Imam Khomeini St and along the waterfront. Alternatively, go west to Sayyadan St for a fast-food extravaganza. This strip of more than a dozen pizza and burger joints is popular with students so is a good place to meet English speakers.

Famus Darya Pizza (Taleqani Blvd; pizzas IR20,000; ⏰ 11am-10pm) Famus serves pizzas and burgers that you eat on the sea wall; it's the one that looks like a giant concrete fire hydrant wearing a hat.

Tanuri Pizza (☎ 224 1988; Sayyadan St; pizzas IR20,000; ⏰ 9am-2pm & 5pm-midnight) This pizza place is one of many along this strip that are reliably good.

Chelokabab Iran (☎ 222 3833; Imam Khomeini St, off 17 Shahrivar Sq; meals IR50,000; ⏰ 11.30am-3.30pm & 7-10.30pm; 🖭) Conveniently located, this unadorned little place serves standard Iranian fare, plus a decent *chelo mahi* (fried fish on rice). Toothless owner Haji Hossain is a nice guy, speaks English and will probably try to tell you about his son the microscopic robot maker – or something.

Sea Restaurant (☎ 334 2205; Hormoz Hotel, Enqelab Sq; meals IR60,000-100,000; ☽ 5.30-11pm) This is the Hormoz Hotel's most interesting restaurant, with a menu loaded with seafood. The patio location is ideal in the cool of evening.

Fish market (cnr Taleqani Blvd & Sayyadan St; ☽ 6.30am-10pm) Self-caterers should head for this fish market for fresh Gulf fish, filleted if you ask. Even if you don't plan to cook, this is a fun place to wander round with a camera.

Come to the waterfront at sunset for *chay*, qalyan (water pipe) and conversation with the locals.

Labkhand Coffee Shop (Imam Khomeini St, off Abuzar Sq; ☽ 5-11pm; ✷) On the night we visited the stylish, second-floor Labkhand was going off like the proverbial frog in a sock. Good fun. It also serves some of the best coffee we drank in Iran.

For the best banana shake (IR4500) on the coast head for the unnamed **shake shop** (Imam Khomeini St), opposite and slightly west of Hotel Ghods.

Getting There & Away
AIR
Iran Air (☎ 333 7170; Beheshti St; www.iranair.com) is inconveniently located east of the centre; use Bala Parvaz Travel Agency (p300) instead. **Iran Aseman** (www.iaa.ir) and **Mahan Airlines** (www.mahan.aero) service international routes.

Domestic Flights
Bandar is, mercifully, fairly well connected by domestic air services. Several smaller airlines fly to Tehran for the same price – ask at the agency.

Destination	Fare (one way)	Flights
Esfahan	IR454,000	3 weekly
Mashhad	IR588,000	2 weekly
Shiraz	IR289,000	daily
Tehran	IR603,000	20 weekly

International Flights
For the short hop to Dubai, you can choose from Iran Aseman (one way IR620,000, 30 minutes, daily) or Iran Air (IR620,000, twice weekly). Mahan Airlines flies to Colombo in Sri Lanka twice weekly, and to Delhi once weekly.

BOAT
Domestic Services
Boats from Bandar to the nearby islands of Hormoz and Qeshm leave from the *eskele* (main pier), near the bazaar.

For Qeshm (for more details see also opposite), you can make the 23km trip in an open fibre-glass speedboat (one way, IR14,000, 40 minutes) or a slightly larger, covered speedboat with padded seats (IR20,000, 25 minutes). If the seas are too rough for small boats try the ferry (IR25,000, 50 minutes, daily), which leaves from the chaotic Shahid Bahonar docks, 5km west of the town centre. You can buy tickets from travel agencies or from the office of **Valfajre-8** (☎ 555 5590; Eskeleh Shahid Bahonar Blvd, near Jahangardi Crossroads), about 1km east of the docks.

Speedboats to Hormoz Island (one way, IR10,000, 30 minutes) leave every 15 to 20 minutes in the morning, and less often as the day wears on. See also p308.

International Services
Valfajre-8 runs boats from Bandar Abbas to Sharjah (one way IR320,000, eight to 11 hours, 233km), usually on Saturdays and Mondays though schedules are notoriously changeable.

BUS
Buses leave Bandar for almost every city in Iran. However, heavy truck traffic, poor facilities along the roads and punishing temperatures can make it an arduous journey. The bus terminal east of town is chock-full of locals who wish they could afford to fly. To join them you'll need to take two shared taxis; one to the corner of Ghadiri Blvd and another to the terminal itself. A taxi *dar baste* costs about IR12,000. There's a handy **bus office** (☎ 223 2917; Imam Khomeini Blvd) in town.

Many routes no longer have *mahmooly* services. The following fares are for Volvo buses except where two fares are listed (which refer to *mahmooly*/Volvo services). Departure times and durations are somewhat approximate.

Destination	Fare	Duration	Departures
Bam	IR30,000/ 40,000	6-8hr	2pm, 4pm, 6pm
Bandar-e Lengeh	IR15,000/ 25,000	3-4hr	hourly 6am-7pm
Bushehr	IR80,000	8-12hr	early morning, 3.30pm, 4pm, 5.30pm
Esfahan	IR45,000/ 75,000	14-16hr	frequent
Kerman	IR45,000	7hr	3pm, 4pm, 5pm, 7pm, 8.30pm, 10pm
Shiraz	IR28,000/ 55,000	8-11hr	frequent
Sirjan	IR30,000	3-4½hr	6 daily
Tehran	IR120,000	14-17hr	frequent
Yazd	IR34,500/ 46,000	11hr	6 daily
Zahedan	IR60,000	17hr	9.30am, 10am, 4pm, 6pm

SAVARI

There are occasional buses to Minab, but most people travel by savari (IR18,000, 75 minutes, 97km). The savaris leave from just south of Abuzar Sq throughout the day. Savaris for Bandar-e Lengeh (Peugeot IR40,000, 2½ hours) leave from the northeastern corner of the huge roundabout outside the Shahid Bahonar docks, about 5km west of the centre.

TRAIN

From Bandar trains run to Tehran, Esfahan and Mashhad, via points in between. The daily 1st-class train to Tehran (IR90,000 for a berth in a six-bed couchette) departs at 2.15pm and, *insh'Allah*, arrives at 9am. It stops at Sirjan (IR29,600, five hours) and Yazd (IR53,000, nine hours), though the arrival time (around 11.15pm) isn't that convenient.

The Ghazal trains offer meals and more luxurious four-berth couchettes. They run to Tehran (IR230,000, 19 hours, 3pm) and Mashhad (IR230,000, 22 hours, 3.30pm), both three times weekly.

An entirely different train goes to Esfahan (IR41,700/66,100 1st/2nd class, Tuesday, Thursday and Sunday), departing at 5pm and arriving at a rather unusually civilised 8.30am.

The train station is 8km northwest of the centre and you'll probably need to charter a taxi (IR15,000). Buy tickets in Bala Parvaz Travel Agency (p300).

Getting Around

It's easy enough to get around Bandar on foot, though shuttle taxis make good sense in summer.

TO/FROM THE AIRPORT

It is easy enough to charter a taxi to or from the airport for about IR15,000. A shared taxi (which is harder to find to the airport) will cost about IR3000.

TAXI

Shuttle taxis are easy to find and cost about IR1000 to IR2000 depending on the distance. To places like the bus terminal, train station and airport, it's far easier to charter one, especially in summer.

The professional **Ani Taxi Service** (☎ 555 5539; Taleqani Blvd; ☽ 7am-9.30pm) has air-con Peugeots for which it charges IR30,000 per hour (including driver) within Bandar Abbas. For a half-day beyond the city limits (eg Minab), expect to pay about IR230,000.

QESHM ISLAND جزیره قشم

☎ 0763 / pop 95,000

The largest island in the Persian Gulf at 1335 sq km, Qeshm boasts attractive beaches bounding an arid, sun-scorched interior of starkly beautiful hills and mountains. The coast is dotted with Bandari villages but the interior is largely deserted.

Qeshm is a duty-free zone – a sort of poor person's Kish – but in a Gulf increasingly full of gleaming skyscrapers it remains refreshingly attached to the traditional Bandari ways. Sure, Qeshm Town is developing pretty quickly. But elsewhere you can still visit boat-building yards turning out *lenges,* the large wooden cargo boats that have criss-crossed the Gulf for centuries. Fishing villages don't come much more traditional than Laft, with its supremely photogenic forest of *badgirs*. The west of the island has been declared Qeshm Geopark in recognition of the quite stunning geology, which includes the world's longest known salt cave.

Qeshm seems destined to grow quickly as a tourist destination, but for now it feels untouched enough to reward the intrepid. And we do mean intrepid. Outside Qeshm Town there are few facilities and much of the southern coast is a naval military zone, evidenced by the hundreds of concrete bunkers being built when we took the road. Going anywhere for longer than a day carries an element of uncertainty – there are no formal lodgings – but that adds to the fun. Just don't be tempted to camp in a military zone.

GETTING THERE & AWAY
Qeshm is accessible by air, speedboat and car ferry.

Air
Qeshm International Airport is about 43km southwest of Qeshm Town. Iran Air has daily flights to Tehran (one way IR633,000, 80 minutes) and flies twice-a-week to Shiraz (IR315,000). **Iran Aseman** (www.iaa.ir) flies daily to Dubai (35 minutes). A taxi from the airport will cost about 70,000, depending on your negotiating skills.

Boat
Regular speedboats (open/closed IR14,000/ 20,000, 40/25 minutes) run between Qeshm's Sangi Pier and Bandar Abbas. There is also usually one ferry everyday to/from Bahman Port (one way, IR25,000, one hour), at the south end of Qeshm Town.

With a vehicle, Qeshm is a good place to lose a couple of days wandering around the quiet roads. A car ferry crosses from Bandar-e Pol to Laft-e Kohneh, near Laft. Departures depend on demand.

GETTING AROUND
Shared taxis, minibuses and occasional *pik-ups* (utilities) take passengers along the north

and south coastal roads. Chartering a taxi for about IR40,000 an hour or IR160,000 a day is recommended if you want to go anywhere beyond Laft, or if you plan a late return to Qeshm Town. Hitching is also possible.

Qeshm Town   شهر قشم

Qeshm Town is the island's largest town and, apart from a single resort, is the only place with accommodation. The town has a long history but not that much to show for it. The main north-south road begins at Pasdaran Sq, near the Eskele Sangi (Sangi Pier) from where speedboats to/from Bandar operate. It's called Montazeri Ave but this road becomes Valiasr Ave and finally Imam Golikhan Blvd as it heads south.

INFORMATION
Bank Melli (Pasdaran Sq; ✆ 9am-1.30pm for exchange) Change money upstairs.
Coffeenet (☎ 524 0575; Felestin St; internet per hr IR10,000; ✆ 10.30am-9pm) Under the Pardis Mall.
Dr S Ahang Pharmacy (☎ 522 8055; Montazeri Ave; ✆ 24hr) Outside Fatima Al Zahra General Hospital.
International Phone Office (Montazeri Ave; ✆ 8am-2pm & 4-10pm Sat-Thu, 4-10pm Fri) Charges IR2000 a minute to most countries.
Jazireh Money Exchange (Valiasr Blvd; ✆ 8am-1pm & 6-8pm Sat-Thu) Under Pardis Mall.
Post Office (Valiasr Ave)

SIGHTS & ACTIVITIES
The crumbling **Ghal'e-ye Portoghaliha** (Portuguese Castle; admission free) is Qeshm Town's

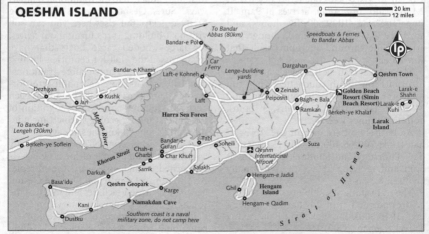

QESHM ISLAND

0 _____ 20 km
0 _____ 12 miles

To Bandar Abbas (80km)
Bandar-e Pol
Speedboats & Ferries to Bandar Abbas
Bandar-e Khamir
1 Car Ferry
Laft-e Kohneh
Lenge-building yards
Dargahan
Qeshm Town
Dezhgan
Kushk
Laft
Zeinabi
Peiposht
Bagh-e Bala
Golden Beach Resort (Simin Beach Resort)
Larak-e Shahri
Larak-e Kuhi
Jan
Harra Sea Forest
Ramkan
Berkeh-ye Khalaf
Larak Island
To Bandar-e Lengeh (30km)
Mehran River
Berkeh-ye Sofian
Khoran Strait
Chah-e Gharbi
Bandar-e Gutan
Char Khun
Tabl
Soheili
Suza
Darkuh
Sarrik
Salakh
Qeshm International Airport
Strait of Hormoz
Basa'idu
Qeshm Geopark
Karge
Ghil
Hengam-e Jadid
Kani
Namakdan Cave
Hengam Island
Dustku
Southern coast is a naval military zone, do not camp here
Hengam-e Qadim

PERSIAN GULF

best-known sight, but once you've photographed the palm tree through a curved hole in the ramparts (like everyone else) it won't detain you for long. We preferred the **Qeshm Geopark Museum** (☎ 522 5930; Valiasr Blvd; admission free; ⊙ 9am-noon & 5-8pm Sat-Thu), with its mix of cultural, natural and geological exhibits. Turtles, Siamese twin goats and a pygmy white-toothed shrew ('the smallest mammal on earth'?!?!) are among the exhibits.

The extensive **Bazar-e Bozorg** (off Pasdaran Sq) and the newer but uninspiring duty-free malls along this strip are the main attractions for Iranian visitors.

Diving

The diving off Qeshm is reportedly far better than that off Kish. Impressive coral reefs in less than 10m can be dived off nearby Larak and Hengam Islands, and the wrecks of three ships sunk during the Iran–Iraq War, at depths of 27m to 43m. Water is flattest during April and May. Diving can be arranged through two operators that run beginners courses and charter dives.

Dolphin Diving School (☎ 021-7763 2085, 0912 193 4194) is a Tehran-based company run by English-speaking Siamak Derakhshan. Boat and shore diving is available. Dives with/without certificate cost from IR250,000/350,000, including equipment and depending on how far the boat needs to go. Contact the school several days in advance.

Alternatively, the Golden Beach Resort (right) has a dive shop that also runs diving courses.

SLEEPING

All but one of the island's sleeping options is in Qeshm Town. The cheapest places are concentrated on Imam Khomeini Ave a short walk from the Eskele Sangi.

Khalija Fars Hotel (☎ 522 3027; cnr Imam Khomeini Ave & Imam Khomeini Sq; r IR100,000; 🌐) One of a couple of cheapies nearby, this is nothing to write home about but the friendly management make up for basic rooms with hard beds. Bathrooms are shared.

Golestan Apartment Hotel (☎ 522 1707; Imam Khomeini Ave; s/tw IR150,000/200,000; 🌐) There are only eight rooms that are relatively attractive (ie, they have attached bathrooms), are reasonably priced and thus often full. Book ahead.

Two midrange options are on a hill overlooking the town about 1km walk from Pasdaran Sq; head west along Imam Khomeini Ave to Jahed Sq, take Sayadan Blvd up the hill and follow Azadegan Blvd about 300m to the right.

Diplomat Hotel (☎ 522 5557; diplomat.hotel@yahoo .com; Azadegan Blvd; s/tw/tr with breakfast IR150,000/ 200,000/250,000; P 🌐 🖳) Diplomat has clean, attractive rooms, some of which are big and have views over the town and the sea. Staff are helpful and some speak English. Good value.

Park Hotel (Qeshm Hotel; ☎ 522 4689; Azadegan Blvd; s/tw/tr IR150,000/250,000/300,000; P 🌐 🖳) Only if the Diplomat Hotel is full.

our pick **Darya Hotel** (☎ 522 8362; Eskele St; r US$35-75; ste US$90-100; P 🌐) Just east of the Eskele Sangi, the Darya is Qeshm's best option for value, location, comfort and service. Rooms are spacious and come with kitchenettes; front rooms (US$40) have water views.

Golden Beach Resort (Simin Beach Resort; ☎ 534 2900; goldenbeach_hotel@yahoo.com; d/tr/q/ste with breakfast US$35/45/60/70; P 🌐) A few kilometres southwest of town and alone on a sandy beach, for now this is the only (vaguely) resort-style place on Qeshm. The bungalows feel like beachside accommodation – which is good – but service isn't fantastic. A dive shop offers equipment and courses and there's a restaurant.

Qeshm International Hotel (☎ 255 4905; 22 Bahman Blvd; d/tr/ste with breakfast US$45/60/100; P 🌐 🖳) This is supposed to be the best hotel on Qeshm, and for facilities it is. But while the rooms are nice enough they're uninspired and the location at the southern end of town isn't great.

EATING

The midrange hotels all have restaurants. There are also restaurants in the shopping centres along Valiasr Blvd.

Seafood Restaurant (☎ 522 4765; meals IR30,000-45,000; ⊙ 6pm-midnight) On the waterfront opposite the Ghal'e-ye Portoghaliha, this simple indoor/outdoor restaurant serves Arabic seafood (no kabab!) in the cool of evening. There is no printed menu, but English-speaking owner Abdul will have shark, crab and/or shellfish dishes.

Island Nights (☎ 524 0458; cnr Valiasr Blvd & Felestin St; meals IR50,000-60,000; ⊙ 11am-4pm & 6-11pm) On the top floor of Pardis Mall, this

Turkish-run place serves the usual range of kabab plus well-prepared fish and prawn dishes. Seating is both indoor and outdoor and the atmosphere fairly upbeat. Access is via the outside lift.

Around Qeshm Island
LAFT & HARRA SEA FOREST

جنگلهای دریای حرا و لافت

The fishing village of **Laft**, 52km west of Qeshm Town, is the best place in Iran to see the fast-disappearing traditional cultures of the Persian Gulf. Perched on a rocky slope overlooking the Khoran Strait, Laft's roofscape is a breathtaking and wonderfully photogenic forest of *badgirs* and minarets. Views are best from the hill near the Portuguese-built Naderi Fort. From here you'll also see dozens of ancient wells and a white-domed cistern, on which the town relied for water. It's a small town that's best seen on foot; there's no formal accommodation.

A few hundred metres north of Laft is one of Qeshm's many **lenge-building yards**. These traditional cargo boats are still used to carry goods back and forth across the Gulf. Other yards are found along the north coast, most notably around Peiposht, Zeinabi and Bandar-e Guran.

From Laft you can see the **Harra Sea Forest**, at 9000 hectares the Persian Gulf's largest mangrove forest. From the town of **Tabl**, south of Laft, it's possible to venture into the forest by rented motorboat or canoe. During spring more than 200 species of migrating birds can be found here.

QESHM GEOPARK   پارک زمین شناسی قشم

In 2006 most of the western half of Qeshm Island, including the Harra mangroves, was declared Iran's first Unesco Geopark (according to Unesco, a Geopark is an area of unique geoscientific significance). Whether you're driving through this area or looking at it on a Google Earth image, the geological significance is easy to see. Nature has carved steep-sided stone canyons, eroded flat-topped hills into sandy dunes and dramatic organ-pipe ridgelines, and dug deep into the island to form caves including **Namakdan Cave** (Khare Namaki), which at 6km is the longest known salt-cave system on earth.

There are plans to develop tourism facilities but for now there is little infrastructure.

Unless you have plenty of time to wait for infrequent transport, you'll need to hire a taxi to take you as these places are hard to find and reach on your own; ask your hotel to find a driver who knows the sights. It's worth doing a full loop (which takes a whole day), perhaps taking in Laft and the *lenge* building-yards on the way. Of particular note is **Char Khuh**, where you can climb up into the narrow canyon to a well that has been used by shepherds for centuries. Further west a dirt road leads south and then heads back along the southern coast. Namakdan Cave is off this road, but is almost impossible to find, so make sure the driver knows the way. Though virtually deserted, this stretch of coast is a naval military zone; you can come here, but be careful with your camera. The beach is also where green turtles lay their eggs.

HORMOZ ISLAND   جزیره هرمز
pop approx 7000

A 30-minute boat ride from Bandar Abbas, delightfully sleepy Hormoz is a world away from the bustle of the regional capital. When your speedboat rounds the sea wall and the captain kills the motor you'll be engulfed by something almost completely unheard of in Bandar – silence.

The only settlement is tiny Hormoz Village, where a richly evocative Portuguese castle slowly erodes at its northern edge and the rest of the largely impoverished village nestles among palm trees, pale-stone mosques and dusty laneways rarely disturbed by traffic. The rest of the 42-sq-km island is virtually uninhabited. The rugged interior is a barren land of forbidding peaks seared by centuries of fierce Persian Gulf sun; not at all inviting.

Hormoz is a fun half-day trip for its mix of history and Bandari village atmosphere; a trip best begun early in the morning to avoid the enervating heat.

History

Until the 14th century this was Jarun Island, while Hormoz was the name of a long-established commercial town on the mainland, probably on the Minab River. That changed when repeated bloody Mongol raids prompted the 15th Amir of Hormoz to seek a home where his head had a better chance of remaining on his shoulders. With many of his subjects in toe the Amir moved first to Kish Island before settling on Jarun Island.

Standing sentinel over the narrow entrance to the Persian Gulf, this new Hormoz soon became a grand emporium attracting immigrants from the mainland and traders from as far away as India and Africa. Visitors to Hormoz described it as heavily fortified, bustling and opulent. European traders arrived and before long the Portuguese took over (below).

The Portuguese were eventually kicked out in the early 17th century and Shah Abbas I relocated the trading hub to the mainland fishing village of Gamerun, which he promptly named after himself. Without commerce the power of Hormoz was shattered and it began a long descent into ruin.

Sights

PORTUGUESE CASTLE   قلعه پرتغالیها

Some 750m to the north of the harbour is the famous **Portuguese castle** (*ghal'e-ye Portoghaliha*), probably the most impressive and ambitious colonial fortress built in Iran (also see the boxed text, below). Centuries of neglect have seen much of the original structure crumble into the sea, but the thick, muscular-looking walls and rusting cannons give it a haunting beauty.

From the port, walk along the waterfront until you reach the castle walls then follow them anticlockwise as far as you can go. You'll come to a pair of rusting cannons and the low arched entrance right on the tip of the cape.

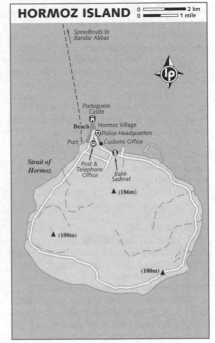

HORMOZ ISLAND

Speedboats to Bandar Abbas

Portuguese Castle

Beach   Hormoz Village

Police Headquarters

Port   Customs Office

Strait of Hormoz

Post & Telephone Office

Bank Saderat

▲ (186m)

▲ (100m)

(100m) ▲

The archway opens onto a wide courtyard facing the sea. On the right as you enter is the ancient armoury. In the middle of the courtyard is a subterranean church that has some splendid vaulted ceilings. Before following the path marked by stones up onto the

---

THE PORTUGUESE ON HORMOZ

In 1507, talented Portuguese admiral and empire builder Afonso de Albuquerque (also known as Afonso the Great) besieged and conquered Hormoz as part of his plan to expand Portuguese power into Asia. The castle of Hormoz (see above), which he started the same year, was completed in 1515.

With Hormoz Island as their fortified base, the Portuguese quickly became the major power on the waters of the Persian Gulf. Virtually all trade with India, the Far East, Muscat (Oman) and the Gulf ports was funnelled through Hormoz, to which the Portuguese, under an administration known for its justice and religious tolerance, brought great prosperity for over a century.

But Portugal's stranglehold over vital international trading routes could hardly fail to arouse the resentment of Persia and the other rising imperial powers. In 1550 Ottoman forces besieged the fortress of Hormoz for a month but failed to take the island. In the early 1600s Shah Abbas I granted the British East India Company trading rights with Persia through the mainland port of Jask, thus breaking the Portuguese monopoly. In 1622 Abbas, who had no naval power with which to challenge the Portuguese, cunningly detained the company's silk purchase until the English agreed to send a force to help liberate Hormoz. The Portuguese put up a brave defence, but ultimately were forced off the island.

ramparts, you can visit the ground-floor room of the watchtower if the door is open. Higher up is another door to the submerged 'water supply', a surprisingly deep and impressive cistern circled by an elevated interior walkway. The crumbling upper levels of the castle offer fine views back over the village to the starkly beautiful mountains, all surrounded by the blue Gulf waters; it's the perfect place to sit, soak up the silence and let your mind wander back a few hundred years.

Officially there is a IR2000 entrance fee, but in three trips we've yet to find anyone to take our money. Entrance fee or not, it's worth finding the old caretaker to let you into the locked doors of the tower and water supply – a tip is appreciated.

HORMOZ VILLAGE   روستای هرمز
This pleasant little **village** is interesting, though there's nothing much to do except ramble through the maze of *kuches* (lanes). In the northern-most corner is the small Sunni **Jameh-ye Imam Shafe'i Mosque**.

There is nowhere to stay or eat on Hormoz Island, though we met two travellers who camped on the beach with some young Tehranis on holiday. Small grocery stores on the road between the castle and port sell bottled water, soft drinks, biscuits and ice creams.

Getting There & Around
The only way to get to Hormoz is by speedboat (one way, IR10,000, about 30 minutes) from the main jetty in Bandar Abbas (p302). Except during winter, Hormoz is witheringly hot and there isn't much shade, so start as early as possible. Boats leave when full – every 15 or so minutes in the morning and less often later. The last boats usually return to Bandar about 4pm, but check this at the port.

Hardy souls who want to get into the island's interior can try talking a local into taking them by motorcycle or, more creatively, chartering a boat to circumnavigate the island. If you choose to do the latter, be wary of tides, leave a trip plan with the police and take enough food and water for a full day, plus a bit extra in case of emergency.

MINAB   میناب
☎ 0765 / pop 81,000
Wedged between a line of rocky desert hills and luxuriant date-palm plantations, Minab was once the biggest town in the re-

gion. Today it has a *mañana* feel except on Thursday, when the famous **Thursday market** (see opposite) draws merchants and shoppers from far and wide. Bandari, Arabic and Indian influences are common, with both the burqa and colourful *shamat* (a finely patterned, gauze-like chador) particularly popular (see Bandari Burqas, p297). One reader described the women of Minab as: 'A truly intoxicating sight after the oppressive uniformity of black "tents" elsewhere.'

Minab is easy enough to navigate. The old town starts at Esteghlal Sq at the south end of the bridge, and stretches away with Imam Khomeini St as the main drag. The bazaar is the most lively part of town, and is mainly to the west of Imam Khomeini St, between Esteghlal Sq and Shohada Sq.

Banks in Minab don't change money, so bring as much as you'll need. **Kara Coffeenet** (Jahangir Amine St; internet per hr IR9000; 🕑 9am-2pm & 5-9pm) is in an arcade about 150m west of Shohada Sq.

The approach to Minab from Bandar Abbas is quite dramatic. As you enter town you'll see the crumbling but picturesque **Hazareh Castle** competing for space on a hill with hundreds of mud-brick houses. It is believed that Minab was built by two sisters, Bibi Minoo and Bibi Nazanin, and the castle is known locally as Bibi Minoo – Bibi Nazanin's castle long ago returned to dust. Traditional custom has couples from the town walk once around this fortress, in the company of their families, before taking their marriage vows.

Sleeping & Eating
Sadaf Hotel (☎ 222 5999; s/d IR115,000/177,000; 🟩) The Sadaf has large, clean rooms that are both comfortable and fair value; with squat toilets and bathrooms. The restaurant serves tasty food, though it's probably not quite good enough to warrant the prices. Sadaf is well signposted on the left about 500m before the main bridge into Minab arriving from Bandar.

Minab Inn (☎ 222 5863; fax 222 5322; Imam Khomeini St; r IR300,000; 🅿 🟩) The location, about 2.5km past the main bridge as you come from Bandar, is a bit away from things, but the adjacent garden is pleasant and the rooms reasonable, though not much better than the Sadaf Hotel.

The restaurant is reliable if not exactly groundbreaking.

THE THURSDAY MARKET OF MINAB   پنج شنبه بازار میناب

Minab's **Thursday market** (panjshambe bazar) is one of the most colourful and well-known in the country; it's well worth timing your visit to include a Thursday. The main market is held on a patch of open ground along the banks of the seasonal Minab River 500m west (downstream) of the main bridge. Buyers and sellers come from surrounding villages, Bandar Abbas and sometimes further. You'll see many women wearing the burqa (p297), as well as bright headscarves and pants.

The panjshambe bazar is actually three separate markets. In the main one you'll find a motley array of makeshift stalls selling everything from fresh fruit, fish, vegetables and clothing to the distinctive zaribafi – a range of items made from local palm leaves including mats, fans, brooms and baskets – and the brocaded strips of cloth used by local women to adorn their clothing. Nearby is a livestock market, which is especially interesting early in the morning when the serious bargaining is done; and a small market for indigenous arts and crafts that is tucked away in the permanent bazaar.

Whether you're there to buy or not, arrive as early as possible to avoid the heat and soak up the atmosphere – a cross between the colour and vibrancy of an African market and the more discreet smiles of an Iranian bazaar.

Minab's range of cuisines is limited, with pizza, sandwich and kabab accounting for something close to all the options. Shohada Sq has several eateries, plus a couple of good ice-cream shops.

Getting There & Away

Savaris to/from Bandar Abbas (IR18,000, 75 minutes, 97km) operate regularly from Esteghlal Sq, at the bazaar-end of the bridge into town, until after dark. If you're heading to Jiroft, first take a savari to Rudan (IR10,000, one hour, 70km).

Big buses leave Minab for Bandar Abbas, Shiraz, Yazd and anywhere else en route. They fill up fast so try to book in advance at the **bus office** (☺ 10am-4pm), opposite and about 200m north of Sadaf Hotel. Even with a ticket, arrive early because services are oversold and competition for seats and luggage space is fierce. Bandar Abbas has more services.

If you're heading to Sirjan, Kerman or Yazd, you could take a bus or savari to the big roundabout with the replica lenge as its centrepiece about 10km east of Bandar and connect with a passing bus.

PERSIAN GULF

Southeastern Iran
ايران جنوب شرقى

This is frontier territory. And like the best frontiers it combines harsh landscapes, periodic banditry and warm welcomes to form a unique and exotic travelling experience. There are real dangers, so it's important to read the boxed text (p325) before heading this way. The region stretches east across ancient Kerman province, through high deserts scarred by brown snowcapped mountain ranges and coloured by occasional oasis towns and seasonal lakes. Kerman is the main city and is, in effect, the cultural border separating the Persians of the central plateau and the more eastern-oriented Baluchis, whose dress and customs feel more Pakistani than Iranian. Following ancient caravan routes southeast across the edge of the forbidding Dasht-e Lut, most travellers will stop in historic Bam and then Zahedan, the capital of Sistan va Baluchestan province (where smugglers criss-cross the deserts and the rule of law is tenuous).

For travellers, the region hasn't been quite so attractive since the Bam earthquake in 2003 flattened the city and wrought havoc upon the monumental adobe Arg-e Bam. Rebuilding work on the Arg is ongoing, and Bam's soothing date groves and strong tradition of hospitality still reward a visit. But taking in a few other places will round out your trip. Sleeping in the cave hotel in Meymand is a fun way to start, and Kerman itself is interesting, and an ideal base for day- and overnight-trips to the small but historic towns of Rayen and Mahan, excursions to nomad communities and camel-trekking trips. But the highlight is surely the journey to Shahdad and the Kaluts, where enormous 'sand castles' stand like broken teeth punctuating the earth for as far as the eye can see and you can sleep in a 'million star hotel'.

HIGHLIGHTS

- Sleep in a cave in **Meymand** (opposite), the troglodyte village without a million tourists
- Marvel at the gardens and historic mausoleum in **Mahan** (p319)
- Lunch in Kerman's **Hamam-e Vakil Chaykhaneh** (p318)
- Watch sunset over the **Kaluts** (p321), then bed down under a million stars
- Wander through the **Arg-e Bam** (p322), still a highlight even after the earthquake
- Check out the less-imposing but more-intact 'new Arg' at picturesque **Rayen** (p321)

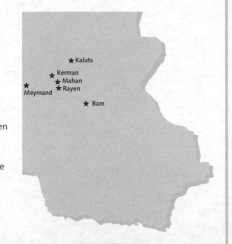

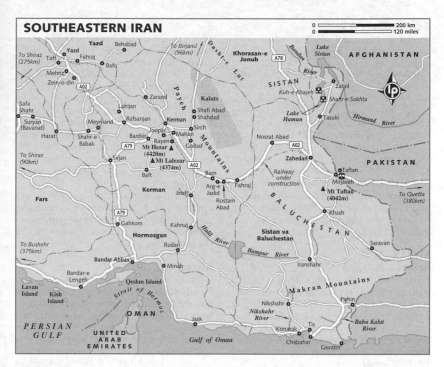

SOUTHEASTERN IRAN

MEYMAND   میمند

pop 60 in summer, 130 in winter / elev 2240m

'This mosque is about 180 years old,' said the guide, 'it's the newest building in the village.' Welcome to Meymand, a troglodyte village about equidistant from Shiraz, Yazd and Kerman. Meymand has been continuously occupied for more than 3000 years and is thought to have originally been inhabited by sun-worshippers. The village consists of 2560 rooms in 406 cave homes dug into the walls of a valley, though most are now uninhabited. It's similar to Cappadocia in Turkey, albeit on a much smaller scale…and without the hordes of tourists.

Meymand isn't exactly busy, but it sees enough day-trippers that the elderly village women have taken to selling locally woven baskets, wild herbs and traditional nomad hats (about IR60,000) made of *namad* (wool soaked and pressed until it mats together). If you have someone to translate for you, the herbs are pretty interesting, too. Dentally challenged Salma prescribed us herbs to treat diabetes and headache, and told us their medicinal use has been understood

by her family for generations. Given her mother is 97 and her father 115, she might be onto something. A university project has built an interesting cave museum and the village *hammam* (bathhouse) was being restored when we visited.

Sleeping & Eating

To get the most from Meymand it's best to stay overnight, sleeping in a cave house that has barely changed in thousands of years. On the west side of the valley near the entrance to town, eight rooms of various size have been converted into the **Meymand Guesthouse** (☎ 0913 356 3442 for Mr Hajirahimi, or 0351 622 5857 in Yazd; www.meymandtour.com; per person full board first/subsequent nights IR350,000/200,000). With *namad* carpets on the floors, beds carved into the walls and warm lighting, it's easy to be transported to another time. Bathrooms are shared but clean, with steaming showers. Mr Hajirahimi is the manager and speaks enough English to answer most questions.

The three meals are prepared by village women and often involve ingredients grown locally.

Getting There & Away

To get to Meymand you first have to get to Shahr-e Babak. Two buses leave Shahr-e Babak every day for Yazd (IR20,000, 4½hours) at 6.30am and 7.30am, returning about 1pm and 2pm; savaris (IR35,000, three hours) leave from Abuzar Sq in Yazd. One or two buses leave every day from Shiraz and Kerman – check times in advance. Savaris from Kerman cost IR40,000, or a taxi *dar baste* (closed door) should cost about IR300,000 to IR350,000 from Yazd, Shiraz or Kerman – Mr Hajirahimi (contact ☎ 0913 356 3442) can help to organise these.

Meymand is 35km from Shahr-e Babak and unless you get very lucky with a hitch or rare savari, you'll have to hire a taxi *dar baste* (IR35,000).

SIRJAN   سیرجان

☎ 0345 / elev 1730m

Sirjan is not really worth a detour, but it's a useful place to break a journey from Kerman to Bandar Abbas or Shiraz, or a staging point en route to Meymand. Sights are few, but if you do stay you might want to see the **Mir-e Zobair mausoleum**, which contains some ancient calligraphy, and the ancient **Firuz Fire Temple**.

For accommodation, the basic **Hotel-e Kasra** (☎ 422 5172; s/tw IR70,000/80,000), down a lane between the main branches of Bank Mellat and Bank Melli, is in the centre of town. Alternatively, the midrange **Sirjan Tourist Inn** (Mehmansara Jahangardi; ☎ 322 7878; sirjan@ittic.com; Khayyam St; d US$25; P ⊠) offers a little more comfort.

Savaris run to Kerman (IR30,000) and back, most frequently before about 2pm, or take a direct bus to or from Kerman, Yazd, Shiraz or Bandar Abbas.

There is no bus terminal, and the individual bus companies are spread all over town. It is best to take a private taxi and ask, for example, for the *terminal-e Yazd* (or wherever you want to go). Trains between Yazd and Bandar Abbas stop here. Trains between Bandar Abbas and Tehran also pass through.

KERMAN   کرمان

☎ 0341 / pop 508,000 / elev 1754m

The desert trading city of Kerman has long been a staging point for people passing between Persia and the Indian subcontinent and today it remains the best place from which to explore southeastern region of the country. Sheltered from the vast Dasht-e Lut by the barren Payeh Mountains to the north, its position and elevation make the weather relatively mild in summer, but cold in winter. The city is something of a melting pot, blending Persians with the more subcontinental way of life of the Baluchis (for details see p315). This mixing is most evident in the historic and very lively bazaar, which is the highlight of any visit. There are enough other sights to keep you for a day or two.

Kerman's environs are extremely dry and the city – and province to which it gives its name – are highly dependent on *qanats* (underground water channels; see the boxed text, p260).

History

Kerman is one of Iran's oldest cities and has always been an important centre on the trans-Asian trade routes. Believed to have been founded in the early-3rd-century AD by Ardashir I, founder of the Sassanian dynasty, its history is a tale of prosperity and plunder, but not that much in the way of peace. From the 7th century Kerman was ruled in turn by the Arabs, Buyids, Seljuks, Turkmen and Mongols, and then until the Qajar dynasty by a further succession of invaders and regional despots. Kerman only gained security under the central government in Tehran during the 19th century.

Kerman's continuity was its commerce, the evidence of which can still be seen in the many caravanserais around the bazaar. As trade moved more to the sea in the 16th century, so Kerman relied more on the production of carpets, a trade that remains important today.

Orientation

The two main squares in Kerman are Azadi Sq to the west and Shohada Sq to the east. Most important offices and sights are on or close to the road between these two squares, or in the bazaar near Shohada Sq. Be on the lookout for that Iranian traffic hazard, the contraflow bus lane along which buses hurtle in the *opposite* direction to the rest of the traffic, particularly along Dr Beheshti St.

DRUG-RUNNING DROMEDARIES

Camels. They're unassuming, a bit thick and no-one seems to care where they go or what they do…sounds like the perfect description for undercover work. And so it is that these ships of the desert have been trained to ship drugs across the deserts of southeast Iran.

Like a homing pigeon, but a lot slower, the camels are trained to know where their home is. They are walked for several days from somewhere near the border to a predetermined place beyond Kerman, thus avoiding the most concentrated police and military surveillance. The process is repeated, with the camels being fed each time they arrive to build an attachment to the destination. When they know where they're going, kilograms of opiates are surgically inserted into their humps and they're left to wander 'home'. Even the government's US$400 million annual war on drugs cannot account for every wandering camel in the desert.

It's a war that's been running for almost 30 years and seen more than 3300 soldiers die in battles with heavily armed smugglers. Iran has erected electric fences, dug desert ditches (to dissuade after-hours motorcyclists) and stationed 30,000 men on the Afghan border, but still an estimated 85% of all Europe's opiates pass through Iran en route from Afghanistan and Pakistan.

Information

EMERGENCY
24-Hour Pharmacy (☎ 245 760; Imam Jameh St)
Police headquarters (☎ 110, 211 3068; Adalat St)
Seyed Shohada Hospital (☎ 252 6280; Esteghlal St) The best in town.

INTERNET ACCESS
There are several other *coffeenets* (internet cafés) between Azadi and Valiasr Sqs.
Alpha Cafe Net (☎ 226 7270; Valiasr Sq; per hr IR10,000; ⏱ 8am-10pm, closed Fri) The best option, with webcams, mics and disc burning available.
Café Net Raap (☎ 244 4917; Jomhuri-ye Eslami Blvd; per hr IR10,000; ⏱ 8.30am-10pm Sat-Thu & 4-10pm Fri) Just west of Azadi Sq; it's below ground level.

MONEY
Changing money in Kerman isn't fun. If these options don't work, Akhavan Hotel (p318) changes money at slightly lower rates.
Bank Melli Central Branch (Adalat St) Nightmare on Adalat St…five signatures, 30 minutes.
Exchange Shop (Qods St) One of two small shops near the corner of Dr Shariati St, easily the best and quickest place to change money.

POST
Post office (Adalat St)

TELEPHONE
Telephone office (Tohid Sq; ⏱ 7am-10pm)

TOURIST INFORMATION
An information office is planned for a restored caravanserai at the east end of Ganj Ali Khan Courtyard.

Tourist information office (☎ 245 5151, 222 8115; cnr Jomhuri-ye Eslami Blvd & Al Qadir St; ⏱ 7.30am-2pm, closed Fri) Helpful staff have brochures etc, but it's too far out of town.

TOURS
These two operators can arrange tours within Kerman and to the surrounding areas, including the Kaluts, Mahan and Rayen. Both charge similar prices and have had mainly positive feedback, though they're not perfect. For desert trips, specify whether you want to sleep in camp or in the desert.
Jalal Mehdizadeh (☎ 271 0185, 0913 142 3174; jalalguesthouse@yahoo.de) Jalal, who also owns Jalal Guesthouse (p317), has a car, speaks German and English and is better organised, but not as fun as, Hossein Vatani.
Vatan Caravan Tours & Travel Agency (☎ /fax 223 7591 0913 343 5265; vatan_caravan@yahoo.com; Ganj Ali Khan St) Hossein Vatani's ancient Jeep seems permanently incapacitated, but he's good fun and can arrange trips to nomad encampments, camel treks and his speciality, trips into the Kaluts to sleep in the 'million star hotel'. Cost depends on the transport you choose.

TRAVEL AGENCIES
Parse Owj (☎ 244 6002/3; parsehowj@yahoo.com; 7 Ayatollah Saduqi St) English-speaking staff sell air, train and bus tickets. Reliable.
Raya Travel Agency (☎ 247 2214; Ferdosi St)

VISA EXTENSIONS
Management of Foreigners Affairs Office (☎ 272 5798; Police Bld No 14, Abbas Pour St; ⏱ 7am-1.30pm, closed Fri) The office is efficient enough but usually only

KERMAN

0 _____ 1 km
0 _____ 0.5 miles

A **B** **C** **D**

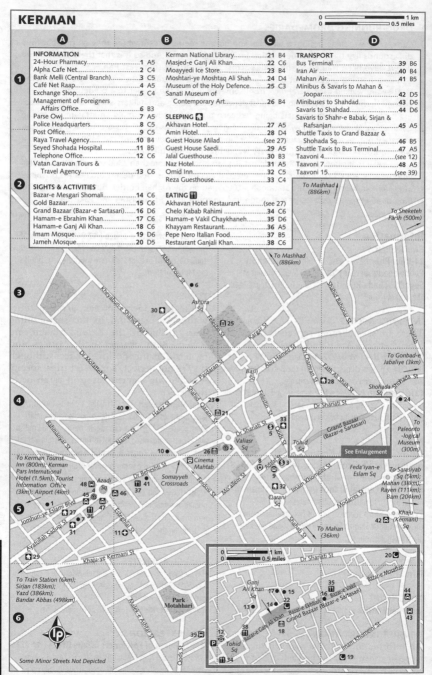

BALUCHIS

Sistan va Baluchestan and, to a lesser extent, Kerman provinces are home to about 1.5 million Baluchis, or about 2% of Iran's population. These Baluchis are among a much greater population whose traditional lands cross the Baluchestan desert deep into Afghanistan and Pakistan, where Quetta is their regional capital. Roughly half of all Baluchis are nomadic, living in tents and migrating in pursuit of seasonal pastures. They speak Baluchi, a language related to Pashtu, and the majority are Sunni Muslims.

Baluchis are easily recognisable for their darker skin and distinctive clothing. You won't see many all-enveloping black chadors in these parts, with women choosing more colourful attire and men wearing the *shalwar kameez*, a long loose shirt and baggy trousers that will be familiar to anyone who was travelled in Pakistan. The Baluchi's handiwork and embroidery are also similar to that found in Pakistan and India. Baluchis are famous for camel races, though you'll be very lucky to find one.

Given they look, dress and worship differently to most Iranians, it's no surprise that Baluchis are widely distrusted in the rest of the country.

issues two-week extensions, and you have to trek back to the Bank Melli Central Branch to deposit your cash. The office is about 300m north of Ashura Sq; look for the pale-green guardhouse on the right-hand (eastern) side of the road. Arrive early and you should have the extension the same day. For more on visa extensions, see the boxed text, p395.

Dangers & Annoyances

Kerman itself is reasonably safe, though there are a lot of drug addicts so it's worth taking extra care, especially walking around at night, particularly in poorly lit parks. The road from Kerman to Bam is busy but has on rare occasions been targeted by kidnappers. If you're cycling or driving alone, consider finding a friend. See p325 for more information.

Sights

GRAND BAZAAR (BAZAR-E SARTASARI)

بازار سرتاسری

Stretching for 1200m from Tohid Sq northeast to Shohada Sq, Kerman's **Bazar-e Sartasari** (End-to-End Bazaar) is one of the oldest trading centres in Iran. This main thoroughfare is made up of four smaller bazaars, and a further 20 or so branch off to the north and south. It is, however, easy enough to navigate and has a vivacity that should keep you interested, especially in the morning and late afternoon.

Starting at Tohid Sq, the first section is the **Bazar-e Ganj Ali Khan**, built in the 17th century for Ganj Ali Khan (the governor of Kerman), which soon opens onto the pretty **Ganj Ali Khan Square**. Built in the Safavid period, this courtyard is home to what was once Kerman's most important *hammam*, the **Hamam-e Ganj Ali Khan** (☎ 222 5577; Gang Ali Khan Sq; admission IR5000; ⊗ 8.30am-6pm, until 7.30pm summer), now restored and transformed into a museum. Wonderful frescoes adorn the walls and wax dummies illustrate the workings of a traditional bathhouse. The reception area, for example, was divided so men practising different trades could all disrobe together. Look for the 'time stones' at the east and west ends of the *hammam*; translucent, 10cm-thick alabaster doorways through which bathers could get a rough idea of the time according to how light it was outside.

On the north side of the courtyard is the photogenic **Bazar-e Mesgari Shomali** (Coppersmith's Bazaar), and at the square's northeastern end is **Masjed-e Ganj Ali Khan** (admission IR2000; ⊗ 8am-sunset), Ganj Ali Khan's lavishly decorated private mosque. A caravanserai next door was being restored when we passed.

From the northeastern corner of the square, the **Gold Bazaar** (Bazar-e Zargaran) leads to a small square with an attractive portal leading to an old (and now closed) madraseh. Follow the steps down into the **Hamam-e Ebrahim Khan** (admission about IR25000; ⊗ 7am-5pm, until 7pm summer), one of Iran's few traditional bathhouses where men can still be rubbed, scrubbed and beaten. The welcoming manager might show women around if it's not busy.

The **Bazar-e Ekhtiari** leads east from the square and passes the Hamam-e Vakil Chaykhaneh (p318) before becoming the

Bazar-e Vakil; both are about 150 years old. After about 600m the covered bazaar ends and the 700-year-old open-air **Bazar-e Mosaffari** begins, though there is little evidence of such antiquity. The Jameh Mosque can be entered from this bazaar, and you can then walk through to Shohada Sq.

JAMEH MOSQUE   مسجد جامع

The well-preserved **Jameh Mosque** (off Shohada Sq) is entered from both Shohada Sq and the bazaar. Its four lofty *iwans* (rectangular halls opening onto a courtyard) and shimmering blue tiles date from 1349 but were extensively modernised during the Safavid period and later. Interestingly, this mosque has no minaret. Instead there is a squat clock tower atop the main entrance (off Shohada Sq).

MOSHTARI-YE MOSHTAQ ALI SHAH
مشترى مشتاق على شاه

The attractive **Moshtari-ye Moshtaq Ali Shah** (Shohada Sq; ☯ 8am-noon & 2pm-sunset) is the mausoleum for Sufi mystic Moshtaq Ali Shah, and other Kerman notables. Moshtaq Ali Shah was renowned for his singing and ability with the *setar* (a four-stringed instrument), and is apparently responsible for adding the fourth string to the *setar* (which literally means 'three strings'). He eventually fell so far out of favour with the local religious community that he was stoned in the Jameh Mosque. Most of what you see, including the prominent blue-and-white-tiled roofs, are from the late Qajar period.

JAMEH MOSQUES

Although every Iranian town has several mosques, the most important one is the Masjed-e Jameh, or Congregational Mosque. This is where men gather for prayers at noon every Friday and where they will listen to the Friday prayer leader preach. In small towns he may be a simple imam (prayer leader) but in bigger towns he might be an *hojattol-Eslam* or even an *ayatollah*, a religious expert who may have studied the Quran for 20 years or more. Jameh also means 'Friday' and Westerners often refer to the Masjed-e Jameh as the 'Friday Mosque'.

IMAM MOSQUE   مسجد امام

The expansive **Imam Mosque** (Imam Khomeini St) is worth a look specifically if you're interested in the process of rehabilitating old buildings. Dating from the early Islamic period, the mosque has suffered considerable damage over the years, not least the destruction of a minaret during an earthquake in the 1970s. But the painstaking restoration goes on with the twin aims of uncovering and restoring early inscriptions while leaving no trace of the recent work. It's quite a challenge. If you get chatting with the architects in charge they might (no guarantees here) let you take a look at the remains of a fine mihrab believed to date from the early Islamic period, locked away in the southwest corner. Also worth finding are the reliefs in the rooms high above the main *iwan*.

SANATI MUSEUM OF CONTEMPORARY ART
موزه صنعتى هنرهاى معاصر

This newly renovated **museum** (☎ 222 1882; Dr Shariati St; admission IR20,000; ☯ 9am-6pm Oct-May, 9am-noon & 3-8pm summer) is a pleasant surprise in a town that can otherwise feel a long way from modern cultural pursuits. In a Qajar-era building set around an attractive courtyard, the museum houses paintings, sculptures and stone inlays by famous local artist Sayyed Ali Akbar Sanati (1916–2006). It also has exhibitions by younger Iranian artists and even a bronze hand by Auguste Rodin. Not surprisingly, it's a good place to meet open-minded young Kermanis.

MOAYEDI ICE STORE   يخچال معايدي

The Safavid-era **Moayedi Ice House** (Abu Hamed St) is a well-preserved, conical adobe structure that was used to store ice. The ice store was, and in some part still is, surrounded by gardens. The gardens would fill with water during winter, and when the water froze the ice would be slid into the Moayedi. It was being transformed into a theatre when we passed and wasn't open to the public.

KERMAN NATIONAL LIBRARY
كتابخانه ملى كرمان

The **Kerman National Library** (Shahid Qarani St; ☯ 7am-8pm) modestly bills itself as the 'greatest informatic research center in the country', but it's the architecture – a forest of columns supporting vaulted ceilings – that is the real attraction. Built in 1929, the style is a harmonious variation on late-Qajar-era design that was purpose built as, wait for it, a textile factory! If only Manchester had been so blessed.

MUSEUM OF THE HOLY DEFENCE

موزه دفاع مقدس

The **Museum of the Holy Defence** (Felestin St; admission IR3000; 🕙 7am-12.30pm & 3.30-6pm) commemorates the eight-year Iran–Iraq War. Symbolism abounds, although much of it won't be obvious without an English-speaking guide. Inside is a gallery of gruesome photos, artefacts, letters and documents from the war, and an animated model re-enacting the Karbala V, a famous battle. Outside, along with a line-up of tanks and missile launchers, is a battlefield complete with bunkers, minefield and sound effects recorded from the actual war. Well worth a look.

PALAEONTOLOGICAL MUSEUM

Located underground in green Park-e Sangi, about 500m east of Shohada Sq, the **Palaeontological Museum** (Park-e Sangi; admission IR5000; 🕙 4-8pm most days) is the passion and life's work of local mountaineer Mohsen Tajrobekar. Mohsen has collected a stunning array of fossils from the mountains around Kerman and his finds have caused scientists to re-assess the origins of some present-day species. They include a perfectly petrified fish believed to be 530 million years old.

GONBAD-E JABALIYE

گنبد جبلیه

At the edge of town is the mysterious, octagonal **Gonbad-e Jabaliye** (Mountain of Stone; admission IR2000; 🕙 8am-6pm Tue-Sun), which houses a mildly interesting and poorly labelled museum of old gravestones. It's mysterious because its age and original function remain unknown – a Kerman Tourism brochure sums it up as 'A big, strange dome in the eastern part of Kerman'. Quite! Some scholars date it to the 2nd century AD and think it may have been an observatory. Others say it was a tomb. Whatever its function, it is remarkable because it is constructed of stone rather than the usual brick; though the double-layered dome, added 150 years ago, is brick. When taking photos (outside only) be careful to point your camera away from the neighbouring army base.

The setting, at the foot of the Payeh Mountains, is picturesque. To get here, try to find a shuttle taxi from Shohada Sq (IR2000), though you might need to go *dar baste*.

Sleeping

Kerman isn't that big but its hotels are scattered inconveniently around town. The rules of supply and demand, or a lack thereof, keep prices relatively low.

BUDGET

Kerman is not blessed with an abundance of good budget options.

Omid Inn (☎ 222 0571; Shahid Qarani St; s/tw/tr IR50,000/70,000/90,000; P) Set around a courtyard (which is ideal for overlanders), the Omid is spartan but provides a warm welcome from the English-speaking manager and his wife. Rooms are basic but they and the shared bathroom and kitchen are clean.

Reza Guesthouse (☎ 226 4012-13; Qods St; s/tw/tr IR60,000/85,000/105,000) This clean, simple guesthouse is ideally located near Tohid Sq. Unadorned rooms have overhead fans; all bathrooms are shared. No English is spoken.

These next two are a longer walk into town.

Guest House Milad (☎ 245 0617; Ayatollah Saduqi St; s/tw IR60,000/90,000; ☒) Drab, functional rooms and shared bathrooms are clean and staff is friendly. Guests can use the kitchen.

Jalal Guesthouse (☎ 271 0185, 0913 142 3174; jalalguesthouse@yahoo.de; 11 Gharbi 3 St, off Ashura Sq; per person €12; P ☒ 🖳) About 3km north of the bazaar, local guide Jalal Mehdizadeh (p313) and his wife have two rooms in their house they open to foreign travellers. It has convenient little luxuries like washing machine, internet and more than 1000 channels of TV, and is a good choice for lone women travellers. Breakfast is IR20,000. Jalal speaks English and German. Book ahead.

Guest House Saedi (☎ 252 0802; Ayatollah Saduqi St; s/tw/tr IR70,000/110,000/140,000; P ☒) Friendly, functional but Spartan; if the others are full.

MIDRANGE & TOP END

Amin Hotel (☎ 222 1954; aminhotel@yahoo.com; Dr Chamran St; s/tw/q US$25/30/50; P ☒ 🖳) Well located near the bazaar, the long-running Amin has larger-than-average rooms with Western bathrooms and soft beds. Front rooms might be noisy.

Naz Hotel (☎ 244 6786; fax 245 0498; Ayatollah Saduqi St; tw with breakfast IR290,000; Ⓟ ✖) The rejuvenated Naz has new, English-speaking management. The 28 largish rooms are very clean, very pink and fair value. It's opposite the Akhavan and comparing is easy.

our pick **Akhavan Hotel** (☎ 244 1411-2; akhavan-hotel@yahoo.com; Ayatollah Saduqi St; s/d with breakfast US$24/34; Ⓟ ✖ 🖵) Staying with the Akhavan brothers is a pleasure. Their rooms are very comfortable at this price and when low-season discounts of up to US$10 are thrown in it's an absolute bargain. They can help with information on visa renewals and organise day trips. Secure parking is popular with overlanders, who use the hotel showers for US$2 per person per day. The restaurant (right) serves delicious food. Highly recommended.

Kerman Tourist Inn (Hotel Jahangardi; ☎ 244 5203-05; www.ittic.com; Jomhuri-ye Eslami Blvd; s/d/ste US$41/50/80; Ⓟ ✖) A fair way from the bazaar, the small, recently renovated rooms are OK but the whole place is a bit soulless. Try Akhavan first.

Kerman Pars International Hotel (☎ 211 9301-32; www.parshotels.com; Jomhuri-ye Eslami Blvd; s/d with breakfast US$72/103; Ⓟ ✖ 🖵) This 200-room behemoth on the edge of town is easily Kerman's best. Rooms are quite luxurious and from the foyer to the facilities – including gym, pool, sauna and three restaurants – it's very much an upmarket business hotel. Good value.

Eating

For cheap eats, there are *kababis* (kabab shops) ice-cream and fruit-shake places, and a pizza place or two on Dr Beheshti and Dr Shariati Sts, particularly around the squares.

Chelo Kabab Rahimi (Tohid Sq; meals IR25,000; ⏱ 11am-3pm & 5-9pm) No-frills place true to its name that also offers a decent *khoresht* (thick meaty stew with rice).

Restaurant Ganjali Khan (☎ 222 7716; Tohid Sq; meals IR20,000-35,000; ⏱ 8am-10pm) This underground place near the bazaar entrance is not nearly as charming as the Hamam-e Vakil Chaykhaneh, but delicious food at very reasonable prices makes it a local favourite. You can also just sit and drink tea. There is no English sign.

Hamam-e Vakil Chaykhaneh (☎ 222 5989; Bazar-e Vakil; admission IR5000 incl tea; meals IR40,000; ⏱ 9am-

7pm Sat-Thu, until 7.30pm summer, 9am-2pm Fri) This architecturally magnificent subterranean teahouse built in 1820 is easily the most atmospheric dining option in Kerman. It's better known for its elegant arches and superb vaulted ceilings than its food (lunch only), though it's not bad. A traditional band plays most days.

Khayyam Restaurant (☎ 245 1417; Ayatollah Saduqi St, off Azadi Sq; meals IR35,000-55,000; ⏱ noon-11pm) This faux-traditional place is convenient to the Ayatollah Saduqi St hotels, though the food quality is inconsistent.

Akhavan Hotel Restaurant (☎ 244 1411-2; Ayatollah Saduqi St; meals IR30,000) What it lacks in atmosphere (it looks like a hospital ward) is amply made up for with the delicious, varied, plentiful and cheap Iranian food; try a bit of everything for the IR50,000 buffet dinner. For a little more romance get it served in your room.

Pepe Nero Italian Food (☎ 244 9716; Dr Beheshti St; meals IR30,000-40,000; ⏱ noon-3pm & 6-10pm) More than 700 years after Marco Polo swung by, Kerman finally has a restaurant (not a pizzeria) serving foreign flavours. And while it's a way off any Michelin stars, the pasta and lasagne we had were surprisingly good.

Shopping

Kermani carpets have been famous for centuries (see p64). The bazaar is a good place to shop for them and if you hunt around a bit you should be able to find good carpets at reasonable prices. The bazaar is also the place to look for Kermani *pate*, a brightly coloured square of cloth with intricate embroidered designs that is unique to Kerman.

Getting There & Away

AIR

Iran Air (☎ 245 7770; Dr Mofatteh St) and **Mahan Air** (☎ 245 0542; Dr Beheshti St) both fly daily to Tehran (one way IR457,000) and Mahan Air also flies to Esfahan (IR335,000, weekly), Kish (IR362,000, twice weekly) and Zahedan (IR258,000, weekly).

BUS, MINIBUS & SAVARI

The bus terminal is in the southwest of Kerman but Taavoni 7 (Volvos only) has an office on Azadi Sq, Taavoni 4 has an office on Tohid Sq. All the other main bus companies have offices at the bus terminal, where Taavoni 15 is the best bet if you want a *mahmooly* bus. The following services are for *mahmooly*/Volvo buses.

Destination	Fare	Duration
Bam	IR12,000/20,000	3–4hr
Bandar Abbas	IR35,000/55,000	7–9hr
Esfahan	IR26,000/55,000	10–12hr
Mashhad	IR85,000 (Volvo)	14–16hr
Shahr-e Babak	IR17,000 (*mahmooly*)	4–5hr
Shiraz	IR23,000/55,000	7–9hr
Tehran	IR90,000 (Volvo)	14–16hr
Yazd	IR15,000/35,000	4½–6hr
Zahedan	IR21,000/55,000	6–8hr

Taavoni 4 has most services to Shahr-e Babak; for Bandar Abbas, see Taavoni 7 first. Minibuses to Mahan (IR1000) leave from around Khaju (Kermani) Sq, though it's worth asking around near Shohada Sq as well. For Shahdad, take a minibus or savari (IR15,000) from Imam Khomeini St, just south of Shohada Sq.

Savaris to Bam (IR25,000) and Rayen (IR15,000) leave from Sarasiyab Sq (about 5km east of Khaju Sq), and to Sirjan from Azadi Sq for IR30,000. Savaris to Mahan (IR5500) leave from Khaju (Kermani) Sq.

If you hire a taxi or guide (see Tours, p313) it makes sense to see Rayen, Mahan and Bagh-e Shahzde as a day trip from Kerman, or en route to/from Bam.

TRAIN

The 1106km line from Tehran has recently been extended to Bam and should run all the way into Pakistan by 2009. The daily train to Tehran (1st class IR63,150; 15 hours) leaves at 4.45pm and stops at Yazd, Kashan and Qom, but not Esfahan. There are also daily 2nd-class trains to Bam (IR10,000, about two hours, 7.30am) and Yazd (IR16,000, five to six hours, 1pm), which make a pleasant break from all the bus travel.

Train tickets can be bought from Parse Owj (p313) or other agencies, saving you the trip to the **train station** (☎ 211 0762), 8km southwest of town. Shuttle taxis (IR2000) leave from Azadi Sq for the station, or go *dar baste* for IR10,000.

Getting Around
TO/FROM THE AIRPORT

There is no airport bus. You can take a shuttle taxi along Jomhuri-ye Eslami Blvd from Azadi Sq, or a taxi *dar baste* for about IR15,000, depending on traffic.

TAXI

Shuttle taxis use Azadi and Shohada Sqs. From Azadi Sq, they run to the bus terminal (IR1500), Bazar-e Vakil and Shohada Sq (IR1000). Taxis all to yourself cost IR10,000 to most destinations around town and at least IR25,000 per hour.

AROUND KERMAN

Mahan and Rayen are easily reached by public transport, but services to Shahdad are less frequent and nothing at all runs to the Kaluts. Some travellers take a tour or hire a taxi for the day. Depending on how far you go, you can expect a half/full day to cost about IR120,000/220,000. Some drivers might charge by the kilometre – IR1000 at the time of writing.

Mahan   ماهان
☎ 0342

Mahan, 35km southeast of Kerman, is a picturesque and low-key town that has long been famous as a summer retreat for the wealthy, and for its two main attractions, the Aramgah-e Shah Ne'matollah Vali shrine and Bagh-e Shahzde gardens. Fed by *qanats* and surrounding natural springs, before the 1979 revolution it was also known for the quality of the locally produced opium. Not any more.

ARAMGAH-E SHAH NE'MATOLLAH VALI
آرامگاه شاه نعمت الله ولی

The splendid dome over the **Aramgah-e Shah Ne'matollah Vali** (admission to museum & roof IR25,000; ☻ 8am-5pm, to 8pm summer), the mausoleum of a well-known Sufi dervish, is one of the most recognisable images of eastern Iran. The mausoleum dates from the early 15th century, when it was built by an Indian king who was an adherent of Shah Ne'matollah Vali's teachings. However, many of the other religious buildings in the surrounding complex were built during the reign of Shah Abbas I and during the 18th century. The mausoleum is renowned for its tiles, the seven Indian doors throughout the building, some inlaid with ivory, and its stunning blue-tiled domes. But we like the small, tranquil prayer room where a dervish, who is said to have stayed in this room on his regular visits, has painted the walls and ceiling with calligraphy in spiral wheel pattern – ask nicely to be let in.

You can see most of the complex without paying, but the entrance ticket allows you into a small **museum** and then up to the roof. The views from here are superb and, assuming the repair work is finished, photographers will be rather excited by the vast (and dented) Safavid-era cupola and Qajar minarets, which can be climbed. There is a decent **bookshop** in the courtyard.

The mausoleum is smack bang in the middle of Mahan, and minibuses (IR1000) and savaris (IR5500) from Kerman will take you straight to it.

BAGH-E SHAHZDE   باغ شازده

Arriving at the handsome **Bagh-e Shahzde** (admission IR4000; ☼ 9am-6pm, 8am-11pm summer) is like being beamed onto a different planet. One second you're in the arid semidesert, the next it's all flowing *qanat* water and tall green trees. The beautifully maintained grounds, built in 1873, contain a series of split-level fountains leading to a dilapidated palace that was once the residence of Abdul Hamid Mirza, one of the last princes of the Qajar dynasty. To the left of the palace there is a well-preserved bathhouse.

The palace itself has been converted into a restaurant (open for lunch and dinner), though it was being renovated when we visited this time. As the sun disappears, the fountains and palace are floodlit, which is a wonderful sight. Occasional music festivals are held in the grounds.

The gardens are a 5km-long walk up Mahan's main road from the mausoleum, and the turn-off is signposted in English. Alternatively, it's easy to get a private taxi.

SLEEPING & EATING

When Robert Byron travelled through Iran in 1934, he stopped in Mahan and stayed in the caravanserai adjoining the Aramgah-e Shah Ne'matollah Vali. According to the caretaker, no foreigners have stayed there since. But that is set to change with the opening, in late 2007, of that same caravanserai...

Aramgah-e Shah Ne'matollah Vali Caravanserai (☎ 0913 340 9375; r about IR70,000) The 170-year-old caravanserai should become one of the most atmospheric – and good value – places

to stay in the region. The small rooms have been faithfully restored, which means all bathrooms are shared, but it adds up to a genuine taste of what travel must have been like years ago. Call English-speaking Hamed Azad Pour, who works at the mausoleum, to book and check the prices.

Mahan Inn (Hotel Jahangardi; ☎ 622 3555; mahan@ittic.com; Gharani Sq; d/tr US$18/22; **P** ✿) The big, tidy rooms here are good value, staff is friendly and the restaurant is decent. The hotel is at a roundabout, a couple of blocks west of the mausoleum and public transport from Kerman takes you past the hotel.

Sultan-e Shabha (☼ 10am-11pm) Opposite the entrance to the mausoleum, a quiet lane leads to this attractive and atmospheric garden teahouse, on the left side. At the end of this lane (about 200m) is a once-grand home called Shotor Galou (Camel Neck), which was built about 200 years ago and served as a home to Qajar period VIPs. It's in a terrible state, but it's fun to wander around and think of how wonderful it could be if it's properly restored – as is the plan.

GETTING THERE & AWAY

About every hour, savaris (IR5500) and minibuses (IR1000) travel the 35km between Khaju (Kermani) Sq in Kerman and Ne'matollahi Sq in Mahan, right in front of the mausoleum.

Shahdad & Around   شهداد

Sleepy Shahdad is the largest town in the Takhab area, a group of about 30 oasis villages wedged between the Payeh Mountains to the south and the vast emptiness of the Dasht-e Lut to the north. Shahdad is fiercely hot in summer, but its oranges (harvested in October) are reputedly the best in Iran.

About 75 minutes northeast of Kerman, Shahdad is mainly of interest as a gateway to the desert. It's only-if-I've-got-plenty-of-spare-time sights are limited to the Safavid-era **Imamzadeh-ye Mohammed Ebn-e Zeid** mausoleum and, to the east of town, two prehistoric archaeological sites: the **Tappeh-ye Kohne**, the archaeological remains of a village settled about 5000 years ago; and 1km further the **Shahrak-e Kotuluha** (City of the Little People) – the name refers to a local Lilliputian legend but its origin is unknown. There's not much to see.

Shafi Abad, an oasis village a few kilometres north of Shahdad, boasts several crumbling caravanserais. The most prominent of these, from the Seljuk-era, has been partially restored and it's possible to climb above the grand gatehouse and the northwest tower, and check out the lodgings along the northern wall where rooms are linked by an unusual arched corridor.

Leaving the Takhab behind, the road to Birjand heads north into the **Kaluts**, a 145km-long and 80km-wide stretch of desert dominated by long lines of five- to 10-storey high 'sand castles'. This stunning landscape is unique on earth and no-one we met was quite sure how it was formed. Theories ranged from simple wind erosion (but why just this north-south stretch?) to the idea that a giant meteorite glanced here, leaving this graze – look at Google Earth (N 30°38'34.63", E 58° 0'58.48") and make your own theory. Whatever the cause, the reality is simply spectacular, especially at dawn and sunset when light and shadows paint a shimmering canvas of gold and brown.

There are no official lodgings in Shahdad, but a desert camp has been set up at the edge of the Kaluts. This is where most people stay, but the bright lights and paved spaces are rather less appealing than real desert camping, which can be arranged (in advance) on a tour with Hossein Vatani (p313). Note that midday temperatures rise to an almost unimaginable 65°C in summer.

Semi-regular minibuses and savaris (IR15,000 per seat) travel between Shahdad and Imam Khomeini St, just south of Shohada Sq in Kerman, but there is no public transport to Kaluts. You can, however, charter your savari to take you to the Kaluts and back to Kerman for about IR120,000 (return), or, as one enterprising traveller did, just go by minibus to Shahdad and put yourself in the care of the locals. Take your passport as there is a checkpoint in Shahdad.

RAYEN　راین

☎ 0342

The demise of Bam has been the rebirth of the **Arg-e Rayen** (admission IR5000; ☯ 7am–sunset), an ancient adobe 'citadel' in Rayen, a small town sitting in the lee of Mt Hezar (4420m) 111km from Kerman. On a hill overlooking the town, the Arg's hotchpotch of architectural styles suggests it is well over 1000 years old, though its exact age is unknown. It had been abandoned for about 150 years before restoration began in 1996.

The structure itself is a story of muscles made of mud, with **outer walls** 3m thick at the base and 1m thick at the top supporting most of the Arg's 15 towers. The entrance leads straight onto the **bazaar** and from the gatehouse you can climb a narrow staircase to the **ramparts** for spectacular views. Coming back down, turn right and you'll come to the **'main walkway'**. About halfway along a door on the left leads to the remains of **public houses** (the sign says 'kommon people'), some of which stood three storeys high and would have been home to several families.

The **governor's complex**, entered from the square, is the highlight. The four separate houses here have been restored (and labelled) and reflect the relative luxury the governor and his family enjoyed; note the subtly different shades of the mud and straw render, reflecting different earth used for each *khan* (home). Climb to the roof for views over the Arg and the mountains beyond. Covered *kuches* (lanes) weave their way through the rest of the Arg, look for the small **zurkhaneh** (literally 'house of strength'; see p52).

Hamid Reza (☎ 662 3644) is the caretaker of the Arg and if you find the doors closed, call him. He is also a sword maker and has a simple workshop just inside the main gate.

Sleeping & Eating

Options are limited.

Rayen Arg Tourist Hotel (☎ 662 3578; s/tw IR60,000/80,000; ❄) This small, new hotel has nine compact but clean rooms above a restaurant, each with bathroom and squat toilet. As you enter town, turn right (west) at the roundabout and it's about 300m along on the right – look for the green façade.

Restaurant Arg (☎ 662 3931; meals IR25,000-35,000) The tasty food here comes in typically large portions. It's about 50m down the hill from the Arg, opposite a park.

Getting there & away

Rayen is 23km south of the Kerman–Bam road, the turn-off being 88km from Kerman. Buses (IR5000) leave Kerman bus terminal every hour or so; Taavonis 3 and 16 are your best bet. Savaris (IR15,000) are more frequent, leaving from Kerman's Sarasiyab Sq and stopping at a square in Rayen about 1km from the Arg, from where they also return to Kerman.

BAM   بم
☎ 0344

Having been all but flattened by a massive earthquake in 2003, Bam is not the tourist attraction it once was. A few years later much of the rebuilding is complete, but the city has undoubtedly changed. Mud-brick homes have been replaced by steel-framed two-storey buildings that are safe but boring. The main attraction, the Arg-e Bam, is obviously a less evocative place than it once was. For all this, however, Bam's thousands of date palms remain and with them the desert oasis feel. If you have the time, Bam is still worth the trip.

Orientation

Bam's bus terminal is in the south of the city near Arg Sq and unless you're packing light you'll need a taxi to get you to any of the lodgings. Once in town, Bam is easy enough to walk around, though taxis make much more sense in summer. What remains of the ancient Arg-e Bam is about 2km north of the centre of town, which is Imam Khomeini Sq. The new bazaar should be finished by the time you arrive, though in earthquake-proof concrete it's unlikely to have the same atmosphere as before.

The Arg-e Jadid free-trade zone is about 14km east of Bam.

Information

Arg-e Bam Reconstruction Headquarters (Arg St)
Bank Sepah (Shahid Sadoqi St) Bank manager changes cash 10am to 12.30pm only, with IR17,000 commission.
Jonub-e Shahr Coffeenet (Pasdaran St; internet per hr IR14,000; ☉ 8am-2pm & 4-9pm) Look out for a building with a green and red façade, the *coffeenet* is on the first floor.
Post office (Shahid Sadoqi St)
Telephone office (Shahid Sadoqi St)

Dangers & Annoyances

A Japanese traveller was abducted from the street in Bam by drug smugglers in September 2007 (see p325). Check the latest situation with other travellers and on the Thorn Tree (www.lonelyplanet.com/thorntree) before you arrive.

Arg-e Bam

The ancient mud city of Bam is the largest adobe structure on earth and, until the 2003 earthquake, it was one of the jewels in Iran's tourism crown. The site has been occupied for almost 2000 years and post-earthquake analysis has revealed the walls were first built using Sassanian-style mud-bricks. Bam was a staging post on the trade routes between India and Pakistan at one end and the Persian Gulf and Europe at the other. Visitors, including Marco Polo, were awestruck by the city's 38 towers, huge mud walls and fairy-tale citadel – the **Arg-e Bam** (admission free; ☉ 24).

Today the Arg is the largest adobe building project on earth. Teams of Iranian and

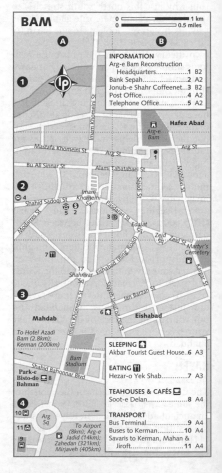

BAM

INFORMATION
Arg-e Bam Reconstruction
Headquarters.................1 B2
Bank Sepah.....................2 A2
Jonub-e Shahr Coffeenet...3 B2
Post Office.......................4 A2
Telephone Office.............5 A2

SLEEPING 🛏
Akbar Tourist Guest House..6 A3

EATING 🍴
Hezar-o Yek Shab..............7 A3

TEAHOUSES & CAFÉS ☕
Soot-e Delan.....................8 A4

TRANSPORT
Bus Terminal.....................9 A4
Buses to Kerman.............10 A4
Savaris to Kerman, Mahan &
Jiroft.............................11 A4

foreign archaeologists, architects and engineers are working to first understand how and when the Arg was built, and then to rebuild it using mainly traditional methods. As team leader Nima Naderi explained, it's a dauntingly complex job.

'We cannot look at the Arg as a single structure,' he told us. 'Every building is different, built at different times using different materials. We must try to rebuild each building using materials as close as possible to those they were originally built with.' In the laboratory opposite the collapsed gate tower, engineers are working to develop a range of mud bricks in line with the differing sizes and densities used in the original buildings. At the same time they are experimenting with different compositions of mud, straw and palm mulch to determine which is the strongest and most flexible.

About 150 people are working on the Arg and its reconstruction is scheduled to take 15 years. But with less than 1000 bricks being made each day, and countless millions being required, Nima's statement that 'the project has no deadline' seems more realistic.

A TOWN BORN OF DUST IS REBORN *Andrew Burke*

When I arrived in Bam on 27 December 2003 to report on the earthquake that had just devastated the city, it was like stepping into a scene from hell. The quake, measuring 6.8 on the Richter scale, had reduced this ancient city of mud-brick homes to dust and rubble. Death was everywhere.

Those Bamis who had survived were in a state of shock. 'After this house collapsed,' one old man told me, pointing to a pile of rubble that was once his home, 'five people were dug out without any injury. But 15 or 16 members of my [extended] family are dead.'

A few metres away, a woman wailed as another body was carted past in a blanket and loaded onto a pink suburban bus, to be taken to the cemetery. As I followed the bus through a gridlock of people trying desperately to escape the carnage, the horror was summed up in a single image. Four large men sat crying in a white Kia Pride while two bodies and two shovels hung out of the boot.

The scene was repeated across Bam. Women wailing and beating themselves; men scrambling through broken concrete in an effort to extract the dead – even then few held out hope of finding anyone alive. That day, and the next, Bam buried most of the 31,000 people who died when their homes had collapsed atop them at 5.30am that bitterly cold morning. With the burying done, the grieving began amid freezing nights spent under Red Crescent canvas.

During several visits since then I've seen Bam deal with an event whose magnitude would have been barely imaginable before it actually happened. Progress has been frustratingly slow, but several years later Bam continues to emerge from the dust and death and depression. Physically, at least.

Bam's progress can be summed up in the progress of the Akbar Tourist Guest House (p324). Manager Panjalizadeh Akbar saw his business flattened and his son's best friend and two guests die in the earthquake, but has rebuilt bit by bit. From the tent on the street I stayed in a few weeks after the quake, to demountable buildings and, as money has become available, a new, two-storey and heavily engineered concrete and brick hotel. As in the rest of Bam, the only constants have been the date palms.

The emotional scars will take longer to heal. When I interviewed a grandmother who had lost all but 11 of her 96-member extended family, I couldn't even imagine such a loss, let alone begin to come to terms with it. For many Bamis, who don't have the luxury of getting on the next bus out of town, solace has come through an opium pipe and addiction has become a serious problem.

Bam is far from perfect, but most people have had their homes rebuilt in some fashion and have their lives back on some sort of track. The loss of tourism has had an impact on the local economy and the loss of the Arg has had an impact on the local identity. But even that is slowly being attended to. As the head of the Arg-e Bam reconstruction project, Nima Naderi, told me: 'What we have here is not just an industrial workshop, re-creating bricks and buildings. This is a psychological workshop for the people of Bam. For them, the Arg is the symbol of their town and as they see us rebuilding it brick by brick, we are also rebuilding their pride.'

For the visitor, it's possible to walk a dusty brown lane from the entrance to the foot of the citadel itself. It's a haunting walk, but even after the *zelzele* (earthquake) the sheer scale of the Arg and the remaining ramparts, arches and supporting walls mean it's not too difficult to imagine its majesty.

There is no shade available, so go early morning or late afternoon.

Sleeping & Eating

The earthquake claimed most of Bam's hotels and restaurants and few have been rebuilt.

our pick **Akbar Tourist Guest House** (☎ 231 4843; mr_panjali@yahoo.com; Sayyeh Jamal od-Din St; dm €5, r with/without bathroom €15/10; ☒) Akbar's has long been the meeting place for overlanders heading to or from Pakistan. And after four years of struggle in tents and prefabricated buildings following the earthquake, a new, earthquake-proof 15-room affair is due to open in 2008. Dorms and a range of rooms with and without bathroom will be available. The easy, social ambience is the main attraction, while laundry, phone and tours to nearby desert and mountain locales often keep people longer than they expect. It's a good place to just hang out and recharge. A restaurant is anticipated during the life of this book.

Hotel Azadi Bam (☎ 221 0095; argbam.2005@yahoo.com; Jahad Blvd; s/d/ste €40/50/70; P ☒ ☐) The earthquake damage is fixed and you'll find spacious, clean and comfortable rooms that are fair value, even if the location of about 6km from the Arg means you'll need a taxi to go anywhere. It's off the left of the main road into Bam from Kerman. The restaurant (meals IR40,000 to IR70,000; open breakfast, lunch and dinner) is one of the best in town.

Hezar-o Yek Shab (meals IR15,000-40,000; ☒ 4-10pm) The name means '1001 nights', and eating on the *takhts* (daybed-style tables) in the rear garden is a favourite Bami experience. The food is excellent, especially the juicy chicken kabab, and it's *bastani* (ice cream) is famous.

Soot-e Delan (Park-e Bisto-do Bahman; ☒ 9am-noon & 4-10.30pm) This indoor/outdoor *chaykhaneh* (teahouse) is a fun place to sit and socialise over *chay* (tea) and qalyan (water pipe) with the young men of Bam. The location deep in a park is not great for solo women.

Getting There & Away

Iran Aseman flies daily between Tehran and Bam's small airport east of town.

Bam's bus terminal is just south of Arg Sq but Arg Sq itself is where most services stop en route to or from Zahedan. Buses to Kerman (*mahmooly*/Volvo IR12,000/18,000, three hours, 204km) leave frequently. The few regular services from Bam include Esfahan (IR70,000, 11 hours, 703km) at 2.30pm and Tehran (IR100,000, 21 hours, 1258km) at 3.30pm. For Zahedan (IR16,000/25,000, four hours, 321km) buses pass intermittently, including one soon after 6am – ask at Akbar Tourist Guest House (left) for schedules.

Savaris for Kerman (IR30,000, two hours), Mahan (IR30,000, 1¼ hours) and Jiroft (IR25,000, 90 minutes) leave Arg Sq when they fill.

BAM TO MINAB

To avoid backtracking, a growing number of travellers are taking the road between Bam or Kerman and the Persian Gulf town of Minab (p308). The major stop along the way is **Jiroft**, which is surrounded by some of the most fertile land in Iran. The nearby Halil Rud Basin has been settled since at least 4000 BC, and two archaeological sites discovered in 2002 have given up thousands of artefacts (many smuggled out to Britain) from this little-understood period. The ziggurat-shaped mounds are 28km from Jiroft but for now it's not really worth the trip. Instead, the **Jiroft Archaeological Museum** (☎ 0348-221 7553; Halil St; admission IR2000; ☒ 9am-noon & 4-6pm), on the north bank of the river, houses several of the finds and has interesting explanations.

If you stay in Jiroft, the **Mosaferkhaneh Valiasr** (Halil St; per person IR40,000; ☒) is the very simple budget option about 100m east of the museum. On the main street, the **Hotel Jaam-e Jam** (☎ 0348-221 0340; Dowlat St, near Setat Sq; r IR180,000; ☒) is a more comfortable, midrange-style place with a restaurant in the lobby.

Savaris to/from Bam (IR25,000, 90 minutes) stop at the central Farmondari Sq, one block south of Hotel Jaam-e Jam. Less-frequent buses to Bam cost IR15,000. Heading south, savaris and minibuses leave the Eskaa Khanuj (Khanuj Terminal) about 2.5km southeast of town. You go first to Khanuj (minibus/savari IR6000/20,000, 1½/one hour) then change for Minab (IR30,000, two hours) or Bandar Abbas via Rudan.

EXTREMISTS & DRUG SMUGGLERS: TRAVEL ANNOYANCES

Sunni extremists operating from Pakistan and drug smugglers who kidnap tourists to use as leverage have added a large degree of annoyance and some danger to travelling in the southeast. The danger is tempered by the fact no tourists have yet been harmed, though that is little comfort to those who have been held.

The Extremists

In 2005 the Jundollah group of Sunni extremists emerged in Sistan va Baluchestan province and in the following years carried out several major terror attacks. First 22 Iranians were shot dead and several taken hostage after the group stopped traffic on the road between Zahedan and Zabol. Then 12 people were killed in a similar operation on the Kerman to Bam road. And in 2007 a Republican Guard bus was blown up in Zahedan, with at least 11 people killed.

So far, the extremists have not targeted tourists, but the government is worried they will and has tightened security in all areas east of Kerman. In Zahedan foreigners are forbidden from staying in cheap hotels and, as we found, are supposed to have a police escort whenever they leave the hotel. An armed police shadow is annoying. We were allowed out unaccompanied if we weren't going too far from the hotel, and even managed to sneak up to Zabol without an escort. The police, however, weren't happy when they found out. Though the threat of kidnap does justify some of their paranoia.

(Some of) The Drug Smugglers

In August 2007 a Belgian couple driving overland were abducted on the road between Bam and Zahedan. The kidnappers were not extremists, but a well-organised group of drug smugglers whose leader demanded the release of his imprisoned son. The woman was released after four days but the man, Stefaan Boeve, was held for 34 days in Iran, Pakistan and Afghanistan before finally being released. Stefaan told us by email he was treated relatively 'well, according to their standard, sleeping open air on hard rocks and with one blanket.' But he urged other travellers to be cautious and travel in groups.

While Stefaan was released, the smuggler's son was not, and three weeks later the smuggler abducted a Japanese traveller from a street in Bam. They again demanded the son's release. As we went to press Satoshi Nakamura was still being held several months later, though he was reportedly in good health.

What to do?

The road from Kerman to Bam, Zahedan and Pakistan is unavoidable if you want to travel overland to or from Pakistan. Clearly it's not completely safe, but people continue to do it, usually without trouble. The best plan is to do your research. Read the Thorn Tree (www.lonelyplanet.com/thorn tree) and the message board (it's called HUBB) of www.horizonsunlimited.com/hubb/middle-east/ferry-to-iran-oman-uae-21170-2 for updates, and ask again at each stop as you head east. If you're driving, you might want to link up with other vehicles in Kerman, or definitely in Bam, where Akbar's (see Akbar Tourist Guest House, opposite) is the place to meet other overlanders.

You could also get your hotel to inform the police and, assuming things are still dangerous, you'll get an armed escort. On our return from Zabol to Zahedan our savari travelled in an escorted convoy, which had the added benefit of keeping the savari driver down to a relatively sane 120km/h. If you're travelling by public transport, take the bus and keep a low profile.

Until there has been a prolonged period without a kidnapping, it's best to play it safe. If you plan to travel in your own vehicle beyond Bam, get an escort. If you're on public transport, try to keep a low profile.

Getting kidnapped can ruin your holiday (understatement alert), but if you do get very unlucky and it happens to you, take some comfort in the knowledge that, so far at least, all the travellers abducted by smugglers have eventually been released unharmed. Finally, help other travellers by writing about your trip on the Middle East branch of the Thorn Tree.

ZAHEDAN   زاهدان

☎ 0541 / pop 534,000

Zahedan is capital of the desolate and near-lawless Sistan va Baluchestan province. It has few attractions of its own (very few), but its proximity to the only legal crossing point between Iran and Pakistan means most overlanders will stop here. Most travellers don't stay long, and restrictive security meant that when we passed there were even fewer reasons to hang around (see p325).

Outside Zahedan there are a couple of worthy day trips, notably to Zabol (p329) and Kuh-e Khajeh (p331). If you're very lucky you might be in town for a **camel race** (*mosabagheh-ye shotor-e davani*), a traditional Baluchi activity usually held in summer.

Orientation

Zahedan is a flat, dusty, featureless town. Most visitors will only worry about getting from the airport or bus terminal to their hotel and back, which is easy to do. Although the whole of Zahedan seems to be one huge marketplace with no particular focus, Bazar-e Ruz is best considered the centre of town.

Information

CONSULATES

Indian Consulate (☎ 322 2337; off Imam Khomeini St; ☾ 9am-1.30pm & 2.30-5pm Sun-Thu) Visas issued in four to five days with a letter from your embassy.

Pakistani Consulate (☎ 322 3389; Pahlavani St; ☾ 9.30am-2.30pm Sat-Wed) No-longer issues visas to non-Iranians; will send you to Tehran.

EMERGENCY

Khatam Hospital (☎ 322 0501; Motahhari Blvd)
Police headquarters (☎ 110) Near the bazaar.

INTERNET ACCESS

Diba Coffeenet (Motahhari Blvd, near Azadi Sq; per hr IR10,000; ☾ 8am-2.30pm & 3-9pm) Not desperately fast.

Esteghlal Grand Hotel Internet Café (Motahhari Blvd, near Azadi Sq; per hr IR15,000) Open on request, maybe.

MONEY

After hours head to the bazaar, where you can also buy Pakistani and Afghan currencies. The Taftan terminal on the Pakistani side of the border offers the best rates for Pakistani currency.

Bank Melli Central Branch (Bank Melli Markazi; Azadi St) Changes US dollars and euros without much fuss.

Bank Saderat (Motahhari Blvd, near Azadi Sq) US dollars and euros changed only between 8am and 1.30pm.

POST & TELEPHONE

International telephone office (Metri-e Kamarbandi St, off Taleqani Sq; ☾ 7.30am-9.30pm) Under the Abuzar Hotel.

Main post office (Emdad St) Better to use the post office in Kerman (p313).

TRAVEL AGENCIES

Khaterat Zahedan Travel (☎ 322 9113; Azadi St)

VISA EXTENSIONS

Some travellers have reported getting help here with recently expired transit visas, but *do not* rely on this. See the boxed text, p395 for details on extending visas.

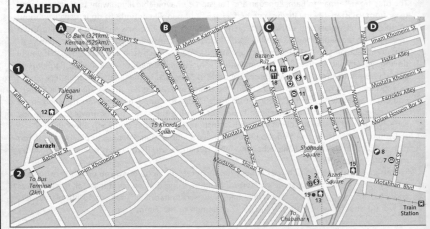

ZAHEDAN

Police Department of Alien Affairs (Motahhari Blvd; ☽ 7am-2pm, closed Fri) Just outside the entrance to the airport, the urbane English-speaking officer of years past has moved on and this office is back to being a bureaucratic event. The middle office will process your application, and extensions should be sorted the same day, or the next. You must deposit your fee at the Bank Melli Central Branch on Azadi St.

Dangers & Annoyances

Zahedan can be dangerous and when we visited it was definitely annoying because almost everywhere we went required a police escort (see the boxed text, p325). At any time it can be a little unsafe at night, and away from the main squares the streets are pretty lonely after dark. Car theft is a problem so if you have a vehicle find a secure place to leave it overnight. Do not venture west of Zahedan in the jagged-looking area known as the Black Mountains, unaccompanied or on foot – they're not known as the Black Mountains for their colour alone.

Sleeping

If you're on a budget, forget Zahedan and head straight through to much-more-pleasant Bam, or Pakistan. When we stayed, foreign guests were banned from Zahedan's cheap hotels (see the boxed text, p325); the first three places wouldn't take foreigners, but this might change. Until it does, your overpriced options are all near Azadi Sq.

Hotel Momtzahirmand (☎ 322 2313; Bazar-e Ruz; s/tw IR45,000/60,000; 🍴) Right in the bazaar, this ultrabasic place is friendly but the plumbing isn't great. To find it, head north along Dr Shariati St from the corner with Imam Khomeini St; take the first left at the edge of the bazaar and it's about 80m along behind a coloured glass door.

Abuzar Hotel (☎ 451 2132; 40 Metri-e Kamarbandi St, off Taleqani Sq; r IR90,000; 🅿 🍴) This well-managed cheapie near the Garazh area, in the west of town, has clean rooms and shared bathrooms and a decent restaurant downstairs.

Kavir Hotel & Restaurant (☎ 326 0137; Motahhari Blvd; s/d IR170,000/250,000; 🅿 🍴) Worn almost to the point of being worn out, and none too clean, avoid the Kavir unless you're an overlander looking for lock-up parking.

Zahedan Tourist Inn (Hotel Jahangardi; ☎ 322 4898; Montazeri St, off Forudgah Sq; r US$47; 🅿 🍴) Away from town but handy if you're en route to or from Pakistan, rooms here are a good size and clean.

Esteghlal Grand Hotel (☎ 323 8068; www.hotelesteghlal.ir; Azadi Sq; s/d/ste IR693,000/988,000/1,386,000 with breakfast; 🅿 🍴 💻) The best place in town by a desert mile, the big Esteghlal has nice-enough three-star rooms with satellite TV, fridge and spotless bathroom.

Eating

There are several good barbecue chicken places around the corner of Dr Shariati and Imam Khomeini streets, and a few *kababis*.

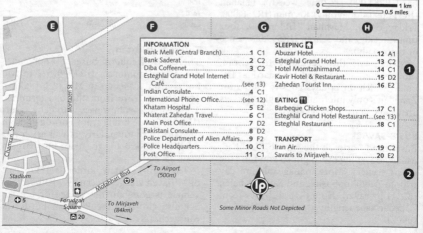

INFORMATION	
Bank Melli (Central Branch)	**1** C1
Bank Saderat	**2** C2
Diba Coffeenet	**3** C2
Esteghlal Grand Hotel Internet Café	(see 13)
Indian Consulate	**4** C1
International Phone Office	(see 12)
Khatam Hospital	**5** E2
Khaterat Zahedan Travel	**6** C1
Main Post Office	**7** D2
Pakistani Consulate	**8** D2
Police Department of Alien Affairs	**9** F2
Police Headquarters	**10** C1
Post Office	**11** C1

SLEEPING 🏠	
Abuzar Hotel	**12** A1
Esteghlal Grand Hotel	**13** C2
Hotel Momtzahirmand	**14** C1
Kavir Hotel & Restaurant	**15** D2
Zahedan Tourist Inn	**16** E2

EATING 🍴	
Barbeque Chicken Shops	**17** C1
Esteghlal Grand Hotel Restaurant	(see 13)
Esteghlal Restaurant	**18** C1

TRANSPORT	
Iran Air	**19** C2
Savaris to Mirjaveh	**20** E2

SOUTHEASTERN IRAN

FROM 'THIEVES' TO 'ASCETICS'... & BACK

Not so long ago Zahedan (meaning 'Ascetics') went under the far-less-inviting name of Dozda (Thieves). The locals offer several explanations for the original name. The more obvious of the two is that the village of Dozda first developed as a place where bandits came to rest. The more romantic version has it that rain soaked straight through the soil, thereby the ground 'stole' the water. Passing through one day, Reza Shah was astonished that, despite its name, the town appeared no more full of thieves than its neighbours. At once he had the name changed to Zahedan in a nod of recognition to the more conspicuous collection of straggly bearded, ascetic-looking men living there.

However, Zahedan's bad reputation seemed fully justified in the days following the Bam earthquake (see p323). No sooner did truckloads of aid arrive than much of it disappeared on *pik-ups* (utilities with canvas covers) going east. Rightly or wrongly, the Baluchis of Zahedan were blamed for stealing as many as 90,000 Iranian Red Crescent tents earmarked for the needy of Bam. And these figures came straight from the government in Tehran.

Other than that, all the hotels have restaurants, with prices reflecting room rates.

Esteghlal Restaurant (☎ 322 2250; Imam Khomeini St; meals IR15,000) Less than no frills, but a decent range of cheap staples in the centre of town. Don't confuse it with...

Esteghlal Grand Hotel (☎ 323 8088; Azadi Sq; meals IR60,000) The indoor/outdoor restaurant out back serves unsurprising but tasty fare in a relaxing setting. The best in town.

Getting There & Away

AIR

Given Zahedan's isolation, flying makes a good alternative to long hours of overland travel. It's also a good idea for northward journeys to Mashhad.

Iran Air (☎ 322 0813/4; Motahhari Blvd), near Azadi Sq, flies from Zahedan to Chabahar (IR284,000, six times weekly), Esfahan (IR512,000, Friday only), Kerman (IR258,000, Friday only), Mashhad (IR436,000, four times weekly) and Tehran (IR599,000, once or twice daily).

Mahan Air flies regularly to Tehran, though you might need to board a Tupolev, which on Fridays goes to Dubai for Zahedan's only international flight. Tickets are available from travel agencies.

BUS & SAVARI

Buses head north all the way to Mashhad, usually travelling overnight so you miss the desert scenery. More manageable are day trips to Zabol (opposite) and Kuh-e Khajeh (p331) by savari. Note that all buses from Zahedan face lengthy stops at checkpoints (p407).

The sprawling terminal in the west of Zahedan is, like so many others in Iran, chaotic in an organised fashion. Buses leave several times a day for the following destinations; longer trips usually leave in the afternoon or evening, for a morning arrival. These days most buses are Volvo or similar (prices here are for Volvos), though if you're prepared to ask around – and wait – a Mercedes will eventually run to most destinations.

Destination	Fare	Duration
Bam	IR20,000	4–6hr
Bandar Abbas	IR50,000	15–18hr
Esfahan	IR90,000	15–19hr
Kerman	IR45,000	6–8hr
Mashhad	IR85,000	13–16hr
Shiraz	IR90,000	15–18hr
Tehran	IR120,000	19–23hr
Yazd	IR65,000	14hr
Zabol	IR12,000	3–4hr

To/From Pakistan

There are frequent buses (IR6000, 1½ hours) and minibuses (IR7500, 1½ to two hours) from Zahedan to Mirjaveh (96km). Most buses leave from the bus terminal. The easiest way, however, is to get a savari (IR20,000, one hour) from Forudgah Sq in the far east of town. Drivers will ask for as much as US$20 for the trip, but bargain your hardest.

The Iran-Pakistan border is 15km east of Mirjaveh village, so clarify whether your vehicle is going to the village or border. See also Crossing the Pakistan Border at Mirjaveh/Taftan, p330.

CAR & MOTORCYCLE

Drivers travelling between Turkey and India often describe the trip between Zahedan and Quetta, across the vast Baluchestan desert, as the worst leg of their journey. The road from Quetta to the Iranian border is barren and lonely, with few facilities and a risk of bandits; consider driving in convoy once on the Pakistan side.

The clearly signposted road between Zahedan and Kerman is good, but short on facilities. Take plenty of water and make sure your vehicle is in good order or risk a potentially long and unpleasant wait for repairs. Petrol is available in Mirjaveh (20L maximum), Zahedan and Fahraj (between Zahedan and Bam).

TRAIN

The new train line linking Bam and Zahedan should open by 2009. Check Raja Trains (www.rajatrains.com) for updates.

To/From Pakistan

The long, remote, dusty, sometimes cold and often uncomfortable train trip between Zahedan and Quetta, in Pakistan, is guaranteed to be a story you'll tell until you die. If you're someone who enjoys meeting people, isn't fussed by hardship (carriages are simple with wooden seats and no sleepers) and has plenty of time, you'll probably enjoy it. If not, take the bus.

Iran and Pakistan have plans to increase cross-border trains between Zahedan and Quetta when the line to Bam is finished (see To the Orient By Train, p404), until then the train is supposed to leave on the 3rd and 17th of every month by the Western calendar at 8.30am, *insh'Allah* (if God wills it). It usually does, but do call the not-exactly-overworked stationmaster in Zahedan's attractive **train station** (☎ 322 4142) to double-check; mornings are best. The trip is scheduled to take 30 hours, but as reader Michael von Kuelmer reported, two days is more likely:

'The speed is 20 to 30km/h, great for viewing and taking pictures. We needed c 47 hours for the whole trip, including about five hours at the border. You can use that time for shopping in Taftan (we bought blankets). Armed guards accompany you on the Pakistani side. The whole staff of the train (more staff than passengers) was very friendly, handshaking with the driver included! The train stops in villages on the way, which gives you the opportunity to meet unbelievably nice people there. It's a ride you won't forget but with warm clothes and enough food and drink it's a pleasant journey as well! And don't be put off if the train is leaving late; ours left with half-a-day delay. It's holiday – you are not in a hurry!'

You pay in rial to Taftan (IR12,000), and in rupees from Taftan to Quetta. Alternatively, you could get yourself across the border and get on the train in Taftan.

Getting Around

A private taxi between the airport and town will cost about IR15,000, if you bargain hard.

You'll be lucky to get a private taxi for less than about IR5000, and from the bazaar to the terminal expect to pay IR7000. Shuttle taxis are available along the main roads for about IR1500 a trip. Around town taxis cost about IR20,000 an hour.

ZABOL   زابل
☎ 0542 / pop 128,000

North of Zahedan, Zabol is a dusty frontier town that's sufficiently close to the Afghanistan border – and far enough away from Tehran – that it's full of smugglers, illicit goods, big-bearded Afghans and the ever-present suggestion of drugs, especially opium. As you wander through the bazaar it becomes clear this is no ordinary town. There are all manner of smuggled goods for sale and there's a good chance you'll see pungent opium smoke wafting out from behind curtained-off sections of stall.

The town has been inhabited for millennia and is known in Iran as the birthplace of Rostam, the mythical hero of Ferdosi's epic poem the Shahnameh. There's little of great historical interest left, though a newly opened **museum** (Ferdosi St; ☼ Sat-Thu) has a small display of archaeological finds. It's housed in the old British consulate, built in 1899, east of the bazaar and opposite the Amin Hotel. Hours are flexible (ie it opens when they feel like it).

Combined with a trip to Kuh-e Khajeh (opposite), and perhaps a brief stop at **Shahr-e Sokhta** (the Burnt City, 56km south of Zabol), Zabol makes a good day trip from Zahedan. How much company you'll have depends on the security situation at the time (see the boxed text, p325). Whatever the situation, they don't see many foreigners out here, so you'll probably stand out. Keep your best weapon – a smile – at the ready.

Sleeping & Eating

Hotel Amin (☎ 222 2823; Ferdosi St; s/tw IR85,000/ 125,000; P) The family-run Amir, near the bazaar, is a good budget sleeping option. English isn't spoken (and there's no English sign) but staff is happy to help and you can use the kitchen. It's about 400m east of Imam Khomeini St, on the northern side of the street – look for the green front and a small yellow sign.

Hotel Aram (☎ 229 5400; Rostam Sq; r IR310,000; ☒) For more luxury, this hotel outside the terminal has squat bathrooms, TV and fridge to go with its pink interior and unmissable octagonal green-glass façade.

For food, there's the usual range of utilitarian *kababis*, pizza, barbeque chicken and sandwich joints.

Getting There & Away

Mahan Air flies between Zabol and Tehran on Tuesdays and Fridays.

Arriving from Zahedan by bus (IR10,000, three to five hours) you'll stop at the new bus terminal, off Rostam Sq (look for the giant statue of Rostam on his trusty steed Rakhsh). Buses leave here for Mashhad (IR60,000, 12 to 15 hours) and all manner of other places, including Tehran. From Zahedan, you're far better off taking a savari (IR25,000, two hours, 216km) if you want to be back in a day.

Savaris leave from Zahedan for Zabol every half-hour or so from 50m west of the Abuzar Hotel (p327), and in our experience the drivers tend to take a disturbingly fatalistic approach to driving. You must bring your passport; if you don't bring your passport the driver won't take you. And there's a good chance you'll have a police escort the whole way.

CROSSING THE PAKISTAN BORDER AT MIRJAVEH/TAFTAN

Crossing the border between Iran and Pakistan at Taftan is a relatively painless process – the painful part is the trip to Quetta. Getting to the border from Zahedan or Mirjaveh is simple, but be aware that Pakistan is 90 minutes ahead of Iran (or maybe just 30 minutes if Iran reinstitutes daylight-saving in summer), meaning the border closes at 4.30pm (Iranian time) in winter, sometimes earlier (1½ hours before sundown). The border usually opens around sunrise Iranian time (about 7am).

Travellers get preferential treatment on both sides so the whole process rarely takes longer than an hour. American travellers might have to undergo a brief but polite interview about their itinerary. People with vehicles have reported similarly smooth crossings.

To change money you will probably have to deal with one of the sharks who circle around both sides of the border. If you don't know the exchange rates you *will* be ripped off, so check them before you arrive or ask someone crossing in the other direction.

Taftan has been described, not unfairly, as hell on earth, especially in summer. On the upside, it's no worse than Zahedan and you don't need a police escort everywhere you go. Buses for Quetta (350 rupees, 617km) leave in the morning (usually before 10am) and afternoon (between about 3pm and 6pm), or whenever they fill to bursting point. If all goes according to plan the bus takes from 11 to 16 hours, so the later evening buses are best if you don't want to arrive in Quetta in the middle of the night. Readers suggest the buses waiting around the square in Taftan are better than those parked at the border itself. A Toyota taxi makes the same trip in 12 to 15 hours for 4000 rupees, or 1000 rupees a seat. From Quetta, most buses depart between 2pm and 6pm.

Coming into Iran, once the paperwork is finished a free shuttle bus will drop you at the edge of the border compound, from where you wait for a *pik-up*/minibus/savari to fill and leave for Mirjaveh or Zahedan. You'll be asked for about IR40,000 per seat in a savari to Zahedan.

If you get stuck at the border, staying in Taftan is preferable to Mirjaveh. Taftan's Tourist Hotel charges about 600 rupees a night, and another hotel costs 150 rupees.

KUH-E KHAJEH   کوه خواجه

The flat-topped mountain that is **Kuh-e Khajeh** rises out of a wide, flat expanse of Sistan that is desolate in winter but swathed in green in spring and summer. It's then that water from the Hirmand River feeds into the lake bed to become the attractive Lake Hamun, though when we last visited only a fraction of the lake had filled. Locals blame water-intensive opium production operations upriver in Afghanistan for 'stealing' their water, and by consequence the 200 or so migratory bird species once found here.

The main attraction is the remains of an ancient town, the crumbling mud-brick dwellings stepping steeply up to the top of the mountain. The town was originally built during the Parthian era, but what remains is thought to date from Sassanid times. Wandering through the arches and squares you'll almost certainly be alone, unless it's a Friday when Zabolis like to picnic nearby. If you have a vehicle, a rough road runs up to the top of the mountain, where there are several more ancient buildings, panoramic views and a radar station; don't take any photos.

On Fridays, the minibus from Zabol runs all the way to Kuh-e Khajeh. At other times it will probably stop in Kuh-e Khajeh village and you'll have to walk the last 4km along a flat, straight road that turns into a causeway at the edge of town. You're unlikely to be troubled by traffic. The minibus runs every 45 minutes or so, takes about 40 minutes and leaves from Mir Hosseini St, just south of the junction with Kargar Blvd – opposite and a bit south of where the savaris from Zahedan stop. If you don't fancy Zabol, ask the savari from Zahedan to drop you at the turn-off to Kuh-e Khajeh – it's on the left about 6km south of Zabol, just before a bridge.

MIRJAVEH   میرجاوه

☎ 0543

Anyone travelling between Iran and Pakistan by land will pass through Mirjaveh. Locals assure us there is little that interests them in Mirjaveh, so there won't be anything to interest travellers. And they're right. There is a hotel if you're desperate, though barely anyone actually stays here. The ITTO-run **Mirjaveh Tourist Inn** (Hotel Ali; ☎ 322 2486; s/tw IR50,000/90,000; Ⓟ Ⓧ) was described by one reader as looking 'like a ghost hotel', it was so quiet. But it is cheap, and you will be desperate, so the room will be welcome. Overlanders can park up in the gated yard for IR40,000.

From Mirjaveh, there is always something about to go to the border or to Zahedan (bus/minibus IR6000/7500, 1½ to two hours, 96km), from where buses go to almost every major city in Iran.

Northeastern Iran
ایران شمال شرقی

Sandwiched between the vast desert emptiness of the Dasht-e Kavir and the steppes of Central Asia, northeastern Iran has a spine of mountains that become more lushly forested as you head west. East of Minudasht the wilderness has been declared the Golestan (Paradise) National Park. Above the overdeveloped Caspian coast rise more forests and the grand Alborz Mountains. A trio of beautiful but busy roads take you across that dramatic range but there are lesser-known alternatives that get you into more remote, less spoilt zones around Alasht and Baladeh. Historically, the area developed as Khorasan (Where the [Iranian] Sun Rises) and Tabarestan/Mazandaran (the southeastern Caspian littoral). Millennia of culture reached a zenith here around 1000 years ago, producing many of the era's great scientists and poet-philosophers. But the 13th- and 14th-century ravages of the Mongols and then Tamerlane were so complete that Tabarestan's settled civilisation was virtually wiped out. Even now the sites of several once-prosperous cities are mere undulations in the steppe. A few marvellously over engineered towers, most astonishingly at Radkan and Gonbad-e Kavus, are the last witnesses of former glories.

The 16th-century Safavid regime's move towards formal state Shiism was a major factor in the growth of Mashhad from a shrine-village to the region's foremost city. Mashhad's extraordinarily grand Haram-e Razavi complex surrounding the tomb of Imam Reza remains Iran's holiest site and draws millions of pilgrims each year. Mashhad is also the logical staging point for visiting Afghanistan or Turkmenistan. But rather than face the bureaucratic hassles of the latter, consider exploring northeastern Iran's own culturally Turkmen areas north of Kalaleh or Gorgan.

HIGHLIGHTS

- Feel the emotion of pilgrims at Mashhad's glorious **Haram-e Razavi** (p354), the Holy Shrine of Imam Reza
- See the magnificent Alborz Mountains at their peaceful best by driving the little-known mountain road through **Baladeh** (p334) to Pol-e Zanguleh
- Go horse-riding and sleep in a Turkmen *öy* (yurt) tent at the **Gharra Tappeh Sheikh** (p343) stud farm
- Ask yourself if a forerunner of NASA didn't help build the incredible 1000-year-old tower Mil-e Gonbad in **Gonbad-e Kavus** (p342)
- Hike across the bald Binalud mountains to the splendid stepped village of **Kang** (p363), nicknamed 'Mashhad's Masuleh'
- Enjoy an incredible Caspian panorama as you wind up through ridge-top forests towards a 'secret valley' hiding the lonely **West Radkan Tower** (p341)

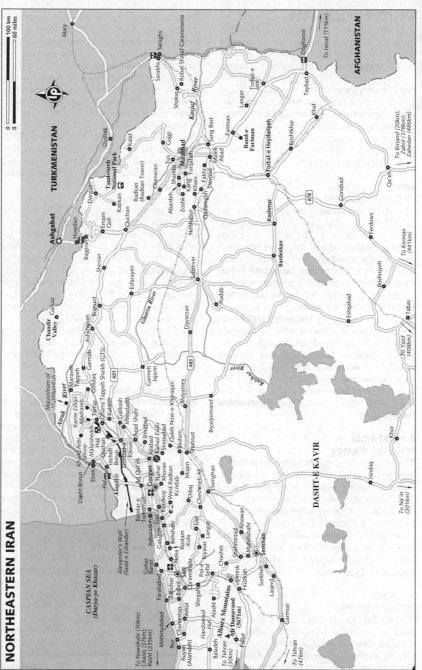

WESTERN MAZANDARAN

A traffic-clogged semi-urban sprawl follows the Caspian's south coast virtually without interruption, except for a fairly pitiful forest reserve at Sisingan. Iranian tourists love the area's rainy climate but few Western tourists find the coast's drizzle and dirty dark-sand beaches a great attraction. The lush green mountain hinterland is contrastingly attractive, with white-top Alborz peaks forming an impressive if distant panorama viewed between Qa'emshahr and Amol (clouds permitting).

Amol   آمل

☎ 0121 / pop 204,000

This drearily characterless sprawl was the capital of Tabarestan (ancient Mazandaran) for a millennium. Sadly, today it retains just a sprinkling of half-forgotten old tomb towers hidden away in unexciting suburban lanes north of the bazaar. **Gonbad Mir Heydar Amoli** (off Andisheh 49th Alley) and the bigger 1623 **Gonbad Mir Bozorg Qarameddin Marashi** (off Mofateh St; admission free). Near the old bridge, the ageing **Mehmankhaneh Tehran** (☎ 222 4534; Beheshti St; s/tw/tr/q IR40,000/70,000/90,000/100,000) is basic but clean-enough. Transport to Tehran, Babol, Sari and Baladeh (IR12,000, two hours, 8am and 2pm only) uses the **terminal** (near Hezar Sangat Sq), way out at Imam Reza St's eastern end. For destinations west, savaris use **Istgah Mahmudabad** (Talib Ahmoli St).

Around Amol

TEHRAN TO AMOL

The tiresomely busy **Haraz mountain road** is less spectacular than the Karaj–Chalus route but skirts right around Fuji-shaped Mt Damavand, which is very briefly visible from west-facing windows when passing through **Pollur** (65km from Tehran). A long, dramatic canyon follows. Above **Vana** (65km before Amol), a long waterfall pours out of cleft cliffs topped by what look like ancient fortress ruins.

BALADEH   بلده

☎ 0122 / pop 9000

A peaceful, lonely road leaves the Haraz road at an isolated tea-shack called Hardowrud. Passing close to Azad Kuh's awesomely vertical north face near **Kalak**, the road zigzags up through some of Iran's very

finest mountain scenery before eventually meeting the Chalus–Tehran road at the lonely Pol-e Zanguleh restaurant.

Baladeh is the only village en route to have accommodation or shops. A 15-minute scramble above Nuri Blvd, 8th Alley, the reasonably extensive towers and fortifications of **Baladeh Castle** offer a fabulous panorama across the fine mountain-backed valley.

Some 10km west in **Yush**, the intriguing **Nima Yushi House** (☎ 433 3491; admission IR3000) has been partly restored, safeguarding fireplaces, chunky plaster-work designs and some multicoloured orosi windows. **Saeed Jamshidi** (☎ 433 3315) has the key.

The route west of Yush is spectacular and delightfully peaceful (only 9km is unasphalted). Azad Kuh's vertical north face is spectacularly visible from **Kalak** (closest approach) and **Khisen**. Between these hamlets, there's a wonderful panorama that incorporates **Mt Damavand** as a conical jewel among a whole collection of mountain peaks: look east approaching **Pil** (28km west of Baladeh). After Khisen the road zigzags up a pass and into an astonishingly vast bowl of white-topped mountains. Fine scenery continues to Pol-e Zanguleh, an isolated restaurant at the junction with the Chalus–Karaj road (p176).

Sleeping & Eating

Mehmanpazir Saeed (☎ 422 3426; Nuri Blvd; s/tw/tr IR50,000/70,000/80,000) Very basic rooms are attached to a sporadically open restaurant in Baladeh village centre. No showers.

Mehmankhaneh Nima (☎ 422 4992; Yush rd; d/tr/ste IR150,000/200,000/500,000) A rural restaurant-teahouse set idyllically above the fork of two mountain streams 3km west of Baladeh. However, its poorly maintained rooms with grotty shared bathrooms are vastly overpriced.

Getting There & Away

Baladeh to Amol buses (IR12,000, two hours) leave at 9am and 1.30pm, with buses to Tehran (via Hardowrud) departing at the same times. The only public transport along the dramatic road via Pil is the daily Tehran–Yush bus leaving Tehran's Chahara Sirus at 5am and returning from Yush around 10am. Rates offered by Baladeh's **taxi agency** (☎ 422 3342; Nuri Blvd) include Yush (single/return IR20,000/30,000), Pol-e Zanguleh (IR120,000), Chalus (IR200,000) and Nur (IR140,000). Very sparse traffic makes hitch hiking unreliable.

Babol بابل
☎ 0111 / pop 208,000
If passing through this busy commercial centre, you could visit **Babol Museum** (☎ 229 2877; Modarres St; admission IR2000; ☾ 8am-2pm & 4-8pm), an attractive colonial-style mansion containing a few ethnographic displays, antique saddles, and dervish paraphernalia. **Marjan Hotel** (☎ 225 0433; fax 225 2189; Keshvari Sq; s/d/tr/q US$30/40/47/54) is a well-tended midrange place, albeit with slightly ageing bathrooms. Eastbound savaris depart from outside once the **Sari terminal** (Qa'emshahr Blvd) closes after

6pm. Westbound, use **Istgah Amol** (Amol Hwy), 2km west of the centre.

SARI ساری
☎ 0151 / pop 262,000
Large but manageable and gently attractive, Sari spent much of the 1st millennium AD as the capital of Tabarestan. After losing ground to Amol, Sari returned to prominence following the building of the railway from Tehran, and became Mazandaran's provincial capital in 1937.

Orientation
The town radiates out from Sa'at (Times) Sq, named for its whitewashed clock tower that looks particularly cute when floodlit

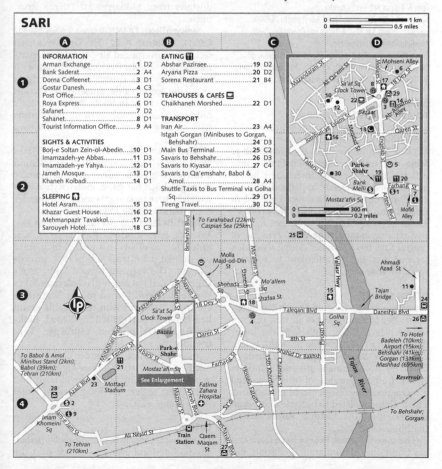

SARI

INFORMATION
Arman Exchange...................1 D2
Bank Saderat.........................2 A4
Dorna Coffeenet....................3 D1
Gostar Danesh.......................4 C3
Post Office.............................5 D2
Roya Express.........................6 D1
Safanet..................................7 D2
Sahanet.................................8 D1
Tourist Information Office.......9 A4

SIGHTS & ACTIVITIES
Borj-e Soltan Zein-ol-Abedin...10 D1
Imamzadeh-ye Abbas.............11 D3
Imamzadeh-ye Yahya.............12 D1
Jameh Mosque......................13 D1
Khaneh Kolbadi.....................14 D1

SLEEPING
Hotel Asram..........................15 D3
Khazar Guest House...............16 D2
Mehmanpazir Tavakkol..........17 D1
Sarouyeh Hotel......................18 C3

EATING
Abshar Paziraee....................19 D2
Aryana Pizza.........................20 D2
Sorena Restaurant 21 B4

TEAHOUSES & CAFÉS
Chaikhaneh Morshed.............22 D1

TRANSPORT
Iran Air.................................23 A4
Istgah Gorgan (Minibuses to Gorgan, Behshahr).........................24 D3
Main Bus Terminal.................25 C2
Savaris to Behshahr...............26 D3
Savaris to Kiyasar..................27 C4
Savaris to Qa'emshahr, Babol & Amol.................................28 A4
Shuttle Taxis to Bus Terminal via Golha Sq.................................29 D1
Tireng Travel.........................30 D2

at night. A few remnant gabled homes in traditional Mazandarani style *(sofal)* are to be found in nearby lanes.

Information

Arman Exchange (Farhang St; 🕙 9am-1.30pm & 4-7pm Sat-Thu) No-fuss moneychangers.

Bank Saderat (Imam Khomeini Sq; 🕙 9.30am-1.30pm Sat-Thu) Exchange desk.

Dorna Coffeenet (Sa'at Sq; per hr IR8000; 🕙 8am-10pm Sat-Thu, 4-10pm Fri) Faster internet connection than nearby Safanet across the square.

Gostar Danesh (Taleqani Blvd; per hr IR8000; 🕙 8am-9pm) Good connection; type to the sound of fizzing neon.

Post office (Enqelab St; 🕙 7.30am-2pm Sat-Wed, 7.30am-1pm Thu)

Roya Express (☎ 325 7720; Mohseni Alley; 🕙 8am-1pm & 4-8pm Sat-Thu) Laundry.

Sahanet (☎ 221 0978; Mofid Alley; per hr IR7000; 🕙 9am-10pm Sat-Thu, 4-10pm Fri) Downstairs with excellent internet connection.

Tourist information office (Edareh Miras Ferhangi; ☎ 229 1001; Jam-e Jam St; 🕙 8am-2pm Sat-Thu) Some guide pamphlets are available, mostly in Farsi.

Sights

TOMB TOWERS

Sari has three famous 15th-century brick tomb towers, all active places of worship. Tucked behind the bazaar, **Imamzadeh-ye Yahya** is a round Rhenish-looking tower onto which a discordant rectilinear new building has been carelessly appended. Within are monstrous chandeliers over a glassed-in sarcophagus. Just behind, **Borj-e Soltan Zein-ol-Abedin** has a square plan and more impressive exterior. **Imamzadeh-ye Abbas**, 2km east of central Sari, has fine inner doors, a wooden sarcophagus and an attendant to sprinkle you with rose water.

OTHER SIGHTS

The restored 125-year-old **Khaneh Kolbadi** (Ab-Anbarno Alley) is reminiscent of an 18th-century khan's palace. Thick walls kept the lower floor warm in winter while the light, bright upper floor could be opened to through drafts for hot summers. Its *orosi* windows (wood-framed puzzles of multicoloured glass) supposedly disorientated mosquitoes. The building is slated to become a museum incorporating the historic **Vasir-e Hamam** (bathhouse) behind.

The unusual **Jameh Mosque** (in the bazaar area) has traditional Mazandarani tiled roofs, but

from outside looks more like a medieval Italian prison.

Sleeping

Khazar Guest House (☎ 222 7231; Jomhuri-ye Eslami St; s/d/tr/q IR35,000/48,500/57,500/71,000) The backyard location looks initially pleasant but walls, ceilings and especially the upper-balcony are all twisted alarmingly off-line. Pillowcases desperately need laundering and whiffy squat toilets are shared.

Mehmanpazir Tavakkol (Sa'at Sq; tw/tr/q IR70,000/100,000/150,000) Clean shared facilities include a shower that sometimes runs hot. Rooms are predictably basic with rock–hard beds and a tap in some rooms. It's friendly, if 100% male, and very central, accessed upstairs from Modarres St. There's Road noise.

Sarouyeh Hotel (☎ 324 5600; Danesh St; s/tw/tr from IR12 0,000/140,000/160,000; P 🔀) The Sarouyeh's hotel section has overpriced air-conditioned apartments (twins/triples IR410,000/470,000) with kitchenettes and droopy curtains. However, the good-value guesthouse section (where the check-in booth is unexpectedly hidden) has sensibly priced fan rooms with small attached bathrooms, towels and top-sheets.

Hotel Asram (☎ 325 5090; fax 325 5092; Valiasr Hwy; s/tw/tr/ste US$35/45/50/55; P 🔀 🖳) Behind a mirrored-glass façade, this professionally managed hotel has good, motel-style rooms with lift, three restaurants and a sauna under construction. Some English is spoken.

Hotel Badeleh (☎ /fax 422 2548; Gorgan Hwy, Angilasam; tw/ste US$65/90; P 🔀) Sari's best hotel (for now) sits in a lush garden amid ivy-draped palm trees, 10km east towards Gorgan. The varnished-wood lobby looks slightly dated but a new glass elevator takes you to fully refurbished rooms. The suites are truly luxurious with remarkably grand bed-heads in part-gilded hardwood. Bathrooms are OK but less impressive. Very friendly.

Two new hotels are under construction on the Qa'emshahr–Gorgan highway. The very grand-looking Hotel Navid is around 10km west of Sari; the more modest Hotel Arab is 4km east.

Eating

Downmarket snack-bars and *kababis* (kabab shops) line Jomhuri-ye Eslami St near the bazaar. Several nicer restaurants lie around a kilometre further on along Azadi Blvd.

Chaikhaneh Morshed (Jomhuri-ye Eslami St; qalyan from IR5000; ☺ 9am-midnight) Easily-missed steps southeast of Dadgar Alley lead up to this semi traditional teahouse. Décor is tasteful apart from the cigarette-smoking stuffed lamb. The boisterous clientele of rockabilly-style 20-something males might get over-excited by a female presence.

Abshar Paziraee (Park-e Shahr; snack meals IR5500-12,000; ☺ 8am-11pm) Marked with a neon swan and a goofy Mr Bean mural, this simple, sunny snack bar is ideal for fresh juices or ice creams while watching the park fountains.

Aryana Pizza (☎ 222 0322; Farhang St; pizzas IR23,000-30,000; ☺ 11am-midnight) This inviting, larger-than-average, new fast-food restaurant has pizzas with excellent, light crusts. For dessert, try the grand pastry-shop eatery next door.

Sorena Restaurant (☎ 222 7069; Ferdosi St; meals IR30,000-60,000; ☺ 11am-3pm & 7-11.30pm) Bright, spacious middle-class *kababi* with big fire-places and fake roses on the tables. Fish dishes are sizeable but laced with bones. Vampires should avoid *zirtoshi*, a side-dish of whole pickled garlic (IR5000).

Getting There & Away

AIR

Iran Air (☎ 226 9400; Azadi Blvd; ☺ 7.30am-4pm Sat-Thu, 8am-noon Fri) flies thrice-weekly to both Tehran (IR315,000) and Mashhad (IR345,000). Tickets are also sold by friendly, English-speaking agency **Tireng Travel** (☎ 222 7973; tirengsary@yahoo.com; Tabarsi St; ☺ 8am-6pm Sat-Thu).

BUS & MINIBUS

From the **main terminal** (northeastern ring rd) regular buses run to Rasht (IR40,000, seven hours) via the coastal cities and to Tehran (IR40,000, five hours) via Amol. Most services to Mashhad (Volvo IR60,000, 11 hours) depart around 7am or 6pm. There's one Taavoni 2 bus to Semnan (via Kiyasar) at 8am. Alternatively, savari-hop via Qa'emshahr.

Savaris to Qa'emshahr (IR2000), Babol (IR5000) and Amol (10,000) leave from Imam Khomeini Sq.

Minibuses/savaris to Gorgan (IR8000/20,000) and Behshahr (IR2500/6000, 45 minutes) use **Istgah Gorgan** (Daneshju Blvd).

Savaris for Kiyasar start across the railway on Keshavarz Blvd. From Kiyasar to

Damghan you'll usually have to pay *dar baste* (closed door).

TRAIN

To travel the trans-Alborz line in daylight, take the 9.10am train *from* Tehran. Trains *to* Tehran run overnight (IR13,750 to IR32,500).

Getting Around

The airport is 15km northeast (IR15,000 by taxi). Shuttle taxis (IR750) start from relevant points around Sa'at Sq. For the bus terminal, use eastbound cars along 18 Dey St that swing north at Golha Sq. For the train station, jump out at the southern end of Artesh Blvd where southbound vehicles turn left.

AROUND SARI
Sari to Tehran

From formless **Qa'emshahr**, another over-busy mountain road climbs up towards the Iranian plateau via Firuzkuh. Scenery starts lush and forested with distant white-topped peaks on the horizon. South of **Pol-e-Sefid** it rises through deep valleys and many a tunnel, shadowing the incredible **trans-Alborz railway**. Building that line was one of the most incredible engineering achievements of the 1930s, as much a political statement by Reza Shah as a means of transport. Arguably it's more attractive to look *at* the line switchbacking up the steep valleys than to actually take the train. The classic glimpse is the 66m-span stone bridge, 110m above **Veresk** village.

Around 15km south of Pol-e Sefid, a peaceful side road branches off towards Shahmir-zad (p348). Scenery is lovely apart from a few unsightly quarries, but there's an un-paved section and a single, rather deep ford. No public transport.

Alasht آلاشت
☎ 0124 / pop 4000

Commanding a wonderfully wide panorama of wooded ridges and peaks across a deep mountain valley, **Alasht** is an increasingly popular summer retreat. It gets deep snows in winter but looks great in spring blossom or autumnal blaze. Alasht's unusual **mosque** has contemporary twin minarets but its central fluted cone-spire tops a central tower that supposedly started life as an ancient church.

Towards the base of the village amid lanes of partly mud-and-timber homes (some with timber-shingled roofs held down by rocks) is the **Khaneh Shah**, a slightly grander house in which Reza Shah Pahlavi was born (1877). Several of the photogenic, moustachioed old men who ride donkeys around the village claim family links with the ex-shah.

Right beside the mosque, the comfortable new **Mosaferkhaneh Darreh** (☎ 533 2022; tw/apt IR250,000/500,000) has great if partly wire-cut views across the valley. The upper apartment includes a spacious sitting room and balcony with barbeque.

Alasht is 35km off the Qa'emshahr–Tehran road, starting 4km south of Pol-e-Sefid, from which taxis want IR60,000/90,000 one way/return. The nicest way to reach Pol-e Sefid from Sari is on the 7.30am local train (IR2000, 1½ hours). Pay onboard.

Behshahr بهشهر

☎ 0152 / pop 78,000

Marginally interesting **Behshahr** was once an R&R getaway for Safavid Shah Abbas I, who built the town's perky little **Safiabad Palace** (Kakh-e Safi Abad; ☽ closed to public) and central **Bagh-e-Shahr** (Shah's Garden; ☽ dawn-6pm). All that remains of his **Abbasabad** pavilion is an arched brick platform in a landscaped lake amid pretty wooded hills (8km east, then 3km inland). In otherwise unprepossessing **Rostam Kola village** (7km west), you could seek out the well-preserved **Farahi Hosseinieh**, a private traditional Mazandarani homestead.

Savaris to Sari (IR6000) and Gorgan (IR10,000) leave from opposite ends of Behshahr town. With your own transport, avoid the thundering main road east of Galugah by using the quietly attractive 'old-road'. For information on Kordkuy, see p341.

GORGAN گرگان

☎ 0171 / pop 253,000

This appealing city has a colourful, ethnically mixed population and an attractive location where the green Alborz Mountains stoop to meet the northeastern steppe. Gorgan was the birthplace of 'eunuch-king' Aga Mohammad who founded the expansionist Qajar dynasty (1779–1925). Architectural heritage is relatively limited but Gorgan makes a fine base for visiting the Turkmen steppes, Golestan's forested mountains or the remote Mil-e Radkan tower (p341).

Orientation

From the bazaar area around Shahrdari (Vahdat) Sq, vibrant Valiasr St leads several kilometres southeast towards Nahar Khoran, an appealingly semi rural scattering of woodland restaurants and hotels. **Honar Stationery** (☽ 7am-2pm & 5-9.30pm Sat-Thu, 7am-2pm Fri) sells reasonably detailed city maps (IR12,500).

Information

Arpa Coffeenet (Valiasr St; internet per hr IR7000; ☽ 9am-3.30pm & 5.30-10.30pm) Near Edalat 10th St.

Golestan Miras (☎ 226 1802; Taqavi House, Taqavi Lane; ☽ 8am-2pm Sat-Thu) Cultural-tourist office. Occupies a splendid, part-renovated 19th-century merchant's house. Plentiful colourful brochures.

Hoshkshuye Asia (☎ 222 6420; Beheshti St; ☽ 8am-2pm & 4.30-8pm Sat-Thu) Laundry. Corner of Behesht 7th Alley.

International telephone office (Beheshti 2nd Alley; ☽ 7am-9.30pm Sat-Thu, 8am-2pm & 4-9.30pm Fri)

Police Foreign Affairs Department (Niwentisdam Atboye Khoreji; ☎ 218 2648; Molaghaty St; ☽ 8am-2pm Sat-Thu) Visa extensions. Staff are helpful despite being sometimes overloaded with Central Asian applicants. Apply by 9.30am; collect around noon. The office is two short blocks from the big Bank Melli tower where you need to pay the IR100,000 fee.

Tourist Exchange (☎ 232 1929; Valiasr St at Edalat 23rd St; ☽ 9am-1pm & 5-9pm) Painless moneychanging.

Sights

Built around a quadrangle in the **bazaar**, the attractive 15th-century **Jameh Mosque** (off Aftab 27th Lane) has blue-tiled portals, sections of traditionally tiled roof and a distinctive Mazandarani-style capped minaret.

Imamzadeh-ye Nur, accessed via Aftab 15th Alley, is a 15th-century brick tomb tower of relatively minor interest, but finding it is a great excuse to poke around Gorgan's most interesting old alleys. The magnificent **Taqavi House** (Taqavi Lane) houses the Golestan Miras cultural-tourist office. Ask to peep inside the 'eight-wife' harem building.

Gorgan Museum (☎ 222 2364; Shohoda St; admission IR3000; ☽ 8am-6pm) has limited, dusty ethnological exhibits, and displays sparse finds from local archaeological sites such as Jorjan (Gonbad-e Kavus) and Turang Tappeh (a large tumulus 22km northeast of Gorgan). The still-growing **Imamzadeh Abdollah** (Shohada Sq) contains dazzling mirror work. Its large blue dome looks especially photogenic viewed through trees from near the bus terminal against a distant backdrop of seasonally snow-topped ridges.

The forest paths of **Nahar Khoran** offer an easy clean-air escape, albeit crowded with weekenders and adorned with litter. The road continues several kilometres through **Ziyarat**. This once-picturesque village has suffered an extensive building boom but remains idyllically set with views up through a cleft green valley to high ridges behind.

Sleeping

BUDGET

Guri Camping (☎ 553 0248; Valiasr St km6; pre-erected tents IR30,000; ☼ No Ruz & summer only) Outside the Guri restaurant-teahouse, a row of seasonal tents are filled on a first-come, first-served basis: there are no reservations. Bring mat and sleeping bag.

Hotel Pars (☎ 222 9550; First Alley, off Panzhdah Metri 2nd Alley; s/tw/tr/q IR52,000/71,000/85,000/100,000) Set around a pleasant courtyard of orange trees, this clean, central yet surprisingly peaceful *mosaferkhaneh* (cheap hotel) lies just a minute's walk from Shahrdari Sq. Ali, the gregarious, philosophical owner, speaks great English, having lived in the UK for nine years.

Hotel Razi (☎ 222 4613; s/tw/tr IR50,000/70,000/80,000, tw with shower IR89,000) Opposite Hotel Pars, this is almost as good.

Hotel Tourist (☎ 335 3797; Jorjan Blvd; tw/tr IR100,000/120,000) These simple, newly tiled rooms have sinks, slightly musty shower booths and ageing beds. Squat toilets are shared. It's close to Istgah Gonbad and rather noisy.

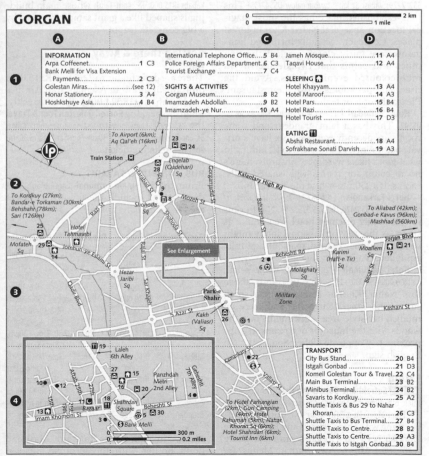

GORGAN

0 — 2 km
0 — 1 mile

INFORMATION
Arpa Coffeenet................................1 C3
Bank Melli for Visa Extension
Payments....................................2 C3
Golestan Miras.........................(see 12)
Honar Stationery............................3 A4
Hoshkshuye Asia............................4 B4
International Telephone Office.....5 B4
Police Foreign Affairs Department..6 C3
Tourist Exchange 7 C4

SIGHTS & ACTIVITIES
Gorgan Museum.............................8 B2
Imamzadeh Abdollah.....................9 B2
Imamzadeh-ye Nur......................10 A4

Jameh Mosque............................11 A4
Taqavi House...............................12 A4

SLEEPING 🛏
Hotel Khayyam...........................13 A4
Hotel Maroof...............................14 A3
Hotel Pars...................................15 B4
Hotel Razi...................................16 B4
Hotel Tourist 17 D3

EATING 🍴
Absha Restaurant.......................18 A4
Sofrakhane Sonati Darvish.........19 A3

To Airport (6km);
Aq Qal'eh (16km)

Train Station

Enqelab
(Qadehari)
Sq

Kalantary High Rd

To Kordkuy (27km);
Bandar-e Torkaman (30km);
Behshahr (78km);
Sari (126km)

Shohoda
Sq

Mozeh St

To Aliabad (42km);
Gonbad-e Kavus (96km);
Mashhad (560km)

Hotel
Tahmasebi

Jorjan Blvd

Mofateh
Sq

Moallem
Sq

Karimi
(Haft-e Tir)

Beheshti Rd

See Enlargement

Hezar
Jaribi
Sq

Molaghaty
Sq

Park-e
Shahr

Military
Zone

Kashani St

Kakh
(Valiasr)
Sq

TRANSPORT
City Bus Stand............................20 B4
Istgah Gonbad 21 D3
Komeil Golestan Tour & Travel...22 C4
Main Bus Terminal......................23 B2
Minibus Terminal........................24 B2
Savaris to Kordkuy.....................25 A2
Shuttle Taxis & Bus 29 to Nahar
Khoran.....................................26 C3
Shuttle Taxis to Bus Terminal.....27 B4
Shuttle Taxis to Centre...............28 B2
Shuttle Taxis to Centre...............29 A3
Shuttle Taxis to Istgah Gonbad...30 B4

Laleh
6th Alley

Panzhdah
Metri
2nd Alley

Shahrdari
Square

Beheshti St

Bazaar

Imam Khomeini St

Bank Melli

To Hotel Farhangian
(2km); Guri Camping
(4km); Hotel
Rahumah (5km); Nahar
Khoran Sq (6km);
Hotel Shahrdari (6km);
Tourist Inn (6km)

300 m
0.2 miles

Hotel Khayyam (☎ 222 4924; Aftab 15th Alley, Imam Khomeini St; s/tw/tr/q IR104,000/218,000/248,000/282,000) A cosy *mosaferkhaneh* whose small but relatively pleasant rooms have attached showers but ageing shared squat toilets. Comparatively overpriced.

MIDRANGE
Most are off Valiasr St, well south of the centre in the Nahar Khoran woodlands.

Hotel Maroof (☎ 442 5591; Jomhuri-ye Eslami St; s/d US$24/32) Although slightly scrappy this is the cheapest option to have en-suite toilets, some Western-style. It's better value than the nearby Hotel Tahmasebi, despite road noise and underlit corridors.

Tourist Inn (Hotel Jahangardi; ☎ 552 0034; fax 552 2279; Valiasr St km8; tw/bungalow US$42/55) This long-established place has the most magical location of several Nahar Khoran forest places. Compact, tastefully furnished bungalows are fairly closely packed through pines and palms that twinkle merrily in multicoloured evening lights. Avoid the tired, cheaper rooms above the restaurant. Pleasant outdoor teahouse.

Hotel Shahrdari (☎ 552 4077; Nahar Khoran Sq; tw US$42) This has a faint grandeur and some rooms are decently equipped. Six have a private bathroom and a Western toilet lurking in what looks like a wardrobe. Absurdly, there's no discount for rooms with shared bathrooms. It's 250m north of the Tourist Inn.

Hotel Farhangian (☎ 552 1652; Valiasr St km4; tr/q/5-bed IR315,555/420,760/525,925; P ⚡) Rooms in this family-oriented hotel aren't quite as smart as the very professional lobby might suggest, but they're new, spacious and fully equipped. No English sign.

Hotel Rahumah (☎ 552 0050; Valiasr St km7; r IR400,000-450,000; ⚡) The 10 rooms above this Nahar Khoran restaurant are small suites with little kitchenettes and there's a modish bar-style area. Back rooms face the woods with the murmur of streams. It's approximately opposite Coffee Soufi café. No English sign.

Eating
ourpick **Sofrakhane Sonati Darvish** (☎ 226 8581; Laleh 6th Alley, off Shohoda St; meals IR25,000-45,000; ☾ 11am-11pm) In a 300-year-old domed chamber hung with ships' wheels and lanterns, the Darvish is by far Gorgan's most intriguing restaurant...if you can find it. Menus are limited but the kababs are superlatively succulent. Around 9pm most evenings there's live traditional Persian music from owner-manager Ahmad Morshe who speaks fluent Romanian plus a little English.

Absha Restaurant (☎ 222 2993; Imam Khomeini St; meals IR20,000-50,000; ☾ noon-4pm & 7.30-10pm) The smartest of many eateries around Shahrdari Sq for decent *polo-morgh* (chicken and rice) and *ghorme sabzi* (green mix of diced meat, beans and vegetables, served with rice). An unpretentious place next door serves ice cream and fresh-squeezed fruit juice.

For pizzerias, head down Valiasr St. Continue all the way to Nahar Khoran for outdoor teahouses, some nicer restaurants and the eccentric **Guri** (☎ 552 4891; Valiasr St km6; kababs IR15,000; ☾ 4pm-1am), whose main building is shaped like a giant samovar topped by a big concrete teapot.

Getting There & Away
AIR
There are daily flights to Tehran (IR315,000) on Iran Air and Iran Aseman. Iran Air flies to Mashhad (IR324,000) thrice weekly. English-speaking **Komeil Golestan Tour & Travel** (☎ 232 6664; komeilgolestan@samopardaz.com; Valiasr St, cnr Edalat 21st St; ☾ 8.30am-7pm Sat-Wed, 8.30am-2pm Thu) sells the tickets.

BUS, MINIBUS & SAVARI
From the big **main terminal** (Enqelab Sq), bus destinations include the following (prices are for *mahmooly*/Volvo):

Destination	Fare	Duration	Departures
Esfahan	IR32,000/80,000	16hr	2-3.30pm
Mashhad	IR31,000/50,000	11hr	6-10am & 6-10pm
Rasht	IR20,000-22,000	9hr	hourly 7.30-1.30am & 8.30-10.30pm Seiro Safar
Shahrud	IR14,000	3hr	7.30, 8am, 1.30pm, 2.30pm Taavoni 14
Tabriz	IR90,000 (Volvo)	14hr	3pm Taavoni 5 & Seiro Safar
Tehran	IR22,000/50,000	8hr	Frequent am & 10-11.30pm
Zabol	IR75,000	25hr	6-7am Taavoni 14
Zahedan	IR42,500	26hr	6am Taavoni 14

Many through-buses to/from Mashhad don't bother with the terminal, instead dropping-off and picking-up passengers at Enqelab Sq and/or just east of Mofateh Sq. A well-organised minibus terminal directly east of the bus terminal has frequent as-full services to Aq Qal'eh (IR1000, 20 minutes), Bandar-e Torkaman (IR2000, 40 minutes), Behshahr (IR3500), Kordkuy (IR1500) and Sari (IR6000, two hours). Savaris to Aq Qal'eh leave from the central reservation at Enqelab Sq.

Minibuses/savaris for Aliabad (IR1750/6000), Azad Shahr (IR3000/12,000) and Gonbad-e-Kavus (IR4000/15,000, 1½ hours) use **Istgah Gonbad** (Blvd Jorjan), a small yard at the eastern edge of town.

TRAIN
Gorgan–Tehran services (IR27,000 to IR40,000, 11 hours) travel overnight in both directions.

Getting Around
Convenient shuttle taxis (from IR750) run from predictable points near Shahrdari Sq. Most city buses start from Panzdah Metri 2nd Alley. However, for Nahar Khoran Sq and upper Valiasr St, savaris (IR1500) and bus 29 (pre-paid ticket IR250, every 20 minutes) start from Valiasr Sq. Getting shuttle taxis back from Nahar Khoran isn't always easy so pre-buy a bus ticket in case.

AROUND GORGAN
Kordkuy   کردکوی
☎ 0173 / pop 31,000
Attractive **Park Jangal** is a popular picnic site 5km behind Kordkuy (locally pronounced Kord-koo). However, the main reason to visit is to organise a beautiful if arduous 4WD ride across the impressive forest escarpment to the Mil-e-Radkan tower.

The relatively high-class new **Bahman Hotel** (☎ 322 1501; www.bahmanhotel.com; Sari Hwy; s/d/ste US$45/65/85) tries a little too hard to be colourfully grand but is comfortable despite the road noise. It's 150m west of Shahrdari Sq where very frequent Gorgan savaris arrive (IR2000, 20 minutes).

Mil-e-Radkan (West Radkan)
میل رادخان
An awkward but highly rewarding 4WD trip takes you right across the near-vertical mountain ridge behind Kordkuy on a seemingly unending ladder of hairpin bends.

Glimpsed Caspian views are fabulous from the top near scruffy Drazno village. Scenery remains appealing as you wind back down out of the forests into a secret valley of traditional mud-and-timber hamlets. **Kondab** and **Latkueh** villages, each requiring a slight detour, are especially quaint. Eventually you find **Mil-e-Radkan**, sitting upon an astoundingly lonely knoll, wistfully gazing at the cliff-edged valley. In English it's sometimes called West Radkan Tower to differentiate it from the better-known Radkan Tower (p364). It was built for a military commander in AD 1020 by the Bavend dynasty of Tabarestan. Along with a small band of Arabic inscriptions it has some stylised Pahlavi letters, virtually the last known use of that ancient script in Iran. Just getting here is a thrill.

Dry-weather 4WD tracks continue from the Radkan Valley to Dibaj (1½ hours) from where you could take a savari to Damghan (IR8000). However, finding transport from Dibaj *to* Radkan is very tough. Better start in Kordkuy.

If all goes perfectly, a return trip from Kordkuy to Mil-e Radkan is just about possible in four hours. Seven hours will be more realistic if transporting an assortment of hitch hiking villagers and their livestock to their diverse destinations en route (an ideal way to visit the valley villages). Forget the trip altogether after snow or heavy rain. To find a suitably sturdy 4WD (preferably with food supplies, snow chains and a shovel packed for eventualities), head to the second *meydan* (town square) south of Kordkuy's central Shahrdari Sq. Getting a shared place on an over loaded early-morning Toyota truck from here is the cheapest way into the Radkan Valley villages. To charter, ask around the surrounding market for a Kordkuy resident who has both 4WD and family in the valley. We've previously had good experiences with humorous, if vaguely manic, **Ali Fagoni** (with relatives in Kondab), and **Mohammad Reza** (who runs a small Kordkuy carpet shop).

Bandar-e Torkaman   بندر ترکمن
☎ 0173 / pop 44,000
This flat, low-rise market town is architecturally tedious and despite the vibrant colours of the Turkmen costumes, the famous Monday morning **market** is just a glorified

car-boot sale. Nonetheless, the tiny *eskeleh* (port) has picturesque views over the Gorgan Gulf from its ultra-basic jetty-side teahouse. From here, occasional motorboats speed across the lagoon to fishing village **Ashuradeh** (IR50,000 each way). The *eskeleh* is 4km west of central Bandar-e Torkaman, behind some oil storage tanks: follow the old train tracks. During holidays this normally peaceful site becomes packed with local tourists browsing through Turkmen scarves at a ramshackle bazaar or getting photographed with colourfully saddled camels.

Frequent Gorgan minibuses (IR2000, 40 minutes) terminate just behind central Kariya Sq, with its copper-coloured statue of Turkmen poet Makhtumkuli. Minibuses to Kordkuy (IR1000, 20 minutes) leave from the southern edge of town.

Other Turkmen Areas

The Turkmen town of **Aq Qal'eh**, 16km north of Gorgan bus terminal, has a celebrated Thursday morning **market**, and a four-span **Safavid Bridge** (Pol-e Safavi) in the town centre. Several tumulus-style **mounds** rise from the flat surrounding fields of rapeseed and wheat. The best known is **Turang Tappeh**, 17km northeast of Aq Qal'eh. Less famous

---

CROSSING THE TURKMENISTAN BORDER AT INCHEH BORUN

The border known as 'Incheh Borun' is actually at Pol. That's 4km off the Gorgan road: turn north, 12km before Incheh Borun village. On the Iran side peddlers sell felt rugs and the nearby lakes are popular with picnickers on Fridays, but there's no public transport. On the Turkmenistan side, 1.5km across no-man's land, there's just a lonely gateway where the queues of Turkish LPG gas trucks wait. You're really in the middle of nowhere, with even the small town of Etrek around 20km distant. There is reputedly a bus to Balkanabat (formerly Nebit-Dag) in the late afternoon but don't count on it. Lonely Planet has only received one report of travellers crossing here in recent years, although they described officials as 'utterly charming'. It's much more common to cross the Turkmenistan border at Sarakhs (p365) or Bajgiran (p345).

Shah Tappeh (12km west of Aq Qal'eh, then 4km south) looks more dishevelled, an appearance that locals blame on WWII excavations after which Nazis supposedly carted off crates of treasure to Berlin. Very Indiana Jones.

The Aq Qal'eh–Incheh Borun road passes within 2km of **Alagöl**, a large if relatively unspectacular lake that's immensely popular with local picnickers at weekends. In season you might see flamingos or Turkmen herders' *öy* tents. Semi-wild camels roam the fast, desolate Incheh Borun–Maraveh Tappeh road, which passes within 3km of the **Makhtumkuli mausoleum** (30km west of Maraveh Tappeh). The modernist mausoleum looks like a gigantic four-stemmed concrete umbrella rising discordantly from the hilly steppe. It commemorates the (disputed) birthplace of Turkmenistan's 'national' poet Fargo Makhtumkuli (aka Pyragu Magtymguly; 1733–83), whose statue appears in virtually every Turkmen town. During No Ruz the monument is over-run by truly vast hoards of patriotic Turkmens. However, it's very peaceful on normal weekdays when humans are heavily outnumbered by scorpions.

Charming, ethnic-Turkmen savari-driver **Abul Halim Qarei** (☎ home 0171-225 4049, call evenings) usually does the Gorgan–Aq Qal'eh run but offers very fair prices on day trips into the Turkmen hinterlands. He speaks a little English.

GONBAD-E KAVUS   گنبد کاووس
☎ 0172 / pop 134,000

Until utterly obliterated by the Mongol and Tamerlane rampages, Jorjan was the region's foremost ancient city. All that remains today of Jorjan are a few lumpy **excavations** behind the huge, ornate **Imamzadeh Yahya** (West Mihan St), 3km west of central Gonbad-e Kavus. This predominantly Turkmen town grew up around Jorjan's one surviving building, the utterly magnificent **Mil-e Gonbad** (admission IR3000; ☯ 8am-8pm). Soaring, 55m tall on 12m-deep foundations, this astonishing tower has the cross-section of a 10-pointed star, and looks like a buttressed brick spaceship. It was built in 1006 for poet-artist-prince Qabus ibn Vashmgir but is so remarkably well preserved that one can scarcely believe it's 100, let alone 1000 years old. Qabus (Kavus), the Zeyarid ruler of surrounding

Tabarestan, had just six years to marvel at his creation before an assassin put him in it permanently. Well, not so permanently, actually. His glass coffin, which originally hung from the tower's dome, vanished long ago. Now there's nothing to see inside, although it's well worth the entry fee for the remarkable echoes both within and even more spookily from the marked circular spot some 40m in front of the tower. Mil-e Gonbad is hard to miss in a park 2½ blocks north of the central Enqelab Sq.

On Friday the hippodrome at the eastern end of town holds *savar kareh* **horse races** (✇ 1pm spring & autumn).

On hot summer days you might want to retire behind the heavy bronze doors of the swish, full-sized indoor **swimming pool** (☎ 555 6909; Peyam St; per hr with/without sauna IR30,000/20,000; ✇ 11am-11pm, Tue, Thu & Sun for women, other days men). It's one block east of Daneshju Blvd near its southern end.

The bearable, central **Mosaferkhaneh Khayyam** (☎ 222 7663; off Imam St; tw/tr/q IR46,000/67,000/79,000; showers IR5000) is just south of Enqelab Sq before East Mihan St. It's signed in Russian as гостиница хям. There's better accommodation in Minudasht (p345) or Azad Shahr (p344).

There are *kababis* and a pizzeria off Enqelab Sq. Facing the great tower, **Safa Café** (☎ 222 0208; ✇ 8am-midnight; ✖) offers ice-cream sundaes (IR4000 to IR9000), floats, espresso (IR7000) and freshly squeezed seasonal juices.

Getting There & Away

Busy Istgah Gorgan, towards Imam St's southern end, has minibuses and savaris to Azad Shahr, Aliabad and Gorgan. For Minudasht and Kalaleh, savaris leave from Basij Sq, 2km directly east of Enqelab Sq. Change in Minudasht for Bojnurd. Change in Azad Shahr for Shahrud.

AROUND GONBAD-E KAVUS

East of Gonbad, the limited-access Golestan National Park includes partly cultivated steppe and contrastingly thick mountain forests of 500-year-old trees in which you half expect to meet Asterix and his cohorts. The region is indistinctly littered with clues to the once vibrant Tabarestan civilisation that lasted from the Neanderthal era right up until the 13th century. Then Genghis Khan's hordes brought it all to an abrupt end.

IRAN'S TURKMEN PEOPLE

Turkmen people (2% of Iran's population) have a truly extraordinary range of facial features from Asiatic (Kazakh-Mongolian) to startlingly blue-eyed Caucasian. Their clans are predominantly Sunni-Muslim and speak their own Turkic dialects. Turkmen women have little patience with black chadors, favouring heavy, full-length dresses in bright colours over trousers and shawls with floral designs. Some older men wear white turban-like headscarves but once-iconic *telpek* hats of shaggy sheepskin are pretty rare these days, as are traditional yurt-style nomad-tents called *öy*. In the last generation most Turkmens have become settled, swapping their famous horses for motorbikes. Although sheep farming remains an economic mainstay, pasture-lands have increasingly been ploughed up by Zaboli immigrants, leaving Turkmen villages amongst the most disadvantaged in post-revolutionary Iran. See www.turkmensahra.com for more about their region.

Much of the steppe population is ethnically Turkmen so if you're lucky you might find yourself invited to a horse milking or for tea in one of the increasingly rare reed-ringed felt *öy* tents. For a hefty fee it's possible to take unique spring and autumn **horse treks** in this fascinating area; book through www.inthesaddle.com/iran .htm. For a riders' experience, read www .equitrek.co m.au/Iran.html.

Gharra Tappeh Sheikh (GTS)   قره تپه شیخ
☎ 0172

A unique stud-farm in the minuscule ethnic-Turkmen village of GTS is home to philosophical US-born Louise Firouz (nee Laylin). Famous for 'rediscovering' (ie selectively back-breeding) the miniature Caspian horse, she also rears classic Turkmen horses, thought to be the genetic forerunners of the thoroughbred. She has lived in Iran for more than 40 years and has an endless wealth of fascinating tales to tell.

By advance arrangement it's possible to stay in a genuine Turkmen *öy* tent on **Louise's farm** (☎ 229 7679; firouz@pinarnet.com; per person US$60). This is a unique, very personal experience and the deliberately high price is designed to keep it that way. Bring a sleeping bag and don't expect luxury: shared facilities include an out door long-drop toilet. The village's flat, steppe position gives a magnificent big-sky panorama edged with a near horizon of high woodland ridges. GTS makes an ideal base for visiting Alexander's Wall and Khalid Nibi Shrine. Louise can arrange transport to these and many other intriguing, little-visited marvels.

GETTING THERE & AWAY

From Gonbad-e Kavus, the shortest route is via Haji Qoshan, once home to ubiquitous Turkmen writer Makhtumkuli. By public transport it's easier to go via Kalaleh. From Kalaleh's Ahmedi Sq, take a Tamar-bound savari, then pay an extra IR20,000 to continue *dar baste* to GTS (20 minutes).

Alexander's Wall   سد اسکندر

Like the Great Chinese and Hadrian's equivalents, **Alexander's Wall** (Sadd-e Eskander) was built to keep out war-like raiders from the north. For the Iranian world it marked the very real edge of civilisation. Being banished beyond was equivalent to capital punishment. Called Qezel Alam (Red Snake) in Turkmen, it stretched over 160km between the Golestan Mountains and the Caspian and probably dates from the 6th century, making any reference to Alexander the Great mere romantic fiction. Comprehensively cannibalised for building materials over the centuries it's now little more than a muddy undulation. However, a relatively recognisable section, conveniently marked by orange concrete bollards, runs along the northern side of the Tamar–GTS road. Raised some 5m above the fields, the outline of a large, square-planned wall-fort is still easy to make out at **Malaisheikh**, around 10km west of GTS.

Khalid Nibi Shrine   آرامگاه خالد نبی

Dramatically perched above a breathtaking sea of badlands sit three small **mausoleums** commemorating Khalid Nibi. Although he was a 5th-century Nestorian Christian, the place now attracts Muslim pilgrims during spring and early summer. From the central shrine, a fairly obvious footpath leads down, then right in about 10 minutes to a grassy knoll dotted with remarkable **pagan grave-markers**. Ancient but of unknown age, these markers include 2m-long spindly phalluses

for men and butterfly-shaped stones for women.

From Tamar (off the Kalaleh–Maraveh Tappeh road), Khalid Nibi is 30km by unsurfaced road (allow 90 minutes). Taxis from Minudasht want around IR170,000 return, but they struggle with the steep last kilometre. A 4WD from GTS costs around IR200,000 return.

Aliabad   علی آباد

☎ 0173 / pop 45,000

Fan-shaped **Kabud Waterfall** is accessed by a 20-minute streamside walk through pretty woodlands starting from a clutch of teahouses, 4km south of Aliabad. However, the path becomes a treacherous mudslide when wet.

From **Shirabad**, 8km off the Aliabad–Azad Shahr road (turn at Khanbebin), an essentially similar but quieter (and less steep) path passes gorgeous mossy rocks and limpid forest pools for a 20-minute stroll to a vertical 20m-chute **waterfall** in a grooved cliff. Less accessible falls continue above.

Don't confuse Shirabad with tiny **Shirinabad**, the last village of an attractive 30km forested valley with tantalising glances up to high mountain-pasture settlements in the side valleys. A tough, summer-only track crosses the high mountains from Shirinabad to Qal'eh Now-e-Kharaqan near Bastam (p351), but finding anyone to rent you a suitable 4WD vehicle is a challenge.

The clean, basic **Mehmanpazir Resalat** (☎ 622 2108; Azadshahr Rd; s/tw/tr/q IR50,000/70,000/80,000/ 90,000) is above a restaurant about 150m east of Aliabad's Velyat Sq, almost opposite the attractive park. Sign reads 'Well Come'.

Hotel Kaniyar (☎ 623 0002; tw/tr/q IR300,000/ 400,000/450,000), 2km west, has a stylish open-plan lobby-restaurant and Jacuzzis in some rooms. Standards are high but some décor is overly colourful.

Azad Shahr   آز ادشهر

☎ 0174 / pop 38,000

Connecting between Shahrur and Gorgan you'll probably change savari at this friendly town, formerly known as Shahparsand. At the western end of town, **Hotel Park** (☎ 672 2545; Beheshti Blvd; s/tw/tr/ste IR140,000/180,000/ 240,000/300,000; ⓟ ⌘) is one of the region's best-value hotels, with an understated elegance and very well-kept, fully equipped rooms.

Minudasht مینودشت
☎ 0174 / pop 24,000

Backed by beautiful green hills, Minudasht is a useful transport junction between Gonbad-e Kavus and Bojnurd. On the northern ring road, the new **Mehmanpazir Minu** (☎ 522 3188; Mashhad Hwy; s/tw/tr/q IR52,000/79,000/84,000/97,000, with private bathroom IR62,000/89,000/104,000/119,000; 🖭) is great value, with fancy Achaemenid-motif bed-heads on the hard beds and air-conditioning in most rooms. The ageing **Hotel Esteghlal** (☎ 522 2314; Mashhad Hwy; s/tw/tr/q US$47/55/60/65; 🖭) is hopelessly overpriced and feels spookily like a set from *The Shining*.

BOJNURD بجنورد
☎ 0584 / pop 201,000

Capital of newly established North Khorasan province, Bojnurd sits in a bowl of gentle mountains surrounded by mildly attractive rural villages. If changing buses here, check out **Ainekhane** (Dochenar/Shariati St; admission IR3000), a psychedelically coloured Qajar-era mansion. Get the key from **North Khorasan Tourism** (☎ 224 5388; Dochenar/Shariati St; 🕑 8am-2.30pm Sun-Thu) directly opposite the rather grand **Emarat Mofarkham building**.

Clean, fresh **Mosaferkhaneh Naghizadeh** (☎ 222 2193; Falakeh Kargat, Imam Khomeini St; s/tw/tr IR56,000/64,000/76,000, showers IR4000) is simple but very well kept.

At the far eastern end of town, the plush new **Hotel Negin** (☎ 225 5737; Imam Reza Sq; d with breakfast IR360,000) has fully equipped modern rooms off smart, if slightly underlit, corridors.

Mashhad-bound savaris (IR30,000, 2½ hours) start from Falakeh Mehmansara (aka Azadegan Sq) in front of a conspicuously marked 'Guesthouse'. The main **bus terminal** (Beit-ol Moqqadas Sq), on the western side of town, has regular buses to Gorgan (IR17,000, five hours), Mashhad (IR12,000, four hours), Quchan (IR6000, 2¼ hours), Sabzevar (IR8000, 3½ hours) and Tehran (IR50,000, 12 hours). Savaris to Sabzevar (IR25,000, 2½ hours) and Esfarayan (IR10,000, 45 minutes) depart from Chahara Khoshi at the west end of Beheshti St.

QUCHAN قوچان
☎ 0581 / pop 116,000

If you're heading to Turkmenistan via Bajgiran, you'll probably need to transit Quchan, where a sweet little **Ethnographic Museum** (☎ 223 2757; admission IR2000; 🕑 8am-1pm & 3-7pm Tue-Sun) and a big new hotel (nearing completion) are both on Azadi Sq on the main Mashhad–Bojnurd road.

From here, Sabzevar Bazaar St runs 1.5km north to central Imam Khomeini Sq (*meydan*) where it continues as Eshkabad St through the commercial centre. It ends at Felestin Sq (1.5km further) from which savaris leave for Bajgiran (IR15,000) and Dargaz (IR20,000).

A short walk north of Imam Khomeini Sq, turn right down a quiet side road to find **Mosaferkhaneh Noor** (☎ 222 3464; Nasser Khosrow St; tw/tr IR50,000/60,000), 150m east of Eshkabad St. Simple rooms around a central courtyard are very clean, but there's no shower and doors are usually locked by 10pm. Three blocks further north off Eshkabad St are eateries and an internet café.

Quchan region is famous for *koshti Quchani*, a kind of **wrestling** that's a bit like sumo minus the bellies. However, competitions are rare and mostly held in remote villages, notably at Ravar (1 to 2 April).

Bojnurd–Mashhad buses and some savaris (back/front IR15,000/20,000) use relevant points on Azadi Sq. However, Mashhad–Quchan buses (IR6000, 2½ hours) arrive at the main bus terminal, 1.6km east, then 300m south of Imam Khomeini Sq.

AROUND QUCHAN
Bajgiran باجگیران
☎ 0582 / pop 920

If you're heading to Ashgabat, Turkmenistan's surreal capital, consider sleeping here to get an early start for crossing the nearby border (see the boxed text, p346). Bajgiran village isn't an attraction but a few huddles of archaic mud-houses look faintly attractive amid the arid mountain ridges and communication towers. Savaris from Quchan (IR15,000/60,000 per person/car, 1¼ hours) terminate at the lower border gate. That's 800m beyond the nine-room **Hotel Bajgiran** (☎ 372 3212; tw IR80,000), which has survivable but rather bare rooms with shared toilets.

The prettier of two possible routes from Quchan uses a degraded old road via Emamqoli, descending through a narrow canyon, and rejoining the main new road just beyond the timeless mud-block village of **Dorbadam**.

CROSSING THE TURKMENISTAN BORDER AT BAJGIRAN HOWDAN

From Bajgiran's lower border gate, it's a steady 1.7km climb to the **immigration posts** (☯ 7.30am-3.30pm Iran time, 9am-5pm Turkmen time); taxis want IR10,000. Before crossing the border, change at least US$10 into Turkmen manats (US$1=23,500M) either with traders in Bajgiran village or at the small (slightly hidden) office marked 'taxi' to the right of the Iranian immigration building. Iranian formalities are swift as long as you don't sneeze at the 'Human Quarantine' desk. Turkmenistan immigration is just 50m away. As at any Turkmen entry point you'll need US$12 (in US dollars) to pay for the hologrammed entry card. If arriving on a tourist visa your voucher must be with the immigration officers and the agency representative should be waiting so be sure to synchronise your watches. That's not required if you're on a transit visa.

Turkmen immigration staff are friendly but procedures can be appallingly ponderous, even when everything's in order (two hours to clear six people when we crossed). Beware that Howdan (the Turkmen-side upper customs post, pronounced hovdan) is not a village, has zero facilities and is 25km from the Turkmen lower border gate (Berzhengi Tamozhna). Smart VW minivans charging 150,000M (or US$10 if you've forgotten to exchange money in advance) shuttle across this no-man's land, departing once they have a handful of passengers. After further passport checks here, less plush shared taxis charge 25,000M per person to any address in Ashgabat (whose city limits start 7km further north).

SEMNAN   سمنان
☎ 0231 / pop 129,000

Capital of an eponymous region, booming Semnan lies on the northern edge of the vast Dasht-e Kavir desert, 240km east of Tehran. Since Sassanian times it has been a key stop on the silk route, attracting wealth and regular destruction in equal measure. At first glance it's a diffuse, nondescript city of low-rise modern buildings and wide boulevards. But around the appealing covered bazaar is an interesting complex of historical buildings. A short drive to Shah-mirzad reveals an impressive hinterland of arid mountain peaks.

Information

Aras Coffeenet (Qods Blvd; internet per hr IR6000; ☯ 10am-7pm Sun-Wed)

Semani Coffeenet (☎ 333 8010; internet per hr IR6000; ☯ 8am-10pm Sun-Wed, 8am-8pm Thu) Separate male and female sections.

Semnan Miras (☎ 332 1602; www.semnanmiras.ir; Tadayon House, Taleqani St, btwn 3rd & 5th Alleys; ☯ 8am-2.30pm Sun-Wed, 8am-1.30pm Thu) They speak minimal English but offer bilingual pamphlets and Farsi-only maps from a lovely Qajar-era mansion with Semnan's finest surviving wind tower.

Sights
OLD SEMNAN

The key sites can all be accessed from within the unusually tall **covered bazaar** via the log-pillared **Takiyeh Market Hall**. Most

impressive is the **Imam Khomeini (Sultani) Mosque** founded under Fath Ali Shah in the 1820s. It's one of Iran's finest surviving buildings from the Qajar period. Two of its four courtyard *iwans* offer perfectly measured use of restrained coloured brickwork. There's no such restraint in the dazzling blue tiling of the contemporary **Imamzadeh Yahya**. The extraordinarily high, if austere, west *iwan* of the **Jameh Mosque** dates from a 1424 rebuild, but the mosque's most lovable feature is the gorgeous 21m brick minaret (11th century?). Leaning and kinked it still dominates the town and is floodlit at night in incongruous electric green.

Between vaguely comical tilework portraits of Qajar warriors in the northwest corner of Takiyeh Hall, a doorway leads into an attractive 1452 bathhouse. Within is the **Hazrat Museum** (☎ 333 1204; admission IR2000; ☯ 8am-noon & 3.30-6pm Sat-Thu) displaying 3000-year-old pottery from the nearby archaeological site of Hissar, plus some pretty photos of Semnan Province.

Around the bazaar area, the construction of makeshift car parks and somewhat brutal redevelopment has bulldozed heartbreaking holes into the fabric of the old city. Only a small percentage of mud-built **traditional homes** remain, mostly in back alleyways. Several of these have crumbling Yazd-style wind towers (Taleqani 1st and 13th Alleys, Hafez 31st Alley, Ghafari 30th Alley, Abuzar Sq).

Near Abuzar Sq, Ghafari 9th Alley leads down to the lumpy ruins of the city's ancient mud **fortress**.

OTHER SIGHTS

Spiked with blue-tiled baby minarets, **Darvaza-e Arg** (Arg Sq, Taleqani St) is Semnan's dinky but iconic Qajar-era city gate. Around 500m northeast there's an old **cistern** (Qods Blvd) beside what appears to be a fortress **tower**, but was actually a decorative element from a now demolished cotton factory.

Activities

Some 5km east of Semnan, the **Shabdiz Tourist Complex** (☎ 335 3123; Damghan Hwy) is a 20-horse equestrian centre where tourists can rent horses and guides for trips into the nearby desert and mountains (around US$100 per day; call ahead). A futuristic, eco-friendly five-star hotel plus restaurant, skating rink and sports complex are planned. The knowledgeable, intelligent owner, **Madjid Dadvar** (☎ 0912 231 1077; dadvar madjid@yahoo.it), speaks decent English and better Italian.

Sleeping

Hotel Kormesh (☎ 332 3647; Imam Khomeini 18th Alley, off Imam Khomeini Sq; tw/tr/q IR100,000/140,000/ 170,000) Facing Imam Khomeini Sq across a children's play area, the basic Kormesh is very central but easy to miss: find an un-marked door (usually covered with a towel), go inside then knock on the glass door to the right. Apathetic staff do their best to deter customers, suggesting randomly high prices, hiding the shower room and lock-ing the doors at 10pm. Squat toilets are shared. The cheaper Mosaferkhaneh Cha-harfazl, diagonally across Imam Khomeini St, is only open sporadically. Look for the Pepsi sign.

Ghods Hotel (☎ 332 2177; Imam Reza Sq; d US$30; ⓟ ⓧ) Some rear rooms have cracked win-dows and worn furniture. Front rooms are better with TV and fridge but suffer more from road noise. Overpriced.

Semnan Tourist Inn (Mehmansara Jahangardi; ☎ 444 1433; Basij Blvd; tw US$37; ⓟ ⓧ) Behind a dowdy exterior, this friendly 36-room hotel offers international standard rooms with new furniture, curtained showers, toiletries and freshly laundered towels: good value but 3km from the old-city core.

Eating

Ghandil Sabz (☎ 334 0129; Motahhari St; ☺ 9.30am-1pm & 4-11pm) There's a grotto theme in this curious ice-cream shop about 700m north of Imam Khomeini Sq after 21st Alley.

Sofrakhaneh Sonati Haft Khan (☎ 333 0463; Ma-shahir Sq; breakfast/kabab meals IR10,000/30,000; ☺ 9am-11pm) The menu is a very short list of ordinary kababs but the décor is unique. Achaemenid figures lead down to a cane-vaulted cavern

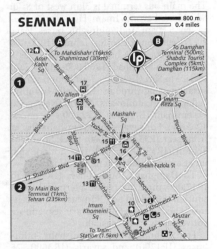

SEMNAN

full of tea-beds, Corinthian columns and an artificial grotto. If that looks fanciful, wait till you see the incredible party room accessed through a secret door between the two gold suns.

Pizza Max (☎ 332 7012; Sa'di Sq; pizzas IR23,000-30,000; ⊙ noon-3.30pm & 6pm-midnight) Good if typically Iranian pizza, mostly for takeaway.

Getting There & Away

The main bus terminal is 3km west of Sa'di Sq, 100m beyond Imam Hossein Sq. Between 5.30am and midnight, buses leave every half hour or so for Tehran (IR20,000 to IR25,000, three hours). Taavoni 2 has a 6am bus to Mashhad (IR60,000) and a 7am service to Sari (IR20,000, four hours) via Kiyasar, passing through seasonally beautiful valleys full of sunflowers. Alternatively, go to Qa'emshahr (IR13,500 IR22,000, 3½ hours, 10 daily). For savaris to Qa'emshahr (back/front seat IR35,000/40,000, three hours) or Tehran (IR35,000/45,000, two hours), sign up at a special office in the terminal.

To Damghan, hourly buses (IR9000 to IR12,000, three hours) use a terminal 100m south of Standard Sq (3km east of the centre). The last is at 6pm. Savaris leave more conveniently from Mashahir Sq.

For Shahmirzad via Mahdishahr, minibuses (IR1200) and savaris (IR3500, 25 minutes) start from Mo'allem Sq.

Three Mashhad–Tehran trains (stopping at Semnan) and two Semnan–Tehran local services (three hours) operate daily. The train station is 1.5km south of Imam Khomeini Sq.

AROUND SEMNAN
Caravanserais

Several partly renovated **caravanserais** lie close to the main Mashhad–Tehran highway either side of town, notably at **Lasjerd** (36km west) and **Ahowan** (42km east). Semnan Miras can get you in by advance arrangement.

Into the Mountains
MAHDISHAHR   مهدي شهر
☎ 0232

Sprawling in arid rocky folds, **Mahdishahr** (16km from Semnan) is dominated by the impressive if mostly contemporary blue-domed **Al-Mahdi Hosseinieh**. The town's other notable building is the 40-year-old Kakh Pal-

ace, now used as the remarkably good-value **Sangesar Hotel** (☎ 362 4280; fax 362 4380; Saheb Zaman St; d/ste US$30/41) with blue tiling, grand lobby and two-storey chandelier of 1970s rope-glass. Take the best suite for full effect.

SHAHMIRZAD   شهميرزاد
☎ 0232

This popular weekend getaway for Semnanis is a quietly charming oasis amid spiky rock ridges. Gushing streams and a few remnant mud-compound houses grace the upper parts of town around Imam Sq. There's enough snow on the ridges 8km behind town to allow impromptu sledging until mid-April. Between Shahmirzad and Mahdishahr, **Darband** is a somewhat scraggy picnic spot behind which a path leads up to a locally famous **cave** in the cliff.

Excellent value even at foreigner prices, **Moshtameh Ferhangi** (☎ 366 4114; local/foreigner d IR70,000/150,000) is a modern, four-storey octagonal tower hotel set in a garden at the top edge of town. It's unmarked but very obvious: follow Motahhari St up from Imam Sq (10 minutes' walk). Rooms are big and although a little bare, have smart bathrooms and good views.

By the chairlift and art-park directly above Imam Sq, a basic **teahouse** spills out into pretty gardens on warm afternoons.

Minibuses (IR2000) and savaris (IR3500) to Semnan leave from Imam St, 500m downhill from Imam Sq. For the picturesque direct route to Pol-e Sefid you'll need to find a taxi driver gutsy enough to ford the unbridged river en-route.

DAMGHAN   دامغان
☎ 0232 / pop 55,000

This historic caravan town sits on the edge of the great desert plateau, attractively backed by parched rocky ridges (the highest are discordantly snow-covered well into April). Damghan's timelessly crumbling mud-walled buildings are rapidly being replaced by modern constructions. However, several ancient religious structures in expertly faceted brick are within easy walking distance of the central area.

The covered bazaar hugs the town's central east–west axis (Imam Khomeini St) for the block between Chaharshir Sq (with its four gilded lions) and Imam Khomeini Sq, where Bank Tejarat changes US$, Euros and

UK pounds. From here, Beheshti St continues northeast towards Mashhad, Motahhari St heads southeast past Tarikhuneh Mosque (400m) to the train station (2km), while the narrow lane due east passes the Jameh Mosque (200m) and Pir Amadar (300m).

Attractive Azadi Blvd leads north from Chaharshir Sq, a pine-lined stream running down its middle. It quickly passes an old (but out-of-bounds) caravanserai to the west and shopping mall (Bazaar Khandaq) to the east. The latter contains friendly but slow **Coffeenet Novin** (internet per hr IR6000; 8.30am-8pm Sat-Thu, 4-9pm Fri).

Sights

The **Tarikhuneh Mosque** (Motahhari St; admission IR3000; 8am-1.30pm & 3pm-dusk Sat-Thu) is a unique, partly ruined mud-brick structure whose 18 extraordinarily sturdy rear columns date from about AD 760. That reputedly makes this the second oldest mosque in Iran, possibly starting life as a Zoroastrian palace-temple. The broken columns and part-renovated arches of a colonnaded courtyard are similarly massive and undecorated. But in striking contrast, the 30m-high AD 1038 brick **minaret** is very finely detailed. Now slightly leaning it's within the yard of a new mosque next door.

The **Jameh Mosque** looks outwardly new but was founded a millennium ago. It has another fine brick **minaret** probably dating from the mid-11th century. Continue walking along the same lane to find the round **Pir Alamdar** tower. Dating from the AD 1020s, its original conical roof has been replaced by a newer brick dome but the Kufic inscriptions are remarkable and if you can get in (hit-and-miss) the interior is reputedly even finer.

The similar **Chehel Dokhtar Tower** hides behind the very photogenic **Imamzadeh Jafar** (Chaharshir Sq), a splendid ancient brick building with round side-towers, arched false-windows and a five-levelled dome culminating in a brick cone. It looks like a movie-set North African castle.

Sleeping & Eating

Amir Hotel (☎ 523 1776; Varzesh Sq; tw/tr IR120,000/ 130,000; P ❄) Above a popular restaurant, the good-value Amir has small, comfortable rooms with bathrooms and a friendly reception in the cosy lobby. Varzesh Sq is identifiable by its 'sport monument' dis-

playing huge footballs in a giant cup. It's 1.5km from Chaharshir Sq, one large block north, then three east.

Hotel Danesh (☎ 523 1121; Beheshti St; s/tw IR200,000/300,000; ❄) If other hotels are full, the Danesh's unfussy, well-maintained rooms are quite acceptable, with fridge, central air-conditioning and new (if slightly uncomfortable) beds. Little balconies offer nice views from east-facing rooms but road noise is a slight problem. It's 1km east of Imam Khomeini Sq.

our pick **Damghan Inn** (☎ 524 2070; fax 524 6800; Azadi Blvd; r US$27; P ❄) With multiple-domed roofs, this remarkably swish hotel is designed to faintly resemble a caravanserai while offering full midrange facilities. It's beside Park-e Shahrdari, five minutes' walk north from Chaharshir Sq.

Caffe Sun City (☎ 524 8131; Beheshti St; coffees IR500-800; 9am-midnight; ❄) Thirty metres northeast of Imam Khomeini Sq, this is an appealing spot for a decent Turkish coffee. Or for a real espresso if they ever fix the machine.

Of several pizza and burger joints around lower Azadi Blvd, the most appealing is **Konj** (Kandagh St; noon-10.30pm; ❄) facing Bazaar Khandaq.

Getting There & Away

Damghan's quiet terminal looks more like a covered bazaar. It's 1km west on 17 Shahrivar St, a IR500 shuttle-taxi hop from outside Imamzadeh Jafar. Buses/savaris run to Semnan (IR12,000/25,000, three hours) and Shahrud (IR3500/14,000, 75 minutes). Arriving in Damghan, incoming transport often leaves passengers obligingly at central Chaharshir or Imam Khomeini Sqs.

AROUND DAMGHAN

Local picnickers love **Cheshmeh Ali** where the skeleton of a lonely Qajar-era pavilion sits amid willow trees in a spring-fed reflecting pool. It's almost worth the taxi fare (IR30,000 each way from Damghan, 30km) for the scenic contrasts en route: high snow-topped ridges, dry rocky outcrops and mud-walled plum orchards.

Along the slowly degenerating ex-asphalt north of here there are some fabulous 360-degree views of a wide mountain-ringed bowl-valley just beyond lonely **Dibaj**. To reach Mil-e Radkan (p341), you'll need a

4WD to get through deep squirming mud around Chamansovar village.

SHAHRUD شاهرود

☎ 0273 / pop 135,000

Shahrud is a pleasant small town with leafy streets squeezed against dusty ridges rising abruptly from the Dasht-e Kavir. It's a useful hub for visiting Bastam (7km northeast) and the stepped village of Mojen (35km west).

Shahrud's axis, 22 Bahman St, leads 1.3km from central Jomhuri Sq to Azadi Sq, passing **Coffeenet Almas** (☎ 223 8419; 22 Bahman St; per hr IR8000; ☯ 9am-11pm), easily missed downstairs, after one short block.

Imam Sq (nicknamed simply 'falakeh') is 300m north of Jomhuri Sq. Here winding Ferdosi St leads up to the small but beautifully presented **Shahrud Museum** (☎ 222 1784; Ferdosi St; admission IR3000; ☯ 7.30am-12.30pm & 4-6pm Sat-Thu), housed in the 1927 former town hall.

Northwest from Jomhuri Sq, Sadeghi St leads towards leafy **Abshar Park** (1km) closely paralleled by the covered **bazaar,** which is lively if less than photogenic.

Southwest of Jomhuri St, Tehran St passes very close to the **tourist office** (Miras Ferhangi; ☎ 223 0760; off 8 Shahrivar St; ☯ 8.30am-8pm Sat-Thu, 4-9pm Fri) after 500m. Look for the wind tower in the side lane (left) behind a shop marked 'Iran Plast'.

Sleeping

Mehmankhaneh Islami Noh (Inn Islam New; ☎ 222 2335; Shohoda St; s/d/tr/q IR48,350/65,900/77,800/89,900; P) Barely 15m southeast of Jomhuri Sq, the location is very handy but the rooms range from bearable (with tap) to highly dishevelled (without). Friendly but no showers.

Hotel Azadi-Sharif (☎ 222 8454; Bahar St; tw/tr/q IR120,000/170,000/220,000, with bathroom IR153,000/220,000/270,000) Rooms are a very mixed bag: some ageing with tight-packed beds and shared toilets; others neat and relatively spacious with newer tiled floors. There's a shared kitchen, family feel and an effusive welcome in approximate-English. To find it, walk 400m down Azadi Blvd from Azadi Sq, take a short block left on Khaqani St, turn left again and it's on your right.

Hotel Nader (☎ 333 2835; fax 333 2836; Daneshju St; s/d/tr/IR140,000/160,000/180,000, with shower 180,000/210,000/240,000; P ✗) Simple but very clean rooms with monogrammed sheets. Toilets are shared. Head two blocks down Tehran

St from Jomhuri Sq, right on Madani Blvd, then take the first left and it's on the right before Daneshju curves left.

ITTIC Shahrud Tourist Inn (Mehmansara Jahangardi; ☎ 222 6078; fax 222 4008; Saderian St; d/tr US$35/40; P ✗) Freshly painted walls and nice new curtains contrast with archaic old bathrooms and a strange mix of old and new furniture. It's peacefully set amid pine trees 300m from Azadi Sq on a street that runs parallel to Ferdosi.

Eating

Note that none of the following have English on their signs, let alone their menus.

Coffee Shop Soorena (off Azadi Sq; sundaes IR12,000-16,000, coffees IR7000-16,000; ☯ 9am-1pm & 5-10pm Sat-Thu, 5-10pm Fri) Though tiny, this mood-lit ice-cream parlour-café is the most stylish of several eateries around the south side of Azadi Sq. Mocha comes thick with chocolate sediment.

Ayaran Restaurant (☎ 224 2540; Abshar Park; meals IR20,000-50,000; ☯ 10.30am-midnight) Unusually good *juje kababs* (grilled chicken pieces) are served in a timber-roofed rotunda constructed around a living tree or outside at tables in the pine woods.

Ferdosi Restaurant (☎ 222 2958; 22 Bahman St; pizzas from IR22,000, kabab meals IR25,000-40,000; ☯ noon-3.30pm & 7-10.30pm) Facing the bazaar entrance the Ferdosi is handy for Jomhuri Sq. Its pine ceilings and wood-effect walls come close to stylish minimalism, and it has a wide-ranging menu.

Getting There & Around

Iran Peyma, Taavoni 3 and Seiro Safar all have handy ticket offices on or near Jomhuri Sq but most long-distance buses actually depart from the hopelessly inconvenient main bus terminal 5km south down Tehran St (IR1500 by shuttle taxi). Iran Peyma services include the following:

Destination	Fare	Duration	Departures
Esfahan	IR60,000 (V)	13hr	5pm
Mashhad	IR16,700	10hr	1pm, 10pm
Gorgan	IR14,000	3hr	10am, 2.30pm
Sari	IR33,000	9hr	3pm via Damghan
Tehran	IR20,000/40,000	8hr	fairly frequent

Savaris to Azad Shahr (IR30,000) and Sabzevar leave from relevant points on Imam Reza Sq, 300m northeast of Azadi

Sq. Just beyond (northeast of the Atlantic Petrol Station) is **Terminal-e Shomal** (☎ 222 3201; Bastam Hwy), a small, hidden yard from which minibuses leave when full to Azad Shahr (IR6000, 1¾ hours; IR10,000 2¼ hours back) plus at 9.30am to Gonbad-e Kavus (IR7000) and at 8am, 9am and 2pm to Gorgan (IR10,000). Savaris and occasional minibuses to Bastam (15 minutes) leave from 17 Shahrivar St just off Imam Sq. Savaris and minibuses to Mojen (30 minutes) leave from 15 Khordat St just off Sadeghi St, two blocks northwest of Jomhuri Sq.

Shahrud train station, on the Tehran–Mashhad train line, is about 3km southeast of Jomhuri Sq.

AROUND SHAHRUD
Bastam   بسطام

Ancient Bastam is now a modest village 7km from Shahrud. It's centred on the quietly photogenic **Bayazid Historical Complex** (Imam Khomeini Sq; admission free; ☯ dawn-dusk), 300m off the main Shahrud–Azad Shahr road up Taleqani Blvd. This collection of mostly 13th-century blue-tiled buildings surrounds the simple grave of Bayazid Bastami (AD 804–874), a philosopher nicknamed 'Sultan of gnostics' who fused Muslim, Mithraic and Zoroastrian ideas in formulating a poetic form of Sufism. Behind the grave, **Imamzadeh Mohammad** has an attractive almost Art Nouveau floral interior. The associated **Bayazid mosque** has a remarkable grey mihrab, glass-protected carved wooden doors and timber pillars supporting a fine log ceiling.

One block behind the complex, the mud-daub walled 1285 **Jameh Mosque** (off Madiyeh St) backs onto the fine 1313 **Borj Kashani**, a circular tomb-tower that possibly doubled as an astronomical observatory like that at Radkan (p364). The mosque reportedly contains superb stucco-work but getting in can be hit-and-miss.

Informal shared taxis pick up passengers outside the historical complex for rides into Shahrud (IR1250).

MASHHAD   مشهد

☎ 0511 / pop 2,965,000

Mashhad is Iran's holiest and second biggest city. Its *raison d'être* and main sight is the beautiful, massive and ever-growing Haram (shrine complex) commemorating the AD 817 martyrdom of Shia Islam's eighth Imam, Imam Reza. The pain of Imam Reza's death is still felt very personally over a millennium later and around 20 million pilgrims converge here each year to pay their respects (and no small amount of money) to the Imam. Witnessing their tears is a moving experience, even if you're not a Muslim yourself. If you notice a lot of lovey young couples, that's because the city's also a haven for honeymooners, who believe sharing it with the Imam will bless their marriage. Away from the Haram Complex there are few sights, but Mashhad is a good place to buy carpets, it's a natural staging post for travel to Turkmenistan or Afghanistan, and offers many interesting excursions into little-touristed Khorasan.

Be aware that during major pilgrim seasons, almost all accommodation and transport will be booked out months in advance (see the boxed text, p358). Contrastingly, at other times Mashhad offers about the best-value accommodation in Iran. Winters can be very cold, with snow on the ground for up to five months a year. Summers are contrastingly hot. April is ideal.

History

Following Imam Reza's burial here, the small village of Sanabad began to attract Shiite pilgrims and soon became known as Mashhad (place of martyrdom). Tus remained a more significant town until 1389 when Timur sacked the whole area. But thereafter it was Mashhad that eventually limped back to life as the new capital of Khorasan. The shrine was enlarged in the early 15th century by Timur's son, Shah Rokh, and his extraordinary wife, Gohar Shad, for whom the Haram's main mosque is named. Once the Safavids had established Shiism as the state creed, Mashhad became Iran's pre-eminent pilgrimage site and Shah Abbas I rebuilt the Holy Shrine's new core around 1612. Politically, Mashhad reached its zenith under Nader Shah (p35) whose empire was focused on Khorasan. Even though Nader was a Sunni of missionary zeal, he continued to sponsor the Haram.

In 1928, nonreligious buildings within 180m of the Holy Shrine were flattened to make way for the Haram's biggest enlargement to date. Prior to the 1979 revolution this religious 'island' was further expanded

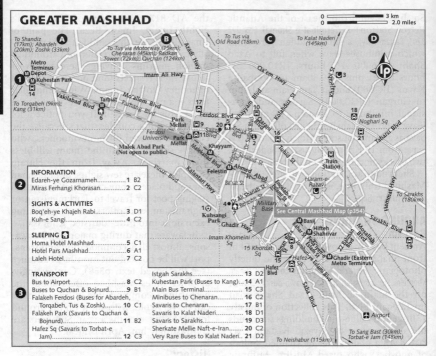

GREATER MASHHAD

to 320m and construction has continued apace ever since. When historians look back on the era of the Islamic Republic, they will point to the Haram as its greatest architectural achievement. Meanwhile, the charitable foundation that manages the shrine, **Astan-e Qods e Razavi** (www.aqrazavi.org), has become a business conglomerate, managing enterprises from baking to carpets, and minerals to transport. But most of the money comes from donations, bequests and the selling of grave-sites: to be buried near the Imam is a great honour and suitably expensive (see Boq'eh-ye Khajeh Rabi, p357).

During the Iran–Iraq War, Mashhad's population ballooned as it was the furthest Iranian city from the front line. Many stayed on and the metropolis is now Iran's second biggest, a huge, unwieldy and rather polluted sprawl.

Orientation

The Haram is Mashhad's physical as well as spiritual centre. Beneath it is a subterranean circular highway loop. A key junction just south of the Haram is Falakeh

Ab, marked on maps as Beit-ol-Moqaddas Sq. Construction around the Haram never seems to end: eventual enlargement plans supposedly include the partial destruction of Andarzgu St's north side.

Information

BOOKSHOPS

Several bookshops stock maps, dictionaries and the odd English book, notably those in **Mahtab Passaj** (Map p354; Sa'di St). The **Friday book market** (Map p354; Modarres St, south side; ☼ 8am-2pm Fri) is good for English-language magazines including the *Economist* (IR10,000). Blind peddlers outside the Haram near Falakeh Ab sell excellent city maps (IR6000).

CONSULATES

Afghanistan (Map p354; ☎ 854 1653; Do Shahid St; ☼ 8am-noon Sat-Wed) An unruly queue of Afghans snakes round the building but foreign visa applicants can walk straight through an unmarked white door part-way down the queue. Apply early with a copy of your passport and two mugshots and in principle the 30-day tourist visa should be ready the same day for a flat €75 fee. However, a few travellers report being refused for no apparent reason.

Pakistan (Map p354; ☎ 222 9845; Imam Khomeini St; ☯ 9am-noon Sat-Wed) Occupies the former British consulate. Unlikely to issue visas.

Turkmenistan (Map p354; ☎ 854 7066; Do Shahid St, off Dah-e Dey Sq; ☯ 8.30am-noon Mon-Thu & Sat) All business is conducted through a tiny hole-in-the-wall window and no English is spoken so if you don't understand Farsi, Turkmen or Russian consider going with a translator. For a five-day transit visa you'll need an onward visa (Uzbek is best, Azerbaijani sometimes accepted). Photocopy that visa and your main passport page, facing each other onto a single sheet of A4 paper. Hand this in, stating the entry and exit points by which you'll transit Turkmenistan (inflexible). Then come back after five days by which time, *insh'Allah*, an approval letter will have arrived for you from Ashgabat. If it has, you may now apply for the visa. This requires two more passport copies and two photos. It normally takes four days but since you'll need your passport for hotel accommodation in Iran, they'll usually handle applications for foreigners within 24 hours (for double the fee; fees vary by nationality). There's a handy photocopy shop three doors from Baghoi Exchange.

EMERGENCY
Imam Reza Hospital (Map p354; ☎ 854 3031-9; Ibn-e Sina St) Good, accessible hospital with 24-hour pharmacy.

INTERNET ACCESS
Aftabshargh Coffeenet (Map p354; Imam Khomeini St; per hr IR5000; ☯ 9am-9pm)
Attar Coffeenet (Map p356; Falakeh Ab; per hr IR7000; ☯ 24hr) Three floors up. Very central.
Coffeenet Dalahoo (Map p356; Imam Reza St; per hr IR6000; ☯ 24hr) Good connection but tends to overheat in the daytime.

MONEY
Banks with foreign-exchange counters are relatively common but the exchange counters are faster and give fair rates.
Baghoi Exchange (Map p354; Imam Khomeini St; ☯ 9am-1.30pm & 5-7pm Sat-Wed, 9am-1pm Thu)
Saraf Exchange (Map p354; Imam Khomeini St; ☯ 9am-2pm & 5-8pm Sat-Thu)
Sepehri Exchange (Map p354; Pasdaran Ave; ☯ 9am-6pm Sat-Wed & 9am-2pm Thu)

PETROL RATION CARD OFFICE
Sherkate Mellie Naft-e-Iran (Map p352; ☎ 7633011; Janbaz Blvd at Blvd Sajjad)

POST
Main post office (Map p354; Tavala'i St) Use for parcels.
Post office (Map p354; Imam Khomeini St) Opposite Bank Melli. OK for stamps, but not parcels.

TOURIST INFORMATION
Information room (bus terminal arrivals area; ☯ 24hr) Library-style sitting room gives you space to think after a long journey. OK free maps indicate several museums that don't yet exist.
Miras Ferhangi Khorasan (Map p352; ☎ 725 9311; Sadeghi Blvd; ☯ 8am-2pm Sat-Thu) Officially you need a letter from these folks before visiting some out-of-the-way sights like Robat Sharaf (p365). They print lavish bilingual brochures for each district in Khorasan.

TOUR GUIDES & TRAVEL AGENCIES
Adibian Travel Agency (Map p354; ☎ 859 8151; www .adibiantours.com; 56 Pasdaran Ave; ☯ 7.30am-8pm) Very

---

THE MARTYRDOM OF IMAM REZA

Within Mashhad's holy shrine, pilgrims break into conspicuous, heartfelt outpourings of grief for murdered Imam Reza as though his assassination (with poisoned grapes and pomegranate juice) were only yesterday. In fact it was in AD 818.

The story starts 20 years earlier with Haroun ar-Rashid, immortalised as the great caliph in the *Arabian Nights* fairy-tales. Less fictionally, Haroun ruled the Abbasid caliphate and was very influential in bringing Greek-style analytic thinking and cosmopolitan sophistication to Arab-Muslim society. His temporal power was unassailable. But he coveted the spiritual pre-eminence of Musa, the seventh Shiite Imam. Musa was eventually slapped into Haroun's Baghdad jail, then killed.

Musa's 35-year-old son Ali al-Raza (Razavi) inherited his father's pious mantle becoming Imam Reza. Meanwhile, after Haroun's death, Haroun's sons Ma'mun and Amin slogged out a civil war to succeed their dad as caliph. Ma'mun, based temporarily in Merv, emerged victorious but needed Reza's help to calm a series of revolts. Having failed to entice the Imam to support him voluntarily in this effort, Ma'mun's agents dragged Reza forcibly across rebellious regions as a symbol of imperial power. However, the ploy appeared to be backfiring. The Imam's charismatic presence captivated the royal court, leaving Ma'mun worried that he'd be upstaged. So out came those deadly grapes. Ma'mun disguised the crime by honouring Reza's body with burial in Sanabad (today's Mashhad) close to Ma'mun's own father (and Reza's father's nemesis) Caliph Haroun.

professional English-speaking agency that sells air and train tickets, provides assistance with visa-extension applications and offers tours in Mashhad (half day with/without guide US$40/30) and well beyond (around US$75/65 per day). Guides speak English, French and Arabic.

Towhid Foroozanfar (☎ 893 7025, 0915 313 2960; towhidfroozan@yahoo.com) A well-informed, engaging driver-guide who has been recommended by readers.

Vali Ansari Astaneh (☎ 851 6980, 0915 100 1324; vali32@imamreza.net) Offers very inexpensive low-tech walking and public-transport based city tours, village visits, mountain walks and a budget homestay.

VISA EXTENSIONS

Edareh-ye Gozarnameh (Map p352; ☎ 218 3907; 45 Metri-ye Reza St, Piruzi Blvd; ✷ 8am-1pm Sat-Wed, 8am-10.30am Thu) Behind fortified green fencing, this

inconveniently located place would look like a prison except that the mad crush of inmates (mostly Central Asians) are all trying to get in. Not the best place to apply. For an additional US$25 service charge, Adibian Travel (p353) can handle the processing for you.

Sights

HARAM-E RAZAVI

Imam Reza's Holy Shrine is enveloped in a series of sacred precincts collectively known as the **Haram-e Razavi** (Map p356; ✷ 24hr), or Haram for short. This magical city-within-a-city sprouts dazzling clusters of domes and minarets in blue and pure gold behind vast fountain-cooled courtyards and magnificent arched arcades. It's one of the marvels of the Islamic world whose moods and glories

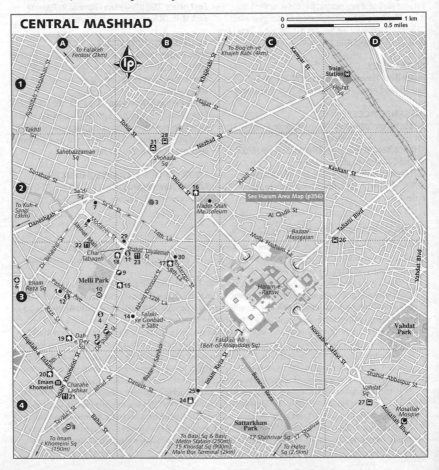

should be fully savoured more than once at varying times of day. Compare the orderly overload of dusk prayer-time to the fairy-tale calm of a floodlight nocturnal wander.

Information

No bags or cameras are allowed within the complex, though curiously snapping photos with mobile phones is accepted. There are left-luggage offices near most entrances. Men and women enter through different carpet-draped portals and are politely frisked. Women must wear a chador: it's sometimes possible to borrow one from your hotel. Dress for either sex should be conservative and clean.

Non-Muslims are allowed in most of the Haram's outer courtyards. They are NOT allowed inside the complex's two holiest buildings, the Holy Shrine and the Gohar Shad Mosque. Technically, non-Muslims are also excluded from the magnificent Enqelab and Azadi courtyards, but you can peep in through relevant gateways. At quieter times, those who act suitably (demure, respectful and soaking up the spiritual rather than the aesthetic) are rarely challenged and might wander through 'by mistake'. However, be particularly careful not to upset Muslim sensibilities: remember, it's a privilege for non-Muslims to be allowed to visit the Haram complex at all.

Friendly, multilingual staff at the **Foreign Pilgrims Assistance Office** (☎ 221 3474; intlrela@ mail.dci.co.ir; 7am-6pm) can show you a 20-minute video about the shrine and shower you with books on all things Shiite. However, once you've visited this office there's no escape from the free, friendly but overprotective guide/minder they assign you.

Outer Courtyards

A good starting point for nonpilgrim visits is Falakeh Ab from which several of the domes and minarets are tantalisingly visible in the middle distance. Enter through the vast, part-constructed **Razavi Grand Courtyard**, which should become grander once the blue, white and gold tiling has been affixed to the courtyard's façades and concrete minarets. Curving east you'll pass the Haram's **museums** (p357) after the unfinished **Imam Khomeini Courtyard** site. Beyond, look northwest across the gorgeous **Azadi Courtyard** to glimpse the exterior of the Holy Shrine building.

Notice the **Naqqareh Khaneh**, a blue-tiled bandstand platform perched above a clock tower gateway. Twice daily (before dawn and dusk) a mesmerising 10-minute fanfare is performed here by drummers and a heptet of gentlemen-hornblowers in faintly comical Salvation Army–style peaked-caps.

Non-Muslims aren't supposed to transit the spectacular **Enqelab Courtyard** with its two gold minarets and fabulous tile-work. So to reach **Jomhuri Courtyard**, the setting for massed evening *namaz* (prayers), infidels should double back via **Qods Courtyard**, which features a miniature version of Jerusalem's 'Dome of the Rock'.

Inner Sanctuaries (Muslims only)

The gold-domed centrepiece of the Haram complex is the revered 17th-century **Holy Shrine** building. Amid tearful prayer and meditation, the emotional climax to any Mashhad pilgrimage is touching and kissing the *zarih* (gold-latticed cage), which covers **Imam Reza's tomb** in the shrine's spectacular interior. The current *zarih*, the fifth, dates from 2001. Non-Muslims are excluded, but

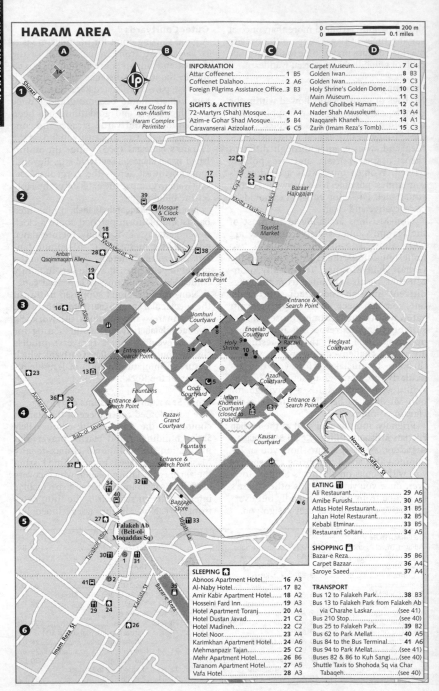

HARAM AREA

| 0 | 200 m |
| 0 | 0.1 miles |

INFORMATION
Attar Coffeenet..........................1 B5
Coffeenet Dalahoo.....................2 A6
Foreign Pilgrims Assistance Office..3 B3

SIGHTS & ACTIVITIES
72-Martyrs (Shah) Mosque..........4 A4
Azim-e Gohar Shad Mosque.......5 B4
Caravanserai Azizolaof...............6 C5

Carpet Museum.........................7 C4
Golden Iwan.............................8 B3
Golden Iwan.............................9 C3
Holy Shrine's Golden Dome.......10 C3
Main Museum..........................11 C3
Mehdi Gholibek Hamam............12 C4
Nader Shah Mausoleum.............13 A4
Naqqareh Khaneh.....................14 A1
Zarih (Imam Reza's Tomb).........15 C3

Map labels
14
Shiraz St
Area Closed to non-Muslims
Haram Complex Perimiter
22
17
25 21
Kyal Alley
Bazaar Hajogajan
39
Mosque & Clock Tower
Molla Hashem La
Sabkat La
18
Mohaberat St
Tourist Market
Anbari Qaqimmaqam Alley
28
38
19
Entrance & Search Point
16
Malek Alley
Entrance & Search Point
Jomhuri Courtyard
Engelab Courtyard
Haram-e Razavi
Hedayat Courtyard
8
Holy Shrine
9
10 11
15
Entrance & Search Point
3
4
23
13
5
Qods Courtyard
Azadi Courtyard
Fountains
36 20
Entrance & Search Point
Imam Khomeini Courtyard (closed to public)
12
7
Entrance & Search Point
Andarzgu St
Razavi Grand Courtyard
Bab-ol Javad
Fountains
Kausar Courtyard
Novab-e Safavi St
37
Entrance & Search Point
34
32
Baggage Store
40
33
27
Falakeh Ab (Beit-ol-Moqaddas Sq)
Idgah La
Tavakoli Alley
30
1 31
41
2
35
29 24
Kalbala St
Bazar-e Reza
26
Imam Reza St

EATING
Ali Restaurant..........................29 A6
Amibe Furushi..........................30 A5
Atlas Hotel Restaurant..............31 B5
Jahan Hotel Restaurant.............32 B5
Kebabi Etminar.........................33 B5
Restaurant Soltani....................34 A5

SHOPPING
Bazar-e Reza...........................35 B6
Carpet Bazaar..........................36 A4
Saroye Saeed...........................37 A4

SLEEPING
Abnoos Apartment Hotel..........16 A3
Al-Naby Hotel..........................17 B2
Amir Kabir Apartment Hotel.....18 A2
Hosseini Fard Inn......................19 A3
Hotel Apartment Toranj............20 A4
Hotel Dustan Javad..................21 C2
Hotel Madineh.........................22 C2
Hotel Noor...............................23 A4
Karimkhan Apartment Hotel.....24 A6
Mehmanpazir Tajan..................25 C2
Mehr Apartment Hotel.............26 B6
Taranom Apartment Hotel........27 A5
Vafa Hotel...............................28 A3

TRANSPORT
Bus 12 to Falakeh Park.............38 B3
Bus 13 to Falakeh Park from Falakeh Ab via Charahe Laskar..............(see 41)
Bus 210 Stop............................(see 40)
Bus 25 to Falakeh Park.............39 B2
Bus 62 to Park Mellat...............40 A5
Bus 84 to the Bus Terminal.......41 A6
Bus 94 to Park Mellat...............(see 41)
Buses 82 & 86 to Kuh Sangi....(see 40)
Shuttle Taxis to Shohoda Sq via Char Tabaqeh...............................(see 40)

can see the previous *zarih* in the Haram's main museum (see below).

You might catch a glimpse of the 50m blue dome and cavernous golden portal of the classic Timurid **Azim-e Gohar Shad mosque** (built from 1405 to 1418). However, non-Muslims aren't allowed within to appreciate its splendid interior hosting the minbar (pulpit) where, according to Shiite tradition, the Mahdi (12th 'hidden' Imam) will sit on the Day of Judgement.

Haram Museums

Bequests and donations from the faithful fill the Haram's fascinatingly eclectic museums. The **Main Museum** (Muze-ye Merkezi; admission IR5000; 8am-5.30pm Sat-Thu, 8am-noon Fri) kicks off with chunks of now-superseded shrine-décor interspersed with contemporary sporting medals presented by pious athletes. The basement **stamp collection** includes a 1983 commemorative featuring the 'Takeover of the US Spy Den'. The 1st-floor **Visual Arts Gallery** offers you the opportunity to shower money (or hats) down onto the top of the Holy Shrine's fourth *zarih* tomb encasement (replaced in 2001). Amid seashells and naturalist landscape-paintings of Surrey, notice Mahmood Farshchian's modern classic *Afternoon of Ashura*. It's a grief-stricken depiction of Imam Hossein's horse returning empty to camp after the Imam's martyrdom. That's an image you'll find repeated as both carpet and giant wood-inlay works in the separate **Carpet Museum** (admission IR5000; 8am-12.30pm Sat-Wed, 8am-11.30am Thu), where rugs range from beautiful classics through to garish coral gardens and a Tabriz-made carpet-portrait of WWI bogey-man Kaiser Wilhelm II. Tying the staggering 30 million knots for *Seven Beloved Cities* took 14 years. Upstairs, beside the shoe-deposit counter, is a two-room **Calligraphy Gallery** displaying priceless Korans, many dating back over a millennium.

OTHER SIGHTS

Just outside the complex's official limits is the splendid 15th-century **72-Martyrs (Shah) Mosque**. In its shadow, **Mehdi Gholibek Hamam** (admission IR3000; 8am-6pm Mon-Thu, 8am-1pm Fri) is one of Iran's most interesting and spacious bathhouse museums. The main delight is the wonderful central dome re-painted for centuries in multiple levels – most recently

in 1922 with naive murals that feature anthropomorphic figures gallivanting between giant bicycles, a Russian vintage car, an early biplane and a curiously unconcerned-looking victim facing a firing squad.

Lanes around the Haram's various entrances are full of tourist trinket sellers but also a selection of real markets. The run-down, century-old **Caravanserai Azizolaof** contains down-market electronics stalls run by Afghans. Hurry to see this area before it's all demolished as the Haram precinct plans to expand yet again.

SIGHTS BEYOND THE SHRINE COMPLEX
Boq'eh-ye Khajeh Rabi   آبقعهخواجه ربیع

This beautifully proportioned, blue-domed **mausoleum** (Map p352) commemorates an apostle of the prophet Mohammad. Coming to pay respects here was said to have been Imam Reza's 'main consolation' in coming all the way out to Khorasan. The tower took its present form after a 1612 rebuild, which added a band of interior Kufic inscriptions by master-calligrapher Ali Reza Abbasi. The jolly floral motifs around it date from a Qajar redecoration. Surrounding the mausoleum is a large cemetery paved with thousands of tombstones. Burial here currently costs from IR8,500,000. That gets you stacked four bodies deep for 30 years before you're dug up again; pay four times that amount per body if you want a 'family room' within

---

MASHTI

Although slightly less significant than pilgrimages to Mecca, Najaf or Karbala, a pilgrimage to Mashhad remains a deeply significant expression of faith for any Shiite Muslim. After *wudu* 'ablutions', the supplicant humbly enters the Holy Shrine asking 'permission' from Imam Reza through specific prayers and recitations. Following tearful meditations and Quranic readings, the pilgrimage culminates with the recitation of the *Ziyarat Nameh* prayer in front of the *zarih* (tomb) of Imam Reza.

In the same way that hajj pilgrims are respectfully known as *haji*, those who have fulfilled the pilgrimage to Mashhad are entitled to attach the prefix *Mashti* to their names.

surrounding arched colonnades. That's still only half what you'd pay to deposit a corpse beneath the Haram.

Get here on bus 34 from Tabarsi Blvd or 38 from Kuh-e Sangi.

Nader Shah Mausoleum   آرامگاه نادر شاه

Elsewhere in the Middle East, Nader Shah is considered something of a historical tyrant. But here he's a local hero for briefly returning Khorasan to the centre of a vast Central Asian empire. Nader's horseback statue crowns his otherwise rather dour 1950s grey-granite **mausoleum** (Map p356; ☎ 222 4888; cnr Shirazi & Azadi Sts; admission IR3000; 8am-6.30pm), which was designed to emulate the lines of a tent (reputedly Nader was born and died under canvas). A small **museum** displays guns, a rhino-hide shield and four-pointed hats that must have made Afshar-dynasty courtiers look like jesters.

Kuh-e Sangi   کوه سنگی

This small but abrupt **rocky hill** (Map p352; admission free, 24hr) rises near Mashhad's southern ring road (the 'Kabul to Paris highway'). Sweeping views show just how huge Mashhad has become. Tastefully set rock steps lead up from a large 'recreation complex' featuring ponds, over-priced ice creams and lots of souvenir shops selling soapstone *dizi* pots and awful porcelain figurines. **Horsecart rides** (IR30,000) do NOT take you up the mountain as they might imply but on a pointless eight-minute trot down some side streets. Within the park there's a sweetly naive loop of **pedal-car monorail** (rides per person IR3500; 9am-1am) for kids.

Buses 86 and 82 run between Kuh-e Sangi and Falakeh Ab. Bus 38 links Kuh-e Sangi to Borq-e Khajeh Rabi.

Gonbad-e-Sabz   گنبد سبز

In its own little traffic roundabout, Sheikh Mohammed Hakim Mo'men's modest, Safavid-era **mausoleum** (Green Dome; Map p354; Falakeh-ye Gonbad-e Sabz; donation appreciated; 8am-11am) isn't very green but makes a useful landmark.

Sleeping

Timing is everything. In peak season, accommodation is jam-packed: prices can rise up to 800% in some cases (especially apartment hotels), though others stay stable. We quote both base rates (April) and peak rates. Some hotels discount in mid-winter.

WHAT ARE MASHHAD'S PEAK SEASONS?

- No Ruz
- summer pilgrim season (June–July)
- the Muslim months of Moharram, Safar and Ramazan
- any major Islamic festival

BUDGET

Vali's Non-smoking Homestay (Map p354; ☎ 851 6980, 0915 100 1324; vali32@imamreza.net; 6th Alley, off Enqelab-e Eslami St, house 277; dm/s/tw IR30,000/50,000/100,000;) Vali is an eccentric and ever-enthusiastic carpet merchant–cum–multilingual guide who offers a twin-bedded guest room in his charming home along with communal carpeted sleeping spaces, some on the open-air terrace. This is the nearest Mashhad gets to a backpacker hostel but it's vastly more personal and inviting. Great home-cooked meals cost only IR15,000 (often vegetarian). Prices stay the same all year. Take bus 85 from near the main terminal or 13 from Falakeh Ab, either way getting off at Charahe Lashkar (Metro Emam Khomeini).

Mehmanpazir Tajan (Map p356; ☎ 222 3243; Baqatavuz Alley, off Sabkar Lane; tw/tr IR50,000/60,000, peak season IR195,000/219,000) Showers are rusty and furniture ageing but for the off-season price this is truly remarkable value. Mehdi speaks very limited English and has a gravity-defying grey-bouff haircut.

Hosseini Fard Inn (Map p356; ☎ 222 5334; Anbari Qaqimmaqam Alley; tw/tr IR80,000/120,000; d/tr/q with private bathroom IR150,000/200,000/300,000) The en-suite rooms are very tatty. Bed-only rooms aren't much better. However, there's a remarkable Haram view and manager Abulfaz can manage a little English. Add 50% in peak season. Other cheaper, ultra-basic options are available nearby.

Hotel Pars (Map p354; ☎ 222 4030; fax 221 4944; Imam Khomeini St 26th Alley; s/d IR100,000/150,000; closes low-season) Mashhad's oldest hotel, the Pars occupies a 1935 brick building and its manager lived nine years in England. Rooms have ageing en-suite bathrooms but are just as good as many midrange equivalents. The basement *sofrakhane sonati* is a lovely vaulted teahouse (qalyan IR10,000; open 24 hours in season) with a tandoori oven providing fresh bread to accompany meals.

Vafa Hotel (Map p356; ☎ /fax 225 8179; Anbari Qaqimmaqam Alley; tw IR100,000-150,000, peak season IR200,000) Modest but new rooms have small, fresh showers and squat toilets.

Razi Hotel (Map p354; ☎ 854 1122; fax 854 4099; Razi St; s/tw with breakfast s/d IR110,000/200,000, peak season IR170,000/300,000; ✖) Characterless, partly-renovated 1960s place with lugubrious front-desk service, ageing bathrooms and pictures akimbo. Passable value in peak season.

Apartment Hotels

Outside peak season many apartment-hotels are often fabulous value but standards vary considerably and pricing is pretty random, rising up to 800% at peak times (when 'standard' hotels are often better value). Save a bundle by seeking out those in forgotten smaller alleys. All those reviewed have hot shower and kitchenette.

Al-Naby Hotel (Map p356; ☎ 222 6981; Molla Hashem Lane; tw IR120,000, peak season IR230,000) This six-storey tower has fewer frills than many apartment hotels, lacking the obligatory waterfalls and columns (do you care?). But the smallish rooms are new and very adequate with absolutely fabulous views across the Haram complex from front-facing upper levels.

Taranom Apartment Hotel (Map p356; ☎ 859 5761; Tavakoli Lane; s/d IR200,000/250,000, peak season r from IR800,000; ✖) Handily right on Falakeh Ab, this very professional eight-storey tower has a cosy mini-atrium with modernist fireplace and comfortably appointed mini-suites with fluffy towels, brilliant hot showers and Western toilets with soft paper.

Hotel Apartment Toranj (Map p356; ☎ 222 0963; Andarzgu St, 11th Alley; s/d/tr IR200,000/250,000/310,000; peak season IR450,000/500,000/600,000; ✖) The lobby has a big modern chandelier and waterfall feature. Rooms are slightly less grandiose but fine value with fully equipped kitchen, choice of toilet-types in some bathrooms and elegant sash curtains.

Amir Kabir Apartment Hotel (Map p356; ☎ 223 1643; Mohaberat St; ste IR250,000, peak season IR360,000; ✖ 🖳) Despite the chandeliers and bulging Corinthian columns this high-service option has great-value if sickly-green suites and fifth-floor views of the shrine complex (for now).

Mehr Apartment Hotel (Map p356; ☎ 851 4797; mehr-apt-hotel@yahoo.com; Karbala St; tr IR250,000, peak season IR550,000; ✖) Bright and somewhat

modernist with reception staff in smart suits and corridors edged in pink marble. Apartments sleep three (double-plus-single) and have a big sitting room but comparatively small bathrooms. *Careless Whispers* plays in the lift.

Karimkhan Apartment Hotel (Map p356; ☎ 854 4077; fax 854 2844; www.karimkhanhotel.8k.com; off Imam Reza St; d/apt IR300,000/450,000; P ✖ 🖳) Rooms and corridors attempt something of a retro, semi Art Deco look and bathrooms are impressive with curtained, seat-showers but there's some wear on the sitting room furniture.

MIDRANGE

In high season this category is usually the best value as prices are comparatively stable year-round.

Hotel Dustan Javad (Map p356; ☎ 223 3791; fax 225 9794; Shahid Golabki Alley, off Sabkar Lane; s/tw/tr IR12 0,000/150,000/180,000, peak season IR210,000/240,000/270,000) Sweet little suites in a small, family pension-style hotel off a lively but mostly pedestrianised shopping street.

Hotel Madineh (Map p356; ☎ 221 2214; Zeiya Lane; tw/tr IR300,000/350,000 year-round) This 100-room bed-factory wallows in nouveau-riche foibles including aquarium, fountain-grotto, musical elevators and Art Deco-effect coffee shop. Overpriced int the low season but good value at peak times.

Hotel Noor (Map p356; ☎ 223 2970; fax 223 2976; Andarzgu St; d IR350,000) The gently trendy 1st-floor lobby is bright and open with highly professional English-speaking staff. Rooms are unfussy business-class affairs with bagged-towels and choice of toilets. Winter discounts 30%, splendid value in peak season.

Iran Hotel (Map p354; ☎ 222 8010; www.irhotel.com; Andarzgu St; s/d/tr/q with breakfast IR331,500/550,000/995,000/1,204,000; ✖ 🖳) This hotel with friendly, English-speaking staff gets it right with a restrained elegance that's personable and not over formal. Bathrooms are small but new and sparkling clean. Excellent value for singles during peak season, if you can get a room.

Hotel Tara (Map p354; ☎ 221 6100; fax 225 9595; www.hoteltara.com; Shirazi St; s/d US$35/55; ✖) Relatively spacious rooms with hints of bed canopy have bath tubs in their slightly outdated bathrooms. In season this is an OK midrange choice with some English spoken.

Pardis Hotel (Map p354; ☎ 222 8095; fax 222 3831; Imam Khomeini St; d/tr US$50/60; P ✕) The friendly multilingual reception is the only real attraction of this overpriced 1970s throwback with antiseptic corridors and dreadfully dated bathrooms.

Laleh Hotel (Map p352; ☎ 840 8047; fax 842 3892; Kuhsanghi St; d US$54 year-round; ✕) Handy for Kuh Sangi but not the shrine, the Laleh's Eastern European idea of style is so outdated that it's almost an attraction. Bedside TV-control panels are worthy of a *Dr No*–era James Bond movie.

TOP END

Abnoos Apartment Hotel (Map p356; ☎ 221 5576; fax 221 5581; apt IR450,000-500,000, peak season IR900,000-990,000) Hidden in a peaceful mini-garden off a tiny alley, the high-class Abnoos offers unusually spacious apartments sleeping four or five people. There are fine Haram views from the roof and from rooms 301 and 302. Manager Mousa Delshad speaks excellent English.

Homa Hotel Mashhad (Map p352; ☎ 761 1001; www.homahotels.com; Khayyam Blvd; s/d/ste US$101/116/140; P ✕ 🖥 ☎) Mashhad's inconveniently located top hotel has a shopping mall–sized lobby whose blue-glass pyramid roof mimics the Louvre's. Rooms are very large and well kept but lack any real style. Women can only use the indoor pool-spa four mornings a week.

Hotel Pars Mashhad (Map p352; ☎ 868 9201; fax 868 9200; Vakilabad Blvd; d/ste US$126/262; P ✕ 🖥 ☎) The main draw of this sprawling, upmarket complex is the full-sized swimming pool (open Sunday to Friday, women 8am to 1pm, men 3.30pm to 10pm), so avoid Saturdays when it's closed. The location, some 8km west of the centre, is awful for the Holy Shrine but comparatively handy for visiting Kang.

Eating

There are plenty of cheap eateries in the lanes off Imam Reza St and pleasant stream-side restaurants can be found on rural roads around Torqabeh, Shandiz and Zoshk. Upmarket, traditional dining options are limited because most visitors eat production-line hotel dinners provided as part of their tour package.

Kebabi Etminar (Map p356; Idgah Lane; meals IR7000-18,000; ✕ 5am-midnight) Bog-standard local eatery whose IR7000 *nun-o panir*

breakfast includes walnuts, raisins and unusually tasty cheese with bread and tea. Kababs from IR4400.

Vitamin Sara (Map p354; ☎ 222 7998; Shahid Diyalemeh (Bahonar) St; ✕ 9am-11pm Sat-Thu, 4pm-11pm Fri) Come to this unpretentious juice-shop for Mashhad's best *maajun* (IR12,000), a fabulous mush of crushed walnuts, pistachios, ice cream, cream, banana and honey, all whizzed through the orgasmatron to form one of Iran's most spectacular desserts. Cheaper but inferior versions are available from Amibe Furushi (Map p356; desserts IR10,000) is open 24 hours on Imam Reza St.

Ali Restaurant (Map p356; ☎ 851 6601; Imam Reza St; meals IR23,000-45,000; ✕ 10am-4pm & 7-10pm) Cavernous downstairs pay-first diner with a giant spoon-and-fork looming above the cashier. The menu is typical but available in English. Fast turnover. Nearby Restaurant Soltani across Falakeh Ab on Andarzgu St is similar in a glittery mirror-tiled basement.

Hafez Restaurant (Map p354; ☎ 754 0768; meals IR25,000-55,000; ✕ 11.30am-3pm & dusk-10pm Sat-Thu) With attractive wrought iron and copperwork, this new, high-ceilinged eatery is a fine choice in the consulate area. For a taste of Central Asia, try their *chelo estanboli* (IR17,000), virtually identical to *plov* (an archetypal if fatty Uzbek lamb-and-rice dish).

Jahan Hotel Restaurant (Map p356; ☎ 225 0085; top fl, Jahan Hotel, Hozeino Alley; meals IR42,000-68,000; ✕ 12.30-2.30pm & 7.30-9.30pm) Kababs, schnitzels or trout (IR49,500) are unremarkable but truly phenomenal views across the Haram make lunch-time dining here a must. Enter via the hotel, easily missed beneath a Bank Mellat sign. Don't be late!

Atlas Hotel Restaurant (Map p356; 1st fl, Hotel Atlas, Falakeh Ab; meals IR50,000-90,000; ✕ noon-3pm & 7-10.45pm) For steak and chips in a middle class setting, this comfortable hotel restaurant opens longer than most and the coffeehouse downstairs has an espresso machine.

our pick **Hezardestan Traditional Teahouse** (Map p354; ☎ 222 2943; Jannat Mall; meals IR60,000-140,000; ✕ lunch & dinner) Hezardestan is one of Iran's most beautiful teahouse-restaurants. Carpets, samovars, antique qalyans, cushions and wooden benches are surrounded by walls adorned with scenes from Ferdosi's *Shahnamah*. There's live music most nights, the manager speaks fluent English and the food is pretty good including vegetarian pos-

WORTH ITS WEIGHT

Cleopatra added it to her mare's-milk baths. Indian Buddhists dyed their robes with it. Romans slapped it on to cure scabies. And Alexander the Great used it to patch up his battle scars. Today saffron adds flavour and colour to Cornish saffron cake and Spanish paella as well as to *chelo* (rice) in Iran where it remains Persia's classic 'spice'. Saffron comes from the delicately dried stigmas of *Crocus sativus* flowers, grown extensively in southern regions of Khorasan. But producing a kilogram of saffron requires around 200,000 flowers. No wonder it's often so staggeringly pricey.

sibilities. Just be prepared for hefty 'service' and 'tea' charges that can double the bill.

Shopping

Mashhad is a great place to buy carpets. Half hidden through deceptively small doorways, both **Bazaar-e Fash** (Map p354; Imam Reza St; 8.30am-1.30pm & 4-8.30pm Sat-Wed, 8.30am-1pm Thu) and **Saroye Saeed** (Map p356; Andarzgu St; 8am-2pm & 4-7pm) are multi-unit carpet markets mostly aimed at bulk dealers so prices can be excellent. Both places have interesting top-floor repair workshops and remarkably there seems to be no sales pressure.

The wobbly, wooden-ceilinged old **carpet bazaar** (Map p356; 13th Alley, Andarzgu St) is more commercial minded but slated for eventual demolition if the shrine's expansion continues.

Upstairs in the 800m-long **Bazar-e Reza** (Map p356; 8am-8pm Sat-Thu), jewellery stalls proffer turquoise (mined at nearby Neishabur) but their sales pitch is often more impressive than their gems.

Around Falakeh Ab, shops sell comparatively inexpensive saffron (see the boxed text, above) in a range of qualities: a highly portable souvenir.

The Haram is surrounded by bazaars and shopping arcades flogging tacky pilgrimage souvenirs. Try to resist the considerable temptation to buy an over saturated photograph of yourself superimposed upon the Holy Shrine.

Getting There & Away

During peak seasons long-distance transport can be booked up months ahead.

AIR
International Services

Iran Aseman (Map p354; 225 8200; Andarzgu St) has flights to Bishkek (Kyrgyzstan, single/return IR2,350,000/3,664,000, Tuesday), Dushanbe (Tajikistan, IR2,020,000/2,840,000, Tuesday), Kuwait (IR1,050,000/1,850,000, Wednesday and Friday) and Kabul (IR1,820,000/2,300,000 Monday). **KamAir** (www.flykamair.ca) also flies to Kabul (IR1,334,000/2,330,000, Saturday). To go further afield, use connections via Bahrain with Gulf Air (IR1,817,000/3,129,000, twice weekly) or Doha with Qatar Airways (IR2,135,000/3,578,000, thrice weekly). Check out **Jazeera Airways** (www.jazeeraairways.com) for budget flights from Kuwait (Wednesday and Friday in season), starting at 15 Kuwaiti dinars (US$52).

Domestic Services

To Tehran there are 63 weekly flights (IR433,000) on six different airlines, including Saha Air, which uses the world's last Boeing 707s still in passenger service. Other direct flights from Mashhad:

Destination	Fare	Flights per week (airline)
Ahvaz	IR625,000	2 (IA)
Bandar Abbas	IR588,000	2 (IA)
Esfahan	IR476,000 (IA)	6 (Eram), 3 (Aria), 2 (Caspian), 2 (Taban)
Gorgan	IR324,000	3 (IA)
Kerman	IR434,000	2 (Mahan)
Kermanshah	IR624,000	(Aria), 2 (As)
Kish	IR714,000	14 (Kish)
Nowshahr	IR329,000	2 (IA)
Rasht	IR497,000	2 (IA)
Sari	IR345,000	3 (IA)
Shiraz	IR540,000 (IA)	7 (As)
Tabriz	IR638,000	2 (IA), 2 (Caspian), 2 (Eram)
Yazd	IR401,000	2 (IA)
Zabol	IR320,000	1 (Taban)
Zahedan	IR436,000	4 (IA)

IA=IranAir, As=Iran Aseman

Arriving in Mashhad by air, the useful hotel reservation counter inside the arrivals hall can book midrange and top-end places. It's well worth using during high season.

BUS, MINIBUS & TAXI

All of Mashhad's numerous transport terminals are well out of the centre. However, most long distance bus services can be pre-booked at relatively central **Binalood Travel** (Map p354; ☎ 852 5580; Imam Reza St).

Main Terminal
Useful services from the bustling **main bus terminal** (Map p352; end of Imam Reza St):

Destination	Fare	Duration	Departures (company)
Birjand	IR21,000/ 40,000	8hr	8am, 8pm-10pm
Esfahan	IR95,000*	22hr	7am, 3pm, 6-8pm
Gorgan	IR26,000/ 50,000	10½hr	6-10am & 6-9pm
Herat (Afghanistan)	IR60,000	7hr	8am, 10am
Kerman	IR70,000*	16hr	3pm Taavoni 14
Sari	IR32,000/ 60,000	12hr	6-8am, 5-7pm
Shahrud	IR17,400	10hr	10pm, Iran Peyma
Tabas (via Birjand)	IR25,100	10hr	7.30pm Saadet Peyma
Tehran	IR40,000/ 70,000	14hr	Frequent
Yazd	IR42,000/ 80,000	16hr	4pm, 5pm, 6pm Saadet Peyma
Zahedan	IR45,000/ 75,000	15hr	9.30am, 7pm Towfik Peyma

*Volvo

For Tabas you'll get many more options by taking a Yazd bus (probably paying full fare). Likewise, consider taking a Tehran bus for Shahrud, Damghan or Semnan.

Check the security situation before taking Mashhad–Zahedan or Mashhad–Kerman buses, which are subjected to frequent drug searches en-route. For Neishabur (IR6000, two hours), Fariman (IR3500, 1¼ hours), Torbat-e Jam (IR10,000, 2½ hours) and Taybad (IR15,000, 3½ hours), buses leave when full from 'stations' five and six within the terminal. Pay on board. Savaris to those destinations usually depart from Hafez Sq.

Other Terminals
For Sarakhs, infrequent buses (IR10,000, three hours) leave from the new **Istgah Sarakhs** (Map p352; Sarakhs Blvd), about 700m east of Sarakhs Sq. More regular savaris (IR30,000, two hours) depart from a point somewhat further east. Get to either by bus 64 from Mosallah Blvd.

For Kalat Naderi, savaris (IR25,000, two hours) leave from Bareh Noghari Sq on the northern ring road, reached by bus 35 from Tabarsi St. Very rare buses to Kalat (IR8000, 3½ hours) leave from a hidden yard 300m to the southeast (Map p352). Savaris to Quchan (back/front IR15,000/20,000, 1½ hours) and Bojnurd (IR30,000/35,0000, three hours) leave from Falakeh Park (Map p352), a 15-minute ride on buses 12 or 25 from the Haram, or on bus 13 from Falakeh Ab via Charahe Lashkar. Buses to Quchan (IR6000, two hours) and Bojnurd (IR12,000, four hours) start 500m further north up Azadi Hwy (beyond Sajjad Blvd) and also pick up at a spot 6km further northwest along the motorway.

Change in Quchan for Bajgiran (and then Turkmenistan).

Buses for Tus (frequent), Torqabeh (122), Abardeh (122, regular) and Zoshk (124, rare) leave from Falakeh Ferdosi (Map p352). That's most conveniently reached by bus 210 from Falakeh Ab or by shuttle taxi (IR1250) from Tohid Blvd at Shohoda Sq. Buses to Kang leave from Kuhestan Park (Map p352) five times daily.

For Radkan Tower, start by heading to Chenaran. Savaris leave from the west end of Ferdosi Blvd, minibuses from the old TBT garage on Garani Blvd (the western extension of Tohid St).

TRAIN
The train offers a wonderfully comfortable alternative to flying, especially if you pamper yourself with a first class berth (comfortable beds, flat screen TV, full meal service included). Book as far ahead as possible.

Destination	Fare	Duration	Departures
Ahvaz	IR110,000	30hr	11.30pm, 5 weekly
Bandar Abbas	IR220,000	22½hr	3.30pm Wed, Fri, Sat
Esfahan	from IR100,000	24hr	6.30pm Mon, Wed, Sat
Sarakhs	IR8500	3hr	10am, 6pm local services
Tabriz	IR210,000	26hr	3.30pm
Tehran	IR200,000	7hr	7am express
Tehran	IR37,000	12hr	10.30am, 2pm old trains
Tehran	from IR72,000	12hr	8 daily, 4-10.30pm
Tehran	IR200,000	12hr	7pm 'Green' train
Yazd	from IR160,000	12hr	9.15pm Mon, Wed, Fri

Getting Around

TO/FROM THE AIRPORT

A semi regular public bus runs between the airport terminal and Basij Mustazafin Sq. Taxis cost IR35,000.

BUS

Pre-buy shiny IR300 tickets from **ticket booths** (6.30am-8.30pm) to use the excellent but complex network of city buses. Most buses stop running after 9pm. A few (eg bus 10) continue later, requiring two tickets at night. From stops near Falakeh Ab (Map p356), southbound bus 84 runs to the bus terminal, buses 13, 62 and 94 wiggle towards Park Mellat. Useful bus 210 passes the Nader Shah mausoleum (first stop), Shohoda Sq (second stop) and Falakeh Ferdosi (one stop beyond the big Saba Hotel). For Kuhestan Park, take bus 10 from Shohoda Sq (Map p354) or Park Mellat.

METRO

The new 19-station metro starts from Ghadir Hwy in the southeast, runs beneath Feda'iyen-e Eslami, Bahar, Enqelab-e-Eslami and Ahmedabad Sts to Park Mellat, then overground down the middle of Vakilabad Blvd rendering that thundering highway almost uncrossable.

TAXI

Shuttle taxis on straight runs usually cost IR1000 (IR1500 for longer hops). However, any deviation requires payment *dar baste*: IR8000 for a short-ish hop, around IR20,000 to cross a larger chunk of the city.

AROUND MASHHAD

Kang کنگ

 0512 / pop 2300

Photogenic **Kang** is 'Khorasan's Masuleh', a wonderfully homogenous **stepped village** of stacked mud-brick homes, most with porch-balconies and earthen roofs. Stairways duck beneath overhangs while steep slate-bottomed streamways run down the middle of alleyways. For the best **overall view**, fork left at the teahouse where the bus terminates, walk 400m, then cross the river and climb for about three minutes.

A very rewarding way to arrive in Kang is to walk (1½ hours) from the Shandiz–Zoshk road. The hike starts up Zoshk 14th Lane, to the left before Zoshk village, signed in yellow Farsi letters on green. This rough 4WD track crosses a bald, low-mountain pass that's lonely but easy-to-follow. Buses from Mashhad's Falakeh Ferdosi are fairly rare to Zoshk but relatively frequent to Shandiz or Abardeh (3km beyond); hitch hiking the last 13km to Zoshk is easy enough, passing a series of idyllic little **stream-side teahouse-restaurants** en route. Doing the trek with Vali Ansari Astaneh (p354), you'll also get to visit local family homes in Abardeh.

From Kang, five daily buses to Mashhad's Kuhestan Park leave at 7am, 11.30am, 2pm, 4pm and 6.45pm. Alternatively, hitch hike via pretty castle-village Noqondar to **Torqabeh** (22km) from which bus 114 (35 minutes, two IR300 tickets) runs to Mashhad's Falakeh Ferdosi every 20 minutes till 7pm. Torqabeh is famous for canework handicrafts, out-of-town riverside teahouse-restaurants and ice-cream sundaes served with nuts and lemon juice on a bed of noodles!

Tus (Ferdosi) (طوس (فردوسي

 0512

Just as Stratford-upon-Avon in England is synonymous with Shakespeare, so Tus is inextricably linked with Persia's 11th-century epic poet Abulqasim Ferdosi (see p74). Domestic tourists flock to the **Ferdosi Mausoleum** (admission IR3000; 8am-6.30pm), set in its own park and topped by a classically styled stone cenotaph. The current mausoleum only dates from 1964 but there's been a tomb of sorts here since Ferdosi's death in AD 1020. He was originally interred in his own garden because the local Muslim cemetery considered his writings too anti-Islamic for burial there. Similar extreme feelings resurfaced very briefly during the earliest throes of the 1979 revolution during which the mausoleum was damaged.

Beneath the main monument a series of reliefs represent Ferdosi's works. A nicely presented but limited **Tus Museum** (266 3339; admission an additional IR2000; 8am-6pm), within the mausoleum's gardens, displays gory paintings, exhibits 'warlike equipment' and sells postcards. In the rear section of the park, the **Razan gate** shows how incredibly thick Tus's original mud-brick city walls once were. Tus had been Khorasan's foremost city before being so comprehensively sacked by Tamerlane's forces (1389) that it was effectively abandoned.

About 1km towards Mashhad, the **Boq'e-ye Hordokieh**' (Gonbad-e Haruniyeh; admission IR2000; ☻8am-4pm) is a massive brick-domed 14th-century mausoleum that looks especially impressive when floodlit at dusk. There are several theories as to the structure's purpose. The most popular (and least likely) is that it was a prison for the assassin of Imam Reza. The rather bare interior displays models of other tomb towers including the impressive **Akhangan Tower** (12km northeast of Tus) with its recently added blue-scalloped 'roof'.

Tus village is now almost a suburb of Mashhad. City buses (two IR300 tickets, 40 minutes) and minibuses leave around three times hourly from Falakeh Ferdosi using two different routes. They terminate outside the mausoleum.

Radkan   رادکان

About 75km northwest of Mashhad, the mysterious 25m-high **Radkan Tower** has baffled visitors for centuries. A tomb? A coronation spot? According to Iranian archaeo-astronomer **Manoochehr Arian** (www .jamejamshid.com), it was actually a highly sophisticated instrument for studying the stars built in AD 1261 by astronomers led by Nasruddin Tusi (Nasir Al-Tusi; 1201–74). The round, conical-topped brick tower was designed so that the sun shines directly through its doors and niches on solstice and equinox days. It was possibly with data collected here and at his more famous observatory at Maraqeh (p145) that Tusi managed to calculate the earth's diameter and explain discrepancies between Aristotle's and Ptolemy's theories of planetary movement.

The tower is in a field, 1km northwest of Qiasabad hamlet or 3km down an unsurfaced road from Radkan village. Radkan village is itself surrounded by a quietly fascinating scattering of old mud ruins, 9km north of the Quchan–Mashhad highway (it's possible to hitch hike). The village taxi agency charges IR10,000 one way to the tower, or IR25,000 if continuing on to **Chenaran** afterwards. Chenaran–Mashhad savaris (IR5000) are very frequent. If you offer IR40,000 *dar baste*, they'll make a side-trip to Tus en route, stopping for long enough to visit the Ferdosi Mausoleum.

Mashhad to Neishabur

Two minor sites, each just 1km north of the busy Mashhad–Neishabur motorway, are easy to tack on as short side visits when chartering a Mashhad–Neishabur savari *dar baste* (IR80,000).

FAKHR DAVOOD   فخرداوود
Visible from the main road this Timurid **robat** (all-weather caravanserai; donation expected; ☻7am-4pm) has an impressive tower-flanked exterior that would make a great movie set. The less exciting domed interior displays a small selection of pottery and an incongruous table-tennis table. It was renovated as headquarters for the Binalud new-town extension, a vast housing development for workers of the Iran Khodro car plant 3km away. That's been shelved for now, sparing the quaint mud-homes of tiny Fakhr Davood village. No taxis available here.

QADAMGAH RAZAVI   قدمگاه رضوی
In Qadamgah village (98km from Mashhad), a two-block scattering of souvenir shops and *kababis* fronts this charming 17th-century octagonal **shrine** (admission free; ☻24hr) with fine blue dome and attractive tiling. It sits in a pretty garden of ancient plane trees and enshrines a black stone slab indented with what are believed to be the **footprints of Imam Reza**. Floods of pilgrims find the site very moving so questioning aloud the authenticity of the Imam's (remarkably large) prints would be rather bad form. Just beside the shrine, steps lead down to a subterranean spring, 'miraculously created' by Imam Reza himself. Behind the shrine, older mud-brick village houses rise up steeply. In front there's a partly restored **caravanserai**. Minibuses run sporadically to Neishabur. The handy **Fajr Taxi-office** (☎ 322 4141) will drive you to Fakhr Davood for IR30,000.

Neishabur   نیشابور
☎ 0551 / pop 231,000

An early capital of Khorasan, Neishabur (Nayshaboor) was first settled around the 3rd century AD. By the Seljuk period it was a thriving literary, artistic and academic centre, notable as the birthplace of the 11th-century poet and all-round good egg, Omar Khayyam (see the boxed text, p74).

OMAR KHAYYAM TOMB COMPLEX
Neishabur's main attraction remains **Khayyam's Tomb** (admission IR3000; ☻8am-9pm). Its present form is a distinctive 1970s-modernist

affair with diamond-shaped lozenges of calligraphic tiling (Khayyam's words, naturally)
set in a curved, airy net of criss-crossed
marble. Don't be surprised to find random
Iranians bombarding you with recitations of
Khayyam's verses as you ponder the monument. A big part of the tomb's attraction is
its manicured garden setting, **Bagh-e Mahrugh**,
with a gently appealing terrace on which to
sip tea (IR10,000 per pot) with Neishabur's famous crystallised sugar while being serenaded
by (caged) birds. Jewellery outlets compete
to sell you Neishabur's equally famous turquoise. In the gardens' free southern section,
the lovely **Imamzadeh-ye Mohammed Mahrugh** is
a fine 16th-century domed mausoleum with
an intricately tiled portal. The octagonal tomb
tower of **Sheikh Attar** (admission IR3000; ⊙ 7am-9pm)
sits in another pretty garden, 1km west (a
popular horse-and-carriage ride).

The tomb complex is 5km from Neishabur's
central Khayyam Sq: take eastbound bus 10
to the end (IR300, 15 minutes).

OTHER SIGHTS

Central Neishabur is a rather unexciting
place, but very close to Khayyam Sq, the restored **Shah Abbas Caravanserai** (Imam Khomeini St)
hosts souvenir shops, the **Sofrakhane Sonati
Abashah** (☎ 222 5168; tea & qalyan IR15,000) traditional teahouse and a small **Nature Museum**
(☎ 224 6690; admission IR3000; ⊙ 8am-1pm & 4-6pm).
Amid the latter's displays of stuffed birds,
local animals, pinned insects and pickled
snakes, notice the bottled human foetuses.

The single-alley Safavid-era **covered bazaar**
(6th Lane, Imam Khomeini St) starts about 300m
further west.

SLEEPING & EATING

Just 30m north of Khayyam Sq, **Hotel
Kamalalmolk** (☎ 224 4277; Modarres St; s/d/tr
IR120,000/150,000/180,000) has five reasonably
tasteful, en-suite rooms, the quieter back
ones looking out across the brilliant little
garden-café that is the place's trump card.
You'd never guess it was there from the
uninteresting front restaurant section.

GETTING THERE & AWAY

Mashhad savaris (IR20,000) and buses
(IR6000, two hours) leave when full from
Neishabur's somewhat hidden **main bus terminal** (11th Alley, 22 Bahman St). That's 2km northeast
of Khayyam Sq. Minibuses for Qadamgah

(IR1500, 25 minutes) leave sporadically from
Bar Sq. Buses to Kashmar use a terminal
that's a circuitous 2km drive south of the
train station (Jafari St), itself about 1km south
of Imam Sq. Coming by Mashhad-bound
train from Tehran you'll arrive in Neishabur
bright and early, allowing plenty of time for
sightseeing before continuing to Mashhad
the same day. However, getting train tickets
FROM Neishabur can be tough.

Mashhad guide Vali Ansari Astaneh
(p354) has pioneered a cross-mountain trip
that allows a Mashhad–Tus–Neishabur–
Mashhad loop by walking (around six hours)
or using a 4WD (when conditions allow)
between Zoshk and the attractive foothill
village of **Kharv** near Qadamgah.

MASHHAD TO SARAKHS

In spring, a miraculous green-grass fuzz dap-
pled with red poppies enlivens the dusty badlands of the Mashhad–Sarakhs road (185km),
providing April grazing for herds of sheep.
Nomad shepherds' tent-camps are easiest to
spot after **Mazdavand**, where the road climbs
an escarpment, then follows a crag-sided
valley of saw-toothed geological uplifts.

In several rural villages, **old mud houses**
consist of three or four adobe domes. A few
such structures still exist in Sarakhs, but a
more impressive collection at **Abravan** is easily spied north of the main road.

A 7km side trip from tiny **Sholoq** village
(130km from Mashhad) reveals the evocatively lonely 1128 **Robat Sharaf Caravanserai**
with twin courtyards and a far *iwan* retaining
some fine stucco patterning and calligraphy.
Deep pits in chambers on either side once
held the water supply. Note that Sholoq has
no taxis. You could try to engage a cranky
old motorcycle (*motor*) but while IR10,000
might be the 'fair price' it's a seller's market
and drivers ask a whopping IR100,000. We
finally settled for IR30,000 return.

Renting a one-way Mashhad–Sarakhs
savari *dar baste* (IR120,000) and paying a little
extra for stops and side trips makes sense.

Sarakhs   سرخس
☎ 0512 / pop 36,000

If heading for Merv and Mary, you can cross
the Turkmenistan border in this strange, flat
town where several redundantly large boulevards don't seem to lead anywhere. A useful
landmark west of the town centre is the new,

CROSSING THE TURKMENISTAN BORDER AT SARAKHS

Using this **border post** (⏰ 8am-4pm Iran Time, 9.30am-5.30pm Turkmen time) allows the shortest cut between Iran and Uzbekistan. A shuttle (IR5000) crosses 2km of no-man's land to the Turkmen post. Bicycles are carried. Turkmen entry formalities are similar to those at Bajgiran (see the boxed text, p345), requiring US$12 in US dollars (cash). From the border it's 3km away as the crow flies to the Turkmen town of Saraghs (no formal hotel) but 10km by a very circuitous road. From Saraghs occasional minibuses run to the fertiliser-factory town of Tejen (with very basic hotel) where you can change for Mary. Moneychangers on the Iran side sell Turkmen manats for nearly full black-market rates (currently US$1=23,500, ie over four times the bank rate of US$1=5200).

dolphin-fronted **Hotel Doosty** (☎ 522 5518; Ghadir Sq; s/d/tr IR150,000/170,000/200,000; P 🖵) whose best rooms are a decent midrange deal and whose restaurant is excellent value (meals IR18,000). From here, Customs Blvd forks right (southeast) off the main road and leads after 800m to the **border gate**. The main road passes the bus terminal (150m beyond the Hotel Doosty) and savari stand (400m) before reaching Pasdaran St (800m). Turn left and follow that street northwest then north for 3km to see the 1356 **Gonbad Sheikh Loghman Baba** (donation appreciated; ⏰ 5.30am-4.30pm) in a wheat-field to your right. That domed brick tomb-tower has a massive, shattered arch support tower and an impressively vast three-storey interior with sections of disintegrating stalactite vaulting held in place by wooden staves.

Buses to Mashhad run roughly hourly till 4pm supplemented by sporadic but relatively regular savaris.

The inconvenient train station is 7km west of town. Trains leave to Mashhad at 6am and 2.30pm but no passenger services cross the Turkmenistan border (it's a different rail-gauge).

KALAT (KALAT NADERI)   كلات
☎ 0512 / pop 8000

Admiring its near-vertical backdrop of mountain cliffs, you don't need to be a mili-tary commander to see why Kalat has historically made the ideal last holdout for rebels on the run. It was one of the only places to have resisted the armies of Tamerlane. And it's still widely called **Kalat Naderi** for Nader Shah who retreated into its impregnable natural fortifications ahead of his considerable band of enemies. Many Kurds were settled here during the Safavid dynasty to guard against northern invaders, and some women still wear Kurdish costumes.

Spring is the best time to visit, when the countryside turns emerald green and nomad tents dot the foothill grasslands, especially along the Kalat–Dargaz road.

Sights

Kalat's foremost site is Nader Shah's **Khorshid Palace** (Kakh-e Nader, Ghasr-e Khorshid; ☎ 272 2239; Imam Khomeini St; admission IR2000; ⏰ 7.30am-6.30pm), 700m beyond the savari terminus. It's not really a palace at all but a distinctively fluted circular tomb-tower, on an octagonal base set in beautifully manicured lawns. The name Khorshid (literally 'sun') refers to one of Nader's wives, not some arcane astronomical purpose. It was never finished, hence the odd proportions and lack of a dome. Intricate exterior panels include pineapple and pear motifs. These fruits were unknown in 18th-century Khorasan suggesting that Nader Shah used foreign artisans he'd engaged (ie kidnapped) during his Indian conquests. The tower's magnificent interior uses gilt and ample colour to bring life to 16 stalactite-vaulted alcoves. Stairs beneath the rear terrace lead down into a graciously cool **ethnology museum** (admission included), graphically depicting Khorasan village life. A gift shop sells Naderabillia.

Facing the complex, an obvious 'Tourist Information' sign attracts visitors to Reza Mortezabi's appealing little **herb shop** (☎ 272 3984; Imam Khomeini St; ⏰ 7.30am-noon & 4-8.30pm Sat-Thu). Reza speaks good English but 'information' means a photocopied page from a pre-historic Lonely Planet guide.

The beautiful blue dome, easily spied from the museum steps, belongs to the otherwise modest 1747 **Kabud Gonbad Mosque** (Imam Khomeini St).

To fully appreciate Kalat's natural impregnability, backtrack 3km to the Mashhad road tunnel. The cliffs here are otherwise only breached by a very narrow gully stream guarded by the fortified **Borg-argavan Shah**, an iconic if small, round, mud-brick tower. Just beyond this (visible from the stream-side below) the **Katibeh Nader** is an inscription on the cliff-face praising Nader Shah with poetry in Turkish and Farsi. Climb to various rocky outcrops for spectacular views across the Darban village area ringed by bright-red laterite slopes.

Sleeping & Eating

Mosaferkhaneh Bahrami (☎ 272 3298; Imam Khomeini St at 13th Alley; d/tr IR80,000/100,000) has pleasant rooms with decent bathrooms and freshly laundered sheets. It's above an unmarked but popular restaurant with black-and-white trim, 200m from the savari stand.

A few snack shops and an un-marked basement for *abgusht* (lamb stew made with lentils, potatoes and tomato paste) cluster round the savari stand.

Getting There & Away

To Mashhad, savaris (IR25,000) are sporadic and buses (IR8000) are rare. For the pretty but very winding road to Dargaz (1¾ hours, 120km) you'll almost certainly need to hire a taxi (Paykan/Saipa IR100,000/120,000). **Talaydaran-e Khesht Taxi Agency** (☎ 272 2637; Imam Khomeini St) can oblige.

DARGAZ   درگز

☎ 0582 / pop 39,000

Whether slithering down the endless hairpins from Quchan or winding past the 'Thousand Mosque' mountains west of Kalat, travelling to Dargaz (Daregaz) is much more interesting than arriving. The sprawling town has one specialist attraction, the **Bandiyan Archaeological Site** (Artyan rd, km 2; admission by invitation; ☼ 7am-7pm), where unusually well-preserved stucco mouldings in white gypsum depict faces and floral patterns on wall and column stumps. Experts believe it was once a particularly fine Sassanian fire-temple complex. Covered with corrugated sheet-roofing, the three adjacent dig sites sit in a cornfield 2km west of Dargaz's northern edge. Annoyingly the caretaker won't let visitors in without permission-letters from Dargaz's **Miras Ferhangi** (☎ 522 5247; Modarres St; ☼ 7.30am-2pm). Near the archaeological site, an abrupt tumulus-style mud hill called **Yarim Tappeh** possibly started life as a Zoroastrian 'tower of silence'.

One block east of central Imam Khomeini St, **Hotel Sarim** (☎ 522 5247; fax 522 5147; Imam Khomeini 29th Lane; s/tw/tr IR160,000/190,000/230,000) has accommodation that is comfortable and would be fairly appealing if they fixed the droopy curtains and threadbare corridor rugs.

THE ROAD TO AFGHANISTAN

There are direct buses from Mashhad to Herat (Afghanistan) but you could add a little spice by doing the trip in bus/savari hops via Fariman, Torbat-e-Jam and Taybad. For intermediate stops you will generally need to pay a private taxi.

Mashhad to Torbat-e Jam

In the scrappy railway-junction village of **Sang Bast** (40km from central Mashhad), you could climb the AD 1028 **Ayaz Minaret**. But don't hope to get inside the **caravanserai** in case your wish comes true: it's now the local prison.

Flat **Fariman**'s unexotic **caravanserai** (Musa Sadr St, 14th Alley) isn't really worth the 2km walk north of central Imam Reza Sq but you might consider a IR20,000 return taxi trip to the **Band-e Fariman**, 10km south. This unusual **dam** was built in pseudo-Safavid style with multiple arches creating an opal-blue reservoir that contrasts strikingly with its arid surroundings. Swap from bus to taxi in Fariman if you want to visit **Langar** en route to Torbat-e Jam (IR40,000 *dar baste*). Pretty Langar village is an archetypal scattering of mud-walled courtyard houses (2.5km off the main road, initially following signs to Mahmoodabad). It's overlooked by the impressive, un coloured **Imamzadeh Qasm Anvar** and an unusually large domed **abambar** (water cistern).

Torbat-e Jam   تربت جام

☎ 0528 / pop 85,000

Where the last ripples of mountain ridge disappear into a vast dusty plain, you'll find this friendly, adamantly Sunni town. White beards and whiter turbans create a street-vibe that's more oriental than in most Iranian cities.

Imam Khomeini Blvd runs 4km from Imam Reza Sq (northwest) to Falakeh Sharak (southeast), passing Shahrdari Sq halfway. The town's central Valiasr Sq is 600m east of Shahrdari Sq along commercial Al Mahdi St. The culture-information office, **Miras Ferhangi** (☎ 222 4790; Robat Karim, Beheshti 3rd Alley; ☑ 7am-2pm) occupies a pretty, mini-caravanserai, two blocks south, then one west from Valiasr Sq, passing **E1 Technology** (☎ 222 8030; Beheshti/Modarres St; internet per hr IR5000; ☑ 8am-10pm) en route.

JAMI MAUSOLEUM آرامگاه جامی

Torbat-e Jam's highly impressive must-see sight is the beautiful **Jami mausoleum complex** (Aramgah St; admission free; ☑ dawn-dusk). Here, 10 religious buildings intertwine around the grave of 12th-century Sunni mystic and poet Sheikh Ahmad Jami. His tombstone rests under a very old pistachio tree, above which soars a particularly impressive blue-tiled **main iwan**. In this *iwan* there are three doors. The one to the right is open to all visitors and leads through a small sanctuary into an inner courtyard across which is the AD 1442 **'New' Mosque**. Look for the magnificent vaulted ceilings and octagonal columns on either side of its prayer hall. It's 'new' compared to the 1302 **Atirgh Mosque** (☑ women-only at prayer times) behind you on the same courtyard, which has double-level arch-vaults and fragments of beautiful calligraphy.

The finest gems are hidden behind the other two locked doors in the main *iwan*. Gatekeeper Qolam Ali Keliddar (who you probably unwittingly met when bagging up your shoes on entering the complex) has the keys. Technically he's only supposed to open the chunky locks for VIPs or those with a letter from Miras Ferhangi. However, foreign tourists are so rare that you'll probably count as the former. The small door on the left leads to the 14th-century **Kermani Mosque**, named after Masoud Kerman who created the splendid mihrab and calligraphy inside. Through the heavy wooden main doors, the 1264 **Khaneh Ghe** sports ancient graffiti and domed ceilings with particularly well-preserved colourful frescoes.

The complex is 700m east of Valiasr Sq via Mirqaveh, then Maadan Sts.

SLEEPING & EATING

Mosaferkhaneh Me'at Dana (☎ 222 7569; Natr St, Al Mahdi St, 2nd Alley; s/tw/tr IR50,000/68,000/80,000, with shower IR59,000/87,000/101,000) Clean simple rooms with camp beds and TV. Very close to central Valiasr Sq.

> ### CROSSING THE AFGHANISTAN BORDER AT DOGHARON
>
> This old Hippie-Trail **border** (☑ 7.30am-4.30pm) is open and remarkably easy. Direct Mashhad–Herat buses run twice each morning either way. Or do-it-yourself in hops via Torbat-e Jam and Taybad. Westbound savaris to the border (135km, 150 Afghanis) leave from Herat's old bus terminal.

Sima Hotel (☎ 222 3377; Behesht 1st St, off Imam Khomeini Blvd; s/tw/tr IR57,000/72,000/82,000, with bathroom IR66,500/98,500/108,000) Very green rooms with ageing linen but the better rooms have private squat toilet and shower.

Sakhteman Sefid (☎ 222 0713; Al Mahdi St; tw IR150,000) At first glance the Sefid appears to have more style than the competition, but much is tatty, road noise can be annoying and the bathrooms are communal. Enter via side stairway. There's a restaurant downstairs and a semi traditional teahouse in the basement.

GETTING THERE & AWAY

For Mashhad, buses (IR10,000, 2½ hours) use a terminal near Imam Reza Sq, accessed by shuttle taxi along Al-Mahdi St from Valiasr Sq. Savaris (front/back IR35,000/25,000, two hours) depart till around 9pm from nearby.

Savaris to Taybad (IR10,000) leave from Falakeh Sharak.

Taybad تایباد

☎ 0529 / pop 49,000

Just 18km from the Afghanistan border post, Taybad's main attraction is the imposing 1444 **Molana Mosque** (☑ 7am-dusk), whose towering *iwan* is of a similar grandeur to that of the Jami complex in Torbat-e Jam. The male-dominated **Municipality Hotel** (☎ 422 2269; Gumruk Sq; tw/q IR120,000/150,000) at the northern edge of town has unsophisticated if fairly spacious box-rooms with bathroom, TV and much too much pink. From a point 300m further north, transport leaves for Mashhad (bus/savari IR12,000/40,000, three hours), Torbat-e Jam (savari IR20,000) and Dogharon, the Afghan border (savari/taxi (IR4000/15,000, 20 minutes). Transport to **Khaf** leaves from near Falakeh Molana, passing the dramatic **Karat Minaret** after 25km.

Directory

CONTENTS

PRACTICALITIES

- Electrical current is 220V AC, 50Hz. Wall sockets are the European, two round-pin type.

- All English-language daily newspapers in Iran are government-run and available only in Tehran and some other large cities. They include the *Iran Daily* and *Iran News,* both of which offer good international coverage; *Kayhan International,* which gives new meaning to 'hardline'; and the *Tehran Times,* which cleaves to the government line.

- All Iranian broadcasters are controlled by the state. However, many Iranians have access to satellite TV, including many stations broadcasting in Farsi from North America.

- On Iranian TV, channels 1 to 4 are national, 5 and 6 province-based. Channel 4 has 10 minutes of news in English at midnight. Most hotels have the 24-hour IRINN news channel, which has a news-ticker in English.

- Good frequencies for the BBC World Service (www.bbc.co.uk/worldservice /schedules) include 11760Hz, 15575Hz and 1413kHz; and for VOA (www .voanews.com) 11740Hz and 15195kHz.

- Iran uses the metric system. A conversion chart is on the inside front cover.

ACCOMMODATION

Iran has a reasonable choice of accommodation, from tiny cells in noisy *mosafer-khanehs* (basic lodging houses) to luxury rooms in world-class hotels. Camping, however, is almost nonexistent, and don't expect anything resembling an eco-resort.

The Orwellian-sounding Ministry of Culture & Islamic Guidance categorises most hotels and decides what they can charge.

Up until recently, in midrange and top-end establishments foreign guests have had to pay more than Iranians for the same room. However, this officially mandated practice of dual-pricing looked like it was coming to an end as this book went to press, which means the prices in this book might serve mainly as a guide, see the boxed text, p388 for details.

Dual-pricing or not, it's possible to engage in a bit of friendly negotiation, especially during the low season between mid-October and early March. Having said that, we found that in most of Iran getting anything more than a nominal discount on an *otagh* (room) seemed as difficult as negotiating an end to the nuclear crisis. If dual-pricing is still happening, you could try asking for a discount for longer stays, or learn the Farsi numbers so you can point out the difference between local and foreign prices (most hotels have Iranian and foreign prices displayed in

---

THE SEASONAL SWING

There are two clear seasons in Iran, with a couple of other spikes. Low season starts in October and continues through winter until shortly before No Ruz (Iranian New Year, on 21 March) and the beginning of spring. From a few days before No Ruz, hotels in popular holiday destinations, such as Kish Island, Esfahan, the Caspian Sea coast and Yazd, are packed, and prices are at their highest. No Ruz also marks the annual government-approved price increase, and after all the madness of the 13-day holiday period is over you'll find prices rise by about 20% from the winter (low season) rate, and stay that way until October. There are a few exceptions. In summer prices along the Caspian Sea coast can skyrocket, while in hot places like Yazd and Bam prices fall with demand. We quote high-season prices (not No Ruz prices) throughout this book.

---

reception). Though this tactic was usually met with a look of 'so?' when we tried it.

The reluctance to bargain is partly because most cities don't have enough hotels to create effective competition. Bandar Abbas, Esfahan and Kashan are among the worst, while notable exceptions include Yazd, Mashhad and Shiraz. The 'hundreds' of new hotels the government has promised will take time to materialise, and will mostly be in the midrange and top-end brackets.

For foreigners, midrange and top-end places often quote their prices in US dollars, and increasingly in euros, though they will accept (and sometimes require to be paid in) rials. The currencies listed in this book are what the hotels were listing when we visited, though the falling US dollar seems to be pushing many back to rial or euros. In the cheapest budget accommodation sheets and mattresses can sometimes be semi-clean and/or stained. Using a light sleeping mat and sheet or sleeping bag can reduce your chances of itchy surprises. In better places soap and (small) towels are usually provided. Most midrange hotels have toilet paper, but you should always carry an emergency stash.

Hotels will almost always keep your passport overnight so keep a photocopy, and get it back if you're heading out of town for the day. Check-out time is usually 2pm. As you get off the beaten track you're likely to encounter heart-warming hospitality that sucks you into 'real' homestays. It's worth coming to Iran prepared with small presents to express your gratitude, as paying cash for such accommodation might be inappropriate.

Sending postcards and photos to your hosts once you get home will be greatly ap-preciated. All accommodation in this book is presented in budget order, from cheapest up; budget is generally up to IR220,000 (about US$25 or €16); midrange is roughly between US$26 (IR242,000 or €17) and $US80 (IR746,000 or €54); top-end listings hover upwards of US$80.

Camping

Iranians love tents, and you'll see them scattered through parks during the No Ruz holiday period. However, there are very few official camping grounds, and unless you can make yourself look like a nomad, camping anywhere else will draw unwanted attention from the authorities. If you do choose to camp rough, steer clear of military facilities and borders.

Long-distance trekkers and mountaineers, who obviously need to camp, should still discuss plans with the provincial tourist information office first (p393) if not accompanied by a recognised guide. The office may be able to write a letter of introduction.

Hotels
BUDGET

As well as *mosaferkhanehs*, basic one- and two-star hotels have rooms that fall into the budget range. In these places you normally have an attached bathroom with at least a shower (usually hot) plus air-con, a TV (Iranian channels only), fridge and maybe a phone. The heating and hot water will almost certainly be working.

Prices in this range start at about IR80,000/100,000 for a single/double and go up to about IR180,000/220,000, depending on your negotiating skills. On the down side, double beds are almost unheard of in the budget range, you're unlikely to get breakfast and some places are not as fastidious as they could be, so watch out for those telltale hairs on your pillow and don't be afraid to ask for fresh sheets.

MIDRANGE

Most two-star hotels, and all three- and four-star places will have a private bathroom with hot shower and toilet, and almost certainly a phone, fridge and TV (sometimes with BBC World and Deutsche Welt). There might even be a reasonable restaurant, and breakfast will often be included. You'll find toilet paper in most places, though bath plugs are a long-shot. Prices start at about US$15/20 for a single/double and go up to as much as US$60/85. Like a 40-something boxer, a lot of places in this range charge rates that reflect a more glorious past than the beaten-around present; try negotiating.

The most charismatic midrange places, and those worth aiming for, are the *sonnati* (traditional) hotels. Yazd has many and the first examples have recently opened in Esfahan and Kashan. The upper end of this range is home to a growing number of modern 'apartment hotels', which can be excellent value outside the high season. Most towns of decent size have a government-run Tourist Inn (Mehmansara Jahangardi). Standards vary considerably but they are usually fair value and often employ at least one English speaker.

TOP END

Many of Iran's top hotels pre-date the 1979 revolution. Several accidentally maintain décor which, like the Bee Gees, is now so out-dated that it's almost retro-cool. Relish these places before they're refitted in typically bland modern-hotel style. Bee Gees–era establishments like to tease you with swimming pools that are never actually filled. Meanwhile those better top-end hotels whose pools do have water will have set segregated swimming times for men and women.

Prices are astronomical by Iranian standards, but pretty reasonable by those of the West, starting from about US$85/100 for a single/double and rising to about US$240/300. Some hotels add 17% for tax and service, though we've included this in the total price.

Mosaferkhanehs & Mehmanpazirs

Iran's most basic accommodation options are *mosaferkhanehs* (literally 'travellers' houses'), a dorm or basic hotel, and similar *mehmanpazirs*. Both are very much male-dominated. Standards vary somewhat but generally you can *not* expect private bathrooms nor spoken English. Some bottom-end places won't even have a communal shower. Prices start at around IR30,000 per bed in a noisy, grotty, male-only dorm. Simple, private rooms, perhaps with a sink, cost IR30,000 (US$3.30 or €2) to IR130,000. Useless old TVs are often added just because it allows the owner to rack up a higher price. In a few cities, including Esfahan, some *mosaferkhanehs* aren't allowed to accept foreigners (see the boxed text, p325). In others, notably Bushehr, Khorramabad and Yasuj, you need written permission from the police to stay anywhere cheap. That's easy enough to organise through a 10-minute visit to the local Amaken – an arm of the police – so long as you don't arrive between 9pm and 6am, when it's shut!

Suites & Homestays

Along the Caspian Sea coast and in those northwestern rural resort-villages most frequented by Iranian tourists, you'll find locals renting out rooms, bungalows and self-contained apartments ('suites') in their homes, gardens or above shops. In the low season prices can be very reasonable, but in summer prices rise by up to 400% and bookings are virtually essential.

Some suites and almost all rooms/homestays are unmarked in Farsi let alone English so it's just a case of asking around for an *otagh*. Food is generally not included.

ACTIVITIES
Beach Going

Iranians are not really sun-worshippers and even if they were, the dress code (women must swim in full hejab) and sexual segregation of the beaches takes much of the potential fun out of lying on them. If you're undeterred by women in orange jumpsuits and scarves, Kish Island (p292) is 'Iran's Hawaii', while Qeshm Island (p303) has a much lower profile and a more local feel.

Iranians love the Caspian coast (p174) because, well, it's a coast and they have little to compare it with. But faced with a scraggy, rubbish-strewn ribbon of black sand, uninspiring architecture and constant rain we think there are better places to spend your visa time.

Cycling

Iran's main highways can be terrifyingly truck-dominated, but the well-surfaced secondary routes are well-suited to cycle touring (p406). You'll find few locals pushing the pedals, but a steady stream of overlanders brave the traffic en route between Europe and Asia.

Diving

Scuba diving and snorkelling is limited to Kish Island (p295) and Qeshm Island (p305) in the Persian Gulf. Readers report the number of dive sites around Kish is limited, particularly when there's more than a zephyr of breeze. More appealing are the range of reefs off Qeshm plus three ships sunk during the Iran–Iraq War.

Mountaineering

It may come as a surprise to learn that Iran boasts several high mountains, some of them permanently snowcapped. Many can be climbed by anyone fit without special equipment, experience or a guide, but you should always check the situation before embarking on a mountain trek. Early June to late August is the best climbing season.

Northeast of Tehran, Iran's highest and best-known peak, Mt Damavand (5671m; p131) has a classic Fuji-esque profile, but reaching the summit is not of great technical difficulty for a mountain of such altitude. The magnificent Alborz Mountains surrounding it contain around another 70 peaks over 4000m. At 4850m Alam Kuh (Mt Alam; p175) is Iran's most technical peak with an 800m near-vertical granite wall on its most difficult northern face: a world-class challenge.

Mt Sabalan (4811m) is an elegantly soaring peak usually approached from Meshgin Shahr (p160), though it's worth arranging guides and equipment in Tabriz (p146) before setting out.

Too tame for climbers, Mt Oshturan (4070m; p212) is the most accessible peak of the splendid Zagros Mountains. It has an attractive lake near the summit and is ideal for mountain walkers.

There are thousands of other mountains in Iran, but they are very seldom, if ever, climbed. If you fancy yourself as a trailblazer, you could investigate Mt Zardkouh (4337m) in the Zagros Mountains, west of Esfahan, or the Dena range, northwest of Shiraz, with 37 peaks over 4000m, the highest of them being Mt Gash Mastan (4460m). Until things settle down security-wise, Mt Hezar (4420m) and Mt Lalezar (4374m) in the Payeh Mountains, south of Kerman, and the snowcapped Mt Taftan (4042m) volcano, near the Pakistani border in Sistan va Baluchestan, are best avoided.

Helpful websites:

Mountaineering Federation of Iran (www.iranmount fed.com in Farsi) The Iran mountain federation's site; English page due soon.

Mountain Zone (www.mountainzone.ir) Mostly in Farsi, but has some trip logs in English and a long list of local climbing clubs and their contact details. See also opposite.

Peakware (www.peakware.com) Including summit logs for several Iranian peaks, including Mt Damavand and Mt Sabalan.

Summit Post (www.summitpost.org) Search 'objects' for 'Iran' and you'll find excellent trip reports – some with maps – by 'Nader', whose love for the Iranian mountains is wonderful to read. Highly recommended.

EQUIPMENT RENTAL & PURCHASE

Camping and climbing equipment can be bought relatively inexpensively in Iran. Well-stocked shops include **Varzesh Kooh** (Map pp102-3; ☎ 021-830 1037; 4th fl, cnr Enqelab Ave & Ferdosi St, Ferdosi Sq) in Tehran and the Nakhajir Camping Shop (p177) in Qazvin. A limited range of equipment can be rented at Darband (p113) and from some mountain guides.

GUIDES & PORTERS

The cost of a guide depends on your bargaining skills, the number of climbers in the group, the equipment needed, the length of the trip and the difficulty of the route you want to undertake. An English-speaking guide will charge about US$50 a day, and a donkey and handler will cost between US$25 and US$80 a day to carry your equipment, depending on how remote your location and whether the donkey is needed for other work.

MAPS

There are few trekking or mountain-climbing maps on Iran available in English, though climbing maps for the Alam Kuh area are available at the climbing centre in Rudbarak (p175). Elsewhere, spend the money you saved on maps on a local guide. For hiking in the valleys behind Gorgan the commonly available *Golestan Province* map gives a basic outline, while Gita Shenasi (p386) in Tehran has a map of the Alborz Mountains with some peaks and walking routes marked.

Rock Climbing

If clambering about on rocks is more your thing, there are several excellent and accessible places to try. Closest to Tehran is Band-e Yakhchal (N 35°85'58.0", E 51°44'48.0"), where several low walls and the 200m-high Shervin wall await; there's a hut here called Shervin Hut. The lower 25m have been set up for climbing and reports are that in summer it's a difficult but not especially technical climb to the summit, with stunning views of Tehran. It's busy on Fridays.

Further afield, there are some awesome rocks, sink-holes, sheer cliffs and overhangs around Kermanshah. The cliffs culminate at Bisotun where, just beyond a collection of ancient inscriptions, Farhad Tarash (p200) rock-face is the region's classic climbing challenge. The Kermanshah tourist infor-mation office (p195) can put you in touch with the local climbers club for support and equipment.

The rocky canyons around Maku (p137), Bijar (p189) and Khorramabad (p208) are easy to reach and tempting to climb, although few locals seem to do so. You'd be wise to check with police or tourist information offices before setting out as certain innocuous looking climbs can overlook sensitive military posts. The 800m-high wall of Alam Kuh (Mt Alam; p175) is a major expedition; there is a thorough description of routes at www .mountainzone.ir. Many waterfalls become good ice-climbs in winter, most accessibly at Ganjnameh (p205), near Hamadan. A good place to meet people who know these climbs is online at www.summitpost.org.

Skiing

There are more than 20 functioning ski fields in Iran. The season is long, the snow is often powdery and, compared with Western fields, skiing in Iran is a bargain. Four downhill fields near Tehran – (p132), Shemshak (p133), Dizin (p133) and Tochal (p133) – are easily accessible, have reliable facilities and equipment for hire. There is

---

OUTDOOR & ADVENTURE AGENCIES

Some of the travel agencies listed under Tours (p415) can arrange walking and climbing trips. We've had positive feedback about the following companies, which specialise in trekking, mountaineering and eco-tourism in Iran. If you have good (or bad) experiences with these or other agencies, please let us know at www.lonelyplanet.com/contact.

Aftab Kalout (☎ 021-6648 8374; www.kalout.com) Professional Tehran-based outfit specialising in eco-tourism, desert trips, trekking and eco-cum-sociological tours.

Araz Adventure Tours (Map p110; ☎ 021-7760 9292; www.araz.org; 1st fl, 1 Chahar Baradran Alley, North Bahar St, Tehran; ☉ 8am-4pm Sat-Wed, 8am-12.30pm Thu) This helpful outdoor tourism agency has been recommended by readers. It offers a wide range of mountaineering, climbing, horse- and camel-trekking, plus cultural tours. Director and experienced climber Mohsen Aghajani speaks English. One reader who climbed Mt Damavand with Araz wrote that 'even the cook had made it within 45 minutes of the Mt Everest summit'. Most equipment is provided.

Kassa Mountaineering & Tourism (Map pp102-3; ☎ 021-7751 0463; www.kassa.ir/tourism; 9 Naghdi Alley, off Sharlati St, Tehran) This private trekking agency offers a full range of trekking and climbing tours, desert expeditions and more. Mountains include Damavand, Sabalan, Zardkouh and 'any mountain you want to climb'. It is run by Ahmad Shirmohammad, an experienced climber who speaks English.

Mountaineering Federation of Iran (Map p94; ☎ 021-2256 9995-96; www.iranmountfed.com in Farsi; 15 No 17, 8th Baharestan Ave, off Pasdaran St, Tehran; ☉ 8.30am-6.30pm Sat-Wed) Experts in anything relating to mountain climbing and trekking, the Mountaineering Federation people are a mine of information and advice. Staff speak English, or can find someone who does.

Sepid Mountaineering Company (☎ 0711-235 5939; 0917-313 2926; www.sepidtour.com or www.iran sightseeing.com) Based in Shiraz, Abdollah Raeesi and crew organise mountaineering, cross-country skiing, nomad and tours by horse back.

also good downhill skiing available near Tabriz (p152) and Ganjnameh (p205), and smaller fields in the Zagros Mountains near Sepidan (p253) north of Shiraz, and Chelgerd (p252), west of Esfahan.

The ski slopes are also some of the most sexually equal areas of Iran outside of the family home; skiing was banned after the revolution, and after the ban was lifted in 1988 the images were of women skiing in manteaus. But with Khatami's rise to the presidency in 1997 came a considerable easing of restrictions on the slopes. Women must still keep their heads covered, but on higher slopes there is usually plenty of hair to be seen. Needless to say, skiing is very popular among the affluent young.

The season in the Alborz Mountains (where most slopes are located) starts as early as November and lasts until just after No Ruz (ie late March); around Tabriz and at Dizin it can last until mid-May. The slopes are busy with Iranians on Thursdays and Fridays, and with diplomats and expats on Saturdays; other days it should be pretty quiet.

All the resorts have lodges and hotels, which charge from about US$30 to US$100 for a room. Ski lifts cost as little as IR40,000 a day. You can hire skis, poles and boots, but not clothes, at the resorts.

For more information, contact the **Skiing Federation** (Map p94; ☎ 021-2256 9595; www.skifed .ir; Shahid Iran Ski Federation, 17 Baharetan 8 Alley, off Pasdaran Ave, Tehran). For reviews and comments about some slopes, see www.goski.com; and for a history of skiing in Iran see www.iran mania.com/trave l/tours/ski/history.asp.

Trekking

Trekking is arguably the single best way to experience a country and Iran is no exception. Trekking information, however, can be hard to come by. Nader's descriptions of various routes on www.summitpost.org are probably the best place to start, while for something more organised see the boxed text (p373) for listings of companies.

Iran offers many excellent one- and two-day walks. Possibilities exist in the mountains north of Tehran, around Darband (p113) and Tochal (p133); at Kelardasht (p175), Masuleh (p171) and Nahar Khoran (p339) in the Caspian region; around Mashhad (p353); from Gazor Khan (p182) and around Orumiyeh (p140) and Takht-e Soleiman (p187). Day

and overnight desert treks can be easily arranged from Yazd (p257), while longer expeditions can be organised on demand.

For the more adventurous, or those with more time, Iran also offers several longer routes across mountains and through forests.

The Alamut area is rich in trekking options, including some taking you across the Alborz Mountains and down to the Caspian (see p183). There are two main routes and many possible variations, but even for the easiest it's advisable to take a guide.

In remote regions, especially near borders, you may stumble across military/police/security areas; an Iranian guide or a few phrases of Farsi should smooth over any misunderstandings. Drinking water is often scarce, so take your own supplies in desert regions, and purification tablets or water filters elsewhere.

BUSINESS HOURS

Opening and closing times can be erratic, but you can rely on most businesses closing Thursday afternoons and Friday (the Iranian weekend). During summer, many businesses close during the hot afternoons, from about noon until about 4pm; along the blistering Persian Gulf coast, doors stay shut until about 5pm. The most likely time to find anything open is between 9am and noon, daily except Friday. In this book hours will accord (more or less) with the following list unless stated otherwise.

Airline offices Open 9am to 4pm, Saturday to Wednesday, and Thursday mornings.

Banks Open 7.30am to 1.30pm Saturday to Wednesday, 7.30am to 12.30pm Thursday.

Government offices Open offices 8am to 2pm Saturday to Wednesday, 8am to noon Thursday.

Museums Tend to open 8.30am to 6pm summer, 4pm or 5pm winter, with one day off, usually Monday or Tuesday.

Post offices Generally 7.30am to 3pm Saturday to Thursday, some main offices open later.

Private businesses Conduct business 8am or 9am to 5pm or 6pm Saturday to Wednesday, until noon Thursday.

Restaurants Offer lunch noon to 3pm, dinner 6pm or 7pm to 11pm, or whenever the last diner leaves.

Shops Open 9am to 8pm Saturday to Thursday, but likely to have a siesta between 1pm and 3.30pm and possibly close Thursday afternoon.

Telephone offices Operate 8am to 8pm or 9pm; earlier in small towns.

Travel agencies Generally 7.30am to 5pm or 6pm Saturday to Thursday, 7.30am to noon Friday.

CALENDARS

Three calendars are in common use in Iran: the Persian solar calendar is the one in official and everyday use; the Muslim lunar calendar is used for Islamic religious matters; and the Western (Gregorian) calendar is used in dealing with foreigners and in some history books. As a result, Iranian newspapers carry three dates; 23 May 2007 also appeared as Khordad 2 1386 (Persian) and Jamada I 6 1428 (Muslim). The Zoroastrians also have their own calendar (see below for details).

When entering Iran if you're planning to use the whole visa time allocated don't forget to make a note of the Western date for your own reference: the stamp in your passport will usually be in the Persian calendar (and in Farsi numerals). When book-ing public transport or extending your visa try to double-check the Gregorian date with a calendar (most calendars in Iran show Persian, Gregorian and Islamic dates) or online at payvand.com/calendar.

CHILDREN

In Iran, foreign children will be the source of much amusement and curiosity, which may drive them (and you) to despair after a while. Nappies (diapers), powders, baby formula, most simple medications and so on are available in most cities, although you might want to bring your own to save having to hunt about. The hardest thing will be trying to keep children entertained in a country where journeys are often long and the attractions often rather 'adult'. Parents would want to relate fairly clearly to their

---

IRANIAN CALENDARS

Persian Calendar

The modern Persian solar calendar, a direct descendant of the ancient Zoroastrian calendar, is calculated from the first day of spring in the year of the Hejira, the flight of the Prophet Mohammed from Mecca to Medina in AD 622. It has 365 days (366 every leap year), with its New Year (No Ruz) usually falling on 21 March according to the Western calendar. The names of the Persian months are as follows:

Season	Persian Month	Approximate Equivalent	Season	Persian Month	Approximate Equivalent
spring	Farvardin	21 Mar-20 Apr	autumn	Mehr	23 Sep-22 Oct
(bahar)	Ordibehesht	21 Apr-21 May	(pa'iz)	Aban	23 Oct-21 Nov
	Khordad	22 May-21 Jun		Azar	22 Nov-21 Dec
summer	Tir	22 Jun-22 Jul	winter	Dei	22 Dec-20 Jan
(tabestan)	Mordad	23 Jul-22 Aug	(zamestan)	Bahman	21 Jan-19 Feb
	Shahrivar	23 Aug-22 Sep		Esfand	20 Feb-20 Mar

Muslim Calendar

The Muslim calendar, which is used to some extent in all Islamic countries, starts from the month before the Hejira, but is based on the lunar year of 354 or 355 days, so it is currently out of step with the Persian solar calendar by some 40 years. The names of the 12 Muslim calendar months in Farsi are: Moharram, Safar, Rabi'-ol-Avval, Rabi'-ol-Osani (or Rabi'-ol-Akhar), Jamadi-l-Ula (or Jamadi-ul-Awai), Jamadi-I-Okhra (or Jamadi-ul-Sami), Rajab, Sha'ban, Ramazan, Shavval, Zu-l-Gha'deh and Zu-l-Hejjeh. The handy website www.rabiah.com/convert converts Islamic (Hijri) dates to Western (Gregorian) ones and vice versa.

Zoroastrian Calendar

The Zoroastrian calendar works to a solar year of 12 months of 30 days each, with five additional days. The week has no place in this system, and each of the 30 days of the month is named after and presided over by its own angel or archangel. The 1st, 8th, 15th and 23rd of each month are holy days. As in the Persian calendar, the Zoroastrian year begins in March at the vernal equinox. Except for Andarmaz, which replaces Esfand, the months of the Zoroastrian calendar are the same as those in the Persian calendar.

daughters aged nine or older that they'll have to wear hejab, and pray there are no tantrums.

Eating with the family is the norm in Iran, and taking your kids into a restaurant will not only be welcome but often bring you more-attentive service. While few menus include special meals for children, staff will usually tailor the size of the meal to the size of the child. Most food is not spicy.

If you have small children and plan on using taxis, you'll probably have to bring your own baby seat. Very few vehicles have seatbelts in the back seats, so it might also be worth insisting on a car that does. At least one bewildered agent we met was forced to have seatbelts fitted in the back seat of his car before his clients would drive anywhere. High chairs, childcare agencies and nappy-changing facilities are scarce indeed. As for breastfeeding in public, it's not a great idea.

CLIMATE CHARTS

Because of its size, topography and altitude, Iran experiences great climatic extremes. Winters (December to February) can be unpleasantly cold, especially in the north and west, and in most of the rest of the country the nights are very cold. In summer (June to August) temperatures as high as 50°C are nothing out of the ordinary along the Persian Gulf coast and southern provinces.

Regular rainfall is more or less restricted to the far north and west – the area north of the Alborz Mountains receives an annual average of about 1300mm of rain, but although year-round cloud helps keep summer temperatures manageable the high humidity makes summer pretty muggy on the Caspian coast. In western Iran winter temperatures are regularly well below zero and snow frequently remains until early spring, making some mountain routes impassable.

Unless you're a mad dog or an Englishman, it's best to avoid the Persian Gulf coast between early May and mid-October, when the double whammy of high temperatures and oppressive humidity take much of the fun out of travel. Further inland, summer temperatures are very warm indeed, but low humidity makes life more bearable. See also When to Go (p15).

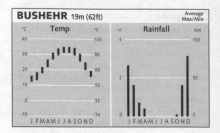

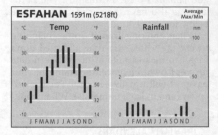

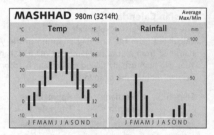

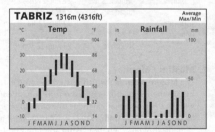

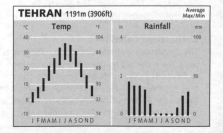

COURSES

There are not a lot of courses aimed at foreigners. Farsi teachers can be arranged through your embassy or one of Tehran's English-language newspapers, which also advertise private schools. However, these options are mainly for diplomats who don't have to fret about visa extensions.

Or you could arrange it all in advance and come to Iran on a student visa. For free online Farsi classes, try the excellent www .easypersian.com.

Two schools have good reputations for intensive courses.

Dehkhoda Institute (Map p94; ☎ 021-271 1902; icps@ut.ac.ir or dehkhoda@ut.ac.ir; Bagh-e Ferdows, off Valiasr Ave, Shemiran, Tehran) The International Center for Persian Studies at the institute offers five-week and 3½-/seven-month courses. Tuition is inexpensive, but you'll need to find your own accommodation.

University of Isfahan (Map p233; ☎ 0311-793 2039-41; www2.ui.ac.ir or int-office@ui.ac.ir; Hezar Jerib St, Esfahan) This sounds like a good bet. Bob, a traveller who completed a three-month course here in 2007, reported that his US$2000 paid for 3½ hours of lessons each morning and comfortable accommodation in the university guesthouse on campus, where foreign students share a floor with views over the city. Apply about three months before you intend to arrive (longer for UK and US passport holders) and the university's International Office looks after the rest. One-month courses cost US$1000. The final word from Bob: 'Needless to say, learning the language takes you into new worlds you might not otherwise see (eg two nights ago I spent a day and night with nomadic shepherds on the summit of Shah-e Kuh above Paveh – priceless)'.

CUSTOMS

Contrary to popular belief, Iranian officialdom is fairly relaxed about what foreigners take into and out of the country; at airports, your bags probably won't be searched at all. However, don't take this to mean you can load your luggage with vodka, bacon and skin mags. You are allowed to import, duty-free, 200 cigarettes and 50 cigars, and a 'reasonable quantity' of perfume. And of course zero alcohol, which remains strictly illegal.

You'll probably get away with any book, no matter how critical of the government, as long as it doesn't have too much female skin or hair visible on the cover.

You should have no trouble bringing in your laptop, shortwave radio, ipod and anything but the largest video equipment. Visitors are supposed to declare cash worth more than US$1000. In practice few people do and the authorities aren't really interested.

Export Restrictions

Officially, you can take out anything you legally imported into Iran, and anything you bought, including handicrafts other than carpets or rugs up to the value of US$160 (hang on to your receipts), as long as they are not for 'the purpose of trade'. Many traders are willing to undervalue goods on receipts issued to foreigners. In our experience, we've never been asked to show any paperwork when carrying (small numbers of) rugs out of Iran.

You can take out a reasonable, non-commercial number of Persian carpets, 150g of gold and 3kg of silver, without gemstones. If you want to exceed these limits, you will need an export permit from the local customs office. Officially you need permission to export anything 'antique' (ie more than 50 years old), including handicrafts, gemstones and coins, so there is always a slight risk that anything vaguely 'antique' looking could be confiscated. If you are worried that an expensive item might be confiscated, speak with the customs office before buying. No more than IR200,000 in Iranian cash is allowed to be taken out of Iran.

American sanctions in theory mean you can't take more than US$100 worth of goods purchased in Iran into the US.

DANGERS & ANNOYANCES
Earthquakes

Earthquakes happen every day in Iran (see Shaking Iran's Confidence, p86), but most travellers will never feel one. If you are unlucky enough to be in the wrong place when a big quake strikes, the following precautions might help.

The greatest danger is from falling debris, so if you're indoors stay inside and try to take cover under a sturdy desk, table or other furniture. Hold on to it and be prepared to move with it. Hold the position until the shaking stops and you can move to a clear area outside. Stay clear of windows, appliances and heavy furniture (such as freestanding wardrobes) that might fall over. In a hotel room, use the pillow to protect your head.

In a mud-brick building it's important to create space (under a bed, perhaps) that won't

DIRECTORY

BIG JUBS

In almost every Iranian city the main streets are lined with *jubs* (canals, pronounced jubes, like tubes), which originally served to distribute drinking water through the city but now serve as channels for rainwater and water running off nearby mountains. At the best of times they're a pleasant urban feature, with water spreading through the city and trees usually nearby. However, they can also be a hazard for anyone crossing a road without looking carefully, and after rain they can quickly turn into raging torrents.

If you're driving, *jubs* can be even more hazardous. In many towns the road drops straight into the *jub* without any form of kerb whatsoever. In Mashhad, we saw one reverse-park go horribly wrong when the back wheel dropped into the *jub*. The anxious driver tried to drive his way out of the *jub* before his boss, whom he'd just dropped off, returned, but only managed to drop the front wheel in as well. They were still trying to lift it out three hours later.

---

be filled with dirt and dust, which could lead to suffocation – which was the primary cause of death in Bam (see the boxed text, p323).

If you're outside, get into the open, away from buildings and power lines.

Scams

BOGUS POLICE

The most notable of Iran's mercifully few organised scams is the bogus police sting. The good news is that a concerted effort by police, particularly in Tehran and Esfahan, has largely ended the problem. Still, it pays to be aware… The usual procedure is for men in plain clothes and an unmarked car to pull up beside you, say 'police' and ask to see your passport or for you to hand over your bag/camera. The usual motive is theft of passports, cameras or money. The best advice it to ignore the 'policemen' and they'll probably leave. If they are real police they will take you to the station or your hotel, otherwise they will eventually disappear. *Never* hand over your passport or anything else to un-uniformed officers until you are at one of these places.

Security

'Iran? Is it safe?' It's a question you'll almost certainly be asked before you come to Iran…and often. But the perception of Iran as an unpredictable, dangerous destination couldn't be further from the truth. Violent crime against foreigners is almost unheard of, and the idea that as a Westerner you won't be welcome is plain wrong. If you do your best to fit in with local customs, you are unlikely to be treated with anything but courtesy and friendliness – that applies to Americans, too.

Of course, crime does still exist, so it pays to take the usual precautions, though in fairness we've heard of very few travellers being robbed. When travelling long distances by public transport, especially on international services, keep your passport, money and camera with you at all times. The occasional pickpocket operates in some crowded bazaars.

Theft from a hotel room is very unlikely, since staff keep careful watch over visitors and residents. This level of observation sometimes extends to hotel staff going through your bags – and 'sampling' your toiletries – while you're out; keep your bags locked. Hotels are locked or guarded at night. Most places have a safe for guests' valuables.

If you're driving, try to avoid parking on the street overnight in Zahedan or anywhere near the Afghani, Pakistani and Iraqi borders.

The most valuable possession Westerners usually bring to Iran – and the hardest to replace – is a foreign passport. Largely because of the difficulty Iranians face in travelling to Western countries, there is a booming black market in forged and stolen foreign passports. If you're carrying it, keep your passport strapped to your body. However, you'll simply have to trust your hotel or *mosaferkhaneh*, which will inevitably demand that you deposit your passport overnight.

Several individual and groups of tourists have been kidnapped in the southeastern provinces of Sistan va Baluchestan and Kerman since 1999. In 2007 the situation became so bad that foreigners were banned from travelling in Sistan va Baluchestan. The kidnappings are believed to have been in response to government successes in their war with powerful drug smugglers who ship huge quantities of opiates from Afghanistan and Pakistan to Europe through these areas. See the boxed text, p325 for details.

Drug smugglers generally aren't interested in the trouble that comes from harming foreign tourists, so if you stay out of their way you shouldn't have any problem. The threat from the People's Resistance Movement of Iran (PRMI; formerly known as Jundallah of Iran) terrorists isn't quite so cut and dried. These guys, who staged bloody attacks in Sistan va Baluchestan in 2005 and 2007, have so far not targeted tourists, but the authorities are very nervous that a foreigner might get caught up in the trouble. Remember that these dangers do NOT apply to any other areas of Iran.

Western embassies (p381) advise their nationals to register with them on arrival, especially if you will be in Iran for 10 or more days, or plan to visit remote places.

POLICE & SECURITY FORCES
It is unlikely you'll have any problem with the Iranian police. The majority of those you'll see will be busy in a fruitless effort to improve the traffic flow, and they really have no interest in hassling foreigners.

In popular tourist destinations such as Esfahan, Shiraz and Mashhad you'll find Tourist Police in conveniently located booths. One of them should be able to speak English, or at least find someone who does.

Thankfully, the truly dreaded Komiteh (Komiteh-ye Enqelab-e Eslami; the Islamic Revolutionary Committee, or 'religious police'), who used to bail up tourists for less than rigorous adherence to Islamic dress codes, is no more. However, the Basij and Sepah religious militias do sometimes get a bit carried away (see A Night With the Basij, below).

SECURITY CHECKS
Although soldiers and policemen roam the streets and patrol the highways checking on the movements of pedestrians and road users, they rarely trouble foreigners. You can expect the usual inspections at airports and in some public places, such as the shrines of Imam Reza in Mashhad and Imam Khomeini in Tehran. Foreigners are expected to carry their passports with them at all times.

A NIGHT WITH THE BASIJ *Andrew Burke*

When the first two bikes screeched to a halt we thought it was another instance of Iranian hospitality. These young guys would ask the lost foreigners looking at the map where they were going and directions would be given. But when the next two pulled up, one with a Hezbollah-style scarf around his face and a gun tucked into his pants, it suddenly looked more sinister. 'Police, police!' one of the bearded men shouted, holding aloft a tatty plastic card that for all we knew could have been his ID for the local video rental store. It was 1am on a large but very quiet Tehran street, and this had all the hallmarks of a robbery. Andrew, a fellow traveller riding his large motorbike from Dhaka to London, decided it was time to split. Alas, a man snatched the keys from his bike and we were going nowhere.

For the next hour we argued by the side of the road. Uniformed police arrived, but it was the young guys in beards and black leather jackets who seemed most agitated. Our frustrated pleas that 'we are Australian tourists' were met with demands that they take the bike, and take us to separate police stations. This didn't sound like a good idea. Eventually, after one guy just rode off on the bike, we and 13 others went to the station. We were under arrest.

After two fruitless hours we were back at the hotel with some idea of what was going on. The original assailants turned out to be members of the Basij ('volunteer'), a hardline militia who see themselves as 'defenders of the revolution'. As Basijis argued with uniformed police at the hotel's front desk, we learned we'd been accused of being British spies and of taking pictures of sensitive sites (at 1am?), and of being on an illegal motorcycle (Iranians are limited to 200cc bikes, but as Andrew's was in transit, it was legal). The real police were as apologetic as the Basijis were enthusiastic with their allegations. Eventually, the Basijis were persuaded that we were not working for MI6, Andrew's bike was returned and we were released, promising next time to get a better map!

This can be tricky as hotels also like to hang onto them throughout your stay. However, as the hotel only needs your passport at night you can retrieve it by day: highly advisable if you're planning any excursion beyond city limits. It's also worth having a couple of photocopies of the front and visa pages handy just in case.

In the eastern provinces, or if travelling late at night, your transport is likely to be stopped more frequently by police searching for drugs and other smuggled goods.

Traffic

Forget religious fanatics, gun-toting kidnappers or any other threats you've associated with Iran, you're more likely to get into trouble with the traffic than anything else. Iranians will tell you with a perverse mix of horror and glee that Iran has the highest per-capita number of road deaths on earth – in 2006 that was nearly 28,000 people, with another 270,000 injured. Somewhat ironically, Iran's president Ahmadinejad holds a PhD in traffic management. He has promised to reduce the death toll: 'The rate of accidents is below our nation's dignity and should be reduced,' he said in 2007.

If you've travelled elsewhere in the region Iran's traffic chaos may come as little surprise, but if you've arrived from the West you will likely be horrified. No-one pays any notice to road rules. The willingness of a car to stop at a busy intersection is directly proportional to the size of the vehicles in its path; that's right, it's survival of the biggest. Playing on this, some cunning motorists have fitted deafening air horns, usually found on trucks and buses, to their Paykans and Prides. A quick blast sees other traffic suddenly screech to a halt, fearing they've been outsized. Meanwhile, the modest little Paykan/Pride sails through the intersection. Size (or at least the perception that you're big) matters.

Some cars and all motorbikes also use the contraflow bus lanes (along which buses hurtle in the *opposite* direction to the rest of the traffic). Motorbikes speed through red lights, drive on footpaths and careen through crowded bazaars.

While traffic in major cities rarely goes fast enough to cause a serious accident, never underestimate the possibility of dying a horrible death while crossing the road. Vehicles never stop at pedestrian crossings. You will quickly realise that there's little alternative to stepping out in front of the traffic, as the Iranians do, and hoping that the drivers will slow down. It may not be much consolation, but the law says that if a driver hits a pedestrian the driver is always the one at fault and the one liable to pay blood money to the family of the victim. Until you've got your head around the traffic, perhaps the best advice comes from one pragmatic reader: 'Cross a busy street with an Iranian person, but make sure the Iranian is closest to the approaching traffic.'

Unmarried Foreign Couples

There was a time when unmarried foreign couples found getting a room in Iran difficult. Recently, however, hotel staff are starting to understand the weird wishes of foreigners and don't usually ask too many questions – if you are asked it's most likely to be in a low-budget establishment.

EMBASSIES & CONSULATES

It's important to realise what your own embassy – the embassy of the country of which you are a citizen – can and can't do to help you if you get into trouble. Generally speaking, it won't help if the trouble you're in is remotely your own fault. Remember that you are bound by the laws of the country you are in. Your embassy will not be sympathetic if you end up in jail after committing a crime locally, even if such actions would be legal in your own country. Don't expect support for feminist or political statements you make in Iran, for example. In genuine emergencies you might get some assistance, but only if other channels have been exhausted. For example, if you need to get home urgently, a free ticket is exceedingly unlikely – the embassy would expect you to have insurance. If you have all your money and documents stolen, it might assist with getting a new passport, but you can forget a loan for onward travel.

Iranian Embassies & Consulates

This is an abridged list of Iranian embassies and consulates abroad. For a full, reasonably up-to-date list see www.irania nvisa.com.
Afghanistan Kabul (☎ 020-210 1390/4; Charahi Sherpur, Shahr-e Nau, Kabul); Herat (040 220015; Jad-e Walayat, Herat)

> ### YOU'VE BEEN WARNED
>
> Check these websites for the latest (usually quite conservative) travel warnings and advice:
>
> **Australian Department of Foreign Affairs & Trade** (www.smartraveller.gov.au)
>
> **Canadian Department of Foreign Affairs & International Trade** (www.voyage.gc.ca)
>
> **Japan Ministry of Foreign Affairs** (MOFA; www.mofa.go.jp)
>
> **Netherlands Ministry of Foreign Affairs** (www.minbuza.nl)
>
> **New Zealand Ministry of Foreign Affairs & Trade** (www.safetravel.govt.nz)
>
> **UK Foreign & Commonwealth Office** (www.fco.gov.uk/travel)
>
> **US Department of State** (www.travel.state.gov)

Australia Canberra (☎ 02-6290 2421; www.iranembassy.org.au; 25 Culgoa Crt, O'Malley, Canberra, ACT 2606)

Azerbaijan Baku (consular section ☎ 012-4980766; www.iranembassy.az; Cəfər Cabbarli küç 44, Baku); Nakhchivan (☎ 0136-50343; Atatüurk küç 13, Nakhchivan; ⊙ 10.30am-noon Mon-Thu)

Belgium Brussels (☎ 2-627 0380; www.iranembassy.be; Ave Victoria 3, behind Franklin Roosveltlaan 15, Brussels B1050; ⊙ 9am-noon Mon & Fri, 1-4pm Wed)

Canada Ottowa (☎ 613-233 4726; www.salamiran.org; 245 Metcalfe St, Ottawa, Ontario K2P 2K2)

Denmark Copenhagen (☎ 39 16 00 73; www.iran-embassy.dk; Engskiftevej 6, 2100 København)

France Paris (☎ 01 40 69 79 60-65; www.amb-iran.fr; 4 Ave d'Iena, 75116, Paris)

Germany Berlin (☎ 030-84 3530; www.iranembassy.de; Podbielskiallee 67, Berlin D-14195); Frankfurt (☎ 069-5600 0739; www.irangk.de; Raimundstr. 90, Frankfurt 60320); Hamburg (☎ 040-514 4060; www.generalkonsulatiran.de; Alsterkrugchaussee 333, Hamburg 22297)

India Delhi (☎ 91-011-23329600; www.iran-embassy.org.in; 5 Barakhamba Rd, New Delhi, 110001); Mumbai (☎ 3630073; www.iriconmumbai.com; 1st fl Swapnalok, 47 Nepean Sea Rd, Mumbai)

Ireland Dublin (☎ 01-288 0252; iranembassy@indigo.ie; 72 Mount Merrion Ave, Blackrock, Dublin)

Japan Tokyo (☎ 3-3446 8022-23; www.iranembassyjp.com; 10-32-3 Chôme Minami Aazabu, Minato-ku, Tokyo)

Kazakhstan Almaty (☎ 0272-541974-75; 31-33, Luganski St, Almaty)

Netherlands The Hague (☎ 070-354 8483; www.iranianembassy.nl; Duinweg 20, 2585JX, The Hague)

New Zealand Wellington (☎ 04-386 2976; www.iranembassy.org.nz; 151 Te Anau Rd, Hataitai, Wellington)

Pakistan Islamabad (☎ 051-2276270; fax 2824839; House 222-238, St 2, G-5/1 Diplomatic Enclave, Islamabad); Karachi (☎ 021-5874371; fax 5874633; 81 Shahrah-i-Iran, Clifton, Karachi); Lahore (☎ 042-7590926-29; fax 757 0374; 55-A Shadman II, Lahore); Peshawar (☎ 091-845403; 18-C Park Ave, University Town, Peshawar); Quetta (☎ 081-843527, fax 829766; 2/33 Hali Rd, Quetta)

Spain Madrid (☎ 6135 9642; 28016 Calle Jeres 5, Madrid)

Syria Damascus (☎ 011-222 6459; Autostraad al-Mezzeh, Damascus)

Tajikistan Dushanbe (☎ 0372-210072-74; Kucai Bokhtar 18 aka Tehran St, Dushanbe)

Turkey Ankara (☎ 0312-468 2820; Tahran Caddesi 10, Kavaklidere, Ankara); Erzurum (☎ 0442-316 2285; Yenishehir Girisi, just off Atatürk Bulvarı, Erzurum); İstanbul (☎ 0212-513 8230; Ankara Caddesi 1/2, Cağaloğlu, İstanbul); Trabzon (☎ 0462-326 7651; Taksim Caddesi, Kizil Toprak Sok, Trabzon)

Turkmenistan Ashgabat (☎ 012-34 14 52; fax 35 05 65; Tehran köçesi 3, Ashgabat)

UK London (consulate ☎ 020 7937 5225; www.iran-embassy.org.uk; 50 Kensington Court, London W8 5DB)

USA Washington The Iranian Interests Section is in the Pakistan embassy (☎ 202-965 4990; www.daftar.org; 2209 Wisconsin Ave, NW, Washington, 20007)

Embassies & Consulates in Iran

The embassies of many European countries, plus the USA, Canada, Australia and New Zealand, were asking travellers to register their presence by phoning in and asking for the consul. If you do, be sure to let them know when you leave. In the event of a genuine emergency (not to ask about the embassy swimming pool), call the number listed here, wait until the message gives you the emergency number, and call that.

Afghanistan Tehran (Map p110; ☎ 021-8873 5040; fax 8873 5600; cnr 4th St & Pakistan St, off Beheshti Ave, Tehran; ⊙ 8am-2pm Sat-Wed) Thirty-day tourist visas cost €75 and are issued in two to three days; Mashhad (Map p354; ☎ 0511-854 1653; Do Shahid St, Mashhad; ⊙ 8am-noon Sat-Wed)

Armenia (Map pp102-3; ☎ 021-6670 4833; 1 Ostad Shahriar St, Razi St, Jomhuri-ye Eslami Ave, Tehran; ⊙ 9am-noon Sun-Thu) Tourist visas issued in nine to 11 days for US$50, in three to five days for US$80. Bring three photos. Call between 2pm and 4pm (not other times) for visa information. Note that visas are also available on arrival at the Armenian border or Yerevan airport.

Australia (Map p110; ☎ 021-8872 4456; www.iran.embassy.gov.au; 15 Eslamboli St, 23rd St, Tehran) Register at www.smarttraveller.gov.au.

Azerbaijan Tehran (Map p94; ☎ 021-2224 8770; www.azembassy.ir; Nader Sq, 15 Golbarg St, Chizar, Tehran;

☺9am–noon Sun, Tue, Thu); Tabriz (☎ 0411-333 4802; Mohabarat St, Valiasr, Tabriz; ☺ 9am–noon Sun–Thu) Single-entry tourist visas issued in three working days for around US$80 to US$101. Visas are also available on arrival by air at Baku airport but *not* at the land borders.

Canada (Map p110; ☎ 021-8873 2623; www.dfait-maeci .gc.ca; 57 Shahid Sarafraz St, Motahhari Ave, Tehran)

France (Map pp102–3; ☎ 021-6670 6005-08; www .ambafrance-ir.org; 85 Nofl Loshato St, Tehran)

Georgia (Map p110; ☎ 021-2260 4154; www.iran.mfa .gov.ge; No 9, 8th Alley, off Shahid Qalandari, Sadr Expressway, Tehran; ☺ 9.15am-1.30pm Sun, Tue, Thu) Two-week tourist visas cost US$40 and take four days (US$60 for two-day service). However, most Westerners don't need visas at all.

Germany (Map pp102-3; ☎ 021-3999 0000; www .teheran.diplo.de; 324 Ferdosi St, Tehran)

India Tehran (Map p110; ☎ 021-8875 5103-5; www.indi anembassy-tehran.com; 46 Mir-emad Ave, cnr Ninth & Dr Beheshti Sts, Tehran; ☺ 8.30am-5pm Sun-Thu); Zahedan (Map pp326-7; ☎ 0541-322 2337; off Imam Khomeini St, Tehran) Visas (IR370,000) issued in four days with a letter from your embassy.

Iraq (Map pp102–3; ☎ 021-8893 8865-66; Valiasr Ave, Tehran) Just south of Valiasr Sq. Not issuing tourist visas.

Ireland (Map p94; ☎ 021-2280 3835; tehranembassy@ dfa.ie; 8 Nahid Alley, Kamraniyeh Ave, Kamraniyeh, Tehran)

Japan (Map p110; ☎ 021-8871 7922; www.ir.emb -japan.go.jp; cnr Bucharest & Fifth Sts, Tehran)

Lebanon (Map p110; ☎ 021-8890 8451; 30 Afshin St, off Nejatollahi St, Tehran) If you need a visa, it costs about US$40.

Netherlands (Map p110; ☎ 021-2256 7005-7; www.mfa.nl/teh; 1st East Lane, 33 Shahrzad Blvd, Darous, Tehran)

New Zealand (Map p94; ☎ 021-2280 0289; www .nzembassy.com/iran; cnr 2nd Park Alley, Sosan St, Nth Golestan Complex, Aghdasiyeh St, Niavaran, Tehran)

Pakistan Tehran (Map p94; ☎ 021-6694 4888; fax 6694 4898; Block No 1, Etemadzadeh Ave, Jamshidabad, Dr Hossein Fatemi Ave, Tehran; ☺ 9-11am Sat-Wed) Single-entry visas about US$35 issued in two days with a letter of introduction from your embassy. Consulates in Mashhad (Map p354; ☎ 0511-222 9845; Imam Khomeini St, Mashhad) and Zahedan (Map pp326-7; ☎ 0541-322 3389; Pahlavani St, Zahedan) were not issuing visas when we asked.

Sweden (Map p94; ☎ 021-2229 6802; www.sweden abroad.se/tehran; 2 Nasdaran St, cnr of Boostan St, Nth Pasdaran, Tehran)

Switzerland (Map p110; ☎ 021-2200 8333; www.eda .admin.ch; Yasamin St, off Sharifi Manesh, Elahieh, Tehran)

Syria (Map p110; ☎ 021-2205 9031-32; Afriqa Hwy, Arash Blvd, Tehran) If you need one, visas in one or two days for about IR500,000.

Tajikistan (Map p94; ☎ 021-2283 4650; 10, 3rd Alley, Shahid Zeinaly St, Niavaran, Tehran) North of the Niavaran Palace; issues tourist visas for IR280,000 in about four days.

Turkey Tehran (Map pp102-3; ☎ 021-3311 5299; www .e-konsolosluk.net; 314 Ferdosi St, Tehran); Orumiyeh (☎ 0441-222 8970, Beheshti St, Orumiyeh); Tabriz (☎ 0411-300 1070, Firoudi St, Tabriz)

Turkmenistan Tehran (Map p94; ☎ 021-2220 6731; 5 Bavati St, off Vatanpour St, off Lavasani St, Farmanieh, Tehran; ☺ 9.30am-noon Sun-Thu); Mashhad (☎ 0511-854 7066; Do Shahid St off Dah-e Dey Sq, Mashhad; ☺ 8.30-noon Mon-Thu & Sat) You need an invitation letter (eg from www.stantours.com) to apply for a tourist visa. Transit visas are sometimes possible without such documentation if you show a valid onward visa for Uzbekistan. Either way your application will normally be referred to Ashgabat which usually takes at least a week. Once approval has been given, speed of stamping depends on the price paid.

United Arab Emirates Tehran (Map p110; ☎ 021-8678 1333; 355 Vahid Dastjerdi Ave, Tehran); Bandar Abbas (☎ 0761-222 4229; Nasr Blvd, Bandar Abbas)

UK (Map pp102-3; ☎ 021-6670 5011; www.british embassy.gov.uk/iran; 198 Ferdosi St, Tehran)

US Interests Section (☎ 021-8878 2964; 59 Farzan-e-Gharbi, Africa Ave, Jordan, Tehran) Part of the Swiss Embassy, it cannot offer full consular services.

Uzbekistan (Map p94; ☎ 021-2229 1519; 15, 4th Dead End, Aqdasieh St, off Pasdaran St, Aqdasieh, Tehran) Most countries need a letter of invitation (LOI) from Uzbekistan. If you have one, a normal 15-day tourist visa takes about two weeks to arrange (US$65), or US$93 for urgent service. Alternatively, use a travel agency in Tehran. The embassy is near the Sadaf Shopping Centre.

FESTIVALS & EVENTS

The majority of Iran's festivals are religious (see Holidays, opposite). Iran's few major festivals are concentrated in Dahe-ye Fajr, or the 10 Days of Dawn (1 to 11 February), which commemorates the lead-up to Ayatollah Khomeini's coming to power.

Keep an eye on www.tehranavenue.com for new festivals. Festivals worth noting:

Fajr Film Festival (www.fajrfestival.ir) Held 1 to 11 February. Iran's premier arts festival, it features Iranian and international films in several cinemas across Tehran.

International Fajr Theatre Festival (en.theater.ir) Held 1 to 11 February, primarily at Tehran's Tezatre Shahr (City Theatre; p122).

International Festival of Ritual and Traditional Plays (en.theater.ir) August or September.

Tehran Short Film Festival (www.shortfilmfest-ir.com) Usually held in October or November. Organised by the Iran Young Cinema Society.

FOOD

Restaurants often add 10% or 15% to the bill in the name of service, though the waiter will rarely receive anything unless you add a further amount. In this book the 'service charge' has usually been included in the overall meal price (see also Tipping, p389). For lots more on Persian cuisine see p78.

GAY & LESBIAN TRAVELLERS

Despite what President Ahmadinejad might like to say, Iranian gays and lesbians do exist. Unlike most other places, however, in Iran homosexuality is not only illegal but punishable by hundreds of lashes and even death. In 2005 two men were hanged in Gorgan for the 'crime' of having consensual sex. Barbaric laws aside, there is no reason why gay and lesbian travellers shouldn't visit Iran. There are no questions of sexuality on visa application forms, and we have not heard of any homosexual travellers being treated badly as long as they refrained from overt signs of affection.

Arranging meetings with Iranian gays and lesbians will, however, be tough. With so many cultural and legal constraints, it's no surprise that the nearest thing to a gay 'scene' are a few nervous-looking men sitting alone in Daneshgu and Laleh parks in Tehran. For lesbians it's even more difficult; most Iranians would probably deny the existence of women who prefer women.

The best way to contact the gay and lesbian communities, such as they are, is through the internet, which can open up all sorts of doors more safely than chancing it in the park. The website of the Iran Gay, Lesbian, Bisexual and Transgender Organisation (www.homanla.org) has interesting articles on homosexual life in Iran plus plenty of links.

Of course, it makes sense not to advertise that you're part of a same-sex couple. Most hoteliers will accept that you're 'just good friends', though you might find in some places that discretion is the better part of valour when seeking a double bed. In Yazd there is one smooth hotel in the old town noted for being more gay-friendly than others.

HOLIDAYS

Public holidays commemorate either religious or secular events. It's worth staying aware of the dates, especially if you are planning to extend your visa. Government offices and just about everything else will close for the morning, at least, on a holiday, but often small businesses will open after lunch. Transport functions fairly normally and hotels remain open, but many restaurants will close. Holidays are sometimes extended for a day if they fall near the Iranian weekend.

At the time of writing the Majlis (parliament) was considering cutting five dates from the holiday roster, including 15 Khordad (Anniversary of Ayatollah Khomeini; p385), 30 Safar (Death of Imam Reza; below), 25 Shavval (Death of Imam Jafar Sadegh; below) and 13 Rajab (Birthday of Imam Ali; below).

Religious Holidays

Religious holidays follow the Muslim lunar calendar, which means the corresponding dates in the Western calendar move forward by 10 or 11 days every year.

Tasua (9 Moharram)

Ashura (10 Moharram) 7 January 2009, 27 December 2009, 16 December 2010, 6 December 2011. The anniversary of the martyrdom of Hossein, the third Shiite imam, in battle at Karbala in October AD 680. This is celebrated with religious theatre and sombre parades.

Arbaeen (20 Safar) The 40th day after Ashura.

Death of the Prophet Mohammed (28 Safar) 24 February 2009, 13 February 2010, 3 February 2011, 22 January 2012

Death of Imam Reza (30 Safar)

Birthday of the Prophet Mohammed (17 Rabi'-ol-Avval) 14 March 2009, 3 March 2010, 20 February 2011, 10 February 2012

Anniversary of the death of Fatima (3 Jamadi-I-Okhra) 28 May 2009, 17 May 2010, 7 May 2011, 25 April 2012. Fatima was daughter of Prophet Mohammed.

Birthday of Imam Ali (13 Rajab) 6 July 2009, 26 June 2010, 15 June 2011, 3 June 2012

Mission of Holy Prophet (27 Rajab)

Birthday of Imam Mahdi (15 Shaban) 6 August 2009, 27 July 2010, 17 July 2011, 5 July 2012

Death of Imam Ali (21 Ramazan) 21 September 2008, 11 September 2009, 1 September 2010, 21 August 2011, 10 August 2012

Eid al-Fitr (1 Shavval) 1 October 2008, 20 September 2009, 10 September 2010, 31 August 2011, 19 August 2012. The Festival of the Breaking of the Fast that marks the end of Ramazan. After sunset on the last day of Ramazan large meals are consumed across the country.

Death of Imam Jafar Sadegh (25 Shavval)

Eid-e Ghorban (10 Zu-l-Hejjeh) 8 December 2008, 27 November 2009, 17 November 2010, 6 November 2011, 26 October 2012. Marks the day when Abraham offered

DIRECTORY

to sacrifice his son. Expect to see plenty of sheep being butchered.

Qadir-e Khom (18 Zu-l-Hejjeh) The day Prophet Mohammed appointed Imam Ali as his successor while returning to Mecca.

RAMAZAN (RAMADAN)

During the month known in Iran as Ramazan, Muslims are expected to perform a dawn-to-dusk fast that includes abstaining from all drinks (including water) and from smoking. This is seen less as an unpleasant ordeal than a chance to perform a ritual cleansing of body and mind. Some people, especially in cities, don't fully observe the fast, but most do for at least part of the month. Some Muslims are exempted from the fast (eg pregnant and menstruating women, travellers, the elderly and the sick), as are non-Muslims but they mustn't eat or drink in front of others who are fasting.

Ramazan can be a trying period, particularly if it falls in summer when the days are that much longer and the heat and hunger tend to shorten tempers. Businesses and shops keep odd hours and very little serious business gets done. However, public transport continues to function and travellers are exempt from the fast so you don't need to worry about finding

food on flights, trains or bus trips, and many hotels keep their restaurants open. Other restaurants either close altogether or open only after dark. Many shops selling food remain open throughout Ramazan, so you can buy food to eat in your room.

Although you shouldn't have many problems in larger cities, in rural areas finding any food might be difficult during daylight hours.

Secular Holidays

Secular holidays follow the Persian solar calendar, and usually fall on the same day each year according to the Western calendar.

Magnificent Victory of the Islamic Revolution of Iran (11 February; 22 Bahman) The anniversary of Khomeini's coming to power in 1979.

'APPROXIMATE' DATES FOR RAMAZAN:

- 1 to 30 September 2008
- 22 August to 19 September 2009
- 12 August to 9 September 2010
- 1 to 30 August 2011
- 21 July to 18 August 2012

IRAN'S AGE-OLD CELEBRATION OF THE NEW YEAR

No Ruz literally means 'new day' and while the celebration is for Persian new year, much of the traditional ceremony is about renewal and hope for the future. The roots of the No Ruz tradition stretch deep into history, with the spring equinox (usually 21 March) having been celebrated since before Achaemenid times. It's a peculiarly Persian tradition that has nothing to do with Islam – a fact that many Iranians are proud of but which doesn't sit well with the Islamic theocracy.

No Ruz festivities stretch for about three weeks. Apart from frenzied shopping, the outward sign of No Ruz is street-side stalls selling the *haft seen*, or seven 's'es; seven (or more) symbolic items with Farsi names starting with the letter 's'. They are supposed to be laid on a table at home, though you'll see them everywhere from TV news studios to taxi dashboards. Today's most commonly seen *seen*, and their symbolic meanings:

- *sabzi* (green grass or sprout shoots) and *samanu* (sweet wheat pudding) represent rebirth and fertility;
- *seer* (garlic) and *sumaq* (sumac) symbolise hoped-for good health;
- *sib* (apple) and *senjed* (a dried fruit) represent the sweetness of life;
- *sonbol* (hyacinth) is for beauty

On many tables you'll also see *sekeh* (a gold coin, symbolising adequate income), *serkeh* (vinegar to ward off bitterness), a mirror, a Quran and candles. You'll also see sorry-looking goldfish in tiny bowls. No-one we asked knew how or why the goldfish found its way into this tradition. Fish might have represented Anahita, the ancient god/angel of fertility, or perhaps it simply symbolises

Oil Nationalisation Day (20 March; 29 Esfand) Commemorates the 1951 nationalisation of the Anglo-Iranian Oil Company.

No Ruz (21 to 24 March; 1 to 4 Farvardin) Iranian New Year.

Islamic Republic Day (1 April; 12 Farvardin) The anniversary of the establishment of the Islamic Republic of Iran in 1979.

Sizdah be Dar (2 April; 13 Farvardin) The 13th day of the Iranian New Year, when Iranians traditionally leave their houses for the day.

Heart-Rending Departure of the Great Leader of the Islamic Republic of Iran (4 June; 14 Khordad) Commemorates the death of Ayatollah Khomeini in 1989. About 500,000 Iranians flock to Tehran, Qom (where he trained and lived) and the village of Khomein (where he was born).

Anniversary of the Arrest of Ayatollah Khomeini (5 June; 15 Khordad) In 1963 Khomeini was arrested after urging the Muslims of the world to rise up against the superpowers.

NO RUZ

No Ruz (see the boxed text, opposite), the Iranian New Year, is a huge family celebration on a par with Christmas in the West. From a practical point of view, Iran virtually shuts down from 21 March (the beginning of new year) and Sizdah be Dar (2 April).

Finding hotel accommodation (especially midrange and top end) is very tough from about 18 March until 2 April and all forms of long-distance public transport are heavily booked, though savaris run more frequently making some shorter-hop trips easier than at other times. Most businesses, including many restaurants, close from 21 to 25 March inclusive. It's not impossible to travel during No Ruz, but you should think twice, then think again, before heading to popular tourist destinations, such as Esfahan, Mashhad, Yazd, Shiraz and anywhere on the Persian Gulf or Caspian coasts. Mountain areas like rural Kordestan and primarily business cities like Tehran and Kermanshah, remain relatively uncrowded. And on the positive side museums and tourist sites stay open much longer hours while some normally closed attractions open specially.

INSURANCE

A travel insurance policy to cover theft, loss and medical problems is a good idea. Some policies specifically exclude dangerous activities, which can include scuba diving, skiing, motorcycling, even trekking.

You might prefer a policy that pays doctors or hospitals directly rather than you

---

life – and the poor goldfish is the easiest 'living' being to put on a table – an estimated five million live, and then die, on Iranian tables every No Ruz.

On the Tuesday night before the last Wednesday of the year another pre-Islamic tradition is played out. *Chahar shanbe-soori* (Wednesday Fire) sees people sing, dance (men only) and jump over fires. The jumping symbolises the burning away of ill luck or health, to be replaced by the healthy redness of the flames. Unfortunately, actually finding a fire can be tough. *Chahar shanbe-soori* is viewed as a pagan festival by the government. When we went fire jumping outside Mashhad the animosity between revellers and the (often half-hearted) Basij militiamen was instructive. Basijis would arrive and order fires to be doused and dancing to stop. After being ignored for a few minutes they would leave, accompanied by laughter and fire-crackers hurled in their direction. Some towns do now have grudgingly 'approved' fire-sites but visiting these can become deafening and rather hazardous due to the uncontrolled impromptu displays for fireworks thrown by excitable youths.

After all this No Ruz itself finally arrives. Families gather around the *haft seen* table to recite a prayer seeking happiness, good health and prosperity, before eating *sabzi polo* (rice and vegetables) and *mahi* (fish). Mothers are also expected to eat symbolic hard-boiled eggs, one for every child. At the moment of the equinox (announced on every radio station) people kiss and hug and children are given *eidi* (presents). For the following two weeks Iranians cross the country to visit relatives and friends in their home towns, before No Ruz celebrations finish on the 13th day of the year, *Sizdah be Dar* (usually 2 April). Everyone leaves home to go picnicking out of town, taking their *haft seen sabzi* with them. The *sabzi* is either thrown into water or, in some cases, left to blow off the roof of the car. Either way, the *sabzi* is meant to have soaked up the bad aspects of the previous year, so this ceremony symbolises getting rid of bad luck.

DIRECTORY

having to pay on the spot and claim later. Check that the policy covers ambulances or an emergency flight home. Make sure the policy covers Iran and adjacent countries if you're travelling on. Some insurers, particularly in the USA, consider the region a 'danger zone' and either exclude it altogether or insist on exorbitant premiums.

INTERNET ACCESS

In Iran, internet cafés are known as *coffeenets*, though you'll rarely find coffee on the menu. You can get online in all Iranian cities and big towns, and a growing number of smaller centres. Most *coffeenets* charge about IR10,000 an hour; more in hotels. Speeds are variable, but most cities now have ADSL connections. If you plan to use a messenger service, note that Yahoo! Messenger (www.yahoo.com) is used almost everywhere, but MSN Messenger (www.msn.com) is harder to find. Skype (www.skype.com) is growing in popularity, but many *coffeenets* don't have headsets.

Unfortunately, Iranian *coffeenets* are badly infected with viruses. During this research trip our USB memory stick picked up more than 50 viruses, worms, Trojan horses, key-loggers and other nasties. So be careful about doing internet banking unless the anti-virus software is up to date, and scan carefully before sticking anything into your own computer that has been in an Iranian machine.

One way to avoid viruses is bring your own computer and connect to dial-up from your hotel. In most cases you'll need an adaptor to plug into the phone line. Most are unusual two-pin types that your RJ-11 plugs into the back of; they're available in electronics stores.

Even with the adaptor, you'll still have work to do to get online. First, you need to find out if your hotel has a switchboard sophisticated enough to allow long local calls (many switchboards look like they've been around since Alexander Graham Bell's day). If they do, you'll then need to buy a pre-paid access card, which costs about IR10,000 for five hours. Unfortunately, most of these have access numbers for local areas only, so you'll need to buy a new one in each city – it won't break the bank. The cards are available at *coffeenets* and newsstands.

LEGAL MATTERS

Like most things in Iran, the legal system is based on Islamic principles. The system, however, is not the strictest interpretation of Sharia law. Most of the same activities that are illegal in your country are illegal in Iran. The main difference is that the penalties can be much harsher. For most minor crimes, foreigners will probably be deported, though this is not an absolute. A few years ago a German businessman was sentenced to death for having sex with an unmarried Muslim woman, though he was eventually released after serving about two years in jail. The penalties for drug or alcohol use and smuggling are harsh. Carrying the smallest amount of hashish can result in a minimum six-month jail sentence; don't expect assistance from your embassy or a comfortable cell. Trafficking heroin or opium carries the death penalty.

There are two 'crimes' that foreigners may not be aware of. Homosexual activity is illegal and has resulted in the death penalty for some Iranians. Deliberate refusal to wear correct hejab (the Islamic dress code for women) can also result in a public flogging (although a foreigner will probably be deported).

In the unlikely event you are arrested, it's best not to reply to, or appear to understand, any questions in Farsi. If you do choose to answer questions, do so politely, openly and diplomatically. In our experience – yes, we have been arrested a couple of times (see the boxed text, p379) – the primary motives for arresting a foreigner are usually curiosity, mild suspicion and the desire to appear powerful. Answer your interrogators so that their curiosity is satisfied, their suspicion allayed and their sense of their own self-importance flattered. Take special care not to incriminate yourself or anyone else, especially anyone Iranian, with a careless statement, and get in contact with your embassy in Tehran as soon as possible if things get heavy.

In Iran, people are legally allowed to vote at age 15, can legally drive when they are 17, and can legally have sex when they're married – girls can be married when they turn 13 and boys when they are 15. Premarital and gay sex are both illegal.

MAPS

The undisputed king of Iranian map-making is **Gita Shenasi** (Map pp102-3; ☎ 021-6670 9335;

www.gitashenasi.com; 15 Ostad Shahrivar St, Razi St, Valiasr Crossroads, Enqelab-e Eslami Ave; ☼ 8am-6pm Sat-Wed & 8am-1pm Thu) in Tehran, which publishes an impressive array of maps covering all the major towns and cities and some of the mountain ranges. A growing number of its maps are in English, while many others list the names of major streets, suburbs and squares in English, although everything else, including the text and indexes, is in Farsi. Maps are harder to find outside Tehran.

Gita Shenasi's *Iran Road Map* (1:2,250,000) is updated annually and is highly detailed, but annoyingly it doesn't have any route numbers on the major intercity roads. Finding maps outside Iran isn't easy; look for the excellent *Reise Know-How Iran* (1:1,500,000).

Gita Shenasi publishes climbing maps, such as *Central Alborz, The Peaks of the Sabalan* and *Damavand and its Ridges,* but their usefulness is limited because many places are marked only in Farsi.

MONEY

The official unit of currency is the Iranian rial, but Iranians almost always talk in terms of tomans, a unit equal to 10 rials (see Rials or Tomans?, below). We can't emphasise enough how important it is to get your head around the idea of tomans as soon as you can. Throughout this book we use the abbreviation 'IR' to indicate Iranian rials. For an idea of costs see p16; and for exchange rates see the inside front cover.

For all intents and purposes, Iran is a purely cash economy. No credit cards. No travellers cheques. Just bring cold, hard cash – preferably in high-denomination

euros or US dollars. Apart from some hotels, carpet shops and tour agencies where you can pay in dollars or euros, all transactions are in rials (or tomans). In this book, we've listed prices in the currency in which they are quoted. You'll obviously need to carry a mix of rials and dollars or euros – you'd need a wheelbarrow to cart around everything in rials.

Which brings us to the question of what sort of cash you should bring to Iran. It used to be, somewhat ironically, that the US dollar was king in Iran. But in response to strong US condemnation of Iran's nuclear program and falling US dollar, the Ahmadinejad government has encouraged Iranian banks and businesses to turn away from the dollar and toward the euro. So much so that some banks won't even change dollars anymore. On this research trip we had no problem changing dollars (as long as the notes were printed since 1996), but if you have to choose between one or the other then it's safer to go for euros. UK pounds get decent rates in most bigger towns too, but can't always be exchanged at borders or in smaller moneychangers, so have at least a few dollars or euros for emergencies.

There is a thriving business in UAE dirhams along the Persian Gulf coast. However, Turkish lira are treated with the utmost scorn everywhere except close to the Turkish border; ditto for the Afghan, Azerbaijani, Turkmen and Pakistani currencies.

Whichever currency you choose, the most important thing to remember is to bring as much cash as you're likely to need, then a

---

RIALS OR TOMANS?

No sooner have you arrived in Iran than you will come up against the idiosyncratic local practice of talking about prices in tomans even though the currency is denominated in rials. While most travellers eventually get used to this, at first it is completely bamboozling. One toman is worth 10 rials, so it's a bit like shopkeepers in Europe asking for 10 cents whenever they wanted €1.

To make matters worse, taxi drivers and *bazaris* (the shopkeepers in the bazaar) will often say 'one' as shorthand for IR10,000. However, before you consider cancelling your trip to Iran on the grounds of commercial confusion, rest assured that after a few days you'll understand that the two fingers the taxi driver just showed you mean IR20,000. And as you start to get a feel for what things cost, you'll understand that if something sounds too good to be true – or too bad – it probably is.

In the interim, you can always have the price written down, and then to double-check ask whether it's in rials or tomans (written prices are usually expressed in rials) – using a calculator is handy, too, as the numbers show in Western rather than Arabic numerals.

bit more. Getting your hands on money once you're inside Iran is a nightmare.

ATMs

Although Iran has a functioning network of ATMs (cashpoint machines), they can only be used with locally issued bank cards, so are useless to travellers unless you open a local account.

Banks

Although it sometimes seems as if every fourth building in Iran is a bank, only a few banks will actually change your money and then usually only US dollars, euros or, less often, British pounds in cash. Your best bet will always be the central branch *(markazi)* of Bank Melli (BMI) in whichever town you are in. In larger cities you may also be able to change money at the central branches of the other major banks: Bank Mellat, Bank Tejarat, Bank Sepah and Bank Saderat. Banks that offer foreign-exchange facilities nearly always have the sign 'Exchange' or 'Foreign Exchange' displayed in English near the entrance. At these banks there should be someone who speaks English. You will need to take your passport with you when changing money in a bank, and in some smaller cities a Farsi-speaker will help you to get through the mountains of paperwork. Often it takes around 30 min-utes or longer and requires five different signatures.

While banks usually open at 7.30am, most will not change money until the day's rates have been faxed through from Tehran between 9am and 10am.

Cash

Although there are coins for IR1, IR2, IR5, IR10, IR20, IR50, IR100, IR250 and IR500, only the latter four denominations are at all common. Indeed, so rare are IR1 coins (no longer minted) that they are considered lucky despite being utterly worthless. There are notes for IR100 (rare), IR200 (rare), IR500, IR1000 (two varieties), IR2000 (two varieties), IR5000 (two varieties), IR10,000, IR20,000 and, since March 2007, a IR50,000 note bearing the three-elipse nuclear symbol. The red-coloured IR20,000 and IR50,000 notes look confusingly similar. Hang on to your filthy IR500 and IR1000 notes to pay shared taxi fares.

Most of the time no-one seems to care what state rial notes are in, then out of the blue someone will reject one on the grounds that it has a tiny tear or is too grubby. Note that this tolerance doesn't apply to foreign currencies, which need to be clean and without any tears whatsoever. If they're not falling apart, Iranian banknotes are easy to read as the numbers and names are printed

---

DUAL-PRICING

First, we'd like to applaud the Ministry of Culture & Islamic Guidance for abolishing the practice of charging foreigners 10 times the Iranian price to see historical monuments and museums. Entry fees are now the same for everyone, except at a few privately run places that don't receive government funding, such as Vank Cathedral in Esfahan and Bagh-e Eram (Garden of Paradise) in Shiraz.

However, as we went to press officially sanctioned dual-pricing was still happening...just. The practice of charging foreigners 30% to 50% more than Iranians for the same hotel room looks like it might finally be coming to an end. In early 2008 the government tourism organisation ordered all hotels to use one rate for all – a policy called *yeksansazi*. Not surprisingly, hoteliers were not happy about this new directive, and a months-long argument ensued while some hotels obeyed and others did not. The outcome remains unclear. The most logical conclusion would be a single price that sits between the old Iranian and foreign prices.

What does this mean for you? Well, the hotel prices listed in this guide will be indicative more than literal, with rampant inflation also playing its part.

In the unlikely event that the hoteliers win and dual-pricing continues, it's worth keeping it all in perspective. A small but growing number of hotels do charge the same rates for everyone, and elsewhere you'll find the vast majority of transactions will be perfectly fair. Indeed, there's a good chance you'll be humbled by someone for whom IR20,000 is a fortune insisting on paying your share of a meal.

SHOW ME THE MONEY

So you've been robbed, lost your wallet, maybe bought one too many carpets and you're out of cash. Don't despair. What is described here is definitely not something to build into your travel plan, but if you need money sent from abroad, this system should work – assuming sanctions haven't cut off Iranian banks entirely.

1 Go to the nearest Bank Melli (BMI) central branch, preferably in Tehran where Mr Abdollahi at counter 13 speaks English and has helped many travellers out of such situations.

2 Find an English speaker, *insh'Allah*, outline what you want to do and give them your local contact details.

3 Get the Swift identification code for this particular BMI branch (eg Tehran central branch is MELIIRTH060); and ask whether there is a BMI branch in your home country (these are listed at www.bmi.ir), or which bank in your country has a relationship with BMI (eg in Australia, it's ANZ).

4 Ask your saviour at home to go to a branch of the nominated bank (eg ANZ) with your full name, passport number and the Swift code, and deposit the money.

5 Between two and four days later, the cash should arrive at your branch in Iran.

Be warned that the charges in your home country can be high. But if you're desperate, this is the least of your worries. Once you're in the money again, don't forget to pick up a decent souvenir for your saviour.

---

in Farsi and English. However, coins are only marked in Farsi.

Credit Cards

The 'war on terror' and the US trade embargo mean you cannot use any credit card in Iran. You cannot pay for a hotel, a plane ticket, nothing. You cannot draw cash on your credit card, despite what one German bank told a traveller we met, who then had to spend 10 traumatic days getting money sent from home. While a handful of carpet shops and travel agencies with foreign accounts will take credit cards, it's not worth relying upon. Better to just file away the plastic and be sure to bring enough cash.

International Transfers

It should be possible to have money transferred from overseas to a bank or an individual's account in Iran; for details, see Show Me the Money, above. Note, however, that economic sanctions might mean banking relations with some countries are cut completely, in which case transfers will become almost impossible.

Moneychangers

The quickest and easiest way to change cash is at an official money-exchange office, where the whole deal is done in seconds, unlike in most banks where half an hour is

fast. Exchange shops can be found in most cities, usually signed in English.

Changing money in an exchange shop is much safer than doing so with a street moneychanger. If you do change on the street, expect to be treated like a total moron with no idea of current rates. You should demand the same rate as you'd get in the bank and expect the changer to take a IR10,000 'service fee'. Count the money carefully, and don't hand over your bill until you're sure it's correct. If you can't find a bank or exchange office, carpet shops, jewellers or someone in the bazaar should be able to help.

Tipping

Tipping is not a big deal in Iran. In upmarket restaurants (mainly in Tehran) a 10% gratuity might be expected – on top of the 10% service charge that's often built into the bill. But everywhere else any money you leave will be a pleasant surprise. It's normal to offer a small tip to anyone who guides you or opens a building that is normally closed. If your offer is initially refused, you should persist in making it three times before giving up (see Ta'arof, p45). You'll be relieved to hear there is no culture of baksheesh' in Iran.

Travellers Cheques

American Express. Leave home without it! Like credit cards, travellers cheques are useless in Iran. Only a couple of banks attached to international hotels in Tehran can (unofficially) change travellers cheques, but even this could change at any time so don't rely on it.

PHOTOGRAPHY & VIDEO

Iran has jumped on the digital photography bandwagon as much as any other country and that's good news for travellers. Many *coffeenets* have card readers so you can upload your images to the internet and/or burn them to CD or, less often, DVD. Memory cards in all but the very latest formats are available at reasonable rates in the larger cities, the widest range being in Tehran.

If you're still using film then you'll have no problem finding garden variety films at good prices. Higher speed films are now much harder to find, and slide film almost impossible outside Tehran, so bring all you're likely to need. Note that airport X-ray machines are not exactly state-of-the-art so it's worth getting the security guards to hand-check your film; they'll usually do so if you ask (or plead) nicely.

Photographing People

Most Iranians are happy to have their picture taken provided you ask first. However, where lone women are concerned it doesn't matter how nicely you ask, the answer will almost always be no. If you point your lens at a woman without permission you can expect her to quickly disappear into her chador or scarf. Exceptions might be made for women photographers.

Offering to take pictures of your Iranian friends and post or email to them later is greatly appreciated – as long as you remember to post or email them. If you don't plan to keep the promise, don't make it.

Restrictions

In Iran it is especially important to avoid photographing government buildings, airports, naval dockyards, nuclear reactors, roadblocks, military installations, embassies/consulates, prisons, telephone offices or police stations – basically, any government building at all. We know of a group of Polish travellers who were detained for hours in Bandar Abbas for taking a picture of the port, and we can speak from first-hand experience of being arrested in Howraman-at Takht (p194) for unknowingly taking a photo of a hill that happened to be the Iraq border. When you see a 'No Photography' sign, take heed. If you're in doubt, ask. If you get caught, don't try to be anything except a dumb tourist.

Technical Tips

The sunlight can be strong during the day, so think about underexposing by a third or half a stop between about 11am and 3pm. A polarising filter will also help to cut out some of the glare, which can be particularly bad in cities such as Tehran, where the pollution is so bad. If hazy, polluted sky is ruining your pictures – such as in Imam Sq in Esfahan – consider coming back at night when the lighting means it's just as beautiful but you can't see the smog.

POST

Postage is very cheap. The cost of sending an airmail postcard to anywhere is IR1000. The cost for a normal-sized letter by airmail to anywhere outside Iran should be IR4000. The service is reliable and reasonably swift. Postcards usually reach Europe in four or five days. In contrast, the domestic postal service is reliable but slow, and sending a letter across the world is often quicker than getting it across the country.

If you're sending mail to a complicated address or to somewhere remote, try to get someone to write the address in Farsi on the envelope. Post boxes are few and far between, except outside post offices. Poste restante is little used and, according to readers, unreliable.

Parcels

Sending a parcel out of Iran can be a frustrating exercise in form shuffling, but it's reasonably priced and your package will usually arrive. Take your unwrapped goods to the parcel post counter (*daftar-e amanat-e posti*) at the main post office (*postk-huneh-ye markazi*) in a provincial capital – the bigger the better. There it will be checked, packaged and signed for in triplicate. There are three parcel services – *pishtaz* (express), *havayi* (airmail) and surface. Rates tend to vary depending on who is quoting them, but a 5kg parcel to anywhere by surface mail should cost less than

US$20. The customs officer on duty at the post office generally has discretion over what can be posted abroad, so be nice (see also p377 for customs regulations). You will usually be asked for a photocopy of your passport.

SHOPPING

Iran has plenty of products that make good souvenirs, with the widest selection sold in Esfahan and Shiraz. Prices are low and quality ranges from cheap rubbish, such as plaster of Paris griffins at Persepolis, aimed at domestic tourists, to high-quality carpets. If you are prepared to search through old stuff in smaller bazaars you should come away with a great souvenir and a good story as to how you found it. If you'd prefer to do it all at once and aren't too worried about price, the bazaars in Esfahan and Shiraz are for you.

Various places in Iran specialise in specific products. Often, knowing the best place to buy something is as important as getting a good price. Export restrictions apply to some goods (see p377). Persian carpets are the ultimate souvenir and are available almost everywhere – see p61 for much more on carpets.

Minyaturha (miniatures; see p69 for more information) are another popular, distinctly Iranian souvenir, and Esfahan is probably the best place to buy them. What constitutes a 'real' miniature is widely debated (should they be painted on paper or camel bone?), however most of what you see will be on camel bone. Better miniatures are likely to cost at least US$50 for a tiny work, climbing into the thousands for the best pieces. Apart from Esfahan, Manuchehri St in Tehran has some good examples. Tehran Bazar, Khorramabad and Orumiyeh are also good for miniatures, and *qabha-ye aks* (picture frames) are good in Orumiyeh.

There are dozens of shops and factories selling *sefalgari* (pottery) and *moza'i-ha* (mosaic tiles) at Lalejin, near Hamadan; Maraqeh, near Tabriz; Minab, near Bandar Abbas; and around Rasht and Masuleh.

Traditional clothes can make great souvenirs. *Givehs* (lightweight shoes) and *abas* (traditional coats without sleeves) are available in the Kermanshah and Khuzestan provinces. Uniquely embroidered *abas* from

villages near Bandar Abbas and Bushehr are especially impressive. All sorts of beautiful garments and fabrics called *termeh* are found in Yazd province. Traditional woollen Kurdish coats and hats from Kordestan and Ilam provinces are popular, and the women of Masuleh will probably attempt to fleece you for their fine woollen socks.

Intricate *shisheh alat* (glassware) can be bought in Yazd and Tehran.

Be wary unless you know what you're doing when buying *javaher alat* (jewellery). If you do, there are plenty of gorgeous choices: traditional jewellery from Kordestan, turquoise from Mashhad, and silver filigree necklaces and earrings from villages in Zanjan province.

Bags made from *charmineh* (leather) from Hamadan and Yazd are popular, and Tabriz is renowned for its *abrishom* (silk).

Some interesting metalwork souvenirs to pick up include knives from Zanjan, anything made of silver or gold from Khuzestan province, Kerman or Shiraz, and *servis-ha-ye chay* (tea sets) and qalyans (water pipes) made from *mes* (copper) and *beronz* (bronze).

Za'faran (saffron) from Mashhad, and *hanna* (henna), particularly from Tabriz and Yazd, are readily available.

Woodwork is widely available, but for carvings and *moarraq* (marquetry inlaywork), some of the best deals come from Sanandaj and Esfahan.

Most cities have bookshops selling at least a couple of inexpensive English-language coffee-table books about Iran. Finally, another popular souvenir that's available in every bazaar in the country is the qalyan. Prices start at about IR40,000 for a smaller pipe with wooden accessories, and a stock-standard pipe with some long-dead shah on the bowl will set you back about IR80,000. Prices rise fast when you step into a souvenir shop.

TELEPHONE

Phone numbers and area codes continue to change with disconcerting regularity in Iran. For example, in 2005 all Tehran landlines had an extra digit added. Fortunately, you didn't need to be a rocket scientist to work out the change; the first number was repeated, so 123 4567 became 1123 4567. If you find the numbers in other big

WHAT A BARGAIN!

As a general rule, the prices of groceries, transport (except private taxis) and most things with a price tag attached are fixed, and fixed prices are undoubtedly more prevalent than they were a few years ago. On the other hand, virtually all prices in the bazaar are negotiable, particularly for souvenir-type products and absolutely always for carpets. In touristed areas, such as Imam Sq in Esfahan or the Bazar-e Vakil in Shiraz, bargaining is essential.

Bargaining can be tough if you're not used to it, so here are a couple of pointers. First, when you find something you like be sure not to show too much interest. Vendors can smell desperation a mile away. Second, don't buy the first one you see; subtly check out a few alternatives to get an idea of the price and quality. With this knowledge, casually enquire as to the price and then make a counter-offer, thus beginning the bargaining process. The vendor will often beseech you to make a better offer: 'But I have nine children to feed'. However, having looked at the competition you know what is a fair price so only edge up slowly. If you can't agree on a price you could try walking out of the store, but if the shopkeeper calls your bluff you'll struggle to knock the price down any further than you already have.

Remember that bargaining is not a life and death battle. A good bargain is when *both* parties are happy and doesn't necessarily require you to screw every last toman out of the vendor. If you paid more than your travelling companion, don't worry. As long as you're happy, it was a good deal. Remember, too, that no-one is forcing you to buy anything. Your money will stay in your pocket until you decide to take it out. And, unlike at home, if you do get ripped off in Iran the damage won't be too great.

cities have changed, they might have followed this method.

Some old-style payphones still work and take IR50 and IR100 coins. Cards for newer payphones are available in newsstands and come in denominations of IR5000, IR10,000 and IR20,000. Calls are so cheap that you'll need to really like the sound of your voice to get through the larger card. Local calls are just IR42 per minute, though it's more if you're calling a mobile or long distance. In our experience, however, every second card phone is broken and you can't make international calls from them. In some cities international calling cards are available from newsstands, grocery stores and *coffeenets*, where you dial a local number and punch in a code.

Local calls are so cheap that if you ask nicely most hotels will let you make a few free of charge. Airports and major bus terminals usually have at least one public telephone permitting free local calls.

International calls are also relatively cheap – just IR1700 per minute to most countries. These rates can be had at small, private telephone offices (usually open from about 7.30am until 9pm). The process is pretty simple: give the number you want to the front desk and wait for a booth to become available. You'll normally be charged a minimum of three minutes.

You can't make reverse-charge (collect) calls to or from Iran. Iran's country code is ☎ 98, to dial out of Iran call ☎ 00; if calling from outside Iran, drop the initial 0 from all area codes. See also the inside front cover for some useful numbers.

Mobile Phones

Iran has three mobile-phone networks. Government-run MCI and private Thaliya have very extensive coverage but are for residents only and their whopping sign-up costs average US$300 (down from US$1000 a few years ago). For travellers, a much better option is Irancell (www.irancell.ir) whose pay-as-you-go SIM card costs just IR300,000. We just had to show our passports to get one, though in some places you might need a local friend to fill the (all Farsi) papers and provide a local address. To top up your credit, buy scratch cards from vendors displaying yellow and blue MTN signs, who usually charge more than the card's face value (haggle). At the time this book went to print calls cost about IR850 a minute domestic, and IR4000 a minute international. Irancell also offers a 'Data SIM', which only allows SMS messages, at IR100 locally and IR1500 for international. Irancell is growing fast and in early 2008 had coverage in all but three provinces – Kerman, Sistan va Baluchestan and Khuzestan.

Thuraya satellite phones also work in Iran.

TIME

Compared with some of their Middle East neighbours, Iranians are fairly punctual and will expect you to be the same.

Time throughout Iran is 3½ hours ahead of Greenwich Mean Time (GMT), so noon in Tehran is 3.30am in New York; 8.30am in London; 10.30am in Turkey; 11.30am in Azerbaijan; noon in Afghanistan; 1.30pm in Pakistan and Turkmenistan (note this when preparing to cross borders); and 6.30pm in Sydney. For more, see the World Time Zones (Map pp450–1).

For years Iranians enjoyed daylight saving between No Ruz (usually 21 March) and mid-September. But in 2007 conservatives within the government decided that daylight saving was too disruptive to prayer times, and it was scrapped. If the government changes, daylight saving might be back – check online for the latest.

TOILETS

Most Iranians have squat toilets at home, but the majority of better hotels have thrones or a choice of loos. Almost all public toilets are squats and while some are regularly cleaned, others are very definitely not. Still, there are usually enough options that you won't have to enter anywhere too stinky. Mosques, petrol stations, bus and train stations and airport terminals always have toilets, *sans* TP.

Fortunately, buying toilet paper is easier than it once was. Most of the bit-of-everything grocery stores stock it, and if you can't find any there's always the ubiquitous box of tissues. Many midrange hotels have joined their top-end counterparts in supplying toilet paper, though sometimes you'll need to ask. Most plumbing is not designed for paper so put your used sheets in the bucket next to the toilet.

TOURIST INFORMATION

The ominous-sounding Ministry of Culture & Islamic Guidance is responsible for 'cultural affairs, propaganda, literature and arts, audiovisual production, archaeology, preservation of the cultural heritage, tourism, press and libraries'. As the list suggests, tourism is not its top priority, though it's rising.

In 2007 the first national tourism website (www.tourismiran.ir) was launched. It's planned to eventually be available in 11 languages, but at the time this book went to press was still largely useless. Cultural Heritage offices, universally known as *Miras Faranghi* in Farsi and often housed in restored historic buildings in provincial capitals, dispense information. They don't see too many walk-in tourists but will usually try to find someone who speaks English and search around in filing cabinet drawers until you have a showbag full of brochures, maps, postcards and other promotional paraphernalia. Some cities also have more proactive private or semi-private tourist offices, where basic information is available in English and guides and tours can be arranged, usually at reasonable prices.

There are small information booths in train stations, where staff are usually good on timetable information, and international airports, where they might speak English and have a map, but little else. Information offices in bus terminals are generally useless.

TRAVELLERS WITH DISABILITIES

Facilities are rare, but as long as you are healthy and come with the right frame of mind there is no reason why travellers with disabilities shouldn't enjoy Iran. Wheelchair ramps are starting to appear, largely to cater to disabled veterans from the Iran–Iraq War, though it will be a long time before you can depend on the ramp's presence. Only the more upmarket hotels are guaranteed to have elevators big enough for wheelchairs and European-style sit-down toilets. Bring your own medications and prescriptions.

For more information on travelling with disabilities, see these websites:

Access-Able Travel Source (www.access-able.com)
Radar (www.radar.org.uk)
Society for Accessible Travel & Hospitality (www.sath.org)

VISAS

Perhaps the biggest reason more people don't come to Iran is that getting a visa can be unnecessarily frustrating. Even though part of the Iranian government is trying to attract international tourists, with the ambitious if spectacularly deluded target of 20 million tourists by 2020, suspicion bordering on paranoia elsewhere in the government makes getting a visa such a protracted hassle that a lot of people either don't bother or give up.

Trying to work out the best way to get your visa isn't easy because the rules seem to change without warning or explanation. Sometimes this change results from actions on a bigger political stage. If, for example, your nation has diplomatic trouble with Iran, as happened with Canada following the death in a Tehran prison of Iranian-Canadian journalist Zahra Kazemi in 2003, then getting your visa will become that much harder. Canadians have been struggling to get visas ever since.

At the time of writing it was actually harder to get a visa than it has been for several years. When we visited in 2003 and 2005 it was simply a matter of applying to the embassy, paying the money and waiting (admittedly, several weeks) for the visa – we were even granted 45 days in 2005. But by 2007 the embassy told us to not even bother submitting the forms unless we had a 'sponsor'. This requirement for an Iranian sponsor has become almost universal in the past couple of years. Fortunately, it's not as big an obstacle as it sounds. For most people, their 'sponsor' will be a visa agency or travel agency. The good news is that using an agency should (this is not guaranteed) make the process faster and simpler – for us, we had the visa in our passport nine days after contacting the agency. See below for all the details.

So before you shut the book and start planning a holiday to Turkey instead, take comfort in the knowledge that most people do eventually get a visa, usually for 30 days (which can then easily be extended – see the boxed text, opposite). And once they've been to Iran, almost everyone thinks the hassle was worth it.

For details on the back-door route through Kish Island, see Ministry of Foreign Affairs Kish office, p293.

Applications for Visas

Turkish passport holders can get a three-month tourist visa on arrival. Everyone else will need to pay and apply well ahead of departure; to be safe that means at least a month but usually longer. Israelis (and anyone with an Israeli stamp in their passport) are not allowed in under any circumstances. Contrary to popular misconception, US citizens are welcome, but need to be on a tour (an organised group or private guide) or be prepared to badger the Iranian-interests section in Washington for many months.

PROCESS

All visa applicants must be 'approved' by the Ministry of Foreign Affairs in Tehran. At the time of writing the official approval times were about five to seven working days, unless you're using a British, Canadian or Danish passport (10 to 15 days) or a US passport (45 days!). If you're approved, the MFA sends an approval number to the relevant embassy by telex, which can take a couple of days (why not by email? We don't know either). When the relevant embassy or consulate has this number, take or send your passport in, with the fully completed paperwork, photos and fee, and (if you are using an agency – see Sponsors, opposite, for more details) a note with your approval number. The visa should then be issued in a day or two.

Don't be put off if you're refused a visa the first time you apply. Although it won't help future applications, some travellers have been successful at a second attempt even at the same consulate, notably by using a different agency.

Note that all applications stall when the MFA in Tehran closes for holidays. That includes two full weeks between about 21 March and 3 April for No Ruz.

Once visas are issued you must enter Iran within 90 days. If you're on a long trip this can be a hassle, so we recommend contacting an agency about two months before you want to enter Iran, nominate an embassy/consulate nearer to Iran (in Turkey, Azerbaijan or Pakistan, for example), and get your approval number sent to that embassy.

Getting the Paperwork Right

However you choose to apply, you'll need to supply full personal details, copies/scans of your passport, an outline of your itinerary and photographs. For women, you'll probably need to have your hair covered (any scarf will do) in the photo. Some embassies/consulates even require you to be covered when going to collect your visa.

While we don't advocate lying on your application form, don't complicate matters

---

MORE TIME, PLEASE

First the good news: there is *usually* little difficulty in extending a tourist visa to 60 days, or even 90. This is how it works.

Head for the provincial police headquarters *(shahrbani)* or Foreign Affairs office, often called Aliens Bureau or passport office *(edareh gozannameh)*, in your city of choice. Take your passport, two or sometimes three mugshots of yourself, photocopies of the picture page of your passport and your existing Iranian visa, and IR100,000 for the extension, plus about IR3000 for the processing.

Once you've filled out the appropriate form (twice) you'll be asked to deposit your IR100,000 at a specific (hopefully nearby) branch of Bank Melli – just turn up and say 'visa' and the bank staff will usually fill the deposit forms for you. When you return with your bank receipt, you might be lucky and be able to collect your passport with new extended visa immediately, but it rarely works as quickly as this.

Instead, you'll probably have to wait a few hours or, in some cases, several days. As such, it's worth carefully choosing the city where you plan to extend and trying to tailor your itinerary to suit. In general, cities familiar with tourists are the best places: Shiraz was easiest for us, with Esfahan, Gorgan and Rasht not far behind. Second-string options include Kerman, Bushehr and Tabriz. Smaller cities often take longer to issue the extension, if at all, and are less likely to grant you a full 30 days.

Timing is also important: you can only apply for an extension two or three days before your existing visa is due to expire, and your extension starts on the day it's issued, not the end of your original visa. In theory you can extend as many times as you like up to a total stay of 90 days.

The bad news is that transit visas cannot be extended, so those crossing Iran in five days can face real problems. However, if your visa is up and you've not yet made it to the border, here are a couple of tips we received from a helpful visa official:

■ A doctor's note on official stationery stating you were unwell and needed, say, two days rest will act as a quasi-extension once you get to the border, or can be used to extend for a couple of days in the nearest Aliens Bureau.

■ If you are heading east and are only a couple of days over, officers at Zahedan have been known to collect a small fine and extend your visa on the spot before you leave, just to make it all legal.

It's best not to rely on these last-gasp options. Everything here is subject to sudden change so ask other travellers and check the Thorn Tree (thorntree.lonelyplanet.com) before making firm plans.

---

unnecessarily by claiming you're something unloved like a journalist or, according to one woman we heard from, anything to do with fashion (very dangerous!). It's better just to say you're a teacher, student or nurse. Having said that, be aware that the MFA might Google your name and we heard of one woman whose application was rejected when the authorities recognised her photo on her website and the stories didn't gel. If you have a website, consider taking it or your picture down during the application process.

Similarly, keep controversial places like Bushehr and Natanz off your itinerary. Whatever you have written on the application, you'll be able to go anywhere in Iran with the tourist visa once it's issued.

SPONSORS

If you know someone in Iran they can sponsor your application, but it's much easier to use an agency that is used to dealing with the MFA, and indeed often has close relationships with people within the ministry. Usually agencies are worth the money.

Visa Agencies

The following agencies have been recommended by readers or have been used by the authors themselves. Not one is perfect and there have also been complaints. Problems usually arise when the applicant has no time left and their application isn't approved as quickly as they'd hoped, or been promised. You don't need a degree in nuclear physics to work out that to avoid trouble you do need to apply as early as possible.

Iranianvisa.com (www.iranianvisa.com) Charges €30 (€32 with charges) and operates through an easy-to-use website.

Pars Tourist Agency (www.Key2Persia.com) Charges US$30 but offers discounts if you book tours/tickets through its Shiraz-based agency (p271), and a 50% refund if you're rejected.

Persian Voyages (www.persianvoyages.com) More expensive at UK£70, but reliable even when other agencies have failed. Usually quite fast.

WHERE TO APPLY

Iran would prefer you to apply in your home country, but if you're using an agency this isn't necessary. If you don't use an agency, you'll have to deal with the peculiarities of individual Iranian missions. Check Lonely Planet's Thorn Tree forum (thorntree. lonelyplanet.com) for recent feedback from travellers.

The best embassies hand out one-month tourist visas in a week or two (if you've got the right passport). The worst (like Delhi in India) will only issue transit visas to non-Indians, and then only after you've waited weeks.

Costs

Visa costs vary from place to place. Most Iranian embassies (p380) in Europe have websites detailing costs and what you need to supply. For example, in their home countries in December 2007 Brits were being charged UK£61/68 for a transit/single-entry tourist visa, Canadians C$47/70 (insh'Allah), and Germans, French, Dutch and Swedes €40/60. Iranianvisa.com has an incomplete list of visa fees.

Visa Extensions

What if you overstay? Don't. You'll be fined IR300,000 for each day you overstay, and you could be stuck for up to a week sorting out paperwork. For emergency overstay procedures, see the boxed text (p395).

Other Visa Types

BUSINESS VISAS

Business visas can be harder to get than tourist visas. To get a two-week or one-month (extendable) business visa you must have a business contact in Iran who can sponsor your visit through the MFA in Tehran.

TRANSIT VISAS

A five-day transit visa is really a last resort. Transit visas cost almost as much as tourist visas and while in theory processing could be quick, in reality it often takes two or three weeks. One advantage is that you don't need an agency-sponsor but you might need a letter of recommendation from your embassy, which might actually cost more. The main disadvantage? Iran is a big country, five days is a very short time and Iran *does not extend transit visas*.

VISAS ON ARRIVAL

Iran introduced the visa-on-arrival in 2005, designed mainly for business people. In theory, you can fly into Tehran, Esfahan, Shiraz, Mashhad or Tabriz and be issued a seven-day visa at the airport. In practice, this service is unreliable, at best. Indeed, we have heard of people being unceremoniously turned around and sent back to whence they came even though they met all the requirements. And citizens of several countries – including the UK, US, Australia and Ireland – cannot get this type of visa under any circumstances. All up, these are only good for desperate last resorts.

WOMEN TRAVELLERS

The overwhelming majority of Iranians can't do enough to help travellers and to make them feel welcome – this applies to both women and men. Most women travellers enjoy Iran and have few problems.

Attitudes towards Women

As unusual as Iranian culture is to Westerners, Western culture is to Iranians. Half-truths and stereotypes exist on both sides: some Westerners assume all Iranian women are black-cloaked, repressed victims, while some Iranians see Western women as 'easy' and immoral. These perceptions of Western women are created largely by foreign movies and media. They're also rooted in the fact that most Iranian women don't travel without men; the implication is that if you're doing so then you must be of dubious moral standing.

It is inevitable that some men will look at you with an unnerving mix of curiosity, lust and hope. It will rarely go beyond just looking, or a hopeful 'hello, missus!' or perhaps some suggestive comment in Farsi. Reply-

NEVER REALLY ALONE IN IRAN *Kerryn Burgess*

I was enjoying tea in the mountain village of Masuleh. As I popped a sugar cube into my mouth, the Iranians at the next table invited me to join them – why was I alone, they asked?

In a month of travelling in Iran, I never reconciled my experience of unending hospitality with the perceptions of my friends back home in Australia. According to them, I should have received a bravery award for holidaying alone as a woman in a country where, they believed, women wore *burqas* (a mask with tiny slits for the eyes) to scuttle to the market in between terrorist attacks.

My new teahouse companions were two scrawny men and a young, superbly athletic woman carrying an enormous backpack and ropes for rock-climbing. Samira, from Tehran, spoke perfect English. 'I was watching you before,' Samira said to me, 'and wondering why you were alone. I thought, I hope one day I can be as brave as her.'

Despite Samira's perceptions of my bravery, in a practical sense I faced no challenges to equal the vertical rock faces she planned to climb and hungry wolves she was hoping to avoid while camping in the mountains with her fiancé. The summer heat, my limited Farsi skills, and the proliferation of awful fast-food restaurants were my biggest 'problems', none of them specific to women. In every other practical way, Iran is an easy destination for women travelling with a companion, whether male or female.

In a social sense, it's not always the easiest country if you're alone, particularly for women. Take the stigma factor of the solo female diner at a restaurant in the West and multiply it by 100. One of my journal entries reads: 'Another desultory dinner time alone; have waited 15 minutes for a waiter to come within shouting distance, while everyone around me stares.' The waiter probably assumed I was waiting for someone else, because Iranian women never, ever eat out alone.

That said, Iranians were unfailingly welcoming and helpful, even those who were puzzled at my strange lonesome behaviour. Every day, strangers invited me to join them for tea, or to share their picnic, or just to chat. I soon learnt what to say in response to the ubiquitous line of questioning: 'Where are you from? Are you married? (No.) Are you alone? (Yes.) Why? *'Man odat daram. Injaree lezat mibaram.'* ('I'm used to it. I enjoy it.').

Despite the solo dining, the pleasures and surprises of travelling in Iran far outweighed the inconveniences. I discovered, for example, the sense of camaraderie that exists in the women's section of a mosque. In a *hammam* (bathhouse), another woman massaged my back, then showed me how to rub my heels against the rough concrete floor to slough off the dead skin. In the bazaar, a mother of six told me how to make *bastani* (Iranian ice cream). And before I left the teahouse in Masuleh, a woman I'd never met wordlessly handed me a gift, a silver statue of Fatima (the daughter of the Prophet), smiled sympathetically at my aloneness, kissed me three times, and walked away.

Kerryn Burgess is Lonely Planet's Middle East commissioning editor.

ing with a cheerful 'hi, how are you?' will sometimes surprise your 'suitor' into silence. Other times, depending on his proficiency in English or yours in Farsi, it will lead to an interesting, friendly and entirely platonic exchange that might even extend beyond 'where are you from?', if you're lucky. Don't assume that your every interaction with local men will be awkward or threatening or intimidating in some way, or have sexual overtones. Many men will be delighted to chat, and you'd be missing out if you always ignored them. That said, the male attention can become wearing. If it does, it can be refreshing to seek out the company of local women.

You will, of course, be accepted into female society far more than any man (Iranian or foreign), and this is one of the huge advantages women travellers have. Most Iranian women will open up to you far more in exclusively female company than in mixed company. The women's sections of mosques, public parks where groups of women congregate to chat, read, study or relax, women's clothing stores staffed by women, and the food sections of bazaars are all good places to meet local women.

You might feel happier travelling in a group or with a male companion, but neither is essential. Some travellers suggest wearing a wedding ring even if you're not married, but be aware that you're then likely to be quizzed with genuine fascination about your 'husband's' occupation, why he's not with you, why you don't have children, or if you do, how old they are... You might feel more comfortable simply being honest. In general, Iranians understand that foreigners have different rules.

If you're travelling with a man, you might find that Iranian men (and Iranian women in the company of Iranian men) will talk almost exclusively to the foreign man. This can be unsettling, especially if the conversation lasts for several hours over dinner, and you, as a woman, are rarely even acknowledged. However, attitudes like this are slowly changing. As their awareness of the world increases, Iranians are becoming more accepting of women travellers and more prepared to approach and engage them, especially in cities. As a foreign woman you will sometimes be considered an honorary male and be accepted into all-male preserves, such as teahouses, in a way that most Iranian women could not dream of being.

Some restaurants and teahouses have separate areas set aside for women and families. Where that's the case, you'll be directed straight to them. In some people's homes, men and women eat separately when guests are present, although as a foreign woman you will often be regarded as an 'honorary man' in this situation.

On city buses, women have their own entrance in the middle of the bus, and must sit at the back. You give your ticket to the driver through the front door, then get on through the back. On intercity buses, Iranian women never sit next to men unless they're related, and you should follow suit unless you want to give an Iranian man an embarrassing shock. Women should not shake hands, or have any other physical contact, with unrelated men. However, Iranian men who are accustomed to dealing with foreigners will sometimes make an exception to this rule.

Safety Precautions

Violence against foreign women is almost unheard of in Iran, even if the odd grope in a shared taxi is not. And while there's a reasonable chance your bum will be pinched by some guy during the course of your trip, it's important to remember that not every man who speaks to you has ulterior motives. Foreign women who've travelled through Pakistan, Turkey, Egypt or Morocco say they've felt more comfortable in Iran where the level of harassment is lower.

Of course, you should take normal safety precautions and avoid staying in the cheapest *mosaferkhanehs*. Sharing a room with a foreign man shouldn't be a problem, even if he's not your husband.

Try to avoid looking men in the eye unless you know them well, as this will almost certainly be interpreted as a come-on. If you're travelling alone or with female friends, then to avoid the possibility of misunderstandings on anyone's part, it's best to be cautious about accepting invitations to 'tea' at a man's house unless at least one of his female relatives will also be present.

If you are harassed, tell your persecutor firmly, but politely, to desist (English will do; your meaning will be clear from your tone), and try to enlist the sympathy of other Iranians. If they think someone is behaving badly towards you, they will probably stop him out of shame. Try to avoid screaming blue murder; it might make the situation worse. If the problem persists, a mere mention of the police ('polis') should have a sobering effect.

What to Bring

If you use tampons, take enough to last your whole trip. They're hard to find in Iran and expensive. Sanitary pads are widely available. It's also handy to take some plastic bags for carrying out your toilet paper, tampons and pads from toilets that don't have rubbish bins.

What to Wear

Since the revolution of 1979 all women in Iran, including foreigners, have been required *by law* to wear long, loose-fitting clothes to disguise their figures, and to cover their hair. This form of dressing is known as hejab, a term that refers in general to 'modest' dress, and is also used to refer specifically to the hair-covering.

Signs in public places show officially acceptable versions of hejab: the chador (literally 'tent' in Farsi), an all-encompassing, head-to-toe black garment held closed with hand or teeth; or a manteau (a shapeless trench coat or shirt dress) with loose trousers and a *maqna'e* (a nun-like head scarf, or wimple).

In reality the dress code is more relaxed and open to interpretation. It's not unusual to see young Tehranis wearing figure-hugging manteaus, tight jeans, and colourful headscarves perched on the back of their dyed hair. Foreign women are not usually judged as harshly as Iranian women when it comes to hejab, and few Iranians will bat an eyelid if you have your fringe showing. Though as anywhere, it pays to look at what women around you are wearing; for example you'll probably want to dress more conservatively in Qom than you would in Tehran. For an idea of the diversity of Iranian women's fashion, search Google images for 'women's fashion Iran'.

Wearing any scarf and a man's long-sleeved shirt several sizes too large should get you through immigration and your first day or two. However, you'll probably want to buy a manteau as soon as possible because otherwise you'll feel dowdy around so many stylish Iranians. They're easy to find and cheap at about US$15 to US$30. Younger travellers can go for a mid-thigh version but older women may want something longer. Wear your manteau over jeans or comfortable trousers suitable for the season.

If you're coming to Iran from Pakistan or India a *shalwar kameez*, a long, loose men's shirt worn over baggy trousers, is also acceptable (albeit far from fashionable), provided it completely covers your bottom. Some travellers wear long Indian skirts with baggy hippie tops, but locals perceive this as sloppy.

Hejab in summer is hell. At this time of year manteaus in light, natural fabrics are strongly recommended, though they can be oddly difficult to find in Iran. It's coolest to wear nothing underneath your manteau except a bra, but this could be embarrassing if you're invited to someone's house and are expected to remove your manteau. In such situations Iranian women carry a blouse to change into. Alternatively, some readers suggest wearing a synthetic sports top or a light shirt in any material that wicks away sweat, such as CoolMax or Dry-FIT. Even inside someone's home, tight, strappy tops, singlets and plunging necklines are usually inappropriate. If you're thinking about the bra-only option, pack a few safety pins to hold together the parts of the manteau that might gape. They're also good for pinning your headscarf under the chin if you get tired of it slipping too far back.

Very fine, light silk scarves stay in place more easily than slippery polyester or heavy silk. They're hard to find in Iran, so shop before you arrive for a summer trip. Sandals without socks are fine for summer wear.

The only times when foreign women must wear a chador are when visiting some shrines and mosques. These can almost always be borrowed onsite. If you choose to struggle with a chador more generally you run the risk of being thought of as try-hard by women in smaller towns and being laughed at by more 'modern' women in cities, such as Tehran.

If you're hiking or camping, you should still wear hejab. Your guide might suggest it's OK to remove your manteau and headscarf if there's no-one around and you're in a remote area. However, you should always wear them as you approach or stay in villages, even if your guide says (because he wants to make you happy) it's not necessary.

Transport

CONTENTS

GETTING THERE & AWAY

ENTERING THE COUNTRY

Arriving in Iran is usually straightforward. Assuming you have a visa, most immigration and border officials are efficient and tourists rarely get too much hassle. If you're flying in, you should be negotiating with a taxi inside an hour. Land borders can take longer if you're on a bus or train. Of course, women need to be adequately covered from the moment they get off the plane or arrive at the border (see p398, for details).

Passport

Iran has issues with Israel. If you're travelling on an Israeli passport you'll be turned away at the border (and you won't even get onto a flight coming into Iran). Similarly, having an Israeli stamp in your passport will see you turned away or put on the next flight out (for details see Applications for Visas, p394).

AIR
Airports & Airlines

The vast majority of international flights come to Tehran. However, a growing number of travellers are choosing to start or end their trip in Shiraz, thus saving some backtracking.

Tehran has two international airports, the old Mehrabad International Airport (THR) and new Imam Khomeini International Airport (IKA). As of late 2007, all international flights except those to/from Medina, Jeddah and Damascus fly into IKA. As IKA isn't that big, delays on arrival are very possible. A second terminal is being built and can't come soon enough.

Elsewhere in Iran, Shiraz, Esfahan, Bandar Abbas and Kish are (in that order) potentially useful arrival or departure points, while Abadan, Ahvaz, Mashhad, Tabriz and Zahedan are less useful.

Iran Air is the national airline and has the Homa, a mythical bird, as its symbol. It has a reasonably good reputation. As the government-owned carrier, it offers service with an Islamic flavour (ie no pork, no alcohol and no exposed hair on the hostesses).

ESPECIALLY IN IRAN, THINGS CHANGE...

You don't need to be a rocket scientist to know that the information in this chapter is particularly vulnerable to change. Where we have listed prices, they should be read as a guide only. In a country where inflation was running at about 25% and fuel costs rising sharply when we were researching, prices on the ground will almost certainly be higher than those listed here.

Such economic factors are particularly trying for small businesses, so don't be surprised if some services have closed altogether. Having said that, we're confident we've listed strong businesses wherever possible. We're also confident that on the ground you will be able to get the latest taxi/bus/train fares yourselves, just as you check with airlines or travel agents to make sure you understand how a given airfare (and ticket) works. Shop carefully, of course, and for more up-to-date details ask other travellers on the Thorn Tree (www.lonelyplanet.com/thorntree).

Women flying on Iran Air used to have to wear hejab from the time they arrived at the departure airport, but these days most women don't put on the headscarf until the plane has landed; if you're unsure, just watch what other women do. The same applies to all other airlines.

Use the following lists when looking for direct flights to/from Iran. For airline offices in Tehran, see p123.

IRANIAN AIRLINES & THEIR INTERNATIONAL DESTINATIONS

All airlines are based in Tehran except for Taban Air, which is in Mashhad.

Caspian Airlines (code RV; www.caspian.aero) Beirut, Budapest, Damascus, Dubai, İstanbul, Kiev, Minsk, Yerevan.

Iran Air (code IR; www.iranair.com) Amsterdam, Ankara, Bahrain, Baku, Beijing, Caracas, Cologne, Copenhagen, Damascus, Doha, Dubai, Frankfurt, Geneva, Gothenburg, Hamburg, İstanbul, Kabul, Karachi, Kuala Lumpur, Kuwait, London, Milan, Moscow, Mumbai, Paris, Rome, Seoul, Stockholm, Tashkent, Tokyo, Vienna.

Iran Aseman(code EP; www.iaa.ir) Bishkek, Dubai.

Kish Air (code Y9; www.kishairline.com) Damascus, Dubai, İstanbul.

Mahan Air (code W5; www.mahan.aero) Arbil, Almaty, Bahrain, Bangkok, Dammam, Damascus, Delhi, Dubai, İstanbul, Kochi, Lahore, Seoul, Sharjah, Tokyo.

Taban Air (code TBM; www.tabanair.ir) Almaty, Damascus, Dubai.

FOREIGN AIRLINES & THEIR DESTINATIONS

Aeroflot (code SU; www.aeroflot.com) Moscow.

Air Arabia (code G9; www.airarabia.com) Sharjah; budget airline.

Air France (code AF; www.airfrance.com) Paris.

Air India (code AI; www.airindia.com) Delhi.

Alitalia (code AZ; www.alitalia.com) Milan.

Ariana Afghan Airlines (code FG; www.flyariana.com) Kabul.

Armavia (code U8; www.u8.am) Yerevan.

Austrian Airlines (code OS; www.aua.com) Vienna.

Azerbaijan Airlines (code J2; www.azal.az) Baku.

British Airways (code BA; www.britishairways.com) London.

China Southern (code CZ; www.cs-air.com/en) Beijing, Urumqi.

Emirates (code EM; www.emirates.com) Dubai.

Etihad Airways (code EY; www.etihadairways.com) Abu Dhabi.

Gulf Air (code GF; www.gulfair.com) Bahrain.

Iraqi Airways (code IA; www.iraqiairways.co.uk) Baghdad.

Jazeera Airways (code J9; www.jazeeraairways.com) Kuwait.

KLM (code KL; www.klm.com) Amsterdam.

Kuwait Airways (code KU; www.kuwait-airways.com) Kuwait City.

Lufthansa (code LH; www.lufthansa.com) Frankfurt, Munich, Zurich.

Pegasus (code LH; www.flypgs.com/en) İstanbul.

Qatar Airways (code QR; www.qatarairways.com) Doha.

Syrian Arab Airlines (code RB; www.syriaair.com) Damascus.

Tajik Air (code 7J; www.tajikair.tj) Dushanbe.

Turkish Airlines (code TK; www.turkishairlines.com) İstanbul.

UM Airlines (code UF; www.umairlines.com) Kiev.

Tickets & Routes

If you're going to Iran you probably know how to find a fair-priced plane ticket, so we'll keep this brief.

Most travellers fly into Tehran, though Shiraz is a good alternative if you want to avoid back-tracking. Buying tickets in Iran for flights from Iran is best done through an agent; Iranian airlines have yet to master internet bookings or even reservations.

The Middle East is a popular staging point, with several airlines connecting Tehran, Esfahan, Shiraz and Kish to the rest of the world via various Gulf airports. Iran Air and other Iranian and regional airlines fly to/from Abu Dhabi (UAE), Bahrain, Beirut (Lebanon), Damascus (Syria), Doha (Qatar), Dubai (UAE), Kuwait, Sharjah (UAE), İstanbul and Ankara, among others. It's worth checking whether your airline flies to Shiraz, Bandar Abbas, Qeshm or Kish Islands, because shorter flights are cheaper and it could save you doubling back to Tehran.

Flights to Central Asia are less frequent and more expensive than you might expect, though things are getting better. Iran Air, Iran Aseman and Caspian Airlines fly between Tehran and Almaty (Kazakhstan), Ashgabat (Turkmenistan), Baku (Azerbaijan), Bishkek (Kyrgyzstan), Dushanbe (Tajikistan) and Tashkent (Uzbekistan), and the respective national carrier usually does too. Ariana flies to Kabul.

Elsewhere in Asia, India, Pakistan, China, Japan, Thailand and Singapore are all connected by direct flights to Tehran. Travellers from Australia and New Zealand usually stage through these (usually Singapore or

TRANSPORT

CLIMATE CHANGE & TRAVEL

Climate change is a serious threat to the ecosystems that humans rely upon, and air travel is the fastest-growing contributor to the problem. Lonely Planet regards travel, overall, as a global benefit, but believes we all have a responsibility to limit our personal impact on global warming.

Flying & Climate Change

Pretty much every form of motorised travel generates CO2 (the main cause of human-induced climate change), but planes are the worst offenders, not just because of the sheer distances they allow us to travel, but because they release greenhouse gases high into the atmosphere. The statistics are frightening: two people taking a return flight between Europe and the US will contribute as much to climate change as an average household's gas and electricity consumption over a whole year.

Carbon Offset Schemes

Climatecare.org and other websites use 'carbon calculators' that allow travellers to offset the level of greenhouse gases they are responsible for with financial contributions to sustainable travel schemes that reduce global warming – including projects in India, Honduras, Kazakhstan and Uganda.

Lonely Planet, together with Rough Guides and other concerned partners in the travel industry, support the carbon offset scheme run by climatecare.org. Lonely Planet offsets all of its staff and author travel. For more information see www.lonelyplanet.com.

Getting to Iran Without Taking to the Skies

Of course, it's possible to come to Iran without getting on a plane and a good number of people do. Getting to Tehran by road or rail from, say, London will create less CO2 per passenger than the 610kg created by air, though it's hard to say exactly how much less. That depends on a huge array of factors, including the type of transport (electric or diesel train?), how new/old your vehicle is, when it was last serviced, and how heavy is your driver's foot.

Bangkok) or the Middle East. Connecting to Africa is best done on Emirates or Etihad in the UAE.

There are no direct flights from North or South America. Instead, most people come through Europe, where a host of airlines have regular flights to Tehran, or the Middle East. As usual, less direct routes (eg via Moscow) are usually cheaper.

LAND

People have been crossing Iran by land for thousands of years, from the earliest merchants seeking fortunes on the Silk Road (see p34) through to those seeking something altogether different on the 1960s and '70s 'Hippy Trail'. The relative laissez faire of '70s travel came to an abrupt end when things got heavy, man, with the revolution in Iran and the Soviet invasion of Afghanistan, not to mention the Iran–Iraq War.

Well, the good news is that, the 'war on terror' notwithstanding, it's easier to cross in and out of Iran than it has been for 25 years. The border with Afghanistan

is open; routes into Armenia, Azerbaijan and Turkmenistan are do-able with varying degrees of hassle, and Turkey is a piece of cake. Most overlanders say the Pakistan crossing is straightforward if not necessarily comfortable. In theory it's possible to cross into Iraq, but think 20 times before you try it.

In recognition of Iran's pivotal position in trans-Asian travel, in this book we've summarised the details of all the crossing points available to foreigners in 'Crossing the Border at…' boxes within the text. General points are given here, but for the specifics follow the cross-references to the relevant chapter. All legal crossing points are marked on the colour map.

Bicycle

There is no reason why you can't ride in and out of Iran at any of the land borders. A small but steady stream of cyclists cross between Turkey and Pakistan, and we have had no reports of trouble at those borders, or any others.

Car & Motorcycle

To bring your own vehicle into Iran, you must be more than 18 years old and have a current international driving permit. For the vehicle, you'll need a *carnet de passage* (temporary importation document), which can be obtained from the relevant international automobile organisation in your country.

Most people with vehicles have reported hassle-free crossings in and out of Turkey and Pakistan. As long as everything is in order it's just a matter of following and waiting. Officials will probably note your vehicle's details in your passport to make sure you don't leave the country without it. Third-party insurance is compulsory for foreign drivers, but can be difficult to obtain outside Iran (if you do get it, make sure the policy is valid for Iran and accredited with Iran Bimeh, the Iranian Green Card Bureau). If you need it, buying the insurance in Maku (p136) is cheaper than at the border.

No-one but the police is allowed to have a motorbike over 150cc. Foreigners, however, are allowed to ride bikes of any size so long as they take the bike with them when they leave. With big bikes so rare, expect to attract a great deal of attention if you're on one. For information about driving around Iran, see p409.

Shipping bikes across the Persian Gulf is time-consuming, annoying and relatively expensive, but a reasonable number of people do it nonetheless. Rules and ferry times change regularly. Try the following websites for details.

Africa Overland Network (www.africa-overland.net) Asia branch has links to blogs by overlanders.

Horizons Unlimited (www.horizonsunlimited.com) Aimed at motorcyclists, but good for anyone with a vehicle. For the most up-to-date detail, search the Middle East thread on its HUBB forum, which has detail on borders, fuel, shipping and repair shops. The overlander's Bible.

Border Crossings

AFGHANISTAN

The border at Dogharon, 20km east of Taybad, is open and straightforward. Daily buses between Herat and Mashhad make the trip even simpler still. Visas are *not* issued here. See the boxed text (p368) for more information.

ARMENIA

The border between Iran and Armenia is only 35km long, with one crossing point in Iran at Norduz. Armenian visas are issued at the border for US$30, though sometimes the bus leaves before you have your visa – apart from that it's pretty smooth. See the boxed text (p158) for more information.

AZERBAIJAN

The Azeri border has two recognised crossings: between Astara (Azerbaijan) and Astara (Iran; see the boxed text, p166), and Culfa (Azerbaijan) and Jolfa (Iran; see the boxed text, p157), the latter leading to the exclave of Nakhchivan, from where you cannot enter Armenia and must fly to get to Baku. Visas are *not* issued here. When we crossed the Astara border for this book it was thoroughly straightforward.

Bus

These days direct buses between Tehran and Baku, via Astara, are as rare as rocking-horse shit. Which is a good thing, because if you're not on a cross-border bus you'll avoid a three- to seven-hour delay as your conveyance gets a full cavity search, which is considerably less interesting than it sounds. Crossing as a pedestrian is *much* easier.

Train

A train linking Qazvin to the Azeri border at Astara, via Rasht, will allegedly begin service during the life of this book.

IRAQ

Until there is a dramatic improvement in the security situation, you'd need to have rocks in your head to even consider crossing into southern Iraq. And anyway, the border posts at Mehran and Khosravi – servicing the holy cities of Najaf and Karbala in Iraq – are open for locals only. Further north, the Haj Omran border near Piranshahr is the gateway to Iraqi Kurdistan and opens fitfully; see the boxed text (p144) and check Lonely Planet's Thorn Tree (www.lonelyplanet.com/thorntree) for the latest information.

PAKISTAN

Along the 830km border with Pakistan, the only recognised crossing for foreigners is between Mirjaveh (Iran) and Taftan (Pakistan). For border details see the boxed text (p330). For bus information, see p328; for train options, see p329.

TRANSPORT

TO THE ORIENT BY TRAIN

After decades of frustration for trainspotters and travellers alike, it will soon be possible to climb aboard a train in London, or almost anywhere in Europe, and travel exclusively by rail all the way to India. It will be possible when the missing length of track, across the barren deserts between Bam and Zahedan, is finished – supposedly in late 2008.

The new, standard-gauge track will link Zahedan to the rest of the Iranian network via Bam and Kerman. In Zahedan it will change bogies to connect with the wide-gauge Pakistani railway, though there are plans to standardise the entire Pakistani network to allow trains to run directly through to India and China. If the oft-talked about but much-delayed Trans-Asian Railway comes to fruition, Kunming in China will be linked to Kapikule in Bulgaria via an 11,460km line. And if politicians can get their act together, you'll be able to continue through to Thailand, Indochina and Singapore by rail…but hang on a minute, now we're getting *way* ahead of ourselves.

For now, getting to India shouldn't be too tough. Sure, we're not talking about the expensive luxury of the modern-day *Orient Express* trains, which only run as far as Venice. Indeed, there is little 'express' about it. But for scenery, comfort and the chance to meet the locals, it's hard to beat going across Asia by train. If you fancy it, see www.seat61.com to plan your itinerary.

TURKEY

There main road crossing to/from Turkey is at Gürbulak (Turkey) and Bazargan (Iran), where there are hotels, moneychanging facilities and regular transport on either side of the border, though staying in nearby Maku (p136) is more pleasant; see the boxed text (p136) for details.

Foreigners can also cross at Esendere (40km from Yüksekova, Turkey) and Sero, near Orumiyeh in Iran. There is nowhere to stay on either side and transport can be infrequent; see the boxed text (p140) for further information. Motorists usually cross at Gürbulak and Bazargan.

Bus

Travelling by bus you have two options. The easier is to take a direct long-distance bus to, say, Tehran or Tabriz from İstanbul, Ankara or Erzurum.

Buses to/from Tehran cost about IR250,000 to İstanbul (about 36 to 42 hours), but IR300,000 to Ankara, which is nearer. They leave from both the central and western bus terminals; several bus companies offer the service, but usually it's just one bus that runs (see p124 for bus departures). Those in the know swear it's better to take the Ankara bus, which is full of students and embassy workers, rather than the İstanbul bus, which is full of traders and therefore more likely to be taken apart at customs.

Alternatively, take it more slowly and enjoy some of eastern Turkey and western Iran along the way. By taking a bus to – but not across – either border you'll avoid having to wait for dozens of fellow passengers to clear customs. It's usually possible to cross from Erzurum (Turkey) to Tabriz (Iran) in one day if you start early.

It takes longer in winter when high mountain passes near the border are frequently snowbound.

Train

The train from İstanbul to Tehran via Ankara and Tabriz is called the *Trans-Asia Express*. It runs weekly in either direction and, at the time of writing, trains on the 2968km journey left Tehran at 8.15pm on Thursday (IR577,300), and departed İstanbul at 10.55pm Wednesday (about €40). It takes about 70 hours and seating is in comfortable 1st-class couchettes with four berths. Check www.rajatrains.com or the Turkish railways website at www.tcdd. gov.tr for the latest timetables and prices, and www.seat61.com for trip reports. (See also p125 for train departures from Tehran.)

The *Trans-Asia Express* is two trains; an Iranian train between Tehran and Van, on the shores of Lake Van in eastern Turkey, and a Turkish train from Tatvan to Ankara and İstanbul. It's evoked some strong feelings among readers, usually relating to the concept of 'express', though complaints have been fewer in recent years. Delays are likely in winter when snow can block the tracks and low temperatures can freeze the plumbing. However, there's a distinctly romantic touch to such a long train trip, as one reader reported:

This was one of the most enjoyable trips I have made. I was the only foreigner on the train, and once this was discovered I had not nearly enough time to visit all the different compartments full of people wanting to chat (and feed me! Oh, so much food…). It is quite a spectacle to watch the (largely middle-class) female passengers switch from coats and scarves into T-shirts and hairpins as soon as you cross the border. The men, of course, fetch beer and the whole thing has a bit of a party atmosphere. I spent the days learning to sing the poems of Hafez and being pursued by the suddenly liberated single girls (Valentines apparently being in the air). All in all, a very, very interesting trip – definitely a journey.

Joshua Smyth

Readers report that although you need to pay for the whole trip even if you are planning to get off at Ankara, the ticket is valid for six months and it is possible to make a new reservation on the same ticket for a later trip to İstanbul. Food on the Turkish train has been criticised for its price and quality. When changing from the ferry to your new train the berth numbers are usually ignored, so you could just grab anything you can find.

TURKMENISTAN

There are three border posts open to foreigners along this 1206km-long frontier. From west to east, there is inconvenient and little-used Incheh Borun and Gyzyl-Etrek (see the boxed text, p342), Bajgiran and Howdan (see p346) linking Mashhad and the Turkmen capital Ashgabat, and Sarakhs and Saraghs (see p366) for those heading east. You must change transport at all three crossings.

The paperwork and organisation involved in travelling to Turkmenistan is still a big hassle; the people at **Stantours** (www.stantours.com) seem to be the best at making it all go as smoothly as possible.

SEA

Iran has 2410km of coastal boundaries along the Persian Gulf, Gulf of Oman and Caspian Sea, but there are relatively few ways to enter or leave Iran by sea.

Caspian Sea

Boats with passenger berths do cross the Caspian, but that's about as definitive as we can be. Schedules are non-existent and most travellers have neither the time, the patience nor the requisite degree of masochism to bother. If you're still keen, start sniffing around in Noshahr (p173).

Persian Gulf

The main shipping agency for trips across the Persian Gulf is Valfajre-8. Valfajre-8 operates car ferries and catamarans from Bushehr (p291), Bandar Abbas (p302) and Bandar-e Lengeh (p298) in Iran to destinations including Sharjah, Kuwait City and Bahrain. Services are not exactly frequent and not that much cheaper than flying; for departure details see www.irantraveling center.com/valfajr8_persian_gulf.htm.

TOURS

Many travellers visit Iran on an organised tour, a situation likely to continue as long as visas are hard to come by. Apart from the convenience, having an English-speaking guide can be worthwhile.

The following are some experienced and reputable agencies that offer organised tours to Iran from outside the country (for adventure tours, see the boxed text, p373). Note that almost all of these companies use local operators once you get to Iran. If you can live without that foreign tour leader, consider booking direct through an Iranian operator (p415).

Australia & New Zealand

Equitrek (☎ 02-9913 9408; www.equitrek.com.au) Tailor-made horse riding tours of the northeast.

Passport Travel (☎ 03-9500 0444, www.travelcentre .com.au) Standard highlights trip, plus a more exotic tour of northwest ethnic groups.

Continental Europe

Catai Tours (www.catai.es) For Spanish speakers.

Clio (☎ 01 53 68 82 82; www.clio.fr) French operator of cultural tours.

Pars Travel (☎ 069-230882) In Frankfurt, mainly flights and some tours.

UK

Ace Study Tours (☎ 01223-835 055; study-tours.org) Ace Study provides infrequent study tours with professional lecturers.

TRANSPORT

TRANSPORT

Magic Carpet Travel (☎ 01344-622 832; www.magic
-carpet-travel.com) Established, Iranian-owned operator
specialising in Iran tours.
Persian Voyages (☎ 01306-885 894; www.persian
voyages.com) Iran specialist with a range of tours; Nasrin
is very helpful.

USA & Canada
Americans often use organised tours as it's
difficult to get a visa otherwise.
Bestway Tours & Safaris (☎ 800 663 0844; www
.bestway.com) Upmarket trips, some combining nearby
'stans.
Distant Horizons (☎ 800 333 1240; www.distant
-horizons.com) Small groups accompanied by a scholar.
Geographic Expeditions (☎ 800 777 8183; www
.geoex.com) Mainly bespoke tours aimed at the upper end.
Silk Road Tours (☎ 888 881 7455; www.silkroadtours
.com) Regular package and tailor-made tours.

GETTING AROUND

Most visitors are pleasantly surprised by
the transport system in Iran. Once you
accept that the driving is...erm...more
imaginative than what you're used to at
home, you'll appreciate that services on
most forms of public transport are frequent, fairly punctual and very cheap.
For planes and trains it's worth booking
ahead if you're travelling on a weekend
or any public holiday, especially No Ruz,
Ramazan and Eid al-Fitr. At No Ruz bus
fares usually rise by about 20%. For more
information on holidays, see p383.

AIR
The days of US$5 flights from Tehran to
Esfahan are gone, but domestic air fares in
Iran are still cheap; Tehran to Shiraz, for
example, is just IR245,000. Happy days!

Airlines in Iran
Iran Air is the largest among a growing
roster of domestic airlines and boasts an
extensive network of flights, covering most
provincial capitals. Domestic prices are
set by the government, so it doesn't matter which airline you fly the price will be
the same. Flight details are included in the
relevant Getting There & Away sections
throughout this book.

Of the others, Iran Aseman and Mahan
Air fly the most routes, while Caspian Airlines, Kish Air and Taban Air have fewer.
For website details, see p400. Generally
speaking, Iran Air is the most reliable, but
whichever airline you choose you stand a
good chance of being delayed. On this trip
all three domestic flights we took were delayed by more than an hour. Despite this,
it's worth trying to get to the airport a good
hour ahead of domestic departures (just in
case it leaves on time).

Except for Iran Air, which has unnecessarily large offices across the country, airline offices can be hard to find. It's much
easier to visit one of Iran's thousands of
travel agencies, which can book you onto
any airline. When making a booking, check
the aircraft type and avoid, wherever possible, the clunking old Tupolevs still struggling through Iran's skies.

Booking domestic flights from outside
Iran can be difficult in some places and
nigh-on impossible if the flight is on a
smaller airline. None of the airlines yet do
online bookings. However, some readers
report it's possible to book domestic flights
by calling an Iran Air office outside Iran.
They give you a booking reference which
you take to an Iran Air office in Iran or
to Tehran domestic terminal...you pay for
it then.

BICYCLE
Excellent roads, friendly people and a relatively small risk of theft mean Iran sounds
like an ideal cycling destination. And indeed, there are usually one or two travellers
pedalling across the country and report-
ing a fantastic experience full of selfless
hospitality. It's not, however, all easy. Vast
distances, dodgy traffic and hot, tedious
stretches of desert road – not to mention
seasonal winds – can get tiring. You'll need
to carry plenty of water and food to last the
long desert stretches, camping equipment
if you are not sticking to major towns, a
decent map, and a phrasebook.

If you arrive in a village or small town
and find either nowhere to stay or only a
hotel you can't afford – and if you can't
persuade the caretaker at the local mosque
to take you in – you might have to load
your bike on a bus or truck and head for
the next big town.

The biggest drawback with cycling, as
with most other activities in Iran, is the

need to stay covered up. We have received varying reports from travellers: some say that it's fine to wear cycling gear when actually on the road, as long as you have clothes at hand to cover up as soon as you stop; others say that women in particular must be covered at all times.

Spare parts can be hard to find and there is nowhere to rent bicycles for long distances, so bring your own.

BOAT

The only places you're likely to use a boat are between the mainland and some islands in the Persian Gulf (see p287).

BUS

In Iran, if you can't get somewhere by bus (or minibus), the chances are no-one wants to go there. More than 20 *taavonis* (bus companies) offer hundreds of services all over the country, so business is highly competitive, fares cheap and, on busier routes, departures are frequent. Most buses are comfortable, with your own cushioned seat and, except on very short trips, standing is not allowed. Fares don't vary much between companies, but they do vary between classes of bus – see One Habitat, Two Species: Mahmooly or Volvo? (p408).

Don't be confused by the names of the destinations on a bus. It's common for a bus travelling between, for example, Khorramabad and Ahvaz, to have 'Tehran–İstanbul' written on the front or side in English. Similarly, phrases like 'Lovely bus' are not always a fair reflection of reality. There are no bus passes.

Bus Companies

Most bus companies are cooperatives and until recently they were referred to simply as Cooperative Bus Company No X (Sherkat-e Ta'avoni Shomare X), or whatever number it is. In recent years most have taken on more varied names, but in the terminal they'll still direct you to, for example, 'ta'avoni hasht' (cooperative number 8). The best *ta'avonis*, with the most extensive network of services, are TBT (Taavoni 15) and Iran Peyma (often with the word 'Ta'avoni' or 'Bus No One' written on it).

For a bit more comfort Seiro Safar and Hamsafar offer newer, better buses for a little more, though most travellers don't bother seeking out a specific company and just take whichever is the next bus going their way. The exception is with bus types – see the boxed text (p408).

Bus Terminals

Most bus terminals are located at the edge of town and are easy to reach by shuttle or private taxi, less so by local bus. In some cities there's more than one bus terminal; if in doubt, ask at your hotel or charter a taxi to the relevant terminal. Tell the driver '*terminal-e* (your destination)' and he'll know where to drop you – pronounce 'terminal' with a prolonged 'aal' at the end.

Bus terminals are filled with the offices of individual bus companies, though

---

CHECKPOINTS

If you're travelling to or from the Pakistan or Afghan borders, or from Bandar Abbas, you're likely to have to stop at checkpoints designed to catch smugglers. In some cases a customs official or policeman will get onto the bus and walk up and down, presumably looking for obvious smugglers or 'illegal aliens', before waving the bus on. However, searches can be much more thorough and time consuming.

Taking the bus from Zahedan to Bam we witnessed both the reasons for and effect of such searches. Each of our bags had our ticket number written onto it, just in case we tried to deny it later on. Then we had to wait an hour before we departed while a couple of men, clearly with the understanding of the bus staff, used a knife to pry open the underneath of several seats and stuff contraband within. At the checkpoint, after waiting an hour while other buses were searched, we got off the bus and, like everyone else, took all our luggage to a nearby table. The officers didn't pay too close attention to our bags once they realised we were travellers, but they did spend 45 minutes opening and searching everything else on the bus, as well as sniffing around inside. Apparently they didn't find whatever had been secreted inside the seats, as the grinning smugglers retrieved it soon after we moved on.

timetables are rarely in English. Just ask 'Shiraz?', 'Esfahan?' or wherever and you'll be directed to the right desk, or listen for your destination being screamed out when a bus is about to leave. When you hear that a bus is 'leaving now', 'now' can be defined as sometime within the next 45 minutes or so.

Terminals always have somewhere to buy food, and some larger terminals have a post office, police station, left-luggage facilities and maybe even a hotel. The information desks are basically useless; as the woman working behind the desk at one Tehran terminal told us with a frustrated shake of her head: 'We'd like to be able to help, but the companies never give us their timetables, so we can't'.

If you're leaving a junction town, such as Zanjan or Kashan, you may need to flag down a passing bus on the road instead of going to the terminal. Position yourself near enough to the passing traffic that you can shout out your destination without being run over – a combination that is not as simple as it sounds. Roadblocks, roundabouts, service stations and junctions are the best places to hail passing buses – locals will point you to the right place.

Costs

Mahmooly buses usually cost a bit more than half what a Volvo costs. For example, the 1024km trip from Tehran to Kerman costs IR52,000/90,000 by *mahmooly*/Volvo, while the 440km journey between Tehran and Esfahan costs about IR23,000/50,000. Either way, it's cheap, though expect prices in this book to rise steadily.

Reservations

It's possible to buy tickets up to a week in advance, except at No Ruz when most people don't bother. Between major cities, such as Esfahan and Tehran, buses leave at least every half-hour between about 5am and 1am. In medium-sized towns, such as Hamadan and Kerman, buses to nearer locations leave every hour or so, but longer trips (and any cross-desert trip) will often be overnight. In smaller places, where there may be only one or two buses a day to your destination, it is essential to book ahead.

There are often no-shows for bus trips, so seats can magically appear on otherwise full buses just before departure. Alternatively, you might be offered the back seat. If you're desperate, then looking like it, plus helpless and lost, usually helps.

Tickets are almost always in Farsi, so learn the Arabic numbers to check the day of departure, time of departure, bus number, seat number, platform number and fare. If it's incomprehensible someone at the terminal, should point you in the right direction.

ONE HABITAT, TWO SPECIES: MAHMOOLY & VOLVO

Iran's roads are home to two main species of bus, the *mahmooly* (mercedus antiquus) and the Volvo (bus invita Minerva). Both enjoy a wide range of habitats, happy to roam relentlessly across deserts or forage through remote mountain roads in search of prey, known as passengers. They are seldom seen without an accompanying crew of three Iranian men (quem pilosus). But while the *mahmooly* and Volvo coexist fairly peacefully within the bus kingdom, they do boast some important differences.

Mahmooly

Apart from the odd throwback, *mahmooly* (or 'normal' in Farsi) buses share a common gene stock that can be traced back to the Mercedes family in Germany. Herded by salesmen, they began an epic migration during the 1960s and within two decades had come to dominate the Iranian roadscape. They were celebrated for their beauty and comfort, notably their curvaceous bodies, colourful hides, generous legroom and large windows. And while some remain in rude health even into their 40s, with working air-conditioning and carefully groomed curtains, the herd as a whole is in decline. By the late 1990s, the *mahmooly* had slowed so much that it began to be replaced, particularly on longer journeys, by new predators that came thundering in from far-off Scandinavia....

The Journey

Don't count on averaging more than 60km/h on most bus journeys. Buses often arrive in a town in the early hours of the morning, which can be a hassle. On most trips of more than three hours you'll stop at roadside restaurants serving cheap food. Ice-cold water is normally available on the bus and is safe to drink. Every two hours or so the driver will stop to have his tachograph checked by the police as a precaution against speeding. If it's summer, try to get a seat on the side facing away from the sun.

CAR & MOTORCYCLE

A small but steady stream of travellers take vehicles across Iran as part of a trip between Europe and the Indian subcontinent. Most report the country driving is great and the city driving is not. If you're considering an overland journey check out www. africa-overland.net/asia-overland, or www. horizonsu nlimited.com.

Iranian roads can be dangerous; see p98 for the shocking figures.

Bring Your Own Vehicle

If you are driving your own vehicle, you should always slow down and get ready to stop at roadblocks. Usually if you wind down your window, smile nicely, and give the officials your best 'I-don't-know-what-to-do-and-I-don't-speak-Farsi' look, you will be waved straight through. At worst you'll have to show your passport, licence and vehicle documents, and if your papers are in order you shouldn't have any hassles.

Keep to the main roads near the Pakistan, Iraq or Afghanistan borders to steer clear of suspicious drug smugglers or equally suspicious customs and police officials. Be sure to find a hotel with safe parking when in the southeast, where your vehicle might be stolen, stripped, driven across the border of Afghanistan or Pakistan and bought by a drug smuggler, before you've finished your plate of kabab. Of course, ensure there is sufficient height clearance before checking in; most places marked with a parking symbol in this book have enough clearance for 4WDs.

Driving Licence

To drive in Iran you need an international driving licence. Get one from the national automobile association in your home country.

Fuel & Spare Parts

For Iranians the price of fuel is always a hot topic (see Inflation, Rising Prices & You, p25). For you, however, if you use diesel it's likely to be the source of incredulity and, let's face it, unbridled joy. That's because diesel costs a whopping IR165L (that's

---

Volvo

The first of these was the Volvo. Bigger, faster and with a respiratory system evolved to breathe ice-cold air more reliably, Iranian passengers were soon lining up to roam with the Volvo even though it cost almost twice as much to do so. Volvo herders learnt new hunting techniques, luring passengers with boiled lollies, packaged cakes, biscuits, a steady stream of Zam Zam (soft drink) and deafeningly loud Bollywood movies.

Seeing the success of the Volvo, other European sub-species began to appear in the Iranian habitat. MAN, Scania and similar boxy European breeds rolled in, and Iranians began calling these sub-species different names depending on their age and location. Some older buses, their air-conditioners no-longer working and their engines weak with age, are called 'lux', or 'super-lux', and cost slightly less to roam with, while in some areas newer Volvos are called 'super', an apparent reference to the awe in which they are held. In this book, we refer to all new buses, be they Volvo, MAN, Scania or even some exotic Korean breeds, as Volvos. Passengers unsure of which herd to saddle up with should consider these points. Seats in *mahmooly* buses are usually just as comfortable as those in Volvos, are cheap enough you can buy two for the price of one Volvo seat, and the air-con usually works. Speed and cost are the real differences, as was illustrated during a migration from Shiraz to Tehran. We ranged with a Volvo while a fellow traveller chose a *mahmooly*, telling us 'there's really not that much difference – save the money'. Alas, his *mahmooly* took 19 hours, our Volvo 12½.

TRANSPORT

about €0.01), meaning you can fill up and get change out of a euro. Happy days! However, the price of petrol has recently taken a steep hike, though it remains very reasonable; see What Fuel Cards Mean For You (opposite).

Once you're on the road, you'll find large towns at least every 100km except in the remote deserts of eastern Iran. But *benzin* (petrol) stations can be hard to find, so it's worth keeping your tanks topped up. Not all stations sell diesel and there is usually nothing written on the pump to differentiate it from *benzin* – be sure to ask. Readers have complained that while fuel is dirt cheap it can also be just plain dirty – especially near the Pakistan border – so don't expect the same mileage as you would at home. More problematic, though, are the eternal shortages and long queues in towns within 100km or so of a border, where well-organised smuggling operations leave little for locals. Somewhat ironically, Iranian motor oil can also be of dubious quality. International brands are safer.

Even the tiniest settlements have repair shops. The price for repair work is open to negotiation but you might not have much say over the quality of the spare parts – unless you're driving a Paykan or Pride. In the height of summer, scalding heat makes tyre blowouts fairly common.

Hire
The concept of car rental barely exists in Iran, not least because without a functioning system for accepting credit cards it's hard for anyone leasing a car to be sure they can make good any damage. Instead, 'car rental' here means chartering a taxi, either privately or through a travel agency. Local drivers-cum-guides are mentioned throughout this guide.

Insurance
Your vehicle will need a *carnet de passage* and a green card, both of which you should organise before you arrive. It's possible to get into Iran without a green card from Pakistan, but getting into Turkey can then be problematic.

Road Distances (km)

	Ahvaz	Ardabil	Bandar Abbas	Bushehr	Esfahan	Gorgan	Hamadan	Kerman	Kermanshah	Khorramabad	Mashhad	Orumiyeh	Qazvin	Rasht	Shiraz	Tabriz	Tehran	Yazd	Zahedan
Ahvaz	---																		
Ardabil	1310	---																	
Bandar Abbas	1280	1930	---																
Bushehr	490	1610	930	---															
Esfahan	750	1030	960	580	---														
Gorgan	1270	770	1730	1630	840	---													
Hamadan	640	670	1420	1050	470	730	---												
Kerman	1230	1630	490	880	660	1440	1130	---											
Kermanshah	490	790	1770	970	650	920	190	1290	---										
Khorramabad	380	930	1330	860	370	900	260	1030	320	---									
Mashhad	1770	1330	1380	1650	1220	570	1230	890	1420	1390	---								
Orumiyeh	1060	530	2030	1550	1070	1300	610	1740	580	870	1800	---							
Qazvin	880	480	1650	1360	560	530	230	1220	420	490	1080	770	---						
Rasht	1040	270	1660	1520	760	500	400	1360	590	670	1070	800	170	---					
Shiraz	660	1520	620	300	490	1320	950	570	1110	860	1380	1320	1050	1250	---				
Tabriz	1080	220	1930	1560	1040	1000	610	1640	590	880	1500	310	480	490	1530	---			
Tehran	870	590	1330	1230	440	400	340	1040	530	500	890	910	150	330	930	600	---		
Yazd	1080	1270	660	730	300	1080	730	360	950	670	920	1380	830	1000	450	1280	680	---	
Zahedan	1760	2160	740	1400	1190	1520	1660	530	1820	1560	950	2270	1760	1900	1100	2170	1570	890	---
Zanjan	970	380	1650	1340	760	720	330	1360	420	590	1210	590	180	350	1240	280	320	1000	1890

WHAT FUEL CARDS MEAN FOR YOU

After years of multi-billion dollar government subsidies and much debate, Iran's state-regulated and ridiculously low *benzin* (petrol) prices were finally raised in mid 2007. The price hike is tied to a new rationing system, by which drivers are entitled to a per-day quota. The quota depends on whether the vehicle is used for private or commercial use. The whole system is underpinned by an ambitious system by which every vehicle owner is issued a ration card, which is swiped through a machine to record the date and quantity of every litre bought. At the time of writing, motorcycles were allowed the equivalent of 1L per day, standard cars 4L a day and taxis about 20L a day. So what does this mean if you're driving your own vehicle in Iran?

Diesel

If you use diesel then start cheering now! Prices are fixed and are not subject to rationing, so you can buy diesel across the country for IR165 a litre. Diesel stations can be hard to find, but you'll know one when you find it by the long line of trucks parked outside.

Benzin (Petrol/Gasoline)

In theory, without a ration card you can't buy *benzin*. After much initial confusion, foreigners can now buy ration cards for 100L (IR500,000) or 300L (IR1,500,000) at the National Iranian Oil Products Distribution Company (usually called NIOPDC) office in each major town. Yes, that's five times what Iranians have to pay. Present the card at the *benzin* station and pay an additional IR1000 for each litre you buy (that's so the station gets the local rate).

Okay, so where do I get a card? Coming from Turkey, the NIOPDC office in Maku (at 39° 17'06.43" N, 44° 32'20.47" E) is the place to go. Take your ownership documents. Elsewhere you'll have to ask for the local NIOPDC office; this system was introduced after we researched so they're not marked on our maps. Overlanders who have travelled with this system report that in larger cities, especially Tehran, it's very difficult to buy petrol without the card. However, a thriving black market operates elsewhere, which you'll probably need to use to avoid running your card dry.

Iranians pay IR1000 per litre for their rationed amount, and can then buy extra for IR3000 a litre – still half of what foreigners must pay. The result is a black market where *benzin* sells for between IR3000 and IR4000 a litre, except near borders where it can be three times that much. The sellers will be petrol station owners, other drivers (usually taxi drivers because of their larger ration) and even, according to one driver, the police themselves. Going to a *benzin* station and looking lost seems to be the best method. If this sounds like a big hassle, then the good news is that you're in Iran...if you run out of gas, some random, kind-hearted Iranian is guaranteed to help out.

Road Conditions

Road surfaces are generally excellent. On the other hand, driving at night is more dangerous because of occasional unmarked potholes and the risk of running into tractors and other vehicles crawling along the road with no lights. On intercity roads most signs are in English and Farsi, including directions to most cities, towns and villages. Within cities, street signs vary between non-existent (quite rare these days) and thorough to the point of telling you when a street is a dead end!

Road Hazards

Iranian drivers in the cities. Camels in the deserts. Unmarked speed bumps everywhere.

The last are both highly annoying and dangerous, and you'll often be completely unaware they exist until your car suddenly lurches and jumps as you launch over the bump. Such speed bumps are often at the edge of towns, so watch for brake lights ahead.

If you're in an accident the Iranian involved will probably call the local traffic police. If you're alone, call the emergency number – ☎ 110 for police, ☎ 115 for ambulance. You should never move the vehicle from the road until the police have come to make their report. As a foreigner, you'll probably be held responsible.

Road Rules

Lanes? What are they? Driving across Iran is not a task to be taken lightly. In theory, the rule is that everyone drives on the right, but this can't be depended upon; faced with a one-way street going the wrong way, the average Iranian driver sees nothing wrong with reversing down it. In theory, you give way to the traffic coming onto a roundabout, though this seems a tad unimportant when some drivers simply drive the wrong way around it. Take 10 Iranian car drivers and an otherwise deserted open road and you can be sure that all 10 will form a convoy so tightly packed that each of the rear nine can read the speedometer of the car in front. The phrase 'optimum braking distance' is not widely understood in Iran.

However, take comfort in the knowledge that Iranian drivers are almost unfeasibly adept at avoiding accidents, and most foreign drivers make it across Iran without too much trouble.

HITCHING

Hitching is never entirely safe in any country, and we don't recommend it. Travellers who decide to hitch should understand that they are taking a small but potentially serious risk. However, many people do choose to hitch, and the advice that follows should help to make their journeys as fast and safe as possible. Women, however, should never hitch in Iran.

Hitching, as understood in the West, is a novel concept in Iran. Although you will often see people standing by the roadside waiting for a lift, they are actually waiting for space in a bus, minibus or shared taxi, for which they expect to pay. Occasionally drivers will offer foreigners a free ride in return for English practice or out of simple hospitality. Like anywhere, you're most likely to find rides in more remote areas. We heard of one traveller who hitched the Howraman valley with his 12-year-old son, and loved it. And as we found hitching through the Dasht-e Lut, host drivers will be typically generous; ours bought us food, shared their smoke, even tracked down some rocket fuel in a tiny desert town because they thought we wanted it, and refused all attempts to pay them. In such a case it's nice to have something small to thank them with.

LOCAL TRANSPORT

Bus

Most Iranian towns and cities have local bus services. Because local buses are often crowded and can be difficult to use unless you know exactly where you're going, most travellers use the ubiquitous shared and private taxis instead.

Bus numbers and destinations are usually only marked in Farsi, so you need to do a lot of asking around – most people will be happy to help (even if you don't entirely understand their reply). Except in Shiraz and on one new private operator in Tehran, tickets must be bought at little booths along main streets, or at local bus terminals, before you get on the bus. Tickets on state-run buses cost between IR100 and IR500. Private companies cost a bit more.

Small children of both genders and all women have to sit at the back of the bus. This segregation can be complicated if you are travelling as a mixed couple and need to discuss when to get off. You must give your ticket to the driver either before you get on or after you get off, depending on the local system. Women must pass their tickets to the driver while leaning through the front door of the bus and then board the bus using the back door.

Metro

Metros are the great hope for Iranian cities slowly being strangled by traffic. The Tehran Metro (p127) is growing and similar systems are being built in Mashhad (p363), Shiraz (p279) and Esfahan (p232); the first two of which should, *insh'Allah* (god willing), be operational during the life of this book.

Minibus

If you think using local buses is a hassle, don't even bother trying to use the infrequent and desperately crowded minibuses. Quite often they are so crammed with passengers that you can't see out to tell where you're going. You normally pay in cash when you get on – about IR1000 a ticket depending on the distance. Men and women get a seat anywhere they can; there is no room for segregation. Minibuses stop at normal bus stops or wherever you ask them.

Taxi

A shared or private taxi is the quickest and most hassle-free way of getting around a town or city, unless there's a Metro going your way.

IS THIS SEAT FREE?

Choosing where to sit on Iranian transport is fraught with difficulty. On city buses, even married couples must sit separately; men at the front of the bus, women at the back.

In contrast, on intercity buses and minibuses, seating is generally arranged so that women sit next to women and men next to men, unless they're couples or family. A woman is not expected to sit next to an unrelated man even if there's only one spare seat left on the bus, and people will move around until the gender mix is right.

If you decide to take a shared taxi you will find people hopping in and out of the front and back like yo-yos in an attempt to ensure that unrelated men and women don't end up side by side. Despite this, often it's impossible to arrange and you'll end up sitting next to someone of the opposite sex without anyone getting too upset. On the Tehran Metro women have the option of the women's only carriage or squeezing in with the men. And on sleeper trains you might find yourself in a mixed compartment if you don't specify that you want a single-sex compartment.

SHUTTLE (SHARED) TAXI

In most towns and cities, shared or shuttle taxis duplicate or even replace local bus services. They usually take up to five passengers: two in the front passenger seat and three in the back. Until recently shared taxis were always Paykans (see the boxed text, p414), often coloured orange, or with a dash of orange somewhere. But these are slowly being replaced by smaller Kia Prides (or similar). Either way, after a while you will get used to using shuttle taxis, especially if you try them out somewhere other than Tehran first.

Shuttle taxis travel between major *meydans* (squares) and along main roads, so the key to using them is to learn the names of the *meydans* along your intended route. They sometimes make slight detours for passengers at no extra charge; for a longer detour, you may be charged IR500 or IR1000 extra. You'll usually find them outside bus terminals, train stations, airports and near major *meydans,* or you can hail one on the street.

There is a certain art to finding a shuttle taxi going your way. Start by stepping onto the road far enough for the driver to hear you shout your destination, but close enough to the kerb to dash back in the face of hurtling traffic. If the driver has a spare seat, he will slow down for a nanosecond while you shout your one-word destination – usually the name of a *meydan.* If he's going your way he'll stop.

When you want to get out simply say *kheili mamnun* (thank you very much) or make any other obvious noise. Drivers appreciate exact change, so try and keep plenty of those filthy IR500 and IR1000 notes handy; you normally pay when you get out.

Fares, which are fixed by the government, range from about IR500 for the shortest trip to IR5000 for long trips in Tehran, depending on the distance and the city (Tehran's fares are naturally the most expensive). Try and see what other passengers are paying before you hand over your money, though most drivers are straight enough.

If you get into an empty shuttle taxi, particularly in Esfahan and Tehran, it might be assumed you want to charter it privately. Similarly, if everyone else gets out the driver might decide you are now a private fare. Clarify what you want by saying *dar baste* (closed door) or *nah dar baste* (for details, see below).

PRIVATE TAXI

Any taxi without passengers, whether obviously a shared taxi or a more expensive private taxi (usually yellow), can be chartered to go anywhere in town; an act usually called '*service*' or '*agence*'. Unless it's a

---

NAH DAR BASTE!

If you hail an empty taxi the driver will probably think you want to hire it privately. He might ask you: '*Dar baste?*', which literally means 'Closed door?', or perhaps '*agence?*' If you want to share, then make your intentions clear by leaning in and telling him simply '*Nah dar baste*', or 'No closed door'. He'll soon let you know if he's interested or not.

THE PERENNIAL PAYKAN

For more than 35 years the Paykan was almost the only car you'd see on Iranian roads. The Paykan (which means Arrow – don't laugh) is a replica of the 1966 Hillman Hunter, an uninspiring vehicle if ever there was one. But it was exactly the sort of cheap, no-frills car Iran needed when it was first sold there in the late 1960s. The boxy white Paykan, the very definition of utilitarian, went on to dominated the roadscape more than any other car since the Model-T Ford. Indeed, it became so well loved that in the years before production was finally stopped in 2005 there was a two-year waiting list to get one.

But while Iranians respect the Paykan's ability to get the job done – just – they are also aware of its diabolical impact on the environment. The Paykan burns, on average, between 12L and 15L of leaded petrol per 100km. That is at least double the exhaust most modern cars pump out, and with no catalytic converter, the poisons are even greater. So bad that, according to reports, the Iranian government actually paid Iran Khodro to shut the factory. Still, with more than two million Paykans on Iran's roads (more than 40% of all vehicles) they'll be around for decades yet. And if reports are to be believed, the Paykan will live on in Africa, where the production line has been sold to a Sudanese company.

complicated deal, including waiting time, simply hail the vehicle, tell the driver where you want to go, and ask *'chand toman?'* Immediately offer about 60% of what he suggests but expect to end up paying about 75% or 80% of the originally quoted price. Taxi drivers are probably the most likely people in Iran to try to rip you off, but the prices are still pretty reasonable.

AGENCY TAXI

Agency taxis, also known as 'telephone' taxis, don't normally stop to pick up passengers; you have to order them by telephone or at an agency office. There are agency-taxi offices in even the smallest towns and hundreds of them in Tehran. Some of the top hotels run their own taxi services, and any hotel or *mosaferkhaneh* (lodging house) can order a taxi for a guest. Naturally, this is the most expensive way of using taxis, but you get a better car, the comfort of knowing there will be someone to complain to if anything goes wrong and, possibly, a driver who speaks English. One reader wrote to say that lone women are advised to get someone to call them a taxi if they're travelling after dark, thus avoiding being hooted at or ignored by dozens of drivers as they try to hail one. Demand is such that Tehran now has a women-only taxi company (p129) – female drivers, female passengers, no groping.

MINIBUS

Minibuses are often used for shorter distances linking larger cities and towns to surrounding villages. Sometimes they're an alternative to the bus, but usually there's no choice; just take whatever is going your way. Minibuses are particularly popular along the Caspian Sea coast, and between Caspian towns and Tehran.

Minibuses are marginally more expensive than buses, but not enough to worry about. They are often faster than larger buses and because they have fewer passengers they spend less time dropping off and picking up. On the downside, they're not at all comfortable and usually leave only when they're full, which can mean a long wait.

Minibuses sometimes leave from a special terminal and sometimes from the main bus terminal. If in doubt, just charter a taxi and tell the driver you want to go to the terminal-e Rasht, Tehran or wherever. Arriving in a town, they have an annoying habit of depositing you in the middle of nowhere. Luckily, hopeful taxi drivers will probably be waiting.

PRIVATE TAXI

Almost every single taxi in the country is available for private hire. Needless to say, prices are open to negotiation. One excellent way to avoid getting ripped off is to ask the driver of a savari (see opposite) for the price per person of a certain trip then multiply it by four or five.

If you prefer to hire the taxi and driver for the whole day you are looking at somewhere between about IR150,000 and IR500,000 – depending on a long list of factors, including your ability as a negotiator, the quality of the car, the distance you plan to drive and where you are. The smaller the town, the cheaper the price. Some drivers charge by the kilometre, with IR800 being the usual rate.

SAVARI (SHARED TAXI)

You can almost always find a savari for a trip between towns less than three hours apart. Savari means 'shared taxi' and is usually applied to intercity versions of the species. Speed is the main advantage because savaris are generally less comfortable than buses. Sometimes two people will be expected to squeeze into the front passenger seat, though for longer journeys four passengers all up is the norm.

Savaris rarely leave with an empty seat unless a passenger (or all passengers) agrees to pay for it. These days most savaris are Kia Prides (or the rebadged Saipa Saba) and bigger Peugeot 404s, though there are still plenty of Paykans around. Peugeots usually cost a bit more.

As a general rule, savaris cost about three times more than *mahmooly* buses. This is still cheap and worth using for quick trips, especially through dull stretches of countryside. As usual, lone women will normally be given the front seat.

Savaris usually leave from inside, or just outside, the relevant bus terminal, or at major squares at the beginning of whichever road they're about to head down. If in doubt, charter a private taxi and tell the driver *'savari'* and your destination.

TOURS

Most organised tours start and finish in Tehran, with a quick look around the capital before concentrating on the mustsees: Shiraz, Esfahan and Yazd, with either Tabriz or Mashhad, or possibly Kerman and Rayen, thrown in.

The handful of Iranian travel companies listed here have been recommended by readers. Most offer standard itineraries plus something different, and can organise tailor-made trips to suit particular interests. They can help with visas if you give enough notice. Guides who speak English, French, German, Japanese and sometimes Spanish or Italian can be arranged. Costs depend on the length of the tour, the mode of transport, the type of accommodation and the current exchange rate. Expect to pay in dollars or euros.

These companies often act as local handlers for foreign-based agencies selling tours to Iran, so booking direct should give you the same tour (without the foreign tour leader) for significantly less than foreign agencies charge. Feedback on these or other operators is welcome and will help us keep this list as helpful as possible; see www .lonelyplanet.com/contact. See also the boxed text (p373) for specialist adventure agencies.

Abgin Cultural Tours of Persia (☎ 021-2235 9272; www.abgintours.com) Based in Tehran; offers wide range of fixed tours plus flexible, personalised trips. Great feedback from travellers.

Adibian Travel Agency (Map p354; ☎ 0511-859 8151; www.adibiantours.com; 56 Pasdaran Ave, Mashhad) Long-established agency specialising in Khorasan province, but able to arrange tours across Iran.

Aftab Kalout Eco-Tour (☎ 021-6648 8374/5, 0912 612 3768; www.kalout.com) Eco- and adventure-tour specialists, particularly desert tours. Based in Tehran.

Arg-e-Jadid (Map p110; ☎ 021-8883 3583; www.atc.ir; 296 Motahhari Ave, Tehran) Large organisation with lots of tour options; mixed reports on guides.

Caravan Sahra (Map p110; ☎ 021-8881 1970; www .caravansahra.com; Caravan Sahra Bldg, 29 Qaem Maqam-e Farahani Ave, Tehran) Big group with a big range of tours.

Pars Tourist Agency (Map p268; ☎ 0711-222 3163; www.key2persia.com; Zand Blvd, Shiraz) Highly professional, well-organised outfit dealing purely with foreign travellers. Has literally dozens of tour options, from highlights through cultural to mountaineering. Offer free online chat consultations in English, German and French.

Freelance guides can be found in most cities around the country. Some are mentioned in relevant chapters, and these few have been highly recommended.

Ali Taheri (☎ 4443 1105, 0912 134 9345; www.iran -tehrantourist.com) Tehran-based driver and guide with is own car.

Arash Sadeghzadeh (☎ 0917 317 1652; travelling toiran@gmail.com) Young Shiraz-based guide with deep knowledge of and enthusiasm for Iranian history.

Gholamreza Shahdadian (☎ 0912 121 3969; www .wwguides.net/g_shahdadian) Experienced guide based in Tehran and specialising in tours to the northeast and the southern deserts.

Mohsen Hajisaeed (☎ 0913 351 4460; yazdguide@ yahoo.com) Young, well-organised and connected guide based in Yazd.

TRAIN

Travelling by train is an inexpensive way to get around Iran and meet Iranians, many of whom approach their rare rail trips with some excitement.

Iran's first line was the trans-Iranian railway, built in the 1930s to connect the Caspian Sea at Bandar-e Torkaman with the Persian Gulf at Bandar-e Imam Khomeini. Passing through mountains and passes, it is one of the great engineering achievements of the 20th century. It will soon be joined by other engineering marvels. First among them is the track between Esfahan and Shiraz, which will quite literally bore its way through the Spartan mountainscapes of the Zagros as it links these two historic cities.

The line is part of an ambitious program to expand Iran's rail network. Recently completed lines include Qazvin to Astara via Rasht and Mashhad to Bafq. The long-awaited Bam to Zahedan (see the boxed text, p404) stretch is set to open late 2008, and other lines either being built or proposed by Raja Trains, the national rail network, include Arak to Kermanshah and Khoramshahr to Basra, in Iraq.

Tehran is the main hub and most services begin or end in the capital. There is at least one daily service to Mashhad, Esfahan, Tabriz, Bandar Abbas and Kerman. Trains usually depart on time, but departure and arrival times for stops en route are often in the middle of the night. For the latest routes and prices, see www.rajatrains.com.

The average age of passenger carriages is 26 years but they're still fairly comfortable, efficient, reasonably fast and always cheap. For overnight trips a 1st-class sleeper is a delight, and while they cost a bit more than a Volvo bus, the comfort level is about 10 times greater. And, of course, trains are much safer than buses.

On most 1st-class services meals are served in your compartment and aren't too bad. Long-distance trains also have a restaurant car, and iced water is available. Security is better than in most other countries in the region, but it's worth asking someone to look after your luggage (or chaining it to something solid) before leaving your compartment.

Classes

The majority of trains have two classes, though a significant minority have only one. If you decide a 2nd-class compartment is too crowded for you, you can often upgrade to 1st class along the way, provided there's space.

On overnight trains (usually to/from Tehran) the 1st-class carriages have sleepers with four or six bunks. They are not all sexually segregated and one reader wrote to complain of having a man in another bunk stroking her arm in the night; women might want to ask specifically for a single-sex sleeper. Some trains on the Tehran to Mashhad route, Iran's busiest, are very comfortable indeed. The *Simorgh*, for example, is more expensive than other 1st-class options but includes dinner, breakfast, a very comfortable bed and the mixed blessing of a TV. You can ask to be seated in a non-smoking compartment.

Costs

As a rough guide, a seat in 2nd class costs about the same as a *mahmooly* bus, and a 1st-class seat is about 1½ times the price of a Volvo bus, depending on the class of train; see www.rajatrains.com for specifics.

Reservations

Train ticketing is on an integrated system, so you can book tickets at stations and travel agencies around the country up to a month in advance. Especially for trains leaving on Thursday, Friday and public holidays, it's worth booking ahead.

Health

CONTENTS

Due in part to its dryness and relative isolation, your chances of getting seriously ill with a virus or other infectious disease in Iran are fairly small. The most common reason for travellers needing medical help is as a result of accidents – the quality of Iranian cars and, more to the point, Iranian driving is dangerously low. If you are unfortunate enough to need a hospital, the good news is that Iran is home to some of the best in the Middle East. Many doctors have been trained in Europe or North America and, especially in the larger cities, you shouldn't have too much trouble finding one who speaks English. In remoter areas, medical facilities are more basic.

BEFORE YOU GO

A little planning before departure, particularly for pre-existing illnesses, will save you a lot of trouble later. See your dentist before a long trip; carry a spare pair of contact lenses and glasses (and take your optical prescription with you); and carry a first-aid kit.

It's tempting to leave it all to the last minute – don't! Many vaccines don't ensure immunity for two weeks, so visit a doctor four to eight weeks before departure. Ask your doctor for an International Certificate of Vaccination (otherwise known as the yellow booklet), which will list all the vaccinations you've received. While yellow fever is not a problem in Iran, if you're arriving from a country where it is a problem you might be asked to show proof of yellow fever vaccination before you're allowed in.

Travellers can register with the International Association for Medical Advice to Travellers (IAMAT; www.iamat.org). Its website can help travellers to find a doctor with recognised training. Those heading off to very remote areas may like to do a first-aid course (Red Cross and St John Ambulance can help), or attend a remote medicine first-aid course such as that offered by the Royal Geographical Society (www.rgs.org).

Bring medications in their original, clearly labelled, containers. A signed and dated letter from your physician describing your medical conditions and medications, including generic names, is also a good idea. If carrying syringes or needles, be sure to have a physician's letter documenting their medical necessity.

INSURANCE

Find out in advance if your insurance plan will make payments directly to providers or reimburse you later for overseas health expenditures (in many countries doctors expect payment in cash); it's also worth ensuring your travel insurance will cover repatriation home or to better medical facilities elsewhere. Your insurance company might be able to locate the nearest source of medical help, but it's probably faster to ask your hotel or, in an emergency, call your embassy or consulate. Travel insurance usually covers emergency dental treatment. Not all insurance covers emergency aeromedical evacuation home or to a hospital in a major city, which may be the only way to get medical attention for a serious emergency.

RECOMMENDED VACCINATIONS

The World Health Organization recommends that all travellers regardless of the region they are travelling in should be covered for diphtheria, tetanus, measles, mumps, rubella and polio, as well as hepatitis B. While making preparations to travel, take the opportunity to ensure that all of your routine vaccination cover is complete. However, in Iran outbreaks are rare.

MEDICAL CHECKLIST

Following is a list of other items you should consider packing in your medical kit.

- Acetaminophen/paracetamol (Tylenol) or aspirin
- Adhesive or paper tape
- Antibacterial ointment (eg Bactroban) for cuts and abrasions
- Antibiotics (if travelling off the beaten track)
- Antidiarrhoeal drugs (eg loperamide)
- Anti-inflammatory drugs (eg ibuprofen)
- Antihistamines (for hay fever and allergic reactions)
- Bandages, gauze, gauze rolls
- DEET – containing insect repellent for the skin
- Iodine tablets (for water purification)
- Oral rehydration salts
- Permethrin – containing insect spray for clothing, tents, and bed nets
- Pocket knife
- Scissors, safety pins, tweezers
- Steroid cream or cortisone (allergic rashes)
- Sun block
- Syringes and sterile needles (if travelling to remote areas)
- Thermometer

INTERNET RESOURCES

There is a wealth of travel health advice on the internet. The World Health Organization (www.who.int/ith) publishes a superb book, *International Travel and Health*,

which is revised annually and is available online at no cost. MD Travel Health (www.mdtravelhealth.com) provides complete travel health recommendations for every country, updated daily and free. The Centers for Disease Control and Prevention website (www.cdc.gov) is also useful.

FURTHER READING

Lonely Planet's *Travel With Children* is packed with useful information including pretrip planning, emergency first aid, immunisation and disease information and what to do if you get sick on the road.

Other recommended references include *Traveller's Health* by Dr Richard Dawood (Oxford University Press), *International Travel Health Guide* by Stuart R. Rose, MD (Travel Medicine Inc) and *The Travellers' Good Health Guide* by Ted Lankester (Sheldon Press).

IN TRANSIT

DEEP VEIN THROMBOSIS (DVT)

Deep vein thrombosis occurs when blood clots form in the legs during plane flights, chiefly because of prolonged immobility. The longer the flight, the greater the risk. Though most blood clots are reabsorbed uneventfully, some may break off and travel through the blood vessels to the lungs, where they may cause life-threatening complications.

The chief symptom of DVT is swelling or pain of the foot, ankle, or calf, usually but not always on just one side. When a blood clot travels to the lungs, it may cause chest pain and breathing difficulty. If this happens to you seek medical attention. To prevent DVT on long flights you should walk about the cabin, perform isometric compressions of the leg muscles (ie contract the leg muscles while sitting), drink plenty of fluids, and avoid alcohol and tobacco.

JET LAG & MOTION SICKNESS

Jet lag is common when crossing more than five time zones; it results in insomnia, fatigue, malaise or nausea. To avoid jet lag try drinking plenty of fluids (nonalcoholic) and eating light meals. Upon arrival, seek exposure to natural sunlight and readjust your schedule (for meals, sleep etc) as soon as possible.

Antihistamines such as dimenhydrinate (Dramamine) and meclizine (Antivert, Bonine) are usually the first choice for treating motion sickness. Their main side effect is drowsiness. A herbal alternative is ginger, which some people swear by.

IN IRAN

AVAILABILITY & COST OF HEALTH CARE

There are few, if any, reciprocal medical arrangements between Iran and other countries so be prepared to pay for all your medical and dental treatment. The good news is that costs are negligible. The quality of hospitals varies from place to place, but in Tehran, Esfahan and Shiraz, in particular, you'll find international-standard hospitals and well-trained doctors.

But, seriously, medical care is not always readily available outside major cities. Medicine, and even sterile dressings or intravenous fluids, may need to be bought from a local pharmacy. Nursing care may be limited or rudimentary as this is something families and friends are expected to provide. The travel assistance provided by your insurance may be able to locate the nearest source of medical help, otherwise ask at your hotel. In an emergency contact your embassy or consulate.

Standards of dental care are variable and there is an increased risk of hepatitis B transmission via poorly sterilised equipment. Travel insurance usually only covers emergency dental treatment.

For minor illnesses such as diarrhoea, pharmacists can often provide advice and sell over-the-counter medication. They can also advise when more specialised help is needed.

INFECTIOUS DISEASES
Diphtheria

Diphtheria is spread through close respiratory contact. It causes a high temperature and severe sore throat. Sometimes a membrane forms across the throat requiring a tracheostomy to prevent suffocation. Vaccination is recommended for those likely to be in close contact with the local population in infected areas. The vaccine is given as an injection alone, or with tetanus, and lasts 10 years.

Hepatitis A

Hepatitis A is spread through contaminated food (particularly shellfish) and water. It causes jaundice and, although it is rarely fatal, can cause prolonged lethargy and delayed recovery. Symptoms include dark urine, a yellow colour to the whites of the eyes, fever and abdominal pain. Hepatitis A vaccine (Avaxim, VAQTA, Havrix) is given as an injection: a single dose will give protection for up to a year while a booster 12 months later will provide a subsequent 10 years of protection. Hepatitis A and typhoid vaccines can also be given as a single dose vaccine, hepatyrix or viatim.

Hepatitis B

Infected blood, contaminated needles and sexual intercourse can all transmit hepatitis B. It can cause jaundice, and affects the liver, occasionally causing liver failure. All travellers should make this a routine vaccination. (Many countries now give hepatitis B vaccination as part of routine childhood vaccination.) The vaccine is given singly, or at the same time as the hepatitis A vaccine (hepatyrix). A course will give protection for at least five years. It can be given over four weeks, or six months.

HIV

HIV remains mercifully rare in Iran but the growing use of prostitutes and, more problematically, the large number of intravenous drug users, means the HIV rate is rising. For some visa types Iran requires a negative HIV test.

Leishmaniasis

Spread through the bite of an infected sand fly, leishmaniasis can cause a slowly growing skin lump or ulcer. It may develop into a serious life-threatening fever usually accompanied with anaemia and weight loss. Infected dogs are also carriers of the infection. Sand-fly bites should be avoided whenever possible.

Malaria

There is very little malaria in Iran. Still, it's worth knowing that malaria almost always starts with shivering, fever and sweating.

HEALTH

Muscle pains, headache and vomiting are common. Symptoms may occur anywhere from a few days to three weeks after the infected mosquito bite. The illness can start while you are taking preventative tablets if they are not fully effective, and may also occur after you have finished taking your tablets.

Poliomyelitis
Generally poliomyelitis is spread through contaminated food and water. It is one of the vaccines given in childhood and should be boosted every 10 years, either orally (a drop on the tongue), or as an injection. Polio may be carried asymptomatically, although it can cause a transient fever and, in rare cases, potentially permanent muscle weakness or paralysis.

Rabies
Spread through bites or licks on broken skin from an infected animal, rabies is fatal. Animal handlers should be vaccinated, as should those travelling to remote areas where a reliable source of post-bite vaccine is not available within 24 hours. Three injections are needed over a month. If you have not been vaccinated you will need a course of five injections starting within 24 hours or as soon as possible after the injury. Vaccination does not provide you with immunity; it merely buys you more time to seek appropriate medical help.

Tuberculosis
Tuberculosis (TB) is found in Iran, especially in the southeast. TB is spread through close respiratory contact and occasionally through infected milk or milk products. BCG vaccine is recommended for those likely to be mixing closely with the local population. It is more important for those planning on a long stay or mixing closely with local people. TB can be asymptomatic, although symptoms can include cough, weight loss or fever months or even years after exposure. An X-ray is the best way to confirm if you have TB. BCG gives a moderate degree of protection against TB. It causes a small permanent scar at the site of injection, and is usually only given in specialised chest clinics. As it's a live vaccine it should not be given to pregnant women or immunocompromised

individuals. The BCG vaccine is not available in all countries.

Typhoid
This is spread through food or water that has been contaminated by infected human faeces. The first symptom is usually fever or a pink rash on the abdomen. Septicaemia (blood poisoning) may also occur. Typhoid vaccine (typhim Vi, typherix) will give protection for three years. In some countries, the oral vaccine Vivotif is also available.

TRAVELLER'S DIARRHOEA
While water is safe to drink almost everywhere in Iran, avoiding tap water unless it has been boiled, filtered or chemically disinfected can help you avoid diarrhoea. Eat only fresh fruits or vegetables if cooked and avoid dairy products that might contain unpasteurised milk. Freshly prepared meals are best; while pre-prepared dishes like *khoresht* should be avoided by anyone with a fragile stomach.

If you develop diarrhoea, be sure to drink plenty of fluids, preferably an oral rehydration solution containing lots of salt and sugar. A few loose stools don't require treatment, but if you start having more than four or five stools a day, you should start taking an antibiotic (usually a quinolone drug) and an antidiarrhoeal agent (such as loperamide). If diarrhoea is bloody, persists for more than 72 hours, is accompanied by fever, shaking, chills or severe abdominal pain you should seek medical attention.

ENVIRONMENTAL HAZARDS
Heat Illness
Heat exhaustion occurs following heavy sweating and excessive fluid loss with inadequate replacement of fluids and salt, and travellers will be especially susceptible during Iran's oven-hot summers, particularly if you are engaging in a greater level of exercise than you usually would. Be especially careful on desert treks out of places like Yazd.

Symptoms include headache, dizziness and tiredness. Dehydration is already happening by the time you feel thirsty – aim to drink sufficient water such that you produce pale, diluted urine. The treatment of heat exhaustion consists of fluid replacement with water or fruit juice or both, and cooling by cold water and fans. The treatment of the salt loss component consists of salty fluids as in soup or broth, and adding a little more table salt to foods than usual. Electrolyte replacement sachets are the easiest and fastest way to treat dehydration.

Heatstroke is much more serious. This occurs when the body's heat-regulating mechanism breaks down. An excessive rise in body temperature leads to sweating ceasing, irrational and hyperactive behaviour and eventually loss of consciousness and death. Rapid cooling by spraying the body with water and fanning is an ideal treatment. Emergency fluid and electrolyte replacement by intravenous drip is usually also required.

Insect Bites & Stings

Mosquitoes may not carry malaria but can cause irritation and infected bites. Using DEET-based insect repellents will prevent bites. Mosquitoes also spread dengue fever.

Bees and wasps only cause real problems to those with a severe allergy (anaphylaxis). If you have a severe allergy to bee or wasp stings you should carry an adrenaline injection or similar.

Scorpions are frequently found in arid or dry climates. They can cause a painful bite, which is rarely life threatening.

Mercifully, Iran doesn't seem to suffer too badly from bed bugs, though occasionally they do pop up (as opposed to appearing – who's ever seen one of the critters?) in hostels and cheap hotels. They lead to very itchy, lumpy bites. Spraying dubious-looking mattress with insecticide will help get rid of them, or use a sleep sheet.

Scabies might also be found in cheap accommodation. These tiny mites live in the skin, particularly between the fingers. They cause an intensely itchy rash. Scabies is easily treated with lotion available from pharmacies; people who you come into contact with also need treating to avoid spreading scabies between asymptomatic carriers.

Snake Bites

Your chances of getting bitten by a snake in Iran are microscopic. To make them even smaller, don't stick your hand into holes or cracks. Half of those bitten by venomous snakes are not actually injected with poison (envenomed). If bitten by a snake, do not panic. Immobilise the bitten limb with a splint (eg a stick) and apply a bandage over the site, firm pressure, similar to a bandage over a sprain. Do not apply a tourniquet, or cut or suck the bite. Get to medical help as soon as possible so that antivenin can be given if necessary.

Water

Tap water is safe to drink in most of Iran, though many travellers stick to bottled water, which is widely available. Do not drink water from rivers or lakes as this may contain bacteria or viruses that can cause diarrhoea or vomiting.

TRAVELLING WITH CHILDREN

All travellers with children should know how to treat minor ailments and when to seek medical treatment. Make sure the children are up to date with routine vaccinations, and discuss possible travel vaccines well before departure as some vaccines are not suitable for children aged under one year old.

In hot, moist climates any wound or break in the skin may lead to infection. The area should be cleaned and then kept dry and clean. Remember to avoid contaminated food and water. If your child is vomiting or experiencing diarrhoea, lost fluid and salts must be replaced. It may be helpful to take rehydration powders for reconstituting with boiled water. Ask your doctor about this.

You won't see many dogs in Iran, but if you do, children should avoid them, and other mammals, because of the risk of rabies. Any bite, scratch or lick from a warm-blooded, furry animal should immediately be thoroughly cleaned. If there is any possibility that the animal is infected with rabies, immediate medical assistance should be sought.

WOMEN'S HEALTH

Emotional stress, exhaustion and travelling through different time zones can all contribute to an upset in the menstrual pattern. If using oral contraceptives, remember some antibiotics, and diarrhoea and vomiting can stop the pill from working and lead to the risk of pregnancy – remember to take condoms with you just in case.

Emergency contraception is most effective if taken within 24 hours after unprotected sex. Apart from condoms you should bring any contraception you will need. Tampons are almost impossible to find in Iran, but sanitary towels are available in cities.

Travelling during pregnancy is usually possible but there are important things to consider. Have a medical check-up before embarking on your trip. The most risky times for travel are during the first 12 weeks of pregnancy, when miscarriage is most likely, and after 30 weeks, when complications such as high blood pressure and premature delivery can occur. Most airlines will not accept a traveller after 28 to 32 weeks of pregnancy, and long-haul flights in the later stages can be very uncomfortable. Antenatal facilities vary between cities in Iran and there are major cultural and language differences. Taking written records of the pregnancy, including details of your blood group, are likely to be helpful if you need medical attention while away. Ensure your insurance policy covers pregnancy, delivery and postnatal care.

Language

CONTENTS

Farsi (also often referred to as Persian) is the official language of Iran. Travelling in the country without at least a basic grasp of Farsi will prove difficult, as English speakers are few and far between.

FARSI

Farsi is an Indo-Iranian language and a member of the Indo-European language family. While it is written in Arabic script, which runs from right to left, the language itself isn't related to Arabic at all.

There are a number of mutually intelligible dialects spoken in Iran. The words and phrases in this language guide are based on the Tehrani dialect, and reflect mostly colloquial, everyday speech. Tehrani is considered to be the standard dialect, and the one spoken by most Farsi speakers. This is distinct from Classical Farsi, which is not an everyday language, but a literary form, normally used only in books or speeches.

LEARNING THE LANGUAGE

Lonely Planet's compact, but comprehensive *Farsi Phrasebook* is a good way to get started and will prove invaluable during your stay. You can also advance your language skills before you head off by working through the excellent free lessons available online at Easy Persian (www.easypersian.com). Another great resource is *Teach Yourself Modern Persian* (by Narguess Farzad), consisting of a 304-page course-book and two audio CDs. If nothing else, you should familiarise yourself with the modified Arabic aphabet used to write Farsi. The chart on p424 shows all the Farsi letters in their various guises (according to position within a word), plus the nearest-sounding Latin letters used to represent them.

TRANSLITERATION

Transliterating from non-Roman script into the Roman alphabet is always a tricky affair. Formal transliterations of Farsi are overly complicated in the way they represent vowels, and they do not accurately represent the spoken language. In this language guide the system used is designed to be as simple as possible for spoken communication, even at the expense of absolute accuracy.

PRONUNCIATION

In general, the last syllable of a multisyllable word is stressed, unless the last vowel in the word is a short vowel.

Vowels
a	as in 'father'
e	as in 'bed'
i	as in 'marine'
o	as in 'mole'
u	as in 'rule'

Consonants
The letters **b**, **d**, **f**, **j**, **m**, **n**, **p**, **sh**, **t** and **z** are pronounced as in English.

ch	as in 'cheese'
g	as in 'goose'
gh/q	a guttural sound like a heavy French 'r' pronounced at the back of the mouth; can appear in transliterations as either **gh** or **q**
h	as in 'hot'
kh	as the 'ch' in Scottish loch

THE FARSI ALPHABET

Final	Medial	Initial	Alone	Transliteration	Pronunciation
ا			ا	a	short, as in 'act', long, as in 'father'
ـب	ـبـ	بـ	ب	b	as in 'bet'
ـپ	ـپـ	پـ	پ	p	as in 'pet'
ـت	ـتـ	تـ	ت	t	as in 'ten'
ـث	ـثـ	ثـ	ث	s	as in 'set'
ـج	ـجـ	جـ	ج	j	as in 'jet'
ـچ	ـچـ	چـ	چ	ch	as in 'chat'
ـح	ـحـ	حـ	ح	h	as in 'hot'
ـخ	ـخـ	خـ	خ	kh	as the 'ch' in Scottish loch
ـد			د	d	as in 'dot'
ـذ			ذ	z	as in 'zoo'
ـر			ر	r	as in 'run'
ـز			ز	z	as z above
ـژ			ژ	zh	as the 's' in 'measure'
ـس	ـسـ	سـ	س	s	as s above
ـش	ـشـ	شـ	ش	sh	as in 'shed'
ـص	ـصـ	صـ	ص	s	as s above
ـض	ـضـ	ضـ	ض	z	as z above
ـط	ـطـ	طـ	ط	t	as t above
ـظ	ـظـ	ظـ	ظ	z	as z above
ـع	ـعـ	عـ	ع	'	a glottal stop (see below)
ـغ	ـغـ	غـ	غ	gh/q	a rough, guttural sound (see p423)
ـف	ـفـ	فـ	ف	f	as in 'fact'
ـق	ـقـ	قـ	ق	gh/q	as **gh/q** above
ـک	ـکـ	کـ	ک	k	as in 'kit'
ـگ	ـگـ	گـ	گ	g	as in 'get'
ـل	ـلـ	لـ	ل	l	as in 'let'; the common sequence l+a becomes ﻻ
ـم	ـمـ	مـ	م	m	as in 'met'
ـن	ـنـ	نـ	ن	n	as in 'net'
ـو			و	u/w	as in 'rule'/as in 'wary'
ـه	ـهـ	هـ	ه	h	as in 'hot'
ـی	ـیـ	یـ	ی	i/y	as in 'marine'/as in 'yacht'

l	always as in 'leg', never as in 'roll'
r	trilled
s	as in 'sin'
y	as in 'yak'
zh	as the 'g' in 'mirage'
'	a very weak glottal stop, like the sound made between the words 'uh-oh' or the 'tt' in Cockney 'bottle'

Note: doubled consonants are always pronounced as two distinct sounds, as in 'hat'-

'trick' not 'battle'; the sole exception is *Allah* (God), in which the l's are swallowed as in English 'doll'.

ACCOMMODATION

Do you have any rooms available?
otagh khali darin

I'd like a ... room.	*ye otagh e ... mikham*
single	*taki*
shared	*moshtarak*

How much is it for ...?	baraye ... che ghadr mishe?
one night	ye shab
a week	ye hafte
two people	do nafar

We want a room with a ...	ma ye otagh ba ye ... mikhayim
bathroom	dastshuyi
shower	dush
TV	televiziyon
window	panjere

CONVERSATION & ESSENTIALS

The all-purpose greeting in Iran is *salam aleykom*, which does duty for 'good morning', 'good afternoon' and 'good evening'. The same expression is used throughout the Muslim world, so if you learn only one phrase in Iran, this is it!

When addressing a stranger, especially one older than you, it's polite to include *agha* (sir) or *khanom* (madam) at the beginning of the first sentence, or after one of the standard greetings. *Agha ye* and *Khanom e* are the equivalents of Mr, and Mrs/Miss/Ms *Agha* can be used before or after the first name as a title of respect, eg Mohammad Agha or, more likely, Agha Mohammad.

The pronoun *shoma* is the polite form of 'you' singular, and should be used when addressing people you don't know well – *to* is only generally used when talking to close friends and relatives of the same generation or older, and to children and animals.

Welcome.	khosh amadin
Greetings.	salam aleykom
Hello.	salam
Good morning.	sob bekheyr
Good day. (noon)	ruz bekheyr
Good evening.	shab bekheyr
Goodbye.	khoda hafez
How are you?	haletun chetor e?
Fine – and you?	khubam – shoma chetoin?
Yes.	bale
No.	na
Please.	lotfan
Thank you.	dastet darnakone
Thank you (very much).	(kheyli) mamnum (also common is dastet darnakone)
You're welcome.	khahesh mikonam
Excuse me/I'm sorry.	bebakhshid
I like ...	man ... dust daram
I don't like ...	man ... dust nadaram

What's your name?	esmetun chi ye?
My name is ...	esmam ... e
Where are you from?	kojayi hastin?
I'm from ...	man ahl e ... am
It is God's will.	mashallah

mother	madar
father	pedar
sister	khahar
brother	bavadar
daughter	dokhtar
son	pesar
aunt	khaleh (maternal)/ ameh (paternal)
uncle	dai (maternal)/ amu (paternal)
wife	zan
husband	shohar

SIGNS

ورود	vorud	Entrance
خروج	khoruj	Exit
باز	baz	Open
بسته	baste	Closed
ممنوع ورود	vorud mamnu'	No Entry
ممنوع دخانيات	dokhaniyat mamnu'	No Smoking
ممنوع	mamnu'	Prohibited
توالت	tuvalet	Toilet
مردانه	mardane	Men
زنانه	zanane	Women

DIRECTIONS

Where is the ...?	... koja st?
Can you show me (on the map)?	mishe (tu naghshe) be man neshun bedin?
Is it far from here?	un az inja dur e?
Go straight ahead.	mostaghim berin
To the left.	samt e chap
To the right.	samt e rast
here	inja
there	unja

behind	posht
in front of	jeloye
far (from)	dur az
near (to)	nazdik be
opposite	moghabele

HEALTH

Where is the ...?	... koja st?
chemist	darukhune
dentist	dandun pezeshk
doctor	doktor
hospital	bimarestan

LANGUAGE

EMERGENCIES

Help!	komak!
Stop!	ist!
Go away!	gom sho!
Call ...!	... khabar konin!
a doctor	ye doktor
an ambulance	ye ambulans
the police	polis o

I wish to contact my embassy/consulate.
mikham ba sefarat/konsulgari khod am tamas
begiram
Where is the toilet?
tuvalet koja st?
Shame on you!
khejalat bekesh! (said by a woman to a man
bothering her)

I'm sick.	mariz am
antiseptic	zedd e ufuni konande
aspirin	asperin
condom	kandom
contraceptive	zedd e hamelegi
diarrhoea	es-hal
medicine	daru
sunblock	kerem e zedd e aftab

I have ...	... daram
anaemia	kam khuni
asthma	asm
diabetes	diyabet

I'm allergic to ...	be ... hassasiyat daram
antibiotics	antibiyutik
aspirin	asperin
bees	zanbur
peanuts	badum zanini
penicillin	penisilin

LANGUAGE DIFFICULTIES

Do you speak English?
shoma ingilisi baladin?
Does anyone here speak English?
inja kesi ingilisi balad e?
I understand.
mifahmam
I don't understand.
na mifahmam
How do you say ... in Farsi?
... ro dar farsi chetori migin?
What does ... mean?
ma'ni ye ... chi ye?
Please write it down.
lotfan un o benevisin

NUMBERS

Unlike Arabic written text, numbers are written from left to right (as in English). The numbers four and six can be written two different ways depending on the calligraphic style

0	sefr	•
1	yek	١
2	do	٢
3	se	٣
4	chahar	۴ or ٤
5	panj	۵
6	shish	٦ or ۶
7	haft	٧
8	hasht	٨
9	noh	٩
10	dah	١٠
11	yazdah	١١
12	davazdah	١٢
13	sizdah	١٣
14	chahardah	١٣
15	punzdah	١۵
16	shanzdah	١۶
17	hifdah	١٧
18	hijdah	١٨
19	nuzdah	١٩
20	bist	٢٠
21	bist o yek	٢١
22	bist o do	٢٢
30	si	٣٠
40	chehel	۴٠
45	chehel o panj	۴٠
50	panjah	۵٠
60	shast	۶٠
70	haftad	٧٠
80	hashtad	٨٠
90	navad	٩٠
100	sad	١٠٠
167	sad o shast o haft	١۶٧
200	divist	٢٠٠
300	sisad	٣٠٠
400	chaharsad	۴٠٠
500	punsad	۵٠٠
1000	hezar	١٠٠٠
2000	do hezar	٢٠٠٠
3000	se hezar	٣٠٠٠
4000	chahar hezar	۴٠٠٠

one million	yek milyon

QUESTION WORDS

Who?	ki?
What?	che?

When?	key?
Where?	koja?
Which?	kodam?
Why?	chera?
How?	chetor?

SHOPPING & SERVICES

Where is the ...?	... koja st?
bank	bank
church	kelisa
city centre	markaz e shahr
consulate	konsulgari
embassy	sefarat
hotel	hotel
lodging house	mosaferkhùneh
mosque	masjed
market	bazar
police	polis
post office	edare ye post
public telephone	telefon e umumi
public toilet	tuvalet e umumi
tourist office	edare ye jahangardi
town square	meydun a shahr

I'd like to buy ...	mikham ... bekharam
How much is it?	che ghadr? (you can also say chand toman? – literally 'how many tomans?')
I don't like it.	az un khosh am nemiyad
May I look at it?	mishe negali esh konam?
I'm just looking.	faghat negah mikonam
I think it's too expensive.	fekr mikonam un kheyli gerun e
I'll take it.	un o mikharam

more	ziyad
less	kam
smaller	kuchiktar
bigger	bozorgtar

TIME & DATES

What time is it?	sa'at chand e?
today	emruz
tomorrow	farda
yesterday	diruz
tonight	emshab
morning, am	sob
afternoon, pm	ba'd az zohr
day	ruz
month	mah
year	sal

Saturday	shanbe
Sunday	yek shanbe
Monday	do shanbe
Tuesday	se shanbe
Wednesday	chahar shanbe
Thursday	panj shanbe
Friday	jom'e

TRANSPORT
Public Transport

Where is the ...?	... koja st?
airport	furudgah
bus stop	istgah e utubus
train station	istgah e ghatar

What time does the ... leave/arrive?	... che sa'ati harekat mikone/mirese?
boat	ghayegh
bus	utubus
plane	havapeyma
train	ghatar

What time is the ... bus?	utubus e ... key miyad?
first	avval
last	akhar
next	ba'di

I'd like a	... mikham
one-way ticket	belit e ye sare
return ticket	belit e do sare

1st class	daraje yek
2nd class	daraje do

How long does the trip take?
in mosaferat cheghadr tul mikeshe?
Does this bus go to ...?
in utubus be ... mire?
Do you stop at ...?
dar ... tavaghghof darin?
Could you let me know when we get to ...
mishe vaghti be ... residim be man begin?
Where does the ... bus leave from?
koja mitunam utubus e ... ro savar sham?
I want to go to ...
mikham be ... beram
How much is it to ...?
be ... che ghadr mishe?
Does the bus stop for toilet breaks?
in utubus baraye dast shuyi negah midare?

Private Transport

I'd like to hire a ...	mikham ... keraye konam
car	mashin
4WD	patrol
motorbike	motorsiklet
bicycle	docharkhe

Is this the road to ...?
in jadde be ... mire?

Where's a service station?
pomp e benzin e ba'di kojast?

Please fill it up.
lotfan bak o por konin

I'd like ... litres.
... litr benzin mikham

diesel	*gazoyil*
leaded petrol	*ma'muli*
unleaded (petrol)	*bedun e sorb*

How long can we park here?
che ghadr mishe inja park kard?

(I/We) need a mechanic.
ye mekanik (mikhaham/mikhayim)

The car/motorbike has broken down at ...
mashin/mororsiklet dar ... kharab shode

I've run out of petrol.
benzin am tamum shode

I had an accident.
man tasadof kardam

TRAVEL WITH CHILDREN

Is there a/an ...?	*yek....hast?*
I need a ...	*man yek....lazem daram*
baby change room	*otaghe avaz kardane bachche*
car baby-seat	*sandaliye bachche*
children's menu	*liste ghazaye bachche ha*
disposable nappies/ diapers	*pushak*
formula (infant milk)	*shire khoshk*
highchair	*sandaliye boland*
potty	*lagane bachche*
stroller	*kaleske*

Are children allowed? *bachche ha ejaze darand?*

Also available from Lonely Planet:
Farsi Phrasebook

Glossary

Here, with definitions, are some unfamiliar words and abbreviations. Generally the Farsi words in this book are transliterations of colloquial usage. See Language (p423) for other useful words and phrases. See also the food glossary (p84) for culinary terms.

agha – sir; gentleman
Allah – Muslim name for God
aramgah – resting place; burial place; tomb
arg, **ark** – citadel
astan-e – sanctuary; threshold
ateshkadeh – a Zoroastrian fire temple where a flame was always kept burning
ayatollah – Shiite cleric of the highest rank, used as a title before the name; literally means a 'sign or miracle of God'
azad – free; liberated
azadi – freedom

badgir – windtower or ventilation shaft used to catch breezes and funnel them down into a building to cool it
bagh – garden
bandar – port; harbour
Bandari – indigenous inhabitant of the Persian Gulf coast and islands
bastan – ancient; ancient history; antiquity
bazar – bazaar; market place
bazari – shopkeeper in the bazaar
behesht – paradise
boq'eh – mausoleum
borj – tower
bozorg – big, large, great
burqa – a mask with tiny slits for the eyes worn by some Bandari women

caliphate – the dynasty of the successors of the Prophet Mohammed as rulers of the Islamic world
caravanserai – an inn or way-station for camel trains; usually consisting of rooms arranged around a courtyard
chador – literally 'tent'; a cloak, usually black, covering all parts of a woman's body except the hands, feet and face
coffeenet – internet café
cuneiform – ancient wedge-shaped script used in Persia

dar baste – literally closed door, used in taxis to indicate you want a private hire
darvazeh – gate or gateway, especially a city gate
darya – sea
dasht – plain; plateau; desert, specifically one of sand or gravel

enqelab – revolution

Farsi – Persian language or people
Ferdosi – one of the great Persian poets, born about AD 940 in Tus, near Mashhad; wrote the first epic poem, the *Shahnamah* (see p74)
fire temple – see *ateshkadeh*

gabbeh – traditional rug
golestan – rose garden; name of poem by *Sa'di*
gonbad – dome, domed monument or tower tomb; also written 'gombad'

Hafez – one of the great Persian poets, born in Shiraz in about AD 1324; see the boxed text (p74)
haj – pilgrimage to Mecca
halal – permitted by Islamic law; lawful to eat or drink
hammam – bath, public bathhouse; bathroom
Hazrat-e – title used before the name of Mohammed, any other apostle of Islam or a Christian saint
hejab – veil; the 'modest dress' required of Muslim women and girls
Hossein – the third of the 12 *imams* recognised by Shiites as successors of the Prophet Mohammed (see the boxed text, p56)
Hosseinieh – see *takieh*

imam – 'emam' in Farsi; religious leader, also title of one of the 12 descendants of Mohammed who, according to Shiite belief, succeeded him as religious and temporal leader of the Muslims; see the boxed text (p56)
Imam Reza – the eighth Shiite *imam* (see the boxed text, p353)
imamzadeh – descendant of an *imam*; shrine or mausoleum of an *imamzadeh*
insh'Allah – If God wills it
istgah – station (especially train station)
iwan – 'eivan' in Farsi; barrel-vaulted hall opening onto a courtyard

Jameh Mosque – Masjed-e Jameh in Farsi; meaning Congregational Mosque, sometimes mis-translated as Friday Mosque

kabir – great
kalisa – church (sometimes cathedral)
kavir – salt desert
khalij – gulf; bay
khan – feudal lord, title of respect
khan-e sonnati – traditional house
kuche – lane; alley

Kufic – ancient script found on many buildings dating from the about the 7th to 13th centuries

madraseh – school; also Muslim theological college
Majlis – Iranian Parliament
manar – minaret; tower of a mosque
markazi – centre; headquarters
masjed – mosque; Muslim place of worship
Masjed-e Jameh – see *Jameh Mosque*
mehmankhaneh – hotel
mehmanpazir – a simple hotel
mehmansara – government-owned resthouse or hotel
mihrab – niche inside a mosque indicating the direction of Mecca; in Iran, specifically the hole cut in the ground before the niche
minbar – pulpit of a mosque
Moharram – first month of the Muslim lunar calendar, the Shiite month of mourning
mosaferkhaneh – lodging-house or hotel of the cheapest, simplest kind; 'mosafer' means traveller or passenger
muezzin – person at mosque who calls Muslims to prayer
mullah – Islamic cleric; title of respect

No Ruz – Iranian New Year's Day, celebrated on the vernal equinox (usually around 21 March)

Omar Khayyam – born in Neishabur in about 1047 and famous as a poet, mathematician, historian and astronomer; his best-known poem is the *Rubaïyat*; see the boxed text (p74)

pasazh – passage; shopping arcade
Persia – old name for Iran
Persian – adjective and noun frequently used to describe the Iranian language, people and culture
pik-up – utility vehicle with a canvas cover
pol – bridge

qal'eh – fortress; fortified walled village
qalyan – water pipe, usually smoked in traditional teahouses
qanat – underground water channel
qar – cave
Quran – Muslim holy book

Ramazan – ninth month in the Muslim lunar calendar; the month of fasting
rial – currency of Iran; equal to one-tenth of a *toman*
rud, rudkhuneh – river; stream
Rumi – famous poet (born in 1207) credited with founding the Maulavi Sufi order – the whirling dervishes (see the boxed text, p74)
ruz – day

Sa'di – one of the great Persian poets (AD 1207–91); his most famous works are the *Golestan* (Rose Garden) and *Bustan* (Garden of Trees); see the boxed text (p74)
sardar – military governor
savari – private car; local word for a shared taxi, usually refers to longer trips between cities
shah – king; the usual title of the Persian monarch
shahid – martyr; used as a title before the forename of a fighter killed during the Islamic Revolution or the Iran–Iraq War
shahr – town or city
shuttle taxi – common form of public transport within cities; they usually run on set routes

ta'arof – ritualised politeness; see the boxed text (p45)
takht – throne, also the daybed-style tables in teahouses
takieh – building used during the rituals to commemorate the death of Imam Hossein during Moharram; sometimes called a *Hosseinieh*
tappeh – hill; mound
terminal – terminal; bus station
toman – unit of currency equal to 10 *rials*

vakil – regent

yakh dan – mud-brick ice house

zarih – the gilded and latticed 'cage' that sits over a tomb
ziggurat – pyramidal temple with a series of tiers on a square or rectangular plan
Zoroastrianism – ancient religion, the state creed before the Islamic conquest; today Zoroastrians are found mainly in Yazd, Shiraz, Kerman, Tehran and Esfahan
zurkhaneh – literally 'house of strength'; a group of men perform a series of ritualised feats of strength, all to the accompaniment of a drumbeat; see the boxed text (p52)

The Authors

ANDREW BURKE
Coordinating Author, Tehran, Central Iran, Persian Gulf, Southeastern Iran

Andrew has spent eight months travelling in Iran in recent years. Apart from enjoying endless tea and unforgettable hospitality, he has written about Iran for the previous edition of this book, for Lonely Planet's *Middle East* guide, and reported the 2003 Bam earthquake and Iran's last two general elections for major newspapers. Despite 'misunderstandings' that have led to occasional short stays with the constabulary, Andrew believes Iranians are among the most hospitable people on earth. This is Andrew's 15th book for Lonely Planet. When he's not travelling Andrew lives in Bangkok, Thailand.

MARK ELLIOTT
Western Iran, Northeastern Iran

Mark has been captivated by Iran's hospitality since his first visit in 1984. On one early trip he found himself caught up in the middle of a vast 'Down with America' demonstration celebrating the anniversary of the storming of the US embassy. Far from being a threatening experience, demonstrators merrily welcomed him along, took him for tea and reminded him that lacking discos, this was the nearest Tehran came to entertainment. Mark is best known as a travel writer and tourism consultant and he specialises in Iran's neighbour, Azerbaijan, about which he has written several books.

CONTRIBUTING AUTHORS

Dr Caroline Evans wrote the Health chapter. Having studied medicine at the University of London, Caroline completed general practice training in Cambridge. She is the medical adviser to Nomad Travel Clinic, a private travel-health clinic in London, and is also a GP specialising in travel medicine. Caroline has acted as expedition doctor for Raleigh International and Coral Cay expeditions.

Kamin Mohammadi contributed to The Culture chapter. Kamin is based in London, where she grew up, but she travels back to Iran frequently. She has written and broadcast on all aspects of Iran and is working on a family memoir about Iran called *The Cypress Tree*, to be published by Bloomsbury in 2009.

LONELY PLANET AUTHORS

Why is our travel information the best in the world? It's simple: our authors are independent, dedicated travellers. They don't research using just the internet or phone, and they don't take freebies in exchange for positive coverage. They travel widely, to all the popular spots and off the beaten track. They personally visit thousands of hotels, restaurants, cafés, bars, galleries, palaces, museums and more – and they take pride in getting all the details right, and telling it how it is. Think you can do it? Find out how at lonelyplanet.com.

Behind the Scenes

THIS BOOK

This fifth edition of *Iran*, like the fourth edition, was researched and written by Andrew Burke and Mark Elliott. Mark was responsible for the Western Iran and Northeastern Iran chapters. Andrew coordinated the book and was responsible for all the other chapters. The Culture chapter was written by Kamin Mohammadi for the fourth edition, and updated this time by Kamin and Andrew. The Health chapter (p417) is based on information supplied by Dr Caroline Evans. The section on Women Travellers (p396) was written by Kerryn Burgess and Miriam Raphael. Lonely Planet is grateful to Danny Rogers for his assistance in providing information for the Environment chapter, and to Matt Dickie for background information on rugs and carpets for the Arts chapter. *Iran* was first published in 1992. The first edition was written by David St Vincent, the second by Paul Greenway, and the third by Pat Yale and Anthony Ham.

This guidebook was commissioned in Lonely Planet's Melbourne office, and produced by the following:

Commissioning Editor Kerryn Burgess
Coordinating Editor Gina Tsarouhas
Coordinating Cartographer Amanda Sierp
Coordinating Layout Designer Indra Kilfoyle
Managing Editor Geoff Howard

Managing Cartographer Shahara Ahmed
Managing Layout Designer Celia Wood
Assisting Editors Susie Ashworth, Judith Bamber, Victoria Harrison, Katie O'Connell, Helen Yeates
Assisting Cartographers Alissa Baker, Daniel Fennessy, Erin McManus, Lyndell Stringer
Cover Designer Yukiyoshi Kamimura
Colour Designer Jacqui Saunders
Project Manager Fabrice Rocher
Language Content Coordinator Quentin Frayne

Thanks to Melanie Dankel, Yavar Dehghani, Diana Duggan, Lauren Hunt, Lisa Knights, Katie Lynch, Raphael Richards

THANKS
ANDREW BURKE

There are many people in Iran to whom I owe a heartfelt *kheyli mamnun* for their warm hospitality and selfless generosity that helped make this book possible. In Tehran, Paul Bellamy was a generous host (good luck with the book), as were Ali Taheri and family, Ali Solhjoo and Hamid Mousavi. Thanks also to patient Hossein Hosseiny, Khosrow Hasanzadeh, Houman Najafi, Hamid Tavassoli, and Nader Zarrin and Mahshid Jahangiri. Heading south, thanks to Mahdi and Mohammad in Kashan, Hossein Fallahi and family, Sufi Shahidzadeh and

THE LONELY PLANET STORY

Fresh from an epic journey across Europe, Asia and Australia in 1972, Tony and Maureen Wheeler sat at their kitchen table stapling together notes. The first Lonely Planet guidebook, *Across Asia on the Cheap*, was born.

Travellers snapped up the guides. Inspired by their success, the Wheelers began publishing books to Southeast Asia, India and beyond. Demand was prodigious, and the Wheelers expanded the business rapidly to keep up. Over the years, Lonely Planet extended its coverage to every country and into the virtual world via lonelyplanet.com and the Thorn Tree message board.

As Lonely Planet became a globally loved brand, Tony and Maureen received several offers for the company. But it wasn't until 2007 that they found a partner whom they trusted to remain true to the company's principles of travelling widely, treading lightly and giving sustainably. In October of that year, BBC Worldwide acquired a 75% share in the company, pledging to uphold Lonely Planet's commitment to independent travel, trustworthy advice and editorial independence.

Today, Lonely Planet has offices in Melbourne, London and Oakland, with over 500 staff members and 300 authors. Tony and Maureen are still actively involved with Lonely Planet. They're travelling more often than ever, and they're devoting their spare time to charitable projects. And the company is still driven by the philosophy of *Across Asia on the Cheap*: 'All you've got to do is decide to go and the hardest part is over. So go!'

desert dwellers Maziar, Ariane and Hadi Aledavoud in Garmeh, and Noushin and Manijeh in Baghestan-e Olia. Thanks to Yazdis Massoud Jaladat, Sebastian Straten and Shohreh, and to Mohsen Hajisaeed and Pegah for a whirl-wind road trip. In Shiraz, Arash Sadeqzadeh and Hossein Soltani were a huge help, as were Kazem Salehi, Majid Piroozmand and Massoud Nematollahi. Good luck rebuilding to Beate Boekhoff, Nima and the team in Bam. Travelling was a joy with Tayfun Guttstadt, Horst Brutsche, Robert Luck, Yasminah and especially my wife, Anne Hyland. For assistance by correspondence, thanks to mountain man Nader Seyhoun, environment man Danny Rogers, authors Kamin Mohammadi and Paul Clammer and language lady (and friend) Maryam Julazadeh. In Lonely Planet world, a huge thanks to Mark Elliott and Kerryn Burgess for being as passionate as I am about Iran, and to the editors and cartographers for transforming it all from digital bits into this book.

MARK ELLIOTT
Iran is a land of where uplifting, random acts of kindness to foreigners are so common that it's easy to overlook just how much help one has received. It's impossible to thank everyone as fully as they deserve. Nonetheless, let me pass on my special appreciation to Delsuz Rahmanzadeh and the gang in Paveh, Amin, Maziyar and father in Gorgan, Saeid Banoi in Malayer, Tahereh Ramezani Moghaddam in Khanbebin, Akbar 'the giant' Khorashadi in Aliabad, Vali in Mashhad, Shane 'taxifish' Warne, Louise Firouz in GTS, Amin Alizadeh in Orumiyeh, Nasrin Harris, Hassan Mohit in Rasht, Seyyid Mojtaba and Meisam, Ali and Ahmad Pishvar, Nasser and Mansur Khan, Ali Reza Yusufzade, Mohammad Pooyayairani, Hossein Ravanyar, Davood Faraji, Amir, Mr Zareie in Tabriz, Firat in Esendere, Edwin and Edward in Sir, Maksud in Sero, Can Yel in Van, Vahdat in Ardabil, Dariush Papi in Dorud, Farhad, Amad, Hossein and Mammad in Shirabad, Saja Banaiqil in Kordkuy, Amin and Hamid in Bijar, Noshin at the Mashhad Haram, Ali Mirzai in Sara'eyn, Shahin Zinati and Mr Saedi in Torbat-e Jam, Ali Sayeedi in Damghan, Ali in Gorgan for his thoughts on God and Barnstable, Abdul Halim and the insidious Mr Azim in Aq Qaleh, Farkhad and Mustafa in Navahand, Mustaffa 'the Iraqi' in Tuyserkan, Azad and Gita in Hamadan. Also many, many thanks to the team at Lonely Planet, notably my super-conscientious colleagues Andrew Burke and Kerryn Burgess, and to managing cartographer Shahara Ahmad for trying so hard to get me detailed maps where none existed. Most of all, unending thanks to my unbeatable wife, parents and siblings for giving me the love and support that make everything worthwhile.

OUR READERS
Many thanks to the travellers who used the last edition and wrote to us with helpful hints, useful advice and interesting anecdotes:

A Aryan Abdollahi, Jan Aengenvoort, Ali Afshar-Oromieh, Ali Akbari, Tariq Al-Aujaili, Anne Apynys **B** Siamack Atiabi, Jo Bakke, Andrew Balakshin, Mary Barry, Hugo Baur, Suzanne Black, Youri Blieck, Sohel Bohra, Michel De Bona, Patricia Brennan, Eline Brilman, Ron Broadfoot, Mirjam Brusins, Joe Bryant, Rana Bysack **C** Bjørn Carlsen, Russell Casey, Andy Chang, Corr Chris, Nick Conway **D** Jeremy Davis, John Davis, Francesca Delany, Matt Dickie, Jasmin Dirinpur, Andrew Dunlop, Hakon Dyrkoren **E** Jochen Ehmann, Linda Eibner **F** Jim Feist, Pascal Fiechter, Fernando Freitas **G** Masih Ghaziasgar, Sammie Gough, David Greenhill, Marti Griera, Bruna Guterres **H** Hassan Hadi, Thierry Haesenne, Manfred Heckl, Gerard Heerebout, Mohammad Heiranian, Annemarie Hekkers, Frederik Helbo, Matthias Henneis, Moritz Herrmann, Petr Hoferek, Steven Den Hond, Eelko Hooijmaaijers, Mojtaba Hosseninasab, Jean-Francois Huertas, Bob Huisken **I** Jan Isaksen, Genta Ishii **J** Sue Johns, Kiran Joshi **K** George Kechagioglou, Caroline Keller, Jeanette Kiefer-Cardinale, Brendan Kilcoyne, Dietmar Klaus, Yvette Knowles-Khaksar, Dietmar Krumpl, Monica Krupenski, Martin Král, Petr Kuca **L** Laurent Labatte, Tillmann Lang, Heydon Letcher, Valere Liechti **M** Simon Maddison, Zahra Mahi, John Malcovitch, Ahmad Marafi, Caroline Mawer, Kayleigh McMahon, Tija Memisevic, Robin Mills, Jennifer Milsom, Karsten Moeckel, Till Mostowlansky, Azam Mousavi, Matthias Müller **N** Serhat Narsap, Henry Newman, Adrian Nordenborg, Francesco Novello, Maider Nuin **O** Koki Odano, Frederic Ouyang **P** Behnam Paksersht, Carol Parkin, John Patterton, Wim De Pessemier, Thekla Pesta, Karl Philpott, Robyn Powell, Jarle Presttun, Clemens Purrucker **R** Haleh Rahjoo, Nis Ranken, Regula Reidhaar, Janis Reinsons, Xavier Riera Renter, Matthew Richards, Milenko Ristic, Richard Robinson, Jef Rosiers **S** Christian Sachse, Mehmet Sahin, Jorge Sanchez-Videgain, Mario Secen, Richard Seinstra, Marty Shams, Katharine Shepherd, Fernando Marques Da Silva, St John Simpson, Cathy Stokes, Jossepe Strano, Eric Sustad, Lisa Sutton **T** Sharon & Abbas Toosarvandi, Kariina Tshursin **U** Paul Ullmann **V** Ivan Aramayo, Ia van Bexecna, Rein van Dun, Egbert van Goudzwaard, Arjan Veersma, Cis Verbeeck, Chris Verres, Veronika Vogelhuber, Marc Vogtman, Ilse Voss-Lengnik **W** Owen Wall, Noé Wiener, Frank Willerton, Lars De Wit, Martyna Wolinska **Y** David Yaghoubian

ACKNOWLEDGMENTS
Many thanks to the following for the use of their content:
Globe on title page ©Mountain High Maps 1993 Digital Wisdom, Inc.

Internal photographs:
p117, p256, p275 Andrew Burke.

Index

INDEX

000 Map pages
000 Photograph pages

000 Map pages
000 Photograph pages

INDEX

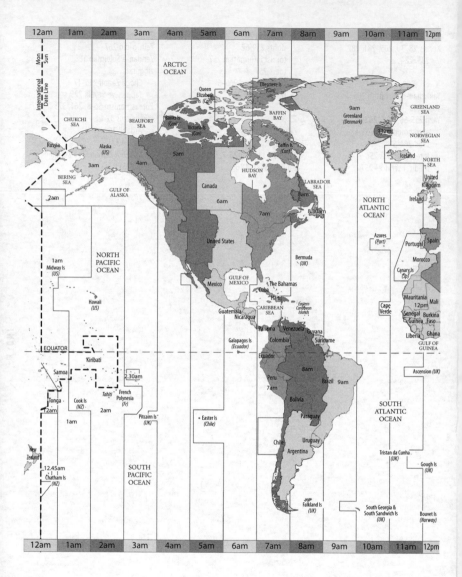

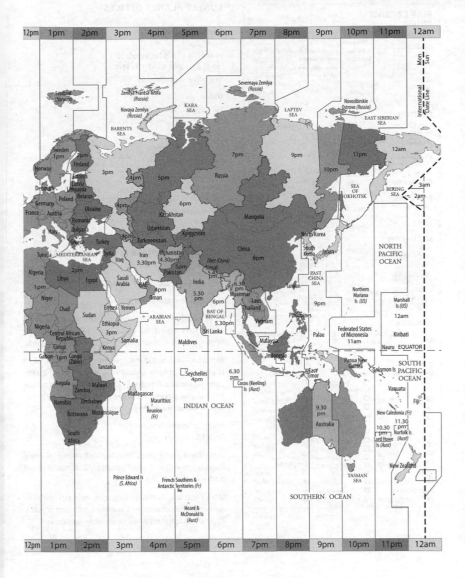

MAP LEGEND

ROUTES

Tollway	Mall/Steps
Freeway	Tunnel
Primary	Pedestrian Overpass
Secondary	Walking Tour
Tertiary	Walking Tour Detour
Lane	Walking Trail
Under Construction	Walking Path
Unsealed Road	Track
One-Way Street	

TRANSPORT

Ferry	Rail (Under Construction)
Metro	Tram
Rail	

HYDROGRAPHY

River, Creek	Canal
Intermittent River	Water
Swamp	Lake (Dry)

BOUNDARIES

International	Regional, Suburb
State, Provincial	Ancient Wall
Disputed	Cliff

AREA FEATURES

Airport	Land
Area of Interest	Mall
Beach, Desert	Market
Building	Park
Campus	Reservation
Cemetery, Christian	Rocks
Cemetery, Other	Sports
Forest	Urban

POPULATION

☉ CAPITAL (NATIONAL)	◉ CAPITAL (STATE)
● Large City	○ Medium City
○ Small City	○ Town, Village

SYMBOLS

Sights/Activities
- Beach
- Castle, Fortress
- Christian
- Islamic
- Monument
- Museum, Gallery
- Point of Interest
- Ruin
- Trail Head
- Zoo, Bird Sanctuary

Eating
- Eating

Entertainment
- Entertainment

Shopping
- Shopping

Sleeping
- Sleeping
- Camping

Teahouses & Cafés
- Café, Teahouse

Transport
- Airport, Airfield
- Border Crossing
- Bus Station
- Cycling, Bicycle Path
- General Transport
- Parking Area
- Petrol Station
- Taxi Rank

Information
- Bank, ATM
- Embassy/Consulate
- Hospital, Medical
- Information
- Internet Facilities
- Police Station
- Post Office, GPO
- Telephone
- Toilets

Geographic
- Lookout
- Mountain, Volcano
- National Park
- Waterfall

LONELY PLANET OFFICES

Australia
Head Office
Locked Bag 1, Footscray, Victoria 3011
☎ 03 8379 8000, fax 03 8379 8111
lonelyplanet.com.au/contact

USA
150 Linden St, Oakland, CA 94607
☎ 510 250 6400, toll free 800 275 8555
fax 510 893 8572
info@lonelyplanet.com

UK
2nd fl, 186 City Rd,
London EC1V 2NT
☎ 020 7106 2100, fax 020 7106 2101
go@lonelyplanet.co.uk

Published by Lonely Planet Publications Pty Ltd
ABN 36 005 607 983

© Lonely Planet Publications Pty Ltd 2008

© photographers as indicated 2008

Cover photograph: children laughing, desert village near Khur, Andrew Burke. Many of the images in this guide are available for licensing from Lonely Planet Images: www.lonelyplanetimages.com.

Printed by Fabulous Printers Pte Ltd
Printed in Singapore